Jin Ping Mei – A Wild Horse in Chinese Literature

NIAS – Nordic Institute of Asian Studies
NIAS Studies in Asian Topics

66 *Departing from Java: Javanese Labour, Migration and Diaspora* • Rosemarijn Hoefte & Peter Meel (eds)

67 *Engaging Asia: Essays on Laos and Beyond in Honour of Martin Stuart-Fox* • Desley Goldston (ed.)

68 *Performing the Arts of Indonesia: Malay Identity and Politics in the Music, Dance and Theatre of the Riau Islands* • Margaret Kartomi (ed.)

69 *Hearing Southeast Asia: Sounds of Hierarchy and Power in Context* • Nathan Porath (ed.)

70 *Asia Through Nordic Eyes: Fifty Years of Nordic Scholarship on Asia* • Geir Helgesen & Gerald Jackson (eds)

71 *Everyday Justice in Myanmar: Informal Resolutions and State Evasion in a Time of Contested Transition* • Helene Maria Kyed (ed.)

73 *East–West Reflections on Demonization: North Korea Now, China Next?* • Geir Helgesen and Rachel Harrison (eds)

74 *Spirit Possession in Buddhist Southeast Asia: Worlds Ever More Enchanted* • Bénédicte Brac de la Perrière and Peter A. Jackson (eds)

75 *Fragrant Frontier: Global Spice Entanglements from the Sino-Vietnamese Uplands* • Sarah Turner, Annuska Derks & Jean-François Rousseau (eds)

76 *From Tribalism to Nationalism: The Anthropological Turn in Laos – A Tribute to Grant Evans* • Yves Goudineau and Vanina Bouté (eds)

77 *Community Still Matters: Uyghur Culture and Society in Central Asian Context* • Aysima Mirsultan, Eric Schluessel and Eset Sulaiman (eds)

78 *Jin Ping Mei – A Wild Horse in Chinese Literature: Essays on Texts, Illustrations and Translations of a Late Sixteenth-Century Masterpiece* • Vibeke Børdahl and Lintao Qi (eds)

79 *Electoral Reform and Democracy in Malaysia* • Helen Ting M. H. and Donald L. Horowitz (eds)

NIAS Press is the autonomous publishing arm of NIAS – Nordic Institute of Asian Studies, a research institute located at the University of Copenhagen. NIAS is partially funded by the governments of Denmark, Finland, Iceland, Norway and Sweden via the Nordic Council of Ministers, and works to encourage and support Asian studies in the Nordic countries. In so doing, NIAS has been publishing books since 1969, with more than two hundred titles produced in the past few years.

UNIVERSITY OF COPENHAGEN

Nordic Council of Ministers

金瓶梅 JIN PING MEI

A WILD HORSE IN CHINESE LITERATURE

Essays on Texts, Illustrations and Translations of a Late Sixteenth-Century Masterpiece

EDITED BY
VIBEKE BØRDAHL & LINTAO QI

Jin Ping Mei – A Wild Horse in Chinese Literature
Essays on Texts, Illustrations and Translations of a
Late Sixteenth-Century Masterpiece
Edited by Vibeke Børdahl and Lintao Qi

Nordic Institute of Asian Studies
NIAS Studies in Asian Topics, no. 78

First published in 2022 by NIAS Press
NIAS – Nordic Institute of Asian Studies
Øster Farimagsgade 5, 1353 Copenhagen K, Denmark
Tel: +45 3532 9503 • Fax: +45 3532 9549
E-mail: books@nias.ku.dk • Online: www. niaspress. dk

© NIAS Press 2022

While copyright in the volume as a whole is vested in the Nordic Institute of Asian Studies, copyright in the individual chapters belongs to their authors. No material may be reproduced in whole or in part without the express permission of the publisher.

Publication of this volume was assisted by generous financial support received from S. C. Van Fonden, Copenhagen, for which the editors express their warm thanks.

 S.C. VAN FONDEN

A CIP catalogue record for this book is available from the British Library

ISBN 978-87-7694-318-9 Hbk

Typeset in 11 pt Garamond Premier Pro by Don Wagner
Printed and bound in the United States by Maple Press, York, PA Cover design: NIAS Press

Cover illustration: Pan Jinlian on a snowy evening toys with her *pipa* (from *Jin Ping Mei*, discussed in detail on pp. 145–146).

Contents

Contributors	xi
Preface	xiii
Foreword Minna Skafte Jensen	xv
Foreword Torbjörn Lodén	xix
Editorial Note	xxv
Introduction Vibeke Børdahl and Lintao Qi	xxvii

Jin Ping Mei and Oral Storytelling

1. *Jin Ping Mei* and the Art of Storytelling
   André Lévy — 1

2. *Pinghua* and *cihua* in *Jin Ping Mei cihua*
   Liangyan Ge and Vibeke Børdahl — 19

3. Language Shifting and the Narrating Instance in *Jin Ping Mei cihua*:
   Some Reflections on the Novel's Usage of Storytellers' Stock Phrases
   Vibeke Børdahl — 29

4. Pan Jinlian as Depicted in the Oral Tradition of the Wang School of
   'Water Margin' from Yangzhou Storytelling
   Ma Wei, translated by Vibeke Børdahl — 58

5. 'Killing Sister-in-law'
   Ma Wei, translated by Loughlin Harrick — 65

Jin Ping Mei and Intertextuality

6. Oral Performing Literature in Traditional Chinese Fiction: Non-
   realistic Usages in the *Jin Ping Mei cihua*
   David L. Rolston — 77

7. The Function and Purpose of Plays Referred to in *Jin Ping Mei*
   Huo Xianjun, translated by Zhang Dahai — 98

v

8. The Historical Value of the Customs of Late Ming Drama as Portrayed in *Jin Ping Mei*
Zhang Tingting, translated by Xu Wei 114

Jin Ping Mei and Print Culture

9. On Chinese Book Graphics and the Illustrations for the Novel *Jin Ping Mei*
Boris Riftin, translated by Sarah Fengler 129

10. Picturing Ximen Qing's World: The Chongzhen Edition Illustrations
Robert E. Hegel 140

11. Pictures and Words as Mirrors: How Woodblock Art and Literary Art in *Jin Ping Mei* Modify Each Other
Zhang Min, translated by Marja Kaikkonen 160

12. The Master Artist of the Newly Re-cut Blocks for the Illustrations of *Jin Ping Mei.*
Liu Kun, interviewed by Zhang Min, translated by Marja Kaikkonen 179

Jin Ping Mei as Forbidden Literature

13. *Jin Ping Mei* as Forbidden Fruit: Ban! Burn! Beat! Punish!
Marja Kaikkonen 193

14. The Portrayal of Sex in *Jin Ping Mei*
Keith McMahon 209

15. The Adaptation of Sex and Sexy Adaptations: Rewriting *Jin Ping Mei* for the Mid-20th Century Anglophone Market
Lintao Qi 226

16. Sex-related Expression or Vulgarism? On the Occurrences of the Word 㑚 in the Two Main Editions of *Jin Ping Mei*
Ondřej Vicher 247

17. A Book that Invites Lust: The Fate of *Jin Ping Mei* during the Edo Period in Japan
Kawashima Yuko, translated by Megan Seal 278

18. The Game of Official Advancement, *Shengguan tu*: A Macaronic Folk Ballad from the Middle of the Qing Dynasty
Martin Gimm, translated and re-arranged by Vibeke Børdahl 294

CONTENTS

Jin Ping Mei in China and in the World

19. A Wild Horse in the History of Chinese Literature: The Value and Influence of *Jing Ping Mei*
    Liu Zhen, translated by Hu Yaowen and Vibeke Børdahl   315

20. The Manchu Edition of 1708, *Gin ping mei bithe*: The Earliest Translation of the Novel *Jin Ping Mei*
    Martin Gimm, translated by Zhenzhen Lu   327

21. About the Life of My Brother and Me
    Artur Kibat, translated by Veronika Bauer   357

22. The Strategy and Process of David Tod Roy's English Translation of *Jin Ping Mei*
    David Rolston   364

23. The Architecture of Ximen Qing's Residence: Visualizing the General Layout and Translating it into a European Language and Culture
    Lucie Olivová   381

24. *Jin Ping Mei* in the World: Its Translation into Foreign Languages
    Wu Gan, translated by Celine Zhijie Ren and Daniel Haocheng Cui 394

Index   403

vii

Figures

3.1 *Jin Ping Mei cihua,* Chapter 39, page 10a, 2nd column — 48

10.1 Illustration from the Chongzhen edition of JPM, Ch. 32b, 'Envious, Pan Jinlian Startles the Child' — 144

10.2 Illustration from the Chongzhen edition of JPM, Ch. 38b, 'Pan Jinlian on a Snowy Evening Toys with Her *Pipa*' — 151

10.3 Illustration from the Chongzhen edition of JPM, Ch. 69a, 'Enjoying the First Tryst with Lady Lin in Her Mansion' — 146

10.4 Illustration from the Chongzhen edition of JPM, Ch. 35b, 'Playing a Female, Shutong Charms the Hangers-on' — 147

11.1 Illustration from *Water Margin,* Ch. 26, 'Wu Song Offers Heads as Memorial Sacrifice' — 172

11.2 Illustration from the Chongzhen edition of JPM, Ch. 87a, 'Captain Wu Kills His Sister-in-law as a Sacrifice to His Elder Brother' — 173

12.1 Liu Kun, woodcut according to the Chongzhen edition of JPM, Ch. 38b — 187

12.2 Liu Kun, woodcut according to the Chongzhen edition of JPM, Ch. 69a — 188

15.1 Translations from the Zhang Zhupo edition of JPM — 227

15.2 Translations from the *Cihua* edition of JPM — 228

15.3 Chinese ST for English excerpts 1, 2 and 3 — 230

17.1 The beginning of *Kinpeibai Yakubun* — 282

17.2 *Kinpeibai Yakubun* Chapter 27 — 283

17.3 Title characters of *Kinpeibai Yakubun* — 285

17.4 Headnotes of *Jin Ping Mei* Chapter 1 — 286

17.5 *Jin Ping Mei* Chapter 27 — 287

18.1 Manuscript No. 2, double page showing verses 24–40 of the *Shengguan tu* — 310

20.1 Hesu (1674–1724), the most likely translator of JPM into Manchu — 337

20.2 *Gin ping mei bithe*, Manchu translation of JPM, printed edition of 1708 — 341

20.3 *Gin ping mei bithe*, Manchu translation of JPM, manuscript — 342

22.1 Page of handwritten notes on the JPM prepared by David Roy — 368

22.2 Scan of pp. 32–33 of David Rolston's personal copy of *Xiaoxiao sheng* 1963 — 370

22.3 Scan of pp. 32–33 of Roy's personal copy of *Xiaoxiao sheng* 1963 — 371

CONTENTS

22.4 Private scan of Vol. 4, pp. 8–9, of Roy's personal copy of *Xiaoxiao sheng* 1963   372

22.5 Professional scan of Vol. 4, pp. 8–9, of Roy's personal copy of *Xiaoxiao sheng* 1963   373

22.6 First of 875 acronym cards made by David Roy   374

22.7 Acronym card for the acronym in the first acronym card   374

22.8 Sample pages from notebook in which Roy kept track of the appearance of characters in the novel   377

Tables

3.1: The 'storyteller's manner' in the novel and short story of the Ming and the Qing   32

3.2: Verse-introductory markers in *Jin Ping Mei cihua*   34

3.3: Markers of narrative transition and progression in *Jin Ping Mei cihua*   36

3.4: Markers of the narrator's comments and appeals to the audience in *Jin Ping Mei cihua*   39

3.5: Main features of the 'manner' in novel, oral storytelling, and written script   41

3.6: Verse-introductory markers in the WESTERN HAN script   29

3.7: Markers of narrative transition in the WESTERN HAN script   44

3.8: Narrator's appeal to the audience in the WESTERN HAN script   44

16.1: The number of occurrences of 合 and 俏 in different sources of both editions   250

16.2: The number of occurrences of 合 and 俏 in the digitized sources (including variants and additions)   251

16.3: The occurrence of 合 in respective chapters and editions, type of incidence, and its speaker   254

16.4: Details on the ten occurrences of 合 that appear only in one of the editions   257

ix

Editors and Contributors

About the Editors

Vibeke Børdahl, PhD., Dr. Phil., is Senior Research Fellow at the Nordic Institute of Asian Studies (NIAS), University of Copenhagen. Specializing in Chinese language and literature, dialectology, and oral performance culture, she has taught at the Nordic Universities of Aarhus, Oslo, and Copenhagen. Her most recent book-length studies in English on Chinese storytelling traditions include *Wu Song Fights the Tiger – The Interaction of Oral and Written Traditions in the Chinese Novel, Drama and Storytelling* (NIAS Press, 2013) and, with Liangyan Ge and Wang Yalong as co-editors, *Western Han. A Yangzhou Storyteller's Script* (NIAS Press, 2017). She has also published a 'Research Database on Chinese Storytelling' on the website www.shuoshu. org. Her major works are currently published in Chinese. Vibeke Børdahl has recently finished her translation of *Jin Ping Mei cihua* (1617) into Danish – *Jin Ping Mei i vers og prosa*, 3000 pages, 10 volumes, published by Vandkunsten Publishers, Copenhagen, 2011–2022.

Lintao Qi is Lecturer in the Masters of Interpreting and Translation Studies at Monash University, Australia. His research interests include literary translation theory and practice, translation and cultural diplomacy, and sexuality and censorship in translation. He is the author of *Jin Ping Mei English Translations: Texts, Paratexts, and Contexts* (Routledge, 2018) and is co-editor (with Leah Gerber) of *A Century of Chinese Literature in Translation: English Publication and Reception* (Routledge, 2020). His most recent book is *Encountering China's Past* (co-edited with Shani Tobias, Springer 2022). Lintao Qi has published widely in internationally recognized journals such as *Target, Translation and Interpreting Studies*, and *Perspectives*. He is a NAATI-certified translator and Co-editor of *New Voices in Translation Studies*.

Contributors

BAUER, Veronika, Monash University, Australia.

BØRDAHL, Vibeke, Nordic Institute of Asian Studies, University of Copenhagen, Denmark.

CUI, Daniel Haocheng, Monash University, Australia.

FENGLER, Sarah, Modern Languages, Jesus College, University of Oxford.

GE Liangyan 葛良彦, East Asian Languages and Cultures, University of Notre Dame, USA.

GIMM, Martin, Department of East Asian Studies, University of Cologne, Germany.

HARRICK, Loughlin, Monash University, Australia.

HEGEL, Robert E., Washington University in St. Louis, USA.

HU Yaowen 胡耀文, Beijing Foreign Studies University, China.

HUO Xianjun 霍现俊, Hebei Normal University, China.

KAIKKONEN, Marja, Stockholm University, Sweden.

KAWASHIMA, Yuko, 川島優子, Hiroshima University, Japan.

KIBAT, Artur (1878–1961), Wilhelmshafen, Germany.

LÉVY, André (1925–2017), University of Bordeaux, France.

LIU Kun 刘坤, Guangling shushe, Yangzhou, China.

LIU Zhen 刘祯, Mei Lanfang Memorial Museum, Beijing, China.

LU Zhenzhen 陆珍槙, Bates College, Maine, USA.

MA Wei 马伟, Association of Yangzhou Quyi Artists, Yangzhou, China.

MCMAHON, Keith, East Asian Languages and cultures, University of Kansas, USA.

OLIVOVÁ, Lucie, Department of Chinese Studies, Masaryk University, Czech Republic.

QI Lintao 齐林涛, Monash University, Australia.

REN, Celine Zhijie, Monash University, Australia.

RIFTIN, Boris L. (1932–2012), Russian Academy of Sciences, Moscow, Russia.

ROLSTON, David L., Asian Languages and Cultures, University of Michigan, USA.

SEAL, Megan, Monash University, Australia.

VICHER, Ondřej, Department of Asian Studies, Palacky University, Olomouc, Czech Republic.

WU Gan 吴敢, Xuzhou Education College, Jiangsu, China

XU Wei 徐瑋, Nanjing Audit University, China.

ZHANG Dahai 张大海, Chongqing College of Humanities, Science and Technology, China.

ZHANG Min 张敏, Nanjing University and Nanjing University Press, China.

ZHANG Tingting 張婷婷, Shanghai Film Academy, Shanghai University, China.

Preface

'[*Jin Ping Mei* was like] a bolting horse running wild over 10,000 miles, shaking off and trampling the morals and principles that people had stuck to scrupulously for ages, displaying frankly and without shame the secrets of human nature and a life of sensual delight [...]'

Jin Ping Mei, long celebrated as 'the number one extraordinary book', is not only one of the most interesting and complex novels of traditional China but is gradually being recognized as one of the greatest masterpieces of world literature. With sovereign contempt for societal and literary conventions, this work by an unknown author came 'bolting like a wild horse' (Liu Zhen, Chapter 19 of this book) into the late 16th century terrain of Chinese literature, from whence it spread in the following centuries to other countries near and far. The present volume is dedicated to contemporary research on this work and its translation into foreign languages. It draws together the diverse and fragmented scholarship on *Jin Ping Mei* and sets out to help future generations better understand and appreciate this important work. We shall explore these goals in greater detail in the Introduction.

This volume came into being during the period when the international symposium '*Jin Ping Mei*: The Oral, the Written and the Pictorial in Late Imperial Chinese Fiction' was being planned in celebration of Vibeke Børdahl's translation into Danish of the first printed edition of the work *Jin Ping Mei cihua* 金瓶梅詞話 (1617), finished in 2021 and published by Vandkunsten Publishers, Copenhagen, 2011–2022. The delays caused by the Covid pandemic, and the generosity of the S.C. Van Foundation allowed us to take the papers to be presented at the symposium and to edit them into a coherent and valuable resource on this Ming Dynasty masterpiece.

We, the editors, did not know each other before the symposium was in the melting pot, but during the initial phase of inviting speakers for this event our ways crossed at several points, and in April 2021 this contact resulted in an agreement to co-edit. With one of us in Melbourne and the other in Oslo, having never met face to face, we certainly can only be thankful for the internet. Søren Møller Christensen of Vandkunsten Publishers followed our efforts with genuine interest from the very beginning and participated in our

xiii

discussions, with helpful insights. The period of this 'triumvirate' was very fruitful and encouraging. When Gerald Jackson of NIAS Press accepted the volume for publication, we became a 'gang of four', and from that point onwards everything progressed quickly and smoothly. We cannot overstate our thanks to Søren and Gerald. With people like them backing you up, creating a book becomes sheer joy.

We want to express our gratitude to the authors and translators of the chapters for this book, which grew into a great collaborative project that could not have succeeded without the ongoing support of the contributors to it. Our special thanks go to Marja Kaikkonen, Sarah Fengler and Zhenzhen Lu, who volunteered to translate difficult texts from Chinese and German. We also had a good deal of help from the translators Hu Yaowen, Xu Wei, and Zhang Dahai from China. We are no less grateful to the younger generation of students from Monash University who offered to translate from Chinese: Daniel Haocheng Cui, Loughlin Harrick, Celine Zhijie Ren; from German: Veronika Bauer; and from Japanese: Megan Seal.

Here we also want to take the opportunity to thank the two anonymous peer reviewers for their encouraging reports on the value of the book and their detailed comments on each chapter. We are no less thankful to David Rolston, who kindly offered to revise some of the chapters translated from Chinese. We are likewise much indebted to the copy editor at NIAS Press, Monica Janowski, who has not only polished the language with meticulous care but has also taken responsibility for many other formal aspects of the book. Don Wagner, typesetting the pages, has placed his mark on the book, which is highly appreciated and has ensured a quality edition.

Last but not least, we want to acknowledge our great indebtedness to the hosts of the Copenhagen Symposium, the Royal Danish Academy of Sciences and Letters, the Nordic Institute of Asian Studies, the Royal Library and the Carlsberg Academy. The symposium was generously sponsored by the Royal Danish Academy, the Carlsberg Foundation and the S. C. Van Foundation. The Van Foundation, a stout supporter of cultural exchange between Denmark and China, has magnificently supported the publication of the Danish translation, the symposium and the publication of the present volume. We are extremely thankful for the support we have received, which is of vital importance for modern scholarship on the masterwork *Jin Ping Mei*.

VB and LQ
Oslo and Melbourne, May 2022

Foreword

Minna Skafte Jensen

On April 27, 2021, Vibeke Børdahl brought her translation of the novel *Jin Ping Mei* to an end after more than ten years of intense study of this Chinese classic. Now the intriguing work is, for the first time, fully accessible to a Danish – and Scandinavian – readership. That the task must have felt overwhelming is easily imagined. The sheer length of the novel – 3,000 pages, 100 chapters, 10 volumes of printed text – could have made anybody lose courage.[1] More importantly, to transplant a text from 17th-century China to 21st-century Denmark means to cover a huge distance in geography, time, culture, language, and morals. Besides, in a critical analysis of three German translations, Yen-Mee Sun maintained that the Chinese language in general and *Jin Ping Mei* in particular are characterised by ambiguity.[2] Add to this that the novel was composed in about 1600 but describes events that took place in the 1120s. The translator's achievement can hardly be overestimated.

Like most speakers of languages spoken by few people, the Danes are relatively well-versed in English and often a couple of other European languages, too; but for literature from 'exotic' parts of the world we are dependent on translations. Often such translations are made on the basis of other translations, but in this case the novel is brought into the Danish reading community directly from the Chinese original. Børdahl's source text is the first printed version, dated 1617. She is explicit about her target readership as non-specialists, people who simply enjoy reading foreign literature. My role here is to act as such a model reader.

I enjoy the foreignness of the story and the community it describes; at the same time, the text develops in a pleasant and balanced language that makes me imagine that I have to some degree understood the story that is being told. The story of the rich and ambitious merchant Ximen Qing is as such recognisable; it is more difficult to get accustomed to his household with his six wives living

---

1   The translator has described the process in Børdahl 2022.

2   'Seine (*Jin Ping Mei*'s) typische Doppelsinnigkeit und die Mehrdeutigkeit der chinesischen Sprache [...].'(Sun Yen-Mee 1978: 272)

each in a separate apartment of the residence and competing to be chosen for the night. At the same time, I find the description of the wives' relationships one of the most entertaining aspects of the narrative, oscillating as it does between friendly solidarity, pleasant companionship, and envious rivalry. Religious conceptions are, of course, also unfamiliar, not least the terrifying ideas about what a person may expect after death; but the reactions of the dying person and his/her relatives when death is close at hand are more easily understood. If the actions and their settings are unfamiliar, the feelings they provoke are similar to what a Danish reader might have.

In order not to weigh down the narrative with learned commentaries, Børdahl gives a minimum of help, mainly in the form of two indexes at the end of each volume, one a list of names of the enormous number of characters taking part, and one of special terms. For instance, every now and then as you read, you have persons arriving and making a *ketou* for the host, and you understand that they are performing a polite greeting. If you are lazy or simply want to get on with the story you are content with that; however, you can learn how a *ketou* is performed in detail by looking into the index. You will find that the newcomers knock their heads on the floor as a sign of deep esteem.

Jin Ping Mei is notorious for its many explicitly erotic scenes, and the translator assures us that she has let them come through as close to the original as possible. To a Danish readership, used to decades of uncensored pornography, they are not as such shocking. To my mind, however, the scenes are too intertwined with the exercising of power to be charming.

What I find most bewildering about reading the novel is coming to terms with the overall feel of the text. Sometimes the narrator suggests satire, but mostly the narrative moves along in a descriptive mood and leaves it to the readers to make up their minds whether to feel attracted, scandalised, envious, amused, or otherwise affected. That somehow the world described must be the narrator's idea of how people were living in the old times does not make the interpretation simpler.

That the novel is closely related to oral storytelling is clear, but exactly how is of course a more intricate question. The organisation of the story follows the rules Børdahl experienced in her field studies of Yangzhou storytelling: the 10 times 10 chapters represent the continued storytelling in the teahouse, where the owner used to engage a storyteller for a week of 10 days. Each chapter ends with the phrase: 'If you do not know what happens next, please listen to the next round of the story', just as if the readers were listeners exhorted to return the next day. In other ways, too, readers are invited to identify with listeners: the narrator approaches them with stock phrases such as 'What a sight!' or 'Let's now turn to...', and they may imagine themselves to be in the teahouse and enjoying the narrative in pleasant company. To me it was very surprising to read that in Børdahl's experience storytellers do not, in real life, use such stock phrases; she suggests that they may actually belong specially to the written novel as a literary convention, enabling the narrator to pose as an oral storyteller.[3]

How closely the translation sticks to the source text I am unable to judge, but the translated novel unfolds in a delightful tension between foreignness and familiarity. Told in a lively, varied and natural prose interspersed with many verse passages, the text is truly enjoyable. Vibeke Børdahl has offered Danish readers a marvellous gift.

References

Børdahl, Vibeke

    2022. 'The translation into Danish of *Jin Ping Mei cihua – Jin Ping Mei* i vers og prosa: personal recollections and reflections.' In L. Qi and S. Tobias (eds), *Encountering China's Past, New Frontiers in Translation Studies*, pp. 185–205. Singapore: Springer.

Sun, Yen-Mee

    1978. *Chinesisch-deutsche Übersetzungsschwierigkeiten am Beispiel des Romans Jin Ping Mei*. München: Ludwig-Maximilians-Universität.

---

3   Børdahl 2022, 189.

Foreword

TORBJÖRN LODÉN

Chinese culture began to attract attention in Scandinavia quite early. Already in the 1690s two academic dissertations on China were presented at Uppsala University.[1] In the 18th century, China was depicted as a country ruled by philosophers and one worthy of emulation. Carl Fredrik Scheffer (1715–1786), a prominent academician and advisor to the court, was important in promoting this idealization of China in Sweden. In a speech before the Academy of Sciences on October 28th, 1772, designed to legitimize the coup d'état that King Gustav III had staged in August that year, he said:

> To the embarrassment of the so-called cultured and well-mannered peoples of Europe we have to admit that in the course of all the changes in our Laws and Customs, which in themselves contained the causes of their impermanence, the Chinese people have lived under a System of Government which has remained stable for several thousand years and which has turned the Chinese realm into the mightiest, most populous and most affluent ever heard of or described.[2]

In the 19th century more critical views, which focused on the ugly aspects of Chinese society, became common. Ever since the late 17th century, perceptions of China in Scandinavia, as in the rest of Europe, have oscillated between the extremes of idealization and demonization.

Historically, images of Chinese culture were first and foremost based on philosophical and historical writings as well as travelogues, while literature – poetry, fiction, drama – played only a very minor role. However, in the 19th century, literature and art, especially poetry, began to attract at least some attention. In 1901 Herbert Giles published his *History of Chinese Literature,* which seems to have been the first attempt in any language to write a comprehensive history of Chinese literature. Previously some translations, especially of poetry, had appeared. In Sweden the first anthology of Chinese poetry – Hans Emil Larsson's *Kinesiska dikter på svensk värs* – came out in 1894. During the first half of the 20th century, Chinese poetry was translated into many

---

1   Locnaeus 1694 and Roland 1697.

2   See Sirén 1950. English translation by Professor Erik Frykman, personal communication.

European languages and attracted considerable interest, not least among many poets and writers, who drew inspiration from the classical masters of poetry in China such as Li Bai and Du Fu. Prose literature was also translated into different European languages but on a much smaller scale and with much less impact than poetry.

In premodern China, fiction did not by any means enjoy the same high status as classical poetry or literary essays. But in the context of the veritable literary revolution that took place in China in the early 20th century as part of the May Fourth New Culture Movement, this changed. From then on, the classical novels written in the vernacular language *baihua,* which was much closer to the spoken Mandarin dialects than the literary language *wenyan,* which required many years of study to master, were described as linguistic models for the new Chinese literature.

In his pioneering work, Hebert Giles devotes a chapter to 'Novels and Plays'. This chapter contains half a page about *Jin Ping Mei,* which he describes as a 'marvellous work' but which he also finds objectionable on moral grounds. He writes:

> The story itself refers to the early part of the twelfth century, and is written in a simple, easy style, closely approaching the Peking colloquial. It possesses one extraordinary characteristic. Many words and phrases are capable of two interpretations, one of which is of a class unfit for ears polite. Altogether the book is objectionable and would require a translator with the nerve of a Burton.[3]

The Swedish sinologist Bernhard Karlgren, whose specialty was historical linguistics and philology, has a short section on classical Chinese fiction in his entry on Chinese language and literature in the Swedish Encyclopedia *Nordisk familjebok* published in 1923–1937. Here Karlgren mentions the *Jin Ping Mei* and sums up the significance of this and the other classical novels he mentions by saying that they give us 'a very schematic and insufficient psychology but instead overwhelming insights into living conditions, customs and ways of thinking'.[4]

This suggests that, while he placed great value on the *Jin Ping Mei* and the other classical novels as sources of knowledge about Chinese culture and society, his attitude to them with regard to their literary merits was rather denigrating.

This perspective on classical fiction seems to have been a striking feature of the reception of Chinese fiction and of modern Chinese literature in the

---

3 Giles 1973: 309. Giles was probably referring to the explorer, polyglot and writer Sir Richard Francis Burton (1821–1890), who was widely known as a ground-breaking translator (*1001 Nights, Kama Sutra* and *The Perfumed Garden* among others) as well as for his sexually explicit writings

4 Karlgren 1923–1937: 743. English translation by the author.

FOREWORD

Western world right up to our own time: these literary works have been read as descriptions of Chinese culture and society rather than as literature. By contrast, classical poetry has always been treated much more as literature. Of course, literature is indeed a very important source for knowledge about China; in some ways it provides us with knowledge that scholarly studies do not. Anyone interested to learn about Chinese culture and society should therefore read Chinese literature. Nevertheless, to approach literary works with this sole purpose reflects a narrow, one-dimensional view of literature. To do so is to close our eyes to the very essence of serious fiction, which is the use of imagination and creativity as a means of seeking truths that cannot be immediately perceived by our observations of real life here and now.

As the quotation from Karlgren shows, the vernacular novels were already known and referred to in Scandinavia in the early 20th century. In 1950 a Swedish translation of the *Jin Ping Mei* from German and English, abridged but still comprising more than 700 pages, appeared.[5] An advertisement from that time characterized it in these words: 'The famous novel about Hsimen [Ximen] and his six wives gives a brilliant picture of Chinese culture, eroticism and morality in general.'[6]

Abridged versions of one or more of the classical novels translated from European languages appeared quite early in all the Scandinavian countries.[7] But it was only when Professor Göran Malmqvist published his translation of the *Shuihuzhuan* in four volumes in 1976–1979, under the Swedish title *Berättelser från träskmarkerna,* that a complete translation into a Nordic language of one of the novels appeared. In 1995–1996 Malmqvist then published his translation of the *Xiyou ji* in five volumes, under the title *Färden till Västern,* and in 2005–2010 the literary scholar Pär Bergman published a complete translation in five volumes of the *Honglou meng,* entitled *Drömmen om röda gemak.*

---

5 *Chin Ping Mei: romanen om Hsimen och hans sex fruar* 1950. This Swedish version was translated from two German versions by Artur and Otto Kibat (*Djin Ping Meh* 1928–1932) and Franz Kuhn (*Kin Ping Meh, oder die abenteuerliche Geschichte von Hsi Men und seiner sechs Frauen* 1930) and the English translation by Bernard Miall (*Chin p'ing mei : the adventurous history of Hsi Men and his six wives* 1939). The English translation was based on Kuhn's German version. These German and English versions were all abridged. Concerning the brothers Artur and Otto Kibat, see Chapter 21 in this volume.

6 The advertisement was in the *Svenska Dagbladet* on 20 October 1950. The English translation is by the author. I am indebted to my friend, the sinological librarian Inga Nyman Ambrosiani, for sharing with me this and many other references in Swedish newspapers to the classical novels.

7 For more information about this, see Børdahl 2022.

These complete translations from the Chinese of three classical novels were very impressive accomplishments, and they did receive praise. Bergman was awarded a prize for his translation by the Royal Swedish Academy of Sciences, and the reviews heaped praise on all three translations. Yet, on the whole, these major accomplishments in the field of literary translation received less attention than one might have expected, and the most prominent literary critics in the major newspapers seem to have stayed away from them, maybe because they felt somewhat at a loss in dealing with Chinese literature, with which they were not very familiar. Rendering these texts into smooth readable Swedish, or into other Scandinavian and Western languages, presents the translator with difficulties of an entirely different order than the translation of modern Chinese works, which are far more similar to Western literature than these books. The translations of these three classic novels were, therefore, really extraordinary feats.

These translations probably marked the beginning of a new era in the reception of Chinese literature in Sweden and Scandinavia. More than we were used to, they captured the critics' attention as *literary* masterpieces, not just as sources of knowledge about Chinese culture and society. In Sweden cultural critics such as Carl Rudbeck and the sinologist and critic Göran Sommardal exemplify this increasing sensitivity to the literary merits of the classical novels in their reviews.[8]

Almost two hundred years have passed since Goethe began to use the term 'Weltliteratur', suggesting that literary works belong to all mankind, not just one nation. It has taken a long time for people in our part of the world to pay due attention to the rich legacy of Chinese literature as part of world literature. However, during the past few decades we have seen an increasing interest in Chinese literature, classical and modern, in the world. Two Nobel Prizes in literature have been awarded to authors who write in Chinese, Gao Xingjian and Mo Yan. In Scandinavia, more and more Chinese works have been translated into the Scandinavian languages and into Finnish.

Now Vibeke Børdahl has completed her ten-volume translation of the *Jin Ping Mei*, an extraordinary accomplishment in the field of literary translation. This means that four of the great classical Chinese novels are now available in unabridged translations from the Chinese into Danish and Swedish, languages that readers throughout Scandinavia can read without too much difficulty. These translations make it possible for readers in Scandinavia to 'discover' the classical Chinese vernacular novels as great multidimensional literary works that belong to world literature.

---

8 See, for example, Rudbeck 1994, 1995, 2006, 2007 and Sommardal 2011, 2012.

FOREWORD

References

Børdahl, Vibeke

2022. 'The translation into Danish of *Jin Ping Mei cihua* – *Jin Ping Mei* i vers og prosa: personal recollections and reflections.' In Lintao Qi and Shani Tobias (eds), Encountering China's Past: Translation and Dissemination of Classical Chinese Literature – New Frontiers in Translation Studies, 185–205. Singapore: Springer Nature.

Chin Ping Mei: romanen om Hsimen och hans sex fruar.
1950. Translated by Elsie and Håkan Tollet. Stockholm: Fahlcrantz and Gumælius.

Chin P'ing Mei: the Adventurous History of Hsi Men and his Six Wives.
1939. Translated by Bernard Miall with an introduction by Arthur Waley. London: John Lane.

Djin Ping Meh
1928–1932. Translated by Artur and Otto Kibat. Gotha: Engelhart. 2 Vols.

Giles, Herbert
1973 [1901]. A History of Chinese Literature. Rutland, Vermont and Tokyo, Japan: Charles E. Tuttle Company.

Karlgren, Bernard
1923–1937. 'Kinesiska språket och litteraturen' (Chinese language and literature). Nordisk familjebok, Vol. 11, 738–746.

Kin Ping Meh, oder die abenteuerliche Geschichte von Hsi Men und seiner sechs Frauen.
1930. Translated by Franz Kuhn. Leipzig: Insel-Verlag.

Larsson, Hans Emil (ed.)
1894. Kinesiska dikter på svensk värs med en inledning om kinesisk kultur och poesi af Hans Emil Larsson (Chinese poems in Swedish verse with an introduction about Chinese culture and poetry by Hans Emil Larsson). Lund: Gleerup.

Locnaeus, Jonas
1694. Murus Sinensis (The Chinese wall). Dissertation presented at Uppsala University on November 11, 1694. 24 pp. Uppsala: Henricus Keyser, S:æ R:æ M:tis and Academ. typographus.

Roland, Eric
1697. De magno Sinarum Imperio (On the Great Empire of the Chinese). Dissertation presented at Uppsala University on June 10, 1697. 59 pp. Uppsala: Holmiæ, ex officina Olai Enæi.

xxiii

Rudbeck, Carl

1994. 'Obscen moralitet från ett svunnet Kina' (An obscene morality from a China long past). Dagens Nyheter 8 April.

1995. 'Bergens onda demoner. Osannolika och spännande kinesiska historier' (Evil demons of the mountains. Improbable and thrilling Chinese stories). Dagens Nyheter 25 October.

2006. 'Jadestenar och röda gemak' (Jade stones and red chambers). Dagens Nyheter 24 February.

2007. 'En magnifik klassiker på svenska. Cao Xueqin tar oss med in i en både förfinad och brutal värld' (A magnificent classic in Swedish. Cao Xueqin brings us to a world both refined and brutal). Dagens Nyheter 3 December.

Sirén, Osvald

1950. Kina och den kinesiska tanken i Sverige på 1700-talet (China and the Idea of China in 18th century Sweden). Lychnos (Lärdomshistoriska samfundets årsbok 1948–1949, 2–84.

Sommardal, Göran

2011. 'Drömmen om röda gemak' (The dream of red chambers). 5 July. Available at archive.org/details/podcast_biblioteket_klassikerrummet-drommen-om-rod_1000095422077

2012. 'Berättelser från träskmarkerna' - om frågetecknen i en kinesisk klassiker' ('Stories from the marshland' – on the question marks of a Chinese classic). 1 September. Available at podcasts.nu/avsnitt/klassikern/berattelser-fran-traskmarkerna

Editorial Note

In this book, 24 essays by authors from all around the world are collected: Australia, China, the Czech Republic, Denmark, France, Germany, Japan, Russia, Sweden, U.S.A. The collection does not only contain original contributions; we have also chosen to include essays written by the late scholars André Lévy (Chapter 1, originally published in 2007), Boris Riftin (Chapter 9, originally published in 1984) and Artur Kibat (Chapter 21, originally published in 1967), as well as some essential studies published in former decades by leading scholars of *Jin Ping Mei* in the West, David L. Rolston (Chapter 6, originally published in 1994) and Martin Gimm (Chapter 18, originally published 2003–2004). Three of these essays were written in German (Chapters 9, 18 and 21). They are here translated into English. Chapter 18 has not only been translated from German but has been rearranged to make this piece more easily accessible for the general reader. Printed between 20 and 60 years ago, it was not always easy to get into contact with the copyright holders for these earlier articles. We have tried our best to approach both publishers, editors, and the authors' relatives wherever possible. The circumstances were different in each case, as described in the *Editors' Notes* to the chapters concerned.

The other 19 chapters are all original works prepared for this volume and published here for the first time. Chapter 20 was written in German and translated into English. Chapters 4, 5, 7, 8, 11, 12, 19 and 24 were all written in Chinese and translated by individual translators from Chinese into English. Sometimes several translators were involved in the translation of the same chapter, and David Rolston offered his expert assistance with the revision of Chapters 7, 8, 19 and 24.

We had to handle a diversity of academic traditions reflected both in the style of discourse and in the formal aspects of presenting the research. We could not just superimpose and demand a Western academic style, such as the North American standard reflected in the widespread *Chicago Manual of Style*. For this reason, we decided to stay as faithful as possible to the style of the individual scholars and only to carry out a superficial streamlining of the notes and references. This may look 'untidy' and less well coordinated, but in our view each individual chapter has its own system, which is easy to grasp, and we do not want to sacrifice individuality for the sake of a pedantic striving for uniformity. In this book, each chapter should be seen as a self-contained unit, including the main text, mostly with notes and references (but not always), and with information on the contributors, i.e. author and translator(s), appended.

For the alphabetic writing of Chinese, the *pinyin* transcription is used, except in quotations from works that use other transcriptions (but some authors have decided to change these into *pinyin*, which is noted where it has been done). As for the use of simplified characters, *jiantizi* 简体字, versus traditional characters, *fantizi* 繁體字, we have left such preferences for the authors to decide, but if there was a discussion about it, we encouraged the use of *fantizi*, since *Jin Ping Mei* is from a time when *fantizi* was the norm. Modern studies in Chinese of the work on which we are focusing are of course often written in *jiantizi*. It is our impression that the readership for a book like this one will be able to cope with both forms of written Chinese without difficulty. It goes without saying that the book is perfectly readable without knowing any Chinese.

Introduction

Vibeke Børdahl and Lintao Qi

Jin Ping Mei 金瓶梅 (*Jinlian, Ping'er and Chunmei*, or *Plum in a Golden Vase*) is a work that puts its readers to the test. For a Western reader especially it presents obstacles, such as the endless number of difficult names and a wealth of exotic things and customs. It is hardly a page-turner or light entertainment either, but it is possible to enjoy it as such. On the other hand, it is no less a serious book of high expectations – a work of humour and irony, of black-hearted witticism, wild enthusiasm, mournful tragedy, riddles, double-entendre, and sheer poetry.

The scene is set in Shandong Province during the final years of the Northern Song (960–1126). But the descriptions are coloured by the society of the last century of the Ming dynasty (1368–1644) and its material culture, perhaps based on the life experience of the author. The author? Well, this is one of the many mystifying aspects of this work. It is attributed to Lanling Xiaoxiaosheng (the 'Scoffing Scholar of Lanling'), an apparent pseudonym. Despite extensive research and enormous energy devoted to the question, there is to this day no consensus in scholarly circles about the authorship of the 100-chapter *magnum opus*.

The story of the novel is an outgrowth from the previous novel *Shuihu zhuan* 水滸傳 (*Water Margin*). With the earliest known printed copies dating to the first half of the 16th century, *Shuihu zhuan* is one of the first of its genre, obviously based on oral storytelling by professional performers in the growing urban entertainment quarters of the Yuan (1279–1368) and early Ming dynasties. The ten-chapter Wu Song 武松 saga, *Wu shi hui* 武十回 (*Ten Chapters on Wu Song*) embedded in this work is one of several core tales about heroes and banditry during the corrupt regime of the Song emperor Huizong 徽宗 (1082–1135).

The story of *Jin Ping Mei* (JPM) begins at the point where storytellers of the Wu Song saga have started since time immemorial, namely with the famous episode where Wu Song slays a tiger with his bare hands. A man and a tiger – a symbolic tale about man and nature, or perhaps rather about male and female principles? Wu Song kills the tiger, but soon he is up against stronger forces. Pan Jinlian 潘金蓮, the wife of his dwarfish brother, falls in love with him, and such an attack is harder to withstand for this giant bulldozer of apparent sexual indifference, who sublimates his sexual energy into bloody and murderous behaviour. While Wu Song is among the main heroes of *Shuihu zhuan*, he has only a supporting role in JPM, in which a story of heroic adventure among outlaws during the Xuanhe 宣和 (1119–1125) reign of the last emperor of the Northern Song dynasty, is developed into a family saga and a novel of manners, the first of its kind in China – and in the world? As David Tod Roy (1933–2016) said in his introduction to the first volume of his remarkable work of 'research-in-translation' (1993, xvii–xviii):

> The *Chin P'ing Mei* (*The Plum in the Golden Vase*) is an enormous, complex, and sophisticated novel, surprisingly modern in its design [...]. The work is a landmark in the development of narrative art, not only from a specifically Chinese perspective, but in a world-historical context. With the possible exceptions of *The Tale of Genji* (1010) and *Don Quixote* (1615), neither of which it resembles, but with both of which it can bear comparison, there is no earlier work of prose fiction of equal sophistication in world literature.

The term 'family saga' might evoke a pleasant, cosy atmosphere that has little to do with JPM and the story of Ximen Qing 西門慶 and his six wives. Although the storyline follows the vicissitudes of a merchant family – much like a Chinese *Buddenbrooks* – there is little family solidarity or social bonding. From the very beginning, the Chinese novel exposes the mutual infighting – the struggle for survival on the part of all the individuals in the story – in the open or undercover. Whether they are rich or poor, man or woman, master or slave, there is a constant battle for status, for riches, for advantages, or just for a meal. The world as a 'slaughterhouse'. Nevertheless, this fearful bass-tone of the story is overlaid with all the wonders of the marvellous Chinese civilization. Moreover, in the universe of this novel there is nothing that is unmentionable. For a Western reader that is probably one of the most disturbing and also one of the most attractive characteristics. The text opens a window on so many aspects of life that have until recently – and probably still to a considerable degree – belonged to the realm of the 'unsayable'. In the 1920s Gertrude Stein told Hemingway to stop writing stories that were *inaccrochables*, i.e. could not be hung on the wall for everybody to see. JPM is *inaccrochable*.

Our novel is a narrative about China during the Song period, but it is just as much, if not more, about the 'China of the day', i.e. the China of the time when the novel was put together. It is possible to analyse the novel as a direct, albeit secret, attack on the emperor and his entourage of powerful ministers, as well as on the ruling class and on the administrative corruption of the late Ming period. Four centuries have passed since the novel's first appearance, but the stories in it still resonate with life in China today, and indeed not just in

INTRODUCTION

China. As a classic, its impact and message transcends time and space. This work speaks to us all – everywhere in the world – *today*.

The Copenhagen Symposium

The Copenhagen symposium 'The Oral, the Written and the Pictorial in Late Imperial Chinese Fiction: *Jin Ping Mei* in Verse and Prose' was postponed several times during 2021–2022 because of the Covid-19 pandemic but at time of writing is scheduled for 26–28 October 2022. Hosted by the Royal Danish Academy of Sciences and Letters, the Nordic Institute of Asian Studies and the Royal Library, a festive occasion is planned that celebrates the translation into Danish by Vibeke Børdahl of *Jin Ping Mei cihua* 金瓶梅詞話 (1617) and its publication in 10 volumes by Forlaget Vandkunsten, Copenhagen, 2011–2022, as *Jin Ping Mei i verse og prosa* (*Jin Ping Mei in Verse and Prose*).

The symposium is intended not only as a meeting for scholars of *Jinxue* 金學 ('Gold studies', i.e., studies of JPM) from all over the world, but also for translators of JPM, more precisely European translators of *Jin Ping Mei cihua* into Czech and Danish. Moreover, artists from China are invited to the symposium – a storyteller from Yangzhou who performs selected episodes that are in common between *Shuihu zhuan* and JPM, and a master of wood-block printing from the old printing house Guangling shushe 廣陵書社, Yangzhou, who will demonstrate his art during the meeting.

Jin Ping Mei – A Wild Horse in Chinese Literature

Fruitful research on JPM has been conducted by scholars around the world from multiple disciplinary backgrounds. More and more informative articles and monographs, many of which dig deep into the meaning of the book, have been published in various languages in the last couple of decades. However, interdisciplinary and transnational exchange, particularly in the form of face-to-face discussions in scholarly fora, remains relatively limited.

The volume draws on this research, including original papers to be presented at the Copenhagen symposium supplemented by seminal papers that were previously published on JPM Studies (mostly in languages other than English). The book will help to present research on JPM from different disciplinary perspectives and increase the global visibility and accessibility of JPM scholarship conducted in different linguistic and cultural contexts in the *lingua franca* of our era, English. The first of its kind, this book has the following unique features:

- Wide geographical distribution: contributors are established or emerging scholars of JPM Studies from around the globe, including America, Asia, Europe, and Oceania.
- Academic diversity: contributions cover a wide range of topics, such as questions of orality/literacy, intertextuality, books and printing, text and illustration, the portrayal of sex, and the impact of translation in China and worldwide. Each chapter approaches its topic from a unique perspective. Chapters in the same section complement each other without being repetitive.
- Representative quality: most chapters have been prepared specifically for this volume and reflect the most up-to-date scholarship in JPM studies; a selection of authoritative texts in other languages and from an earlier period are also reprinted in English translation in this book to benefit researchers worldwide.
- Multidisciplinary scope: the book includes theoretical frameworks and research methodologies from various disciplines including Chinese Studies, Literary Studies, Book History, Print Culture, Translation Studies, History Studies and World Literature.
- Academic and artistic approaches, scholarship from East and West: the book includes contributions by academics as well as by artists; and different traditions of communicating knowledge, East and West, meet in this book.
- Opening up for female scholars and translators: more than a third of the scholars and translators featured in this book are female. Engaging in JPM studies and in translation has been rare among women until recently. The book has been claimed unfit to be read by women ever since its first appearance in China and was generally banned throughout the Qing dynasty. The social mores relating to decency for women and men, both in China and in the West, were different enough to practically exclude women from participation in such studies. In this book the sexes meet around the same academic table.

The essays of the book are arranged into five sections covering five main topics: JPM and oral storytelling; JPM and intertextuality; JPM and print culture; JPM as forbidden literature; and JPM in China and in the world. These five topics were not decided in advance but grew out of the titles that the invited scholars and artists had chosen, so that these topics reflect the interests of the contributors.

INTRODUCTION

Jin Ping Mei and Oral Storytelling

There is a long tradition in both East and West of praising JPM as the first Chinese novel created and written by a genius author from the intelligentsia of the late Ming scholar class, the so-called 'literati'. Undoubtedly the earliest manuscript circulated within a readership that belonged to this class. It was appreciated very early on as a masterful text. However, the connoisseurs who bowed to JPM tended to put it on a par with earlier masterworks, such as *Shuihu zhuan* – a work with strong connections to oral storytelling and a weak identification with 'authorship' in the usual sense. The educated readers of the manuscript versions do not appear to have felt any overt disdain for the oral culture of song, balladry, opera, and storytelling that were the most widespread kinds of entertainment in their time. André Lévy (1925–2017), translator of *Jin Ping Mei cihua* into French (*Fleur en Fiole d'Or*, 1985) – the first complete translation of the *cihua* text into a European language – wrote an essay entitled '*Jin Ping Mei* and the art of storytelling' for a symposium entitled 'The Interplay of Oral and Written Traditions in Chinese Fiction, Drama and Performance Literature' that took place in Oslo 2007. We reprint it here in lightly edited form to pay tribute to this extraordinary scholar and translator, not to mention because we find it a brilliant and 'evergreen' contribution to the discussion about JPM and its relationship to oral culture (see Chapter 1).

JPM is a conglomeration of all kinds of popular entertainment mixed into 100 chapters of novelistic written storytelling. Because of its realistic, unreserved and elaborate descriptions of sexual life (as well as many other aspects of daily life) and its covert attack on dynastic rule, it might have been risky to reveal oneself as the author of this work. Later the book was doomed to belong to the category of forbidden books. But we should also keep in mind that 'authorship' in China at this time was mainly connected to the 'serious' genres of philosophy and high poetry. When it came to entertainment, *xiaoshuo* 小說 ('small talk', fiction), there was no strong tradition of putting one's name to this – it was considered left-hand scribbling, nothing serious, despite its popularity within both higher and lower classes.

The first printed edition of JPM that has come down to posterity was titled *Jin Ping Mei cihua*. The word *cihua* 詞話 (verse and prose, or, in French, *chantefable*) at the end of the title was added to this first block-print version, despite the fact that the work was called *Jin Ping Mei zhuan* 金瓶梅傳 (JPM chronicle) in the manuscript versions. The editors or printers (or the author?) decided on a different category for this book, different from *Shuihu zhuan*. Originating in history-writing, *zhuan* was a genre marker that was much more respectable than *cihua*, which was associated with popular storytelling and

xxxi

story-singing. Can we consider the shift from *zhuan* to *cihua* in the title of the novel as a conscious effort to target a low-brow audience? From another perspective, we can perhaps say that the adoption of *cihua* as part of the novel's title signals a new attitude among some late Ming literati writers toward popular orality. Unlike Jin Shengtan 金聖歎 (1608–1661), the famous critic who was always ready to attribute the merits of a narrative work to a writing genius, the author or editor of JPM *cihua* flaunts the book's ties to popular and performing sources (see Chapter 2). Just like other Ming and Qing novels, JPM is cast in the so-called 'storyteller's manner'. In the first edition of 1617, the *cihua* edition, the meta-narrative formulary idiom, which defines the narrating instance as 'a storyteller' and occasionally specifies the narrator as a storyteller of *pinghua* 評話 (storytelling with commentary, or plain storytelling without music), is much richer and more developed than what is found in earlier novels and stories, such as *Shuihu zhuan*, almost to the point of parody (see Chapter 3).

Is it fruitful to compare the text of JPM with oral storytelling as it is still performed in China today? During the Copenhagen symposium we shall not try to answer a question of this type. But we have invited a storyteller from Yangzhou in China to perform selected episodes from the *Shuihu* 水滸 (*Water Margin*) repertoire of the famous school of Wang Shaotang 王少堂 (1889–1968). We shall experience the way in which storytellers of *Yangzhou pinghua* 揚州評話 (Yangzhou storytelling) perform some of the core episodes in the life of the main female protagonist, Pan Jinlian, episodes that are shared with the narrative of JPM (see Chapters 4 and 5).

Jin Ping Mei and Intertextuality

The *cihua* edition of JPM is not only the oldest edition that has been preserved to our time; it is the version of the text that stands out most clearly as a work of remarkably dense intertextuality. The fact that the novel incorporates the Wu Song saga and some other material from its predecessor *Shuihu zhuan* is of course one of the most obvious signs of intertextual borrowing, but it is also notable that in the composition of the work the quotation of a host of works circulating in the society of the time is a principle, not an exception. The novel can be considered a patchwork quilt. The narrative text is constantly interrupted by verses, songs, arias, theatrical plays, Daoist recitations and Buddhist edifying stories. The way in which these textual ingredients are used in the novel is not homogeneous. Sometimes the inserted texts function as a realistic framework, and sometimes their use is non-realistic (see Chapter 6). The role of opera scripts referred to in the novel implies diverse functions and purposes (see Chapter 7); and moreover, the customs and practices surrounding the

xxxii

INTRODUCTION

performances as described in the novel constitute a rich source for historical research on the theatre in China (see Chapter 8).

Jin Ping Mei and Print Culture

In the late 16th century JPM circulated only in manuscript copies. It was then printed early in the 17th century, apparently in editions on a small scale (with very few copies surviving). There is no doubt that the print culture that developed during the late Ming was decisive in terms of the way in which this work spread during the decades after it was first printed. One of the important developments in the printing of the work was the artwork of the illustrations that were added to the so-called Chongzhen (1628–1644) edition. These pictures were not part of the *cihua* edition but may well have been created at about the same time as this edition saw the light of day. They were published in an edition that was probably based on a manuscript that was roughly contemporaneous with the *cihua* text, although published a few years later. Boris Riftin (1932–2012), one of the foremost sinologists in the field of East Asian and Central Asian folklore and popular literature, was also an eminent scholar of Chinese book illustrations and folk prints. In 1984, he published an essay in German on the block-printed pictures of JPM, which we are reprinting in English translation. Important as it is for us to honour the name of this great scholar, it is equally important to bring his research into the Anglophone world of sinology (see Chapter 9).

The pictures of the Chongzhen edition are the first illustrations created for the work. Exquisite facsimile reprints were produced in the 1930s in China from the *cihua* edition when it first was discovered, and apparently these editions included the illustrations from the Chongzhen edition, even though they did not belong to that edition. When the *cihua* edition was later reproduced in Hong Kong and Taiwan for a general readership, the Chongzhen illustrations were also inserted into the text or were placed separately. These pictures are of a far better quality than those re-cut for later editions, such as the reproductions from 'an old edition of 1755' for the German translation by Otto and Artur Kibat (see below). When the first translation of the *cihua* edition into a European language was published, namely the French translation by André Lévy, it was furnished with the Chongzhen illustrations. This was also the case when David Tod Roy published his English translation (1993–2013). Thereafter, the 200 pictures from the Chongzhen edition became the generally known illustrations for JPM among Western readers, and in a way they were associated more with the *cihua* edition than with the original Chongzhen edition. While JPM is a text of the utmost interest for literary studies, the

xxxiii

pictures are no less interesting and represent a world of their own of art and craft (see Chapter 10).

The JPM illustrations also show how the interplay between text and image creates room for development of the text within the microcosm of the one-page image. The woodcuts, like other pictorial art forms, fix the flowing movement of the physical world for a moment and allow quiet contemplation. With their captions roughly corresponding to the chapter titles of the work, they also serve as a kind of bridge linking the parts of the book. At times the illustrations have been published as separate picture books, evoking the storyline of the written work for the onlooker (see Chapter 11). In the Chinese block-print industry there is a long tradition of re-cutting old blocks that are worn down or destroyed. This is equally true of the blocks used for book illustrations. As was the case with the Chongzhen edition, the first edition of JPM with illustrations, there is a long and unbroken tradition of copying the illustrations in later editions, by having the artists at the printers re-cut the pictures. Such re-cut blocks are not identical to the original set. In the case of JPM, we can see that during the 17th and 18th century the illustrations were re-cut, basically according to the Chongzhen illustrations, but with obvious differences in cutting technique and style. In this book we present a master of wood block cutting from the present time. Mr. Liu Kun 劉坤 has worked throughout his life at the famous 400-year-old printing house, the Guangling Book Society of Yangzhou (Guangling Shushe 廣陵書社). In 2018 he completed his unique series of the 200 pictures from the Chongzhen edition, re-cut, and published using old-style paper and binding, as *Jin Ping Mei banhua* 金瓶梅版画 (*Jin Ping Mei* woodcuts). His technique and the prints themselves will be presented during the symposium, and selected samples of his art are displayed in the present volume (see Chapter 12).

Jin Ping Mei as Forbidden Literature

When JPM circulated in manuscript form at the turn of the 17th century it was extolled by the famous critic Yuan Hongdao 袁宏道 (1568–1610) as one of the foremost works in its time and put on a par with *Shuihu zhuan*. Later, the novel received high praise from a gifted young Chinese critic of the late 17th century, Zhang Zhupo 張竹坡 (1670–1698). Zhang's insightful textual commentary and editing of the text, together with the title he bestowed on the work, *Di yi qishu* 第一奇書 ('The Number One Marvellous Book'), soon made his commented version of JPM a standard edition. However, the erotic descriptions distributed throughout the book soon led to its being harshly suppressed by Qing dynasty authorities. The book was branded 'obscene' and

INTRODUCTION

was strictly suppressed, with one exception: it was translated into Manchu, which enabled the Qing ruling class to enjoy this work in secret.

Despite being classified as a 'forbidden' book, the work has circulated in China for 400 years and has been highly praised by famous literary personalities. During the last four decades the book has won a reputation in China as one of the most outstanding works of the Chinese literary canon. Nevertheless, the book is not generally for sale in complete editions in Chinese bookshops. Only 'purged' editions, devoid of the descriptions of sexual activities, are readily available (see Chapter 13). The explicit portrayal of sex found in the two early editions, the *cihua* and the Chongzhen editions, amounts to only a very small percentage of the entire text, but enough to establish its notoriety. Many later editions, both in China and elsewhere, sought to delete or soften such passages to make the book tolerable in a given context, but can we regard this as anything other than a crippling of the work? Can we afford to close our eyes to the inherent role – linguistic, aesthetic and thematic – that the erotic plays in JPM? (See Chapter 14).

In the West, popular translations of JPM of the first half of the 20th century were effectively 'cleaned' and adapted by popular translators into editions in which not only were the most 'offensive' sexual descriptions suppressed or toned down, but a considerable proportion of the verses and other intertexts were also removed, to create a handier, less 'boring' book. Publishers and translators cooperated in transforming the original work to cater to the tastes of a readership that still clung to Victorian standards but nevertheless had a taste for exotic entertainment. The efforts of the early translators such as Clement Egerton (1884–1960s?) and Franz Kuhn (1884–1961), who translated from Chinese originals, should, however, not be underestimated. What happened to these editions in the hands of *their* translators and adaptors is another story, bringing us into contact with slick European bookstall literature and soft porn (see Chapter 15).

One of the 'dirty' words of the sexual vocabulary, a word that is generally not found in Chinese dictionaries (apart from JPM dictionaries), *ri* 肏 (to fuck), is here scrutinized in relation to its use in the two early editions of JPM – the *cihua* edition and the Chongzhen edition – its sexual and vulgar meanings, and its equivalents in the two main English translations, Egerton (1939) and David Tod Roy (1993–2013). A study such as this would have been practically unheard of until recently. In fact, with this linguistically rigorous approach we gain much insight into the way individual protagonists, such as Pan Jinlian and Wang the Sixth, are characterized through their frequent use of this word, both to swear and to describe the act. What happens in the two translations – half a century apart and created on the two sides of the Atlantic Ocean – is no less interesting (see Chapter 16).

XXXV

In Japan, great Chinese novels such as *Sanguo yanyi* 三国演义 (Three Kingdoms), *Shuihu zhuan*, and *Xiyou ji* 西遊記 (Journey to the West) were very well received and became folk entertainment on a large scale. JPM did not have the same fate but remained what was described as an 'under-the-desk-book' well into the 20th century. Its fame as 'a book that invites lust' placed it in the category of 'obscene books', but in Japan during the Edo period (1603–1867) the authorities did not put a ban on such books, and JPM was relatively well known though few had read it. It should not be forgotten that the educated Japanese of this time were well-versed in Chinese. Around 1750, a learned commentary to the vocabulary of JPM was produced in manuscript, but never printed. Kyokutei Bakin (曲亭馬琴, 1767–1848), one of the most famous novelists of the time, made an adaptation of JPM with pictures, but purged of the sexual descriptions. However, his promotion of the book was probably an important stimulus for its subsequent translation into vernacular Japanese during the Meiji period (1868–1912) (see Chapter 17).

In this section we finally present a rearranged translation of Martin Gimm's article in German (*Oriens Extremus* 2003–4) about a Manchu ballad, *zidi shu* 子弟書 ('gentry tale') with a theme deriving from JPM, dated to the years just before 1800. We shall not lift the curtain in front of this piece but will let our readers see for themselves how the JPM was enjoyed in the bilingual society of the Manchu gentry (see Chapter 18).

Jin Ping Mei in China and in the World

The influence of JPM on the Chinese novel and other literary genres is a long story. Most remarkable is the way in which JPM left its mark on the famous 18th century novel, *Honglou meng* 紅樓夢 (A Dream of Red Mansions, hereafter HLM) (1792) by Cao Xueqin 曹雪芹 (fl. first half of the 18th century). That HLM would soon overshadow its ancestor, JPM, in the Chinese canon, seems closely related to the treatment of the private and the official in the two works. Today, HLM is usually considered the greatest masterpiece of the Chinese novels of the Ming and Qing periods. HLM is a book that lends itself to the enjoyment of young girls and innocent youngsters without much 'harm', and the whole work has a mild and nostalgic tone – far from the harsh social and human realism of its predecessor. In contrast, JPM is compared to 'a wild horse', bolting away over ten thousand miles, shaking off and trampling customary age-old morals and principles. 'Frankly and without shame, the work displays the secrets of human nature and a life of sensual delight and disreputable acts' (see Chapter 19)

INTRODUCTION

The reception of JPM in its own country, in nearby countries and in the West seems to say more about the target readers of the book than about the book itself. The first translation of the novel was into Manchu, the language of the Qing rulers, who were strictly suppressing 'immoral' literature in the enormous area under their jurisdiction during the entire era. However, in 1708, about 100 years after the first printing of JPM, a Manchu translation, *Gin ping mei bithe*, was issued in print, supported by the Manchu nobility, and maybe even translated by an imperial prince (Chapter 20). Step by step, the novel was found and translated into European languages, first from Manchu into German by the learned and highly esteemed linguist, Hans Conon von der Gabelentz (1807–1874). This translation was considered lost after Gabelentz' death, but the manuscript has recently been recovered by Professor Martin Gimm, who has edited and published this fruit of Gabelentz' pioneer achievement (2005–2013). Since the translation was left unfinished and only the family knew about it, it had no impact in European intellectual circles at the time.

Information about Chinese philosophical and literary texts spread from French missionaries in China. JPM was already being discussed in these circles in the middle of the 19th century. The French diplomat Georges Soulié de Morant (1878–1955), well versed in Chinese and a prolific translator of Chinese medical books and love stories, produced the first abridged and adapted version of JPM, *Lotus-d'or* (1912), which was later translated into English. Meanwhile, however, an utterly complete and faithful translation into German, *Djin Ping Meh, Schlehen-blüten in goldener Vase,* (1928–32, 1967) was being undertaken by the brothers Otto Kibat (1880–1956) and Artur Kibat (1878–1961) from East Prussia, based on the Chinese edition by Zhang Zhupo (see above). Otto had spent 18 years altogether in China in German–Chinese trade, and Artur had joined him for some years in China. When both returned to their homeland after World War I, they decided to jointly embark on the production of the first-ever complete translation of JPM into a European language (3,000 pages). After the publication of the initial two small volumes (1928–32), the work was burned by the Nazi government in 1933. The brothers, however, continued their translation in secret, and the complete work was published posthumously (1967). This early initiative could not under such circumstances have any substantial influence among the European readers. But it was and is a monument to the brothers' deep familiarity with Chinese culture and to their diligence and perseverance in accomplishing their aim against all odds. It is a rich source for any student of JPM (see Chapter 21).

As mentioned above, it was only with the German translation (1930) by the lawyer and translator from Chinese, Franz Kuhn that the novel gained a solid readership in the Western world. This translation became the fundamental

xxxvii

text on which a host of translations into other European languages were based. It goes without saying that the erotic and pornographic aspects of the novel were downplayed in order not to offend public decency. However, roughly contemporary with Kuhn's German translation, an edition in English was prepared by Clement Egerton, who worked together with the Chinese author Lao She (1899–1966) and was able to accomplish a translation of fluent style and reasonable accuracy, even though it was also considerably shortened and streamlined according to Western norms of morality. These two translations, by Kuhn and Egerton respectively, both based on the standard 17th-century edition of Zhang Zhupo, were the background for the transmission of JPM into European and American milieux from the 1940s to 1980s.

When, in 1933 in China, the *cihua* edition, *Jin Ping Mei cihua* (1617), came to light, this led to Western translators slowly but steadily turning their attention towards this edition as possibly the most trustworthy source for the original handwritten copies. We have already mentioned Lévy's French translation of 1985 (see Chapter 1). About a decade later, David Tod Roy (1933–2016), professor of Chinese at the University of Chicago, began to publish his American-English translation of the same source text, published as *Chin P'ing Mei, or The Plum in the Golden Vase* (1993–2013). This work grew into a formidable research tool for later generations of students and colleagues, since notes, appendixes and other paratexts swelled to about a third of the complete five-volume edition spanning nearly 4,000 pages (see Chapter 22). As such, Roy's work was very different from both Lévy's two-volume edition in light *papier bible*, and Oldrich Král's (1930–2018) Czech edition, *Jin Ping Mei aneb Slivoň ve zlaté váze* (2012–2018), planned for ten elegant and handy volumes with only sparse annotation. A chapter of our book is devoted to the question of how to translate the architectural surroundings of the Ximen Qing mansion into a European language and culture of the present, in this case the Král translation as continued by Lucie Olivová and Ondřej Vicher (see Chapter 23).

We finish the section about '*Jin Ping Mei* in China and in the World' with a review of the great harvest of translations of this masterwork into numerous languages all over the globe. Since the 47th year of Kangxi (1708), when the first translation of JPM by a Manchu nobleman saw the light of day, the work has been translated (including fragmentary translations) into nearly 30 languages, including Belgian, Czech, Danish, Dutch, English, Finnish, French, German, Hungarian, Italian, Japanese, Korean, Latin, Manchu, Mongolian, Polish, Romanian, Russian, Swedish, Vietnamese, Yugoslavian, and more... (see Chapter 24).

INTRODUCTION

Let us bring our introduction to an end and invite the reader to engage with the real thing, or to borrow one of the stock phrases of Chinese storytelling in the traditional novels: 'IF YOU DO NOT KNOW WHAT HAPPENS THEN, PLEASE, LISTEN TO THE NEXT ROUND OF THE STORY!'

Jin Ping Mei and Oral Storytelling

CHAPTER I

Jin Ping Mei and the Art of Storytelling

ANDRÉ LÉVY

May this chapter stand as just an appetizer! It is presented before the courses of the main meal that is to follow. My aim is to remind readers how much the controversies around *Jin Ping Mei* have been conducive to the neglect of the role of the art of storytelling. Mention of the famous novel was made around 1800 by the Catholic mission at Peking, but it was really brought to the attention of learned sphere when it was quoted by the first Western sinologist, Abel-Rémusat (1788–1832), two years after he was promoted to a chair at the *College de France* in 1814. Let me quote some of the few lines that sent the Western world dreaming of forbidden treasures:

> [...] moral corruption is as widespread in China as in any other country [...] There are a great many books in which the most outrageous cynicism prevails [...] Here we have a book of tales which can be classed in this respect next to Petronius and Martial [...] *Jin Ping Mei*, a famous novel, is said to be above, or rather below anything licentious produced by decadent Rome or modern Europe. I know it only by repute, and although it was condemned by the court in Peking, it did manage to find a translator, one of the brothers of the famous emperor Kangxi; and this prince's version in the Manchu language is regarded as a masterpiece of elegance and fidelity.'[1]

As far as I know, the earliest explicit prohibition of the Manchu version was somewhat later, in the Yongzheng reign. But the Chinese original is said to have been specifically condemned only as late as 1867. Of course, there was

---

1   See Rémusat 1939: 97.

This paper is a slightly revised reprint of the late André Lévy's (1925–2017) contribution to the symposium 'The Interplay of Oral and Written Traditions in Chinese Fiction, Drama and Performance Literature', The Norwegian Academy of Science, Oslo, 5–6 November 2007, printed in Børdahl and Wan 2010, 13–29. Reprint courtesy of NIAS Press and the editors.

an implicit prohibition, which incited daring publishers to multiply rare and costly editions. The Manchu authorities tried, in fact, to stop any attempt to translate it as early as 1635, even before the conquest of China, but to no avail under a more liberal reign, as Kangxi's version, printed in 1708, did exist and a copy of that translation fell into the hands of the German scholar Hans Conon von der Gabelentz (1807–1874) who started putting it in German between 1862 and 1869, leaving us a manuscript forgotten till 1998.[2]

Re-translation via the Manchu language was fairly common among the few early sinologists but disappeared with the generations that followed. However, re-translations from Chinese through other languages were admitted as fair game much later, and still are in my own day. Chinese was reputed to be so much more difficult! Of course, that was some 40 years ago. Étiemble (1909–2002), late professor emeritus of comparative literature at the Sorbonne, chaired the jury before which I had to talk about the rise of vernacular short stories in 17th century China. He thought that he had found, at long last, a fellow who could give him a more complete translation of *Jin Ping Mei* than those then available in French. In short, the novel was a work he admired, as free from the Christian prejudices that afflicted Western society. He planned to get such a translation included in the prestigious collection of world literature called *La Pléiade*, soon after its soon-to-be-published cousin, so to speak, *Shuihu zhuan,* which was called, in French, *Au bord de l'eau* (1978). First Etiemble asked me if I could read German. Somewhat taken aback, I said yes. Then, later, he introduced me to the ageing head of the Gallimard family and mentioned acquiring the rights to translate into French the German version by the brothers Kibat. It was a complete translation of what was, at that time, the current edition of *Jin Ping Mei,* established at the end of the 17th century by Zhang Zhupo 張竹坡. In fact, it was not yet fully published at the time, but was in production by the Swiss firm *Die Waage* in Zürich. The fifth and last volume was to appear in 1982. The first was published in 1967 and was in fact a reissue of the ones burned in Hitler's Germany when I was about 10 years old, in the 30s. I had to point out that it was precisely in the thirties that a different, more ancient edition was discovered in China, and that – besides – I was the lucky owner of a photostat of a slightly better copy of the same rare edition, this time found in Japan. Third, I pointed out that this *cihua* edition was likely to be closer to the original manuscript[3] and was not yet translated

---

2   See Gimm 2005. Conon was the father of the better-known sinologist Georg (1840–1893), the author of the famous *Chinesische Grammatik* (1883). He and his brother Albert (1834–1892) worked with his father, who produced *Eléments de la grammaire mandchoue* in 1832.

3   See Wrenn 1964.

JIN PING MEI AND THE ART OF STORYTELLING

the world over, but only in Japan where the objectionable portions were left in the original Chinese.[4]

Do I need to add that I felt more at ease with Chinese than with German? The arguments hit their target. That is how I was drawn into battling with the not always easy Chinese of the *Jin Ping Mei cihua* text for seven years, pretty long ago. Perhaps the Fates had decided it even earlier. Is it not a strange coincidence that some 10 years earlier I had translated two pieces[5] that happened to be those cleverly woven into the beginnings of the *cihua*? They do stress what the novel will deal with – the dangers of sexual indulgence. But this reminds me that I share now some of the ailments old Zhang found himself afflicted with after he acquired as a new young concubine, Golden Lotus.[6] Let me just mention that my hearing is getting dull and will need your forbearance. I have to confess that seven years translating *Jin Ping Mei* while teaching and managing the centre for Far-Eastern studies at Bordeaux was a pretty short time, meaning that I was often in a regrettable hurry. Fortunately, in a way, the novel was not yet a good field of research to be associated with. So, I was spared a lot of precious or futile readings. After the publication of my translation in 1985, the studies on *Jin Ping Mei* that resumed on the mainland by the eighties turned into an outpouring that I was unable to cope with, as I had to handle many other successive jobs. The level of critical sophistication reached new heights I dared not climb. Still, after 20 years of estrangement from *Jin Ping Mei* it seems that no radical changes have taken place in this field, so that I do not yet feel that the introduction to my translation written a quarter of a century ago is completely obsolete. It seems to me that a radical polarization has taken place between two opposite camps, the one depreciative and the other laudatory. In fact, the two incompatible poles were already germinating much earlier, nearly a century ago.

Students of the early westernization of China may be aware of the long exchange of letters between Qian Xuantong 錢玄同 (1887–1939) and Hu Shi 胡適 (1891–1962). This took place in 1917 and the letters were published with Hu Shi's writings in 1921.[7] Let us cut short the details of their arguments, however much these may be worth considering. From a literary angle, free from common prejudices, Qian Xuantong placed *Jin Ping Mei* in first place, as a verbal monument and an exposure of social hypocrisy, putting it above

---

4   Ono Shinobu and Chida Kuichi 1960.

5   See Lévy 1971b and 1972.

6   See page 27 of David Roy's translation (1993), and page 32 of mine (Lévy 1985), in the first chapter of *Jin Ping Mei cihua*.

7   See Hu Shi, *Hu Shi wencun* 1953: 41–54.

ANDRÉ LÉVY

even *Honglou meng*, as did the ageing Sun Kaidi 孫楷第 (1898–1986) when I was privileged to meet him in the early 80s, praising the forcefulness, the *qi* 氣 of *Jin Ping Mei*.[8] Did not Zhang Zhupo draw on the same line of argument at the end of the 17th century with his *ku shuo* 苦說, the thesis that it was bitterness that was the driver behind the production of a work like this? For Hu Shi, on the contrary, *Jin Ping Mei* belongs to the sort of book that is devoid of any value from a literary viewpoint.[9] Why? Because, he thought, it was of the sort that induces no aesthetic pleasure, no 'feeling of beauty'. Though both were for 'complete modernization' along Western lines, they handled different parameters of questionable validity. Hu Shi called for more translations of foreign material, while hoping for indigenous production some 50 years ahead. Here we may pinpoint the roots of a rather confusing situation in the present day regarding this object of contention.

Why this astonishing paradox, of a 'number one' masterpiece still unavailable in intact condition in its own country?[10] One way out is to deny it any value, as did young Hu Shi 90 years ago. Is this not the same stance taken today by the veteran scholar Liu Shide 劉世德? After a talk on the enigma surrounding the author of *Jin Ping Mei* given this year in February and relayed by *People Online* 人民網,[11] Professor Liu Shide was asked by a female member of the audience why the *Jin Ping Mei*, which requires the attention of so many scholars, was still prohibited. He replied by reiterating the axiomatic saying that a 'great work' (*weida* 偉大) must come out of one great mind and one great artist, denying the qualification of 'great' for a work of such a low value. Is this stance personal rather than official? Whatever the case, the *Encyclopedia of Chinese Classical Fiction* 中國古代百科全書 directed by the same Professor Liu Shide nevertheless has a sizeable entry for *Jin Ping Mei* signed by Liu Hui 劉輝. If *Jin Ping Mei* is not to be counted among the great masterworks, why should it be neither cumulative, *jileide* 積累的, nor collective, *jitide* 集體的? Professor Liu Shide emphatically denied such possibilities. He did not elaborate on this point, which he considered obvious, though he proffered a relentless scepticism about some 15 personalities worth mentioning among the 50 to 60 candidates

---

8 若拋棄一切世俗見解，專用文學的眼光去觀察，則金瓶梅之位置故亦在第一流。Hu Shi 1953, 50.

9 此重書即以文學的眼光觀之，一殊無價值。何則? 文學之一要素，在於《美感》。請問先生讀金瓶梅，作何美感? Hu Shi 1953: 43.

10 See my review of Sun Suyu's aesthetics of *Jin Ping Mei*, Lévy 1986, 528–532, where I pinpointed this paradox, which is apparently keenly felt in China.

11 Liu Shide 2007.

JIN PING MEI AND THE ART OF STORYTELLING

for authorship so far presented in so many inconclusive studies: a quadrupling, I am afraid, since I wrote my introduction a quarter century ago.

There are now two places where the famous *roman-fleuve* is said to have been composed. One is at Yixian 邑縣, formerly Lanling 蘭陵, in Shandong: there you may see the tree above a small cascade under which Jia Sanjin 賈三近 wrote the masterwork. I saw the spot being built with my own eyes when I participated in the first or second international conference on *Jin Ping Mei* in the mid-80s.[12] The other place, in Huizhou 徽州 district, Anhui 安徽 province, is a more recent location. I confess I have not seen nor read the report of the discovery of Gou Dong 苟洞 a few years ago. This attribution to a Wang Daokun 汪道昆 is ignored by Professor Liu Shide, but the tourist attraction under construction is mentioned in the newspaper map introducing Professor Liu Shide. Does it add a touch of ridicule to this fancy idea of how *Jin Ping Mei* was conceived? Professor Liu Shide concludes humorously that it would be better to apply the term *Jinxue* to the studies of Jin Yong 金庸's *wuxia xiaoshuo* and create the term 'scoffing studies', *Xiaoxue*, for those on *Jin Ping Mei,* since the obscure author of *Jin Ping Mei* calls himself Xiaoxiaosheng 笑笑生 and most studies of *Jin Ping Mei* are in search of a likely author.

Jin Yong (Louis Cha, 1924–) himself used to say that most writers, since the Hu Shi/ Qian Xuantong controversy, have produced only Western fiction in Chinese, while he alone has continued to compose real Chinese novels, the secret of his immense popular success. Whatever the stand to be taken regarding this dictum, it recalls a break with traditional fiction that cannot be ignored. Several factors that favoured the rise of fiction in the West were present in China much earlier. This fact is commonly recognised. Even if all of them were similar, it would be fallacious to expect products with western features as the end result of normal evolution. I am afraid today critics do not take sufficiently into account the specificities of different cultures or civilisations. The art of storytelling reached quite early in China a degree of refinement and maturity unknown in the West. But it was an art of entertainment confined to despised ranks of society. Vernaculars did not succeed in pushing out classical culture before the Western intrusion. Europe drew on its own multilingual and multicultural landscape, which added to its dynamism. Did China find something equivalent in its literature of entertainment in the vernacular? Was the 17th century simply an abortive turning point? Well, no simple answers can be provided to questions that are so crude. Still, Qian Daxin 錢大昕 (1728–1804) was not taking *xiaoshuo*, fiction, so lightly. For him, though

---

12 Zhang Yuanfen 1983.

despised, it was a vehicle of evil pervading all ranks of society.[13] Would such a complaint, uttered at the end of the 18th century, apply in the 16th century? Why not, if we challenge the accepted idea, *idée reçue*, of a progressive evolution towards a western model of fiction?

Negative as well as positive evaluations are legitimate as long as we remain aware of their references to extraneous criteria. They are not irrelevant but are, in both cases, of questionable propriety. Is it not by a misappropriation of a sort that *Jin Ping Mei* is passed off as a 'literati novel'? Let us quote at some length from Andrew Plaks before dealing with this notion:

> [...] my readings of these 'amazing books' are based on the conviction that they yield the most meaningful interpretations when viewed not simply as compendia of popular narrative materials, but as reflections of the cultural values and intellectual concerns of the sophisticated literary circles of the late Ming period. I believe that the fullest recensions of each of these novels were composed by and for the same sort of people who gave us the startlingly original achievements of Ming 'literati painting' and the gems of the contemporary 'literati stage', which is why I speak of them with the somewhat pretentious and perhaps misleading term 'literati novels.'[14]

It is true that small but influential circles of literati expressed an unusual interest in many kinds of popular arts. Can we say that by putting their finger on that sort of stuff, they turn it into the gold of higher literature? I am afraid that we have here a response, though not an answer, to the depreciative posture of C.T. Hsia's epoch-making critical introduction to *The Classic Chinese Novel* published by Columbia University Press in 1968. His blunt critical weapon fell harshly on *Jin Ping Mei*. Let us quote from page 166:

> 'Its generous inclusion of songs and jokes, of mundane and Buddhist tales, constantly mars the naturalistic texture of its narrative so that, from the viewpoint of style and structure, it must be rated the most disappointing novel we have thus far considered.'

And from page 169:

> In a sense, the novel is almost a poetic anthology within a narrative framework'. Professor Hsia rejects any attribution to a 'great' author among the literati

---

13 See several derogatory remarks in his *Shijiazhai yangxin lu* 十駕齋養新錄: 'After the Song and Yuan period scholars who could boast of their abilities considered it shameful to produce it (fiction) [...] 宋元以後士之能自立者皆恥而不為矣. What follows is even more clearly disparaging for storytellers. Cf. the remarks in *Guisi cungao* 癸巳存搞; both are reprinted in Kong Lingjing 1982: 258–59.

14 Plaks 1987: ix.

as no 'genius could have fathered a book of such low culture and ordinary mentality.

How can we explain the fact that less than 40 years later the presentation of the novel in an important compendium testifies to a complete reversal of this depreciative judgment shared by both professors C.T. Hsia and Liu Shide? Forgive me for citing at length the entry on *Jin Ping Mei* in the *Encyclopedia of Erotic Literature* edited by Gaëtan Brulotte and John Phillips.[15] Though not signed, it follows fairly faithfully the views of David Roy, the great translator of the *Jin Ping Mei cihua*, now an enterprise in its final stage:

> *Jin Ping Mei*, first published in 1618 or shortly thereafter, is the first major Chinese novel to have a cohesive narrative, to be written by a single author, and to be an original creation. It is unlike almost all earlier novels – which developed from the repertoire of professional storytellers – engaging in new modes of representation. *Jin Ping Mei* is acutely aware of its divergence from the established form of the vernacular novel in China, which allows it to incorporate an almost encyclopedic range of texts and genres, such as jokes, popular songs, comic skits, and short stories, which were all made available to a wider audience than ever before because of the boom of commercial publishing... *Jin Ping Mei* is also a milestone in the development of narrative fiction in world literature. With the possible exception of the *Tale of Genji* (1010) and *Don Quixote* (1615), there is no earlier work of prose fiction of comparable sophistication and depth...

Elsewhere, in the introduction to Professor Roy's translation, the *Jin Ping Mei* is said to be reminiscent of Joyce's *Ulysses* and Nabokov's *Lolita*.[16]

Would you allow a few comments? Abel-Rémusat wrote that it was a Chinese *Petronius;* inspired by a Marxist approach, some Chinese critics evoked a Chinese Zola. I am not sure that such comparisons do justice to the Chinese masterwork. I do not think that the significance of the *Jin Ping Mei* can be negated as flippantly as Professor Liu does, but I do not feel that it should be overstated the way Professor Roy suggests. There is no need to quibble about the different meanings of *Weltliteratur* since the time when Goethe was among the first to handle this notion in his talks with Eckermann in 1827. The status of a milestone can be acknowledged, but should not imply that *Jin Ping Mei* fathered similar offspring or that a kind of Chinese Cervantes conceived and penned this verbal monument seated at his desk or crouched under a tree. The importance of the *Odyssey* in our western culture does not require us to believe it sprang fully armed from a single mind. Since the 18th century the Homeric question testifies to this unsolved

---

15 Brulotte and Phillips 2006: 698–701.

16 See the inner jacket of the first volume of David Roy's translation of *Jin Ping Mei* (1993).

ANDRÉ LÉVY

enigma. Is some degree of comparable sophistication to be found in *Jin Ping Mei* and Joyce's *Ulysses*? Really? I am not inclined to think that the significance of *Jin Ping Mei* would be in the least impaired by dragging it out of the prejudiced clutches of literati, whether practitioners of Chinese traditional high literature or westernized critics. Should we agree that the established form of the vernacular novel in China allowed *Jin Ping Mei* to incorporate an almost encyclopedic range of texts and genres, such as jokes, popular songs, comic skits, and short stories, which were all made available to a wider audience than ever before because of the boom of commercial publishing? Yes, indeed, but to impute to *Jin Ping Mei* an acute awareness of its divergence seems a not very meaningful subjective judgment. I am afraid that the impulses to magnify the novel by reducing the role of storytellers and their art has had a rather negative effect. We may not be fully aware of the extent of our ignorance. Testimonies are very fragmentary throughout the ages, limited to what has come to us in random fashion from popular oral or written materials. How much do we know of those countless popular kinds of entertainment of the past? Probably very little.

After all, *Jin Ping Mei* offers us the first instance of a work for which we have so much information about its prepublication stage and so little about its birth, so as to generate endless speculation. To declare it as having been 'written by a single author, and an original creation' may not be conducive to understanding it in the context of a sphere of entertainment dominated by storytellers and all sorts of jugglers of words. Let us try to sum up the situation in this sort of cryptic way. A small group of eminent literati in the cultural sphere over two decades in the late Ming exchanged and copied impressive manuscripts which never amounted to a complete set. At least two sets were prepared, perhaps three. One was completed differently by two different publishers, the earlier perhaps in 10 instalments. The other, in 20, not yet ready, never went into print. There is not the slightest hint that the author could in fact be a member of the group of literati interested in its publication. The first scholar to mention a manuscript, Yuan Hongdao 袁宏道 (1568–1610), found its reading relaxing and jocular. Later his younger brother, Yuan Zhongdao 袁中道 (1570–1624) thought its content highly incorrect; better to hush it up.[17] There is some irony in the fact that the owner of the first part of the manuscript mentioned above, Dong Qichang 董其場 (1555–1636), was himself the target of a slanderous book which 'soon became popular' and 'found its way into the repertoire of the wandering minstrels.'[18]

I do not mean that we should jump to the conclusion that *Jin Ping Mei* belonged at the start to this genre of slanderous literature, almost entirely lost,

---

17 About this manuscript stage, see Hanan 1962: 39–42.
18 See Nelson I. Wu 1962: 260–293, especially p. 287.

JIN PING MEI AND THE ART OF STORYTELLING

though fairly common at the time.[19] It is not an unlikely possibility. Early connoisseurs mentioned it. Oral or written sources? The one does not preclude the other. Such items circulated long before in manuscripts, occasionally printed, often suppressed. In the West roughly at the same time, for example in France, they had equivalents of a sort in the *nouvelles à la main*, 'hand-written news', mostly scandalous. There must have been an abundant literature, printed or not, sung or told, which is now completely lost, but in a tenor more or less reminiscent of *Jin Ping Mei*. We can even imagine a reversal of the rather conservative thesis of Zhu Xing 朱星[20] defending an originally pure *Jin Ping Mei*, stuffed with obscenities by commercial publishers. *Youxi wenxue* 遊戲文學, sketches, skits, jokes of a sexual nature, typically vulgar, may have been the nutshell, so to speak, the magnet attracting the venomous story-stuff contained in chapters 23 to 27 of the *Shuihu zhuan*.[21] When Zhang Dai 張岱 (1597–1689) remembers listening to a tale told in the Northern slang from *Jin Ping Mei* in 1634, can we be sure that that was a part of our novel, as it was so jocular that the audience bent over and fell down laughing?[22] Must we consider the few *zidi shu* 子弟書 we know of by their titles as being without a doubt derivative, extracted from the written novel, and not from a tradition of oral materials? More investigations are needed.

I am afraid the quest to find a 'great author' for a great work has led us away from the main problem. Should we take the masterpiece as having fallen out of the blue fully equipped, before turning over every stone likely to explain its birth? Why should oral literature tarnish it?

Negative as well as positive appreciation fail for this reason to do full justice to this question. It has been said that Zhang Zhupo gave *Jin Ping Mei* a second skin.[23] Trying to substantiate the comparison with Joyce's *Ulysses* may give it a third one, likely to distort it further. Of course, these skins are not to be despised; they bring new vistas and deserve due appraisal for their sophistication. But are they not misleading?

Are they not liable to divert us from a proper understanding of the complex interconnections between oral and written literature? The market for popular

---

19 See the preface of Ling Mengchu to the *Erke Pai'an jingqi* (1633).

20 Zhu Xing 1980.

21 See Lévy 1971A and 1969.

22 See Zhang Dai, *Tao'an mengyi*, 卷四不係園, 《 用北調說金瓶梅一劇, 使人絕倒。》Cf. Zhang Dai, *Souvenirs rêvés de Tao'an*, traduit et annoté par Brigitte Teboul-Wang, p. 74 : 'Au dixième mois de l'année [...] il nous conta avec l'accent du Nord un passage de *Fleur en Fiole d'Or* qui nous ravit' is a questionable translation of 絕倒 and may not refer to the novel, though it is later than its first publication.

23 See Ding Naifei 2002: 121.

ANDRÉ LÉVY

books began thriving in China much earlier than in Europe. There were already centuries of obscure interrelationships when Zhao Qimei 趙琦美 (1563–1624) related how he had found a rare copy of Duan Chengshi's 段成式 *Youyang zazu* 酉陽雜俎, in his preface to this work, dated at about the time when the *Jin Ping Mei cihua* appeared, the first printed copy of which, by the way, was discovered in the far North, in Shanxi:

> In the busiest part of the shop-market in the centre of Suzhou, documents are always displayed under people's eaves, the so-called bookstalls. What they sell are just short stories, 'affairs behind the door', songbooks and the like. So-called 'affairs behind the door' are entirely of the sort sung and told by boys and girls in the women's quarters...[24]

吳中廛市閙處，輒有書傑籍列人詹劄下，謂之書攤子，所鬻者悉小説門事唱本之類。所謂門事，皆閨中兒女子所唱說也。

I am not sure of my translation, nor of the authenticity of the text as I found it, but it says enough to evoke the complexities of the cultural surroundings in which *Jin Ping Mei* was born.

Let us admit it: the more noticeable the presence of the storyteller in a vernacular story, the more likely is its conventional nature; the more skilful the re-appropriation of the storyteller's language, the more likely it is to be an imitation without real oral sources. In any case it is a testimony of the influence of the art of storytelling, direct or indirect, on traditional fiction in the vernacular as a whole. After all, some half a century ago John Bishop denounced its limiting effects.[25] Whether felt to be negative or positive, these effects are not to be appreciated as if traditional Chinese fiction was born to grow into our sort of modern fiction. Surely, we have to allow for a written stage and a printing stage. But it is not in our agenda to deal further with this here.

Of course, imitation is more common than direct oral origin. By producing a *contrario* to this kind of naïve argument, Pan Kaipei's plea for an oral origin for *Jin Ping Mei* has been easily dismissed.[26] Almost all the reviews of the studies on *Jin Ping Mei* in the last half century mention his failure with a nostalgic

---

24 Zhao Qimei preface 趙琦美序 in Duan Chengshi 1981: 253. See Anne McLaren 1983: 7 and Ye Dejun 1957.

25 See Bishop 1955–6: 239–247.

26 See Pan Kaipei 1959: 173–180. 'It has been adequately rebutted,' considers Patrick Hanan in his epoch-making study on the sources of the *Jin Ping Mei*. Hanan 1963: 24 note 2.

tinge.[27] The tale of Wu Song and the tiger is commonly held to have been copied from an unknown edition of the written novel *Shuihu zhuan*, but in her study of the drum tale Vibeke Børdahl points out that borrowing from the oral tradition is more likely. Besides, any unbiased reader would admit a stylistic gap between Li Yu's *Rou putuan* and *Jin Ping Mei*. Should it be explained by the time interval? Hardly likely, if the texts are less than half a century apart, whether or not we accept David Roy's attribution to Tang Xianzu.[28] Patrick Hanan pointed this out in the preface to his masterful translation of *Rou putuan* 肉蒲團, *The Carnal Prayer Mat*.[29] The differences between this and *Jin Ping Mei* are so patent that they need no elaboration. That is why Xu Shuofang's hypothesis sounds more plausible after all: a refraction and emendation of older storytellers' materials by Li Kaixian 李開先 (1502–1568).[30]

Let us accept this: the sheer difference in size between the two most famous pornographic works of fiction in China makes them hardly comparable. In a way the plot of *The Carnal Prayer Mat* is much more intricate than that of *Jin Ping Mei*. It sounds like an invention of literati for literati. At the other extreme, the intrigues of *Jin Ping Mei* could be the plot of *xiaoshuo* in the Song meaning of storytelling, told in one session. The amplification to some 800,000 characters in one single jump seems all the more unlikely. An oral stage of some length is not to be excluded, nor a leap or a glide from one genre of storytelling to the other. Perhaps some genre belonging to *xiaoshu* 小書. *Xiaoshu*, meaning minor tales – minor in the sense that they concern minor affairs – is defined in opposition to *dashu* 大書, which are about major historical events. Both were pretty long genres. I remember Yao Xinnong 姚莘農 (1905–1991), the playwright of the ill-fated *Qinggong yuan* 清宮怨 (Tragedies at the Qing Court), telling me long ago in Hong Kong how a storyteller spent three months with the heroine of his tale remaining on top of the staircase.[31]

---

27   See Liu Shide 2007, section 6: 'After the refutation by Xu Mengxiang 徐夢湘, the controversy lost intensity until Xu Shuofang revived it.'

28   See Roy 1986: 31–62. For Xu Shuofang, Tang Xianzu only read *Jin Ping Mei*. See Xu Shuofang 1983: 125–132. On the other hand, Xu Shuofang refuted, so to speak in advance, any connection of the 酒色財氣四犯 with *Jin Ping Mei* in his *Tang Xianzu nianpu*; Xu Shuofang 1958: 230. Thirdly, Tang Xianzu does not seem any sort of adept of Xunzi; see Lévy 2001.

29   See Hanan 1990: xi.

30   See articles published in Xu Shuofang 1983: 133–178. Two of these articles are to be found in *Jin Ping Mei yanjiu* 1984: 150–164.

31   See Yao Hsin-nung 1970. The introduction gives the full story of the misadventures of the play before the 1967 campaign aimed at Liu Shaoqi.

Before putting an end to this rather senseless guesswork, let us point out that oral arts tend to be verbose, while good written prose in the Chinese tradition should be terse. The verbosity of *Jin Ping Mei* cannot be denied, nor its connection with oral entertainments of all sorts.

To wrap it in its first skin, publishers had to gather the manuscripts painstakingly and hurriedly. There were several of them in the competition, hoping to make money or fame. A certain number of misprints, mistakes, incoherencies, double endings and so forth may be there on account of haste. None of them ever got the complete set. As no ancient manuscripts have come down to us, we can hardly guess the extent of the tampering needed to produce a book in a neat set of 100 chapters. The word 'cohesive' instead of 'coherent' in the article from *The Encyclopaedia of Erotic Literature* may be a cover for these inconsistencies, but I would take it rather as an avowal of the verbal rhetoric of the storyteller that pervades the book. Its qualification as *cihua*, whatever the extension of the term, underlines its relationship with the rhetoric of prosimetric narrative usually called *chantefable*. Its link with the art of storytelling cannot be more clearly stated. The storytellers' point of view explains the wealth of details and extended descriptions that pervade the novel better than drawing a comparison with a western literary movement like naturalism, let alone with such masterpieces written in parody of western literature as Cervantes' *Don Quixote* or Joyce's *Ulysses*.

Lack of *qing*, excess of *se*, a gang of rascals, a lascivious lass wallowing with profligates, horses, food, drink, dresses, an encyclopaedic level of detail: all of these seem to carry on the narrative when irony does not verge on the burlesque. The role of verses is to create or strengthen a mood. The suspense of the story is called for in order to induce the listeners to come back, listeners who are to some extent spectators, as the term *kanguan* 看官 seems to imply, though it is readily confused with *kan*, meaning silent reading. It is not a novelist speaking to us, but a tale being told through a storyteller putting us in the proper mood. In this light we may disclaim as a western-inspired fallacy the criticism of minor disgraceful discrepancies, as in this quotation from C.T. Hsia:

> Early in the novel, Ximen Qing runs his hands over Lotus' naked body and finds her *mons Veneris* hairless.[32] This brief scene, however, is immediately followed by a poem in praise of her private parts with due reference to her pubic hair. It is such discrepancies of detail that make the reader lose confidence in the novelist. What has happened here is that, in quoting a jocular poem to

32 For the scene referred to here see *Jin Ping Mei cihua,* chapter 4, Dai'an facsimile pp. 98–99, prose: 西門慶摸見濱戶上並無□毛猶如白馥馥鼓蓬蓬軟濃濃紅縐縐緊秋秋, verse: 薄草崖邊是故國. See also translations by Lévy 1985: 95 and Roy 1993: 91.

JIN PING MEI AND THE ART OF STORYTELLING

support his prose description, he has not bothered to check if the two accounts tally. Such oversights may appear trivial, and they are certainly common in traditional Chinese novels...[33]

In fact, we may deny that this is an oversight and argue that the poem 'which brings the testimony', *you shi wei zheng* 有詩為証, celebrates the attraction of the naked female body in poetical images, but does not specifically describe Lotus. For her, the prose turns lyrical, a Chinese way of showing the arousal inside the mind of Ximen Qing. Something similar occurs in western opera. We may claim that the so-called lack of coherence of the storyteller's manner has good points: it enlarges its impact and enlivens the characters by showing contradictory qualities. As the British novelist Forster remarked, the characters succeed in becoming 'round', though a Li Xifan 李希凡 may have complained that the bad Ximen Qing is not bad enough.[34]

The art of storytelling in China reached early on a maturity that calls for a more positive assessment. Its shortcomings may be argued, as may its strengths. Of course, granted the contributions of the storyteller's manner, the *Jin Ping Mei* as a written piece of fiction is a book which had an author, an editor and a publisher, a trinity in one or several persons, who successfully put together diverse sorts of materials. As a number of manuscripts are referred to, but none has come to us, we are reduced to more or less wild guesses. For example, in chapter 51, just after the middle of the novel, was it the impulse of the editor to have stuffed in somewhat too many events or the long-windedness of the storyteller to add this joke told by Ximen Qing to Lotus after making love to her? Or both? In David Roy's translation:

'Fivey' said Hsimen Ch'ing. 'I have got a joke to tell you, which I heard from Brother Ying the Second. A certain man died, and King Yama enveloped his body in a donkey's skin in order to change him into a donkey. Later, however, the Assessor consulted his ledgers and found that he still had thirteen years in the human realm allotted to him, so he was allowed to return to life. His wife noticed that although the rest of his body had reverted to human form, his male organ was still that of a donkey and had not returned to its former dimensions. 'Let me go back to the nether regions and get it changed', the man said. But this threw his wife into consternation, and she replied, 'Brother, if you undertake this journey, I fear that you may not be allowed to return, and what would we do then? Just leave it as it is, and I'll gradually learn to put up with it.'[35]

---

33 See Hsia 1968: 173.

34 See Li Xifan 1959: 185–200, especially 197. See also Forster 1962 / 1927: 67: 'We may divide characters into flat and round.'

35 See Roy 1993, vol. 3: 239. David Roy points out that the anecdote was known to Li Kaixian; see Roy 1993, vol. 3: 568, note 29. Bu Jian infers from this the likelihood of his part in

13

We may observe that this joke, probably well-known at the time, fits well into the story, as Lotus suffered from the effect of the aphrodisiacs Ximen Qing had taken. On the other hand, it may be taken as a hint at Lotus' lasciviousness, which will lead Ximen to his death in chapter 79. Thus, the shadow of the genial author who has cleverly woven all these threads together reappears. It could be somebody fallen into oblivion, from which there is hardly any hope of retrieving him, whether a learned associate of a despised profession or an unmentionable member of the imperial family who had wealth, leisure, taste for popular entertainment and no literati training. Certainly, *Jin Ping Mei*, and traditional fiction at large, owed a lot to the storyteller's manner.

Rather than dwelling on its limitations, is it not more vital to investigate its contribution? It can be argued that the early appearance of printing and refinements in the art of storytelling were both factors shaping a tradition of fiction quite different from, though similar to, the western one. When we come to think about it, starting with the Homeric epos of battles and seafaring, could such different roots produce similar branches? Is it possible? Yes and no. The way we look at *Jin Ping Mei* does involve a conception of the evolution of traditional fiction that is quite different. Did it by its own synergy evolve into a genre of world literature deeply infected by western traditions? Was *Jin Ping Mei* a sort of meteorite fallen from another planet? Our doubts do not entail a denial of the turning point that marked the appearance of the novel. *Jin Ping Mei* is a masterpiece, whatever the criteria involved in judging it 'great' or 'not great'. It is a masterpiece through its link with the art of storytelling and on the same level with the other three 'amazing four books', *si da qi shu* 四大奇書, and above them. Why? Perhaps more patient research, more new discoveries may help to anchor that inescapable feeling. The role of the art of storytelling has to be recognised more fully. An immense field is there to be prospected!

---

the authorship of the *Jin Ping Mei*; See Bu Jian 1988: 277. For the original text see Dai'an facsimile vol. 3: 280: 西門慶笑道五兒我有個笑話兒說與你聽是應二哥說的一個人死了閻王就拿驢皮被在身上交他變驢落後判官查簿籍還有他十三年陽壽又放回來叻他老婆看見渾身都變過來了只有陽物還是未變過來那人道我往陰間換去他老婆慌了說我的哥哥你這一去只怕不放你回來怎了瞪我慢慢的挨罷。 My translation, vol. 2 : 23–4: 'Ma petite cinquième, répond Ximen en riant, laisse-moi te raconter une histoire drôle que je tiens de mon ami Le-comte : un homme était mort. Le roi des enfers le fait recouvrir d'une peau d'âne en vue de sa prochaine réincarnation en cet animal. Mais, quelque plus tard, le juge vérifie ses registres : il annonce qu'il reste à l'homme un laps de treize années ici-bas. On le renvoie auprès sa femme : elle constate qu'il entièrement reprit l'aspect humain : seul son sexe garde la forme de celui de l'âne. Je retourne le faire changer chez les morts, déclare le mari. Son épouse, alarmée, réplique aussitôt: j'ai trop peur qu'ils ne te permettent pas de revenir; laisse, je m'habituerai peu à peu à supporter le nouveau!'

The rambling thoughts I have presented to you are not meant to lead to any conclusion. And I will not conclude. If I have not put you into too sleepy a mood, I shall be satisfied to have aroused your keen interest in so many topics that are to follow. *Xianhua xiufan* 閑話休繁: sorry to have put your long patience to task.

References

Bishop, John
> **1955–6.** 'Some limitations of Chinese fiction.' Far Eastern Quarterly XV: 239–247.

Børdahl, Vibeke and Margaret Wan (eds)
> **2010.** The Interplay of the Oral and the Written in Chinese Popular Literature. Copenhagen: NIAS Press.

Brulte, Gaëtan and John Phillips (eds)
> **2006.** Encyclopedia of Erotic Literature. New York and London: Routledge.

Bu Jian 卜鍵
> **1988.** Jin Ping Mei zuozhe Li Kaixian kao 金瓶梅作者李開先拷. Lanzou: Gansu Renmin chubanshe.

Ding Naifei
> **2002.** Obscene Things: Sexual Politics in *Jin Ping Mei*. Durham and London: Duke University Press.

Duan Chengshi 段成式
> **1981.** Youyang zazu 酉陽雜俎. Beijing: Zhonghua shuju.

Forster, E.M.
> **1962** [1927]. Aspects of the Novel. Place: Penguin Books.

Gimm, Martin
> **2005.** Hans Conon von der Gabelentz und die Übersezung des chinesischen Romans JIN PING MEI. Wiesbaden: Harrassowitz.

Hanan, Patrick
> **1962.** 'The text of the Chin P'ing Mei.' Asia Major IX: 1.
> **1963.** 'The Sources of the Chin P'ing Mei.' Asia Major X: 1.
> **1990** (tr.). The Carnal Prayer Mat. New York: Ballantine Books.

Hsia, C. T.
> **1968.** The Classic Chinese Novel. New York: Columbia University Press.

Hu Shi 胡適
> **1953.** Hu Shi wencun 胡適文存. Reprint. Taipei: Yuandong tushu gongsi.

ANDRÉ LÉVY

Jin Ping Mei yanjiu 金瓶梅研究
1984. Shanghai: Fudan Daxue chubanshe.

Kong Lingjing (ed.)
1982. Zhongguo xiaosho shiliao 中國小說史料. Shanghai: Shanghai guji.

Lévy, André
1969. 'Un texte burlesque dans le style de la chantefable.' Bulletin de l'Ecole Française d'Extrême-Orient LVI, Paris: 119–124.

1971a. 'Notes bibliographiques pour une histoire des "histoires pour rire" en Chine.' In A. Lévy, *Etudes sur le conte et le roman chinois*, 67–96. Paris: EFEO.

1971b. 'Un document unique sur un genre disparu de la littérature populaire, "Le rendez-vous d'amour où les cous sont coupes."'In Études sur le conte et le roman chinois, 187–210. Paris: PEFE.

1972. 'L'honnête commis Tchang.' In L'antre aux fantômes des collines de l'Ouest, Connaissance de l'Orient n°38, Gallimard, Paris: 91–106.

1985 (tr.). Fleur en Fiole d'Or (*Jin Ping Mei cihua*). Paris, Gallimard.

1986. 'Review of Sun Suyu's aesthetics of *Jin Ping Mei*.' Translated in Fang Ming 方銘 (ed.), Jin Ping Mei ziliao huibian 金瓶梅資料匯錄, 528–532. Hefei: Huangshan shushe.

2001. 'Tang Xianzu and the authorship of the novel *Jin Ping Mei* – under the light of some data regarding the play Mudanting.' In Christina Neder, Heiner Roetz and Ines-Susanne Schilling (eds), China in seinen biographischen Dimensionen, Gedenkschrift für Helmut Martin, 83–88. Wiesbaden: Harrassowitz Verlag.

Li Xifan
1959. 'Shuihu he Jin Ping Mei zai woguo xianshizhuyi wenxue fazhan zhong de diwei 水滸和金瓶梅在我國現實主義文學發展中的地位.' In: Ming Qing xiaoshuo yanjiu lunwen ji 明清小說研究論文集. Beijing: Renmin chubanshe.

Ling Mengchu 淩夢初
1633. *Erke Pai'an jingqi* 拍案驚奇.

Liu Shide 劉世德
2007. 'Jin Ping Mei zuozhe zhi mi 金瓶梅作者之謎'. Online talk on Renmin wang 人民網, September 2, 2007.

McLaren, Anne E.
1981/1984. Ming chantefable and the early Chinese novel: A study of the Chenghua period cihua. Ph.D. dissertation, Australian National University. University Microfilms International.

Ono Shinobu 小野忍 and Chida Kuichi 千田九一
1960. Kimpebai. Tokyo: Heibonsha, 3 vols.

JIN PING MEI AND THE ART OF STORYTELLING

Pan Kaipei 潘開沛

1959. 'Jin Ping Mei de chansheng he zuozhe 金瓶梅的產生和作者.' Ming Qing xiaoshuo yanjiu lunwen ji 明情小説研究論文集, 173–180. Beijing: Renmin. Reprinted from Guangming ribao, August 8, 1954.

Plaks, Andrew

1987. The Four Masterworks of the Ming Novel. Princeton, NJ: Princeton University Press.

Rémusat, Abel

1939. Le Livre des récompenses et des peines. Réédition P. Paris: Gruthner.

Roy, David T.

1986. 'The case for T'ang Hsien-tsu's authorship of the *Jin Ping Mei*.' CLEAR VIII, 1–2: 31–62.

1993 (tr.): The Plum in the Golden Vase, or Chin P'ing Mei. Princeton: Princeton University Press.

Wrenn, James J.

1964. A Textual Method and Its Application to the Texts of the Chin P'ing Mei. Ph.D. dissertation, Yale University. University Microfilms.

Wu, Nelson I.

1962. 'Tung Ch'i-ch'ang: apathy in government and fervour in art.' In Denis Twitchett and Arthur Wright (eds), Confucian Personalities, 260–293. Stanford: Stanford University Press.

Xu Shuofang 徐朔方

1958. Tang Xianzu nianpu 湯顯祖年譜. Shanghai: Zhonghua shuju.

1983. Lun Tang Xianzu ji qita 論湯顯祖及其他. Shanghai: Shanghai guji.

Yao Hsin-nung

1970. The Malice of Empire. Trans. Jeremy Ingalls. London: Allen and Unwin.

Ye Dejun 葉德均

1957. Song Yuan Ming jiangchang wenxue 宋元明講唱文學. Shanghai: Gudian wenxue chubanshe.

Zhang Dai 張岱 (Ming-Qing)

1986. Tao'an mengyi 陶庵夢憶 (Recollections of Tao'an's Past Dreams). Taibei: Jinfeng chubanshe.

1995. Souvenirs rêvés de Tao'an,. Trans. and annotated by Brigitte Teboul-Wang. Paris: Gallimard.

Zhang Yuanfen 張遠芬

1983. Jin Ping Mei xinzheng 金瓶梅新証. Jinan: Qi Lu shu she.

Zhu Xing 朱星

1980. Jin Ping Mei kaozheng 金瓶梅考證. Tianjin: Baihua wenyi.

Note on Contributor

André Lévy (1925–2017), Professor, Director of Chinese Studies at the University of Bordeaux, France. Translator of *Jin Ping Mei cihua* (1617) into French as *Fleur en Fiole d'Or* (1985).

CHAPTER 2

Pinghua and *cihua* in *Jin Ping Mei cihua*

LIANGYAN GE AND VIBEKE BØRDAHL

Among the four masterworks of Ming fiction, *Jin Ping Mei* 金瓶梅 occupies a unique position. Unlike *Sanguo yanyi* 三國演義, *Shuihu zhuan* 水滸傳, and *Xiyou ji* 西遊記, *Jin Ping Mei* has no precursor in any known oral storytelling tradition on the same subject matter. While much of the action in the novel is an outgrowth from a portion of *Shuihu zhuan*, *Jin Ping Mei* is generally believed to be China's earliest *written* work in full-length vernacular fiction, albeit published anonymously under the pseudonym 'The joking gentleman from Lanling', Lanling Xiaoxiaosheng 蘭陵笑笑生. On the other hand, however, the novel is permeated by an atmosphere of orality – perhaps even more so than its parent work *Shuihu zhuan*, which took its textual shape from a time-honoured oral tradition (Ge 2001). Indeed, in the 1617 edition of the novel titled *Jin Ping Mei cihua* 金瓶梅詞話 – generally considered the most 'authentic' and in later decades the most translated among the extant versions of the novel – numerous performance genres are mentioned, including *pinghua* 評話 and *cihua* 詞話, two major storytelling genres. The novel presents a couple of scenes of *pinghua* storytelling, and the narrator refers to *pinghua* in one of the recurring stock phrases. In the meantime, *cihua* seems to have been deliberately adopted to become part of the title for the novel. What does all this mean for the novel in particular and for the orality-writing interaction in general? This short essay aims to call attention to an issue that has hitherto not been adequately addressed and provide some fodder for further thinking.

Scenes of *Pinghua* Storytelling

In the text of *Jin Ping Mei cihua* 金瓶梅詞話[1] there are two occurrences of a storyteller's performance. In each case, Abbot Wu 吳道官 invites a storyteller,

---

1 Cf. Facsimile edition of the edition of 1617 – *Quanben Jin Ping Mei cihua* 全本金瓶梅詞話 1982.

shuoshude 說書的, to perform in private for a small group of guests (Chapter 35 and 39). The second time his performance is specified as being an episode of *pinghua* 評話 (Chapter 39). Chapter 35 includes an occasional remark about a storyteller whom Abbot Wu has invited to perform for the 'brotherhood' of Ximen Qing. One of the brothers, the utterly poor Bai Laiqiang, reports the awkward situation when Ximen Qing had not showed up and those few who did attend the feast had had nothing to contribute toward the fee:

> [...] A few days ago, when the Zhongyuan festival of the seventh month was celebrated in the Temple of the Jade Emperor, there were only three or four of us who attended the feast, me included. But none of us could pay, we were all penniless. Abbot Wu had taken great pains, and for our entertainment – after the ceremony for the Heavenly Generals was over – he had even invited a storyteller. That must have been expensive for him! Even if he did not say anything, we all felt sorely embarrassed [...] [2]

> 昨日七月內。玉皇廟打中元醮。連我只三四個人兒。到沒個人拿出錢來。都打撒手兒。難為吳道官。晚夕謝將。又叫了個說書。甚是破費他。他雖故不言語。各人心上不安。

In this passage we learn that it is expensive to invite a storyteller (甚是破費他) and the members of the brotherhood are painfully aware of their own inability to contribute. We know from sources on the famous storyteller Liu Jingting 柳敬亭 (1592–1674), who was active around the 1630s, that it was decidedly expensive to invite him to give performances:

> He told one session of storytelling a day. The price was one silver tael.
> 一日說書一回。定價一兩。   (Zhang Dai 1986: 68)

The text of *Jin Ping Mei cihua* confirms that storytellers of the late Ming were not available for small change but had a status that was respectable enough to require serious payment, even if the price of Liu Jingting was probably higher than the average.

In Chapter 39, Abbot Wu once again invites a storyteller, who performs from the WESTERN HAN saga for Ximen Qing and his friends in the Temple of the Jade Emperor:

> Actually, Abbot Wu had invited a storyteller to come over and tell them the episode of 'Meeting at Swan Gate' from the saga of Western Han.

---

2   In order to highlight the subtleties in the Chinese text, we refrain from using the current English translations.

原來吳道官叫了個說書的說西漢評話鴻門會。

No more is said about this in the two chapters or elsewhere. The episode of 'Meeting at Swan Gate' (*Hongmenhui* 鴻門會) takes place when Liu Bang and Xiang Yu first become rivals. Liu Bang is in danger during a sword dance at Swan Gate but survives. David Tod Roy chooses to translate *Xi Han pinghua* 西漢評話 as the title of a written work, *P'ing-hua on the Western Han Dynasty,* (NB! *italics* for book titles!) which has not survived (*Plum* 2001: 420 and 570, note 74). However, according to the text of *Jin Ping Mei cihua*, it seems more likely that the passage refers to a storytelling performance from an oral tradition about Western Han in the style of *pinghua* 評話 (Børdahl and Ge 2017: 9, 13–14). The passage is short and not spectacular in the least. Apparently, the novelist considers a storytelling performance a commonplace event and does not bother to give it any further description in the fictive world of the work.

Jin Ping Mei cihua was published only slightly later than some still extant Western Han popular narratives from the Wanli reign (1573–1620). It is, however, unlikely that the 'Meeting at Swan Gate from the saga of Western Han' (*Xi Han pinghua Hongmenhui* 西漢評話鴻門會) could refer to any of those works. The mentioning of the telling of Western Han in *Jin Ping Mei cihua* supports the notion of a continuous storytelling tradition on this topic since the Northern Song (Chen Ruheng 1985: 37). In Yangzhou storytelling, *Yangzhou pinghua* 揚州評話, the tradition of Western Han was still active during the late Qing and the early Republic. It only vanished in the late 1950s (Børdahl and Ge 2017, 4; see also Børdahl 2019: 116).

Pinghua in a Stock Phrase

The storyteller's stock phrase *pinghua jieshuo* 評話捷說 ('speed up your storytelling') is found twice in the novel (Chapters 30 and 70). This is the only genre-defining expression among the stock phrases. It is not particularly emphatic or frequently used, but nevertheless this stock phrase defines the story being told as one belonging to *pinghua* storytelling. The stock phrase carries the tone of a command: Speed up the telling of the *pinghua*-saga!

Roy translates this stock phrase in a generalized way: 'To make a long story short', leaving out the specific meaning of *pinghua*.[3] Lévy has two different

---

3   David T. Roy does not differentiate between the various stock phrases in his translation, but applies the same translation, 'to make a long story short', for this stock phrase as well as a number of other metanarrative formulae, such as *hua xiu raoshe* 話休饒舌 (let us not waste more words on that), *hua xiu xufan* 話休絮煩 (let us not get lost in unnecessary details) (*Plum*, vol. 2: 197 and vol. 4: 283).

translations: 'Abrégeons les commentaires' ('Let us shorten the commentaries') and 'Précipitons le récit du roman' ('Let us hurry on with the novel') (*Fleur*, vol. 1: 606, and vol. 2: 516 and 1362, note 1). Obviously, Lévy understands *pinghua* the first time as 'critical commentary' and the next time as 'novel'. For the second occurrence of the stock phrase Lévy has a note:

> *Pinghua*: le terme désigne aussi bien un genre narrative de la literature orale, non chanté, à l'origine, sans doute du 'roman' au sens large: c'est une fiction narrative, de longeur variable. Il est a noter que ce sens dérivé ne semble avoir eu cours qu'entre le XVIe et le XVIIIe siècle; il est ici employé pour la première fois, au lieu de *hua*, tout court, que nous traduisons par 'récit'.

> (*Pinghua*: the term implies more likely a narrative genre of oral literature, originally without singing, pointing no doubt to the idea of 'novel' in a wide sense: it means a fictional narrative of variable length. It is noteworthy that this derived meaning seems to have been in use only between the 16th and the 18th centuries It occurs here for the first time instead of simply *hua*, which we translate as 'story'.)

Has Lévy forgotten that the word *pinghua* has already occurred twice in the text of *Jin Ping Mei cihua*? Maybe he did not notice this, since the occurrences are rare and seemingly insignificant. Roy and the Kibat brothers overlooked or misinterpreted this word.[4]

The Storyteller Persona of the Narrator

In *Jin Ping Mei cihua* we notice that the narrator assumes the 'storyteller's manner' and adopts a storyteller persona at least twice, by addressing himself as *shuohuade* 說話的 (Chapter 1 and 27):[5]

> Storyteller, why are you so eager to tell about the two words love and lust?

> 說話的。如今只愛說這情色二字。做甚。

---

4 The Chongzhen edition used by the Kibat brothers did not include the metanarrative stock phrases of *pinghua jieshuo;* as for the *Xihan pinghua,* they translated the passage as 'Der Priester Wu hatte einen Geschichtenerzähler kommen lassen, der aus dem kritischen Werke über die vestliche Han-dynastie das Zusammentreffen in Schwanentor vortrug.' This translation is in line with Roy's translation and with Lévy's first translation of *pinghua jieshuo*.

5 Lévy in *Fleur*, vol. 1: 21, translates *shuohuade* as 'conteur' (storyteller, teller of stories), while he translates the next occurrence of *shuohuade* in vol.1: 543, as 'cher lecteur' (dear reader), a free translation pointing to the context of communication with the audience/reader. Roy in *Plum*, vol. 1: 15, and vol. 2: 130, renders *shuohuade* as 'narrator', by which translation the connection with Chinese professional storytelling, *shuohua, shuoshu,* is downplayed or even eliminated.

Storytellers used to say: In this world there are three kinds of people who fear the heat, and three kinds of people who do not fear it.

說話的。世上有三等人怕熱。有三等人不怕熱。

This use of the expression *shuohuade* 說話的 is in contrast to the storyteller as a character among other characters in the narrative, *shuoshude* (Chapter 35 and 39). In the Rongyutang edition of *Water Margin, Shuihu zhuan* 水滸傳 (1610), we find occasional markers of appeal to the audience, where the storyteller is called *shuohuade* (Børdahl 2013: 120–121). Apparently the 'manner' of *Jin Ping Mei cihua* here imitates an older set of stock phrases (from *Shuihu zhuan* and other earlier novels), while the prose narration reflects a later stage of the language, where *shuoshude* has taken over as the expression for a storyteller (Lévy 1999: 33 and ff.).

Cihua as a Pseudo-Genre of *Jin Ping Mei cihua*

Cihua 詞話, mentioned in the title before each scroll, *juan* 卷, in the margins of every page and at the end of Chapter 100, seems to be another case of genre definition of the work. It should be kept in mind that *cihua* was not part of the earliest title of this work. In two of the para-texts to the *cihua* edition of 1617, a preface and a postface, the work is mentioned by the title *Jin Ping Mei zhuan* 金瓶梅傳 (The Chronicle of *Jin Ping Mei*), on a par with *Shuihu zhuan* 水滸傳 (The Chronicle of the Marshlands) (*Water Margin*) and other semi-historical narratives (*Quanben Jin Ping Mei cihua* 1982: 3, 15; Wu Gan 2015: 7). The fact that in the title of the earliest extant printed edition the genre name *cihua* replaces the genre name *zhuan* 傳 cannot have been incidental. Since *Jin Ping Mei* was obviously an outgrowth of the *Water Margin* tale (*Shuihu zhuan*), there would be nothing strange in calling the book a *zhuan* like its most obvious forerunner. But the editors of the *cihua*-edition must have speculated about the fact that the two works were significantly different in format, particularly because of the large number of poems and songs inserted in *Jin Ping Mei*.

Cihua had been a genre name of long standing, since the Song and Yuan dynasties. It had been used for a wide spectrum of performance genres and printed texts that had a relationship with performance: tales for singing and telling (McLaren 1998: 7, 17, 58, 116–114, 94–101, 264, 275). None of these genres would appear to have a close parallel in *Jin Ping Mei cihua*. It is clear that the texts found in the tomb of a woman from the Chenghua period (1465–1488) represent one or more oral genres in the verse and prose of the period, *shuochang cihua* 說唱詞話, or 'ballad-stories' for narrating and singing, as they are called by Wilt Idema (Idema 2010: xvi, and ff.) However, the format is very different from that of *Jin Ping Mei cihua,* in so far as the verse and prose of the *Chenghua shuochang cihua* have a regular and simple form.

If these Chenghua prints are considered the most reliable textual exemplars of *cihua,* we have reason to believe that *cihua,* as a form of 'oral text', belonged to a time period much earlier than the advent of *Jin Ping Mei cihua.* By the Wanli period (1573–1620) when Lanling Xiaoxiaosheng's novel was taking its shape, *cihua* may have long passed its heyday and lost some of its clarity as a genre label. To be sure, apart from *Jin Ping Mei cihua* there is another text from the Wanli period that contains the word *cihua* in its title – *Da Tang Qin Wang cihua* 大唐秦王詞話, a prosimetric narrative about the founding of the Tang dynasty compiled by Zhu Shenglin 諸聖鄰. According to Zheng Zhenduo 鄭振鐸 (1898–1958), however, this work is a revamped version of a much earlier textual prototype (Zheng Zhenduo 1984 [1938]: 385). Occasionally, the word *cihua* shows up in some late Ming stories as well. One example is 'Jiang Xingge chonghui zhenzhu shan' 蔣興哥重會珍珠衫 (Jiang Xingge reencounters the Pearl Shirt), collected in Feng Menglong's 馮夢龍 *Yushi mingyan* 喻世明言 (Clear words to instruct the world). In the story, the narrator claims to be telling a *cihua,* but the story, according to Patrick Hanan (Hanan 1973: 44), may have been written by Feng Menglong himself, and indeed it is little different, formally, from other stories by that author.

It is also worth noting that if we consider the Chenghua *shuochang cihua* as most representative of the narrative form in *cihua,* we find that *cihua* features not only an alternation between verse and prose but also a distinct regulation of the metric pattern in the verse lines. Despite the word *ci* in the name of the genre, which often suggests a diversity of metric patterns, the verse portions in a *cihua* text appear overwhelmingly in heptasyllabic lines, which occasionally vary into decasyllabic ones. Unlike *zhugongdiao* 诸宫调 and some other prosimetric performative genres, *cihua* typically does not indicate the tunes for the verse lines, which led Ye Dejun (1911–1956) to make a distinction between *yuequ* 樂曲 ('musical verses' that fit into well-established tunes) and *shizan* 詩讚 ('panegyric verses' that are relatively independent of any musical patterns) (Ye Dejun 1957: 212–17). Additionally, in *cihua* there are no verse-introducing stock phrases, which we frequently encounter in early works of vernacular fiction, including *Jin Ping Mei cihua.* Prose passages in *cihua* are rather parsimonious, in some cases consisting of only one or two exchanges in the characters' dialogue. The story is thus narrated mainly by the lines in verse, which are heavily formulary and therefore must have been relatively easy for the performer to remember or improvise.

Jin Ping Mei cihua, on the other hand, is cast in a format with a very different synthesis of verse and prose: a shifting between a sophisticated prose incorporating a wealth of different styles both in dialogue and narration, and a much less sophisticated conglomeration of verse in endlessly shifting poetical meters and melodies. While the prose sections – apart from obviously borrowed portions, such as ritual texts or official documents – mainly reflect the narrative voice of the work, even in mimicking the dialogue of the characters, the verse sections are by and large imported goods, 'stolen' from here, there, and everywhere. The administration of the 'stolen goods' does imply the work of a mastermind, and in that respect the narrative voice is also active here. But, this said, the verse of the work serves different purposes from that of the prose.

What is then the meaning of *cihua* in *Jin Ping Mei cihua*? Is it the genre name of the work? As mentioned above, the stock phrase *pinghua jieshuo* defines the narrative as *pinghua* storytelling, but the phrase is only used a couple of times, and it is fully possible to consider this formula a light-hearted and playful usage, pointing only to the 'storyteller's manner' as the 'pseudo-framework' of the novel. However, when we consider the many inserted songs and metric performance texts (opera arias, precious scrolls, *baojuan* 寶卷, etc), which alternate with the prose narrative, the term *cihua* seems nevertheless to be reasonably precise as a description of the genre of the work, a short form of *changci pinghua* 唱詞評話 (verse for singing and prose storytelling; or verse and prose; or *chantefable*) which is also the standard definition of *cihua* in modern dictionaries. However, just as the stock phrase *pinghua jieshuo* seems to be a half-ironic, jocular application of the 'storyteller's manner' – not really to be taken literally – likewise the use of *cihua* in the title of the work could have been part of the framework for the 'unreliable narrator' of the work: borrowing the name of a former simple *chantefable* genre and playfully gluing it onto this work as part of the pseudo-storytelling 'manner'.

Pinghua and *Cihua*: A New Narrative Template

To reiterate, both *pinghua* and *cihua* are used in *Jin Ping Mei cihua* as components of a narrative framework, where the narrator puts on different masks on different occasions. They are not as much stringently defined genre names in storytelling performance as designations for two different modes of fiction making. Both concepts were therefore reimagined and remolded by the novelist. *Pinghua*, as a major storytelling form of extended length primarily used in prose, has a natural affinity to the vernacular novel, which arose from the interface between orality and writing. During the Wanli period, *pinghua* storytelling was flourishing, as evidenced by the scenes of *pinghua* performance in the novel itself. The narrator's stock phrase *pinghua jieshuo* and playful self-reference as *shuohuade* clearly suggest a jocular and self-reflexive view, but that does not make *Jin Ping Mei cihua* a *pinghua*. When *Jin Ping Mei cihua* came into existence in 1617, it was predated by several known editions of *Sanguo yanyi, Shuihu zhuan,* and *Xiyou ji.* That is to say, by the late Wanli years, the vernacular novel had become a mature and well-established literary genre, and much of *pinghua*'s influence on *Jin Ping Mei cihua* may have had to be intermediated by its novelistic forerunners. Also, it should be noted that the word *cihua* added to the title of the novel does not change the novel into a *cihua* text, but it serves as a good rubric for all the arias and songs the novelist borrows from various sources of metric and melodic performance. In the novelistic text they can appear in regular heptasyllabic metric verse lines, but often their metric pattern can be closer to the poetic form of *ci* 詞, with no uniform length for all the lines – as the rubric for these borrowings, *cihua*, would suggest on a literal level. The *pinghua-cihua* tandem has a notable impact on *Jin Ping Mei cihua*, which presents a special narrative rhythm and a remarkably rich synthesis of narrative voices, not seen in any earlier works in vernacular fiction.

Take Chapter 8 of *Jin Ping Mei cihua*, for example. After being neglected by Ximen Qing for many days when Ximen is taking another woman for concubine, Pan Jinlian finally reunites with her lover. In anticipation of the dreaded return of Wu Song, they hasten to arrange a memorial service for Wu the Elder (Wu Da). The monks conducting the service are all turned topsy-turvy when they overhear the adulterous couple's erotic dialogue. This plotline for the chapter is narrated primarily in prose, but verse also features prominently. Like other chapters, this one starts with a heptasyllabic poem, and the prose narration in the main body of the chapter is interspersed with verse lines following stock phrases such as *you shi wei zheng* 有詩為證, *dan jian* 但見, and *zheng shi* 正是. However, what makes the novel markedly different from its precursors, such as *Shuihu zhuan,* is its blatant appropriation of materials from performance genres. In Chapter 8, Pan Jinlian sings several songs in different tunes (*shanpoyang* 山坡羊, *jishengcao* 寄生草, and *miandaxu* 绵褡絮), and writes down the arias of another song as a letter to Ximen Qing. With these songs, she expresses her yearning and resentment as a neglected mistress, but it is apparent that the songs remain in their original forms without being adapted into the fictional context, as they contain no reference to any specific figures or events in the novel. Even though it is particularly fitting for Pan, a former singing girl, to sing the songs, they might be sung by any abandoned women from the lower social strata of the time. To that extent, they belong not so much to the *Jin Ping Mei* saga per se as to the social and cultural setting for that saga.

As illustrated in Chapter 8, there are roughly two different storyteller's manners in *Jin Ping Mei cihua*. The main narrative plotline is, for the most part, taken forward in prose, interspersed with verse lines introduced by stock phrases, in the manner of simulated *pinghua* storytelling. For the sake of convenience, we may simply call it the '*pinghua* manner'. In the meantime, on a verbal level the novel borrows all kinds of metric materials from melodic and operatic sources, materials placed under the general rubric of *cihua*, and we may call this the '*cihua* manner'. If the *pinghua* manner can be considered a 'vertical' force taking the narrative plotline forward, the *cihua* manner represents a 'horizontal' force intensifying and elaborating on particular narrative moments, as exemplified by Pan Jinlian's songs in Chapter 8. While the *pinghua* manner is something *Jin Ping Mei cihua* may have inherited from earlier novels, the *cihua* manner, which adds a vocal and melodic dimension to the novel that is separate from the dialogues between the characters, is *Jin Ping Mei cihua*'s unique contribution to the art of fiction creation. These two manners function differently, but they are interrelated and mutually complementary in the novel's panoramic depiction of urban life in late Ming China.

References

Børdahl, Vibeke

> **2013.** *Wu Song Fights the Tiger. The Interaction of Oral and Written Traditions in the Chinese Novel, Drama and Storytelling,* NIAS Press, Copenhagen.
>
> **2019.** 'Revisiting WESTERN HAN in Written Script and in Oral Performance: Language, Style, Length, and the Question of Exegesis.' In *CHINOPERL, Journal of Chinese Oral and Performing Literature,* No. 38(2,): 107–127.

Børdahl, Vibeke and Liangyan Ge (editors and translators in cooperation with Wang Yalong). 2017. *Western Han. A Yangzhou Storytellers' Script.* Copenhagen: NIAS Press.

Chen Ruheng 陈汝衡

> **1985.** *Chen Ruheng quyi wenxuan* 陈汝衡曲艺文选 (Chen Ruheng: Collected Works on the Performance Arts). Zhongguo quyi chubanshe.

Fleur en Fiole d'Or (Flower in Golden Vase) (Jin Ping Mei cihua), vols 1–2. Shortened: *Fleur.*

> **1985.** Edited and translated by André Lévy, Bibliothèque de la Pléiade, Editions Gallimard.

Ge Liangyan

> **2001.** *Out of the Margins. The Rise of Chinese Vernacular Fiction.* Honolulu: University of Hawai'i Press.

Hanan, Patrick

> **1973.** *The Chinese Short Story: Studies in Dating, Authorship, and Composition.* Cambridge Mass.: Harvard University Press.

Idema, Wilt

2010. *Judge Bao and the Rule of Law: Eight Ballad-Stories from the Period 1250–1450,* Singapore: World Scientific.

Lévy, André

1999. 'About the Chinese storyteller's change of name.' In Vibeke Børdahl (ed.), *The Eternal Storyteller. Oral Literature in Modern China,* 33–39. Richmond, Surrey: Curzon Press.

Lévy, André, see *Fleur en Fiole d'Or*

McLaren, Anne E.

1998. *Chinese Popular Culture and Ming Chantefables.* Leiden: Brill.

Plum in the Golden Vase or Chin P'ing Mei, vols 1–5.

1993–2013. Shortened: *Plum.* Edited and translated by David Tod Roy. Princeton: Princeton University Press.

Quanben Jin Ping Mei cihua 全本金瓶梅詞話

1982. Hong Kong: Taiping shuju

Roy, David Tod, see *Plum in the Golden Vase*

Wu Gan 吳敢

2015. *Jin Ping Mei yanjiu shi* 金瓶梅研究史 (A History of Research on *Jin Ping Mei*). Guanzhou: Zhongzhou guji chubanshe.

Ye Dejun 葉德均

1957. *Song Yuan Ming jiangchang wenxue* 宋元明講唱文學. Shanghai: Gudian wenxue chubanshe.

Zhang Dai 張岱 (1599–1684)

1986. *Tao an meng yi* 陶庵夢憶 (Dream Reminiscence of Tao'an). Taibei: Jinfeng chubanshe.

Zheng Zhenduo 鄭振鐸

1984 [1938]. *Zhongguo suwenxueshi* 中國俗文學史. Reprint. Shanghai: Shanghai shudian chubanshe.

Note on Contributors

Ge Liangyan 葛良彥, Professor Emeritus, East Asian Languages and Cultures, University of Notre Dame, USA

Vibeke Børdahl, Ph.D., Dr.Phil., Senior Researcher, Nordic Institute of Asian Studies, University of Copenhagen, Denmark

CHAPTER 3

Language Shifting and the Narrating Instance in *Jin Ping Mei cihua*

Some Reflections on the Novel's Usage of Storytellers' Stock Phrases

VIBEKE BØRDAHL

In Chinese vernacular fiction of the late-imperial period, stylistic features signalling oral/performance aspects and those signalling written/reading aspects seem to intertwine and shift in complicated and many-faceted ways. Here I want to draw attention to one shifting of this kind, namely the usage of a special 'language-within-a-language': the meta-narrative idiom of the so-called 'storyteller's manner'. This intralingual stratum not only constitutes a sub-language among other sub-languages of the linguistic equipment of vernacular fiction; it also serves a genre-signalling function that has important consequences for the narratological framework.

Use of storytellers' stock phrases was widespread in Chinese vernacular fiction from the 14th century to the 20th century, with roots going back even further (Børdahl 2013: 35–44). This meta-narrative sub-stratum in vernacular fiction has a certain homogeneity but has changed over time and has been used in both stereotypical and creative ways. Sometimes it has functioned as a relatively tedious frame that could be added to any story by an editor, as though it were a kind of punctuation. It has mostly evoked a resonance of recognition: once the story begins with 'the story goes', *hua shuo* 話說, the reader knows

---

This chapter was originally written for the workshop 'Intralingual Translation, Language Shifting, and the Rise of Vernaculars in East Asian Classical and Premodern Cultures', Paris, January 19th–20th, 2017, Maison de l'Asie, Ecole Française d'Extrême-Orient, organized by Rainier Lanselle and Barbara Bisetto, as part of the project SCRIPTA PSL. I am much indebted to the two anonymous readers of the chapter, who at the time provided inspiring comments as well as critical notes, which I have tried to incorporate into the present version. Later, my colleagues and friends Margaret Wan and Liangyan Ge also read and commented on the article and gave me insightful criticism for which I am deeply grateful.

perfectly well what to expect (even though he does not necessarily realize this consciously). Sometimes it has furnished a note of humour, and it has also been used ironically or in a self-mocking way.

The focus of this chapter is the presence and function of this meta-narrative language in the famous vernacular novel *Jin Ping Mei cihua* 金瓶梅詞話 (*The Plum in the Golden Vase in Verse and Prose*) (1617) (*Quanben Jin Ping Mei cihua*, facsimile, 1982).

It is clear that 'storytelling' in the Chinese sense, *shuohua* 說話, *shuoshu* 說書, belongs to oral performance. The question of whether there is a 'manner' in Chinese storytelling as an oral event, comparable to the 'storyteller's manner' in vernacular literature, is relevant to an understanding of the 'simulacrum of storytelling' that is usually implied. A related question is how far the storyteller's manner has been part of the style of storytellers' own scripts, i.e. manuals of repertoires, *aides-mémoire*. Oral storytelling events before and contemporary with the creation of *Jin Ping Mei cihua* have of course vanished as performed 'oral texts', although descriptions of the art have been left to posterity. Genuine storyteller's scripts likewise have not survived, to the best of my knowledge. However, the oral traditions that are still alive in China may furnish material for reflection in this respect. In the following, the 'manner' of *Jin Ping Mei cihua* is compared, not only with earlier novels, but also with today's and yesterday's *pinghua*-storytelling, *pinghua* 評話, as performance and as script.

The storyteller's manner in *Jin Ping Mei cihua* is firstly compared to that found in early vernacular entertainment literature – cast in the storyteller's rhetoric – from the time before the publication of *Jin Ping Mei cihua*, namely the 14th century 'plain tale', *pinghua*, the 15th century *chantefable, shuochang cihua*, and the Ming novel, *zhanghui xiaoshuo*, exemplified by *Shuihu zhuan* 水滸傳 (Water Margin) (1610) (Børdahl 2013). Then the data is compared to that of a genuine storyteller's script, *jiaoben*, from the Yangzhou storytelling tradition, *Yangzhou pinghua* 揚州評話, in the late 19th century (Børdahl and Ge 2017) and also with oral Yangzhou storytelling as performed in the late 20th century (Børdahl 1996).

The definition of oral and written registers as intralingual strata within a certain oral or written text will generally imply a layering, i.e. an analysis at different levels of the discourse. While the storyteller's manner as an intralingual stratum in the novel can – in its totality – be categorized as an oral register, because it implies the oral situation of oral performance, we shall see that this sub-language is not uniformly related to spoken/oral style. A minor portion of the meta-narrative vocabulary is tinged by literary/written associations, being coined in *wenyan* 文言 forms. This is also true for *Jin Ping Mei cihua*. Apart from the stratum of the meta-narrative formulas, throughout the work we find

LANGUAGE SHIFTING AND THE NARRATING INSTANCE

a patchwork of styles, representing different linguistic strata and connected to a wide spectrum of spoken and written styles. However, while the intralingual language of the 'manner' is decisive for the narrative posture of the entire text, the same is not true of other registers employed in the work, since they function on various intradiegetic levels of narration, such as letters written by characters in the work (official documents), or genres performed by characters in the work (sutra-recitation, song suites, jokes etc).

The findings have implications for our understanding of how *Jin Ping Mei cihua* – in the usual garb of 'ordinary storytelling' – experiments with the 'narrating instance' (Genette 1980: 212–262) and the definition of its own genre.[1] The long-debated question of the oral roots of the Chinese novel in general and of the kind of authorship it may have had, in relation to *Jin Ping Mei cihua* in particular, is not the main issue here. Nevertheless, the shifting of registers in this novel and the specific inventory of terms in the 'manner' invite some preliminary considerations about the affinities of the novel to the contemporary oral milieu of performance culture.

'Simulating' versus 'Representing' Storytelling

Jin Ping Mei cihua is both a typical and an atypical example of the Chinese novel from the Ming period. It is typical in the sense that it demonstrates what has been termed 'the storyteller's manner' or 'the simulacrum of storytelling' (Idema 1974: XXII, 69–72; Hanan 1977: 87; Meng Zhaolian 1998: 137–152; see also Børdahl 2010a and Børdahl 2013: Chapter 5). It is atypical in the way in which it incorporates material from drama and storytelling (Rolston 1994: 27–36). Here the word 'storytelling' is taken in its broad sense of *shuochang* 說唱 (telling and singing arts).

The storyteller's manner was a convention for written vernacular fiction including the novel, *zhanghui xiaoshuo* 章回小说 (fiction divided into sections and sessions), and the short story, *huaben* 話本 (stories).

This narrative model does not, however, reproduce directly any actual performance or performance tradition, and the written work is not intended for performance, but for reading. Some works may have had a close connection with oral traditions. Some may even have had a former incarnation as

---

1   Gérard Genette (1980, Chapter 5) defines the 'narrating instance' as the posture of the narrator at any given level of the fictional narrative. The storyteller's manner of Chinese fiction, including *Jin Ping Mei cihua*, implies that the narrator is a (third person) extradiegetic, heterodiegetic narrator (corresponding to the type of narrator we find in *Homer*), characterized by the storyteller's stock phrases with which this narrator is openly identified (ibid. 214: 244, 248).

31

VIBEKE BØRDAHL

Table 3.1. The storyteller's manner in the novel and
short story of the Ming and the Qing

Division into sessions	The narrative is divided into 'sessions' (of oral performance) or 'chapters' (of a book), called 'returns' if the setting is oral and *hui* 回, if it is longer than what can go into a single session.*
Prose and verse	Prose and verse alternate.
Storyteller narrator	The act of narrating is couched in the persona of a storyteller (the narrator) and his audience (the narratee).
Simulated dialogue with the audience	Narrator's comment and simulated dialogue with the audience are part of the style.
Stock phrases	A set of so-called storyteller's stock phrases are interspersed throughout the tale.

* With a view to the storyteller's manner of *Jin Ping Mei cihua*, I prefer to translate the dividing unit of the text, *hui,* as 'session', because as part of the manner the *hui* refers to oral sessions or 'returns', something that is also implicit in the use of the stock-phrase at the end of each unit: 'If you really don't know what comes next, please, listen to the explanation in the following session', *bijing wei zhi houlai he ru, qie ting xiahui fenjie* 畢竟未知後來何如 且聽下回分解; the audience is invited to 'listen to the explanation', and the action of listening evokes the session of storytelling rather than the reading of a chapter. In some novels the verb is not 'listen', *ting* 聽, but 'see', *kan* 看, so that the reference to the oral situation is weakened or blurred; it is ambivalent if you are 'seeing' a performance or 'seeing' (reading) a book.

scripts, *jiaoben* 腳本 – *aides-mémoire* – for oral performance, but in general the *zhanghui xiaoshuo* and *huaben* in their early printed form were intended for and used for silent reading, not meant as ancillary tools for oral performance (see the discussion on 'plain tales', *pinghua* 平話, and storytelling in Børdahl 2013: 29–49).

The situation is different with printed texts that stand in close proximity to certain performance genres, such as the Ming Chenghua *chantefables, Ming Chenghua shuochang cihua* 明成化說唱詞話 (1471–1478). These texts from the late 15th century seem to be closely connected to the oral performance traditions with which they share the genre name *shuochang cihua* 說唱詞話 or just *cihua* 詞話 and *changci* 唱詞 (McLaren 1998: Chapter 3). Moreover, the *reading* practice of the printed texts was likely to approach a performance-like *vocalizing* in the family circle.[2] This means that it would be misleading to talk about a 'simulated context of storytelling', because the text 'represents' an orally performable linguistic string of words, just as the hymns of a Christian hymn book correspond to the words as sung in church. The text of the Chinese *chantefables* does reflect *bona fide* the actual performance tradition of these pieces of 'telling and singing'. The words of the *chantefable* in print presumably corresponded to the words as they were performed as closely as anything written can represent anything spoken. The distinction between a text based on a 'simulacrum' of storytelling and one that 'represents' a storytelling performance is essential, but the delineation of the borderline between these two categories of texts is not always obvious or easy to establish (Ge Liangyan 2000: 162).

There can be no doubt that *Jin Ping Mei cihua* in its earliest extant edition (1617), as well as later editions, belongs to the category of vernacular fiction that was meant for reading, not for performance. Therefore, the title designating the work as *cihua* obviously has a different implication from that of the 15th century *shuochang cihua*. Maybe the application of *cihua* in the title should rather be considered part of the 'simulacrum of storytelling'? We shall return to this.

A Language within a Language

Meta-narrative markers of the shifting of mode, time or focus of a tale often seem to be closely associated with conventions of genre. 'Once upon a time...' and we are immediately situated in the genre of fairy tale (if not a mock-fairy tale: 'Once upon a time, and a very good time it was...' [James Joyce]).

In the novels of the Ming and the Qing we mainly find that there are meta-narrative markers with the following functions: 1) verse-introductory markers; 2) markers of narrative transition and progression; 3) formulary phrases with comments and appeals to the audience (the narratee) on the part of the narrator. These markers and formulary phrases constitute the essential equipment of the so-called 'storyteller's stock phrases', *taoyu* 套語. Many of the phrases serve more than one function, however, so that the categories cut across each other. The stock phrases consist mostly of phrases of two or four characters, but some constitute full sentences. While vernacular vocabulary and grammatical structure are preponderant in this sub-language, there are, among the verse-introductory markers, a few instances of expressions in *wenyan*. But overall the idiom of the 'manner' belongs to the vernacular style.

---

2   McLaren 1998: 67–76; see also the pre-modern and modern usages of both professional and amateur performance of 'precious scrolls', *baojuan* 寶卷, along with silent reading, described as 'multifunctionality' by Berezkin 2015: 172–177.

VIBEKE BØRDAHL

Table 3.2. Verse-introductory markers in *Jin Ping Mei cihua*

Behold	*dan jian*	但見	**105**
How did it look	*zen jian / zen jiande*	怎見 /怎見得	**13**
Indeed	*zheng shi*	正是	**364**
Truly	*zhenge shi*	真個是	**3**
Here it is specially expressed	*dan dao*	單道	**13**
*The poem says	*shi yue*	詩曰	**10**
*The song says	*ci yue*	詞曰	**2**
*There is a poem in proof	*you shi wei zheng*	有詩為証	**126**
*There is a verse in proof	*you ci wei zheng*	有詞為証	**4**
There is a poem especially about it	*you shi dan biao*	有詩單表	1
It was predestined	*you fen jiao*	有分教	1

The asterisk * indicates that the marker is in *wenyan*. **Bolding** indicates that the marker is in common between *Shuihu zhuan* and *Jin Ping Mei cihua*. The numbers in the fourth column indicate the number of occurrences in *Jin Ping Mei cihua*.

In Tables 3.2–3.8, I will provide lists of these three categories of markers or stock phrases found in *Jin Ping Mei cihua* Chapters 1–100.[3]

The verse-introductory markers of *Jin Ping Mei cihua* are basically the same as those of the representative *fanben* 繁本 (complex version) edition of *Shuihu zhuan*, the so-called *Rongyutang* 容與堂 edition, ca. 1610. Four of the 11 markers are in *wenyan*, including some of the most high-frequency expressions. The formulas with 曰 are much older than the earliest vernacular literature, going back to the Confucian classics. The formulas with 為 reflect the *wenyan*

---

3   The numbers in Tables 3.2–3.8 indicate the total number of occurrences of each stock phrase in *Jin Ping Mei cihua*. Markers shared with the *Rongyutang* edition of *Shuihu zhuan* are **bolded**. The comparison with the *Rongyutang* 容與堂 edition of *Shuihu zhuan* is restricted to Chapters 23–32, where the tale of the hero Wu Song is told, cf. *Rongyutangben Shuihu zhuan*, 1988: 315–466. This 10-chapter tale, *shihui* 十回, of *Shuihu zhuan* is shared with *Jin Ping Mei cihua*.

LANGUAGE SHIFTING AND THE NARRATING INSTANCE

or *shumian* 書面 style (Norman 1988: 95–96; Yang Bojun 1965: 34–35). These formulas are so frequent in vernacular literature that their *wenyan* origin is hardly noticeable. They are not indicators of a more formal style in what follows, but simply function as a kind of punctuation for poetry and verse, just like the other verse-introductory markers. The marker *you fen jiao* occurs regularly at chapter endings in the *Shuihu zhuan*, but is an exception in *Jin Ping Mei cihua* where *you fen jiao* is only found once, namely in Chapter 4. The marker *dan dao* has a close parallel in the marker *dan ti* 單提 of *Shuihu zhuan*. However, a few markers are not shared with *Shuihu zhuan: zhenge shi, you ci wei zheng* and *you shi dan biao*. These extra verse-introductory markers have their roots, like the others, in the tradition of the 'plain tale', *pinghua* 平話, as well as the *chantefable* (Børdahl 2013: 36; McLaren 1998: 271). Furthermore, the fixed markers shown in Table 3.2 are supplemented with more freely composed verse-introductory expressions, also strongly reminiscent of those found in the plain tale *Xuanhe yishi* 宣和遺事 (*Legends of the Xuanhe Reign* [1119–1126]), *ca* 1300.[4] The variation in 'free' verse-introductory expressions is, however, much greater than in *Xuanhe yishi*.

In the Ming novel it is a general characteristic of the verse-introductory markers that they not only introduce various kinds of metric verse or *bon mot*, but very often the verses that are introduced represent the narrator's comment, providing some general truth or moral lesson to be drawn from the events of the story (Porter 1991: 135–137). However, in *Jin Ping Mei cihua* many of the poems and verses have an ironic function, representing truths or moral views that contrast with those of the narrator, or with those of the person who vocalizes them (Hanan 1963: 52, 60, 67; Carlitz 1986: 117). Other poems and verses are descriptive rather than 'moral', but, set off from the prose narrative, they acquire a special status as 'pictures' to contemplate.[5] A major portion of the verses consists of songs that are introduced either as being sung, then and there, by one of the characters in the novel, or as remembered, dreamt of, or written down by the characters.[6] Songs, defined by their melody, rarely belong to the narratorial mode in the same way as do other poetical texts, and they are as a

---

4   Børdahl 2013: 35–40, 122–124. *Zen jian* (or *zen jiande* 怎見得) and *zhenge shi* are found among the verse-introductory markers of *Xuanhe yishi*. Interestingly, *zen jiande* is also frequent in a storyteller's script in the *Yangzhou pinghua* tradition from the late Qing, cf. Børdahl 2005; Børdahl 2013: 239; Børdahl and Ge 2017: 31.

5   Cf. the discussion of 'set pieces' and *descriptio* as a common feature of oral-related texts in Hanan 1981: 21.

6   For a discussion of the question of so-called 'realistic' versus 'non-realistic' uses of oral performing literature in *Jin Ping Mei cihua*, cf Rolston 1994: 1–2, 14–15, 36.

Table 3.3. Markers of narrative transition and progression in *Jin Ping Mei cihua*

The story goes (tells)	***hua shuo***	話說	**85**
Let's tell now again	***zai shuo***	再說	**1**
Let's tell in particular about	*dan shuo*	單說	2
Meanwhile let's tell	***qie shuo***	且說	**83**
Let's rather tell	***que shuo***	卻說	**49**
Let's just tell	***zhi shuo***	只說	**4**
No need to tell this	*bu bi shuo*	不必說	4
Let's not go into details	*bu bi xi shuo*	不必細說	40
Enough about that	*bu bi yong shuo*	不必用說	3
No need to tell everything	*bu bi jin shuo*	不必盡說	1
Speed up your storytelling	*pinghua jieshuo*	評話捷說	2
Let's leave this track and rather tell	*anxia yitou, que shuo*	按下一頭,卻說	5
Meanwhile let's perform*	*qie biao*	且表	2
Let's rather perform	*que biao*	卻表	10
Let's perform once again	*zai biao*	再表	1
Let's leave … and perform in particular	*anxia … dan biao*	按下 …單表	3
Let's not tell about …but perform in particular	*bu shuo … dan biao*	不說 …單表	12
Let's not speak more of this… but perform in particular	*bu ti … dan biao*	不提 … 單表	12
Let's not continue our performance of this	*bu zai yanbiao*	不在言表	7
Let's not speak more of this	*bu ti*	不題	101
Let's leave this and not speak more of it	*anxia zheli, bu ti*	按下…, 不提	7
This has already been performed, let's not speak more of this	*biaoguo bu ti*	表過不題	12
Let's not speak more of what happened that night	*yisu wan jing buti*	一宿晚景不題	4
Let's not go into boring detail	***hua xiu xufan***	話休絮煩	**3**

LANGUAGE SHIFTING AND THE NARRATING INSTANCE

Let's not waste more words on this	*hua xiu rao she*	話休饒舌	16
The story says no more of this	***bu zai hua xia***	不在話下	**99**
There is no more to tell about that evening	***dang wan wu hua***	當晚無話	**3**
About all that happened that evening we have already spoken	*yisu wanjing tiguo*	一宿晚景題過	13
There's no more to say about the trip	*yilu wu ci*	一路無詞	6
The story divides at this point	***hua fen liangtou***	話分兩頭	**9**
Day and night hastily passed	*guangyin xun su*	光陰迅速	6
Day and night flew like arrows, sun and moon shifted like shuttles	*guangyin si jian, ri yue ru suo*	光陰似箭, 日月如梭	2
Day and night hastily passed, sun and moon shifted like shuttles	*guangyin xun su, ri yue ru suo*	光陰迅速,日月如梭	4
It's slow in the telling, but it happened in a flash	***shuoshi chi, nashi kuai***	說時遲那時快	**4**
When you have something to tell, the story grows long. When you have nothing to tell, it's short	***you hua ji chang, wu hua ji duan***	有話即長, 無話即短	**1**
…then the story would have stopped here	*…bian ba*	便罷	27
…then nothing more in the whole world would have happened	*…wan shi jie xiu*	萬事皆休	5
Just look**	***zhi jian***	只見	Ca. **400**

Bolding indicates that the marker is in common between *Shuihu zhuan* and *Jin Ping Mei cihua*. The numbers in the fourth column indicate the number of occurrences in *Jin Ping Mei cihua*

* The expression 'just look', *zhi jian,* is treated as a stock phrase on a par with the other phrases of Table 3.3., cf. ROLSTON 1993: 129; Børdahl 2013: 117–118. Sometimes *zhi* 只 functions as MSC 'then', *jiu* 就 + verb 'see', *jian* 見 (then he/she saw), but it also has the highly frequently function as a stock phrase reminiscent of the verse-introductory phrase *dan jian*. However, *zhi jian* is never placed at the end of a paragraph, before an indented set piece, such as is the case with *dan jian*. But like *dan jian*, *zhi jian* introduces and emphasizes visual situations, namely prose descriptions that are of a striking nature. In *Jin Ping Mei cihua* Chapter 1, where the story of Wu Song and the tiger is retold, *dan jian* is repeatedly used in shared passages where early editions of *Shuihu zhuan* have *zhi jian,* something that corroborates the understanding of *zhi jian* as a variation *of dan jian*

** Even though *biao* 表 has a wider meaning, such as 'show' or 'express', its meaning in the context of storytelling *shuoshu* 說書, *shuochang* 說唱, is generally 'to perform', *biaoyan* 表演, cf. below, note 8.

rule not framed by the same set of storyteller's stock phrases.[7] This usage is extremely interesting, not only for its 'experimental' (or sometimes just 'irregular') character, but also with a view to the connection between *Jin Ping Mei cihua* and contemporary oral genres of *shuochang* and drama (Rolston 1994: 31–32).

While the verse-introductory markers of *Jin Ping Mei cihua* are very close to those found in the novel *Shuihu zhuan,* this is not the case with the markers of transition and progression. Only about a fourth of these markers are shared between the two novels. The shared markers (**bolded**) are highly frequent in both works, but in *Shuihu zhuan* the constant use of a small number of markers of transition and progression leave an impression of a stereotyped 'manner' that could easily be the result of editorial pre-printing revision. It is noteworthy that the so-called *jianben* 簡本 (simple version) editions of *Shuihu zhuan* are characterized by a still shorter and more stereotyped list of markers of transition. These editions, although the surviving copies are roughly contemporary with the earliest *fanben* editions, seem to bear witness to an earlier stage in the development of the 'storyteller's manner' as a written style of the novel (Børdahl 2013: 327–337). In *Jin Ping Mei cihua* the sheer variation of these expressions, even though each of them has a fixed formulaic form, provides the progression of the tale with a livelier framework. While it is unlikely that this phenomenon would reflect the style of contemporary scriptwriting for performed literature, it exemplifies what is probably the apex of the development of the 'manner' or 'simulacrum of storytelling' for the genre of the novel as written literature.

Another deviation from the novel *Shuihu zhuan* is that many of the markers of transition and progression in *Jin Ping Mei cihua* point to 'performance', *biao* 表, or *yanbiao* 言表. While *Shuihu zhuan* refers to the narrator's activity as 'telling', *shuo* 說, and the object of the telling as 'the story', *hua* 話, *Jin Ping Mei cihua,* besides sharing the activity of 'telling the story', also uses the 'storyteller's manner' as a demonstration of the activity of 'performance'. There are 14 markers composed with the verb *shuo* 說, while the verb *biao* 表 is used in seven expressions. The latter is completely absent from the *Shuihu zhuan*. A couple of times the narrator of *Jin Ping Mei cihua* even uses a meta-narrative marker that adds testimonial evidence about the 'genre' in which the story is supposedly told/performed, i.e. 'speed up your storytelling', *pinghua jieshuo* 評話捷說.

---

7   The most frequently used melody, *Shanpo yang* 山坡羊, is mentioned in total 20 times in the work, 8 times with the addition of the verse-introductory formula 'in proof', *wei zheng* 為證 (there is a *Shanpo yang* song 'in proof'...), but elsewhere without any special verse-introductory marker. The other relatively frequent melodies, such as *Jinzi jing* 金字經, *Suo nanzhi* 鎖南枝, *Shua hai'er* 耍孩兒, *Hongxiuxie* 紅綉鞋, and *Zhu yun fei* 駐雲飛 occur altogether 29 times, but only twice with 'in proof', *wei zheng*, added.

LANGUAGE SHIFTING AND THE NARRATING INSTANCE

Table 3.4. Markers of the narrator's comments and
appeals to the audience in *Jin Ping Mei cihua*

Listen, dear audience	*kanguan tingshuo*	看官聽說	**45**
Storyteller, why do you only love to tell about ...?	**shuohuade**,*rujin zhi ai shuo ...zuo shen*	說話的如今 只爱說 ... 做甚	**2**
Do you think this really happened?	*ni shuo you zhedeng shi*	你說有這 等事	1
In fact	*yuanlai*	原來	**99***
If you really don't know what comes next, please, **listen to the explanation in the following sessi**on	**bijing** *wei zhi houlai he ru,* **qie ting xiahui fenjie**	畢竟未知後 來何如 且聽 下回分解	**98****

Bolding indicates that the marker is in common between *Shuihu zhuan* and *Jin Ping Mei cihua*. The numbers in the fourth column indicate the number of occurrences in *Jin Ping Mei cihua*

*The expression 'in fact' *yuanlai*, occurs altogether 184 times in the work, but 85 times are in dialogues between the characters. In Table 3.4 only occurrences in narrative passages are counted.

**The chapter ending stock phrase occurs regularly after each chapter, except the final chapter 100. However, there is one chapter where this phrase is left out, probably by mistake, so that there are altogether 98 occurrences.

By way of the 'storyteller's manner' – as manifested in the meta-narrative markers – not only is the context of the storyteller narrator 'simulated', but also the *genre* of the work as orally performed *pinghua* is suggested. Through the meta-narrative phrases composed with *shuo, biao, yanbiao* and *pinghua*, the 'narrating instance' of *Jin Ping Mei cihua* identifies the written work with the oral entertainment genre of *pinghua*-storytelling.[8]

The markers of the narrator's comments and appeals to the audience constitute a short list of only five expressions. Four of these are also used in *Shuihu zhuan*. 'In fact', *yuanlai* 原來, is very frequent as the introductory remark for a comment from the narrator, but it functions in general as a time adverb irrespective of whether it has a textual function as a 'comment' or not. The

---

8   The expression *biao* is used both in *Suzhou tanci* 蘇州彈詞 and in *Yangzhou pinghua* 揚州評 話 for 'performing', especially with a view to the narrative portions in contrast to dialogue, cf. Bender 2003: 55–56, and Børdahl 1996: 442.

chapter-concluding phrase 'listen to the explanation in the next session', *qie ting xiahui fenjie* 且聽下回分解, is used in a longer version than that found in *Shuihu zhuan*. It occurs once in every chapter, except the last. This marker, together with 'Listen, dear audience', *kanguan ting shuo* 看官聽說, and referring to the narrator as 'storyteller', *shuohuade* 說話的, just like the expression *pinghua jieshuo* 評話捷說 that we have discussed above, are strongly supportive of the illusion of *pinghua* storytelling as an oral activity with performer and audience in face to face contact. But in contrast to the manner of the 15th century *shuochang cihua,* it is the *illusion* of *pinghua*-storytelling that matters. The work as a whole in its printed form could not, in this form, be regarded as a *bona fide* rendition of a certain storytelling repertoire.

Many passages of the work seem to have been, so to speak, 'cut out' from oral or oral-related performance genres of the time and 'pasted into' the work, more or less directly, just as passages in officialese or religious dogma are inserted into the kaleidoscopic 'realism' of the work. This kind of recirculation of oral and written materials does not basically change the narratological frame of the work, but it all contributes to the impression of a playful and ironic mind lurking behind the narrating instance of the work. Once again one feels the need for the narratological concept of the implied author.[9]

The 'Manner' in *Yangzhou Pinghua*: Oral Performance and Written Script

How far can we relate the function and form of the novelistic 'manner' to oral professional storytelling, as we know it from present day performance practice of storytelling in China, such as Yangzhou storytelling, *Yangzhou pinghua* 揚州評話, and other oral genres of China? Does this kind of manner exist in oral storytelling? Does it exist in written *aides-mémoire* of storytelling? To explore this question, we shall consider a corpus of oral performances of *Yangzhou pinghua* from 1961 to 2003, recorded on tape and video (Børdahl 1996; Børdahl (Yi Debo) 2006 and 2016. See also Børdahl 2003). Further we shall examine a genuine storyteller's script from the Yangzhou tradition of WESTERN HAN, datable to the late Qing (ca. 1880–1910) (Børdahl and Ge 2017).[10]

Let us recapitulate the main features of the storyteller's manner and see how far these features are present/not present in 1) oral performance of Yangzhou storytelling in the 20th century, 2) the script from late Qing.

---

9   Cf. the discussion of the superfluous status of this concept in Genette 1988, Chapter 19.

10   Titles of oral traditions, such as the Yangzhou tradition of WESTERN HAN, are written in SMALL CAPITALS to distinguish them from titles of printed books, written in *italics* as usual.

LANGUAGE SHIFTING AND THE NARRATING INSTANCE

Table 3.5. *Main features of the 'manner' in novel, oral storytelling, and written script*

Storyteller's manner	Novel *Shuihu zhuan*	Novel *Jin Ping Mei cihua*	*Yangzhou pinghua* in oral performance	*Yangzhou pinghua* in written script
Division into sessions	X Session *hui* 回	X Session *hui* 回	X One session of storytelling *yichang shu* 一場書 One day of storytelling *yitian shu* 一天書	0 No division according to sessions
Prose and verse	XX Verse in medium proportion	XXX Verse in high proportion	X Verse in low proportion	XXX Verse in high proportion
Storyteller narrator	X Overt narrator as storyteller *shuohuade* 說話的	XX Overt narrator as storyteller *shuohuade* 說話的	XXX The narrator *is* a professional storyteller *shuoshu yiren* 說書藝人	0 Covert third person narrator
Simulated dialogue with audience	X Storyteller, why was it...? *shuohuade,... yinhe* 說話的 ... 因何	XX Dear audience, listen! *kanguan tingshuo* 看官廳說	XXX Frequent intrusions of simulated dialogue with the audience, but no *real* dialogue	0
Stock phrases	XX	XXX	(0)	XX

X = this feature is found; 0 = this feature is not found or exceedingly rare (0); XX = the feature is frequent; XXX = the feature is highly frequent.

VIBEKE BØRDAHL

Stock Phrases of the Western Han Script

Since storyteller's stock phrases are very rare in the oral tradition of *Yangzhou pinghua*, we shall now concentrate on the features of the Western Han script, a manuscript of 330 handwritten pages in black calligraphy with additions by a later hand[11] in light ink (underlined below).

In the Western Han script, we find about the same handful of frequent verse-introductory markers as in the plain tale and novel, but *Jin Ping Mei cihua* has about twice as many in total. However, the high-frequency markers are the same as those in the script.

In the script, we find a much shorter list of markers for narrative transition than in the novel, particularly in *Jin Ping Mei cihua*. Both in the plain tale and in the novel, we find the formula 'let us just tell', *zhi shuo* 只說, but this form is not found in the Western Han script. Here we find, however, the very similar formula: 'let's now tell about', *zhi yan* 只言. The negative form 'no more of this', *bu yan* 不言, is also a frequent marker of transition. The use of *yan* instead of *shuo* seems to parallel the literary style *wenyan*, which flavours the script throughout. The formula 'the story goes', *hua shuo* 話說, extremely frequent in the novel, is found only once in the script. The formula 'meanwhile, let's tell', *qie shuo* 且說, also very frequent in the novel, is found only twice in the script, and in both instances it is used in passages added by the later hand and marked by underlining. The same is true of the formula 'time passed by like an arrow', *guangyin ru jian* 光阴如箭, seen only once in an added phrase.

Only one formula is found that belongs to the traditional set of formulas for 'simulated dialogue with the audience', namely 'how did it look? / 'what a sight!', *zen jiande* 怎見得. This formula has two functions, both as a signal of verse (usually in proximity to a verse, but not as the ultimate pre-verse marker) and as the narrator's (storyteller's) simulated question to an imagined audience. The form occurs regularly in the plain tale *Xuanhe yishi*, a few times in *Shuihu zhuan* and has a certain frequency in *Jin Ping Mei cihua*. In the Western Han script, *zen jiande* functions mainly as one of the verse-introductory formulas and has hardly any connotation of 'conversation with the audience'.

In a couple of instances, we find in the script the expression 'let me explain' or 'one should explain', *jiaodai* 交待, which is not used in the plain tale or the novel. In the edited book versions of Yangzhou storytelling from the 20th century, this expression is not infrequently found, as a marker of the storyteller's

---

11 The later hand is identified with the last owner of the manuscript, who was a storyteller of this repertoire, the late master Dai Buzhang 戴步章 (1925–2003), cf. Børdahl and Ge 2017: Introduction.

42

LANGUAGE SHIFTING AND THE NARRATING INSTANCE

Table 3.6. Verse-introductory markers in the WESTERN HAN script

Behold	*dan jian* / *dan zhi jian* / *dan jiande*	但見, 但只見, 但見得	**11**
Indeed	*zheng shi*	正是	**107**
There is a poem in proof	*you shi wei zheng*	有詩為証	**57**
The poem says	*shi yue*	詩曰	**1**
How did it look	*zen jian* / *zen jiande*	怎見, 怎見得	**36**
… a stanza as follows	…*yishou*	… 一首*	4

The **bolded** forms are found in the plain tale *Xuanhe yishi*, in *Shuihu zhuan* and in *Jin Ping Mei cihua*; … *yishou* 一首 is shared with the plain tale; the other non-bolded forms are not shared with either plain tale or novel. The numbers in the fourth column indicate the occurrences in the WESTERN HAN script.

* See Børdahl 2013: 36, 124. The use of '[...] a stanza as follows' is reminiscent of the style of the plain tales, where this formula has many variations, all ending with '[...]a stanza as follows'.

address to the audience. But in oral performance of Yangzhou storytelling the expression is exceedingly rare. The two occurrences in the script are both in the added comments and they serve as a reminder to the performer of how to perform a certain passage, not 'simulated dialogue' with the audience.

To sum up the situation in relation to the stock phrases: In the script, we find a regular use of four verse-introductory markers, identical with the high-frequency formulas of the plain tale and the novel, but with some interesting variations. Transitional meta-narrative formulas are sparingly used, and only a couple of terms from the usual set of formulas used in the novel occur. The only traditional formula of the storyteller's simulated conversation with the audience is used primarily as a signal of verse, with only a faint tinge of appeal to the audience.

It seems obvious that the WESTERN HAN script does not intend or pretend to be a 'reproduction' or 'mirror' of actual performance. There is no indication of how much should be told in one session, no division of the text into 'sessions' or 'days of storytelling', no markers of closing a performance or beginning a

VIBEKE BØRDAHL

Table 3.7. Markers of narrative transition in the WESTERN HAN script

Let's now tell about	*zhi yan*	只言	19
No more of this	*bu yan*	不言	14
No more of this	***bu ti***	**不提/題**	**7**
Just look	***zhi jian***	**只見**	**45**
The story goes	***hua shuo***	**話說**	**1**
Meanwhile, let's tell	***qie shuo***	**且說**	**2**
Time passed by like an arrow	***guangyin ru jian***	**光阴如箭**	**1**

Not underlined = first hand of the manuscript; underlined = second hand of the manuscript

The **bolded** forms are found in the plain tale *Xuanhe yishi*, in *Shuihu zhuan* and in *Jin Ping Mei cihua*; the other non-bolded forms are not shared with either plain tale or novel. The numbers in the fourth column indicate the occurrences in the WESTERN HAN script.

Table 3.8. Narrator's appeal to the audience in the WESTERN HAN script

How did it look	***zen jian / zen jiande***	**怎見，怎見得**	**36**

new one. This feature is reminiscent of the plain tale *Xuanhe yishi*, where the text also runs on undivided. It is of course in contrast to the novel and to oral *Yangzhou pinghua*. Oral performances are by necessity divided into sessions lasting a couple of hours, but in *Yangzhou pinghua* this kind of division is usually highly flexible, to fit in with the situation. There is no fixed plan for how a repertoire should be divided into portions to be told. Moreover, in contrast to the 'manner' of the novel, there are no formulas of beginning or ending a session.

The alternation of prose and verse is clearly reflected in the script. The prose portions record the happenings of the story in a short, terse style, with inserted dialogue, while verse and set pieces are inserted with regular intervals. From the oral performance tradition of *Yangzhou pinghua* it seems obvious that the prose portions were meant to be performed at much greater length, while the verse etc. had to be learned by heart (Børdahl 2005, 2013: 240–243). That is consistent with the practice in pre-modern vernacular drama, where prose

LANGUAGE SHIFTING AND THE NARRATING INSTANCE

was not fully textually represented but was meant to be amplified in actual performance (Ge Liangyan 2001: 26–27). Probably dialogues, verses, and set pieces were the *raison d'etre* for the script. Some scripts had only verses and set pieces (Børdahl 2005: 257).

The narrator of the written script is imperceptible (covert, third person narrator). This phenomenon is closely connected to the kind of language used in the script, the simple *wenyan* style of history writing or chronicle. The writer of the script is apparently not interested in reproducing the actual spoken style of storytelling. The fixed portions, such as solemn and portentous dialogues, poems, statements, etc., *do*, as far as we can test from modern performance, reflect the words-in-performance that are actually spoken, but there is little reason to think that the storytellers would also narrate the saga in the *wenyan* style of the script. It is more likely that the compressed style of narration was a kind of shorthand, as well as a habit of written style. This was not a reflection of the actual oral storyteller's linguistic habits, and it was certainly at a distance from the narrative style of the novel, too. But this brief style was closer to that of the plain tale.

In contrast to the plain tale and novel, the WESTERN HAN script does not in any way pretend to mirror the storyteller's direct address to the audience. The few examples of 'explaining', *jiaodai*, are found, not in the hand of the original script writer, but in a couple of notes added by the later hand, in order to remind the *performer*, not the *audience*, of certain portions that need to be told more in detail.

The usage of 'storyteller's stock phrases', *taoyu*, in the script is particularly intriguing. Were the stock phrases part of the linguistic idiom of 'history writing' in simple *wenyan,* adding a few of the most general stock phrases to introduce verse and demarcate transition in the text? Verse and set pieces are marked by indentation in the text, so that the formulas are somehow superfluous. Were the *taoyu* mainly part of a *written tradition of recording oral repertoires?* They could have had very little to do with the actual oral habits of the performers of WESTERN HAN. We know that storytellers of Yangzhou storytelling in the late 20th century hardly used such *taoyu* during performance. Occasionally, there might be a single instance, but the use of such expressions was in general not part of Yangzhou storytellers' idiom of performance. The writer of the script was perhaps giving his text a finish of storytelling ('the storyteller's manner') by using these *taoyu*, but at present we cannot know exactly what the relationship was between these expressions in the written script and the tradition of oral performance during the late Qing.

Interestingly, it is the second hand, the last owner of the script, who occasionally inserts a few stock phrases in the style of the novel into his added remarks, such as 'meanwhile, let's tell', *qie shuo*, and 'time passed by like an arrow', *guangyin ru jian*. Did he try to apply the 'written vernacular style' of the novel when he wrote things into the script – a style that he would not use for oral performance?[12]

The 'Manner' in *Jin Ping Mei cihua* and the World of Oral Storytelling

The oral-related genre of *cihua* 詞話 (*chantefable* or 'prosimetric storytelling') is not a constituent word of the meta-narrative phrases used in the text, but the word is used as a genre appellation in a loose sense in the title of the first edition of *Jin Ping Mei,* the *cihua*-edition of 1617 (David Roy in Nienhauser (ed.) 1986: 849–851). Indeed, the work itself is not an example of the *cihua* genre as we know it from the 15th century (McLaren 1998: 105–114). Obviously, from the point of view of genre and formal characteristics, the *Jin Ping Mei cihua* is written into another stream of entertainment literature, stretching from the Yuan period plain tale, *pinghua* 平話, (Hegel 1998: 24–25; Breuer 2001: 150–169 and passim) and the *yanyi* 演義 and *zhuan* 傳 of the Ming, i.e. the genres that were later subsumed under the concept of the novel, *zhanghui xiaoshuo*. It is, however, perhaps significant that the early edition of *Jin Ping Mei* was not presented as *yanyi* or *zhuan*, but as *cihua*.

For the *Shuihu zhuan,* oral antecedents are documented, both in 'tales of the streets and lanes' from the 13th century and in the plain tale format.[13] Since the *Jin Ping Mei cihua* is explicitly related to the tradition of the Wu Song saga, shared with *Shuihu zhuan,* both novels have distant oral origins. This is of course the case for most vernacular fiction, since recirculation of story-material with ultimate oral roots is a frequent phenomenon. However, this kind of connection to formerly oral traditions is irrelevant for the question of a certain written work of fiction and its possible more *immediate* relationship to oral performance. From the point of view of the 'storyteller's manner' as manifested in the *Jin Ping Mei cihua,* is it at all possible to argue for a relationship with contemporary Ming oral storytelling (16th century), and if so, in what respect?

---

12 Neither *qie shuo* nor *guangyin ru jian* are found in the oral performances by Dai Buzhang that are studied in Børdahl 1996 (Yi Debo 2006) and Børdahl and Ross 2002.

13 The picture eulogies, *huazan* 畫贊, about the 36 heroes of Song Jiang were based on 'hearsay from the streets and lanes' from the 13th century; the section on Song Jiang and some of his men in the plain tale *Xuanhe yishi* was demonstrably based on colloquial narration, most likely associated with oral storytelling (Ge 2001: 37–40; see also Børdahl 2013: 29–33).

LANGUAGE SHIFTING AND THE NARRATING INSTANCE

Oral storytelling, called *pinghua* 評話, has flourished since the Ming (McLaren 1998: 98–100; Lévy 1999: 35) and has continued in modern oral *pinghua* 評話, through the Qing into the 21st century (Børdahl 1996; Yi Debo 2006).[14] When the compilers of the first great Ming novels adopted the storyteller's manner and developed a written vernacular, their immediate source and linguistic model could hardly have been elsewhere but must be anchored in the oral storytelling of their time (Hanan 1981: 21–22). But with the establishment of the genre of the novel and the short story as written genres, it is equally true that the written model became another immediate model for the later compilers and authors of fiction (Hanan *ibid.*). Oral storytelling continued to exist, and in later centuries writers could draw on oral as well as written sources for inspiration, just as the storytellers could. The oral and the written genres of entertainment fiction seem to have gone hand in hand since the Yuan and Ming. This give-and-take – the mutual influence between the oral and the written – is of course a highly complicated issue, and the 'manner' of the novel should certainly not be taken at face value as a mirror of spoken performance (Børdahl and Wan 2010: Introduction; Børdahl 2013: Chapters 2, 3, 5 and 12). But even as a secondary 'imitation of orality', the framework may yield some insights into the question of the kind of *model* envisaged for the work.

What is particularly interesting in this case is that the *pinghua* genre of oral storytelling is mentioned as an oral genre performed for Ximen Qing and his brotherhood in Chapter 39:

Yuanlai Wu daoguan jiaole ge shuoshude shuo Xihan pinghua 'Hongmen hui'.

原來吳道官叫了個說書的說西漢評話鴻門會。

In fact, Abbot Wu had invited a storyteller to come over and tell them the episode of 'The meeting at Swan Gate' from the *pinghua* of Western Han.

This short passage is embedded in the narrative of the chapter as the most natural thing on earth. Nothing more is said about it. That there should be a performance of *pinghua* 評話, is mentioned only *en passant*.[15] A professional storyteller, *shuoshude*, is mentioned twice in the *Jin Ping Mei cihua*, in Chapters 35 and 39, in both cases relating to Abbot Wu, who each time

---

14 We can trace the art back even further to the early 14th century, if we consider the plain tales *pinghua* 平話 (*Xuanhe yishi, Wudai shi pinghua* 五代史平話, etc.) as precursors to *pinghua* 評話.

15 In the French translation by André Lévy it is noted that an oral performance is meant, but in the English translation by David T. Roy there is a misunderstanding of the kind of performance meant by *pinghua* (Lévy 1985: 820, 1228; Roy 2001: 420; see also Rolston 2014: 97, entry 39.514).

了函張卓卓上堆的鹹食齋饌，點心湯飯甚是豐潔。西門慶寬

去衣服同吃了早齋，原來吳道官吽了個說書的，說西漢評話

鴻門會。吳道官發了文書走來陪坐，問哥兒今日來不來西門

慶道正是小厮還小哩，房下恐怕路遠諕着他來不的。到午間

拿他穿的衣服來，三寶面前攝受過，就是一般。吳道官道小道

也是這般計較最好。西門慶道，別的倒也罷了，他是有些小膽

兒家裡三四個丫鬟連養娘輪流看視，只是害怕貓狗都不敢

到他根前吳大舅道孩兒們好容易養活大，正說着，只見玳安

進來說裡邊桂姨銀姨，使了李銘吳惠送茶來了，西門慶道吽

他進來李銘吳惠兩個拿着兩個盒子，跪下揭開都是頂皮餅、

松花餅、白糖萬壽詩糕、玫瑰搽穰捲兒西門慶俱令吳道官收了

金瓶梅詞話　　第三十九回

Figure 3.1. *Jin Ping Mei cihua*, Chapter 39, page 10a, 2nd column

invites a storyteller to entertain the brotherhood. Both passages are short and 'insignificant', which points to the normality of the activity. It is, however, mentioned by one of the brothers that the price for the performance by the storyteller is quite high (Chapter 35).

The *pinghua* of WESTERN HAN has a long tradition of oral transmission among storytellers from Yangzhou (Børdahl and Ge Liangyan 2017: 1–3). The fact that it was also a well-known repertoire in the fictional universe of *Jin*

Ping Mei cihua confirms an even longer existence of the repertoire. The genre of *pinghua* has a 'realistic' existence internally in the work, since it belongs to one of the oral genres of entertainment that are provided for the characters in the narrative. This existence is of course on another level, different from the idea of the narrator of *Jin Ping Mei cihua* posing as a 'storyteller of *pinghua*' as implied by the meta-narrative stock phrases, notably the phrase *pinghua jieshuo*, mentioned above. Through the special variety of the storyteller's manner found in *Jin Ping Mei cihua* the work defines itself not only as storytelling but as *pinghua*-storytelling. While it demonstrates a large amount of material from other contemporary oral entertainment genres, none of these are incorporated into the narratorial model.

However, *Jin Ping Mei cihua* – in contrast to *Shuihu zhuan* – regularly inserts songs, defined by their melodies, and presented mostly as sung by the characters of the work. It would be strange if these were not meant for the ear, but only for the eye of a reader. The insertion of these songs seems to presuppose a reader who can hum the songs to himself or recreate the songs as music in his inner thought. But more importantly they seem to reflect closely the contemporary milieu of song culture in general, songs that were on the lips of everybody concerned with popular music, drama, and performance (Hanan 1963: 63; Jiang Kun and Ni Zhongzhi 2005: 354). From this perspective, the format of *Jin Ping Mei cihua* as a novel invites comparison with oral traditions of storytelling performed with singing and musical accompaniment, as we shall discuss below.[16]

Storytelling, *shuoshu* 說書, as performed by Liu Jingting 柳敬亭 (1592–1674), was sometimes without music or singing (Zhang Dai 1986: 68). This is still the case today for oral *pinghua* as performed in Yangzhou storytelling. We should note, however, that when Zhang Dai (1597–1689) comments on the storytelling of Liu Jingting, 'Liu Jingting as storyteller', *Liu Jingting shuoshu* 柳敬亭說書, he mentions especially that his performance was in prose, *baiwen* 白文. This might well imply that Liu Jingting did not always tell in *baiwen* or that other storytellers did not restrict themselves to prose performance but did perform their tales with music and song. There is still a tradition, for storytellers of *pinghua* as well as story-singers of *tanci* 彈詞, to consider Liu Jingting a founding father. It is obvious that Liu Jingting did not 'invent'

---

16 Chen Liao 1988 argues for a number of 'remnants' of *pinghua* storytelling with song in the *cihua* edition of *Jin Ping Mei*, remnants that were meticulously removed or changed in the Chongzhen edition and later. For a readership that did not know the songs anymore but was reduced to read the passages without having the music in mind, this stuff material had apparently become tedious and superfluous.

the genres for which he became the representative so-called founder or 'great master' (*Zhongguo quyi zhi. Jiangsu juan* 1996: 7). It seems more likely that *shuoshu* as well as *pinghua* were not yet during his lifetime strictly divided into traditions of prose storytelling and storytelling with song and music (Wei Ren and Wei Minghua 1985: 85–88). It is also noteworthy that *tanci* and *xianci* 弦詞 had been recognized genres of storytelling, *shuoshu,* since the late Ming and were considered 'small repertoires', *xiao shu* 小書, dealing with love stories, while the term *pinghua* was gradually reserved for the 'great repertoires', *da shu* 大書, about war and heroic action (Wei Ren and Wei Minghua 1985: 83–85).

The *chantefable* genre as documented from the 15th century has a format that is quite far from the form of *Jin Ping Mei cihua.* The later genres of story-singing could provide interesting comparative material for an understanding of possible oral antecedents or oral models for the format of *Jin Ping Mei cihua.* The present-day oral story-singing genres, like the prose genres, carry with them age-old traditions that can open our eyes to phenomena of the former world of *shuochang.* The oral genres that come to mind are those of *tanci* 彈詞 (Suzhou) and *xianci* 弦詞 (Yangzhou), but also *Fuzhou pinghua* 福州平話, a genre going back to the early Qing period and performed in both prose and verse. For the episode of 'Wu Song Fights the Tiger', *Wu Song da hu* 武松打虎, common to *Shuihu zhuan* and *Jin Ping Mei cihua,* there exists a written text of *Fuzhou pinghua,* dated to the late 19th or early 20th century (Børdahl 2013: 431–447). Here we can see at a glance that this genre – in its oral-related written form – applies a fixed meter for the verse portions, which immediately sets it apart from the style of *Jin Ping Mei cihua* (but makes it closer to the style of the *chantefables*). Nevertheless, there are also interesting parallels in the usage of stock phrases including the term 'performing', *biao* 表, and the description of an erotic milieu of prostitution, which are characteristic of this piece of performance literature (Børdahl 2013: 223–224, 431 ff.). A comparison of the way songs are used in contemporary oral *tanci* and *xianci* vis-à-vis in *Jin Ping Mei cihua* might give further background to an understanding of how far the novel was anchored in or inspired by already existing oral traditions in this respect. *Tanci* and *xianci* as terms for oral genres are generally considered to have appeared only in the 18th century. Before that time, the story-singing genres were called *guci* 鼓詞, *cihua* 詞話, and *changci* 唱詞. In *Jin Ping Mei cihua,* the first two expressions are not found in the text of the novel, (*cihua* only in the title), but in Chapter 100 we find an instance of *changci* as a profession for the impoverished young woman, Han Aijie, who says: 'Because of the chaotic situation, nobody could come with me, and I had to travel on alone as best I could, supporting myself by story-singing... 荒亂中又沒人帶去, 胡亂單身唱詞, 覓些衣食前去'. Whether *changci* points only to the singing of songs

LANGUAGE SHIFTING AND THE NARRATING INSTANCE

or to prosimetric story-singing reminiscent of the later genre of *tanci* is not clear. But in any case, it is a kind of singing by which she can earn her living (clothes and food).

The printed work *Jin Ping Mei cihua*, as it exists in book form, breaks with the genre of modern oral *pinghua* in several ways. First, based on the performance practice of modern *Yangzhou pinghua* we may doubt that the insistent use of stock phrases for meta-narrative remarks had such prominence even in the oral *pinghua* of the Ming (Børdahl 2013: 340–344). The storyteller's manner, ultimately inspired by oral models, is, in *Jin Ping Mei cihua,* handled with a supreme literary flourish. Even if *Jin Ping Mei cihua* was closely connected to oral tradition, the work as we have it bears witness both to adaptation to the novelistic 'manner' and to a burlesque playing around with all kinds of oral genres.[17]

The Yangzhou storyteller's WESTERN HAN script provides evidence that the scribes of such *aides-mémoire* may well have applied a certain number of the stock phrases of the 'manner'; poems, set-pieces, and dialogues reflected words as performed. However, the narrative portions were in a compressed shorthand style, typical in historical chronicles, but not in performed oral storytelling. In this sense, the script is not only far from oral performance, but also far from the style of the novel. A WESTERN HAN storyteller has learned the repertoire by studying with a master for several years, taught orally. The script is only intended to help him, reminding him of stories he already knows. An oral performance will necessarily represent an *amplification* of the narrative text of the script, just as the script represents a *short form* or *condensation* of the oral performance.

The first printed edition of *Jin Ping Mei*, the *cihua* edition, would, according to this evidence be far from a script-like version of an oral repertoire of *pinghua* prose with song. Both the *Shuihu zhuan* and the *Jin Ping Mei cihua* may, however, in their narrative language, both dialogue and narration, have been much closer to oral *pinghua*-storytelling as *performed*. The genre-indicating word of the title, *cihua,* appears to fit well with the specific 'manner' of the narrating instance. I think there is good reason to understand this item of the novel's vocabulary as a short form of *changci pinghua* 唱詞評話. The narrating instance, embedded in the special intralingual stratum of the 'manner', including the title, is therefore *posing* not only as a generalized storyteller, but more specifically as a performer of *changci* and *pinghua,* i.e., *cihua.*

---

17 This feature is typically considered by some scholars to be a sign of the inventiveness and 'experimentation' of the individual author, cf. Rolston 1994: 34–35. By others it is regarded as a 'remnant' of oral *pinghua* storytellers' practice of inserting musical or humorous additions into their narrative performance, cf. Chen Liao 1988: 17–19.

Conclusion

The formation and composition of early novels in China, including *Jin Ping Mei cihua*, are still nebulous questions, despite an enormous research tradition. Here we have only been concerned with a very small detail of the picture: the form and function of the intralingual meta-narrative idiom of the narrating instance as demonstrated in the work. Through the specific inventory of terms used in the 'manner' of *Jin Ping Mei cihua*, the narrator is defined as a performer of *changci* and *pinghua*-storytelling, genres that are also mentioned as entertainment for and by the characters of the novel. We have compared this meta-narrative idiom to that of pre-modern and modern *pinghua*-storytelling in oral (as recorded performances) and written form (as script or *aide-mémoire*). What we have found is an intricate picture of similarities and differences as shown in the tables.

In brief, the meta-narrative formulary idiom of *Jin Ping Mei cihua* is not only far more developed than that of the early plain tales, but also much richer than that of the *fanben* of *Shuihu zhuan*. One could say that this feature of the vernacular narrative is being overdone, almost parodied. Compared to modern storytelling of *pinghua* – *Yangzhou pinghua* – this feature is even more prominent, since 20th century storytellers of this profession hardly used any of the stock-phrases of the 'manner'. Compared to the style of a genuine written storytelling script from late Qing in the *Yangzhou pinghua* tradition, the situation is much the same, but the script – reminiscent of the early plain tales – does intersperse the narrative with a few markers of this kind, mainly verse-introductory markers. The storyteller's manner of the novel *Jin Ping Mei cihua* is therefore much more conspicuous, almost glaring, while in the true storytelling that we are able to record today, 400 years later, there is – considering the feature of stock-phrases – hardly any 'manner' and few 'mannerisms'. This situation seems bound up with the level of narration (the narrating instance) of a real storyteller confronting his real audience in real life. But that is probably not the only aspect, since the oral idiom of the storytellers *as storytellers* is not to be confused with their daily language as ordinary citizens. The idiom of the true storyteller, like that of the simulated storyteller, can be observed as a specific narrating instance.

The authorship of *Jin Ping Mei cihua* has always been controversial. Was the book written by an ingenious (but anonymous) literati scholar with a large library to consult for constant borrowing of passages, plot fragments, poems, songs, sketches, jokes etc.? Or did it grow out of a milieu of oral performance, and if so, how? Was it originally a storyteller's script for performance? Did it have collective authorship, and if so in what sense? Maybe there is no contradiction here, when we consider the role of oral tradition in China. Storytelling for entertainment has had a strong position and a widespread significance in China from the Song dynasty into the 20th century – a milieu of oral transmission that fosters exceptional talents to this day. I think we need to take into consideration the special workings of oral-performed traditions, the mutual borrowings from a common pool of oral storytelling, drama and song traditions, the ability to remember and creatively *retell* large amounts of story-material and constantly bring them into recirculation – something we can still observe in the living genres of today's China. Obviously, we find a lively arena for intralingual translation in the professional activity of the performers.

Storytellers seem to have been a mixed population, with both illiterate and literate people among them. Their audience likewise seems to have always been composite, including not only poor people who had little access to books, but also well-educated people from upper classes. Like the milieu of theatre, that of storytelling in recent times, as we know it from the example of Yangzhou, was attractive for all kinds of aficionados, who took an active part and some of whom entered the ranks of the storytellers themselves or wrote down oral repertoires, sometimes as scripts, sometimes as novels (storyteller's novels).[18]

On the narratorial level, the *Jin Ping Mei cihua* simulates this activity and milieu. The text *as text* – apart from being printed on paper – identifies itself with story-singing and storytelling. Obviously, this is only one of the colours in the linguistic palette of the work, only one strand in the warp and woof of the shifting registers of the entire text. But under the aegis of singing and telling, the story develops in the daily spoken language of the time in dialogue and narrative, including a wealth of low- and high-style literary material, officialese, and religious, dramatic, and musical borrowings or pastiches. The author, from the point of view of the narrating instance, is truly dressed up as a storyteller – a *pinghua*-storyteller – but the historical creation of the work is an entirely different question.

---

18 Examples are some 18th century novels connected to Yangzhou storytelling, such as *Qingfengzha* 清風閘 (Qingfeng Sluice) (1819) and others (Wan 2009: 177–204). In the 20th century, aficionados, scholars and storytellers from Yangzhou all published oral Yangzhou *pinghua* repertoires as novels – cf. the production by local scholars of Wang Shaotang's *Shuihu* 水滸 (Water Margin) repertoire and by Fei Junliang and Fei Li of their own various repertoires (Børdahl 1996: Bibliography).

References

Bender, Mark

2003. *Plum and Bamboo. China's Suzhou Chantefable Tradition.* Urbana and Chicago: University of Illinois Press.

Berezkin, Rotislav

2015. 'Printing and circulating "precious scrolls" in early 20th century Shanghai and its vicinity: Towards an assessment of multifunctionality of the genre.' In Philip Clart and Gregory Adam Scott (eds), *Religious Publishing and Print Culture in Modern China*, 139–185. Berlin: De Gruyter.

Børdahl, Vibeke

1996. *The Oral Tradition of Yangzhou Storytelling.* Richmond, Surrey, UK: Curzon.

2005. 'Storytellers' scripts in the *Yangzhou pinghua* tradition.', *Acta Orientalia* No. 66: 227–96.

2010a. 'Storytelling, stock phrases and genre conventions.' In Vibeke Børdahl and Margaret B. Wan (eds), *The Interplay of the Oral and the Written in Chinese Popular Literature*, 83–156. Copenhagen: NIAS Press.

2010b. 'Dialectal and normative registers in Yangzhou storytelling.' In: *Chinese Language and Discourse*, 1(1): 93–122.

2013. *Wu Song Fights the Tiger – The Interaction of Oral and Written Traditions in the Chinese Novel, Drama and Storytelling.* Copenhagen: NIAS Press.

2011–2021(trans. into Danish). *Jin Ping Mei i vers og prosa.* 10 bøger (*Jin Ping Mei* in verse and prose. Vols. 1–10). Copenhagen: Forlaget Vandkunsten. (Volumes 8–10 in press)

2016. 'Tentative thoughts on the "storyteller's manner" in *Jin Ping Mei cihua.*' *Modrý Jasmín, Dálný východ (Far East)*, Olomouc 6(1): 33–46.

Børdahl, Vibeke and Ge Liangyan 葛良彥 (eds)

2017. *Western Han – A Yangzhou Storyteller's Script.* Copenhagen: NIAS Press.

Børdahl, Vibeke and Wan, Margaret (eds)

2010. *The Interplay of the Oral and the Written in Chinese Popular Literature*, NIAS Press, Copenhagen.

Breuer, Rüdiger

2001. 'Early Chinese Vernacular Literature and the Oral-Literary Continuum. The Example of Song and Yuan Dynasties Pinghua'. Ph. D. Dissertation, Washington University.

Carlitz, Katherine

1986. *The Rhetoric of Chin P'ing Mei.* Bloomington: Indiana UP.

LANGUAGE SHIFTING AND THE NARRATING INSTANCE

Chen Liao 陳遼

1988. '"Jin Ping Mei" yuan shi pinghua zai lun 《金瓶梅》原是評話再論' (Discussing again whether *Jin Ping Mei* was originally *pinghua*-storytelling). *Yangzhou shiyuan xuebao* 揚州師院學報 1988 No. 1: 14–19 + 26.

Ge Liangyan 葛良彥

2000. Book review: Anne E. McLaren. *Chinese Popular Culture and Ming Chantefables. Sinica Leidensia* 41, 161–163. Leiden: Brill.

2001. *Out of the Margins. The Rise of Chinese Vernacular Fiction.* Honolulu: University of Hawai'i Press.

Genette, Gérard

1980. *Narrative Discourse.* Translation by Jane E. Lewin. New York: Cornell University Press.

1988. *Narrative Discourse Revisited.* Translation by Jane E. Lewin. New York: Cornell University Press.

Hanan, Patrick

1963. 'Sources of the Chin P'ing Mei.' *Asia Major* 10(1): 23–67.

1977. 'The nature of Ling Meng-ch'u's fiction.' In Andrew Plaks (ed.), *Chinese Narrative.* Princeton NJ: Princeton UP.

1981. *The Chinese Vernacular Story.* Cambridge Mass.: Harvard University Press.

Hegel, Robert E.

1998. *Reading Illustrated Fiction in Late Imperial China.* Stanford, California: Stanford University Press.

Idema, Wilt L.

1974. *Chinese Vernacular Fiction. The Formative Period.* Leiden: Brill.

Jiang Kun 姜昆 and Ni Zhongzhi 倪鍾之

2005. *Zhongguo quyi tongshi* 中國曲藝通史 (A general history of the *quyi* of China). Beijing: Renmin wenxue chubanshe.

Lévy, André

1985. *Fleur en Fiole d'Or (Jin Ping Mei cihua).* Paris: Gallimard.

1999. 'About the Chinese storyteller's change of name.' In Vibeke Børdahl (ed.), *The Eternal Storyteller – Oral Literature in Modern China.* Richmond, Surrey, UK: Curzon Press.

McLaren, Anne E.

1998. *Chinese Popular Culture and Ming Chantefables.* Leiden: Brill.

Meng Zhaolian 孟昭連

1998. 'Zuozhe, xushuzhe, shuoshuren. Zhongguo gudai xiaoshuo xushi zhuti zhi yanjin 作者, 敘述者, 說書人。中國古代小說敘事主體之演進.' (Author, narrator and storyteller. The development of the narrative form of the Chinese classical novel). *Ming Qing xiaoshuo yanjiu* 清小說研究, Nanjing, 4: 137–152.

Nienhauser, William H. Jr.

1986. *The Indiana Companion to Traditional Chinese Literature.* Indiana University Press, Taiwan edition.

Norman, Jerry

1988. *Chinese.* Cambridge: Cambridge University Press.

Porter, Deborah

1991. 'The Style of *Shui-hu Chuan*'. Ph.D. dissertation, Princeton University.

Quanben Jin Ping Mei cihua 全本金瓶梅詞話 (Complete *Jin Ping Mei cihua*).

1982. Facsimile edition. Hong Kong: Taiping shuju.

Rolston, David L.

1993. '"Point of View" in the Writings of Traditional Chinese Fiction Critics.' *Chinese Literature: Essays, Articles, Reviews* 15: 113–142.

1994. 'Oral performing literature in traditional Chinese fiction: Nonrealistic usages in the *Jin Ping Mei cihua* and their influence.; *CHINOPERL Papers* 17: 1–110.

2014. 'Imagined (or perhaps not) Late Ming music and oral performing literature in an imaginary Late Ming household: The production and consumption of music and oral performing literature by and in the Ximen family in the *Jin Ping Mei cihua* (Plum in the Golden Vase)'. In: 'Supplementary Material to Research Note: Introducing a Resource on Music and Oral Performing Literature in the Ming Novel *Jin Ping Mei cihua* made available in celebration of the completion of David Tod Roy's translation.' *CHINOPERL: Journal of Chinese Oral and Performing Literature,* 33(1): 94–95. Available on CHINOPERL website, www.shuoshu.organdatmingstudies.arts.ubc.ca/2014/06/26/rolstonpreprint/

Roy, David Tod

2001. *The Plum in the Golden Vase or Chin P'ing Mei.* Vol. 2. Princeton, New Jersey: Princeton University Press.

Shi Nai'an and Luo Guanzhong 施耐庵，羅貫中

1988. *Rongyutangben Shuihu zhuan* 容與堂本水滸傳 (Rongyutang edition of *Water Margin*). Shanghai: Shanghai guji chubanshe.

Wan, Margaret B.

2009. 'Local fiction in the Yangzhou region: *Qingfengzha*.' In Lucie Olivová and Vibeke Børdahl (eds), *Lifestyle and Entertainment in Yangzhou*. Copenhagen: NIAS Press.

LANGUAGE SHIFTING AND THE NARRATING INSTANCE

Wei Ren and Wei Minghua 韋人，韋明鏵

1985. 揚州曲藝史話 (*A History of Yangzhou Performed Arts*). Beijing: Zhongguo quyi chubanshe.

Yang Bojun 楊伯峻

1965. *Wenyan xuci* 文言虛詞 (*Empty Words in Literary Chinese*). Beijing: Zhonghua shuju.

Yi Debo 易德波, see Vibeke Børdahl

Yi Debo 易德波 (Vibeke Børdahl)

2006 and 2016. *Yangzhou pinghua tantao* 揚州評話探討 (*The Oral Tradition of Yangzhou Storytelling*). Beijing: Renmin wenxue chubanshe. New edition published in 2016 in simplified characters. Nanjing: Jiangsu renmin wenxue chubanshe.

Zhang Dai 張岱 (Ming-Qing)

1986. *Tao'an mengyi* 陶庵夢憶 (*Recollections of Tao'an's Past Dreams*). Taibei: Jinfeng chubanshe.

Zhongguo quyi zhi. Jiangsu juan 中國曲藝志。江蘇卷 (Encyclopedia of Chinese *quyi*. Jiangsu volume).

1996. Zhongguo ISBN zhongxin chuban.

Note on Contributor

Vibeke Børdahl, Ph.D., Dr.Phil. of Sinology, Senior Researcher, Nordic Institute of Asian Studies, University of Copenhagen, Denmark. Main interests: dialects and oral literature, storytelling, interaction between written and oral genres. Translator of *Jin Ping Mei cihua* (1617) into Danish as *Jin Ping Mei i vers og prosa* (2011–2022).

CHAPTER 4

Pan Jinlian as Depicted in the Oral Tradition of the Wang School of WATER MARGIN from Yangzhou Storytelling

MA WEI
Translated by Vibeke Børdahl

Both in the theatre (*xiju* 戏剧) and in storytelling (*pinghua* 评话), it is very important to portray the individuality of the various characters. In Yangzhou storytelling (*Yangzhou pinghua* 扬州评话),[1] the performance of the character of Pan Jinlian 潘金莲 from the repertory of WATER MARGIN (*Shuihu* 水浒)[2] is centrally important, leaving a profound impression on the audience and resulting in a strong artistic portrayal.

As an inheritor of the Wang School,[3] I performed the Yangzhou storytelling repertoire of WU SONG (*Wu Song* 武松) in 2008 in the storyteller's house of the Wang Family Memorial Hall of Gaoyou 高邮. The event lasted for more than 20 days,[4] and the plot went on as far as the most dramatic part of the story, the

---

1   Yangzhou storytelling, *Yangzhou pinghua* 扬州评话, is a Chinese storytelling genre performed in the Yangzhou dialect, with a history of more than 400 years. In 2006 this oral art was entered with priority into the National Register of Intangible Cultural Heritage.

2   *Editor's note*: In Yangzhou storytelling the oral WATER MARGIN repertoire is called *Shuihu* 水浒 (not *Shuihu zhuan* 水浒传 after the title of the Ming novel).

3   *Editor's note:* The Wang School of Yangzhou storytelling is the main branch of the old Deng School of WATER MARGIN 邓门水浒, which was named after its earliest master, Deng Guangdou 邓光斗 (19th century). Wang Shaotang 王少堂 (1889–1968) became the most famous storyteller in China after 1949, and his descendants and disciples, both from within the family and from outside the family, were called 'storytellers of the Wang School'. Ma Wei 马伟 belongs to the current generation of these performers. WU SONG, also called WU SHI HUI 武十回 (Ten Chapters on Wu Song), is one of the four main sagas of the enormous WATER MARGIN repertoire mastered by Wang Shaotang and his disciples, namely WU SONG 武松, SONG JIANG 宋江, SHIXIU 石秀 and LU JUNYI 卢俊义, which have been orally transmitted for more than five generations.

4   *Editor's note*: Storytelling sessions in the present day usually last two hours. For continuous repertoires, there is one session every day, and the length of the whole performance is counted in 'days of storytelling', i.e., two hours a day.

58

PAN JINLIAN AS DEPICTED IN ORAL TRADITION

episode known as 'Killing Sister-in-law as a Sacrifice to Elder Brother' (*Sha sao ji xiong* 杀嫂祭兄).[5] When I came to the place where Wu Song is lifting his knife to kill his sister-in-law, I suddenly 'cut short the story' (*jiankou* 剪口), creating a point of high suspense (*mai guanzi* 卖关子).[6] After the day's performance, there was an elderly member of the audience who came over to the stage and said to me in a serious tone: 'Master, tomorrow is the Mid-Autumn Festival. Can you, please, let Pan Jinlian enjoy the Mid-Autumn Festival first, and postpone the killing? Of course, she must die, but let her at least enjoy the Mid-Autumn. We feel pity on her!'

I think this is the attitude towards Pan Jinlian among afficionados of Yangzhou storytelling: Although she arouses displeasure, she also arouses pity.

In the Wang School of WATER MARGIN, the character of Pan Jinlian is prominent. Pan Jinlian is portrayed as a 'lewd woman' (*yinfu* 淫妇) in both the earlier novels and in the oral literature of present-day China. However, in the Wang School of Yangzhou storytelling, Pan Jinlian has a multi-layered personality. Besides being 'selfish', 'unrestrained' and 'malicious', she is also 'innocent' and 'infatuated'. Her personality develops in four stages: Pan Jinlian is at the outset a 'poor and defenseless girl'. In the oral WU SONG repertory there is an episode called 'Wu the Elder gets married' (*Wu Da jiehun* 武大结婚), where Jinlian's background is described in detail. She is introduced to the audience as a young maid servant in the household of the Wealthy Pan family from Qinghe district. Since her feet have been well-bound since childhood, she is called Jinlian 金蓮 (Golden Lotus).[7] And since the family name of servants at the time usually followed the name of their master, her full name is Pan Jinlian. Later she is spotted by her master, Father Pan. What kind of a person is he? In the storytelling episode he is clearly portrayed as an 'old itchy bone', a greedy and lecherous fellow, crafty, but afraid of his wife. At the time Jinlian is

---

5   *Editor's note*: The subtitles of individual episodes of the oral saga are generally not used during performance. Sometimes they are used in storyteller's books (published versions of oral repertoires) as subtitles or on the advertisements outside a storyteller's house (*shuchang* 书场). These titles are, however, the same as those used in the titles of dramas drawing on the 'Water Margin' stories, as well as those used in many other performance genres.

6   *Jiankou* and *mai guanzi* belong to the insider argot of the Yangzhou storytellers. The first refers to the way the storyteller ends his performance each day when he is performing a long repertoire, continued for several weeks or months; the second refers to the habit of creating an ending with suspense in order to attract the audience to return the following day.

7   *Editor's note*: 'Golden lotus' (*Jinlian*) is the general name for the small bound feet of Chinese women in the late imperial period. In the case of Pan Jinlian, her given name is based on this expression, since her feet are exceptionally small.

only 16 years old. At this young and tender age, she has no chance of opposing her master, and finally she falls victim to his devilish attacks. At this stage, we cannot blame her for being a 'lewd woman'. This is a stroke of her tragic fate that she cannot prevent. However, as soon as her mistress detects the affair between Jinlian and Father Pan, she becomes full of hatred. To punish Pan Jinlian, she decides to 'give the girl away as a present' to Wu the Elder, a dwarf who looks 'scarcely three parts like a human being and seven parts like a devil'. Pan Jinlian is thrown away like a simple commodity. After she is married off to Wu the Elder, she naturally feels very unhappy, but as a poor, weak girl she has no means of resisting her fate. In order to start a new life, the couple decides to leave Qinghe and to move to another township, Yanggu. At this stage Pan Jinlian is a victim of circumstances and has no choice. Still only a child, she must meekly accept the humiliations that she suffers.

When the performance proceeds to the episode of 'Brothers meet again' (*Dixiong xiangfeng* 弟兄相逢), Pan Jinlian manifests herself in a new role as the 'emotional woman'. In her relationship with Pan the Rich and Wu the Elder there have been no true feelings involved. However, when Wu Song appears on the scene, she is changed into a 'woman in love'. After Wu Song has killed the tiger, he looks for his elder brother in Yanggu Town, and as soon as the brothers have found each other, Wu the Elder takes Wu Song home with him. In the Wang School of Yangzhou storytelling, this episode is unfolded with exceptional insight, and the audience is especially moved when listening to this. At this point, Pan Jinlian and Wu Song meet for the first time. As soon as Wu the Elder knocks on the door, Pan Jinlian opens it, and when she spots Wu Song standing right there, she inadvertently blurts out 'Oh, my!' The moment she utters that sound is the beginning of her 'emotional change'. It is also the point from which the storytellers begin to perform Pan Jinlian as a 'passionate' character of strong feelings. She had never imagined that her brother-in-law, Wu Song, would be so tall and strong, a person of outstanding ability, and she says to herself: 'True enough, one mother may bear nine sons, and the nine sons will all be different. But the difference between these two brothers is too amazing. I thought that I, Pan Jinlian, would be drifting like duckweed, ending up anywhere. But now it looks like I have arrived at this home of the Wu family, and I may still be able to be with him to my heart's content.' As soon as Pan Jinlian has seen Wu Song, she is in love with him. When we perform Pan Jinlian's character, we must be very careful and accurate in order to re-create her vivid personality. Imitating the way she opens the door, the way she lifts her face with a dull expression in her eyes – and then suddenly, in a split-second after she has caught sight of Wu Song, her countenance changes into the liveliest expression as if she has had a shot of hormones, and only then she withdraws

PAN JINLIAN AS DEPICTED IN ORAL TRADITION

and tries to compose herself. When this scene is performed with all the details, it will often result in a chuckle from the audience, visualizing this new 'passionate' Pan Jinlian. In the episode 'Jinlian flirts with her brother-in-law' (*Jinlian xishu* 金莲戏叔), she tries to seduce Wu Song, whose handsome looks and charm touch the strings of her already hopelessly enamoured heart with force. When she is told that her brother-in-law will soon leave on a mission, she takes advantage of a morning when Wu the Elder is not at home and abruptly lets her latent passion flow over.

When the story arrives at the episode 'Flirting by the awning stick' (*Chagan tiaoqing* 叉竿调情), Ximen Qing enters the stage and Pan Jinlian changes again, from being a 'passionate woman' to a 'lewd woman'. From the episodes of 'Madam Wang arranges a tryst' (*Wang Po shuo fengqing* 王婆说风情), to 'Collaborating on evil plans' (*Gouchuan moujian* 勾串谋奸), the story is about a series of love encounters.[8] As Wu the Elder is about to catch the lovers in the act, but is wounded by Ximen Qing, Madam Wang asks Jinlian: 'Do you want to become a long-term wife of His Highness Ximen Qing, or just a casual partner?' At this question Jinlian hesitates, and Madam Wang says: 'If we consider it a casual partnership, the feelings of those concerned can be soothed. After Wu the Elder has recovered, we can just pay him five hundred silver taels. But that means His Highness must from now on forever break his association with you, my lady, and never see you again. We must make a somersault and not speak any more about it. If you aim to become a long-term wife, the plan is clear. We must get hold of two crowns' worth of arsenic and get rid of the old man tonight.' Pan Jinlian finally decides to accept the solution that will cost Wu the Elder his life: 'I want to become a long-term wife of His Highness.' We can say that Pan Jinlian has hitherto appeared as a 'poor and defenseless girl' and then as a 'passionate woman', which is all due to the oppression of Pan the Rich and the unhappy marriage to Wu the Elder. It is understandable if she sometimes oversteps the bounds of what is proper. But her decision in this case leads her to commit an unforgivable sin. She chooses to kill Wu the Elder with arsenic, and thus she allows herself to enter a road of no return. This is what fixes the image of Pan Jinlian as a 'lewd woman' in the minds of the audience.

When the performer of the Wang School arrives at the episode of 'Wu Song returns home' (*Wu Song hui jia* 武松回家), we may notice some differences vis á vis the novel *Water Margin* (*Shuihu zhuan* 水浒传). At this important turning point, Pan Jinlian, in the oral performance, changes again. She changes back

---

8 In the novel *Shuihu zhuan,* this episode describes Pan Jinlian's utterly lewd character. The famous critic Jin Shengtan 金圣叹 (1608–1661) admires the author Shi Nai'an 施耐庵 (Yuan) for 'describing a lewd woman so that she truly comes to life as a portrait of a lewd woman'.

into an 'infatuated woman', and her 'infatuation' is described with particular care. After Pan Jinlian has murdered Wu the Elder, she considers Ximen Qing her only real 'husband'. When Wu Song returns home the second time, she is drinking with Ximen Qing upstairs, dreaming about how the two of them will 'fly in heaven like a pair of lovebirds and intertwine here on earth their branches like a loving couple'. When the 'sixth seven-days' period'[9] is over, she is going to be married into the family of Ximen Qing as a wife. At this point she has changed completely into an 'infatuated woman' (*chi nüzi* 痴女子).

This characteristic is also the main feature of her personality as performed in the episode 'Killing Sister-in-law as a Sacrifice to Elder Brother' of Yangzhou storytelling, but at the same time her person is portrayed with a multifaceted richness of colours. At this junction the audience is also changing from a purely depreciative attitude to one of compassion and sympathy; as the saying goes: 'the most hateful person also has tender spots'. As Wu Song, with an iron knife in his hand, forces Jinlian to confess in front of the neighbours, we witness once more how her 'infatuation' is completely revealed. An iron knife on her neck, she still puts all her faith in Ximen Qing and expects his protection. When she is about to deliver her oral confession, a single word multiplies into ten words and a single sentence grows to ten in her attempt to draw out the time, and she believes the whole time, until her death, that Ximen Qing will surely arrive with some men and deliver her. As she is crying in front of Wu the Elder's spirit tablet, we find an ironic commentary in Wang Shaotang's work, *Wu Song*:[10] 'After Wu the Elder's death, Pan Jinlian had cried quite a lot, but it was all false tears, purely snuffling and snivelling. On this day, however, she surely cries in earnest.' Pan Jinlian is shedding tears and repenting: 'If Wu the Elder had still been alive, my brother-in-law would never dare to lift his knife and kill me.' But even though she is regretting it all in her heart, she whispers at the end: 'I didn't know better than that I had a bond with *him* from an earlier existence. Who could have predicted that my brother-in-law would return home today and send my soul off to the Yellow Springs ...'? She is still convinced that in marrying Wu the Elder she had no choice, but with Ximen Qing it was true love. However, what awaits Pan Jinlian as an 'infatuated woman' is the pitiless iron knife of Wu Song.

Generation after generation of storytellers from the Wang School has continuously 'added flesh' (*duirou* 堆肉)[11] to the portrait of Pan Jinlian, so that she

---

9 42 days after the person has passed away.

10 *Editor's note:* Wang Shaotang's oral WU SHI HUI repertory was recorded and edited into a 'storyteller's book' under the title of *Wu Song* (Wang Shaotang 1959).

11 Another expression from the Yangzhou storytellers' insider argot, meaning to 'enrich', to 'flesh out'.

PAN JINLIAN AS DEPICTED IN ORAL TRADITION

has been sculpted into a many-facetted image of a 'tragic, comic, pitiful, hateful but also sympathetic person', a representative example of the art of character portrayal in Yangzhou storytelling.

Let us return to the beginning: Because of the 'plea for leniency' from the audience, I decided to perform, the following day, a review of the four stages of Pan Jinlian, from 'defenceless girl' to 'passionate woman', 'lewd woman' and finally 'infatuated woman'. In this way I succeeded in letting Pan Jinlian stay 'alive' over the Mid-Autumn Festival.

After all, our art is meant to serve the audience...

References

Jin Shengtan piping ben Shuihu 金圣叹批评本水浒
    2015. Beijing: Beijing Lianhe chuban gongsi.

Wang Litang 王丽堂
    1989. *Wu Song* 武松. Zhongguo quyi chubanshe.

Wang Shaotang 王少堂
    1959. *Wu Song* 武松. Jiangsu renmin chubanshe.

Wang Xiaotang 王筱堂
    1992. *Yihai kuhang lu* 艺海苦航录. Ed. by Jiangsu wenshi ziliao bianjibu and 江苏文史资料编辑部. Zhenjiang zhengban.

Xu Deming 徐德明 and Li Zhen 李真
    2006. 'Cong "Wangpai Shuihu" kan Yangzhou pinghua de yishu xingtai tezheng 从'王派水浒'看扬州评话的艺术形态特征'. *Yangzhou daxue xuebao* 扬州大学学报 (2): 39–44.

Yangzhou quyi zhi 扬州曲艺志
    1993. Ed. by the editorial committee for *Yangzhou quyi zhi*. Jiangsu wenyi chubanshe.

Note on Contributors

Ma Wei 马伟 is a fifth generation storyteller of the Wang School of WATER MARGIN from Yangzhou storytelling and studied with Hui Zhaolong 惠兆龙 and Wang Litang 王丽堂. He is a Member of the China Quyi Artists Association Committee for Storytelling; Vice-chairman of the Association of Young Artists of Jiangsu Province; Vice-leader of the Institute of Yangzhou Quyi; Vice-chairman of the Association of Yangzhou Quyi Artists. He has won the Ninth National Contest of the Chinese Quyi Peony Prize (for best performance), as well as the Second Cultural Prize of Jiangsu Province (for best performance and best script).

Vibeke Børdahl, Ph.D., Dr. Phil. of Sinology, Senior Researcher, Nordic Institute of Asian Studies, University of Copenhagen, Denmark.

CHAPTER 5

Killing Sister-in-law as a Sacrifice to Elder Brother

PERFORMED BY MA WEI

Translated by Loughlin Harrick

'Hey, fellow! Bring me an iron chain, close the door and bolt it, put the chain on, and lock the door.'

'Will do!' The fellow locked the door at once. The three old neighbours, Hu Zhengqing, Zhao Zhengming and Yao Wenqing, looked at each other:

'Old friends, hm...?'

'Yes, Old Wen!'

'What's going on?'

'Hm..., we don't know.'

'I, Yao Wenqing, have lived to 83 and have never heard of a host closing and locking the door and even bolting it! Why is he locking the door?'

'Hm, well, let's just leave it, shall we?'

There were also two freeloaders, one called Xiao Chenghuang, the other called Li Tudi. The two of them looked at each other, chuckling:

'We'll tell you! Do you know why Captain Wu wants the door locked and chained? Our captain, he's a northerner, he's as frank as can be, not like us locals. Today he's prepared wine for us, he's definitely prepared a feast, I reckon four stir-fries, four cold dishes, five main dishes and eight small dishes, and the first dish is sea cucumber! He is aware how old we are and worries we won't be able to finish it all, that we'll just have a bite and be off. That's why he's locking the door.'

The translation of this performance is based on a written version in Chinese provided by Ma Wei as a transcript of his oral performance of 'Killing Sister-in-law as a Sacrifice to Elder Brother' (*Sha sao ji xiong* 杀嫂祭兄), performed 11 September 2017, 23:51 mins, transmitted on the program Guangling xue (广陵雪) which is available on YouTube.

65

The two freeloaders were gluttons and thought of nothing but food.

Madam Wang, the old [teahouse] hostess, looked around: 'Oh my!' She knew something was going on today, best to go upstairs and stay with Pan Jinlian. She went to the kitchen, fetched a serving tray, a pot of wine, two small dishes of food, two pairs of cups and chopsticks, and went upstairs to see Pan Jinlian.

'Young Lady, don't be silly, don't be sad! Of course you're sad! But if you cannot have things your way, you must try another way! Your husband is not here anymore, he's gone, you still have to go on living. He hated to leave you and you him. Come on, today your brother-in-law has come home. Your Auntie will stay with you upstairs and we shall have a cup of wine.'

'You are right!' Pan Jinlian thought to herself: 'Oh, Godmother, good Godmother, you understand that my life is at stake downstairs, that I'll feel more secure upstairs.' So the two women straightened their faces and prepared to go upstairs.

Wu Song looked at them and thought: 'So you are going upstairs! How can I let you two go upstairs? I'm ready to kill!' Lifting his arm, the hero blocked the stairway:

'Godmother, where are you two going?'

'Oh, my! Don't you understand your sister-in-law? How pitiful she is, with her hair uncombed, her face unwashed, no thoughts of tea or food. She is eating her rice mixed with her tears. So you've come home today? Those guests downstairs, they are all male guests, they're all male. But your sister-in-law and me, we're women, we are womenfolk. We're going upstairs for a drink. Please go and attend to the guests downstairs.'

'No, that won't do! You must stay downstairs, Granny! We'll sit together.'

'Oh, my! Can I sit downstairs? We are women. Those downstairs are all men. How can men and women drink together? If people saw it, they would laugh so much, their teeth would fall out of their mouths. Let me tell you, your sister-in-law can sit here, but your auntie cannot, I'm a widow.'

Wu Song stared at her, thinking: 'You are certainly very well-behaved!'

'These neighbours are all elderly gentlemen with white beards.'

'Their beards are white, but even if they live to a thousand, they'll always be men, and we'll always be women! Men and women are different and should not touch or exchange items and avoid suspicion that they are doing so.'

KILLING SISTER-IN-LAW AS A SACRIFICE TO ELDER BROTHER

'Godmother, I told you to stay here downstairs! So please do stay! Why are you so fickle? Sit down!'

'I'll stay, I'll stay! I'll sit down! What are you shouting for? If one behaves correctly, one acts correctly. I'm not afraid of sitting next to a monk!' Madam Wang knew she was in trouble today. She was not even allowed to go upstairs.

The soldier beside them brought out paper money ingots, silver wax, and agarwood incense, placed them in the incense burner, lit them, and placed six large dishes of food and tributes on the table.

'Captain?'

'Yes?'

'The food and wine for the memorial banquet have been served. Please, sir, come over and kowtow.'

'What do you mean? Who are you asking to kowtow?'

'I'm asking you to kowtow. You're commemorating your elder brother. Shouldn't you kowtow?'

'I am not going to kowtow.'

'If you are not, who is?'

'Let her do it!' He pointed at Pan Jinlian who stood beside them.

Why didn't Wu Song want to kowtow? Because the title of this session is 'Killing Sister-in-law as a Sacrifice to Elder Brother'. Only when Pan Jinlian's head and heart are placed on the table will he do his kowtow. When he now asked Pan Jinlian to kowtow, she did not dare to disobey. She came over and kowtowed, shivering. When Pan Jinlian had kowtowed, the three old neighbours kowtowed, and Wu Song bowed in obeisance. The two freeloaders Xiao Chenghuang and Li Tudi also kowtowed, and Wu Song bowed. The four soldiers kowtowed, Wu Song bowed. Madam Wang kowtowed, and Pan Jinlian bowed.

Then the soldier dragged a large table over into the room. At that moment, the three elderly neighbours began to display utter politeness towards each other: 'Please, take the seat of honour, Elder Master! Please, do!'

Wu Song watched them and thought: 'If you are going to be so polite, it will be late in evening before you are finished! Let me handle this!'

'Grandpa Hu and Grandpa Zhao, please sit down in the seat of honour! Grandpa Yao and Godmother, please take the seats opposite them! Master

67

Xiao and Master Li, please sit down on the side, and sister-in-law, please come over here!'

He called her over to sit beside him, working out how to accomplish his murderous plan. Although they were sitting on the same bench, there was still some distance between them, about half a metre, I think.

At that moment, wine was poured.

'Here's to you, Grandpas!'

All of them saw how he finished his cup in one gulp. My goodness, it did not look like drinking wine! He swilled it down like cold water.

'Second Master, you can really hold your liquor, all we can do is appreciate it. We would like to ask you, Captain, why have you invited us here tonight?'

'My three distinguished neighbours, your servant has asked you here tonight to solve a domestic matter.'

'Captain, forgive me for interrupting your noble speech, but your clan patriarch should solve domestic matters; how could we outsiders concern ourselves with the matters of your honourable house?'

'Dear Grandpa, your humble servant is not a local person, I am from Qinghe county, Guangping prefecture in Beizhi. I migrated here, a stranger in a strange land, no patriarch to speak of, I can only ask you elders to discuss this case in public.'

'Very well, no case will escape the scrutiny of a public discussion. This table is square as sure as reason is round. Let's have a discussion in public and let public reason reign! What domestic matter do you have in mind, Captain?'

'I'm glad you asked, Grandpa!'

At this moment, our hero undid his ceremonial robe and let it sweep the floor – shsh... – with one move, the gentleman let his sleeves fall – the robe circled around his head, and then with a leap, he threw it toward the kitchen entrance.

'Catch it!'

'Yes!', a youngster, sharp-eyed and agile, caught it and hung it over a chair.

After removing his outer robe, a short-hilted broadsword in a red, embroidered sheath was revealed at his waist. The eldest neighbour, Yao Wenqing, stared at him and thought: 'My goodness, isn't that a 's-s-saw'...at his waist?' His tongue was stiff with fright, and he could not manage to say 'sword', so he said 's-s-saw'.

'Let me, your humble servant, ask you, Grandpa: In this world there is both life and death, sure enough?'

'Why! Captain, a clever person like you should not ask such a question. Of course there is life and death in this world. If there were no death, the streets would be swarming with people. If there were no life, they would be deserted. So there is both life and death, we are sentenced to death before we're born.'

'Ah! The saying goes that life, death, wealth, and status are fated by Heaven. Life and death happen normally in other families. But that was not the case with my elder brother. My elder brother was murdered!' Wu the Second pointed at Madam Wang and cursed: 'You colluding, worthless, depraved, old slut! You killed my brother! You are the root of misfortune in my house!' Second Master Wu spoke no lies, everything had been planned and directed by Madam Wang.

How did Madam Wang react? Anyone else in her place, being cursed to her face, would, of course, not be able to just sit there! But she, she was different! Crossing her legs and not moving an inch, she said in a steady voice:

'Let me tell you something, Wu the Second! Don't you shout and swear! I have taken good care of your home and house, and this is how you're thanking me today! Young Lady, you're still sitting there, aren't you? Please speak up in public!'

Madam Wang thought to herself: 'My dear Pan Jinlian, are you present or not? Your brother-in-law has laid it all out. He says you cheated on your husband and killed him! What are you doing just sitting there? Say something!'

'Yes, let me tell you something, dear brother-in-law! Don't listen to what onlookers are stirring up! It will hurt our in-law relationship. As the ancients said: In this world, even cats and dogs cherish life, and your elder brother and I enjoyed the marital love like "fish in the water".'

When our hero heard the words 'fish in the water' he felt flames scorching his heart. 'Damned cheap slut! Since you know all about marital love and righteousness, how could you poison him with arsenic!'

'That is slander!'

'Enough!' With one palm, Wu the Second slapped Jinlian and sent her down onto the dirty floor, stepped forward and, like a tiger flashing its claws, caught a handful of Jinlian's black hair.

'Get up!'

Clutching her hair, he dragged her up. He dragged her up, did he? Oh, my! How heavy could Pan Jinlian be? Such a slender woman, who weighed less than 79 pounds! With the 2000-pound strength of Wu Song's arms, he picked up Pan Jinlian the way I pick up a chicken at home, effortlessly. Lifting his arm, he unsheathed his iron sword from its red embroidered sheath and drew it out. The blade was about an arm's length, four fingers wide, chilling cold, ghastly cool and shining brightly. There he stood with the murderous iron sword in his hand, eyebrows raised, rolling pupils and eyes wide! The neighbours beside him began dissuading him. All three of them were scared out of their wits.

'Captain, you can't kill her, you can't!'

One of them grabbed Wu Song's right hand. In actual fact, Wu Song did not mean to kill her that moment. If he had done so, three neighbours, or even 30 of them, would not have been able to stop him. Once his grip tightened, the blade would fall.

As Wu Song had drawn his sword, its flash of cold light was scaring someone to death – who? The freeloader sitting opposite, Xiao Chenghuang! Xiao Chenghuang was sitting there and eating merrily. A dish had just arrived, what was it? Sugar-roasted pig's head! He had just selected a chunk from his bowl – fat and lean meat in stripes like a staircase. Just as he was about to put it into his mouth, Wu Song on the opposite side drew his blade. Its cold flash startled him. The meat quavered in his mouth and stuck in his throat, not going in, not going out; his face changed colour. In mortal fear, he clasped his throat with both hands, feeling constantly choked. Hu Zhengqing stared at him:

'Damn! Either somebody is going to be being killed or somebody is going to be choked to death! Hey! You soldiers, come over here to save him and be quick!'

'What? All right, I'm coming!'

One of the young fellows came over. If you had been one of these youngsters, you would have given the neighbour a slap on the back and been done with it. But this fellow was not like that; he deliberately made the poor man suffer.

'Grandpa, was the food so good that you had to put yourself in such a state? You must slow down a bit! You're choking, right? I told you again and again to stop eating but you still went ahead. You're not doing very well, are you? Having a hard time? I should let you choke a little longer, but you're old and you can't take it, so sit still!'

He lifted his hand and slapped Xiao Chenghuang on the back. Couldn't you have been a little softer? How thoughtless and overly forceful! That bite of pig

KILLING SISTER-IN-LAW AS A SACRIFICE TO ELDER BROTHER

head shot out like a bullet, and lo and behold, perfectly skimmed the tip of Yao Wenqing's nose.

'What was that?'

'Oh, Old Yao, it was a piece of pig's head.'

'Goodness, that piece of pig's head knocked my nose crooked!'

At that moment, Pan Jinlian became terrified: 'Let me confess!'

When Madam Wang heard this, she thought: 'Oh, you will confess! Then you're done for, and so am I! I must leave immediately.'

Madam Wang lifted her hand and pulled out a hairpin, so that her coiffure fell down. This is called 'keeping the pot boiling'. Clapping her hands, she shouted:

'Oh, no! Oh, no! All you worthy neighbours are present. You have all raised sons and daughters, and you must speak up in public! What Wu Song is saying is foul language, slandering his widowed sister-in-law! How could you neighbours know that I have taken care of everything in his house? But I understood: Wu the Elder is gone, sister-in-law is young, and Wu Song is unmarried. He thought it convenient to take her as his wife, but she declined. So, he's using foul language to frame her. You must not believe his barefaced slander. This case is urgent! If you worthy neigbours won't take him to task, I'll have to. I'm going to get the magistrate now!'

With that, she prepared to leave.

Wu Song watched her:

'Young fellows, see how talkative this old biddy is! Grab her for me!'

'That's it! Come on, Granny, our Captain is solving a domestic issue, and you're talking nonsense, come here.'

'I tell you! Don't you touch me!'

'And what if I do?'

'You were born as a man, and if I live for a thousand years, I'll still be a woman. Men and women should not touch or exchange items, and I'm a widow at that! One does not seek shelter from the rain in a widow's house!'

'I'm getting sick of listening to you, I don't know why you're bringing that up! Come on!'

'Stop it! For every grievance someone is responsible, for every debt there is a debtor! If you touch me, I'll risk my life against you.'

71

When the young fellow heard this, he did not dare to move. As the senior squad leader was watching, [he said]:

'Let me take care of this!'

As soon as Madam Wang saw this, [she said]:

'So, *you* are coming, alright! Then I'll risk my life against you!'

With these words, she bent at the waist, lowered her head and charged at the senior leader. He dodged, and Madam Wang stabbed the air and fell flat on the ground. The senior fellow picked her up:

'Brother, try and knock some life into her!'

Madam Wang knew she was in trouble:

'Gentlemen, we're civilised folk, let's use words, not our fists.'

'Then you'd better behave yourself.'

'I don't know how I could behave any better.'

'Then get going!'

'Where?'

'To the kitchen and sit down!'

'Sit where?'

'On the wooden block.'

'Lower your head.'

'Yes.'

'Don't speak.'

'No.'

'Behave yourself.'

'Yes.'

Madam Wang behaved herself.

At that moment Pan Jinlian began to confess:

'On the second of February the trouble began at our home. Madam Wang called me over to make a shroud. Who could tell that when I'd only sewn two stitches, she would bring some wine to warm my hands, and that after drinking it I would become dizzy and pass out? When I woke up, I'd lost my chastity to Ximen Qing. Madam Wang had put a magic potion in the wine.'

What had Pan Jinlian said? She said Madam Wang had put a magic potion in the wine. Did Madam Wang really do that? Let me declare this in public: Pan Jinlian and Ximen Qing's adultery was 'like a general buying a horse – both parties are willing'. However wicked Madam Wang might be, she did not put any magic potion in the wine. Pan Jinlian said this because 'the frog fights for its life, but the snake has to eat its fill, too'. We must all do what we must to survive. Pushing the blame onto Madam Wang, did the old lady hear it? Why should the old granny not hear it? She was cocking her ear, and when she heard it, she stood up, raised her hands and split aside the four soldiers in front of her.

'Let me through.'

The soldiers were pushed aside, and Madam Wang stepped outside, feet thumping on the ground, *da, da, da, da* ... She clapped her hands and pointed at Pan Jinlian:

'How awful! How awful! ... Young Lady, what are you saying? You're spouting nonsense, you! I gave you a magic potion, did I? When did I ever give you a magic potion? Alright, alright, alright, alright! That's what you're saying, come on then! Let me ask you, then! Let's assume that I prepared a magic potion. But that day when you and Ximen Qing were together, and your husband caught you in the act, Ximen Qing refused to beat him, but you still told him to! So he beat the pitiful old man until his nose and mouth bled! You're not going to blame that on your old auntie, are you? Let me ask you something else: After you beat him, I asked you if you were going to stay illicit lovers or be a real husband and wife, and you said ... you said you wanted to be husband and wife! How shameful, how shameful ...! And let me ask you another thing: When your husband came home, he refused to drink that arsenic, but you pushed it into his mouth, didn't you? Heaving his eyebrows, his eyes rolled and his teeth gritted. But you still pushed it in, until blood was pouring out of all his openings, and he died such a pitiful death. You're not putting the blame for that on your old auntie, are you? Is this how a young person should talk? Heaven above knows! May Buddha preserve us!'

Oh, my! She even managed to call on Buddha!

Wu Song was looking at her:

'Drag the old procuress away.'

'Yes, right! Let me through. – But, oh, my! Master...?

'Are you going to start up your nonsense again?'

'I have something I must say, I will not be accused unjustly!'

'Haven't you said it already now?'

'Yes!'

'Then go! Go to the kitchen.'

'To the kitchen? Well ...'

Madam Wang behaved herself.

At this moment Pan Jinlian began confessing, a very long confession. But even a long confession needs an ending. She just went on and on, and the more she talked, the angrier Wu Song got:

'What! Damned cheap slut! You are an adulteress and you've killed your husband! That this blade shall cleave your neck is just! I avenge my brother!' *Slash* ... with one swipe, he killed Pan Jinlian!

Note on Contributors

Ma Wei 马伟 is a fifth generation storyteller of the Wang School of WATER MARGIN from Yangzhou storytelling and studied with Hui Zhaolong 惠 兆龙 and Wang Litang 王丽堂. He is a Member of the China Quyi Artists Association Committee for Storytelling; Vice-chairman of the Association of Young Artists of Jiangsu Province; Vice-leader of the Institute of Yangzhou Quyi; Vice-chairman of the Association of Yangzhou Quyi Artists. He has won the Ninth National Contest of the Chinese Quyi Peony Prize (for best performance), as well as the Second Cultural Prize of Jiangsu Province (for best performance and best script).

Loughlin Harrick is a student translator currently completing his Masters of Interpreting and Translation at Monash University, Melbourne, Australia. He graduated from Monash with a BA and Bachelor of Music with a major in Chinese Studies. During this time, he studied for a year at Shanghai International Studies University and Peking University. As part of his Masters, his research project focused on Orientalism in translation of Chinese science fiction, during which he translated three short stories by Liu Cixin 刘慈欣.

JIN PING MEI AND INTERTEXTUALITY

CHAPTER 6

Oral Performing Literature in Traditional Chinese Fiction

Non-realistic Usages in the *Jin Ping Mei cihua*

DAVID L. ROLSTON

Traditional Chinese fiction is full of references to oral performing literature. It is surely conceivable that some of these references were included in order to lend verisimilitude to the fictional worlds described in these works of fiction. That is to say, the appearance of descriptions of the performance of oral literature in fictional works could perhaps be explained as a reflection of the real world that produced and consumed these works. If we were to argue that the sole purpose of the inclusion of these descriptions was to remind the reader of the real world and to persuade the reader to accept the fictional portrayal of that world as real, such a use of oral performing literature could be characterized as 'realistic'. If we were to argue further that these descriptions were included solely for the purposes of verisimilitude and literary realism, for their ability to signify the 'real', we would be in the realm of what has been called 'insignificant notation', 'useless detail' or 'circumstantial realism', and these descriptions would provide relatively unmediated information on the role of oral performing literature in traditional Chinese culture.

This paper, however, is concerned with 'non-realistic' uses of oral performing literature in traditional Chinese fiction. Although these non-realistic uses

Editor's note: David L. Rolston has kindly allowed us to include this extract from his article, 'Oral performing literature in traditional Chinese fiction: non-realistic usages in the *Jin Ping Mei Cihua* and their influence', originally published in *CHINOPERL Papers*, 17 (1994): 1–36. The rest of the article traces the model outlined in the extract in later editions of the novel and its sequels and in later fiction. A 'road map' of the entire article appears at the end of the introduction, in the paragraph that comes right before the first heading. The extract is reprinted courtesy of Hawai'i University Press, the current publisher of the journal, whose name changed in 2013 to *CHINOPERL: Journal of Chinese Oral and Performing Literature*. The list of references for this reprint only include those relevant for the extract. Minor corrections, with the approval of the author, have been made.

include anachronisms, such as figures that are ostensibly Northern Song dynasty (960–1127) singing the latest hits of the late Ming dynasty (1368–1644), and unlikely events such as fictional characters trading arias with each other, by the word non-realistic I intend to refer to all usages exclusive of the realistic kind outlined above. These non-realistic usages range from content-oriented categories, such as allegory, to form-oriented categories, such as experimentation in the adaptation of dramatic techniques and conventions to the telling of fictional stories. A single instance of the description of a performance can have both realistic and non-realistic aspects; very few descriptions are entirely the one or the other. In any case, with non-realistic usage, our attention is drawn away from the issue of whether the content of the description is in accord with reality or plausibility and towards a different issue: what message is being conveyed by the non-realistic usage.

In China, the relationship between fiction and oral performing literature has always been very close. Recently the tendency of scholars to specialize in either fiction or drama has been criticized and the need for a more unified and dialectical history of their interaction has been stressed. At one time it was thought that the earliest works of vernacular fiction were developed from promptbooks used by professional oral storytellers. Although this view has now been largely discredited, almost all vernacular fiction imitates aspects of oral storytelling, and this is especially true in the conception of the narrator. Many stories and novels were adaptations of plays or prosimetric narratives, while dramatists also turned works of fiction into plays. With the rise of printing in the late Ming, the development of a market for printed popular literature, and the new willingness of literati to compose works in popular genres, one of the major differences between oral performing literature and fiction, the fact that the former was ordinarily performed and not read and the latter was ordinarily read and not performed, became less clear-cut.

Unlike in the West, whose foundational poetics is based on drama, in China the development of a poetics of drama and discussion of the distinguishing characteristics of the genre comes quite late and remained underdeveloped. The criticism of fiction in traditional China was even less systematic, and the description and analysis of non-dramatic oral performing literature was almost non-existent. This lack of theoretical or even analytical literature was compounded by the fact that because neither fiction nor oral performing literature was felt to belong to the realm of 'Literature', bibliographic classification systems tended either to leave them out of consideration, or to include individual works under categories that had nothing to do with creative literature. All of this led to a certain fuzziness over generic boundaries, which was further compounded by the fact that many critics and practitioners worked in several different genres.

NON-REALISTIC USAGES OF ORAL PERFORMING LITERATURE

Ling Mengchu 凌濛初 (1580–1644), for example, wrote plays, dramatic criticism, and two collections of vernacular short stories. Yet a play was included in an edition of one of the story collections and he used the dialogue of a different play for the dialogue of one of the stories. He also incorporated an aria and several poems from a play into his story version of that play. Jin Shengtan 金聖歎 (1608–1661), author of an extremely influential commentary on the novel *Shuihu zhuan* 水滸傳 (Water Margin), wrote an equally influential commentary on the play *Xixiang ji* 西廂記 (Western Chamber), and included both works in his list of *caizi shu* 才子書 (works of genius). The *Xixiang ji* 西廂記 commentary was criticized by Li Yu 李漁 (1611–1680) for exhibiting an almost complete lack of understanding of the play as a work of drama but Li Yu himself, notwithstanding the fact that he was the author of one of the most systematic and comprehensive treatises on drama, has been criticized for not sufficiently distinguishing drama from fiction.

The tendency to conflate oral performing literature with fiction or to include the former under names more properly applied to the latter reached a new height in the 19th century and the beginning of the 20th century. In the 19th century novel *Qinglou meng* 青樓夢, the main character responds to the question 'Among works of fiction [*baishi* 稗史], which do you consider the best?' by putting *Shitou ji* 石頭記 (Story of the Stone) first, and a play, *Xixiang ji,* next. Lin Shu 林紓 (1852–1894), the prolific 'translator' of Western literature into Chinese, would translate dramatic works into fictional form. In the writings of late Qing reformers of fiction, such as Yan Fu 嚴復 (1853–1921) and Liang Qichao 梁啟超 (1873– 1929), and in the journals founded by them and among those influenced by them, works of drama, prosimetric narrative (e.g., *tanci* 彈詞) and fiction all appear under the rubric of 'fiction' (*xiaoshuo* 小說).

Alongside this persistent conflation of oral performing literature and fiction there were additional reasons for writers of fiction to turn to the other forms of popular literature for sustenance. Prior to the composition of the *Jin Ping Mei cihua* 金瓶梅詞話 in the latter half of the 16th century, complex characterization and complicated plot structure divorced from history could be said to have been terra incognita for fiction writers, whereas works of great complexity such as Dong Jieyuan's 董解元 (fl. 1190–1208) version of the *Xixiang ji* story in the prosimetric *zhugongdiao* 諸宮調 style and Gao Ming's 高明 (c. 1301–c.1371) play *Pipa ji* 琵琶記 had been around for centuries. Even though we do have indications that printed works of fiction were sometimes read to the illiterate, fiction reached a far more restricted audience than oral performing literature. While writers of fiction could assume that the average person was familiar with works of oral performing literature, they could not assume the same familiarity with printed works of fiction.

DAVID L. ROLSTON

Of course, Chinese traditional fiction was not alone in featuring non-realistic descriptions of and references to oral performing literature. In Chinese oral performing literature, for actors or narrators to pretend to be someone they are not is non-realistic enough, even without the widespread practice of communicating through song or other metric forms found only rarely in ordinary speech. In any case, performance techniques were borrowed from one form of oral performing literature to another. There are many instances of the presentation of performances of oral performing literature within other works of oral performing literature of the same general type and in works not presented as orally performed. Especially with the rise in social status of oral storytellers after the career of Liu Jingting at the end of the Ming dynasty and the flourishing in the following dynasty of the rather 'literary' style of storytelling known as *zidi shu* 子弟書, it became quite common for plays to feature performers of oral literature as positive characters and to allow them to display their wares.

For the rest of this paper, we will first examine the antecedents to the non-realistic uses of oral performing literature in the earliest edition of the *Jin Ping Mei*, and then proceed to an analysis of the various types of non-realistic usages in that work. We will then turn to the fate of those usages in sequels to that novel and in later editions of the *Jin Ping Mei*. In the final part of this paper, attention will first be turned to works of fiction generally held to have been influenced by the *Jin Ping Mei*, such as the *Honglou meng* 紅樓夢 and its sequels and imitations. Then we will take a look at fiction not typically connected to the *Jin Ping Mei* and at one novel, *Qilu deng* 歧路燈, which positions itself in opposition to the *Jin Ping Mei*. For a conclusion we will try to decide which of the types of non-realistic uses of oral performing literature in the *Jin Ping Mei cihua* were adopted by later authors and became a part of the tradition of fiction composition and which uses were abandoned.

Pre-*Jin Ping Mei* Uses of Oral Performing Literature

The non-realistic uses of oral performing literature we are interested in include descriptions of performances, quotations from and allusions to works of oral performing literature, and the application of techniques from oral performing literature to works of fiction. Prior to the *Jin Ping Mei cihua*, performances of oral performing literature presented directly in the narrative of novels can be found, but they are few in number. In the earliest versions of the *Shuihu zhuan*, performances of this type are included for plot rather than thematic reasons. Yulan sings a famous *ci* 詞 poem by Su Shi 蘇軾 (1037–1101) as part of the plot, to frame Wu Song 武松 for theft, and the author goes to the trouble of showing us Lei Heng watching the performance of a *zhugongdiao* (medley in all keys with

80

interpolated prose) because he gets into trouble when he has no money on him with which to reward the performers. The original version shows no interest in the content of the performance, as is also the case in the mention of the performance of an unnamed *yuanben* 院本 (dramatic skit) later in the novel. Although Zhang Qing lets on that he is afraid of what roving actresses will sing about him and other 'heroes of the greenwood' if not treated kindly, and Yan Qing sings a peddler's (*huolang'r* 貨郎兒) song, there is not a lot of overlap between the world of the novel and those areas of Chinese life, the pleasure quarters, the marketplace, and the homes of the wealthy, where oral performing literature was most common. The most extensive description of dramatic performances in the novel is in a passage of parallel prose describing a banquet put on by the emperor for the Shuihu band in the capital (Zheng Zhenduo 1954: 82.1359–60).

All of us are inclined to break out into song from time to time, so instances of replacing dialogue by song (*yi qu dai yan* 以曲代言) in fiction are not a priori non-realistic. However, when a certain ratio of frequency is reached and it becomes clear that we are dealing with a convention rather than an attempt to portray life as it is lived, I think we are clearly in the realm of the non-realistic. The intended effect is not so clear when characters are shown declaiming oceans of traditional or newly composed poetry to each other. As alien as this is to us today, some fictional works seemed to take this for granted or even generically required it of their heroes and heroines. Prior to the *Jin Ping Mei cihua,* there are many works of literary language fiction that featured declaimed poetry, and even a few in vernacular Chinese, but it is the narrator and not the characters in the *Jin Ping Mei cihua* who is given to quoting poetry.

The use of declaimed or sung *ci* and *qu* 曲 poetry in a non-realistic fashion is a prominent feature in two early vernacular stories, 'Wenjing yuanyang hui' 刎頸鴛鴦會, in which the poems are sung by the narrator, and 'Kuaizui Li Cuilian ji' 快嘴李翠蓮記, in which declaimed poetry, to a certain meter, is spoken by one character alone, the eponymous heroine.

The conventional rather than realistic nature of the use of this verse in both stories is stressed by the prefatory phrases used in the first story and the fact that in the second story the declamation of that type of verse is restricted to one character, who is only allowed a few lines of spoken prose. The first story was used extensively in the first chapter of the *Jin Ping Mei cihua*, although no use was made in the novel of the narrator's songs or of the convention itself. The consistency of the use of the convention in the second story, of having the main character speak almost entirely through rhythmic verse, is also not reflected in the *Jin Ping Mei cihua.*

Passing reference to oral performing literature is made in some early vernacular short stories. For instance, story 39 in *Jingshi tongyan* 警世通言

includes the opening spiel (*kaihe* 開呵) of a Daoist to a street corner audience, complete with an opening poem and the phrase *kanguan tingshuo* 看官聽說 (*Jingshi tongyan* 警世通言 1971: 39.588). In story 33 of *Xingshi hengyan* 醒世恆言 (1978), the telling of the story of an earlier imperial consort surnamed Han by a professional teller of stories, without musical accompaniment (*pinghua* 平話), is instrumental in driving the female protagonist of the story, also a palace consort surnamed Han, into a state of melancholy that leads to a meeting with her future illicit lover (*ibid.*: 33.243).

The Uses of Oral Performing Literature in the *Jin Ping Mei cihua*

The *Jin Ping Mei cihua* describes a world in which the inclusion of descriptions of oral performing literature is quite natural. Oral performing literature was conceived primarily as a form of entertainment and many of its varieties got their start or maintained a permanent home in the pleasure quarters. The main character of the novel, Ximen Qing, is described upon his first appearance as a denizen of the pleasure quarters and well acquainted with the 'minor arts' of that world. His best 'friend', Ying Bojue, makes his living as a sort of travel guide to the pleasure quarters and is on good terms with many of its inhabitants. With Ximen Qing's rise in financial and political status, his household progressively resembles the pleasure quarters. His third wife, Li Jiao'er, is a former prostitute; one of the main attractions for him of his fourth wife, Meng Yulou, is the fact that she can play the *pipa*; his fifth wife, Pan Jinlian, was trained as a performer of popular songs; his first and sixth wives, Wu Yueniang and Li Ping'er, both become courtesy mothers to singing girls, Li Guijie and Wu Yin'r respectively; his personal body servant, Shutong, can sing and act in the Southern manner; his acquaintance Miao Qing sends him a pair of singing boys; and his maids take lessons in popular songs and music from Li Guijie's brother, Li Ming. He has the financial resources to hire entertainers to perform everything from skits to full-blown plays in his household and does so not only to celebrate birthdays and holidays, but even for quite ordinary occasions. The women of his household are also permitted to enjoy performances of oral performing literature, whether from behind bamboo curtains or in their own quarters.

Throughout the present century the mining of the *Jin Ping Mei cihua* for information on the history of oral performing literature, particularly drama and song, has been one of the continuing focuses of interest in studies of the novel. It is certainly a safer topic than trying to deal with the descriptions of sexual activity in it. Studies of this kind are slightly complicated by the fact

NON-REALISTIC USAGES OF ORAL PERFORMING LITERATURE

that, by strict definition, the majority of the uses of oral performing literature in the novel are non-realistic. I refer here to the fact that the novel is set in the last years of the Northern Song, but the specific examples of oral performing literature described or alluded to are more typical of the late 16th century than of the 12th. Taking seriously the idea that these portions of the novel refer to Song dynasty practice is quite absurd, either from the point of view of modern scholars or that of contemporary readers. The easiest way to drive this home is to point out that scholars have used the description of drama in the novel to establish the outside limits for the period of time during which the novel was composed. Since we have taken pains above to make clear that under our rules any specific use of oral performing literature can have both realistic and non-realistic aspects, we are not obliged to consider the bulk of references to oral performing literature in the *Jin Ping Mei cihua* as primarily non-realistic, but can regard them, rather, as deliberately anachronistic, intended to create a distancing effect – an important feature to which we will return below. On the other hand, scholars interested in the novel as an historical source on popular entertainment in the late Ming are sometimes worried about the opposite problem, that the descriptions of performance in the novel might be anachronistic from the point of view of the late Ming. It is therefore necessary for these scholars to argue, for instance, that, according to contemporary accounts, the Yuan dynasty *zaju* 雜劇 plays mentioned in the novel were still in the performance repertory of the late Ming.

The study of the rhetorical uses of oral performing literature in the *Jin Ping Mei cihua* and the influence of oral performing literature on the composition of the novel has grown and deepened, particularly in the last 15 years. We can identify two broad approaches in this body of work. One approach is to point to the existence of substantial quotation and imitation of oral performing literature in the novel as evidence that the novel itself is an (imperfect) revision of earlier renditions of the same story in a genre of oral storytelling created collectively by practitioners of that genre. The opposite approach, influenced both by traditional Chinese commentaries on fiction and by the tenets of New Criticism in the West, assumes that everything in the novel was carefully selected by the literati author for various rhetorical purposes.

Although I tend to disagree with the conclusions drawn by scholars of the first approach, I am greatly indebted to the work of both groups, as well as those interested in the *Jin Ping Mei cihua* as a record of Ming dynasty performance of oral literature. I doubt that anything that I can say about the *Jin Ping Mei cihua* itself cannot be found in this collective body of scholarship. The originality of this paper is better found in its focus and its attention to subsequent developments.

83

DAVID L. ROLSTON

Non-realistic Uses of Oral Performing Literature in the *Jin Ping Mei cihua*

We can take the scholarly interest in this general topic as evidence of the importance of oral performing literature in the *Jin Ping Mei cihua* and proceed to a brief analysis of its non-realistic uses in the novel. As intimated above, these non-realistic uses can be divided into (1) a level at which it is the content or secondary associations of the material described or alluded to that is important, and (2) a level of formal experimentation involving the incorporation into the novel's repertory of techniques and conventions employed in oral performing literature, such as the use of self-revelatory comic verse from secondary actors on their first appearance on stage in drama or the use of song to replace dialogue. Of course, there are many instances where both levels are present.

Content-Centred, Non-Experimental Uses

The content-centred level can be involved with characterization or an implied authorial commentary on specific characters. Characters' thoughts can be conveyed indirectly to the reader or fairly directly to other characters through their requests for the performance of particular works of oral literature. Likewise, a character's preference for or reaction to works of oral performing literature can be used to convey additional information to us about that character. Thus the desire by the eunuchs Liu and Xue in Chapter 31 to hear a pessimistic song suite ('Tan fusheng you ru yi meng li' 嘆浮生有如一夢裡 [Ah, Life is but a Dream]), a song suite from a drama featuring an heroic eunuch who saves the crown prince, and a song suite about separation (31/14b–15a); and their criticism of romantic Southern plays as implausible, but more to the point, having nothing to say to their condition (64/6b); all help the reader get a better picture of their mental world. At the same time, the very same material is used to comment on the general situations in which oral performing literature is discussed, and to foreshadow future plot developments. The requests in Chapter 31 are made at a banquet to celebrate the birth of Ximen Qing's son by Li Ping'er, and his new official post, commemorated in the baby's name, Guan'ge (literally, 'Office Boy'). The references in the song suites to life being but a dream and to separation cast a pall over the ongoing celebration of Ximen Qing's posterity and official promotion, resonating with what the second-time reader already knows: all three, Guan'ge, Li Ping'er, and Ximen Qing, will die prematurely. The play about the eunuch is related by the astute reader to the fact that there is dissension in the household over the fact that Guan'ge is being treated like a crown prince. The skit about Wang Bo (650–676) quoted in its entirety in the

NON-REALISTIC USAGES OF ORAL PERFORMING LITERATURE

same chapter (31/13a–14b), is generated from a misreading of Wang Bo's 王勃 'Tengwang ge xu 滕王閣序' (Preface to Prince Teng's Pavilion), which contains a reference to a crown prince.

Although the eunuch's comments on drama are later mocked by Ying Bojue and Ximen Qing (64/8a–b), it is common for the author to put perceptive comments in the mouths of generally unreflective characters. This brings us to another kind of point made by the author through references to oral performing literature. As discussed in depth by Katherine Carlitz, the author of the *Jin Ping Mei* was sometimes critical of the values and conventions of oral performing literature itself and used the contrast between them and his work to point out shortcomings in the former. For instance, the convention of the prostitute with the heart of gold so popular on the Chinese stage is made problematic in the novel by contrast with his more realistic prostitutes. Finally, implicit comments are made about the characters in the novel by the author working references to specific works of oral performing literature into the text, which either act as a sharp contrast to, or an implied simile for, the state of the world of the fictional characters. An example of the first is the contrast implied between the positive figure Cai Bojie from the play *Pipa ji* and Ximen Qing in Chapter 27 through the device of quoting extensively from the play in that chapter. As an example of the second type, the extensive quotation from the play *Yuhuan ji* 玉環記 (The Jade Ring) in later chapters (and particularly in Chapters 63–64) is set up to allow the disorder in Zhang Yanshang's household in the play to mirror that in Ximen Qing's.

In all of the uses outlined above, oral performing literature is used as a kind of yardstick for measuring the character of people who request or listen to it or as a kind of language or code by means of which messages can be conveyed from character to character or from author to reader. Is this a misreading or an over-reading of what is going on in the novel? This possibility is significantly lessened when we take into account that characters in the novel are clearly shown to be consciously making similar uses of oral performing literature themselves, divining similar intentions behind the actions of others, and noticing both disparities and similarities between their world and the world of oral performing literature. In Chapter 21, Pan Jinlian has a song suite sung from a play (only the title of the scene is given, 'Jiaqi chonghui' 佳期重會) to satirize the reconciliation of Wu Yueniang and Ximen Qing and the part that the former's burning of incense at night had in that reconciliation (21/8b–9a). The point is not lost on Ximen Qing, who immediately asks who had the suite sung and explains the satiric import to Meng Yulou the following day (21/16b–17a). In the previous chapter, Pan Jinlian incited Wu Yueniang against Li Ping'er by pointing out the implications of the performance of a scene from the play

DAVID L. ROLSTON

Cailou ji 彩樓記. This scene celebrated the union of a man and his main wife at a banquet honouring Li Ping'er, who is only Ximen Qing's concubine but whose favoured treatment by him is a continual source of dissension in the household (20/10b). The inauspiciousness of the eunuchs' choices is immediately pointed out by Commander Zhou and Xia Yanling (31/14b–15a). In Chapter 52, Ying Bojue cracks jokes commenting on the incongruity between Li Guijie and the goodhearted person who figures in the song suite she is singing (52/9b–11b). During the performance of the early scenes of the *Yuhuan ji* (63/10b), Li Guijie tries to get her own back by pointing out the similarity between Ying Bojue and a character portrayed in the play. In the same chapter, similarities between the world of this play and that of the novel are again brought to mind: a ruckus is set off when one of the maids is teased for having the same name, Yuxiao, as the heroine-prostitute of the play (63/11a). On occasion, the narrator himself explains why a character asks for the performance of a particular piece of oral performing literature (96/7a).

Perhaps the paradigmatic example of the content category of non-realistic use of oral performing literature in the novel is the performance of a song sequence from scene 27 of Li Kaixian's 李開先 (1502–1568) *Baojian ji* 寶劍記 (The Precious Sword) at a banquet attended by Ximen Qing at Zhu Mian's mansion in the capital (70/13a–b). The song sequence, a clever parody of traditional songs of praise composed for use on such occasions, is actually a detailed rehearsal by the singer of the crimes of Gao Qiu, a prominent member of the political faction to which Zhu Mian belongs. Functionally, to curse Gao Qiu is the same as cursing the host, Zhu Mian. The unrealistic nature of this section of the novel is universally agreed upon, but it has also been pointed out that we are not justified in trying to hold the author to conventions of mimetic realism that we have bought into but that we have no reason to believe were dear to the novelist.

It is inconceivable that the song sequence was part of an oral storyteller's version of the story. Oral storytellers show far more concern for surface plausibility and less interest in the structural arrangement of materials. The quotation of the song sequence is set up earlier in the same chapter by the quotation of a description of Gao Qiu's mansion from scene 3 of the *Baojian ji* and by explicit commentary on Zhu Mian from the narrator (70/12b). The desire to satirize Zhu Mian and all he stands for as strenuously as possible has won out over plausibility. Although Lu Xun 魯迅 and Wu Zuxiang 吳組緗 held that satire has to be realistic (*xieshi* 寫實), for many Western critics satire and realism are often antithetical.

In this example from Chapter 70, the author quoted material from a play in order to make a comment on characters in the novel. For this effect to work, it is important that the reader be aware of the source of the quotation. In this particular instance, the characters at the banquet are portrayed as oblivious to the import of the songs sung for their entertainment, but the author surely did not expect the same reaction from his readers.

Space does not permit either a full listing of examples or a detailed analysis of their use, what must be done here is to give an idea of their range and general characteristics.

Besides the types of oral performing literature already mentioned (skits, drama, song sequences, and popular songs), a couple of other types should be pointed out. *Baojuan* 寶卷 (sacred scrolls; stories told alternately in verse and prose illustrating Buddhist dogma) are performed or referred to several times in the novel. Some of the *baojuan* used are similar to extant *baojuan*, some are not. Some are quoted at great length, but the performances tend to be interrupted and left unfinished. This last fact makes it clear that the author was not interested in proselytizing Buddhism through quotation of *baojuan* in the novel, but in showing Wu Yueniang's credulity, her willingness to associate with nuns of unsavoury background, and to set up her giving away of her only son to a monk at the end of the book. *Daoqing* 道情, basically the Daoist equivalent of *baojuan*, also figure in the novel, though the texts of the performances are not quoted. Jokes are told on many occasions in the novel. They often are used by their tellers to indirectly criticize members of the audience.

Subtle quotation (and sometimes misquotation) of and allusion to pre-existing literary works has a long tradition in China. The *Jin Ping Mei cihua* was quite innovative when it extended this tradition to prose fiction and treated popular literature as a suitable object for quotation and allusion. Some of the references to popular literature in the novel work the same way as *xiehou yu* 歇後 語 (literally, 'words that come after a pause'), a rhetorical technique in Chinese whereby the quotation of a certain amount of text is designed to bring into the reader's mind a separate section of text closely associated with the first but not explicitly referred to in it. In English, for instance, we could get someone to say the phrase 'he's my brother' by giving him the cue 'he ain't heavy'. What we really want the other person to concentrate on is not said. The reader's attention is explicitly directed to the use of this technique in the realm of references to popular literature when Wu Yueniang praises Pan Jinlian's knowledge of drama and popular song by saying that all you need is to mention the beginning and she'll know the end (*titou zhiwei* 提頭知尾; 73/10b). Sometimes the quotation of a segment of text in the *Jin Ping Mei cihua* is designed to call up the original context of the quotation. It should also be pointed out that although the first printed edition of the novel suffers from editorial dereliction of duty, material is not quoted carelessly or in huge unchanged blocks. Comparison of the text of the novel with original sources shows that the author has made many minor changes in the material quoted so as to increase its relevance to his concerns.[1]

Sometimes works of oral performing literature are referred to only once in the novel, but perhaps more interesting is the author's clear concern with a relatively small number of plays, which show up over and over in the text: *Yuhuan ji* (and the earlier *zaju* play on the same material, *Liangshi yinyuan* 兩世因緣), *Xixiang ji,* and *Baojian ji,* all of which have already been mentioned above. Some sense of the non-realistic use of their content in the novel should already be apparent. References to performances of the *Xixiang ji* (whose plot could be summarized as the story of an unorthodox betrothal and marriage) are very frequent in Chapter 41, the time of the betrothal of the daughter of the Qiao family to Ximen Qing's son, Guan'ge, a match that is presented in the novel as ill-considered.[2] This play and *Baojian ji* also exerted a strong influence on the way the story is told in parts of the *Jin Ping Mei cihua,*[3] a subject to which we now turn.

Experimental, Formal Uses

When the formal conventions of oral performing literature are used non-realistically in the *Jin Ping Mei cihua,* there are, of course, many occasions in which the content of the sequence is used to achieve the same range of effects discussed above, but new effects are achieved as well. If a character sings when we would more likely expect normal speech, the content of the songs can be the straightforward expression of the character's thoughts or feelings, and thus a rather direct way for the novelist to get into the character's head without recourse to western-style internal views. This is one of the main features of songs used as dialogue or soliloquy in oral performing literature, and there are examples of this in the *Jin Ping Mei cihua.* However, the songs are sometimes borrowed from previous sources and almost always deal in popular stereotyped images. The majority of the time there is the same kind of disjunction, between the character's true personality and the stereotyped images in the songs, that we have seen in the case of Li Guijie, a mercenary and calculating professional entertainer, singing about good-hearted prostitutes. Comparison of the content

---

1   See Kang-i Sun Chang 1980: 30 and Cai Dunyong 蔡敦勇 1989: 333–36, 345.

2   For further discussion, see Carlitz 1986: 104–105.

3   Bu Jian 卜健 believes that the *Baojian ji* and the *Jin Ping Mei cihua* were written by the same person, Li Kaixian. He stresses several points of convergence between the two (such as their revisionary relationship to the *Shuihu zhuan*) and presents the idea that the novel was an attempt to accomplish some of the goals of the play in another medium (Bu Jian 1988).

NON-REALISTIC USAGES OF ORAL PERFORMING LITERATURE

of the songs and what we know about the characters' past actions often reveals that the singers have an unrealistic and benighted view of themselves.[4]

How many times does the author make his characters sing instead of speak? Excluding minor examples or those that are perfectly natural, instances in which only one character sings include the following: Pan Jinlian sings many songs in Chapter 8, but one of them (8/2a) describes what she is doing as she sings, while another occurs when she is talking to Dai'an, Ximen Qing's servant (8/3b–4a); in Chapter 38 Pan Jinlian sings first to herself and her maid[5] and then to Ximen Qing and Li Ping'er about her loneliness and how she is wasting away (38/8a–12b); Li Ping'er sings two songs to the tune of 'Shanpo yang' 山坡羊 (Sheep on the Mountain Slope) in mourning for her dead son (59/16a, 19b–20a)[6]; a quack doctor sings about his drug for inducing abortion (85/2b); a jealous maid questioned by her master sings to the tune of 'Shanpo yang' (91/13b); and Chen Jingji sings the story of his life to his fellow beggars (93/2b–4a).[7]

There are scenes in which more than one character sings to relieve his or her own emotion without any sense that the songs are in response to each other: Wu Yueniang and Meng Yulou sing at Ximen Qing's grave in memory of him (89/4b–5a); Pang Chunmei and Meng Yulou sing in memory of Pan Jinlian at her grave (89/8b, 11b–12a)[8]; and Chen Jingji's two 'wives', Ge Cuiping and Han Aijie, take turns reciting quatrains in mourning for him (100/5a–6a). The most 'dramatic' sequences, in which dialogue between several parties is sung instead of spoken, include: Ximen Qing in an aria accuses a bawd of deceiving him and she defends herself with an aria to the same tune (20/15a–b); Ximen Qing gives his deathbed instructions to Wu Yueniang in an aria and she replies in an aria to the same tune (79/20a–b); and, in the process of the consummation of the adulterous and technically incestuous love affair between Chen Jingji and Pan Jinlian with the aid of the maid Chunmei, they sing songs to one another (82/3a–b, 83/5b–7a, 8b).[9] In Chapters 82–83, many references are made to

---

4   For instance, in Chapter 8 Pan Jinlian presents herself as powerless and abandoned in the songs that she sings, but a moment later she tortures her stepdaughter, Ying'r, savagely (8/2b–3a) and Li Ping'er, who is responsible for her husband's death, sings that she has never hurt anyone and cannot understand why she is so ill-fated (59/16a). See Carlitz 1986: 116–17.

5   An interesting feature of their interaction is that the maid, Chunmei, asks her mistress questions that are answered in song. This is a very common occurrence in Yuan *zaju*.

6   Many of the songs of mourning in the novel are sung to this tune. See Cai Dunyong 蔡敦勇 1989.

7   As we will see later, beggars often sang when they went on their begging rounds, so this sequence has perhaps more of a basis in ordinary reality.

8   These four songs are sung to the tune of 'Shanpo yang', followed by 'Bubu jiao' 步步嬌.

9   In this sequence, songs are also written down and used as love letters, something that happens frequently in the novel, but, because they cannot be considered to be performed orally and

89

DAVID L. ROLSTON

the *Xixiang ji* (Chunmei is compared by the narrator to the go-between maid in that play, Hongniang, and she quotes dialogue from Hongniang), and it seems likely that the whole conception of the sequence was coloured by a rather jaundiced understanding of the play as championing sexual and moral disorder. There is a certain element of parody involved as well.[10]

Entrances are very important in traditional Chinese drama, and, like the convention of using song for dialogue when strong emotion is involved, the conventions governing stage entrances are highly non-mimetic. In a typical entrance, time is taken out for the character to recite verse and/or sing a song and then to introduce him or herself in prose, all of which is addressed to the audience, not to other characters on stage. Perhaps under the dual principle of economy and keeping the audience from moral perplexity, devious or morally deficient characters will generally, upon their entrance to the stage, tell the audience wherein they are devious or what part of their moral armour needs repair. It is possible to achieve the same basic effect in vernacular fiction by exploiting the narrator's license to quote poems or set-pieces critical of the character being introduced.

It therefore makes a difference whether the description is in the first person (as in drama), or in the third (as in fiction).[11] What is striking about the *Jin Ping Mei cihua*, however, is that frequent use of the dramatic style entrance is also made. Self-mocking entrance verse is recited by Midwife Cai (30/8a),[12] Tailor Zhao (40/9a–b), and Doctor Zhao (61/22b). In the last instance, we are told that Zhao's recitation of the verse provokes general laughter, something that would be natural in the theatre. Some of these 'dramatic' introductions are borrowed from extant works of drama.[13] A similar self-mocking set-piece is recited by Li Gui (90/2a).[14]

---

tend not to have known sources in oral performing literature, I have not included discussion of them in this paper. Kang-i Sun Chang characterizes the use of song in the first 20 chapters of the novel as 'expressive' and 'dramatic' in the last 20 chapters (Sun Chang 1980: 27–28, 30–32).

10 See Carlitz 1986: 118.

11 For an example of where the author of the *Jin Ping Mei cihua* takes this route, see the parallel prose describing Scholar Wen, 58/4b–5a. The comic poem quoted at the entrance of Tailor Zhao (40/9a–b), which is written as if it were spoken by him, is said by the narrator to have been composed by the tailor's contemporaries (*shiren* 時人).

12 Wu Yueniang, who is miffed that she has arrived late, tells her to cut the small talk.

13 Material in the entrance of Doctor Zhao is either quoted from or modelled on scene 28 of the *Baojian ji*. A self-mocking entrance poem suitable for a midwife is used in the chapter-opening-poem for Chapter 7. It shares text with an entrance poem in scene 30 of the same play. Quotes from self-introductions in works of drama are also used to describe characters in the novel. See Carlitz 1978a: 281.

14 The text is borrowed from scene 14 of *Yuhuan ji*. Portions of 'self-introductions' from the same play show up elsewhere in in the novel (100/3a, 4b–5a). See Carlitz 1978a: 281, 283.

NON-REALISTIC USAGES OF ORAL PERFORMING LITERATURE

Not only is the idea of having characters introduce themselves with self-mocking verses borrowed from drama, the formula introducing these sections and certain orthographical conventions are influenced by dramatic texts as well. The lyrics to songs in Chinese oral performing literature were almost always set (*tian* 填) to tune matrixes (*pai* 牌) that involve restrictions on numbers of lines, syllables per line, which lines must rhyme, etc. This information is very important for the purposes of performance or even scansion, so texts (but not performances) include the names of the tune matrixes for each song within brackets on the same approximate level of discourse, vis-à-vis the reader, as stage directions. In the *Jin Ping Mei cihua*, when more than one song is sung in sequence without prose interruption from the narrator or characters in the scene, the name of the first tune matrix is usually made clear by the narrator or in conversation between the singer and other characters. This is perfectly natural within the conventions of the prose novel in traditional China. For the subsequent songs, however, the names of the matrixes are given parenthetically in the exact same manner as in drama texts. Other conventional formulas used in printed texts to indicate the repetition of the previous song matrix (*qianqiang* 前腔, etc.), singing in harmony (*he* 合), and the insertion of refrains (*heqian* 合前) all appear in the novel. Not only is the common dramatic technique of having a character break up the lines of a single song by interpolated prose comments or exclamations (*daibai* 帶白) used in the novel when Pan Jinlian is singing about her loneliness in Chapter 38; the orthographic convention of printing the interpolations in smaller characters in double columns is also imitated (38/8b–9a).[15] Although not a case of experimentation with dramatic conventions, the description of the skit about Wang Bo (31/13a–14b) and the performance of a scene from the Southern version of *Xixiang ji* (74/8a–b) also show the preservation of the conventions of written dramatic texts (stage directions written in smaller characters, reference to characters in the stage directions by role-type only, etc.) instead of having the narrator give us the equivalent information in a style more suited to prose fiction.

Perhaps because the novel was being experimental in this regard, there is considerable confusion in the way that songs sung by the characters are introduced into the narrative. Most often the songs are introduced by the narrator or the singer. They use formulas adapted from those used by the narrator to

---

15 The related convention of having the prose interpolations come from a different character than the singer (*chabai* 插白) also appears in the novel (52/9b–11b). In both cases, the interpolated unsung dialogue was added by the author and does not appear in extant versions of the songs in other sources. On the other hand, the omission of interpolated material, which often consisted of questions to which the songs are responses, sometimes makes the quoted material hard to understand, as is the case of the use of the songs only from Act 3 of *Fengyun hui* (71/3a–5b).

91

DAVID L. ROLSTON

quote poems, in what Patrick Hanan has termed the commentarial mode,[16] taking the general form of *'you x wei zheng'* 有X為証, in which X is either the name of a genre (*shi* 詩, *ci* 詞) or a tune matrix.[17] This formula seems to carry the presumption that the poem or song is quoted rather than composed extemporaneously, which does not work in all contexts.[18] The second problem is that sometimes the songs given after this type of formula from the narrator are in the first person and can be taken to be sung by a certain character present, but this is not explicitly indicated to the reader.

Sometimes the formulas are just plain garbled (83/10b).[19] On other occasions, lines that should belong to the singer's song are set off orthographically and placed in the narrator's voice (38/8b).

The models for the above instances of borrowing from oral performing literature are primarily dramatic, but formal conventions of narrative oral performing literature are also experimented with in the novel, in Chapter 86. The main difference between narrative and drama in this case is that, because the former makes use of a narrator, dialogue is often embedded within narration instead of being directly quoted and independent.[20] In one section of the chapter (86/10b), the dialogue between Dame Wang and Pan Jinlian suddenly turns into rhymed and rhythmic prose. There is a section earlier in the chapter (right before Wu Yueniang turns on Chen Jingji and he resorts to the novel

---

16 Hanan 1974: 305.

17 This basic formula is also sometimes used by characters in drama to introduce a song they are about to sing, but the practice is rare, and seems to be used more often with *ci* than with *qu* songs. For examples from scenes 3 and 5 of *Baojian ji* and the proposal that this is the source of the *Jin Ping Mei*'s use of the formula and of using song for dialogue, see Bu Jian 1988: 69–70. In the *Xiyou ji* 西游記 play cycle, which probably dates from the late Ming, it is common for intrusive arias to be introduced with formulas that include the name of the tune. For example, see Sui Shusen 隋樹森 (ed.) 1959: 17.679, where Sun Wukong sings a song to the tune of 'Jisheng cao' 寄生草. In Yuan drama, interpolated songs and arias (songs not belonging to the song suites of the individual acts) occur but are not prefaced by set formulas. The contexts for the interpolated arias tend to be more 'realistic' than for the other arias. See Zhang Qichao 張起超 1988: 209–60.

18 For instance, see the formula used to introduce Pan Jinlian's song addressed to Dai'an (8/3b).

19 Xia Chunhao 夏春豪 believes that almost all of the instances of using song for speech are actually cases where the quoted material is in the voice of the narrator and not that of the characters, but that the formulas have gotten left out. He also argues that appropriate punctuation would make it clear that Ximen Qing and Wu Yueniang do not sing to each other on his deathbed. See Xia Chunhao 1992: 12–13.

20 There can be a lot of mutual borrowing between narrative and dramatic oral performing literature, as in the case of the *zhugongdiao* and *zaju* versions of the *Xixiang ji*.

92

NON-REALISTIC USAGES OF ORAL PERFORMING LITERATURE

device of dropping his pants in order to escape from her and the other women of the household, who are poised to beat him) that is introduced by the following line: '*Yueniang bian dao, you changci wei zheng*' 月娘便道, 有長詞為証 (Yueniang then said, 'There is a long doggerel poem as evidence'; 86/7b). The text that follows is actually told by a narrator, not Wu Yueniang. It consists of rhythmic lines, set off orthographically, containing description and dialogue, and it conforms to the general practice of narrative oral performing literature of the prosimetric variety. This is surely a breach of realism; but then again, the whole conception of this part of the novel is farcical rather than realistic.

It is not unusual for oral performing literature to influence the development of fiction,[21] but it is, I think, unusual for the borrowings to appear to be so imperfectly assimilated.[22] There is, of course, a variety of ways to try to account for this state of affairs. One is the theory that the novel is a written version of the treatment of the same story in oral performing literature and that the transformation to prose fiction was incomplete or sloppily done. The 'remnants' of orality are then censured as detrimental to the realism that the novel is supposed otherwise to be in accord with.[23]

A related approach is to take the words *cihua* 詞話 in the title of the novel as a generic designation that indicates that we are dealing with a narrative with doggerel verse.[24] *Cihua* as the title of a genre appears in the chapter on penal law in the *Yuan shi* 元史 (History of the Yuan Dynasty), but the only information given there on the formal nature of this genre are the verbs used to speak of its performance (*yanchang* 演唱 [act] and *banchang* 搬唱 [sing]).[25]

---

21 See, for instance, Genette 1980: 172–73, for a summary of the influence of ideas from drama (mimesis, scene, etc.) on Western fiction. For general remarks on the mutual influence of drama and fiction on each other in China, see Liu Hui 1988: 17–54 and 55–77, respectively.

22 Some of the difficulty in following the dialogue in the *Jin Ping Mei cihua* might also be because of interference from the model of written dramatic dialogue, which was traditionally slighted and often incomplete, but could also be written in a skeletal style that would require padding out on stage by the skilled actor through facial expression, tone of voice, etc.

23 See, for instance, Guo Licheng 郭立誠 1984: 274, on the use of songs to the tune of '*Shanpo yang*' sung by characters, and Liu Hui's preface to Cai Dunyong 蔡敦勇 1989: 4, on Ximen Qing and Wu Yueniang's deathbed duet. To explain the heavier concentration of non-realistic uses of oral performing literature in the last 20 chapters, Liu Hui put forward the idea that the first 80 and the last 20 chapters were printed from two different manuscripts 1986: 3–5.

24 Those who argue for collective authorship tend to point to the title of the novel to buttress their claim, but, as we will see, the idea that the non-realistic uses are 'left-overs' from an oral tradition and the idea that the novel itself is a *cihua* in the sense of a narrative with doggerel poetry are not very compatible.

25 Yu Tianchi 于天池 and Li Shu 李書 1983: 47. See also Li Shiren 李時人 1986.

93

There are extant works that call themselves *cihua:* several of the prosimetric texts printed in the Chenghua reign period (1465–1487) found in a tomb near Shanghai do so, and there is a late Ming work, *Da Tang Qinwang cihua* 大唐秦 王詞話, by the otherwise unknown author, Zhu Shenglin 諸聖鄰.[26] Both types use substantial sections of even line poetry (*shizan* 詩讚) for narrative purposes as a regular conventional feature. Two things set the *Jin Ping Mei cihua* apart from them: (1) while poetry (primarily *ci* and *qu*) is used to replace dialogue, in only one instance (86/8a) are narrative and dialogue mixed the way they are in the poetry of the other *cihua*, and (2) the material borrowed from oral performing literature is not used according to any one overriding convention but is experimental and largely unassimilated.

A different approach, the one that I favour, is to treat the non-realistic uses as experiments aimed at broadening the capabilities of prose fiction,[27] and to treat the 'distancing' effect of these uses as part of the author's overall strategy.[28] Of the three foundation genres, Earl Miner has described drama as the most 'estranging', because its basic premise, someone pretending to be someone else, is irredeemably fictional. Furthermore, according to him, 'The greater estrangement of drama precludes narrative's drawing on plays in any direct way.'[29] This estrangement is naturally greater in a non-mimetic theatre, like that of China. But not only is Chinese theatre not as mimetic as western theatre,[30] the same can be said of Chinese prose fiction as well, especially as it began to absorb literati values and to relate itself to Chinese literati poetics, described by Miner as 'affective-expressive' rather than mimetic.[31] In this conception of fiction, breaches in 'realism' can be functional: they prevent over-identification with

---

26 For Liu Hui, the presence of the convention of using both narrative prose and sung poetry (*you shuo you chang de yishu xingshi* 又說又唱的藝術形式) in fiction is the main criterion for deciding whether a work of fiction is a collective composition from among the people or a literati creation (see Liu Hui 1988: 386). Whatever shape the original work took, the extant *Da Tang Qinwang chihua* was revised by a literatus. Even the *shuochang cihua* 說唱詞話 from the Chenghua reign period might be written imitations of oral performances. See Roy 1981: 97–128. For an early Qing interpretation of *cihua* in *Jin Ping Mei cihua,* see note 118 in the original article.

27 Hanan described the novel in this respect to be a 'strange and isolated experiment' (Hanan 1963a: 59). Mainland scholars presently taking this approach include Bu Jian and Li Shiren (see Bu Jian 1988: 19 and Zhou Juntao 1991: 54).

28 Katherine Carlitz has consistently maintained this view. For representative statements, see Carlitz 1978a: 263; 1978b; 1986: 87–89, 144. Andrew Plaks is also sympathetic to this approach. See his remarks on the deathbed duet in Chapter 79 (Plaks 1987: 128–29).

29 Miner 1990: 72.

30 An exception must be made for western opera, of course.

31 *Ibid.,* pp. 24–25.

the characters in the fictional world[32] and draw the reader's attention to the message that the author is trying to convey. In the *Jin Ping Mei cihua*, besides the non-realistic use of oral performing literature, 'breaches' of realism occur on a variety of levels, from the anachronistic use of Ming customs and history to details such as the description of the foreign monk as a penis (49/13a) and the provision of impossible horoscopes for many of the characters.[33]

To sum up, non-realistic uses of oral performing literature in the *Jin Ping Mei cihua* can be divided into two main categories, depending on whether it is the content (and meaning) of the description or quotation that is focused on, or a matter of the borrowing of formal conventions. The content (and associated meaning) of the descriptions and quotations is used as a symbolic language by the author and the characters to convey new information about what characters are thinking, to foreshadow future events, to make comments on characters and general situations by analogous or antithetical contrast, and to draw ironic attention toward the thematic and plot conventions of popular literature. The most striking of the formal conventions borrowed from oral performing literature are the use of song for dialogue and soliloquy and the manner of handling the entrances of comical secondary characters. There is also, however, one instance of borrowing techniques for handling dialogue from orally performed narrative and many instances of orthographic conventions borrowed from written versions of oral performing literature. These conventions are used intermittently, with little regard for consistency or the assimilation of the material into the predominant style of the narrative. There is also one instance in which Chen Jingji, after dreaming of the past, sings the story of his life (93/2a–4b), which represents a partial recapitulation of the plot of the novel.

References

Bu Jian 卜健

1988. *Jin Ping Mei zuozhe Li Kaixian kao* 金瓶梅作者李開先考. Lanzhou: Gansu renmin chubanshe.

Cai Dunyong 蔡敦勇

1989. *Jin Ping Mei cihua juqu pintan* 金瓶梅詞話劇曲品探. Nanjing: Jiangsu wenyi chubanshe.

---

32 This is very important in a novel like the *Jin Ping Mei,* where positive characters are few and far between.

33 See Carlitz 1986: 54–55 and Plaks 1987: 127 n 214.

Carlitz, Katherine

1978a. 'The Role of Drama in the Chin p'ing mei: The Relationship Between Fiction and Drama as a Guide to the Viewpoint of a Sixteenth-Century Chinese Novel.' Ph.D. thesis, University of Chicago.

1978b. 'Allusion to drama in the *Chin P'ing Mei*.' *Ming Studies* 6: 30–35.

1986. *The Rhetoric of* Chin p'ing mei. Bloomington: Indiana University Press.

1989. 'The role of song in the *Jin Ping Mei cihua*.' Paper presented at the international conference on the *Jin Ping Mei*, Xuzhou, China (abstract in Chinese: *Jin Ping Mei cihua* zhong gequ de suoyin 金瓶梅詞話中歌曲的索引, *Jin Ping Mei yanjiu* 金瓶梅研究 1 (1990): 163–65).

Genette, Gerard

1980. *Narrative Discourse: An Essay in Method.* Jane E. Lewin, tr. Ithaca: Cornell University Press.

Guo Licheng 郭立誠

1984. '*Jin Ping Mei* zhong de xiqu yu zaqu' 金瓶梅中的戲曲和雜曲. In Guo Licheng, *Zhongguo yiwen yu minsu* 中國藝文與民俗, pp. 271–86. Taipei: Hanguang wenhua chubanshe.

Hanan, Patrick

1963a. 'Sources of the *Chin P'ing Mei*.' *Asia Major,* n. s., 10(1): 23–67.

1974. 'The early Chinese short story: A critical theory in outline.' In Cyril Birch (ed.), *Studies in Chinese Literary Genres,* pp. 299–339. Berkeley: University of California Press.

Jingshi tongyan 警世通言

1971. Taipei: Dingwen shuju.

Li Shiren 李時人

1986. 'Cihua xinzheng 詞話新証.' *Wenxue yichan* 文學遺產 1: 72–78.

Liu Hui 劉輝

1986. 'Cong cihua ben dao shuosan ben 從詞話本到說散本.' In Liu Hui, *Jin Ping Mei chengshu yen banben yanjiu* 金瓶梅成書與版本研究, pp. 1–39. Shenyang: Liaoning renmin chubanshe.

1988. 'Yishu xingshi de jiejian yu jiaoliu: Zhongguo xiaoshuo yu xiqu bijiao yanjiu 藝術形式的借鑑與交流: 中國小說與戲曲比較研究.' In Liu Hui, *Bijiao xiju lunwen ji* 比較戲劇論文集, pp. 383–416. Beijing: Zhongguo xiju chubanshe.

Miner, Earl

1990. *Comparative Poetics.* Princeton: Princeton University Press.

Plaks, Andrew H.

1987. *Four Masterworks of the Ming Novel.* Princeton: Princeton University Press.

Roy, David T.

1981. 'The fifteenth-century *Shuo-ch'ang tz'u-hua* as examples of formulaic composition.' *CHINOPERL Papers* 10: 97–128.

Sui Shusen 隋樹森 (ed.)

1959. *Yuanqu xuan waibian* 元曲選外編. Beijing: Zhonghua shuju.

Sun Chang, K'ang-i

1980. 'Songs in the *Chin P'ing Mei tz'u-hua*.' *Journal of Oriental Studies* 18(1): 26–34.

Xia Chunhao 夏春豪

1992. '*Jin Ping Mei* zhong shi de yishu xiaoyong 金瓶梅中詩的藝術效用.' Unpublished paper from the 1992 international conference on *Jin Ping Mei*.

Xingshi hengyan 世恆言

1978. Taipei: Dingwen shuju.

Yu Tianchi 于天池 and Li Shu 李書

1983. 'Cihua 詞話.' In *Xiqu quyi* 戲曲曲藝, pp. 47–48. Beijing: Dabaike quanshu chubanshe.

Zhang Qichao 張起超

1988. '*Yuan zaju de 'chaqu' yanjiu*' 元雜劇的插曲研究. *Xiaoshuo xiqu yanjiu* 小說戲曲研究 1: 209–60.

Zheng Zhenduo 鄭振鐸 (ed.)

1954. *Shuihu quanzhuan* 水滸全傳. Beijing: Renmin wenxue chubanshe.

Zhou Juntao 周鈞韜

1991. *Jin Ping Mei sucai laiyuan* 金瓶梅素材來源. Zhengzhou: Zhongzhou guji chubanshe.

Note on Contributor

David L. Rolston is Professor of Chinese Language and Literature in the Department of Asian Languages and Cultures at the University of Michigan. After working and publishing on traditional Chinese fiction (with an emphasis on traditional Chinese fiction commentary), he turned his attention primarily to traditional Chinese theatre in general and *Jingju* (Peking opera) in particular.

CHAPTER 7

The Function and Purpose of Plays Referred to in *Jin Ping Mei*

HUO XIANJUN
Translated by Zhang Dahai

The exact number of opera scripts referred to in *Jin Ping Mei* is not known. According to Feng Yuanjun 馮沅君 (1900–1974) (1947), 10 plays are mentioned.[1] Apart from these, a further 25 or so plays are referred to.[2] Among them, some belong to the genre of *zaju* 雜劇 of the Yuan and early Ming dynas-

---

1 *Han xiangzi shengxian ji* 韓湘子升仙記 (Han Xiangzi rises to immortality); *Xixiang ji* 西廂記 (The Story of the Western Wing); *Wang Yueying yuanye liu xie ji* 王月英元夜留鞋記 (Wang Yueying Loses her Shoe on the First Night of the New Year); *Hanxiangzi du Chen Banjie shengxianhui* 韓湘子度陳半街升仙會 (Chen Banjie Rises to Immortality with the Help of Han Xiangzi); *Weigao Yuxiao nü liangshi yinyuan yuhuan ji* 韋皋玉簫女兩世姻緣玉環記 (The Story of the Jade Ring); *Hongpao ji* 紅袍記 (The Story of the Red Robe); *Pei Jin gong huan dai ji* 裴晉公還帶記 (Duke Pei Jin Returns the Belt); *Xiao Tianxiang banye chaoyuan* 小天香半夜朝元 (Little Tianxiang Goes to Court at Midnight); *Sijie ji* 四節記 (The Story of the Four Seasons); and *Shuangzhong ji* 雙忠記 (Two Loyal Generals).

2 *Bei xixiang ji* 北西廂記 (The Story of the Western Wing: A Northern Version); *Liangshi yinyuan* 兩世姻緣 (The Bond of Two Generations); *Fengyun hui* 風雲會 (The Gathering); *Bao zhuanghe* 抱妝盒 (Carrying the Dressing Case); *Qiannü lihun* 倩女離魂 (Qiannü's Soul Leaves her Body); *Liu hongye* 流紅葉 (Flowing Red Leaves); *Yuexialao ding shijian peiou* 月下老定世間配偶 (The God of the Moon decides on a Match); *Zimu yuanjia* 子母冤家 (Enmity Between Sons and Mothers); *Lin zhaode* 林招得 (Lin Zhaode); *Pipa ji* 琵琶記 (The Story of the Pipa); *Baojian ji* 寶劍記 (The Story of the Precious Sword); *Shagou ji* 殺狗記 (The Story of the Lilling of a Dog); *Xiangnang ji* 香囊記 (The Story of the Scent Bag); *Cailou ji* 彩樓記 (The Story of the Painted Pavilion); etc.

Editors' note: This chapter is a translation of excerpts from Chapter 5 '*Jin Ping Mei* yu juqu 金瓶梅与剧曲' (*Jin Ping Mei* and play arias) in Huo Xianjun (2010). The translation is based on the work of Zhang Dahai, revised by the editors according to the principles of the present book. We gratefully acknowledge the assistance of David Rolston in revising the pre-final version of this chapter. Some of the notes are also added by the editors. For quotations from *Jin Ping Mei cihua*, the translator has mainly based himself on the English versions in Roy 1993–2013, and the editors have followed up in this respect and changed many remaining passages according to Roy for the sake of consistency.

PLAYS REFERRED TO IN *JIN PING MEI*

ties, some to the *nanxi* 南戲 genre of the Song and Yuan dynasties, and some to the *chuanqi* 傳奇 genre of the Ming dynasty. About half of these plays are represented by unstaged singing (*qingchang* 清唱) of arias from them, the other half by staged performances.

The main purpose here is to point out the roles the plays listed above have in *Jin Ping Mei*, not to sort out how much they have been used. Therefore, I will not examine the plays one by one. In general, however, one can say that the author exhibits a clear purpose through his insertion of these items, which serve a variety of functions in the work.

Revealing the True Message through Wisecracks

In Chapter 61 of *Jin Ping Mei cihua*, Ximen Qing is in a state of panic because of Li Ping'er's extreme physical weakness. After calling a number of doctors, he finally calls Dr. Zhao, alias Zhao Longgang, nicknamed Zhao the Quack. The doctor's self-introduction, which he delivers after 'entering the stage', is very hilarious:

> I'm a doctor whose surname is Zhao,
> At my gate people constantly clamor.
> I sport placards and rattle my bell,
> With no genuine article to peddle.
> In healing, I abjure the best nostrums,
> In pulse-taking, I say what comes to mind.
> Incompetent at pharmacology and medicine,
> I'm inept even at relieving constipation.
> For headaches I use tightened headbands,
> For eye ailments I rely on moxibustion.
> For heart trouble I recommend surgery,
> For deafness I would advise acupuncture.
> For money I'm prepared to do anything,
> I'm out for profit rather than results.
> Those who consult me are less likely to be fortunate than
> unfortunate.
> Wherever I appear there is likely to be weeping rather than
> laughter   (Chapter 61)[3]

This kind of 'self-introduction' is indeed borrowed and adapted from traditional opera, in this case from scene 28 of *Baojian ji*, written by Li Kaixian 李開

---

3   All quotations from *Jin Ping Mei* are based on *Jin Ping Mei cihua* 金瓶梅词话. Taiwan: Tianyi chubanshe 1982. *Editors' note:* The English translations in this chapter, unless otherwise indicated, are quoted from Roy 1993–2013.

HUO XIANJUN

先 (1502–1568).[4] The earliest extant edition of this opera, which is loosely based on *Shuihu zhuan* 水滸傳 (Water Margin), is the 1549 original printing. The title of the opera is not mentioned in *Jin Ping Mei,* but the piece has a unique relationship to the novel and is more important than other operas. Both works borrow content from certain episodes of *Shuihu zhuan,* developing them along new lines to express the authors' feelings toward contemporary society and to criticize governmental corruption, and this connects them. Furthmore, as for *Jin Ping Mei*'s borrowing from previous authors' works, it is very clear that *Baojian ji* is the closest source.

Jin Ping Mei copies and adapts more passages from *Baojian ji* than from any other play.[5] Among those passages, Dr. Zhao's self-introduction is particularly important. 'Dr. Zhao' in *Baojian ji* is a non-descript way to refer to him; the play does not provide his full name, native place, of family background. But when *Jin Ping Mei* made use of him, these details were very clearly given:

> 'And my surname is Ying,' said Ying Bojue. 'May I venture to ask, sir, what is your distinguished name; where do you reside; and what is your profession?'

> 'Unworthy as I am,' the newcomer replied, 'the dwelling of your humble servant is located outside the East Gate (*Dongmen* 東門), on the First Alley (*Toutiao xiang* 頭條巷), beyond the Temple of Erlang (*Erlang miao* 二郎廟), across the Three Bends Bridge (*Sanzhuan qiao* 三轉橋), in the Quarter of the Four Wells (*Siyan jing* 四眼井). I am none other than the celebrated Zhao the Quack and have practiced medicine all my life. My paternal grandfather was an administrative assistant in the Imperial Academy of Medicine (*Taiyi yuan* 太醫院), and my father is currently serving as a medical officer in the mansion of the Prince of Ru. For three successive generations we have devoted ourselves to the study of the medical arts. Every day I pore over the works of Wang Shuhe, Li Gao and Wu Tingzi, as well as such texts as *Yaoxing fu* 藥性賦 (Rhapsody on the Properties of Drugs), *Huangdi suwen* 黃帝素問 (Essential Questions Regarding the Yellow Emperor's Inner Classic [of Medicine]), *Nanjing* 難經 (The Classic of Difficult Issues), *Huoren shu* 活人書 (The Book on Preserving Human Life), *Danxi zhuanyao* 丹溪纂要 (Essential Teachings from Danxi [by Zhu Zhenheng]), *Danxi xinfa* 丹溪心法 (Quintessential Methods from Danxi [by Zhu Zhenheng]), *Jiegulao maijue* 潔古老脈訣 ([Zhang Yuansu's Commentary on Wang Shuhe's] Secrets of Pulse Diagnosis), *Jiajian shisan fang* 加減十三方 (Thirteen Alternative Prescriptions), *Qianjin qixiao liangfang* 千金奇效良方 (Beneficial Prescriptions of Unusual Efficacy Worth a Thousand Pieces of Gold),

---

4   *Editors' note:* Cf. note 3.

5   Cf. *Jin Ping Mei* Chapters 33, 61, 67, 68, 70, 74, 92 etc.

PLAYS REFERRED TO IN *JIN PING MEI*

Shouyu shenfang 壽域神方 (Divine Prescriptions for the Realm of Longevity), and *Haishang fang* 海上方 (Overseas Panaceas from the Isles of the Blest). There is no text I have not perused; there is not a text I have not read.' (Chapter 61)[6]

On the surface, this is a kind of textual game, which is extremely humorous and jocular, and apparently just for fun. It is, however, a realistic text. The author lodges serious content in wisecracks and humor and hides what is true within that which is false. When reading, people burst out laughing, but afterwards they forget why. This is one of the brilliant techniques used in *Jin Ping Mei*. 'Zhao the Quack' is a babbling character, as such, readers would perhaps not pay attention to that he is chosen by the author to reveal true information.

Qinghe County and Yanggu County of *Jin Ping Mei* are two small counties of the Ming Dynasty, with only a few streets. Common names such as First Alley, *Toutiaoxiang* 頭條巷 and Erlang Temple, *Erlang miao* 二郎廟, might be found in Qinghe and Yanggu, but there would hardly exist such rare names as Halfside Street, *Banbian* jie 半邊街.[7] No other place except Beijing includes all those four places: First Alley, Erlang Temple, Three Bends Bridge (*Sanzhuan qiao* 三轉橋) and the Quarter of the Four Wells (*Siyan jing* 四眼井).[8] The *Jin Ping Mei* is constructed like a 'circular network'. All of the content in this round network is mutually connected and mutually defining.

For example, Ximen Qing's alternative name is Four Springs, *Siquan* 四泉. In Chapter 51 he explains: 'It was chosen because my country estate, *xiaozhuang* 小莊, has four wells on it.' This corresponds with the Quarter of the Four Wells mentioned by Zhao the Quack, because it also is a name found only in Beijing. *Xiaozhuang*, 'my humble country estate', is an ironic way to indicate, through indirection, the Great Capital, *Dadu* 大都. Cai Yun, Cai Jing's adopted son, has an alternative name, One Spring. *Yiquan* 一泉; Shang Xiaotang, the son of Shang Liutang, who was a judicial official of Chengdu Prefecture in Sichuan Province, has the alternative name of Two Springs, *Erquan* 二泉; and Wang Yixuan's son, Wang Cai, is named Three Springs, *Sanquan* 三泉. These names, taken together with Ximen Qing's alternative name of Four Springs, all precisely correspond to the names of the four wells in Beijing. Thus, Bejing has one through four wells, and has one through four

---

6   *Editors' note*: For information about these medical works, cf. Roy 1993–2013: Chapter 61, notes 70–84.

7   *Editors' note*: Mentioned in *Jin Ping Mei cihua*, Chapter 7.

8   Cf. the geographic descriptions of the streets of Beijing in *Jingshi wucheng fangxiang hutong ji* 京師五城坊巷衖衕集 (A Collection of Streets and Lanes in Five Major Districts of Beijing) (Ming) and *Jingshi fangxiang zhigao* 京師坊巷志稿 (A Draft Record of Beijing's Streets and Lanes) (Qing).

springs; that the geographical background of the novel is Beijing is not only implied, it is basically spelled out.

Dr. Zhao in Chapter 61 mentions that his father was a good doctor in the Ru Mansion, *Rufu* 汝府, an imperial mansion belonging to the eleventh son of Ming Emperor Xianzong 憲宗 (1465–1488). Such mansions had 'good medical clinics', *liangyi suo* 良醫所, which were in the charge of a chief doctor and his deputy. Zhao also relates that his grandfather was the *yuanpan* 院判, an official in the Royal Hospital, *Taiyi yuan* 太醫院. The Royal Hospital has one *yuanshi* 院使 (chief doctor), and two chief assistants. The subordinates include four imperial doctors, *yuyi* 御醫, and one minor officer, *limu* 吏目. Judging from Dr. Zhao's family background and his familiarity with traditional medical books, his identity would have been that of an imperial doctor of the Royal Hospital. He and many other imperial doctors served the Ximen family, and Ximen Qing's identity may be deduced from this.

The title 'royal doctor', *taiyi* 太醫, of traditional opera was an honorary title given to doctors, but judging from their actual descriptions, they are almost all quacks. When they take the stage they have to perform a humorous self-introduction. But no royal doctor in a Chinese opera would introduce his hometown and family background in such detail as Dr. Zhao Longgang in *Jin Ping Mei*. From this we can draw the conclusion: *Jin Ping Mei*'s borrowing Dr. Zhao from *Baojian ji* is just like it borrowed Ximen Qing from *Shuihu zhuan*, all that was borrowed was the name, not the true circumstances.

The insertion into Chapter 31 of *Jin Ping Mei* of *Chen Lin bao zhuanghe* 陳琳抱妝盒 (Chen Lin carrying the dressing case) is also like this. After Ximen Qing has been promoted and had a son, he invites the two eunuchs, Eunuch Xue and Eunuch Liu; Commandant Zhou; and Judicial Commissioner Xia to a feast. The boy actors Li Ming and Wu Hui pluck their instruments and sing for the guests. During the dinner, Commandant Zhou asks the two eunuchs to select the items they prefer for entertainment. After several rounds of modest declining the honour on both sides, Eunuch Liu first selects an item, namely the non-dramatic song suite beginning with the line 'Alas, this floating life of ours is like a dream', *Tan fusheng youru yimengli* 歎浮生有如一夢裡.[9] The central idea of this song concerns seeing through the illusion of the mortal world, a pessimistic outlook that turns ones back on the human world and escapes from making judgments. Therefore, Commandant Zhou says:

---

9   This is a song suite written by Lü Zhi'an 呂止庵 (14th century) found in the *Yongxi yuefu* 雍熙樂府 (1566) and other collections, originally titled 'Sighing over the World', *Tanshi* 歎世. *Editors' note:* Cf. Roy 1993–2013: Chapter 31, note 57 and pp. 467–70 of the appendix (for information on the suite and a complete translation).

PLAYS REFERRED TO IN *JIN PING MEI*

'Senior Eunuch Director, that is a piece about the life of retirement and disillusion with the world. Today we are celebrating His Honor Ximen's happy event, and the happy birth of his son. It wouldn't do to sing that.' (Chapter 31)

Then Eunuch Liu orders the song suite beginning with 'Though I am not one of the eight ministers entitled to wear the purple sash, I command the denizens of the six palaces with their golden hairpins.' Commandant Zhou objects again:

'That is from the *zaju* drama *Chen Lin bao zhuanghe*. Today is a celebratory occasion. It wouldn't do to sing that.' (Chapter 31)

Why does Eunuch Liu choose these items? What is the author's real intention behind this arrangement? This play describes how the eunuch Chen Lin and the female palace attendant Kou Chengyu loyally save the life of the crown prince. The crown prince is the son of Emperor Zhenzong (r. 998–1022) and Consort Li, but the jealous Empress Liu wants to kill the crown prince (who will eventually take the throne as Emperor Renzong 仁宗 (r. 1023–1064)). The empress orders Kou Chengyu to kill the crown prince, but she meets Chen Lin, who agrees to smuggle the crown prince out of danger by hiding him in the imperially sealed dressing case.[10] Ming Emperor Wuzong's 武宗 (r. 1506–1522) birth and parentage were very similar to that of Song Renzong. Both of these emperors were controlled by their empresses. When they had an imperial son with other women, they had to be sent to be raised elsewhere. Only after some years, when the imperial sons became emperors, could the true circumstances of their birth and parentage be disclosed. Because they involved the birth and parentage of the crown prince, there were extremely sensitive stories. Looked at superficially, Eunuch Liu should never have selected an aria from *Bao zhuanghe* on a festive occasion celebrating Ximen Qing (the emperor) having gotten a son (prince), to do so will make people easily draw connections between Emperor Renzong and Emperor Wuzong. The author deliberately arranged for the reference to this play, and his real purpose lies here.

As for the selection of items to be sung at this banquet, the author's arrangement is very sequenced. Next, Eunuch Xue orders a song beginning with the line 'It seems that in this life the hardest thing to bear is separation'. At this, Judicial Commissioner Xia laughs out loud and says:

'Senior Eunuch Director, that is a piece on the subject of separation. It's even more inappropriate for this occasion.'

'Our responsibilities as eunuchs are such', responds Eunuch Director Xue, 'that all we know how to do is to wait upon the pleasure of the Lord of Ten Thousand

---

10 Editor's note: Cf. Roy 1993–2013, Chapter 31, note 58.

Years. We have no taste for the subtleties of lyrics and songs. Let them sing whatever they want.'   (Chapter 31)

These words are ironic. Everyone among the common people, no matter how uneducated, knows what 'separation' means, not to mention the eunuchs who had been educated in the palace. They of course know that they should not pick such unlucky songs to be sung on this occasion. When the two eunuchs Liu and Xue time and again select such disheartening songs, could it be that they are not afraid of Ximen Qing's anger? Finally, Judicial Commissioner Xia orders a song from a suite called 'Thirty Melodies', a set of auspicious birthday songs, appropriate for the atmosphere described in the novel.

The episode of 'selecting songs' seems, on the surface, to be great fun, but it is an example of 'revealing the true message through jesting'. Through this kind of 'playful', casual narrative, the author reveals his true message.

Unveiling the Personalities of the Characters

Jin Ping Mei is a work based on the realities of life. It carefully uses a variety of artistic techniques not only to create different types of characters, but also to display the complexity of their personalities, overcoming the unsatisfying simplicity of the personalities in previous fiction. Behind this technique is a very intriguing phenomenon: the author uses the performance of plays by characters in the novel to show the personalities of different characters. Different plays are used to reveal characters' personalities, and this goes so far as to draw analogies between characters in the plays and in the novel. It can be said that in the history of the Chinese novel this unusual artistic method began in *Jin Ping Mei* and reached its peak in *Honglou meng* 紅樓夢 (A Dream of Red Mansions).

In Chapter 63 of *Jin Ping Mei* we find an example of this technique. During the first seven days after the death of Li Ping'er, Ximen Qing hires a troupe of Haiyan actors to perform. What they perform is *Yuhuan ji* 玉環記 (The Story of the Jade Ring), a *chuanqi* opera in 34 scenes.[11] In *Jin Ping Mei*, there are

---

11 For the full title of the opera, cf. note 1. The story is set in the Tang dynasty. The student Wei Gao travels to Chang'an, the capital, to take the examination. He is expelled from the examination because of arguing with the examiner. His friend tries to comfort him by introducing him to a brothel where he meets Yuxiao, a beautiful prostitute. The two fall in love at first sight and get engaged. Later, the penniless Wei Gao is driven out of the brothel and is unable to redeem Yuxiao. Before leaving, Wei Gao presents Yuxiao with a jade ring from his family, while he himself keeps a similar ring. After their separation, Wei Gao marries another girl. Yuxiao longs for Wei Gao's return, and finally dies keeping the jade ring in her mouth. After all kinds of hardships, Wei Gao finally makes a great contribution to the country and is named governor-general of Sichuan province by the

PLAYS REFERRED TO IN *JIN PING MEI*

about 10 plays whose titles are mentioned, but among them there is only one whose plot is somewhat outlined, namely *Yuhuan ji*. Together with *Baojian ji*, mentioned above, this opera has a very unusual relationship to the novel.

The author's cleverness resides in how passages from *Yuhuan ji* are embedded into the plot of the novel so that they become an organic and inseparable part of it. In this chapter, after the *tiedan* (secondary female role) playing the part of Yuxiao sings for a bit, she then proceeds to sing: 'In this life we are unlikely to meet again. For this reason, I bequeath this self-portrait to you,' and the novel then has this narration:

> [I]t suddenly brought to mind the image of Li Ping'er on her sickbed, and his heart was so moved that he couldn't help starting to shed tears, which he wiped away constantly with a handkerchief. This was spotted at once by Pan Jinlian, who was gazing with a sardonic eye through the lowered blinds and pointed it out to Wu Yueniang, saying,

> 'First Lady, just look at that feckless good-for-nothing! Why on earth should he have started to cry while drinking wine and watching the performance of a play?'

> 'Smart as you are,' said Meng Yulou, 'it's a wonder you don't understand such things. Music expresses man's sorrows and joys, partings and reunions. I imagine that on seeing this episode of the drama, his heart was moved. "Upon seeing an object, one remembers its owner; Upon seeing a saddle, one thinks of one's horse." That is why he started to shed tears.' (Chapter 63)

In the *Jin Ping Mei*, Ximen Qing is a lascivious rascal who cares only for whoring and affairs and who seduces and abandons lovers and just plays around with women. People called him 'the foreman of the wife-beaters, and the leader of the lotharios' (Chapter 17). He hunts women only for the sake of satisfying his instinctive sexual desire. Does he have anything called feelings? But then: Why does he love only Li Ping'er so much, crying for her when he watches the play?

Many readers think that this is because when Li Ping'er married Ximen Qing, she brought him a fortune so that 'his affairs became more prosperous than ever. On his country estate outside the walls and in his residential compound, everything was put on an entirely new footing' (Chapter 20).

---

emperor. 15 years later, Yuxiao is reborn with the jade ring in her mouth, into a family with the name Jiang, and now she marries Wei Gao as his second wife. Wei Gao is ennobled as Prince of Zhongwu, and his second wife is raised to the status of First Lady. Apart from the *chuanqi* version, there is also a Yuan *zaju* by Qiao Ji 喬吉 on the same theme. The opera as presented in *Jin Ping Mei* is, however, closer to the Ming *chuanqi*.

105

Therefore, when Li Ping'er dies, Ximen Qing is overwhelmed with sorrow. When he cries so bitterly over Li Ping'er, this action is regarded as hypocritical: he loves the money and does not care for the person. In fact, this is not the case. Li Ping'er has already died, but the fortune she brought with her still belongs to Ximen Qing. It does not disappear with her. Why then is Ximen Qing so deeply unhappy?

Ximen Qing is mostly cold and ruthless towards women, but his personality is definitely not purely simple, nor does it never change once it has been developed, instead it is complex and changes a lot. Among all Ximen Qing's women, it is only Li Ping'er whose love for him was deep, and it is her sincere and deep love that moved him. Especially when she was at death's door and so weak that her crying was soundless, she still hugged Ximen Qing with her skinny 'silver bar' arms, with unlimited affection for her 'karmic enemy' (lover), and said:

> 'Taking advantage of what time is left before my eyes are closed, I'd like to say a few words to you. Your household wealth is extensive, and you are without paternal relatives to rely on, or anyone to assist you in managing it. You must consider carefully whatever you do, and not give way to the impulse of the moment. [...] Moreover, you occupy an official post. From now on, you ought not to go out drinking so often and should endeavor to come home earlier when you do. Your household responsibilities are important. The situation will not be the same as when I was here to admonish you. If I die, who will there be to deter you with bitter tasting but well-meant advice?'

> When Ximen Qing heard these words, he feels just as though a knife were slashing his heart and liver, and he wept, saying,

> 'My sister, I understand what you're saying. Don't you worry yourself about me. I, Ximen Qing, must have been bereft of affinity and short on fortune in a former existence, to be unable to remain husband and wife to the end with you in this incarnation. It pains me to death! Heaven is destroying me!'

> (Chapter 62)

From this we can see that Ximen Qing is not devoid of human feelings, and we understand better why he is so utterly sad when watching the play. What is revealed here is another aspect of his character. But perhaps the selection and performance of the entire *Yuhuan ji* in *Jin Ping Mei* has a deeper meaning? Is it that Ximen Qing wants to, with this sixth concubine, Li Ping'er, who loves him in both life and death, have a matrimonial ties with her across two incarnations?

In *Jin Ping Mei* only one sentence from *Yuhuan ji* is quoted. However, this sentence arouses a number of different reactions from the audience: Ximen

Qing's sorrow, Wu Yueniang's indifference, Pan Jinlian's coldness, and Meng Yulou's calmness, etc. From this we can come to a conclusion: as for the borrowing and insertion of plays in *Jin Ping Mei*, the purpose for their selection is clear, their main purpose is to work toward the creation of the characters in the novel. What is especially worth our attention is how, when *Yuhuan ji* is borrowed in *Jin Ping Mei*, the characters in the play and in the novel are compared with each other; this is a very unique and engaging phenomenon.

> Below them drums and music began to sound, as the players came on to perform another scene in which the *sheng* (male role), playing the part of Wei Gao, and the *jing* (comic-villain role), playing the part of Bao Zhishui, paid a visit together to the bordello in which the singing girl Yuxiao is employed. When the madam came out to receive them, Bao Zhishui said, 'You go and call out that girl for me.' 'Master Bao,' responded the madam, 'you don't know how to treat people properly. My daughter is not accustomed to come out for just anybody. Are you incapable of uttering the word "please"? How can you speak of simply calling her out?' (Chapter 63)

The above passage is based on scene 6 of *Yuhuan ji,* but in the original script the text is slightly different:

> The *jing* role says, 'Well, call out that girl for me.' The *chou* (clown) role says, 'Monsieur Bao, you are so rude. My daughter is more gorgeous than the most beautiful flower of spring, dimming all others in the garden. Her charm is like that of Bodhisattva. She is not accustomed to come out for just anybody. Are you not able to say the word "please" rather than simply calling her out?'[12]

The novel does not finish the copying of the dialogue between Bao Zhishui and the madam but instead inserts evaluation of characters in the novel. This transition is very natural:

> At this, Li Guijie turned to the company and laughed, saying,
>
> 'This character named Bao is just like Beggar Ying, a lame donkey who doesn't know the score.'
>
> 'If I don't know the score,' said Ying Bojue, 'how is it that the madam of your establishment likes me so much?'
>
> 'What she likes is for you to keep out of the way,' responded Li Guijie.
>
> 'Let's watch the play,' said Ximen Qing. 'What are you dithering about anyway? If you say another word, you'll have to drink a large bumper of wine as a forfeit.'

---

12 (淨)也罷，叫他出來見我。（醜）包官人，你好輕人。我女兒麗春園逼邪氣鶯鶯花賽壓眾芳。美嬌嬌活豔豔的觀世音菩薩，等閒不便出來。你說不得一個請字，你到說叫他出來。

Only then did Ying Bojue consent to remain silent, while the players finished the scene they were performing and went offstage. (Chapter 62)

Ying Bojue and Bao Zhishui are go-betweens who arrange prostitutes for others, while Li Guijie is a prostitute. The comparisons in the novel are very apt. Moreover, Wu Yueniang's maidservant is called Yuxiao, exactly the same name as that of the heroine Yuxiao in *Yuhuan ji*. Judging from his use of the special technique, the author must have been a talented scholar of exquisite artistic accomplishments; this is not something a low-level writer or performer could have been capable of.

Pushing the Development of the Storyline Forward

Drama performance is one of the indispensable components of daily life in the Ximen mansion, therefore, it has become part and parcel of the fictional episodes that concentrate on describing family life. If the arrangement of the theater programs is just right, they will serve to stir up conflicts among the characters and to push the development of the storyline forward.

There are many examples of this in *Jin Ping Mei*. In Chapter 20, after Ximen Qing has married Li Ping'er, he holds a party at home on the 25th of the eighth lunar month. Friends and relatives, such as Ying Bojue and other sworn brothers, as well as Second Uncle Wu, gather in the Ximen mansion to watch performers display acrobatics and perform plays. Ying Bojue forcibly gets Li Ping'er to come out to meet the guests, while the other wives watch what happens from the back of the hall:

> To resume our story: Meng Yulou, Pan Jinlian, and Li Jiao'er clustered around Wu Yueniang behind a hanging screen in the reception hall to see what they could hear and see of the proceedings. They heard the singing girls perform the song to the tune 'Clever Improvisation' that begins with the words 'How pleased we are by your success,' and then continues, 'Heaven has made this perfect match; Like male and female phoenix are husband and wife.' They then proceeded to the next song in the suite, to the tune 'Flirtatious Laughter,' which begins with the words 'Gaily laughing we celebrate this happy occasion. By raising our phoenix goblets on high. To the sound of ivory clappers, silver psaltery and a jade flute, let them bring on, in cups and platters, the fruits of sea and land, to grace the auspicious feast.' The song concluded with the words, 'May they live happily together, as husband and wife, forever and ever.' At this point Jinlian turned to Yueniang and said,
>
> 'Elder Sister, listen to what they're singing. She's only a concubine, after all. That really isn't an appropriate song suite to sing on a day like this. If they're

PLAYS REFERRED TO IN *JIN PING MEI*

to be like fish in the water, and "live happily together as husband and wife for ever and ever", where does that leave you?'

Now although Yueniang was a good person by nature, when she heard these words she couldn't help being somewhat dismayed and feeling resentful in her heart. She also observed the way in which Ying Bojue, Xie Xida, and the rest of the company carried on when Li Ping'er came out to greet them. It seemed as though they wished they had more mouths than nature had provided, the better to praise her with.

'This sister-in-law of ours,' rhapsodized Ying Bojue, 'is truly something seldom seen in the universe, and without peer in this world. Quite aside from the fact that she is compliant and virtuous by nature, and dignified and stately in demeanor; she cuts such a striking figure that in all the world you could hardly hope to find the like. Who else but our elder brother deserves to enjoy such good fortune? We who have been privileged to see her today will have been the gainers though we should die tomorrow.'

[...] When Wu Yueniang and the others overheard this speech they cursed him unremittingly for a rot-talking, glib-tongued jailbird. (Chapter 20)

The above quotation, 'How pleased we are by your success', is the first line of a song suite named *He Sheng* 合笙 in chapter 16 of *Yongxi yuefu,* with the original comment 'A Happy Family Gathering' (*Hejia huanle* 合家欢乐). It is also recorded in *New Sounds of the Flourishing Age. Thirteen Musical Notations of Nanjiugong* (*Nanjiugong shisan diaopu* 南九宫十三调谱), in which two of those songs, 'Harmonious Dao' (*Daohe* 道和) and 'Plum Blossom Wine' (*Meihua jiu* 梅花酒) are both mentioned as belonging to *Cailou ji* 彩楼记 (The Story of the Painted Pavilion). *Cailou ji* is a play in the genre of *chuanqi* 传奇. It is an adaptation of the Southern opera *Poyaoji* 破窑记 (The Story of the Pottery Kiln) from the Ming Dynasty.

The irony is that while the theme of the song suite is 'A Happy Family Gathering', Ximen Qing's wives and concubines experience an 'unhappy family gathering' after listening to the play. Subsequently several other conflicts break out as a result of listening to the song suite. First, Wu Yueniang, provoked by Pan Jinlian, becomes extremely jealous. She curses people unremittingly in public, sweeping away her original image as a 'warm and modest' wife and maximizing her original conflict with Ximen Qing. Then Pan Jinlian instigates Wu Yueniang to get into a rage with Li Ping'er.

Jinlian also speaks ill of Yueniang in front of Li Ping'er, saying Yueniang cannot accommodate others, easily tricking Li Ping'er into trusting her. The uproar from this instance of listening to (the song suites from) a play has a profound impact on the evolution of the subsequent happenings, continuously causing contradictions and conflicts between the characters. This also foretells and lays the foundation for later events such as Wu Yueniang showing off by 'sweeping snow and cooking tea', and the bitter fighting—both in the open and in secret—between Pan Jinlian and Li Ping'er.

Adding Colour to the Atmosphere of the Surroundings

In *Jin Ping Mei* great importance is attached to the depiction of the surroundings through adding on layers. Since the activities of the characters necessarily take place in certain surroundings, therefore the author, when incorporating material from operas—often combined the descriptions of external 'scenes' and 'realms' of the plays with descriptions of the 'scenes' and 'realms' in the novel, obtaining the effects of adding colour to the atmosphere and illuminating the character.

In Chapter 76 of *Jin Ping Mei* we are told how Ximen Qing, after listening to the plays for a whole day at home, had still not had enough. After seeing off all the officials, including Grand Coordinator Hou Meng and Censor Song Qiaonian, he listens to the performance of *Sijie ji* 四节记 (Story of the Four Seasons):[13]

> After Ximen Qing had seen them off and come back inside, he dismissed the musicians and, seeing that it was still rather early, directed that the tables should be left in place, and that the caterers should set what remained of the various dishes and delicacies in order. He then sent page boys to go and invite Uncle Wu, Licentiate Wen, Ying Bojue, his managers, Fu Ming and Gan Jun, Ben Dichuan and Chen Jingji to come and join him, and enjoy a dramatic performance. He also had two table settings of wine and savories provided for the troupe of Haiyan actors to eat while he waited for the guests to arrive, after which he told them to be ready to perform the winter scene entitled '*Han Xizai yeyan*' 韩熙载夜宴 (Han Xizai's Nocturnal Banquet), from the *chuanqi* drama *Sijie ji*. In addition, he had pots of plum blossoms brought out and displayed on the tables to either side, so they could enjoy the plum blossoms while consuming their wine.

> Uncle Wu [...] went back to the front compound, where the wine had already been provided, and he could have a drink. [...] At this juncture, Uncle Wu, together with Wu the Second, Ying Bojue and Licentiate Wen, took their places

---

13 Another name for *Sijie ji* is *Si you ji* 四游记 (The Story of the Four Journeys) by Shen Cai 沈采 of the Ming Dynasty, recorded in Lü Tiancheng 吕天成: *Qupin: Jiu chuanqi* 曲品·旧传奇 (A Study of Opera: Old *Chuanqi* Dramas). In *Baneng zoujin* 八能奏锦 (A Collection of Music Scores played by the Eight Categories of Musical Instruments in Ancient Orchestras) the drama is also called *Si you ji*. A fragment is also included *Ming Qing chuanqi gouchen* 明清传奇钩沉 (A Collection of *Chuanqi* Dramas from the Ming and Qing Dynasties).

PLAYS REFERRED TO IN *JIN PING MEI*

as guests, while Ximen Qing sat down in the host's position, and managers Fu Ming, Gan Jun, Ben Dichuan and Chen Jingji took their places to either side, making a total of five tables in all; while below, the troupe of actors began to play their gongs and drums and then proceeded to perform a scene from the *Sijie ji* entitled '*Han Xizai yeyan: youting zhuyu*' 韩熙[载]夜宴·邮亭住遇) (Han Xizai's Nocturnal Banquet Exposes the Tryst in the Relay Station). [...] That day, by the time the actors had performed two scenes from the play about 'the tryst in the relay station', it was already the first watch. (Chapter 76)

The play takes the four scenes of spring, summer, autumn and winter, and matches up each of them the story of a famous person. The winter scene is titled '*Tao xiushi youting ji* 陶秀实邮亭记' (The Story of Tao Xiushi in the Relay Station), which tells how the scholar Tao Gu 陶谷 of the Song Dynasty was sent on a diplomatic mission to the state of Southern Tang, and the minister of Southern Tang, Han Xizai 韩熙载, hosted a banquet in the wintry night. A famous prostitute, Qin Ruolan 秦弱兰, served him. During the banquet, Tao Gu presented her with a poetic song to the tune '*Fengguang hao* 风光好' (The Scenery is Beautiful). The winter scene in this story coincides exactly with the eve of the 'first day of the twelfth lunar month' mentioned in *Jin Ping Mei*. Thus, when Ximen Qing and Uncle Wu '[...] had pots of plum blossoms brought out and displayed on the tables to either side, so they could enjoy the plum blossoms while consuming their wine', this may be considered 'an appropriately matched scene'. The selection of this play also matches the time of the party in *Jin Ping Mei*, namely 'the first watch', and in this respect it is also highly appropriate. *Sijie ji* is about literati and scholars, while those listening to the play are Ying Bojue, Licentiate Wen and the whole group of so-called 'aficionados of art and culture', which is also very much to the point. Obviously, the author was not randomly throwing things together, but instead carefully selected passages to match the development of the plot.

Of course, the author wrote about this performance not just to add colour to the atmosphere, but more importantly to throw light on the characters. Although the performance of this play adds a sort of refined bookish flavour to Ximen Qing, Licentiate Wen and the rest, the irony is that just as the merrymaking is at its height, Qiaotong, a servant in the Qiao family, is sent over 'to deliver the customary fee of thirty taels of silver for the purchase of a position as an honorary official, which he has sealed up here, together with an additional sum of five taels, to be distributed to the staff of the personnel office.' This 'smell of money' is incompatible with the 'nobleness' of learned literati and gentry. Immediately afterwards, Licentiate Wen's sodomizing of the page Huatong is discovered and Ximen Qing expels him from his house. The opera performance creates an excellent background for setting off the outward refinement but inward dirty filth of the family.

References

Feng Yuanjun 馮沅君
>**1947.** '*Jin Ping Mei* zhongde wenxue shiliao.' In 金瓶梅詞話中的文學史料. Shanghai: shangwu yinshuguan.

Guo Xun 郭勋
Yongxi yuefu 雍熙乐府 (The Music Department of Yongxi) Photorepint in *Sibu congkan Xubian* of woodblock edition with preface dated 1566.

Huo Xianjun
>**2010.** *Jin Ping Mei yishu lunyao* 金瓶梅艺术论要 (Essential Artistic Features of *Jin Ping Mei*), Tianjin: guji chubanshe.

Lanling Xiaoxiao Sheng 兰陵笑笑生
>**1982 [1617].** *Jin Ping Mei cihua* 金瓶梅词话. A photocopy of the block-printed edition, Dingsi year of the Ming Wanli period. Preface dated 1617. Taipei: Tianyi chubanshe.

Jin Ping Mei cihua jiaozhu 金瓶梅词话校注
>**2000.** Collated and annotated by Tao Muning 陶慕宁. Beijing: Renmin wenxue chubanshe.

Li Kaixian 李开先
>**1649.** *Baojian ji* 宝剑记 (The Story of the Sword). An original block-printed edition. Preface dated 1649.

Liu Hui 刘辉 and Yang Yang 杨扬
>**1989.** *Jin Ping Mei zhi mi* 金瓶梅之谜 (The Mysteries of *Jin Ping Mei*). Shumu wenxian chubanshe.

Roy, David Tod (tr.)
>**1993–2013.** *The Plum in the Golden Vase or* Chin P'ing Mei (5 vols). Princeton: Princeton University Press.

Zang Xian 臧贤
>**1955.** *Shengshi xinsheng* 盛世新声 (New Sounds of a Flourishing Age). Wenxue guji kanxingshe.

Zhang Lu 张禄
>**1955.** *Cilin zhaiyan* 词林摘艳 (Excerpts of Lyrics). Wenxue guji kanxingshe.

Note on Contributors

Huo Xianjun 霍现俊: Professor and doctoral supervisor in the School of Chinese Language and Literature, Hebei Normal University. PhD in Chinese Literature. His academic part-time positions include that of Vice President of *Jin Ping Mei* Research Association of China; Vice President of Hebei Yuan Song Research Association; Sub-President of The Society of 'A Dream of Red Mansions' in Hebei Province, etc. Research interests: ancient Chinese novels and operas.

Zhang Dahai 张大海: Associate Professor, School of Foreign Languages, Chongqing College of Humanities, Science and Technology, China.

CHAPTER 8

The Historical Value of the Customs of Late Ming Drama as Portrayed in *Jin Ping Mei*

ZHANG TINGTING
Translated by Xu Wei

With the sprouting of the 'buds of capitalism' during the Ming dynasty, a movement of enlightenment began in Chinese social philosophy. In the field of thought, there was a shift from the School of Principle (*lixue* 理學) founded by Zhu Xi 朱熹 (1130–1200) to the School of the Mind (*xinxue* 心學) of Wang Yangming 王陽明 (1472–1529).

Continuing to extend and expand Chinese culture on the basis of the doctrines of Confucius 孔子 and Mencius 孟子, the School of the Mind flourished in Shaoxing and particularly in Taizhou, where Wang Gen 王艮 (1483–1541) and his disciples were devoted to the popularization of Confucianism, insisting on preaching the ethical principles of Confucianism among the lower classes. Wang Gen proposed that '"the way" (*dao* 道) exists in the people's daily practices' (百姓日用即道) and even common people 'can know and practice' (能知能行) the way. In contrast to the orthodox learning of the past, Wang Gen advocated that for humans to desire to eat when hungry, to drink when thirsty, and to love the opposite sex was naturally 'the nature of human beings' (人性之軆). Thus, he promoted the liberation of the individual, attacked the stifling of desire, and in the world of thought opposed the feudal orthodoxy that proclaimed the need to 'preserve heavenly principle but suppress human desires' (存天理, 滅人欲). Tang Xianzu 湯顯祖 (1550–1616), the famous playwright, studied under Luo Rufang's 羅汝芳 (1515–1588), a member of the Taizhou School of the Mind. Tang thought that 'the great *dao* exists only in oneself' (大道只在自身), explaining that 'we Confucians in our daily life are dependent

---

The translation is based on the work of Xu Wei, revised by the editors according to the principles of the present book. We gratefully acknowledge the assistance of David Rolston in revising the pre-final version of this chapter.

on our instincts, but we do not realize it. Why?' (See the continuation of this line of thought in the note).[1]

The School of the Mind and the later philosophy derived from it won great popularity and became the dominant social thought. Its influence covered almost all fields at the time—political, moral, cultural, artistic, and other areas. A new trend arose in the field of literature, with works depicting urban themes and reflecting the interests of townspeople. Through seductive erotic descriptions and depiction of passionate feelings, these works focused on the people's personalities and emphasized the ego, to show the mental state of the 'true self' and the 'true nature'.

The Rise of the School of the Mind and the Narrative Perspective of the JPM

Literary creation and philosophy are not separated from each other, with no connections. This enlightenment movement of the late Ming society affirmed the reasonable nature of human desire, advocated personal liberation, and used the ideas of 'human desire' to fight against the long repression of human nature in feudal orthodoxy. However, the movement went to the opposite extreme, that is, excessive emphasis on 'desire', one-sided exaggeration of 'lust' and 'material desire' encouraged social fad favoring extravagance and decadence. Although *Jin Ping Mei*, a product of the late Ming Dynasty when Wang Yangming's School of the Mind and its later offshoots flourished, focuses on the rise and fall of the Ximen Qing 西門慶 family during the Song Dynasty, it actually describes the living world and the spiritual state of the late Ming.

Jin Ping Mei depicts exquisitely the scenery of life during the late Ming. Government affairs, social activities, family life, human emotions, etiquette, festival customs, food, daily life, drama performances and other activities: all are vividly described, just like a picture scroll. The rise of material culture allowed people a new extravagance and they were infatuated with the most beautiful and exquisite things. In a social atmosphere where everybody was 'going the pace' and 'showing off', there was, on one hand, an extreme pursuit of material things, and on the other hand, a fanatic desire for sex. All of this is reflected in the novel in its aesthetic appreciation of the abnormal, the 'strange among the ordinary', as Xie Zhaozhe 謝肇淛 (1567–1624) put it, in his postscript to *Jin Ping Mei*:

---

1 Tang Xianzu 1962, 1165: 吾儒日用性中而不知者, 何也? '自诚明谓之性', 赤子之知也。'自诚明谓之教', 致曲是也。隐曲之处, 可欲者存焉。致曲者, 致知也。

Affairs between the government and the people, contact between official and private spheres, frivolous talk between couples, street slang, nepotistic behaviour, apparent cordiality combined with sneering behind people's back, seeking occasions for illicit love, drunken words of lovemaking on the pillow, cynical profit mongering, rivalry among the womenfolk, flattering platitudes of prostitutes, servants' calculating talk, all of this is described in lifelike detail. How amazing and amusing!

其中朝野之政务, 官私之晋接, 闺阃之媒语, 市里之猥谈, 与夫势交利合之态, 心输背笑之局, 桑中濮上之期, 尊罍枕席之语, 驵侩之机械意智, 粉黛之自媚争妍, 狭客之从谀逢迎, 奴伙之稽唇淬语, 穷极境象, 骇意快心.[2]

In the description of this pleasurable lifestyle, we are also shown drama performances and the actors' living conditions in the late Ming Dynasty. We get a glimpse of the performance of various performing arts such as *nanxi* 南戲 (Southern drama), *zaju* 雜劇 (comedies), *chuanqi* 傳奇 (operas), *xiaochang* 小唱 (unstaged singing of arias), *zashua* 杂耍 (acrobatics), and *buxi* 步戲 (a kind of skit), and can also observe the popular *Haiyan qiang* 海鹽腔 (Haiyan style of opera)[3] and Yiyang qiang 弋陽腔 (Yiyang style of opera)[4], styles that were spreading to all classes. We are introduced both to performances by private and commercial troupes. From this point of view, *Jin Ping Mei* is not only an important novel of particular significance for literary history, but it also has an extremely great importance for the history of the performing arts.

---

2   Zhu Yixuan 朱一玄 2002: 179.

3   *Haiyan qiang* was one of the four *Nanxi sheng qiang* (vocal styles of the Southern drama) named after Hanyan in Zhejiang. It was first formed in the Southern Song dynasty, and during the Jiajing and Longqing periods (1522–1572) of the Ming dynasty, it spread to Jiaxing, Huzhou, Wenzhou, Nanjing, Taizhou, Suzhou, Songjiang, and even as far away as Yihuang in Jiangxi Province and Beijing. The singing was accompanied only by percussion instruments, the tone was clear and soft, and the style was much beloved by bureaucrats and scholars. See Wu Xinlei 吳新雷 (ed.) 2002: 17.

4   *Yiyang qiang* (abbreviated as *Yi qiang*) was another of the *Nanxi sheng qiang*, named after Yiyang in Jiangxi Province. It appeared in the late Yuan Dynasty. During the Jiajing period of the Ming, it was popular in present-day Nanjing, Beijing, Hunan, Guangdong, Fujian, Anhui, Yunnan, Guizhou and other places. It is characterized by solo singing accompanied by choral amplification (*bangqiang* 幫腔), accompanied only by percussion instruments. Due to the combination of *Yiyang qiang* with the local language and folk tunes, under its direct and indirect influence, many types of dramas were produced, or became part of local opera forms, forming a wide range of 'vocal cavity' systems, generally known as *gao qiang*. In the Ming and Qing dynasties, *Yiyang qiang* evolved and developed into one of the main vocal styles among the folk during the Ming and Qing dynasties. See ibid., 17–18..

The Height of Sound and Beauty, Performances by the Music Office

The Music Office (*Jiaofang si* 教坊司) and the Bell and Drum Office (*Zhonggu si* 鐘鼓司)[5] were set up by the Ming government to take care of the performances inside and outside the court. The Music Office, which belonged to Ministry of Rites (*Libu* 禮部), 'was in charge of the provision of music and dance performances, which were performed by members of registered entertainer households'.[6] It was solely responsible for the performances of the inner court, and was also in charge of the performances for ceremonial, honorific, and entertainment feasts of the outer court. 'In the outer court, they were used to provide performances at banquets for foreign envoys when military and civil officials were instructed to be in attendance.'[7] At first, the Office mainly choreographed and performed orthodox 'refined music' (*yayue* 雅樂), but later items for entertainment were added; in addition to music and dance, there were also performances of *zaju* and acrobatics and skits (*baixi* 百戲). The Bell and Drum Office, also known as the Drama Supervision Bureau (*Yuxi jian* 禦戲監), belonged to the palace and was responsible for 'drumming when the emperor goes to the court', as well as for all kinds of variety performance such as *neiyue* 內樂 (palace music), *chuanqi* 傳奇 (opera), *guojin* 過錦 (sketch), *dadao* 打稻 ('threshing' dance).[8] The musicians were mainly eunuchs, who performed for the palace, and the Office was generally in charge of performances inside the palace. The Music Office also handled official entertainment outside the court, such as performances in the officially run entertainment quarters that included the various entertainment quarters of the cities. These places were provided for patronisation by princes and noblemen, but it was also permitted for distinguished officials and aristocrats to watch the performances. In addition, some dignitaries could also engage performers from the Office to

---

5   *Jiaofang si* was a government agency in China during the Ming Dynasty. It already existed during the Tang Dynasty but changed name to the *Jiaofang si* during in the Ming Dynasty and was established under the Ministry of Ceremonies, responsible for welcoming and entertaining important guests with music. There was also an official brothel with both male and female musicians (official prostitutes). During the Qing Dynasty, emperor Shunzhi abolished female musicians and replaced them with performing eunuchs. Emperor Yongzheng abolished the *Jiaofang si* and established a harmony office. *Zhonggu Si* was a eunuch institution, mainly responsible for the bells and drums of the court, as well as for music and dance, acting, juggling and other activities in the palace.

6   Shen Defu 1959: 271–72.

7   ibid.

8   Zhang Tingyu et al. 1974: 1820.

their mansions to entertain prominent court officials and aristocrats of sufficient status. In *Jin Ping Mei*, there are several descriptions of performances by the Music Office. For example, in Chapter 32, after Ximen Qing has been promoted and has been blessed with a newborn son, he hosts a special banquet to entertain the high officials from Qinghe County: Magistrate Li Datian 李達天, Vice-magistrate Qian Cheng 錢成, Assistant Magistrate Ren Tinggui 任廷貴, Secretary Xia Gongji 夏恭基 and Eunuch Xue 薛內相. During the dinner, Ximen Qing invites entertainers from the Music Office to perform:

> Beneath the steps, drums and music begin to sound, pipes and voices rise in concert. Wine was served, and someone from the Music Office presented the program from which Eunuch Xue picked the four scenes of the *zaju* drama entitled *Han Xiangzi shengxian ji*. A number of ensemble dance pieces were also presented, performed with superb execution. Eunuch Xue was delighted by this and called on his attendants for two strings of cash with which to reward to the performers. (Chapter 32, translation according to Roy 2001: 245)

阶下鼓乐响动，笙歌拥奏，递酒上坐。教坊呈上揭帖。薛内相拣了四摺《韩湘子升仙记》，又队舞数回，十分齐整。薛内相心中大喜，唤左右拿两吊钱出来，赏赐乐工。

There is another example in Chapter 65: Censor Song 宋巡按 and some of the local officials borrow the Ximen mansion to set up a banquet to welcome Eunuch Huang 黃太尉. The front hall is decorated with peacock screens, the floors are covered with carpets, the tables draped with brocade, the chairs with embroidered cushions – everything is luxurious, elegant and extravagant. Ximen Qing has specially invited performers from the Music Office to play at the welcoming ceremony. When Eunuch Huang's party passes from Dongping Prefecture into Qinghe County, the musicians from the Music Office let their drums sound, making an earsplitting noise. When Eunuch Huang enters the hall to take his seat, all the other officials, together with Ximen Qing, sit down, according to their status. At this point the director of the troupe presents an album with a list of items for the guests to pick and choose from:

> When a director of the Music Office had presented an album listing the program of pieces they were prepared to perform, the music commenced. Every one of the performances, including both instrumental and vocal music, and ensemble dance pieces, was presented in appropriate order, displaying to maximum advantage the beauties of sound and colour. During the feast, after a scene from the *chuanqi* drama *Pei Jingong huandai ji* (The story of Pei Du's Return of the Belts) had been performed, the chef came out to preside over the carving of the entrées of roast venison and pork, served with a soup of a hundred ingredients,

HISTORICAL VALUE OF THE CUSTOMS OF LATE MING DRAMA

and steamed open-topped dumplings. After this, four of the musicians, playing psaltery, mandola, *pipa*, and harp, without any percussion instruments, sang a song. (Chapter 65, translation according to Roy 2011: 146)

教坊伶官递上手本奏乐，一应弹唱队舞，各有节次，极尽声容之盛。当筵搬演《裴晋公还带记》，一折下来，厨役割献烧鹿、花猪、百宝攒汤、大饭烧卖。又有四员伶官，筝、琵琶、箜篌，上来清弹小唱。

According to *Jin Ping Mei*, the musicians of the Music Office at that time were recruited into the outer court, mainly performing on solemn occasions or grand ceremonies, and were used for the banquet of Ximen Qing and his official colleagues to entertain important officials of the imperial court. Based on the description of the performance, the Music Office, according to the circumstances, would prepare a number of plays from which the guests could choose. If the occasion was a celebration of the completion of the first month of a new born baby or a birthday feast, then plays about immortals and celebration of long life would be performed. If the ritual occasion was on the order of a welcoming ceremony or one of congratulation, the story of Pei Du becoming top graduate might be chosen in order to praise the integrity of the Ming officials. This play was about Pei Du 裴度, a young man from the Tang Dynasty, who returned a treasure to its owner, thereby saving the lives of several people. At this time, the Music Office still followed the practice of performing *zaju*. During the performance, various large-scale dances with song, instrumental music, and singing accompanied by stringed instruments were inserted in between the four acts of the *zaju*, that were staged sequentially according to the progress of the banquet; 'the height of sound and beauty' was used to enrich the spectacle and solemnity of the congratulatory ceremonies, and to adjust the balance between quietude and liveliness. As Gu Qiyuan 顧啟元 (1565–1628) of the Wanli period said in 'Ke zuo zhui yu' 《客座贅語》: 'In Nanjing before the Wanli period, if local gentry or rich families held a smaller banquet, they would mostly make use of 'free music' (*sanyue* 散樂) where three, four or more singers performed *Beiqu* 北曲 (Northern songs); if it was a large banquet, performers from the *Jiaofang* would be invited to perform y*uanben* 院本 which consisted of four acts of *Beiqu*, with *cuodianjuan* 撮墊圈 (gasket tricks), *wu Guanyin* 舞觀音 (Guanyin dance), *baizhang qi* 百丈旗 (dance with a very big flag) or *tiao duizi* 跳隊子 (group dance) during the intervals.'[9] It is evident that such banquets were very extravagant, and the use of musicians from the Music Office to create auditory and visual

---

9　Gu Qiyuan 顧起元 2012, 204.

spectacle had become the custom, and an irreplaceable item in the ordinary social intercourse and rituals of officials.

Keeping Private Troupes to Provide Music and Song

Private troupes (*jiaban/jiayue* 家班/家樂) first appear in the Jiajing and Wanli reign-periods (1522–1620) and prospered during the Tianqi and Chongzhen reign-periods (1621–1644). The families of officials, nobles, and rich merchants, all would maintain drama troupes in their homes to entertain guests. They would buy child actors from among the people, bring them home to raise, and would hire music teachers to teach them to sing and act.

After Ximen Qing took Li Ping'er 李瓶兒 into his home as a concubine, he gradually became so prosperous that he began to plan to establish his own private troupe. He chose four of his maid servants: Chunmei 春梅 from Pan Jinlian 潘金蓮's apartment; Yuxiao 玉簫 from Wu Yueniang 吳月娘, his first wife's apartment; Yingchun 迎春 from Li Ping'er 李瓶兒's apartment; and Lanxiang 蘭香 from Yulou 玉樓's apartment, had clothes and jewelry made for them, and organized then into a private troupe. He also hired Li Ming 李銘, a performer from the Music Office, to teach the four girls to sing while they play instruments. Chunmei studied the *pipa* 琵琶 (a kind of lute); Yuxiao the *zheng* 箏 (a kind of zither), Yingchun the *xianzi* 弦子 (a three-stringed banjo), and Lanxiang the *huqin* 胡琴 (a two-string fiddle). Apart from meals and tea, Li Ming was also paid five taels of silver a month. Soon after the establishment of the troupe, it began to perform at Ximen Qing's daily family banquets for social entertainment. For example, in Chapter 21, Ximen Qing's concubines arrange a joint party. After a round of drinks, Pan Jinlian invites the four maids to perform the song suite whose first song is to the tune matrix 'Southern Pomegranate Blossoms (*Nan shiliuhua* 南石榴花) and whose first line is 'It was the night of their assignation' (*Jia qi chong hui* 佳期重會). By choosing this song, she is mocking the hypocrisy of the first wife, Wu Yueniang, for 'burning incense on a moonlit night' in order to make up with Ximen Qing.

Ximen Qing was just a local bully in Qinghe County, so the scale of his family troupe was still small. Those who had higher status, such as Eunuch He 何太監, Wang Huangqin 王皇親 (Imperial Relative Wang) and Prime Minister Cai Jing 蔡京, had larger family troupes. Eunuch He had a male troupe of 12 boys. Wang Huangqin also had a male family troupe but with 20 young boys, who could perform *Xixiang ji* 西廂記 (The Story of the Western Wing), and the Prime Minister's family troupe was still bigger, with only female performers:

> His Honor has had these female musicians trained, altogether twenty-four of them in his troupe. They know how to perform the Dance of the Daughters of

HISTORICAL VALUE OF THE CUSTOMS OF LATE MING DRAMA

Mara, the Dance of Rainbow Skirts, and the Dance of Guanyin. They perform before his Honor during breakfast, at lunch, and at evening banquets. I imagine that at present they are entertaining him at breakfast. (Chapter 55, translation according to Roy 2006: 353.)

这是老爷教的女乐，一班二十四人，都晓得天魔舞、霓裳舞、观音舞。但凡老爷早膳、中饭、夜宴，都是奏的。如今想是早膳了。

These twenty-four beauties were good at singing and dancing, had excellent skills, and their performance made people 'feel like in heaven'.

In *Jin Ping Mei,* in the spectacular material way of life presented, the self-importance and arrogance of the imperial relatives and aristocrats, the court eunuchs and big officials, are reflected in all aspects of their daily life. Every social banquet was accompanied with music, song, wine, and other pleasures. They immersed themselves into the experience of their own sensibilities, intoxicated themselves in the sound and spectacle of performance. They do not hesitate to spend huge amounts of money producing gold and silk to have clothes and accessories made for their family troupes to stimulate sensory desire by their gorgeous performances, displaying the spectacle of a deformed and extravagant culture.

Elegant and Vulgar for Different Tastes: Haiyan and Yiyang Styles

Jin Ping Mei describes life in the Jiajing period from a realistic angle. At that time, Chinese indigenous theatre was very popular, and various vocal styles (*shengqiang* 聲腔), especially the Haiyan style and Yiyang style, became popular but they were distinguished as to whether they were thought to be vulgar or refined. Haiyan style, because it used Mandarin, was very particular about enunciation and pronunciation, its prosody was very lively, and its emotional expression very evocative, 'people in both capitals patronised it,' and it became very fashionable near and wide in literati circles in the capitals.[10] Before the Wanli period, most scholar-officials preferred the Haiyan style at their banquets to entertain guests. If Yiyang or Yuyao style (*Yuyao qiang* 余姚腔)[11] were used, it was disrespectful.'[12] The Yiyang style had strong local features. After enter-

---

10 Lu Can 陸粲 et al. 1987: 303.

11 *Yuyao qiang* is another of the four Southern vocal styles of Southern Drama. It originated in Yuyao, in Zhejiang Province. It was mostly performed among ordinary folk and was despised by scholars. After the end of the Ming Dynasty, it declined. See Wu Xinlei (ed.) 2002: 17.

12 Zhang Mu 張牧 2004: 414.

ing the capital, because of its mixed use of local languages, it was considered particularly rustic. Although 'people from various places liked to hear it' and it was welcomed by the lower classes, it was despised by scholars and literati. In *Jin Ping Mei*, Ximen Qing loves Haiyan style plays. Whenever he spent money to recruit commercial drama troupes at home, or welcomed high-grade senior officials, he only wanted Hanyan troupes. He refrained from inviting Wang Huangqin's family troupe, which was good at performing Northern *zaju*. In Chapter 74, for example, Secretary An 安主事 hosts a banquet at Ximen qing's residence to entertain Magistrate Cai Jiu 蔡九 (Cai the Ninth):

> The troupe of Haiyan actors, including Zhang Mei 張美, Xu Shun 徐順, and Gou Zixiao 苟子孝, arrived bearing their costume trunk, and, along with the four boy musicians, Li Ming 李銘 and company, who had come earlier, they all proceeded to kowtow to him. (Chapter 74, translation according to Roy 2011: 425–26).

海盐子弟张美、徐顺、苟子孝都挑戏箱到了，李铭等四名小优儿又早来伺候，都磕头见了.

Before the main guests, including Cai Jiu, arrived, the actors only sang some song suites, such as *Yichun ling* 宜春令 (A Song of Spring) as wine was drunk. But when the guests were properly seated, the Haiyan boys presented their programme, for the main guest to choose a play, and began in earnest their performance of the piece *Shuang Zhong Ji* 雙忠記 (The Loyal Pair). Haiyan actors did not only perform *chuanqi* drama but also sing song suites as an accompaniment to toasting with wine, which became a high-level entertainment habit for dignitaries to show off their wealth, power, and taste. A similar example is found in Chapter 63 after Li Ping'er's death. The mourners arrive at Ximen Qing's home to pay tribute, and at night relatives and friends keep vigil. A troupe of Haiyan actors are asked to perform the drama *Liangshi yinyuan Yuhuan ji* 两世姻缘玉环记 (The Marriage of Two Lifetimes).

In *Jin Ping Mei*, the elegant or vulgar taste of the characters is often portrayed in a few strokes, namely through how far they are able to appreciate Haiyan style opera. For example, in Chapter 64, Ximen Qing invites Eunuch Xue and Eunuch Liu into his summerhouse for a theatre performance and has specially invited a troupe of Haiyan actors for the entertainment. However, Eunuch Xue doesn't like the Southern drama, which he finds pretentious. He remarks:

> What with that barbarous accent of theirs! Who knows what they are singing about? Their plots are only concerned with those poor discontented scholars who endure hardships for three years within their unheated chambers and

HISTORICAL VALUE OF THE CUSTOMS OF LATE MING DRAMA

then wander abroad for nine years, carrying their zithers, swords, and book boxes on their backs, making their way to the capital in order to compete in the examinations, in the hope of obtaining an office. They don't even have the consolation of wives or children by their sides. What do the vicissitudes of such people mean to celibate old eunuchs like ourselves? We can do without them. (Chapter 64, translation according to Roy 2011: 114)

蛮声哈刺，无非是酸子每在寒窗之下，三年受苦九载遨游，背着琴剑书箱来京应举，得了个官，又无妻小在身边，便希罕他这样人，你我光身汉老内相，要他做甚么？

Due to the special fate of court eunuchs, the themes of 'candidates passing the examinations' and 'scholars meeting with beauties' as commonly found in Southern drama, are not interesting to them. Therefore, they bluntly criticize Haiyan opera of which Ximen Qing is so proud. The way the eunuchs talk about it reveals their vulgarity. Another example is found in Chapter 49, where Ximen Qing holds a banquet to entertain Censors Song Qiaonian and Cai Yun. Ximen Qing, well aware of the shady conduct of these two officials, does not dare to neglect them, and he especially recruits two musicians to perform Haiyan opera for them. However, Censor Song doesn't like Haiyan opera and soon leaves. Censor Cai, on the other hand, is well acquainted with the Haiyan style and the elegance of the art. He not only enjoys the play with Ximen Qing, but also orders the actors to sing *Yujia ao* 漁家傲 (The Fisherman's Pride) and other suites, which clearly demonstrates his taste. The two men are in sharp contrast, and their different characters are cleverly depicted by this method. Haiyan opera serves as a cultural symbol, affixing a striking label indicating the level of taste of a character.

Conclusion

During the late Ming when society was in transformation, Wang Yangming created a new Confucian school with an emphasis on dynamic subjectivity of the mind. His followers came up with a new interpretation of the relationship between principle and desire, one that did not lack the affirmation of the reasonableness and necessity of desire. This brought with it a series of thoughts and behavior contrary to the traditional idea of control through ritual. The pursuit of 'desire' in *Jin Ping Mei* is a vivid manifestation of the outlook of this era. The novel's description of the myriad complex relationships between people, between people and things, and between things can be interpreted from multiple perspectives. However, if we just unroll the corner of the novel that includes the scenes of extravagant performances of plays and look at what stimulates 'the desires of the eye and the ear,' what can be seen is the ugliness of social 'desire for pleasing songs and pleasing forms', under the stimulus of such things as the decline of the control of ritual, the blooming of self-consciousness, the boom of commodity economy, and the rise of urban culture. In any epoch, when people's desires for pleasure know no bounds, selfish desire metastasises, and material desires overflow, but the kind of moral ethics necessary for restraint is lacking, then the truth, goodness and beauty of the world will be completely shattered, then it will be inevitable for society to move toward extremes of the filthy and ugly. Perhaps *Jin Ping Mei* is, by painting a group portrait of a society of rampant desire, searching for a point of balance between 'heavenly principle' and 'human desire', in order to awaken the people of this world, and repair public morals.

References

Dai Hongsen 戴鴻森 (ed.)
> **1992.** *Jin Ping Mei cihua* 金瓶梅詞話. Beijing: Renmin wenxue chubanshe.

Gu Qiyuan 顧起元
> **2012.** *Ke zuo zhui yu* 客座贅語. Shanghai: Shanghai guji chubanshe.

Huang Lin 黃霖 (ed.)
> **1987.** *Jin Ping Mei ziliao huibian* 金瓶梅資料彙編 (A Compilation of *Jin Ping Mei* Materials). Beijing: Zhonghua shuju.

Li Shiren 李時人
> **1987.** '*Jin Ping Mei: Zhongguo liushi shiji houqi shehui fengsu shi*' 金瓶梅: 中國十六世紀後期社會風俗史 (*Jin Ping Mei*: History of Chinese Social Customs in the late 16th Century). *Wenxue yichan* 文學遺產 (Literary Heritage) No. 5: 103–112.

Liu Hui 劉輝
> **1986.** '*Jin Ping Mei zhong xiqu yanchu suoji*' 金瓶梅中戲曲演出瑣記 (Interpretation of Chinese Opera Performance in *Jin Ping Mei*). *Juyi baijia* 劇藝百家, No. 2: 106–107.

Lu Can 陸粲
> **1987.** *Kezuo zhuiyu* 客座贅語 (Chattering in the parlour). 卷九'戲劇'條 (Volume 9, Drama), Beijing: Zhonghua shuju.

Peng Jing 彭晶
> **2011.** *Jin Ping Mei shengri miaoxie zhong yunhan de minsu xianxiang* 金瓶梅生日描寫中蘊含的民俗現象 (Folk customs in the descriptions of birthday parties

in *Jin Ping Mei*). *Yichun xueyuan xuebao* 宜春學院學報 (Journal of Yichun University), No. 10: 78–82.

Qi Yan 齊煙 and Wang Rumei 王汝梅 (eds)

1989. *Xinke xiuxiang piping Jin Ping Mei* 新刻繡像批評金瓶梅 (*Annotated Edition of the Xinke xiuxiang text of Jin Ping Mei*). Jinan: Qi Lu shushe.

Roy, David Tod (trans.)

2001. *The Plum in the Golden Vase.* Vol. 2. Princeton: Princeton University Press.

2006. *The Plum in the Golden Vase.* Vol. 3. Princeton: Princeton University Press.

2011. *The Plum in the Golden Vase.* Vol. 4. Princeton: Princeton University Press.

Shen Defu 沈德符

1959. *Wanli yehuo bian* 萬曆野獲編 (Miscellaneous Notes of Wanli). Beijing: Zhonghua shuju.

Sun Chongtao 孫崇濤

1989. *Jin Ping Mei xiju shiliao jishuo* 金瓶梅戲劇史料輯說 (On historical sources of drama in *Jin Ping Mei*). *Wenxian* 文獻 (Literature) No. 3: 3–29.

Tang Xianzu 湯顯祖

1962. *Tang Xianzu ji* 湯顯祖集 (Tang Xianzu Collected Works). Beijing: Zhonghua shuju.

Tian Xiaofei 田曉菲

2019. *Qiushuitang lun Jin Ping Mei* 秋水堂論金瓶梅 (Autumn Lake Studio: On *Jin Ping Mei*). Guilin: Guangxi shifan daxue chubanshe.

Wu Xinlei 吳新雷 (ed.)

2002. *Zhongguo kunju da cidian* 中國昆劇大辭典 (Dictionary of Chinese Kunqu Opera). Nanjing: Nanjing daxue chubanshe.

Yang Lin 楊琳

2012. *Jin Ping Mei minsu zhishuo* 金瓶梅民俗摭談 (*Talking about folk customs in Jin Ping Mei*). *Wenxue yu wenhua* 文學與文化 (Literature and Culture), No. 1.

Zhang Mu 張牧

2004. *Lize suibi* 笠澤隨筆 (Jottings from Lize). In Zhang Guohua 張國華 (ed.), *Haiyan qiang yanjiu lunwen ji* 海鹽腔研究論文集 (Collection of Haiyan Qiang Research). Xuelin chubanshe.

Zhang Tingyu 張廷玉

1974. *Ming shi* 明史 (A History of the Ming Dynasty). Beijing: Zhonghua shuju.

Zhu Yixuan 朱一玄 (ed.)

2002. *Jin Ping Mei ziliao bian* 金瓶梅資料彙編 (Compilation of Sources on *Jin Ping Mei*). Tianjin: Nankai daxue chubanshe.

Note on contributors

Zhang Tingting 張婷婷 is Doctor of Literature and Professor at the Shanghai Film Academy, Shanghai University, China.

Xu Wei 徐瑋 is Lecturer at Nanjing Audit University, China.

JIN PING MEI AND PRINT CULTURE

CHAPTER 9

On Chinese Book Graphics and the Illustrations for the Novel *Jin Ping Mei*

BORIS RIFTIN
Translated by Sarah Fengler

When the balladeers in Germany sang their heartbreaking songs on the streets and illustrated their recitals with picture series, they could not, of course, know that the recital of stories based on pictures had emerged in ancient India, and that it was from there, some scholars believe, that it had reached China. In fact, storytelling monks in eighth- and ninth-century China portrayed the life of Buddha and his disciples on murals in Buddhist cave temples, depicting the deeds of Buddhist saints. And for centuries, almost to the present day, professional storytellers in China used to say: 'Look here!', when they came to the description of a hero's physical appearance or some house, palace, or festival procession. There had been no pictures for a long time, but the expression had remained as a formula. The idea of connecting the text of a story with a picture had also remained, only in another form. There is a series of five folk books (*pinghua*) that has survived to the present, printed in block printing during the early twenties of the 14th century. In these books, the upper third of each page contains a woodcut illustration, with the text written below. However, these editions did not maintain a close correspondence between text and picture. Often, the text would precede the pictures or trail behind them.

Chinese painting was, from its early beginnings, linked to a text, an inscription. The inscription could be a poem, an explanation of the occasion for which the picture was made, the name of the painter, or the time of its creation. Next to human figures on stone reliefs and in some cases on polychrome murals from before CE, the artists added the name and sometimes also the rank of those depicted in Chinese characters. This is also the way in which the creators of early book graphics proceeded. They indicated the names of

---

Editor's note: This chapter is a translation from the German version (Riftin 1984). Courtesy of the Riftin family and Gera Riftin.

the figures so that the reader would not confuse them. In addition, they also gave the illustrations themselves short titles, which corresponded to certain episodes of the story.

From folk books, this style – editions with illustrations at the top of each page – spread to novels and dramas. For example, all early editions of *Shuihu zhuan*, published in the 16th and early 17th centuries, replicate this style. (Unique examples of such editions are stored in various libraries, both in the GDR – in Berlin and Dresden – and in the FRG – in Munich and Göttingen.)

We do not know exactly when the art of printed graphics arose in China. It appears to have been the woodcut that came first, not later than during the Tang dynasty (618–907). Old Chinese works mention graphic printing from the sixth century, but only examples of book illustrations from the ninth century have survived to our time, such as the title pages of Buddhist sutras, embellished with a woodcut each, for example the *Diamond Sutra (Jinggangjing)*, printed in 868. This woodcut depicts Buddha in a sitting position, teaching his doctrine to Subhūti, one of his ten best disciples, who is listening to the teacher in a kneeling position. There are various protective spirits and monks on Buddha's left and right. The text begins on the same sheet, to the left of the woodcut. The woodcut itself has been cut quite artfully – this kind of art was a centuries-old tradition, not based on woodcuts, but on stone reliefs, the cutting of ceramic bricks, and the cutting of a variety of seals. These did not only include the written name of the owners, in artistic calligraphy, but also representations of birds, insects, and animals in general, as well as human figures and scenes taken from real life. Decorative seals like these had already emerged around the beginning of the Common Era. However, the idea of cutting wood and printing these cuts had, as already mentioned, first arisen during the Tang dynasty.

According to Chinese scholars, the art of woodcutting originated in monasteries, just like the professional art of storytelling. The Buddhist sutra editions contain the oldest surviving examples of book illustrations.[1] Initially, pictures were only featured on the title pages, but later, illustrations also accompanied the text – it was in such illustrations that the key moments in the biographies of the saints that were being related were presented in graphic form. At the same time, certain principles for the layout of book illustrations emerged. Some 'publishers' put the pictures at the top of the page and the text below, others put the illustration on the left part of the sheet, with the text on the right (we should not forget that the Chinese used to write in columns,

---

1   The previous and contemporary art of illustrating handwritten books with drawings or painted pictures will not be discussed here.

ILLUSTRATIONS FOR THE NOVEL *JIN PING MEI*

from the right to the left), and still others generally put the illustration in the middle of the page, bounded by the text. However, the editions with an illustration at the top of each page had the widest distribution. This is obviously related to the fact that that many ordinary, illiterate people belonged to the Buddhist worshippers; they could recite the prayers by heart but not read the sacred sutras. They simply looked at them, and since they had a rough idea of their content it gave them a special aesthetic pleasure to recognise constellations of topics they knew from oral sermons for laymen (the so-called *sujiang*). In this way, the kind of editions that became characteristic of early Chinese folk books emerged, as mentioned above.

Between the 10th and the 13th centuries, when the Song dynasty ruled over China, city life saw a revival. It was a time of rapid book production. Block printing was no longer used exclusively to print sacred writings, but also for historical works, collections of poetry and prose, treatises on medicine, botany, law, etc. In the context of this practice of book production, the illustrated editions of the classical books of Confucianism have a prominent place. The special editions contain clear explanations of the old texts, as well as illustrations that are supposed to give the reader a vivid idea of the musical instruments and implements described. Other treatises with descriptions of plants, books on craftsmanship, and military treatises are also amply illustrated. Although the woodcut illustrations in all these books had a clear practical purpose, they helped to develop the masterly art of woodblock cutting and the ability to adjust the picture and highlight the peculiarities of one object or another. In general, however, all these depictions are static.

Based on the few surviving book copies that we know about, it was precisely in these folk books from the beginning of the 14th century that the first woodcut illustrations with a dynamic subject emerged.

However, it is the Ming dynasty that must be considered the golden age of the development of Chinese book illustrations, especially from the end of the 15th century, when book graphics appeared, perhaps for the first time, printed from blocks and then coloured by hand (a procedure that has survived until today in the production of New Year pictures). It must be noted that two-colour printing has been known in China since the 14th century. In 1498, the bookshop of the Yue family in Beijing published an edition of the famous drama *Xixiang ji* (The story of the Western Wing), which contained 150 illustrations, but these were, unlike in previous editions, presented in different formats. Now, the illustrations no longer covered only the upper third of each page, but half a page or even more: to link picture and text as accurately as possible, the formats of the illustrations were modified for the first time. In a few cases, the illustrations are as 'long-drawn' as those from the Chinese picture scrolls and cover several subsequent pages (three to eight pages).

With their artistic style, these illustrations are very different from the pictures of the 14th-century folk books, but they are clearly still connected with them, for example through the strong contrast between the self-contained black and white areas. The magnification of the illustrations involves the magnification of the persons and objects depicted, which leads to a more meticulous elaboration of the details and an accurate representation of the interior and exterior views of the living rooms.

Towards the end of the 16th century, a new kind of edition emerged – with illustrations covering an entire page. For example, there is an annotated edition of the drama *Xixiang ji*, published in 1573 in Jian'an in the province of Fujian, the same city where the folk books were printed at the beginning of the 14th century. Liu Longtian, the editor of the book, created a new type of woodcut illustrations: the pictures are no longer on the same page as the corresponding text, as was common in previous editions, but seem to have a more independent status. In his edition of the drama, illustrations accompany single acts, foregrounding large figures of the acting characters. The economical elaboration of the details and the abundance of 'air' are striking. This is reminiscent of illustrations in modern books. The only difference is that the captions, following the old tradition derived from the stone reliefs, are not placed at the bottom, as they are today, but on the margins and in the form of long inscriptions, evocative of poems. In addition, a special small frame at the top contains the title of the picture. And although these illustrations continue the 14th-century tradition of book graphics in terms of how black and white are arranged over the surface, their independent place in the book and the magnification of the figures depicted bear witness to the beginning of a new stage in the development of Chinese book illustrations.

In China in the second half of the 16th century, two woodcutting schools concerned with book illustrations emerged – the Jinling school (this is the old name of the city of Nanjing), where the masters of the bookshops owned by the houses of Tang and Chen worked, and the Huizhou school, named after a city in the province of Anhui. Both schools specialised in the publication of dramas and novels, but in those of the masters of the Jinling school, the compositions of the drawings are based on a principle that resembles a theatre stage – the plot unfolds in the foreground and close to the viewer, while the background forms a second layer, with blurred outlines. The masters of this school widely used a method called *da dao kuo fu*, which literally means 'big knife, broad axe', and refers to broad strokes without fine lines, but with frequent juxtapositions of white and black areas (white clothes vis-à-vis head gear

ILLUSTRATIONS FOR THE NOVEL *JIN PING MEI*

in black ink, as well as individual components of the house, walls, furniture, and the like).

In contrast to the Jinling school, which, with its fine, 'naive' simplicity, essentially continued the tradition of earlier book illustrations, the masters of the Huizhou school created a completely different style of book graphics. In the 16th century, Huizhou was still a large trading hub, and paper and ink had been produced there since time immemorial. In today's China, ink is still traded in tablets, usually ornamented with a pattern or calligraphic inscription. In the past, the ink tablets were embellished with the finest ornaments. This was done as follows: master engravers crafted small wooden forms with grooved ornaments, which were then filled with a paste-like mixture of ink. After hardening, the ink had the relief of the design. These engravings were drawn very tenderly – hence the fine main lines in the woodcut illustrations of the Huizhou school, which emerged from this art of wooden ink forms (and partly from meticulous seal cutting).

Not far from the city of Huizhou, in the district of Shexian, was the village of Jiucun, famous for its woodcutters from the Huang clan. The names of about 40 people have survived, from whom the illustrations for a large number of dramas, novels, and other books stem. For almost 200 years, from the second half of the 16th century to the middle of the 18th century, the woodcut masters from the Huang clan were known throughout the country. Many of these masters moved to other centres of the printing industry, to Hangzhou and Suzhou. And it was precisely in Suzhou that, Chinese scholars of art believe, the illustrations for the novel *Jin Ping Mei* were printed. We know very little about their creators. Looking at the *Jin Ping Mei* illustrations, we can see tiny Chinese characters in the margins of some of the woodcuts – the names of the woodcutters. It is difficult to say whether the woodcutters were also the artists who created the drawings for the woodcuts. This, too, belongs to the history of Chinese woodcutting.

In illustration 2a of *Jin Ping Mei*, we see the name Huang Zili. It is known that this was the pseudonym of the famous master Huang Jianzhong, who later worked with and outlived the famous artist Chen Hongshou (1598–1652).[2] It is evident from this fact that Huang Zili was still very young when he was involved in the creation of the illustrations for our novel. In his family, the art of woodcutting was passed on from generation to generation: his grandfather Huang Yingjue created the illustrations for the *Selected Yuan Dramas* from the 13th or 14th century, and his father Huang Yibin, together with other family members, had become famous for illustrating books of poetry. In the twenties

---

2   *Editor's note:* For the Chinese characters of the names of the woodcutters, please, see Chapter 10 by Robert E. Hegel.

133

BORIS RIFTIN

of the 17th century, he created woodcuts for the above-mentioned *Xixiang ji*. Huang Zili's uncle was also a woodcutter: the portraits of the heroes of the *Shuihu zhuan*, published by Chen Hongshou, are connected to his name. All the older members of Huang Zili's family were still alive and actively working when he created these various woodcuts for *Jin Ping Mei*.

In a corner of illustration 48a, the name of another woodcutter is shown, Huang Ruyao. We know that it was he who created the illustrations for *Huanghe qing* (The Yellow River turns clear), but his family relationship with the Huang clan cannot be established. Illustrations 5b, 7a, and 64b state that Liu Qixian cut them, and even though he did not belong to the famous Huang clan, it is known that he worked with one of them, Huang Zhenqi, who, between 1628 and 1644, created an illustrated volume of *Shuihu zhuan*, to which the development of *Jin Ping Mei* is linked.

In illustrations 38b, 44b, and 82a, tiny Chinese characters say: 'Cut by Hong Guoliang'. Little is known about this master. He came from the same area near Huizhou where the Huang woodcutter clan used to live. He is known to have been one of the masters who created the woodcuts for the *Fragments of Southern Drama*, which were published in 1628 and are somewhat reminiscent of those in *Jin Ping Mei* in their style.

Of the woodcutter Liu Yingzu, who made illustration 1b, we only know that he came from the same area as the Huang clan, because he preceded his name with the place name Xin'an. Xin'an is an older name for the area surrounding Huizhou. (In most of the 18th- and, it would appear, also the 19th-century editions made with the old woodcuts, the names of the woodcutters were removed.)

So we know the names of five woodcut masters who created illustrations for *Jin Ping Mei*, but if we look at the woodcuts themselves, we can hardly distinguish between their individual styles (that it could have been many more masters is, of course, not excluded). This is quite easy to explain – we are not dealing with works in which the individual artists expressed themselves. What was appreciated was not an individual style that differed from that of others, but faithfulness to one's own 'school'. In a peculiar way, individual mastery was absorbed into tradition.

We do not know exactly when these illustrations were made; they did not yet exist in the earliest and most complete edition of the *Jin Ping Mei*, which emerged around 1617. They appeared for the first time in an edition from the years between 1628 and 1644, at the very end of the Ming dynasty.

The illustrations follow the division of the text. For each of the 100 chapters of the original, there are two illustrations inserted on a double-folded page. The structural unit of the old Chinese (and, in a broader sense, the Far Eastern) block printed book was not the single page, as in Europe, but the folded page.

ILLUSTRATIONS FOR THE NOVEL *JIN PING MEI*

The unfolded sheet of thin paper would be placed on the printing block and folded in the middle after printing, whether it contained an illustration or text. The open ends of all the sheets were on the spine of the book, which was bound together with a thread. The folded sides of the sheets were on the opposite long side where one turns the pages. Normally there were all kinds of inscriptions at the fold: the book title, the number of the chapter or section (of the 'scroll'), and the page number. Each folded sheet was counted as a single page. The illustrations were treated in the same way.

In an earlier illustrated edition of *Jin Ping Mei*, a double-folded page with two illustrations preceded each chapter. In the later reprints, all illustrations were compiled in the first or final volume of the edition. Each fold of the illustrations of the present edition includes the title of the novel at the top, the number of the chapter to which the illustrations belong in the middle, and two vertical, parallel lines at the bottom, both of which consist of seven Chinese characters; when folding and tacking, one of them appears on the 'front side', the other on the 'back side' of the sheet. It is not hard to guess that these are the captions. But such captions were not common. The chapter titles of the Chinese epics and novels of former times consisted of two parallel rhythmic lines. However, here the artist reused these titles as captions for the pictures at the folds of the sheets, the first line for one illustration, the second for the other. We remember that in the traditional Chinese novel a chapter usually consists of two episodes, the main content of which is reflected in the two chapter titles. And now the artist has chosen to illustrate each of the two episodes. Take, for example, the illustrations of the second chapter, 2a and 2b. The chapter is titled: 'Under the bamboo blind, the beautiful Mrs Pan hitches a lover' and 'In her tea house, Madam Wang talks about how to make advances'. Consequently, in the first illustration we see Jinlian who looks out from behind a curtain, Ximen Qing who bows in greeting, and on the ground a stick with a fork-shaped top that has fallen from the hand of the beauty and hit Ximen Qing who passed under it. This episode is the real starting point of the novel. The second part of the chapter tells the story of how Ximen Qing pleads with Madam Wang, the owner of the tea house where he now turns up (she is the one we have already seen in the first illustration, in a sitting position next to the entrance to Jinlian's house), to help him get together with the beautiful woman in whom he has taken pleasure. In this way, the artist illustrates both episodes of the second chapter.

Let us revisit the different editions of the book. The woodcuts in the first chapter and the titles of the two episodes at the fold prove that the present sequence of woodcuts was not crafted for the oldest surviving edition of the novel, but for a text version edited by an unknown literary figure in the first half of the 17th century. The title of the first chapter of the oldest surviving edition is

135

'Wu Song kills a tiger on Jingyang Ridge' and 'Pan Jinlian disdains her husband and plays the coquette', but the illustrations in the revised version, on which also Kuhn's translation is based, are captioned 'Ximen Qing cordially welcomes the ten brothers' and 'Second Brother Wu meets his brother's wife with coolness'.

The events described in *Jin Ping Mei* belong to the 12th century, but the heroes of the story actually live during the Ming dynasty, when the book was written. The illustrations reinforce this illusion of a temporal proximity to the life of the reader at the end of the 16th and beginning of the 17th century. A recognised specialist in the history of Chinese costumes, the painter L. P. Sytschow, has drawn our attention to the details of the clothes that were characteristic of the fashion of the late Ming dynasty. (In China, the cut of the clothes used to change with the beginning of a new dynasty.)

Look carefully at the robe of the beautiful Jinlian in the above-mentioned illustration from the second chapter, but also at the representation of her and the other beauties to whom Ximen Qing was married, for example in illustration 18b, where we can see a button on the high collars of the robes in the form of a black dot. In China, such collars came into fashion during the reign of Emperor Wuzong (1506–1521). Illustration 31b shows some district officials who are going to a feast in Ximen Qing's house. The one on the right wears a so-called *bufang* on his back, an appliqué patch, a badge of rank for officials introduced during the Ming dynasty. Depending on the rank, the illustration of a quadruped (for military officers) or a bird (for civil servants) would be embroidered. In the case of the official on the left, a broad stripe of ornaments can be made out at knee height, a detail characteristic of officials' robes during the Ming dynasty. Some woodcuts show another detail of the officials' robes, a large insertion of cloth, a gusset on each side, wide at the belt and narrowing downwards. This cut came into fashion during the reign of Emperor Xiaozong (1488–1505). This costume with the gusset from the waist down is clearly observable in illustrations 72b and 92b. Finally, another seemingly insignificant feature of the time: In the Middle Ages Chinese officials wore caps with 'wings' (in Chinese they were called *zhanjiao*, 'stretched horns'). During the Song dynasty, these wings were strictly horizontal. During the Ming dynasty, the prongs were bent upwards, as illustration 18a of the official in the capital shows.

All the other characters of the novel are dressed in robes without features typical of a certain period of time. For example, in illustrations 10b and 11a and b the protagonist of the novel, the owner of a pharmacy, can easily be recognised by his characteristic angular headgear (*walengmao*, 'tiled roof cap'). This headgear has more of a social than a temporal function; it was worn by urban merchants and artisans.

ILLUSTRATIONS FOR THE NOVEL *JIN PING MEI*

The *Jin Ping Mei* illustrations familiarise the reader with the details of the everyday life in Imperial China: they show how the Chinese ground grain with an ox-powered stone mill (illustration 87a), what an old Chinese pharmacy, which had to have a cabinet with many drawers, looked like (illustration 19a), how a new-born is washed (illustration 79b) and how the laundry was done (illustration 72a), what a rich Chinese man's round grave, surrounded by a stone wall, looked like (illustration 89a), what the shoe-shaped silver bars that represented wealth looked like (illustration 80b), and much more.

Jin Ping Mei features quite a few naturalistic and erotic scenes. They are also visible in the woodcuts. This was not unusual in China at the time, but neither was it a very common phenomenon either. We must remember that the novel and its illustrations are both products of their time, and that the work is satirical. With a candid representation of all the passions, the author, who has not coincidentally chosen the pseudonym The Joking Scholar from Lanling, attempts to show how disastrous Ximen Qing's lack of restraint is. To warn those who do not want to die of exhaustion at the age of 33, he exposes him with all his weaknesses.

It must be noted that the Chinese had an attitude to illustrating sexual intercourse that was different from what was common in the Western world. On a journey through China in 1907, a young Russian sinologist, the later academy member W. M. Aleksejew, saw erotic popular prints displayed in the kitchen (!) of a house. His hosts explained to him that such illustrations prevented fire. In this context, one must know that old Chinese beliefs identify the sky with the male and the earth with the female principle, while rain symbolises the fusion of sky and earth: it fertilises the earth, which gives birth to all the grasses and plants. At the same time, rain is water from the sky that extinguishes fires and blazes. According to the old way of thinking, intercourse between man and woman is an allegorical performance of this cosmic act, taking place under earthly circumstances. It is not for no reason that the author so frequently uses the poetic image of 'cloud and rain' to describe love scenes in the novel. However, the thought that the revealing *Jin Ping Mei* illustrations might have been created as measures of fire prevention is nevertheless highly farfetched.

On the other hand, it must be mentioned that the graphic representation of sensual love was not a smaller, but perhaps even a greater achievement in medieval China than in medieval Europe. Even the most chaste depiction of love, for example in the literati novels written by Yuan Zhen, Ju You, and other authors, was rebuked by Confucian rigorists. Thus, both *Jin Ping Mei* and its illustrations are so much the more extraordinary memorials of their era, the end of the 16th and first half of the 17th century. Indeed, they must be considered monumental testimony of their own time.

In order to show life in all its richness and even in its nakedness, the creator of the illustrations (or, more likely, the *creators*) use a special trick: in the fashion of a theatre stage, they remove the front wall of the room where the plot unfolds. Another typical technique is to show the actions through a large, round window, for example as in illustrations 50a and 60a. In Chinese architecture, there were round windows, but they were neither as large nor were they located in the inner quarters, but on verandas, etc.

Often the *Jin Ping Mei* illustrations show several situations at the same time. In illustration 9b, we see a tavern without a house front, with a kitchen on the ground floor and a lounge on the first floor. In the background, we see a genre scene: Ximen Qing is fleeing from Wu Song's revenge, ending up in Doctor Hu's backyard and startling a maid who has come outside to relieve herself. It is striking that the characters in the foreground and background are almost the same size, creating the illusion that the foreground and background, equally distant, are equally important.

The creators of these illustrations applied various techniques. The most specific one is the representation of dreams or phantasms in the form of a peculiar 'cloud of steam' that springs from the head of the sleeping person, with the figures emerging in the dream depicted on the white background. This can be easily seen in illustrations 67b and 71a. The procedure is amazingly reminiscent of modern comics, isn't it?

In general, the characters are depicted on a background of different architectural constructions, surrounded by trees, flowers growing in the soil or in flowerpots, and towering artificial mountains made of strangely eroded boulders. Some interesting rules have come down to us (recorded in the form of poetry), according to which the woodcut master first had to cut the figures of the persons and then the natural background and other accessories.

The illustrations for *Jin Ping Mei*, as well as for other Chinese books at the time, are typical line woodcuts. The lines are in high relief, not the background; the woodcut replicates the principle of block printing, which was also the basis for Chinese letterpress printing, with the Chinese characters of the wooden printing block carved out in high relief.

Earlier, in the case of the first woodcuts of Chinese book illustrations made for Buddhist sutras, the artists strove to fill the entire space of the woodcut with human figures or decorative details. By contrast, the masters of the Ming dynasty attempted to leave as much 'air' in their woodcuts as possible, so that the design of the characters in the novel would stand out more clearly.

When the illustrations for *Jin Ping Mei* were created, Chinese book graphics had been developing for almost 1000 years from its beginnings to the start of the 17th century. From static, iconic-like illustrations to Buddhist sutras, the painters and woodcut masters had arrived at the representation of the most complicated

ILLUSTRATIONS FOR THE NOVEL *JIN PING MEI*

forms of life, including those scenes that normally remain hidden from the eyes of outsiders. When the lithographic printing process found its way into the book industry in the 1870s and spread rapidly, publishing old novels with this technique, which allowed a smaller print run and a higher number of copies, new principles for the illustration of these works came to the fore. The new, however, was mainly constituted by the layout of the illustrations; stylistically, they did not differ from the traditional line woodcuts. As a rule, several full-page portrait illustrations (*xiang*) now preceded a book, mostly group portraits of three fictional characters standing upright; the pictures (*tu*), which were the actual illustrations, with scenes from the plot, were placed at the beginning of each chapter or the larger sections, which were called 'scrolls' (*juan*, a term taken from the earlier form of written records). In most cases, there were two illustrations on the same page, one above the other. The Hong Kong edition of *Jin Ping Mei* from 1906 was also decorated in this way. The book begins with eight group portraits with three characters each, followed by two illustrations for the first chapter, which fill the entire page and are arranged one above the other: in the upper illustration, the fraternisation between Ximen Qing and his friends is depicted, though the figures do not sit, as they do in the early woodcut, but stand; in the lower illustration, the encounter between Ximen Qing and Pan Jinlian, the subject is also designed differently from the early woodcut. In this case, however, *different* does not mean better. Artistically, the woodcuts created by the masters of the 17th century are on a much higher level.

References

Riftin, Boris

1984. 'Über die Chinesische Buchgraphik und die Illustrationen zur Roman Djin Ping Meh.' In *Kin Ping Meh oder die Abenteuerliche Geschichte von Hsi Men und seinen sechs Frauen*, 485–503. Translated by Franz Kuhn. Leipzig-Weimar: Kiepenheuer Verlag. Second edition 1988, pp. 507–522.

Note on Contributors

Boris L. Riftin (1932–2012), Academician of the Russian Academy of Sciences, Moscow, Russia. Researcher of Chinese folk prints, novel and drama, storytelling, rare books.

Sarah Fengler is a DPhil student in Modern Languages at Jesus College, University of Oxford. She has a Master of Arts in Comparative Literature, Goethe University, Frankfurt, Germany. Her research focuses on biblical tragedies in the Age of Enlightenment.

CHAPTER 10

Picturing Ximen Qing's World
The Chongzhen Edition Illustrations

ROBERT E. HEGEL

The 'Chongzhen Edition', *Jin Ping Mei (Plum in the Golden Vase), Newly Carved and Illustrated, with Commentary* (*Xinke xiuxiang piping Jin Ping Mei* 新刻繡像批評金瓶梅), has 100 chapters of text; in the Beijing University Library copy, every chapter is prefaced by two narrative half-folio illustrations, each of which is captioned with one line of the couplet that serves as its chapter title.[1]

All of the *Jin Ping Mei* images depict at least one incident from the chapter with sufficient specificity to indicate that the illustrators had read the text carefully and attempted to represent actions as narrated.[2] However, unlike illustrations in late Ming imprints of other books, these artists did not hesitate to leave blank space to balance densely realized details.

All follow conventions of representation shared with literati painting during the late Ming: people and objects represented in ink outline drawings (*baimiao* 白描 or *baihua* 白畫) but with little filling in, objects at the top of the image are considered farther away from the viewer (with no necessary difference in size), and often the images 'read' from lower right to upper left.[3] These illustrations

---

1 The edition published by Sanlian shudian in Hong Kong (Joint Publishing (H.K.) in 1990 based on the Peking University Library copy is the source for all the illustrations discussed here, referred to simply as *Jin Ping Mei*. For this and other editions based on this version, see Hu Wenbin (comp.)1986: 30–35. Later editions, with more characters per page and in a smaller format, roughly copy some of these illustrations but group them at the head of the text, in 'capping illustration' (*guantu* 冠圖) format. All 200 illustrations are scattered through David Tod Roy's complete translation of the unillustrated 1618 *Jin Ping Mei cihua* 金瓶梅詞話 (Roy 1993–2013).

2 Most illustrations (abbreviated as 'Ill.') portray only one incident. However, Ill. 28a, 'Chen Jingji Teases Jinlian', shows two: Jinlian's punishment of the maid Qiuju for failing to find her missing shoe (the maid is forced to kneel in the courtyard with a rock on her head), and, subsequently, Chen teasing Jinlian with the missing shoe (in an upstairs room where she has just finished arranging her hair).

3 Western-style perspective was introduced through the imperial court painters only later, during the middle Qing.

PICTURING XIMEN QING'S WORLD

are replete with details of the setting of each scene, whether this is the street (Ill. 1b), a wineshop (Ill. 2b), an official *yamen* (Ill. 35a), or a bedroom (Ill. 5b). Even though some images may have objects that are out of scale compared to the human figures, these images preserve aspects of late Ming material reality that might not have been mentioned in the text. This decorative function in most pictures consists of trees, rocks and architectural features that do not necessarily add to, or comment on, the acts being represented.

The conventional perspective for book illustration, as in the *Jin Ping Mei* images, is that of a somewhat distant viewer who is above and to the right of the action. Large round openings in the buildings allow the reader to see into the most private spaces (Ill. 7b, 22a, 23b, 50a, 52a for example); in other images, screens and blinds are carefully carved to allow viewers to glimpse what goes on inside (in many, someone in the image is spying on that action; see Ill. 13b, 95a).

These illustrations are the work of Anhui School (Hui *pai* 徽派) specialists, both the artists who drew the outlined images and the craftsmen who carved their drawings onto the printing boards. Anhui (or Huizhou 徽州) artisans became prominent during the Wanli era around 1600 and quickly dominated the market for illustrations, supplanting in popularity the earlier Jianyang (建陽 or Fujian) and Jinling (金陵 or Nanjing) schools. By imitating conventions of literati painting, the Anhui professionals produced more sophisticated and attractive images than other schools.[4] Many of these experts traveled around the major Jiangnan cities plying their crafts, with the result that illustrations of this type were seen in books produced throughout the region during the late Ming. The Anhui style inspired the development of other styles, of Hangzhou (Wulin 武林), Wuxing 吳興, and Suzhou 蘇州, as well.[5] Compared with the images, the text itself was probably carved by far less skilled artisans, as was the usual practice.

Compared with illustrations drawn by Jianyang or Jinling school artisans, the images in this edition of *Jin Ping Mei* are generally attractive and carefully executed. Most meet or exceed late Ming standards for 'good' (but not exquisite) book illustrations; they are rather less elegant than illustrations that grace the finest contemporary imprints of plays and poetry collections. The focus of attention in each illustration is the people in it. Although landscape is of less importance, the reader/viewer is provided with enough visual information to make identifying the setting where that action takes place quite easy.[6] The

---

4 See the discussion of 'modular painting' among literati in Ledderose 2000: 202–12.

5 Zhou Xinhui and Wang Zhijun (comp.) 2000: 9–10. See Zhou Wu 1983: 1–52 on the development and characteristics of the Anhui school of artisans and their art.

6 Plays and fiction imprints that enlist 'capping illustrations' to constitute a separate fascicle at the head of the text often use two half-folios (a 'b' side and the following 'a' side of the

figures here are presented in a variety of lifelike and, for the most part, quite expressive poses. But there is little individuality to be found in most faces; the bodies of the human figures are generic as well (even the gender of naked bodies is distinguished only by hairdo and prominent genitalia).[7] Often enough, identifying who the characters are is difficult unless the reader has skipped ahead and has read the text in advance. Because they precede the text, one function of the illustrations is to serve as 'teasers' to encourage further reading. One would assume that the titillating effect of the erotic pictures would spur at least some readers to seek to find out 'what happened next' – as the reader is encouraged to do in the concluding phrases of every *Jin Ping Mei* chapter in the earliest, *cihua* 詞話, edition.

By placing the illustrations two at a time separate from each other, this edition forecloses the option of reading them as an album of 'capping illustrations' where all of the images are grouped in a fascicle that precedes the text (as they are in at least one of the surviving copies from this period).[8] Because the separate fascicle for illustrations was becoming the more common format in novels and plays, spacing the images throughout the book seems like a deliberate choice on the part of the printer, if not by those involved earlier in the production process.[9]

What We See

Private spaces are the most common settings, as is appropriate for a novel in which most scenes take place indoors. Some are relatively consistent in their representation. For example, Wu Da's house, in which Ximen Qing carries out his seduction of Pan Jinlian and where she subsequently murders her ill-shapen husband, has several connected rooms with a tall tree and a pile of rocks midway along the side of the structure (Ill. 3b, 4ab, 5a, 8b). Government buildings are regularly portrayed as having wide steps from ground level up to the building proper, where the authority sits behind a high bench (Ill. 18a, 30a, 35a, 92b). Wineshops have open outside walls to allow conversation between patrons and

---

folded pages) to depict one scene. This greater space allows far more landscape scenery or architectural structures than can be incorporated into a half-folio. For examples from late Ming play imprints, see Zhou Xinhui and Wang Zhijun (comp.) 2000: 89–96, 194–207.

7   For examples of the images in deliberately erotic texts, see *Huaying jinzhen* nd.: 2.

8   Liu Hui 1984: 91.

9   For an illustrated Chongzhen period description of the woodblock printing process, see *Tiangong kaiwu* 1957: 945–59; modern descriptions: Tsien 1984: 16–25 and Tsien 1985: 146–83, 196–201. Capping illustrations: Hegel 2001: 74.

passersby, with tables and chairs inside (Ill. 2b, 3a, 6a). All of these elements appear elsewhere here and in the illustrations for other books.

Fully 40 of the 200 illustrations here portray sexual activities involving a variety of actors. Nearly 30 others represent physical violence, primarily beatings (Ill. 8b, 11a, 19a, 28b, 58a – a dog, 72a, 86a, 91b, 94a, 99a), but also destruction of property (Ill. 20b), vicious and humiliating punishments (Ill. 12a, 28a, 35a, 41b, including in 74b, self-punishment), and even murder (Ill. 5b, 47a, 87b). Suicide is not illustrated (Ill. 26b), but sexual violence is (Ill. 27b, 61a). Most of these images would seem to be vulgar by any standard. One can only wonder whether the artists who drew them meant to titillate, or to shock, their viewers. They are excessively explicit, far more so than the text, leaving little to the imagination.[10]

Most illustrations contain decorative objects that are not mentioned in the text and are often irrelevant to the incident being depicted. This is true, as we will see, of the erotic images as well. Most elements were conventional in both book illustration and literati painting at that time. Servants are generally portrayed as being somewhat smaller than their masters (Ill. 7a, 10b, 21a, 48a). (This presents some difficulties in representing Chunmei, who is a servant but who becomes a central figure – as the title of the work suggests – and increases in height in relation to Ximen's wives; compare Ill. 27b with 41b, 76a, 82a, and 96a.) Emotions are represented here through the positions of bodies and the poses in which they are represented – not what might be seen on their faces. Characters cover their mouths with their sleeve-covered hands to suppress sadness (Ill. 85b), embarrassment (Ill. 27b), or to suppress a giggle (Ill. 31a), for example. Many of these positions were exemplified in the model books that served as inspiration for book illustrators and elite amateur painters as well.[11]

---

10 Park 2010: 189 discusses the criteria for 'elegant' erotica for 'discerning viewers'; such images do not feature nudity, and in many, the woman is alone in a suggestive setting. See also Hegel 2004 for observations on the greater appeal of suggestive text in contrast to explicit visual representation. A century and a half later, Japanese color prints in the *ukiyo-e* 浮世繪 tradition known as *shunga* 春畫 became popular. Although they were explicit in their presentation of (often oversized) genitalia, they were elegant in style, in marked contrast to illustrations such as these, which presumably served as models; see Gulik 1951: 127–28. About the simple representations of the naked human body, Mark Elvin (1989: 267) remarks: 'Considered from the outside, the Chinese body (*shen*) is a peg-doll whose role it is to be a carrier of corporal and/or sartorial attributes.'

11 For a somewhat later collection of painters' models of human subjects, see the early Qing *Jieziyuan huazhuan* 2010: 1.221–57. On conventionality in decorative elements, etc., see Hegel 2001: 65–66. Examples of the use of models can be seen in Ill. 7b, where all the male figures have identical left legs.

Figure 10.1, from Chapter 32, the second illustration: 潘金蓮懷嫉驚兒 (Envious, Pan Jinlian Startles the Child)

For the first 30 chapters, Ximen Qing is presented wearing a colourless cap; thereafter, once he receives his commission as Assistant Judicial Commissioner in the Qinghe office of the Shandong Provincial Surveillance Commission, he often wears the black official hat and the official robes that he has tailored in Chapter 31.[12] Other male characters wear a variety of head coverings, as they might have in late Ming society (see Ill. 69b). Ximen Qing is represented in a variety of poses as we learn more about his character. Readers see him first as he forms his brotherhood with 10 other men (Ill. 1a) and then as he bows before Pan

---

12 See *Jin Ping Mei* 1: 396; Roy 1993–2013: 2.214–15. For Ming – compared to Song – clothing styles, see Zhou Xun and Gao Chunming 1984: 176–95 and 240–55.

PICTURING XIMEN QING'S WORLD

Jinlian, having just been struck by her awning pole (Ill. 2a). In Ill. 2b he leans back casually in a wineshop as he speaks with Old Woman Wang about a plot to get together with Jinlian.[13] Later we see him in proximity to superiors, servants and his various lovers and friends, in particular Ying Bojue. We also see him naked, although in some of those illustrations (eg., Ill. 8b) he keeps his hat on.

Readers learn little about Pan Jinlian, the novel's central character, through the illustrations. That is, although we do see her in the nude and clothed somewhat differently depending on the occasion, her face in each image is all the same. Nor is she significantly different in appearance from the other women. Partly this is due to the small size of individual persons in these illustrations (in images 16 cm high, individuals stand at no more than 3 cm in height, their faces around 5 mm). Considering the printing technology of the time (carving away from a board all of its surface that is not covered by the narrow lines of the illustration), to carve out very fine details required great skill on the part of the block carver.

An illustration for Chapter 32 exemplifies many common features in these images. Figure 1 (Ill. 32b), 'Envious, Pan Jinlian Startles the Child' (Pan Jinlian huaiji jing er 潘金蓮懷嫉驚兒), represents Jinlian in the lower left quarter, in an open space, as if to draw attention to her by leaving her alone onstage. The rest of the illustration is relatively full, with other female figures involved in various tasks. A stylized gnarled pine tree angles upward to the left from the lower right corner; the upper left quadrant apparently indicates a distant location with shrubs visible in three places – but one set is upside down. Roof tiles, worktables, food items, a decorative panel and a hanging lamp are all drawn and carved with attention to consistency and delicacy. At first glance the illustration is attractive, given its quotidian activities and decorative touches. Only when one reads its caption and then the ensuing text can the reader realize the violence latent within this image. The meaning of the upper left quadrant is left unclear.

Figure 2 (Ill 38b), 'Pan Jinlian on a Snowy Evening Toys with Her *Pipa*' (Pan Jinlian xueye nong pipa 潘金蓮雪夜弄琵琶), is another highly attractive image. Its focus is on the only action represented here, the female figure sitting on her bed at night, playing the *pipa* by the light of a single candle on a table beside her. A fine wooden stool is nearby, and on both sides of the opening through which we viewers look are mounted decorative carvings. Details of the structure, the balustrade outside, with a maid coming in through a door on the left: all are delicately realized. But what makes this illustration stand out is its effective representation of heavy snow on the roofs and especially on the trees, shrubs, and the rock outside the balustrade in the foreground of the picture. Unsurprisingly, the image is signed by its carver Hong Guoliang 洪國良 (about whom more below).

---

13 This is an unusual position: Ximen is sitting, leaning back, his elbows resting on a table. For a similar pose, see *Jieziyuan huazhuan* 2010: 4.75.

145

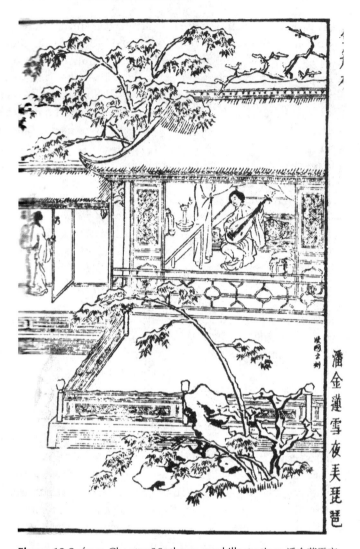

Figure 10.2, from Chapter 38, the second illustration: 潘金蓮雪夜弄琵琶 (Pan Jinlian on a Snowy Evening Toys with Her *Pipa*)

Given the propensity of some illustrators to use images as a form of commentary on or interpretation of narrative texts, it is not surprising to find that this practice is seen here as well.[14] Figure 3, Ill. 69a seems to comment on the situation. In this chapter Ximen Qing enjoys a secret tryst with Lady Lin in

---

14 For example, illustrations for *Further Adventures on the Journey to the West* (*Xiyou bu* 西遊補, 1641) draw out the essential Buddhist messages of the text. See Hegel 2006; Li Qiancheng (ed.) 2011: 33–47.

PICTURING XIMEN QING'S WORLD

Figure 10.3, from Chapter 69, the first illustration: 招宣府初調林太太 (Enjoying the First Tryst with Lady Lin in Her Mansion)

her own mansion; the illustration shows the couple passionately making love, ignoring the table before them with heaping dishes of food. Above, a gigantic rock overhangs the roof that slants down on their action; a curtain threatens to shut off the view. To the left especially are closed shutters, dark with their tight lattice, over a huge and bizarre Taihu rock with a twisted tree behind it. Wide stairs seem to lead directly to their curtained chamber, which draws attention as an avenue of exposure and discovery. It is also the avenue Ximen takes to his other commitments as soon as their intercourse comes to a halt.

ROBERT E. HEGEL

This setting seems to encapsulate and limit their affair, as does Ill. 76a, in which we see Ximen Qing trying to seduce Chunmei, again with architectural details crowding around, as if hemming them in.

The Hands That Shaped the Images

At least 18 of the *Jin Ping Mei* images bear a personal name, usually of the carver, although some well-known artisans drew and carved their own illustrations. Five names appear here; probably all are from families traditionally specializing in book illustration, all well known for their work on other major publishing projects in the Jiangnan region:

Hong Guoliang 洪國良: Ill. 30b, 37a, 38b, 41a, 82a
Huang Ruyao 黄汝耀: Ill. 31a, 48a
Huang Zili 黄子立 (Huang Jianzhong 建中, b. 1611): Ill. 2a, 4a, 35b
Liu Qixian 劉啟先; Ill. 7a, 22a, 26b, 27b, 46a, 47a, 64b
Liu Yingzu 劉應祖: Ill. 1b

Huang Zili was the son of the Hangzhou artisan Huang Yibin 黄一彬 (b. 1581) who carved Wanli editions of the well-known plays *The Lute in Southern Style* (*Nan Pipa ji* 南琵琶記) and *The Western Wing in Northern Style* (*Bei Xixiang ji* 北西廂記). Scholars have speculated that Liu Qixian and Liu Yingzu were the same person; artisans of the time often did use more than one name professionally.[15] Ill. 1b reads 'Drawn (*xiu*) by Liu Yingzu of Xin'an' 新安劉應祖綉; Xin'an is another name for Shexian 歙縣 in Anhui. Since only he is identified as having *drawn* the image, perhaps he and his assistants drew all of them; other names identify outstanding carvers. Apprentices would not sign their work; it is likely that the bulk of the unsigned images here were drawn and/or carved by less skilled artisans under the supervision of the masters.[16] And yet they all followed the same models: most illustrations are similar to each other in style, general composition, types and appearance of decorative details, how human figures are realized, and other details, whether they bear an artisan's name or not.

---

15 Zhou Wu 1983: 73, identifies the two; Bussotti 2001: 102, agrees. For examples, see Zhou Xinhui and Wang Zhijun (comp.) 2000, 341–44. Bussotti 2001: 71 note 44 notes that Huang Zili also used the name Huang Jianzhong 黄建中. Zhou Wu 1983: 32 identifies these five artisans as well. I have been unable to learn more about Huang Ruyao; he is not among the Huang family of carvers (Zhou Wu 1983: 44–45). He may have been a brother or cousin of Huang Yisong 黄一松 (b. 1599, professional name Ruguang 黄汝光).

16 Ledderose 2000: 4–5 and 75–101, has a fascinating discussion of modular, 'factory', production of goods of all sorts, including art.

PICTURING XIMEN QING'S WORLD

All names appearing on these *Jin Ping Mei* illustrations are identified with the Huizhou school of illustration.[17] Except for Ill. 1b, names here indicate who carved, rather than drew, the images. It is unclear whether late Ming readers understood the term 'carved by' (*ke* 刻) as indicating both roles in image production. In addition to finely detailed human subjects, Anhui school illustrations generally include decorative elements that are precisely rendered and are usually quite attractive. These objects included architectural details, 'Taihu' limestone boulders, and trees of several varieties. Compared to other Huizhou-style illustrated books, the images in the Chongzhen edition of *Jin Ping Mei* are rather less crowded with details.[18]

Hong Wenyuan 洪聞遠 (more frequently identified – as he is in *Jin Ping Mei* – by his alternate name Hong Guoliang) from Huizhou along with the very active Hangzhou craftsman Xiang Nanzhou 項南洲 (also known as Xiang Zhonghua 項仲華) carved many of the images created by Lu Wuqing 陸武清, one of the best known among Jiangnan illustrators. The three worked together on illustrations for the vernacular novel *The Shrew* (*Cu hulu* 醋葫蘆), which, like several of their other projects, was printed in Hangzhou.[19] Lu Wuqing illustrated the notorious Ruan Dacheng's 阮大鋮 (1587–1646) very popular romantic play *The Swallow's Letter* (*Yanzi jian* 燕子箋); its illustrations were like-

---

17 Zhou Xinhui and Wang Zhijun (comp.) 2000, 10: differences among illustrations of this school and the Wulin 武林 or Hangzhou school can be slight.

18 Compare the examples in Zhou Wu 1983, especially the plays and poetry collections, and in Zhou Xinhui and Wang Zhijun 2000: 93–96 (Huizhou school) and 190–91 (Hangzhou school). Human figures are larger in the illustrations in the contemporaneous Rongyutang edition of *Outlaws of the Marsh* (*Shuihu zhuan* 水滸傳); see *Ming Rongyutang ke Shuihu zhuan tu* 1965; Zhou Xinhui and Wang Zhijun (comp.) 2000: 192–93 list this among the Hangzhou imprints, as they do the Chongzhen edition of *Jin Ping Mei* (ibid.: 341–44). Zhou Wu (1983: 32) points out that another fictional text with similar illustrations (small human characters, rich architectural details, decorations) is *The Bell in the Still of the Night, Stories Newly Carved and Illustrated* (*Xinjian xiuxiang xiaoshuo Qingye zhong* 新鐫綉像小說清夜鐘), a collection of tales narrating the fall of Beijing to the bandit Li Zicheng and other mid-century disasters; Zhou Xinhui and Wang Zhijun 2000: 366–67 identify this as a Hangzhou publication of about 1645; its carvers were Anhui school artisans, Liu Qixian 劉啟先 and Huang Zihe 黃子和, who presumably was a brother or cousin of Huang Zili 黃子立. That its illustrations follow the same models as those for *Jin Ping Mei* is hardly surprising, with these artisans in charge.

19 Zhou Xinhui and Wang Zhijun 2000: 359; for comments on its contents and sample illustrations, see McMahon 1995: 75–80. Bussotti 2001: 282, mentions Hong Guoliang as Xiang Nanzhou's collaborator. Zhang Xiumin (1989: 501) identifies Hong as a Huizhou native. *Cu hulu* bears a preface by Zui Xihu Xinyue zhuren 醉西湖心月主人, who also wrote a preface for the homoerotic story collection *Bian er chai* (and *Yichun xiangzhi* 宜春香質, another homoerotic novel) under his name; see *Zhongguo tongsu xiaoshuo zongmu tiyao* 1990: 224.

ROBERT E. HEGEL

wise carved by Xiang Nanzhou together with Hong Guoliang.[20] The trio also collaborated on the 1640 collection of vernacular stories *Tales of Outstanding Figures from Seventy-two Reigns, Organized According to [Quotations from] The Four Books* (*Qishier chao Sishu renwu yanyi* 七十二朝四書人物演義).[21]

Lu Wuqing drew round illustrations for the 1642 poetry (*qu* 曲) collection *Suzhou Tunes* (*Sumen xiao* 蘇門嘯) collected by Fu Yichen 傅一臣, which were then carved by Hong Guoliang.[22] Lu's illustrations also appear in the stories of gay romance collected in *Hairpins Beneath His Cap* (*Bian er chai* 弁而釵).[23] In Lu Wuqing's figure portraits especially, the influence of the distinctive style of the famous late Ming painter Chen Hongshou 陳洪綬 (1599–1652) is readily visible. Chen Hongshou's illustrations for other books were also carved by Xiang Nanzhou and the Huizhou carvers Huang Junqian 黃君倩 and Huang Zili (who worked on *Jin Ping Mei*).[24] Named illustrators and carvers seemingly did not form long term partnerships; they may have signed on individually for specific projects. Many were itinerant, at least during parts of their working lives; others settled down in Hangzhou, a cultural centre.

Although Hong Guoliang may have been the most widely known artisan to have carved images for this Hangzhou edition of *Jin Ping Mei*, Huang Zili was similarly involved in other prestigious productions after he moved to Hangzhou.[25] Huang Zili reportedly took over the project to illustrate the 'Outstanding Figures from the Past' (*Bogu yezi* 博古葉子) playing cards series when artist Chen Hongshou died unexpectedly.[26] Three, or perhaps five, of

---

20 Zhou Wu (comp.) 1985: 232–33; Zhang Mangong (comp.) 2004: 2.78–79; their style is very much like that of *Jin Ping Mei*.

21 Zhou Wu 1983: 123. For a description and synopsis, see *Zhongguo tongsu xiaoshuo zongmu tiyao* 1990: 261–65. These illustrations, too, are very much like those of *Jin Ping Mei*.

22 The original was printed by Qiaoyuezhai 敲月齋 in Suzhou; see Zhou Xinhui and Wang Zhijun 2000: 498–99. Copies of a 1930s reprint are available in several North American libraries.

23 For examples of the *Yanzi jian* illustrations, see Zhou Xinhui and Wang Zhijun 2000: 304–07; Zhou Wu 1985: 232–33. Sample images from *Bian er chai* appear in Zhou Xinhui and Wang Zhijun 2000: 331–32; Zhou Wu (1985: 233) identifies Lu as its illustrator. McMahon 1998: 73–78 discusses this 'homosexual romance'; Wang Wei 2022 discusses *Bian er chai* and its illustrations.

24 At least one image attributed to Chen Hongshou appears in *Xixiang ji zhenben* 西廂記真本 1640, also published in Hangzhou during the Chongzhen period. See Zhou Xinhui and Wang Zhijun 2000: 319–21.

25 Zhou Wu 1983: 45.

26 See Bussotti 2001: 113. Zhou Wu 1983: 45 notes that Huang also worked on *Exemplars of the Women's Quarters* (Guifan 閨範), the Wanli *Shexian Gazetteer* (*She zhi* 歙志), and the Chongzhen anthology of selected scenes from *chuanqi* plays, *A Roster of Subtle*

PICTURING XIMEN QING'S WORLD

Figure 10.4, from Chapter 35, the second illustration: 書童兒作女粧媚客 (Playing a Female, Shutong Charms the Hangers-on)

Huang Zili's illustrations appear in this *Jin Ping Mei*; two specify that he was the carver, leaving the identity of the artist ambiguous. Two of his signed images are among the first that readers see, Ill. 2a and 4a. Both have delicately evoked tile roofs, conventionally aged trees, and clearly defined rooms. The same is true of Figure 4, Ill. 35b, 'Playing a Female, Shutong Charms the Hangers-on' (Shutong'er zuo nüzhuang mei ke 書童兒作女粧媚客), also signed by Huang. Although its roof is of a different style, it is carefully rendered, as is

---

Ameliorations, Newly Carved and Illustrated, with Commentary (*Xinjuan xiuxiang piping Xuanxue pu* 新鐫繡像批評玄雪譜).

the conventional craggy tree arching into the upper left quarter of the image. There it balances the highly detailed banana-palm in the lower right.

Only two of the *Jin Ping Mei* erotic images (27b and 83b) have a name: Liu Qixian as carver. The first depicts the sweltering day of drinking and sex spent by Ximen Qing, Pan Jinlian, and Chunmei in the grape arbor. The image presents the drunken Jinlian helplessly tied to the arbor by her foot wrappings, her legs spread wide, with Ximen Qing poised to throw a chilled plum at her. Decorative elements in the image are few; only the grape arbor, Ximen, his maid, the rock they are sitting on, and a pile of clothing are rendered in detail. As commentary on the scene, Chunmei is covering her mouth with her sleeve, indicating her embarrassment. The upper third of the image is attractive decoration, perhaps the bank of a body of water, but it is merely visual filler, utterly irrelevant to the activity below. Why the artist chose to leave this essentially blank space is not clear; perhaps to enhance the visibility, hence the violation of normal behavioral standards, of the action portrayed.

Ill. 83b is a more complex and better integrated picture. The lower half is devoted to the activity of the scene of Chunmei helping Chen Jingji penetrate Jinlian as they try out a variety of sexual positions. All three are stark naked. The maid Qiuju is partly discernable behind a banana-palm near the Taihu rock at centre left. Her head is not visible, but this activity is what she sees when she makes a hole in a paper window pane and peeks through, the text explains. The surroundings of the three actors are comprised of the rock, a gnarled tree, and the broad-leafed plant outside in the garden where the maid has come to relieve herself; she is drawn to spy on them when she hears sounds emanating from Jinlian's apartment.

The structure is similarly carefully rendered, with fine parallel lines to delineate the roof tiles and the decorative cap along the roof ridge; inside, the actors are surrounded by a large folding screen painted with leaves and a bird. On the table beside the trio lies the lover's manual and a candlestick, with wine cups to indicate that the three have been drinking. All of these details have been described or alluded to in the text. The roof ridge of the residence divides the image horizontally in half. But the top half is well integrated into the rest by its tall trees, seemingly standing on the other side of Jinlian's chambers. Leaves and limb patterns represent two kinds of trees, broad leafed and narrow leafed, and a tiny moon in the sky indicates that the scene takes place at night. Except for the crude figures, this image is exquisitely rendered.

Figure 2 above (Hong Guoliang's Ill. 38b) is yet better integrated. Here Pan Jinlian occupies the right side of the centre section, where she plays the *pipa* and sings. She is balanced on the left side of the image by a faceless maid who opens a door, balancing Jinlian's open – and lonely – space with this closed room. Above and below are carefully executed decorations. Jinlian's isolation is made yet more palpable by the cold but beautiful snowy setting, making an altogether convincing, even moving evocation of her state of mind.[27]

Reflections

Discerning book buyers of the mid 17th century would have found this illustrated edition to be quite exceptional. The narrative content was extraordinarily dense, its characters unexpectedly complex, its theme uniquely bleak. But as a material object they would have noticed both ordinary and less ordinary aspects of the book. To judge from the copy in the Beijing University Library, although its many sections (*juan* 卷) would make a great pile of paper, its pages were of a standard size for that period. The printed area (the *bankuang* 板框) of each half-folio measures 20.8 by 13.6 cm, slightly smaller than the average for late Ming printed fiction editions.[28] Its half-folio pages have 10 lines of text, each with 22 characters, a not unusual format. As we have seen, the small images, the fine details of screens and of the figures seen through those screens, all necessitated extraordinary skill and care on the part of the printing block carvers. Seeing the names of some of the best-known illustrators and image carvers of the whole Jiangnan region would suggest to late Ming readers that this was an expensive production: hiring well known craftsmen was relatively costly. If it had been for sale, the book would have brought a high price.

However, since apparently only one copy of this printing exists, it seems likely that very few were ever produced.[29] This supposition is supported by the clarity of the print in this exemplar, as if it had been pulled from new or barely used blocks. Parallels with private printing during the 17th century suggest that this edition of *Jin Ping Mei* was never intended to be a commercial product. Copies may have been provided to a special self-selected audience of prospective readers who had paid in advance to allay printing costs. It may even have appeared in installments: the text is divided into 20 sections of five chapters each, a convenient division for production in stages.[30] Given the strong interest in this novel by the

---

27 This illustration is also reproduced in Zhou Xinhui and Wang Zhijun 2000: 343.

28 For the *Jin Ping Mei* measurements, see Hu Wenbin 1986: 30; for average sizes, see Hegel 1998: 115–21, the entries with late Ming dates. Hu: 34–35, notes that later 17th century editions of this version had 11 lines of 28 characters per half-folio; the printed area was 20 by 11.5 cm.

29 In addition to the Peking University Library copy, Hu Wenbin (1986: 30) speculates that two copies in Japan may also be of this edition, although comparisons make this unlikely.

30 See Son 2018, esp. 20–54, 127–41.

ROBERT E. HEGEL

Yuan brothers Hongdao 袁宏道 (1568–1610), Zhongdao 袁中道 (1570–1624), and Zongdao 袁宗道 (1560–1600), leading scholar–administrators of their day, it is likely that this edition was produced for an exclusive audience of appreciative literati;[31] its intended audience would have to be experienced enough as readers to apprehend the political and social criticism embedded in the text and its ongoing pastiche of snippets from popular culture, even if some might have enjoyed it as a 'lewd book' (*yinshu* 淫書). For their subscriptions, these readers were treated to a meticulously-produced book, exceptional as a relatively fine material object and rare for extraordinarily frank and brutal narrative.

But what of the illustrations? Because the conventional decorative elements – trees, rocks, architectural elements – are so carefully drawn and carved, one can only conclude that they are meant to be attractive, *artistic,* in that they are standard visual components shared with literati painting, even if they would not be considered *art*.[32] By comparison with the decorative elements, the erotic images are simplistic and naïve; little effort was expended in realistic depictions of bodies or their parts. Among commercial artists, some specialized in background details while the master painters focused on the central elements and presumably established the overall design.[33] Might the erotic images have been wholly assigned to apprentices? This might explain the simple and uniform representations of the human body, assuming that no craftsman specialized in drawing nudes as he might be in creating elegant tall evergreens, impressive buildings, and massive Taihu rocks.

The last century of Ming rule was the 'apex of painting manual culture' of the elite and would-be elite of middle classes, those who failed in the civil service examinations, the wealthy educated merchants, students, women, managers of shops that sold high culture items – all of whom would be literate and familiar with high cultural values. Potential and implied readers of this novel would have been familiar with the conventional elements of literati painting, even if their experience were indirect, through viewing manuals and other illustrated

---

31 See documents in Zhu Yixuan (comp.)1986: 267–70.

32 See Hegel 2001: 77.

33 Cahill 1994: 102–05. Gulik 1951: i-ii, 155–62, discusses erotic paintings during the Ming; on p. 163 he comments: 'The attempts made by the book illustrators at depicting the nude human figures are not based on actual observation. They took the *ti-pen* [*diben* 底本, artist's printed or painted model] for human figures draped in clothes and tried to construct a nude body within this outline. The result was that their nudes are clumsily rendered [...] It is understandable that these illustrators did not dare to try their hand at large nude figures; their nudes in the book illustrations seldom exceed two inches.' The late Ming erotic album *Huaying jinzhen* has larger, somewhat better proportioned nudes than in *Jin Ping Mei* illustrations; likewise, the decorative details in this exotic album are even more exquisitely rendered.

PICTURING XIMEN QING'S WORLD

books.[34] The more artistic aspects of these illustrations such as Figure 2 might then be seen as imitations of 'elegant' (*ya* 雅) art even though the pornographic images were not only vulgar' (*su* 俗), but worse yet, 'lewd' (*yin* 淫), as if intended to offend.[35] From this distance in time, one can only speculate, but surely in addition to the intended and implied readers of the novel, the real readers and viewers included people who brought a variety of perspectives to the text. Some readers might have read moralistic messages into these pictures; some may have found them shocking. For some readers, the images must have been titillating.

Late Ming reading practices suggest that the text took precedence in establishing the scene; illustrations played a secondary role, confirming the text they accompanied.[36] Leaving aside the erotic images, what do the illustrations contribute? With this edition of *Jin Ping Mei*, a reader gets a lengthy, relatively carefully produced book, of which only a very few copies were available. This scarcity would appeal to the collector's sense of exclusive privilege. It is a book graced – by and large – by attractive illustrations that allow the reader to experience elements of high art even as these pictures represent places, people, clothing, and cultural values that readers might have experienced themselves or at least could imagine encountering. The combinations of familiar objects, beautifully portrayed, with morally reprehensible and shocking activities made this edition unique for its time, a significant factor in the widespread and continuing notoriety of the novel. And for prurient minds, these crudely drawn naked bodies gave ample material for the imagination as well.

References

Bussotti, Michela

2001. *Gravures de Hui: Étude du livre illustré chinois de la fin du XVIe siècle à la première moitié du XVIIe siècle* (Woodcuts from Huizhou: A Study of Illustrated Chinese Books from the End of the Sixteenth to the First Half of the Seventeenth Century). Paris: École Française d'Extrême-Orient.

Cahill, James

1994. *The Painter's Practice: How Artists Lived and Worked in Traditional China.* New York: Columbia University Press.

---

34 Park 2010: 3: about 25 painting manuals were published between 1570 and 1620.

35 On *su* and *ya* evaluations, see Park 2010: 119, 189.

36 See Hegel 2002: 287–89.

Elvin, Mark

1989. 'Tales of *shen* and *xin*: Body-person and heart-mind in China during the last 150 years.' In Michael Feher (ed.), *Fragments for a History of the Human Body,* Part 2. New York: Zone.

Gulik, Robert H. van, comp.

1951. *Erotic Colour Prints of the Ming Period* 秘戲圖考. 3 vols. Tokyo: Privately printed; rpt. Taipei, ca. 1975.

Hegel, Robert E.

1998. *Reading Illustrated Fiction in Late Imperial China*. Stanford, Calif.: Stanford University Press.

2001. 'Painting manuals and the illustration of Ming and Qing popular literature.' *East Asian Library Journal* 10(1): 53–84.

2002. 'Images in legal and fictional texts from Qing China.' *Bulletin de l'École français d'Extrême-Orient* 89: 277–90.

2004. 'Imagined violence: Representing homicide in late imperial crime reports and fiction.' *Zhongguo wenzhe yanjiu jikan* 中國文哲研究季刊 (Bulletin of the Institute of Chinese Literature and Philosophy, Academia Sinica) 25: 61–89.

2006. 'Picturing the monkey king: Illustrations and readings of the 1641 novel *Xiyou bu*.' In *The Art of the Book in China*, pp. 175–91. London: London University School of Oriental and African Studies.

Hu Wenbin 胡文彬, comp.

1986. *Jin Ping Mei shulu* 金瓶梅書錄 (A *Jin Ping Mei* Bibliography). Shenyang: Liaoning renmin.

Huaying jinzhen 花營錦陣 (Flowery Encampments and Brocade Battle Arrays).
n.d. In Robert H. van Gulik (ed.), *Wulin yanghaozhai* 武林養浩齋繡梓.

Jieziyuan huazhuan 芥子園畫傳 (The Mustard Seed Garden Painting Manual),
2010. Ed. Wang Gai 王概, et al. 4 vols. Changchun: Jilin chuban jituan.

Ledderose, Lothar

2000. *Ten Thousand Things: Module and Mass Production of Chinese Art*. Princeton, NJ: Princeton University Press.

Li Qiancheng 李前程 (ed.)

2011. *Xiyou bu jiaozhu* 西遊補校注 (An Annotated *Further Adventures on the Journey to the West*). Beijing: Kunlun.

Liu Hui 劉煇

1984. *Jin Ping Mei chengshu yu banben yanjiu* 金瓶梅成書與版本研究 (Studies on the Compilation and the Editions of *Jin Ping Mei*). Chaoyang: Liaoning Renmin.

McMahon, R. Keith

1995. *Misers, Shrews, and Polygamists: Sexuality and Male–Female Relations in Eighteenth-century Chinese Fiction.* Durham, NC: Duke University Press.

1988. *Causality and Containment in Seventeenth-Century Chinese Fiction.* Leiden: Brill.

Ming Rongyutang ke Shuihu zhuan tu 明容與堂刻水滸傳圖 (Illustrations from the Rongyutang Edition of *Outlaws of the Marsh*).

1965. Shanghai: Zhonghua shuju.

Park, J. P.

2010. *Art by the Book: Painting Manuals and the Leisure Life in Late Ming China.* Seattle: University of Washington Press.

Rolston, David L. (ed.)

1990. *How to Read the Chinese Novel.* Princeton, NJ: Princeton University Press.

Roy, David Tod (trans.)

1993–2013. *The Plum in the Golden Vase or, Chin P'ing Mei.* 5 vols. Princeton, NJ: Princeton University Press.

Son, Suyoung

2018. *Writing for Print: Publishing and the Making of Textual Authority in Late Imperial China.* Cambridge, Mass. and London: Harvard University Asia Center.

Tiangong kaiwu 天工開物

1957. In Zheng Zhenduo 鄭振鐸 (ed.), *Zhongguo gudai banhua congkan* 中國古代版畫叢刊 (A Collection of Classical Chinese Printed Illustrations), Vol. 3, 635–1094. Shanghai: Shanghai guji, 1985.

Tsien Tsuen-Hsuin 錢存訓

1984. 'Technical Aspects of Chinese Printing.' In Soren Edgren (ed.), *Chinese Rare Books in American Collections*, pp. 16–25. New York: China House Gallery, China Institute in America.

1985. 'Paper and printing.' *Chemistry and Chemical Technology,* in Joseph Needham (ed.), *Science and Civilisation in China*, Part 1 of Vol. 5. Cambridge, Eng.: Cambridge University Press.

Wang Rumei 王汝梅

1990. 'Qianyan' 前言 (Foreword). In *Xinke xiuxiang piping Jin Ping Mei*, 1.

Wang Wei 王蔚

2022. *The Lure of Visual Complexity: Narration, Decoration, and Symbolization in Illustrated Fiction during the Ming–Qing Transition.* Ph.D. diss., Washington University in St. Louis.

ROBERT E. HEGEL

Wu Yinghui 吳穎慧

2022. 'Figures in Print.' (Forthcoming essay)

Xinke xiuxiang piping Jin Ping Mei 新刻繡像批評金瓶梅 (Newly Carved and Illustrated *Jin Ping Mei*, with Commentary).

1990. Ed. Qi Yan 齊煙 and (Wang) Rumei 王汝梅. 2 vols. Hong Kong: Sanlian shudian.

Xu Shuofang 徐朔方

1988. *Lun Jin Ping Mei de chengshu ji qita* 論金瓶梅的成書及其他 (On the Composition of *Jin Ping Mei* and Other Topics). Jinan: Qi Lu shushe.

Zhang Mangong 張滿弓 (comp.)

2004. *Gudian wenxue banhua* 古典文學版畫 (Illustrations from Classical Literature). 4 vols. Kaifeng: Henan daxue.

Zhang Xiumin 張秀民

1989. *Zhongguo yinshua shi* 中國印刷史 (A History of Printing in China). Shanghai: Shanghai renmin.

Zhongguo tongsu xiaoshuo zongmu tiyao 中國通俗小說總目提要 (A General Bibliography of Chinese Popular Fiction, with Abstracts).

1990. Ed. Ouyang Jian 歐陽健 and Xiao Xiangkai 蕭相愷. Beijing: Zhongguo wenlian.

Zhou Wu 周蕪

1983. *Huipai banhua shi lunji* 徽派版畫史論集 (Collected Essays on the History of Book Illustrations of the Anhui School). Hefei: Anhui renmin.

Zhou Wu (comp.)

1985. *Zhongguo guben xiqu chatu xuan* 中國古本戲曲插圖選 (Selected Illustrations from Early Editions of Chinese Plays). Tianjin: Tianjin renmin meishu.

1982. *Zhongguo gudai banhua bai tu* 中國古代版畫百圖 (One Hundred Early Chinese Book Illustrations). Beijing: Renmin meishu.

Zhou Xinhui 周心慧 and Wang Zhijun 王致軍 (comp.)

2000. *Huipai, Wulin, Suzhou banhua ji* 徽派武林蘇州版畫集 (Collected Book Illustrations from the Anhui, Hangzhou and Suzhou Schools). Beijing: Xueyuan chubanshe.

Zhou Xun 周汛 and Gao Chunming 高春明 (comp.)

1984. *Zhongguo lidai fushi* 中國歷代服飾 (Chinese Clothing through the Ages). Shanghai: Xuelin.

Zhu Yixuan 朱一玄 (comp.)

1986. *Gudian xiaoshuo banben ziliao xuanbian* 古典小說版本資料選編 (Selected Materials on Editions of Classical Fiction). 2 vols. Taiyuan: Shanxi renmin.

Note on Contributor

Robert E. Hegel is Liselotte Dieckmann Professor Emeritus of Comparative Literature and Professor Emeritus of Chinese at Washington University in St. Louis, Missouri, USA, where he taught for 43 years before his retirement in 2018. Professor Hegel is the author of *The Novel in Seventeenth Century China* and *Reading Illustrated Fiction in Late Imperial China*. In collaboration with others, he has published English translations of short stories, novels, plays, and crime case reports from the Yuan, Ming and Qing periods.

CHAPTER 11

Pictures and Words as Mirrors

How Woodblock Art and Literary Art in *Jin Ping Mei* Modify Each Other

ZHANG MIN
Translated by Marja Kaikkonen

The general public and academia have gradually grown aware of the wood-cut illustrations of *Jin Ping Mei* 金瓶梅 (JPM).[1] Advances in research on book culture during the Ming and Qing dynasties, which have been text-centred research, have focused mainly on other essential aspects of the work, such as its author, the time of writing, and its ideological tendencies. Among contemporary research works on JPM, Zhejiang Ancient Books Publishing House 浙江古籍出版社 (Zhejiang Guji Chubanshe) has published *Li Yu quanji* 李漁全集 (Collected Works of Li Yu), including JPM, with Li Yu's (1611–1680) commentary, in two volumes, and prefaced them with the complete illustrations from the Chongzhen edition.[2] In the collection *Zhongguo Gudian*

---

1 This chapter is mainly based on the illustrations in the collector Wang Xiaoci 王孝慈 (1883–1936) copy of *Xin ke xiuxiang piping Jin Ping Mei* 新刻繡像批評金瓶梅, in *Li Yu quanji* 李漁全集 (*Collected Works of Li Yu*), Vol. 12, Hangzhou: Zhejiang Guji Chubanshe 浙江古籍出版社, 1991. Photoprinted *Quanben Jin Ping Mei cihua* 全本金瓶梅詞話 (Unabridged), Hong Kong: Taiping Shuju 太平書局, 1992. The information in the chapter about the technique of woodcutting is from my visit to Yangzhou Guangling Shushe Diaoban Yinshua Chuanxisuo 揚州廣陵書社雕版印刷傳習所 (Yangzhou Guangling Book Company's Woodcut Heritage Studio), where I had the opportunity to follow the production of *Muban shuiyin Jin Ping Mei quan tu* 木版水印金瓶梅全圖 (*Complete Jin Ping Mei Watercolour Woodcuts*) by woodcutting master Liu Kun 劉坤.

2 The many editions of *Jin Ping Mei* are roughly divided into three systems: 1. The oldest version, *Jin Ping Mei in Verse and Prose* (*Jin Ping Mei Cihua* 金瓶梅詞話) (JPMCH), 2. the version of *Jin Ping Mei, Newly Engraved and Illustrated, with Commentary* (*Xin ke xiuxiang piping Jin Ping Mei* 新刻繡像批評金瓶梅) or Chongzhen 崇禎 1628–1644 edition, and 3. the version with Zhang Zhupo's commentaries (*Zhang Zhupo pingdian Jin Ping Mei* 張竹坡評點金瓶梅). Despite the widely divided opinions about the chronology of the JPMCH edition and the Chongzhen edition, it is undisputed that the woodblock illustrations of the Chongzhen edition were created approximately simultaneously with the two editions. As

160

PICTURES AND WORDS AS MIRRORS

Xiaoshuo Mingzhu Ziliao 中國古典小說名著資料 (Materials on the Best Chinese Ancient Novels), the cover of the fourth volume, *Jin Ping Mei yanjiu ziliao huibian* 金瓶梅研究資料彙編 (Collection of Studies on *Jin Ping Mei*), used the illustration from Chapter 2 of the Chongzhen edition, 'Beautiful Ms. Pan Evokes Feelings beneath the Awning' (*Qiao Pan niang lian xia gou qing* 俏潘娘簾下勾情) as an element of its background design. Both works apply illustrations from the Chongzhen edition woodcut series. Woodcuts enter the reader's field of vision before writing does, which indicates that JPM research and the reception of the work have recognized the aesthetical efficacy of the woodcut illustrations of the Chongzhen edition.

On its way from JPMCH to the Chongzhen edition and again to the edition commented by Zhang Zhupo 張竹坡 (1670–1698), the text of JPM has been in a fluid state of additions and deletions, polishings and interpretations, but in every edition of the text the work's intrinsic style has more or less fallen into a pattern. The words of literary historians and critics of the past communicate their shared impression: platitudes of the marketplace, fragmentary words in the boudoirs, language involving the unrefined, all living creatures of every kind, an illusory leitmotif, slick and sly, overripe... To generalize, in the text we can see how the dividing line between the written style and the daily vernacular has almost been lost; the conventional tension between the refined and the vulgar, the rash and the calm, the individualistic and the epoch-determined, is dissolved. But our excessive pursuit of the meaning of the text may turn into something other than what we desired. In short, the contents of the text still leave literary criticism and literary theory plenty of leeway.

In comparison, research on the woodcuts seems to lack deeper thinking. The size, position, and characteristics of woodcuts are often seen as the one important proof in the study of the editions, but those that take woodcuts as an independent object of study are still very few. The Indian poet Tagore (1861–1941) said: 'Painting is the language of silence; it is the one among the

---

texts of the Chongzhen edition system have been incessantly discovered both in China and abroad, it appears that woodblock illustrations, inserted into the text more or less before there were chapter titles, were included in the book in two different ways. The versions of the Chongzhen edition differ as to the number of illustrations: they come with 50, 100 or 200 pictures, and there are small deviations on the side of the printed area, but when it comes to the central contents and style of carving, they are largely identical, with only minor differences, something that reflects some kind of continuous modelling of, or technical improvement on, versions carved still earlier. Since the editions in Beijing University Library and Tianjin Library as well the one edited by Zheng Zhenduo 鄭振鐸 (1898–1958) have the most complete illustrations and the quality of carving is the clearest, they together make up the stable features of the Chongzhen edition, not considering the texts. Therefore, this article chooses to analyze the woodblock illustrations primarily in these works.

161

arts that best can offer people peace of mind.' (Tagore 1988: 5) The German philosopher E.G. Lessing's (1729–1781) work *Laokoön: An Essay on the Limits of Painting and Poetry (Laokoon; oder, Über die Grenzen der Malerei und Poesie)* (1766) deals with the aesthetic relationship of ekphrasis; the Greek-Spanish painter El Greco (1541–1614) portrayed 'Laokoön' in oils, and contemporary musicians and cartoonists continue to use the story of Laokoön or his image... A picture gives in an instant a more long-lasting effect than what writing does, while the temporal sequence of writing engenders meanings in images of dynamic conditions. No matter which era, east or west, pictures are an art form that depends on spatial change and differs from the temporal art of writing with its consecutive and parallel order. Their differences allow for mutual influences.

During the past hundred years, the research on the woodcut illustrations of JPM can be divided into mainly two broad categories. The first is concerned with the study of the Ming printmaking in general.[3] The second relates to the overall study of works of popular literature during Ming and Qing. In the first place, illustrations, forming part of the literary products in their entirety and serving complementary and auxiliary narrative functions, gained attention in literary research as literary *noumena* (Kant's (1724–1804] definition). Composite research in texts-with-illustrations has now arrived at the point where the concept and the function of illustration have been defined through a comparison with text versions.[4] The illustrations of JPM, for example, have provided time-specific proofs and microcosmic demonstrations for the entire text-with-illustration field of the Ming Dynasty, and at the same time, added new evidence and interpretational possibilities for the prints of the JPM Chongzhen edition.

Based on this common knowledge and the new research, this article takes the illustrations of the Chongzhen edition as a case through which to investigate how woodcut illustration intervenes in the artistic conception and the reader's acceptance, and how the tension between picture and text influences the literary work.

---

3   During the first half of the 20th century, Lu Xun 魯迅 and Zheng Zhenduo 鄭振鐸 collected and edited prints. Between 1980 and 2000, Zhou Wu 周蕪, Zhou Xinhui 周心慧, Du Xinfu 杜信孚 and other art historians viewed the illustrations of JPM as preeminent among woodcuts.

4   For example, Wang Liqi's 王利器 (1912–1998) *Historical Materials on Forbidden Novels and Operas in the Yuan, Ming and Qing Dynasties (Yuan Ming Qing san dai jinhui xiaoshuo xiqu shiliao* 元明清三代禁毁小說戲曲史料) and Zhang Yuanfen's 張遠芬 (1939-) *Preliminary Study on the 'Newly Discovered'* Jin Ping Mei (*'Xin'faxian de* Jin Ping Mei *yanjiu ziliao chu tan* '新'發現的金瓶梅研究資料初探). The viewpoints of Patrick Hanan 韓南 (1927–2014), Andrew H. Plaks 浦安迪 (b. 1945), Toi Kuyasushi 鳥居久靖 (b. 1911), Wang Rumei 王汝梅 (b. 1935), Mei Jie 梅節 (b. 1928), as well as some unpublished theses.

PICTURES AND WORDS AS MIRRORS

In the Handwritten Copies only the Text was Relevant

Research has always focused on the assessments of JPM by famous literati such as the Yuan brothers Hongdao 袁弘道 (1568–1600) and Zhongdao 袁中道 (1570–1624), Dong Qichang 董其昌 (1555–1636), Yu Yue 俞樾 (1821–1907), Wang Shizhen 王世貞 (1526–1590), Li Yu 李漁 etc., and the order in which they wrote their evaluations, but usually they can be summed up as differences between the outlook of the day and the writers' personal thinking. Very little has to do with the concrete paper version that the critic had read or the form of that version. Of the two big systems from the Ming Dynasty, JPMCH is the most complete version, while the editions of the Chongzhen system are characterized by deletion and revision. These editions are, however, more widespread and have more offshoots. From the amount of the included illustrations, it is very hard to draw conclusions about the chronological order of the two systems, so this question awaits the discovery of more material. On the other hand, it is easy to infer that in addition to the printed texts of the two editions, there must have existed great numbers of handwritten copies.

By re-examining the critical comments by Yuan Hongdao, Yuan Zhongdao, Dong Qichang and others, we may get some clues. From the insider's judgement that JPM is a book that 'promotes licentiousness', we can see that for a long time, handwritten copies had functioned as forerunners for the full work in book form. At present, the earliest evaluation of JPM can be found in Yuan Hongdao's letter to Dong Qichang (1596):

> Where did you get the *Jin Ping Mei*? I glance at it from time to time, while lying in bed, and find this full of interest, and far superior to Mei Sheng's *Seven Stimuli*. Where is the latter part? Please let me know where I can return it to you, once it has been copied, and exchange it for the other part.[5]

《金瓶梅》從何得來，伏枕略觀，雲霞滿紙，勝於枚生《七發》多矣。後段在何處。抄竟，當於何處倒換，幸一的示. (Yuan Hongdao 1981: 289)

The copy that Yuan Hongdao refers to and which Dong Qichang knew about must have been a handwritten copy. Yuan Zhongdao also says in his *Supplement to Collected Texts from the Jade Snow Studio* (*Kexuezhai ji Wai ji* 珂雪齋集 外集), volume nine, item 'Records of Leisurely Tours' ('You ju fei lu' 游居柿錄):

> Sibai said: 'Quite recently there has been a novel called *Jin Ping Mei* which is extremely fine.' I had heard of it myself; later I got half of the work from

---

5 *Translator's note*: English translation from Hanan 1962: 40.

Zhonglang while he was in Zhenzhou. Broadly speaking, it is a detailed description of lovemaking... Sibai said that this book must absolutely be burnt. Thinking of it today, I feel it is not necessary to burn it, nor admire it; it is enough to listen to it.

思白曰近有一小說名《金瓶梅》極佳，予私識之。後從中郎真州，見此書之半，大約模寫兒女情態具備 … 思白言及此書曰，決當焚之，以今思之，不必焚，不必崇，聽之而已。　　　　　(Yuan Zhongdao 2019: 1401)

From Yuan Zhongdao's description it is not possible to determine whether it was a printed or hand copied text. But somewhat later, Shen Defu 沈德符 states in his *Gathered and Edited in the Country (during the Wanli Reign Period)* (*Wanli Ye huo bian* 萬曆野獲編), volume 25, item '*Jin Ping Mei*':

...By now, the only person who possesses the complete work is Liu Chengxi, style Xianbai, of Macheng. No doubt it was copied for him from the manuscript of Xu Wenzhen, to whose family his wife belongs. Three years later, when Xiaoxiu [Yuan Zhongdao] came to the capital to take the examinations, he had the book with him. I borrowed it from him to copy and brought it back with me. My friend from Suzhou, Feng Youlong [Feng Menglong 馮夢龍], was both surprised and delighted when he saw it. He said a bookshop should buy it for a high price and have it engraved. At that time Ma Zhongliang [Ma Zhijun 馬之駿] had been appointed to the Customs in Suzhou, and he, too, urged me to accede to the publisher's request, and thereby satisfy my needs. But I told him that although eventually someone was bound to publish the book, once published it would circulate from person to person and from household to household, corrupting men's minds. And if one day Yama would tax me with setting off this catastrophe, what excuse should I be able to offer? How could I possibly risk all the torments of Niraya for the hope of a paltry profit? Zhongliang entirely agreed with me, and so I locked the novel securely away. Yet in no time at all it was on sale all over Suzhou. However, the original text was short of Chapters 53 to 57; a search was made for them everywhere, but they could not be found. Some ignoramus supplied them so that the work could be printed.[6]

…今惟麻城劉涎白承禧家有全本，蓋從其妻家徐文貞錄得者。又三年小修上公車，已攜有其書，因與借抄挈歸。吳友馮猶龍見之驚喜，慫恿書坊以重價購刻。馬仲良時榷吳關，亦勸予應梓，人之求可以療饑。予曰此等書必遂有人板行，但一刻則家傳戶到，壞人心術。他日閻羅究詰，始禍何辭置對，吾豈以刀錐博泥犁哉。仲良大以為然，遂固篋之。

6　*Translator's note*: English translation, slightly modified, from Hanan 1962, 47.

PICTURES AND WORDS AS MIRRORS

未幾時，而吳中懸之國門矣。然原本實少五十三回至五十七回，遍覓不得。有陋儒補以入刻。 (Shen Defu 2012: 550)

Between the lines one can see that Shen Defu first had seen a handwritten copy, and first after that came great amounts of forgeries or sequels that book dealers had produced for commercial ends. The above persons had not even seen an entire engraved version, and since handwritten copies depended entirely on manual work, there were no woodblock illustrations among the early handwritten copies that circulated, and evaluations of the early JPM texts followed a trend constrained by preconceptions. The texts seen in Macheng (now Macheng, Hubei 湖北 Province), Zhenzhou (now Yizheng 儀徵, Jiangsu 江蘇 Province) and by the famous official Xu Wenzhen during this period were all handwritten copies. Consequently, the early evaluations of the text that came to determine the tendency with which the novel was assessed even later, were based on the text only. In addition, writing carried a more serious purport in classical China. Within the system of appraisal of classical literature, writing was seen as more often related to personal accomplishments and engagement in the 'economic' undertakings of society, whereas 'idle arts' such as calligraphy and painting, were mainly means of pleasure and moral cultivation; therefore, writings had more authority. Although later readers have been able to survey JPM with both text and pictures, the text has remained a foundation much more accepted than the illustrations. In a word, before the Wanli era when JPM was printed in large quantities, the widespread circulation of the handwritten copies resulted in a thematic evaluation of the text as serious 'admonition'. By fully depicting reality, the text as such became a precursor to the novel of manners, although Yuan Hongdao and other famous literati affirmed its artistic level and praised it as 'far better than Mei Sheng's *Seven Stimuli*'. JPM contains plenty of trifling details, but the plot displays such great variegation that it could only have been written by a person of wide knowledge.

Adherence to the Text and Control over the Text

The writing in JPM is skillful and smooth, reading it makes one feel as if listening to a lively storyteller in the marketplace and viewing a scene of bustle and excitement, just what the Yuan brothers appreciated but Shen Defu worried about. The text of the entire novel of JPM opened a wide field to the 'ways of the world [世情]' and the images supported the mental reception. However, the idea that the text governs the book's entire function of circulation does not accord with stated facts nor with the basic laws of communication between the arts. Let us reflect upon the style of JPM that has caused so much controversy, that is, *realism*. Realism imbues the world that JPM is constructing. Through the ages there have been people with a certain training in Buddhism and Daoism, who have, with a more rational attitude in their commentaries, given JPM credit for its realism by praising its 'genuineness' and 'ease'. But this has put even higher demands on the reader.

It cannot be denied that from the middle of the Ming Dynasty, novels of manners and erotic novels flourished, and erotic pictures abounded on the markets. When novels were printed to attract a broader group of readers, it was inevitable to utilize the existing erotic picture resources. When JPM entered the commercial publishing stage, the expansion of the readership and the appearance of fakes, inferior copies and sequels on the market also contributed to JPM being rejected by readers with moralizing views. As illustration is essentially a marketing tool used for attracting a larger readership, the erotic elements were partly responsible for this shift in attitude. In Chapter 15 of the novel *Lantern at the Crossroads* (*Qiludeng* 歧路燈), the main character states:

...novels in bookshops, such as *Jin Ping Mei*, are books that promote licentiousness. Although apparently only talking about former troubles, and writing about future hopes, the inserted pictures showing erotic situations are sure to weaken the youth of the world. *Water Margin* is a book that advocates turmoil and revolt and harms the people; it not only talks about enforcing justice on behalf of Heaven, it even takes bandits whose heads have been displayed on execution grounds and gets ignorant people to view them as valiant heroes; this results in an even bigger disaster. Therefore, the author's descendants in three generations will all turn out dumb, but bad *karma* seems not to have reached its maximum hereby....

…但坊間小說如《金瓶梅》，宣淫之書也，不過道其事之所曾經，寫其意之所欲試，畫上寫秘戲圖像，殺卻天下少年矣。《水滸傳》，倡亂之書也，叛逆賊民，加上替天行道四個字，把一起兒市曹梟示之強賊，叫愚民都看成英雄豪傑，這貽禍更大了。所以作者之裔三世皆啞君子，猶以為孽報未極。　　　　　　　　　　　　　　　　(Li Lüyuan 1998: 666)

The erotic pictures mentioned in the quotation may refer to the pictures in the Chongzhen edition, or at least to pictures that Qing booksellers had produced for profit according to the illustrations of JPM. But the later illustrations can hardly be regarded as equal to the first originals that were executed with strict adherence to and mastery of the text.

Let us now consider how the woodcuts present the secret love scenes of the text. If we contemplate how the characters and plots in the woodcuts relate to the chapter titles of the text, we must ask: was there really no way for the woodcuts to

PICTURES AND WORDS AS MIRRORS

avoid these details? If they did, was it in order to add to or to indirectly diminish the beauty of the sexual descriptions of the text? Already the titles in twenty-one chapters out of the one hundred touch upon such descriptions.[7] In these twenty-one chapters, the titles deal with secret trysts that are being overheard. They draw support from the main characters' words and from the description of the listeners' psychology. These passages belonged to the most controversial part of JPM. The woodcuts are closely bound to the chapter themes and to the narrative structure, and therefore they have to portray the main characters. Consequently, they lose the function of indirectly constructing an artistic conception and can only by using the most obvious details of the plot manage to disclose the main theme. Compared with painting, poetry or music, woodcut art is more limited by the medium of its wooden material and engraving tools. The woodcuts of the Chongzhen edition are nevertheless able to express methods of realism and concretization when developing the details of the characters' actions – this is demanded by the episodic quality of woodcuts in a novel.

A close reading of the illustrations in the Chongzhen edition reveals that both with a view to the general plot and to the details, they closely follow and use the text to their advantage. This is manifested in many cases where the text deals with erotica, as well as in the formulaic representation of the atmosphere of the ancient material culture. The 'controlling' function of woodcuts has to do with the strict adherence to the text content. The JPM woodcuts account fully for the story line of the text, but here and there can be found some minor deviations from the textual version. The serial quality and number of woodcuts were enough to sustain their later circulation as separate editions. For a novel of manners that relies on narration, each woodcut shows figures based on the main characters, and compared to woodcut illustrations in contemporaneous novels, they seem extraordinarily methodical and rigorous in style. The woodcuts, even if circulated as separate editions, could still confer the main plot to readers familiar with the novel JPM, as it was rewritten from the *Water Margin* story. Therefore, plenty of leeway was left for the separate publication of text and pictures. During Ming and Qing, great numbers of literati praised JPM in every possible way as soon as they had seen it. It is conceivable that the illustrations through visual means rectified the reputation of a controversial book.

The adherence to and control of the text by the woodcuts is demonstrated in the portrayal and composition of the natural surroundings and material aspects. Further, the woodcuts as such assist the episodes of the plot through the titles of the chapters; the episodes are condensed into the chapter titles; the feelings and even philosophical thoughts that the chapter titles want to

---

7   The chapters 2, 3, 4, 5, 8, 13, 28, 50, 51, 52, 61, 65, 77, 78, 79, 82, 83, 85, 86, 93, 97.

convey are mainly transmitted through the verses in the text. The titles are usually composed of six or seven characters and are formulated with antithetical parallelism. Seven-character poems in the novel are a sign of adaptation to the literati style (文人化); their language accounts concisely for the plot and serves a material and cultural atmosphere. Both the titles and the verses in the text are by themselves often able to create an atmosphere that embodies the entire chapter, and it is indeed done with refined artistic conception. Poems are generally full of allusions connecting feelings and objects with historical happenings. Using allusions is also an important method to show literati influence, i.e., refinement. For the woodcuts of the novel, the chapter titles help to establish order and serve almost as literary quotations. Except for the more complicated episodes, the titles serve as the red thread and the fixed points. The woodcuts' adherence to text content reflects the ingenuity of the carving masters. 'During their work, the illustrators did not regard *Jin Ping Mei* as a 'pornographic book' but created the pictures on the basis of a total grasp of the theme of the novel' (Zhao Xianzhang 2020 [ed.]: 661). In this edition of the novel, we find a concentrated expression of the cream of the Chongzhen period as it was manifested in ancient musical annotation, opera and book engraving.

Text Refined by Images

In a field of vision that does not possess rational perspective, things turn to their opposites when they reach the extreme, and thus the world that the text constructs is even more likely to create feelings of disgust in the reader. But in woodcuts, by contrast, this kind of fatigue from clamorous discourse seems to be diminished. Woodcuts derive a split second from the irregularly changing world, making the conditions calm down, making the complicated gentle. By examining JPM's woodcuts we can discover how they through various dimensions, voice and countenance, activity, elegance and vulgarity, develop the text.

The strokes of the JPM illustrations are dominated by fine lines, flexible changes in the creation of characters and environment. The white areas and the thin deep traces in the woodcuts highlight the fact that characters and surroundings have symbolic details but hide more complicated elements. As the woodcuts in general comply with the description of characters, the arrangement of things, and the seasons of the landscape in the text, they manage to restore the personalities, times, and spaces, but without forfeiting creativity.

The 'refining' function of woodcuts is connected to the intrinsic quality of their graphic art, stemming from the history of printmaking in classical Chinese art, and to identifying the most suitable theory correlating the respective artistic essences of printmaking and text. Scholars both Chinese and foreign have often talked about 'synesthesia' (*tonggan* 通感), meaning that the different sensory pathways can be transformed.[8] The theory of synesthesia maintains that man is naturally endowed with synesthesia, and the reason is that man is a part of this world just like the myriad things. Another view bases itself on the common results of different art forms that mold human mind and develop feelings; therefore, when it comes to affecting human feelings, they reach the same goals by different means. These two reasons are a question of which came first, the occurrence of art or the concept of art; together they confirm that synesthesia can be awakened. Great amounts of classical Chinese poems inscribed on paintings, stories in Dunhuang frescoes based on illustrations in Buddhist sutras, lyrics and scores of musical compositions, writings, pictures, sounds – when searching for tallying points, many great pieces of art were born. All this substantiates that synesthesia is in action when we discuss both classical Chinese literary and pictorial arts.

The special qualities of JPM's woodcuts merge with the tradition of Chinese painting, and are expressed when contrasted with other kinds of art, such as poetry, calligraphy, music, dance etc. The idea of 'appearance', *xiang* 象, arose very early in Chinese painting. Already the pre-Qin *Six Classics*[9] (*Liu Jing* 六經) and the various schools of thought contained the concept of 'appearance', its basic meaning being 'figure', *tuxing* 圖形. The arrival of picture into the literati-officialdom culture happened relatively late. The Six Dynasties 六朝 (222–589) was a period imbued with philosophical thinking. Deep and serene philosophical thoughts and exquisite painting were all linked to the flourishing of Six Dynasties' literature in the south. During the period when the *Six Classics* were formed, pictures were not a part of any one of them. This meant that pictures attained a sort of freedom, thereby complementing the tradition of the *Six Classics*, and this kind of relative artistic freedom had a close connection to Confucian philosophy and, beyond it, to the aesthetic

---

8   Su Shi 蘇軾 (1037-1101) says: 'Savoring Wang Wei's [701-761] poetry one feels that the poems conjure pictures, and his paintings teem with poetry' (Wei Mojie shi, shi zhong you hua, hua zhong you shi. 味摩詰詩, 詩中有畫, 畫中有詩). (Kong 1998, 111). Qian Zhongshu 钱钟书 (1910-1998) defined it: In everyday experience, the senses of sight, hearing, touch, smell and taste can often quicken or communicate with each other; it is not necessary to draw dividing lines between the functions of the eye, ear, tongue, nose, and body. It is as if colour can have temperature, sound can have form, cold and warm can have weight, smell can have sharp edge. 在日常經驗裡, 視覺、聽覺、觸覺、嗅覺、味覺往往可以彼此打動或交通, 眼、耳、舌、鼻、身各個官能的領域可以不分界限。顏色似乎會有溫度, 聲音似乎會有形象, 冷暖似乎會有重量, 氣味似乎會有鋒芒 (Qian 1988, 56).

9   I.e. *Book of Songs* (*Shijing* 詩經), *Book of Documents* (*Shujing* 書經), *Book of Rites* (*Yili* 儀禮), *Book of Changes* (*Yijing* 易經), *Book of Music* (*Yue* 樂), and *Spring and Autumn Annals* (*Chunqiu* 春秋).

appreciation influenced by Buddhism and Daoism.[10] During the Tang 唐 and Song 宋 dynasties, both Buddhism and Daoism supported the spread of woodcuts to the people through the printing of Buddha images, illustrations to the canonical texts and religious stories, and picture talismans; around the Yuan 元 dynasty they became illustrations interspersed in books. Before woodcuts took the step from the world of religions into books of daily use, the tradition of Chinese painting incorporated elaborations on the philosophical connotations of 'appearance': in the evaluation of the elite class, when pictures were seen as art, they were closely connected to moral quality, nature, and philosophy, something that widely surpassed the deconstructed impression of the form itself.

Among contemporary woodcuts, the JPM illustrations also held an appropriate position. Novels of the Ming and Qing dynasties were the foremost literature of their time; this was also the prime time of book illustration woodcuts. The greater approachability of illustrations compared to the text alone increased the popularization of the illustrated books, and the combination of the two became a phenomenon of the time. The flourishing of woodcut illustrations aided the development of the craft in Jinling 金陵, Wulin 武林, Huizhou 徽州, Jianyang 建陽 etc., and promoted the appearance of the critique of woodcut art. The most widespread impact was left by Wulin woodcuts, centered around Hangzhou 杭州, through the support by woodcut engraving masters from Huizhou, who resided there for a long time, and at one point through the encouragement by literati such as Li Zhi 李贄 (1527–1602), Xu Wei 徐渭 (1521–1593), and Wang Jide 王驥德 (1540–1623). During the Chongzhen period, there was *A Complete Catalogue of the Superior Famous Mountains of the World* (*Tianxia ming shan sheng gaiji* 天下名山勝概記), which already reveals unprecedented characteristics of excellent quality.

In the Chongzhen edition, signatures of five engravers of Xin'an 新安 appear on the frames near the middle fold: Liu Yingzu 劉應祖, Liu Qixian 劉啟先, Hong Guoliang 洪國良, Huang Zili 黃子立 and Huang Ruyao 黃汝耀.[11] The place of origin of the engravers, Xin'an, has discernibly been under the influence of Wulin

---

10 The earliest woodcut in China is the 'Dharani Sutra Charm' (*Tuoluonijing zhoutu* 陀羅尼經咒圖) from the Suzong 肅宗 period (756–761) of the Tang Dynasty. The earliest woodcut where the exact year of engraving is noted is from 868, on the title page of the Diamond Sutra (*Jin'gangbanruojing* 金剛般若經), an illustration of Sakyamuni's teachings (Zhou Wu 1988: 3).

11 The dates of birth and death of the artisans are not known, but they were all active in the early 17th century, since the book was printed sometime during 1628–1644.

PICTURES AND WORDS AS MIRRORS

engraving. The five engravers were masters at that time,[12] with experiences of many artistic skills of printmaking, amply exhibited in the illustrations of JPM.

While the Chongzhen period carried on the remnants from the Wanli 'golden age' of engraving, rapid fragmentization of the main tradition set in with consequent great disparities between the styles of different localities and different workshops. For a comparison, in Chapter 40 of *Outstanding Figures from Seventy-two Regions, Organized According to the* Four Books (*Qishier chao Si shu renwu yanyi* 七十二朝四書人物演義) (Zhou Wu 1988: 552), which was printed during the same period, the woodcuts use plenty of wide line, the contrast between heavy and pale black is very strong, and the colour of trees, auspicious clouds, and human expressions all display a state of vivid brushwork and not realism. In contrast, the JPM illustrations stand out with their clear style and appropriate composition level between complex and simple.

Enhancing the Artistic Conception

Let us then compare JPM with the illustrations in the Sanduozhai 三多齋 edition of *The Loyal and Righteous Men of Water Margin, with Mr. Li Zhuowu's comments* (*Li Zhuowu Xiansheng piping Zhong Yi Shuihu zhuan* 李卓吾先生批評忠義水滸傳, hereafter *Water Margin*).[13] Both novels start from the *Water Margin*, and Pan Jinlian 潘金蓮 is murdered in both texts, but the circumstances are widely different, something that is also reflected in the illustrations. In the illustration of *Water Margin*, Chapter 26, Wu Song 武松, as if blown by the wind, is standing up on the rooftop, holding the chopped-off head of the adulteress in his hand. It is clear that the woodcut focuses the viewer's vision on the main theme, 'punishment'. Comparing in detail how JPM treats the same main theme in text and in woodcut, one arrives at the following impression: in the text of *Water Margin*, the death of Pan Jinlian and Ximen Qing 西門慶 is placed in Chapter 26, and the revenge action happens quickly as lightning. The movements are described in a few words, the sensation of the image is forceful. The entire chapter gives the impression of the text being simple, but the matters complicated. JPM writes about Pan Jinlian's death only in Chapter 87, and the description of both psychology and action, direct description and indirect setting in equal measure, express tactfully Pan Jinlian's pleas for mercy

---

12 Hanan states that 'The same signatures are also found in the songbook *Wu-sao hebian* 吳騷合編, which has a Chongzhen preface. It seems reasonable, therefore, to take this as a Chongzhen edition.' Hanan 1962: 6.

13 Reproduced in Zhou Wu 1988, 319–20. With signature 'Carved by Liu Junyu' 刘君裕; in the style of the Anhui school woodcuts.

171

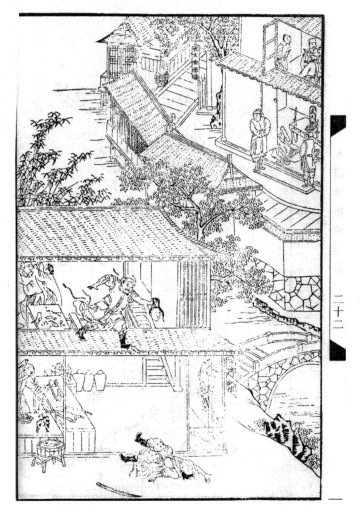

Figure 11.1. Illustration from *Water Margin,* Ch. 26, 'Wu Song Offers Heads as Memorial Sacrifice'

and fear as well as the onlooker, the girl Ying'er's 迎兒 various reactions. In both cases, the woodcuts echo the text, and much attention is drawn to details: in *Water Margin* the scene is a restaurant along a canal of the small town, and in the upper right part of the picture almost one third is covered by buildings, among which Wu Da's home is clearly discernable with the spirit table and two of Wu Song's men on guard. In the middle and lower part of the picture, Wu Song, Ximen Qing, and the waiter Xiao Er 小二 are all arranged according to the circumstances in the text so that the entire picture in its density comes close to a realistic representation of the scenery. In the Chongzhen edition

PICTURES AND WORDS AS MIRRORS

Figure 11.2. Illustration from the Chongzhen edition of JPM, Ch. 87a, 'Captain Wu Kills His Sister-in-law as a Sacrifice to His Elder Brother'

illustrations, Wu Song and Pan Jinlian as main characters are also placed in the middle of the picture, just slightly lower; the space under the eaves in the middle is quite small, and the surrounding trees and window lattices on the right and the full moon in the sky are in no way differentiated as primary or secondary. The figures in the pictures are fewer and equally distributed to the middle of the scene with the long candles on the altar, the memorial tablet with Wu Dalang's name carved on it, and the horizontal hanging lock on the left side of the room's door. The representation of the main theme of the text is both subtle and sophisticated, to a certain degree diminishing the implied moral

173

admonishment found in the text ever since the *Water Margin*, playing down the marketplace atmosphere and making use of the customary objects that carry symbolic significance in the text. By displaying a few stylized everyday objects and scenery, JPM's woodcut closely echoes the text and conveys richer information than the text.

With their tastefulness and calm, woodcuts bestow new connotations on the illustrated text. After the technique of engraving and printing developed, illustrated volumes became a new art form that brought benefit to literati, engravers, and readers. The period when the illustrations of JPM were created was exactly during the golden age of Chinese woodcuts – around the Wanli period, and therefore these specimens of illustrations are both typical and representative. If we look at the engraving trends in contemporaneous literary works in general, illustrated novels followed the continuous development of the narrative themes and flourished as bamboo shoots after spring rain. The course of development of the novels was also the course of maturation of the woodcut art and their commercialized selection. As soon as the texts of the long chapter novels *zhanghui xiaoshuo* 章回小說 had been stabilized, there were seldom big changes in their plots or characters. The basis for the creation of woodcuts was the relatively stable primary text of the novel; a rather small number of illustrations would lay bare the written text, and through the transformation into another art form, the contents of the written text would gain new connotations and artistic conceptions, the precondition and basis of the illustrations being a selective appropriation of the contents of the text. Therefore, woodcuts influenced the textual contents by adding, deleting, and even remodeling.

The use of line in the woodcuts, the utilization of harmonious combinations of straight and curved lines, attained the artistic effect of coupling hard and soft. In the one hundred woodcuts the overall use of straight line has above all assumed the function of dividing the tableau so that the main theme can be concentrated into a smaller area of the picture. At the same time, the frequent use of straight line creates a general impression of orderliness, something that accords with the mainstream aesthetic appreciation of regularity. Straight line is even used to construct courtyards, doors and windows, corridors and pillars, steps, wattled walls, temples, and everyday tables, beds, couches, and long candles. But there are also cases of curved lines, e.g. as used in Chapter 71: 'Li Ping'er Appears in a Dream in Battalion Commander He's House' ('Li Ping'er jian He jia tuo meng' 李瓶兒見何家托夢), one of the two chapters that in detail retell things in a dream; the two curved lines restrict the characters onto a space of approximately two thirds of the picture; this method to express a dream is really a precursor to modern cartoons. The specific usage of line cannot be

PICTURES AND WORDS AS MIRRORS

separated from the medium and the tools of woodcuts as such; straight line is the type that is most easily employed in woodcuts, and when it is used in illustrations of regular collections of poems or prose, such as *Illustrations of Tang Poems* (*Tang shi huapu* 唐詩畫譜), *Pictures Beyond Poems* (*Shi yu huapu* 詩餘畫譜), the classical quality of the texts causes the reader to pay less attention to the effect the illustrations have on the text. But in the novel JPM, where the text is very controversial, the illustrations made with prevalent technique first enter the reader's vision generating only low expectations, but then turn into a contrasting impression instead; this is an active result of the great ingenuity of woodcut art.

The great amount of everyday scenery and objects in the woodcuts even overshadowed the textual description of the 'ways of the world'. The judgement of which category of novels JPM should be counted into belongs to the domain of literary criticism, and it came after the creative process. But in the text, we can find grounds for why it was characterized as 'a novel of manners': one reason is that the author generously made use of popular customs and slang, ditties, novels, folk songs, Daoist exhortations to do good, Buddhist persuasions and songs, including lots of direct quotations. The main characters of the text are taken from the *Water Margin*; they belong to the rising economic middle class of the Song, Yuan, and Ming societies, with a certain distance to the cultured middle class, and although the text is not lacking in elegant scenes or rich and ornate rhetoric, on an ideological level we can still see how classical elites in the noisy world of the novel are losing their voice. At the same time, due to the use of dialects, an impression is created of the text not being particularly elegant. In the woodcuts, however, one can see how the choice and arrangement of everyday scenes is made more tasteful. E.g. in Chapter 1, 'A Hearty Gathering of Ten Brothers' ('Re jie shi xiongdi' 熱結十兄弟), the story is set in a Daoist temple, but in the woodcut it is only symbolized by towering buildings far away and part of a bell visible in the picture; the teahouses, wineshops in numerous chapter titles are simply represented by the words 'Wineshop', and 'Teahouse' on their hanging signs; when the text touches on paintings, they are also specially inscribed on the woodcuts, but 'pictures in the pictures' are mediated not realistically but by symbolic methods; natural landscapes are expressed in the woodcuts by making use of seasonal trees and changing forms of branches and leaves of flowers and grass; if we look closer, we will also note that rosy clouds covering the moon suggest late night. So, rosy clouds reflecting the moon also set off the bustling scene of the night of the Lantern Festival. A great number of interior milieus in the woodcuts make use of symbols as method, such as when the wineshop where He Jiu 何九 accepts a bribe from Ximen Qing conveys its position in a desolate corner of the city, while the houses and courtyards of distinguished families are extensive, often embellished with coiled dragons and other building decorations. Especially when woodcuts picture Ximen Qing's residence and scenes of get-togethers, there appear vases with cherry blossoms, tables, long scroll paintings, and other elements of literati style – these things are quite seldom touched upon by the narrative text.

Epilogue

We know that in Chinese history, already since the elite influence on popular manners during the Song Dynasty, general aesthetic appreciation had developed toward ever greater sophistication. No attention was thus paid to the fact that in culture, the gap between refined and vulgar still existed, a gap that could hardly avoid being unfair, but in JPM woodcuts we see that the boundary between refined and vulgar can be transformed through a switch to another art form. The reality that has been concealed by the leitmotif of the text and its appraisals can emerge through the illustrations, which again are refined: this is exactly how woodcut art exerts an influence on texts. It is indeed as Lu Xun 魯迅 said:

> A so-called creative woodcutter does not imitate, nor does he re-cut, he grasps the knife and directs it to the wood and cuts away – a person from Song, probably Su Dongpo, asked someone to paint plum blossoms to a poem with a line: 'I have a bolt of good silk from the east, please put your brush to it and have a go!' This putting one's brush to it and going ahead is just what creative woodcutting mostly needs; it is different from painting in that a knife replaces a brush, wood replaces paper or silk. Chinese woodcuts, although they are 'embroidered woodblocks', they were for a long time, considered of hardly any worth, only someone who cuts stone seals with an iron pen might come close to that spirit.

> 所謂創作的木刻者，不模仿，不復刻，作者捏刀向木，直刻下去——記得宋人，大約是蘇東坡罷，有請人畫梅詩，有句云：'我有一匹好東絹，請君放筆為直幹！' 這放筆直幹，便是創作的版畫首先所必須，和繪畫的不同，就在以刀代筆，以木代紙或布。中國的刻圖，雖是所謂 '繡梓'，也早已望塵莫及，那精神，惟以鐵筆刻石章者，仿佛近之。

> (Lu Xun 2005: 335)

Woodcutting is different from painting, and painting is different from writing. But they can borrow from each other. This spirit of the 'new woodcut' had of course been brewing since a long time in the ancient tradition of woodcut.

References

Hanan, Patrick D.

1962. 'The Text of the Chin P'ing Mei.' *Asia Major* 9(1): 1–57.

Kong Fanli 孔凡禮

1998. *Su Shi nianpu* 蘇軾年譜 (*Su Shi Chronology*). Vol. 5. Beijing: Zhonghua Shuju 中華書局 (Zhonghua Book Company).

Li Lüyuan 李綠園

1998. *Qiludeng* 歧路燈 (*Lantern at the Crossroads*). Zhengzhou: Zhongzhou Guji Chubanshe 中州古籍出版社 (Zhongzhou Classics Press).

Lu Xun 魯迅

2005. 'Jindai muke xuanji (Yi) Xiao Yin 近代木刻選集（一）小引' (Foreword to *A Selection of Modern Woodcuts* 1). In *Lu Xun quanji* 魯迅全集 (*The Complete Works of Lu Xun*), Vol. 7. Beijing: Renmin Wenxue Chubanshe 人民文学出版社 (People's Publishing House).

Qian Zhongshu 錢鍾書

1988. *Qi zhui ji* 七綴集 (*Seven Compositions*). Shanghai: Shanghai Guji Chubanshe 上海古籍出版社 (Shanghai Classics Press).

Shen Defu 沈德符

2012. *Wanli ye huo bian* 萬曆野獲編 (*Gathered and Edited in the Country during the Wanli Reign Period*). Shanghai: Shanghai Guji Chubanshe 上海古籍出版社 (Shanghai Classics Press).

Shuihu zhuan jiaozhu 水滸傳校注 (*The Annotated Water Margin*)

2009. Annotated by Wang Liqi 王利器. Shijiazhuang: Hebei Jiaoyu Chubanshe 河北教育出版社 (Hebei Educational Publishing House).

Tagore, Rabindranath 泰戈爾

1988. *Taigeer lun wenxue* 泰戈爾論文學 (*Tagore on Literature*). Shanghai: Shanghai Yiwen Chubanshe 上海譯文出版社 (Shanghai Translation Publishing House).

Yuan Hongdao 袁宏道

1981. *Yuan Hongdao ji jiao jian* 袁宏道集校笺 (*Yuan Hongdao: An Annotated Collection*). Shanghai: Shanghai Guji Chubanshe 上海古籍出版社 (Shanghai Classics Press).

Yuan Zhongdao 袁中道

2019. *Kexuezhai ji Wai ji* 珂雪齋集 外集 (*Supplement to Collected Texts from the Jade Snow Studio*). Vol. 9. Shanghai: Shanghai Guji Chubanshe 上海古籍出版社 (Shanghai Classics Press).

Zhao Xianzhang 趙憲章 (ed.)

    2020. *Zhongguo wenxue tuxiang guanxi shi* 中國文學圖像關係史 (*The History of the Relationship between Chinese Literature and Illustration*). Nanjing: Jiangsu Fenghuang Jiaoyu Chubanshe 江蘇鳳凰教育出版社 (Jiangsu Fenghuang Educational Publishing House).

Zhou Wu 周蕪 (ed.)

    1988. *Zhongguo banhua shi tulu* 中國版畫史圖錄 (*A Pictorial Record of the History of Woodcuts in China*). Shanghai: Shanghai Renmin Meishu Chubanshe 上海人民美術出版社 (Shanghai People's Fine Arts Publishing House).

Note on Contributors

Zhang Min 张敏, Ph.D. candidate, Nanjing University; editor, Guangling shushe, Yangzhou, and Nanjing University Press, China.

Marja Kaikkonen is Professor Emerita of Sinology, Stockholm University, Sweden.

CHAPTER 12

The Master Artist of the Newly Re-cut Blocks for the Illustrations of *Jin Ping Mei*

LIU KUN, INTERVIEWED BY ZHANG MIN
Translated by Marja Kaikkonen

Zhang Min Q: What made you choose to work with the engraving of woodcuts? Were you motivated by family traditions or a personal interest?

Liu Kun A: I think it was a personal interest. I was born in Yangzhou 揚州, a famous historical city that was established more than 2500 years ago. In both economic and cultural growth Yangzhou was ahead of the rest of the country; an unprecedented flourishing together with stimulation from salt merchant culture intensified the cultural atmosphere in Yangzhou and spurred on a brisk development of the publishing and printing industries. The place where I spent my childhood was the Old Town of Yangzhou, a district with a concentration of traditional handicrafts and trades. There were also some folk craftsmen, seal engravers and New Year picture makers, among our neighbours, and under the imperceptible influence of what I constantly saw and heard, I grew deeply interested in traditional folk handicrafts such as woodcutting, seal engraving, and New Year pictures.

Q: During your years as an apprentice, how would you characterize the state of the art of wood engraving in China?

A: When I was an apprentice, the art of wood engraving in China was going through a period of renewed appreciation and recovery. Chinese woodblock printing artistry includes Yangzhou printmaking, Jinling 金陵 [Nanjing 南京] sutra engraving and printing, Taohuawu 桃花塢 New Year pictures in Suzhou 蘇州, the Dege Parkhang Sutra Printing Institute 德格印經院 in Sichuan 四川 Province, Rongbaozhai 榮寶齋 watercolour woodcut prints [in Beijing 北京], Yangjiafu 楊家埠 New Year pictures in Weifang 濰坊 [in Shandong 山

The translator wishes to express her warmest thanks to Dr. Mette Siggstedt for her kind help with terminological questions. The notes to this text are added by the translator.

179

東 Province], Nantou 難头 New Year pictures [in Hunan 湖南 Province], Fengxiang 鳳翔 New Year pictures [in Shaanxi 陝西 Province], and Huaxian 滑縣 New Year prints in the stencil technique [in Henan 河南 Province].

Yangzhou is one of the birthplaces of Chinese woodblock printing, and it is also the only city in China where the ancient wood engraving and printmaking craft has been preserved in its entirety. When applications for the status of World Intangible Cultural Heritage were sent in, Yangzhou woodblock printing artistry was the main applicant. From the Qing Dynasty to the Republic of China, the areas that managed to preserve the woodblock printing craft were already very few, only Yangzhou, Beijing, Wuhan 武漢, Nanjing, Xuwan 許灣 in Jiangxi 江西 Province, and Sibao 四堡 in Fujian 福建 Province. After 1949, wood engraving and printmaking were recognized as traditional crafts, and Yangzhou succeeded quite well in preserving and passing on the tradition. This has been particularly true since the year 2000, when the woodblock printing craft was enrolled into the first list of National Intangible Cultural Heritages. Inspired by the national Rare Editions Project, people regained their love for traditional culture and the need to display national characteristics to outsiders. This gave the art of wood engraving an excellent opportunity to recover and develop, and all kinds of activities were conducted with enthusiasm and achieved plenty of results.

In 1978, the Guangling Ancient Books Engraving and Printing Society (*Guangling guji keyin she* 廣陵古籍刻印社) was re-established, and not only managed to re-employ some specialists, but also to train a group of newcomers. That was when I applied to join the training class for engraving and printmaking artistry at Guangling. China and Japan had normalized their diplomatic relations in 1972, and since Yangzhou City had a cultural bond with Japan through Great Master Jianzhen 鑑真 (688–763),[1] the Guangling Society received engraving assignments for ancient books from Japan's Institute for Zen Studies (*Chan wenhua yanjiusuo/Zen bunka kenkyūjo* 禪文化研究所). For example, I participated in the engraving work of the four volumes of *Stretching and Yawning* (*Qian shen gao/Kanshinkō* 欠伸稿)[2] and the 31 volumes of *Collected Engraved Works by Zen Master Baiyin* (*Baiyin chanshi zibi keben jicheng/Hakuin zenji jihitsu kokuhon shūsei* 白隱禪師自筆刻本集成). During my studies and during my work career I have participated in sorting out, conserving, reprinting, and re-engraving a large number of ancient and new books and have tried to contribute my meagre effort to the development and transmission of the artistry of woodblock engraving and printing in our country, and to

---

1   A short presentation of Jianzhen/Ganjin in Japan: www.youtube.com/watch?v=5c4Lv400XlE.

2   17th century work of facsimiles of calligraphy by Kōgetsu Sōgan 江月宗玩.

MASTER ARTIST OF THE NEWLY RE-CUT BLOCKS

the rescue of unique extant copies and rare books. Something that makes me greatly gratified and proud is that in the late 1990s my colleagues and I at the Society made a great effort to lay bare, study, and finally restore the traditional craft of movable type printing.

Q: What kind of threshold does this craft have? Are there mandatory requirements as to scholarship or personality, such as some background in seal engraving or drawing? What did you rely on during your first years as an apprentice – diligence or natural gifts or what?

A: I feel that if one wants to pursue woodblock engraving and printing artistry one must first and foremost ardently love this craft, as this is after all a traditional branch. Today's scientific and technological developments have long since moved the printing business from ink printing through laser printing to 3D printing. Woodblock engraving and printing, on the other hand, belongs to the most traditional printing methods; besides the fact that it uses huge amounts of time, labour and material, it also places high demands on the craftsmanship of the worker. It is not like today's printing industry, where you only need to know how to operate a machine and understand the necessary computer software and that is all there is. If you lack a love for traditional Chinese cultural crafts, you will never be able to persevere in learning, much less carry this on as a profession.

When I was an apprentice, my master used to say that in this art 'three years get you started, five years make you feel familiar, ten years set you achieving'. I have also taught many people, but only very few of them have been able to persist, and the reason is that staying in this profession places tough requirements on you: besides love, you need a lot of patience, and that is very hard to live up to in today's society with its rapid pace. If you want to learn the skills thoroughly, you have to sit down and keep practising, there are no shortcuts whatsoever. When I was an apprentice, the engraving training meant that you would keep cutting all day; every day you simply kept engraving vertical and horizontal strokes on a woodblock. Only when you had mastered the vertical and horizontal ones could you move on to learn other strokes, and only when you had mastered all the individual strokes could you move on to engraving entire characters, and only when you had mastered characters could you start training to engrave pictures. I think the fact that I was able to persevere at that time was due not only to my deep love for the craft but also to the fact that people's thinking at that time was quite unassuming, it was easy to immerse oneself in one single thing that absorbed one.

When using the engraving knife, your left thumb must support the knife blade steadily, and match the swirling (*xuan* 旋), raising (*tiao* 挑), gouging

181

(*wa* 挖), cutting (*qie* 切), etc. movements of the point of the knife. You must maintain firm control of the pressure you direct onto your wrist and fingers, otherwise you risk damaging the woodblock or hurting your fingers. If you cut your finger, it only hurts a little and bleeds a bit. After some years you cannot avoid your left thumb accumulating a callus from all the cuts. Today very few people can tolerate pain or bleeding that can even leave scars and a thick callus.

If you want to learn this handicraft, besides love and patience you also need vigilance. If you damage a woodblock too much during engraving, the whole block will be wasted; especially if you happen to damage it when you are cutting the last character, then the entire block will be discarded as useless, and you have to start again from the beginning.

A complete woodblock engraving and printing process is divided into the following parts: choosing the wood, producing the block, writing the model and proofreading, engraving, printing, and binding. Each stage is very important and requires painstaking practice for days on end. And after painstaking practice you are just at a beginner's level and have the skills, you have not achieved success yet. The reason why an engraving master can be called a master is that he is able to completely re-create other people's characteristic calligraphy and style of painting in the woodblock print. This is something that places heavy demands on the cultural self-improvement and artistic inspiration of those engaged in the craft – faculties that take years to accumulate and polish.

Q: Which school did your master belong to? Have there been changes in the foremost schools these years, or has there just been one main trend all the time?

A: The transmission of tradition within woodblock printing can be divided according to organizational forms, into official engraving (*guan ke* 官刻), commercial engraving (*fang ke* 坊刻), and private engraving (*jia ke* 家刻). The ways in which these have been transmitted are different. Official engraving employed the best woodblock printers in the whole country. During the Kangxi 康熙 period of the Qing Dynasty, Cao Yin 曹寅 (1658–1712), the paternal grandfather of Cao Xueqin 曹雪芹 (1715–1763),[3] received an assignment to establish the Yangzhou Poetry Bureau (*Yangzhou shiju* 揚州詩局) at the Tianning Temple 天寧寺 in Yangzhou. There he assembled the most talented woodblock printers of the nation to engrave and print the *Complete Tang Poems* (*Quan Tang shi* 全唐詩). The history of Yangzhou's official engraving stretches from the Yangzhou Poetry Bureau to the Yangzhou Book Bureau (*Yangzhou shuju* 揚州書局) and to the Huainan Book Bureau (*Huainan shuju* 淮南書局), all of which engraved

---

3   The author of the 18th-century novel *Dream of the Red Chamber* (*Honglou meng* 紅樓夢).

countless books, and whose representative artistry has been transmitted and developed in Yangzhou.

Commercial engraving focused on generating profit. The workshop owner gave employment to established woodblock craftsmen, who concentrated on engraving and printing books and pictures in the workshop. Gradually this resulted in certain workshops developing an engraving and printing style of their own, or, in some areas, in the appearance of various schools of commercial engraving. For example, in the middle of the Republican period in Yangzhou, the Chen Henghe Book Forest (*Chen Henghe shulin* 陳恆和書林), created by Chen Henghe (1883–1937) and his son, was praised as the rising star of Yangzhou commercial engraving.

Among the books engraved in Yangzhou during the Qing Dynasty, the greatest number was produced through private engraving, which also created the largest number of products of the best quality. In Yangzhou, private engraving can be divided into three types. The first is engraving commissioned by Yangzhou salt merchants, the most famous representatives being the 'Ma editions' (*'Ma ban'* 馬版) of the [bibliophile] brothers Ma Yueguan 馬曰琯 (1687–1755) and Ma Yuelu 馬曰璐 (1697–1766) of the Yongzheng 雍正 (1723–1735) and Qianlong 乾隆 (1736–1795) periods of the Qing Dynasty. The second type is engraving for literati, who were authors, bibliophiles, and collators all at the same time. This type of engraving was the most widespread of Yangzhou private engraving. The third type is engraving commissioned by calligraphers or painters, for example the Eight Eccentrics of Yangzhou (Yangzhou Ba Guai 揚州八怪). They personally wrote the texts that were then meticulously engraved onto woodblocks, and thus they brought calligraphy into woodblock printing. This was the case with *Poems by Banqiao* (*Banqiao shichao* 板橋詩鈔), which I re-engraved and printed in 2013: it was a collection of Zheng Banqiao's 鄭板橋 (or Zheng Xie's 鄭燮) (1693–1766) earlier poetry that he had assembled and written down in his own handwriting to be engraved.

After the end of the Qing Dynasty, because of changing times and the blow that modern printing techniques caused, these forms of transmission, together with woodblock printing as such, were declining. In that situation, the 'Yang Gang of Hangji' (*'Hangji Yang Bang'* 杭集揚幫) became the main force in transmitting woodblock printing artistry in Yangzhou. When it comes to succession, my woodblock craft belongs to the Yang Gang of Hangji.

At the end of the Qing and in the early Republic, a large group of woodblock printing craftsmen gathered in Hangji of Yangzhou, including model writers, engravers, printers and binders. Their families had worked with woodblock-printed books for generations and had passed on the techniques from father to son, from son to grandson, with masters training apprentices, apprentices again training apprentices. Whenever someone in Jiangsu or Zhejiang Province needed people for important engraving work, they usually asked these craftsmen to come in a team to do the work. People in the engraving circles called them 'the Yang Gang'. Because the majority of the craftsmen in the Yang Gang were from Hangji, and they were the most skilled and took leading positions, the group was called the Yang Gang of Hangji 杭集揚幫. Their artistry was comprehensive, exquisite, simple and elegant, and during long years of practice and transmission, they cultivated a unique style of their own.

In 1960, the Small Group for Reparation and Binding of Ancient Books (*Gu jiu shu xiubu zhuangding xiaozu* 古舊書修補裝訂小組) was established in Yangzhou. It was later to become the Guangling Ancient Books Engraving and Printing Society. Practically all of their master craftsmen of woodblock printing were successors to the Yang Gang of Hangji. Chen Zhengchun 陳正春, a second-generation leader of the Yang Gang, travelled to Jinling Sutra Engravery (*Jinling ke jing chu* 金陵刻經處) in Nanjing and spent some time there helping them restore the art of woodblock printing.

Yang Gang's first-generation leader was Chen Kailiang 陳開良, Chen Zhengchun's father; both father and son had superior skills in engraving and repair of woodblocks; their outstanding family specialty was engraving of illustrations. Wang Yilong 王義龍 was Chen Kailiang's apprentice, and he had become thoroughly proficient in repairing woodblocks; Master Wang was able to repair old blocks, so they became as new. While I stayed at the Guangling Society, I followed Master Wang Yilong so as to learn the art of woodblock repair.

Chen Yishi 陳義時, Chen Zhengchun's son, was a National Representative Transmitter of the Intangible Cultural Heritage Project of Woodblock Printing Artistry. He was expert in engraving all kinds of character types, particularly Song typeface and Regular script, and developed a profound mastery of the variations in the six different strokes of Song typeface characters. When Master Wang Yilong retired, I became one of the five apprentices of Chen Yishi, and learnt from him the art of engraving.

I have learnt things on a wide scale; I think there are very few people in this country that have truly mastered all of the techniques of block production, engraving, printing and binding. After 2010 I also focused my research on the art of printing, and on my own I mastered and restored the techniques of water-colour block printing (*shuiyin* 水印, *douban* 餖版) and embossed printing (*gonghua* 拱花), gradually establishing and perfecting my own style of artistry.

Q: At what stage of your career did you start engraving *Jin Ping Mei*? How difficult was it, and how was its artistic quality, compared with other projects?

MASTER ARTIST OF THE NEWLY RE-CUT BLOCKS

A: *Jin Ping Mei* was a job I did at a turning point in my engraving career. In early 2013 I finished re-engraving the Ming Dynasty *Old Letter Papers from the Wisteria Studio* (*Luoxuan bian gu jianpu* 蘿軒變古箋譜) and the Qing *Poems by Banqiao*, and in the course of these projects my own artistry improved a lot. Having finished the *Old Letter Papers from the Wisteria Studio* and mastered and restored the techniques of water-colour and embossed printing, I set my heart on perfectly recreating the foremost works in China's woodblock printing history, the *Painting Manual of the Ten Bamboo Studio* (*Shizhuzhai huapu* 十竹齋畫譜) and the *Letter Papers from the Ten Bamboo Studio* (*Shizhuzhai jianpu* 十竹齋箋譜), engraved by Hu Zhengyan 胡正言 (1584–1674) in the Ming Dynasty. But Hu Zhengyan had learnt the art of the Six Script Styles from Li Ruzhen 李如真, and his seal, clerical, regular and running scripts were all perfectly correct and outstanding; besides, he excelled in painting landscapes and human figures, and he excelled even more in flowers and plum blossoms in ink. I felt that I could not yet live up to that level of artistry, so I thought I would first engrave the Ming Chongzhen version of *Jin Ping Mei*, which is contemporaneous with Hu Zhengyan's *Painting Manual of the Ten Bamboo Studio*, and draw lessons from that work.

The Ming Chongzhen version of *Jin Ping Mei*, or *Jin Ping Mei, Newly Engraved and Illustrated, with Commentary* (*Xin ke xiuxiang piping Jin Ping Mei* 新刻繡像批評金瓶梅), also called the *Illustrated Version* (*Xiuxiang ben* 繡像本), differs from the Wanli period version *Re-engraved Jin Ping Mei in Verse and Prose* (*Xin ke Jin Ping Mei cihua* 新刻金瓶梅詞話), also called *Verse and Prose Version* (*Cihuaben* 詞話本), and from the Kangxi period version *The First Marvellous Book Jin Ping Mei, Commented by Zhang Zhupo* (*Zhang Zhupo piping di yi qi shu Jin Ping Mei* 張竹坡批評第一奇書金瓶梅), also called the *Zhang Commentary Version* (*Zhang ping ben* 張評本), in that it includes 200 illustrations with the names of engravers – Liu Yingzu 劉應祖, Liu Qixian 劉啟先, Huang Zili 黃子立 and Huang Ruyao 黃汝耀 and others. These professionals, active during the Chongzhen period, were famous wood engravers from Xin'an 新安 (today's Shexian 歙縣 county in Anhui 安徽 Province). The ancient towers and pavilions in the book are accomplished with utmost precision, elegance, and glee; the style of calligraphy is vigorous and distinct, the lines of the human figures are soft and mellow, the clothing smooth and sumptuous, buildings and stones are forceful and clear – all these elements are an enormous challenge for a master engraver.

Consequently, in addition to the original basic methods of moving the knife, such as pushing (*tui* 推), raising (*tiao* 挑), circling (*yun* 暈), trembling (*chan* 顫), wavering (*yao* 搖), shoveling (*chan* 鏟), scraping (*gua* 刮) and carving sloping lines (*dan*[*dao*] 單[刀]), I adopted the specialized methods of brush

185

movements from Chinese painting: stable (*ping* 平), round (*yuan* 圓), lingering (*liu* 留), heavy (*zhong* 重) and light (*qing* 輕); and then, depending on the material of the woodblock and the contents of the picture, I focused on grasping the form, the structure and the special characteristics of the objects, gave free rein to the effects of the touch of the knife and its trace, and portrayed fully the model of the thing being engraved so as to strengthen its appeal.

Besides, due to the tints of the water-colour prints, their layers of colour, and their consequent charm, if one wants to attain a result practically identical with the original one must have perfect control of the moisture of the woodblock and the paper, and through meticulous matching of blocks, engraving and set printing one can finally create a result with forceful lines, ink, and colour, and the use of colours with the correct moisture so that the tones become neither too deep nor too light. Through the engraving work one also has to display clearly the three-dimensionality of the motif, and skillfully use absence of colour to interpret the relationship between 'concave and convex', 'existing and nonexistent', 'strength and softness', and to completely master 'lightness within depth' and 'depth within lightness' of the colours, so that the picture in its entirety is manifested as simple but elegant. All of these things are difficult to give expression to when engraving and printing any work of plain text.

Q: What kind of principle have you adhered to during the engraving work? Totally identical imitation? And what have been the concrete technical methods and tools for imitation? Or have you, after having formed a concrete impression of the original, recreated it according to your approximate impression? Printing in colour is also a sort of new creation, isn't it? What made you change the black print of the original to coloured set printing? When using coloured set printing, is there a need to choose the ideal scheme, or is there a great degree of freedom and fortuity?

A: Woodblock engraving in itself is both very complicated and has a rather high degree of artistry. For the engraver it means that one must not only grasp the style of calligraphy and the mood of the painting, but also thoroughly understand their structural patterns, and comprehend the writer's style of writing and his brush movements. When engraving, one must be particular about holding the knife in the correct position, and one must concentrate one's mind, watch attentively, start each cut with precision and move the knife steadily, stopping in the middle and defining the beginning and the end of each cut. Especially when engraving pictures, the lines have to be smooth; the facial expressions and hand gestures of the human figures are very subtle, so if the engraver happens to make the slightest deviation from the desired goal, the facial and hand expressions will be altered; for example, if two figures look at

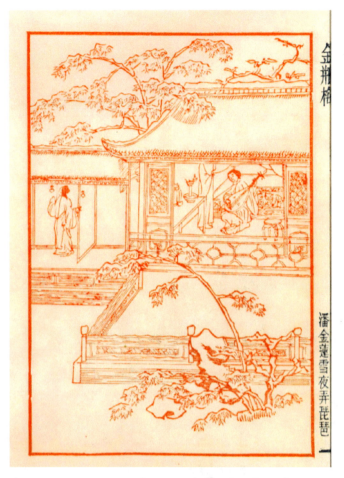

Figure 12.1. Liu Kun, woodcut according to the Chongzhen edition of JPM, Ch. 38b

each other – with the slightest change, their glances will be directed in totally different directions. In Chinese painting, expression of the essential idea (*xieyi* 寫意) is important, and if there is so much as one tiny error the mood will not be expressed, or it will be entirely changed. Therefore, the highest level that a finished engraving can attain is to reproduce the style and features of the original.

Consequently, the only principle that I follow in my engraving work is to restore, to reproduce a total likeness of the original. Re-engraving to reproduce and engraving an original are, after all, two different things. The picture to be re-engraved was once created with a high artistic and technical quality of its own, and my aim is to display it again with all its original qualities. The

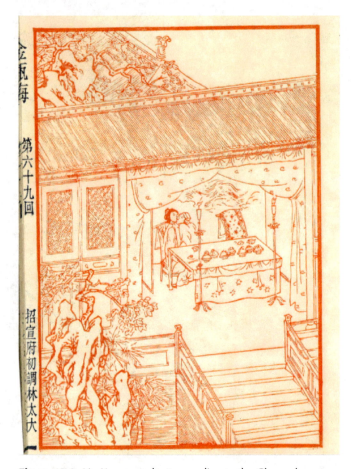

Figure 12.2. Liu Kun, woodcut according to the Chongzhen edition of JPM, Ch. 69a

woodblock prints from the Ming Dynasty are so old that they only exist in paper books, while the original woodblocks have long since disappeared into the long river of history. Through my efforts I hope to make these woodcuts appear anew; that would also be a kind of preservation of ancient books, since if the original is somehow damaged, it can be given new life through the woodcut that I engrave. So I strive with all my ability to make my engravings identical with the originals, not adding a single cut or leaving out a single dot.

Before printing, I had many considerations about changing the black print of the original into coloured set printing. One idea was that using coloured set printing would make the images even more bright and lively, and better highlight the appearance and the sense of contrast of human figures and buildings. Another point of view had to do with the receptivity of the public in our

MASTER ARTIST OF THE NEWLY RE-CUT BLOCKS

present society. A third thought was that by using set printing with colours I would accumulate experience for a later printing of the *Painting Manual of the Ten Bamboo Studio* and the *Letter Papers from the Ten Bamboo Studio*.

Q: Aside from the technical demands with *Jin Ping Mei*, did you and your apprentices practice division of labour or cooperation?

A: I did not cooperate with other people; all the work was done by myself; the engraving and printing took four years altogether to finish.

Q: How much work did *Jin Ping Mei* require? Did it put special demands on the tools you used?

A: The workload was huge as the book has 200 illustrations, and engraving illustrations is much more difficult than plain text engraving. There were no special requirements in relation to engraving tools, just traditional tools for engraving woodblocks such as scrapers (*guatie* 刮鐵), burins (*kedao* 刻刀), ring chisels (*quanzao* 圈鑿 or *wanzao* 剜鑿), chisels (*tixianzao* 剔綫鑿 and *wanyuanzao* 彎圓鑿), large clearing chisels (*da ping chandao* 大平鏟刀) and mallets (*muchui* 木槌). A scraper has a blade at one end – it is a special tool used for preparing the woodblock before the pattern is pasted on it. Burins, or beveled carving knives (*xiekoudao* 斜口刀), have the functions of incising (*fa* 發) and raising (*tiao* 挑). They are used for engraving all kinds of lines, crooked, straight, arched, long or short, coarse or fine, or crisscrossed, according to the requirements, and they come in many different models. *Quanzao* is used for engraving full points and similar symbols. Chisels include the different models *tikongzao* 剔空鑿, flat chisels (*pingkouzao* 平口鑿), and u-shaped gouges (*yuanzao* 圓鑿), all in different sizes; they are supplementary tools of the engraving process and clear out unwanted wood. *Wanyuanzao* is used for trimming contours and cleaning up. *Da ping chandao* are special tools for trimming the stencils of seal-like forms, and for the occasions in woodblock printing process when an area of the woodblock needs to be repaired.

Q: How many times, up to now, have you engraved *Jin Ping Mei*? Do you have further plans to continue engraving *Jin Ping Mei* in the future?

A: So far, I have only engraved *Jin Ping Mei* once. In my future work plans right now *Jin Ping Mei* is not included, since the *Chongzhen Version*, the *Verse and Prose Version* and the *Zhang Commentary Version* have so many volumes and characters that it would take a great deal of mental and physical effort and energy to accomplish it alone. To organize people to do it together, from organization to coordination, and guaranteeing that the end product would have a coherence and integration, would present quite some difficulties. Therefore, for the time being there are no such plans.

189

Note on Contributors

Liu Kun 刘坤 is Master Woodcutter, Shizhuzhai Painting Institute Co. Nanjing; Guangling shushe, Yangzhou, China.

Zhang Min 张敏, Ph.D. candidate at Nanjing University; editor, Guangling shushe, Yangzhou, and Nanjing University Press, China.

Marja Kaikkonen is Professor Emerita of Sinology, Stockholm University, Sweden.

Jin Ping Mei as Forbidden Literature

CHAPTER 13

Jin Ping Mei as Forbidden Fruit

Ban! Burn! Beat! Punish!

MARJA KAIKKONEN

... Niemand will es besitzen, aber jeder hat es, keiner will es gelesen haben,
aber jeder kennt es ...
(Wilhelm Grube 1909: 431)

··· 政府一直將其列為禁書, 而一般讀者的心裡卻視閉門讀禁書為人生
的一大樂事 ···
... governments have always wanted to designate it as a forbidden book,
but in the mind of the general reader, poring over forbidden books on
the sly is one of the greatest pleasures of life ...
(Sun Chao 2021: 66)

Jin Ping Mei 金瓶梅 is a grand piece of Chinese traditional vernacular
literature with a widespread reputation for explicit descriptions of sex.
'These descriptions have caused the first great novel of Chinese morals to be
forbidden, inaccessible to the public at large, although it has been recognized
throughout Chinese literary history as a masterpiece.' (Lévy 2000: 140) The
erotic contents of the book have led to its treatment as an object to condemn,
forbid, destroy, expurgate, and criticize, but also to covet, copy, hide, falsify,
comment, extol and admire. Academic and political discussions have flared up
about whether it demoralizes the people, or whether it should be viewed and
respected as one of China's foremost literary treasures and one of the world's
earliest examples of coherent novel structure. Its defenders have calculated that
only a tiny proportion of the huge book – 20,000 out of one million characters
– deals with sex, while the rest of the work is of high literary and cultural value,
a view that has legitimized expurgation. Its cultural and historical value appears
obvious, as it offers a detailed description of the various activities of a number
of individuals in close interaction with one another in their local community,
their careers, economy, corruption, daily life, joys and sorrows. Ever since the
appearance of JPM, scholars have argued that it has been forbidden not because

of its vulgarity but because it reveals the ways corruption works all through the highest social groups, and because of all the immoral acts of its characters. On the other hand, it also lays strong emphasis on illustrating retribution, how evil deeds do get their punishment in the end – something that should have appeased the faultfinders.

Generations of commentators and researchers have investigated the pros and cons, the bans and expurgations of the novel, and produced a wealth of material to consult. It is indeed difficult to write anything new on this topic. Let me here just briefly summarize the situation of earlier prohibitions of this 'forbidden fruit' and illustrate some more recent cases of how this 'thorn in the flesh' has been handled.

Ban! Burn! Beat! Banish! – Imperial China

The treatment of JPM can partially be explained by the traditional status of fiction in premodern China. JPM is a *xiaoshuo* 小說, a piece of fiction from the late 16th century. At that time the traditional literati attitude toward fiction was contemptuous, a view they adopted through the education system, which for centuries had concentrated on teaching high moral qualities to a select group of men through the study of exemplary literary works – the literary canon – from two millennia. One of the main requirements for respectable texts was that they had to be true. Only that way could they teach and encourage readers to function in a useful way. As fiction per definition is not true, it could not be respected as worthy literature. Further, authoring texts that told the truth was a challenge, while inventing things freely from imagination was seen as something anyone could accomplish – it required no education. Consequently, fiction was seen as mainly inducing adultery and banditry. Earlier fiction writers felt obliged to present their texts as historical (Idema and Haft 1997: 52–60; Kaikkonen 2006: 37–40). This applies to JPM as well, 'retell' as it does a story from the Song Dynasty four centuries earlier. However, its 'historicity' appears to have been so thinly veiled that its contemporaries had no trouble connecting its irony to contemporaneous maleficence.

This kind of understanding of what fiction is and is not prevailed to a great extent up to the 20th century, when it only gradually receded (Kaikkonen 2006: 45–69). This mindset paved the way for a disdainful attitude toward a book like JPM, and it legitimized various sanctions along the way. None of this kept fiction from being consumed as entertainment. While fiction in written form was primarily produced and consumed by members of the elite – the literati – ordinary people, mainly illiterate, were mostly entertained by oral performances of various kinds.

JIN PING MEI AS FORBIDDEN FRUIT

That books have been banned and destroyed all through Chinese history, at least since the Qin Dynasty (秦), is a well-known fact. But looking into the details, it is hard to see the forest for all the trees. The Ming Dynasty (明) was a time when novels flourished, even erotic ones, but apparently not everyone enjoyed them. The first time that JPM was banned seems to have been in 1611, well before the first printed edition that has come down to us, *Jin Ping Mei cihua* 金瓶梅詞話 (JPMCH) (1617). The title appears in a list of forbidden books put out by the Board of Rites during the Ming Wanli (萬曆) period (1573–1620) (Li Mengsheng 2008: 35–6). How effectively the early bans were executed remains unclear.

The Qing Dynasty (清), on the other hand, is notorious for its book bans. Books could be banned when authorities so decided, and at least 20 lists of prohibited novels were circulated during the dynasty (Song Shinan 2017: 100).[1] In 1714, an addition was made to *The Great Qing Code* (*Da Qing lüli* 大清律例 2010), which banned the sale of obscene novels (Ma 1980: 203, 212). *The Code* decreed that the sale of such novels was strictly forbidden. When discovered, both the woodblocks and books would be confiscated and burnt. Were an official found guilty of authoring or commissioning printing of such books,

> he would be dismissed from office. Were he a military man, he would be flogged 100 blows with heavy bamboo and banished to a distance of 3000 li.[2] Anyone who sold such books in a market would be sentenced to 100 blows and three years of penal servitude, and those who bought such books for reading would [also] be flogged 100 blows 係官革職軍民杖一百流三千里市賣者杖一百徒三年買看者杖一百 (*Da Qing lüli* 2010: 256.02).

The Qianlong emperor 乾隆 (r. 1736–1796) decreed further that even renting out such books was forbidden: anyone who rented them publicly should be punished in the same way as those who sold them; were he an official, the first time he would be fined six months' salary, the second time one year's salary, and the third time he would be demoted one rank and removed to another post (Yang Hongtai 1991: 27). In practice, the punishments were often far more severe, depending on the emperors' or censors' whims, and could be the death penalty (Wang Fan-sen 2016: 634).

Besides, it was not only imperial decrees that prohibited the availability of certain books:

---

1   The main object of bans on the part of the Qing emperors was not, however, pornography but books that referred to the Manchus in negative terms.

2   Today 3000 li equals 1500 km.

[...] officials were responsible for the protection and, if possible, the improvement of public morals. They had – and used – the power to censor the books, plays, and so on that the people under their administration were likely to come in contact with, and to punish anyone involved in the performance or dissemination of material they believed to be subversive to public morality. (Johnson 1985: 48)

As many as over 150 'obscene' books, probably mainly works of fiction, were banned and destroyed, and more than one hundred persons received punishments (Yang Qi 2006: 57). Of course, the bans did not apply to everyone. Some research claims that the Kangxi emperor 康熙, who prohibited 'obscene' novels, allowed his brother to translate the work into Manchu (Xiu Yun 秀雲 2015: 194–6; Egerton 1988 vol. 1: x). And the Qianlong emperor's seal can be found on a JPM picture book ('Wan Qing jin shu zhengce ji dui wenxue chuban de yingxiang' n.d.: 2).

There seems to be agreement that the bans proved ineffective. Handwritten copies certainly continued to circulate in private hands, while much of the printing and sales went underground to satisfy the demand, which remained brisk. Booksellers used various tricks to avoid destruction of the valuable wood blocks. If the newest blocks had to be handed in, they used older blocks to continue printing. Another favourite method was to change the title of the book into something different; this was effective, as the inspectors had long lists of books to take care of and could not possibly read all of them. JPM is known to have been printed with titles such as *Illustrated Eight Talents in Verse and Prose* (*Xiuxiang ba caizi cihua* 繡像八才子詞話), *Number Four of the Four Big Marvellous Books* (*Si da qishu di si zhong* 四大奇書第四種), *The First Marvellous Book Newly Engraved Illustrated Romance* (*Xin juan hui tu di yi qishu zhongqing zhuan* 新鐫繪圖第一奇書鍾情傳), *Lessons of Polygamy* (*Duo qi jian* 多妻鑒), and *Corrected and Annotated Collected Lessons of Polygamy* (*Jiao zheng jia pi duo qi jian quanji* 校正加批多妻鑒全集) (Song Shinan 2017: 100). The printers could also add a false mark of passed imperial inspection, *jingben* 京本, to pretend that their version was officially approved (Zhang Xia 2014: 15). At the same time, expurgated editions of JPM started appearing. What was possibly the earliest one was a shortened version from the Jiaqing 嘉慶 period (1796–1820), titled *The Re-Engraved Marvellous Book Jin Ping Mei* (*Xin ke Jin Ping Mei qi shu* 新刻金瓶梅奇書) (Zi Yang 1985: 95).

As local officials did not only execute imperial orders in different ways but also declared bans of their own,[3] the penalties must have varied a lot from place

---

3   One of the most ambitious officials was Ding Richang 丁日昌 (1823–1882), Provincial Governor in Jiangsu 1867–1870. See Zhang Xiansheng 1994.

to place and time to time. During late Qing in Shanghai, where foreign influence was strong, traditional punishments were changed into imprisonments and fines. In 1907, a man named Zhao Guangyao 赵广耀 was caught selling JPM: he was fined 10 silver dollars and his books were burnt (Zhao Xingqin 2016: 171).

The popular support for bans had always been nourished by stories circulating about the cruel fates that writers, printers and sellers of forbidden books had met with, or conversely, the great (financial) luck that had befallen individuals who had burnt banned books. As a sign of modern times, in the late 19th century such stories started appearing in newspapers (Zhao Xingqin 2016: 171).

Ban! Punish! Bowdlerize! – Republican China

The Republic of China exercised censorship widely and actively, but the main object of this was politically sensitive works. The prevalent moral outlook, however, was conservative, while there was a widening market for JPM. It took quite some time before any national regulation was in place, so generally speaking Qing practices continued. This meant lists of banned books – in which JPM was usually included – and inspections. Two bookdealers in Fuzhou Street, Shanghai, of Laiqingge 來青閣 and Cuihua 粹華 bookshops, were in 1922 apprehended selling JPM and other 'obscene' books, and were consequently arrested and fined 50 silver dollars each, besides having their books confiscated and burnt. In another case two men, He Songyu 何松玉 and Ma Ronggen 馬榮根, had set up a book stall at Baxianqiao in the French Concession in 1926 and sold JPM and other 'obscene' books. They were imprisoned, fined 50 silver dollars, and had their books confiscated (Zhao Xingqin 2016: 171).

A wealth of expurgated editions, at least six or seven different versions, appeared in the early 1900s. In 1916 Cunbaozhai 存寶齋 put out *The Illustrated Authentic Jin Ping Mei* (*Hui tu zhen ben Jin Ping Mei* 繪圖真本金瓶梅), set in lead type, and possibly a reprint of an 1864 version. Another edition, *Ancient Version of Jin Ping Mei* (*Guben Jin Ping Mei* 古本金瓶梅), possibly a reprint of the above version, was published in Shanghai in 1926 (Zi Yang 1985: 96).

In 1931, an unknown, old block printed version of JPM, *Re-cut Jin Ping Mei in Verse and Prose* (*Xin ke Jin Ping Mei cihua* 新刻金瓶梅詞話) was discovered in Shanxi 山西 province, causing a sensation. In Beiping 北平, a photoprint of 104 numbered copies was soon accomplished, naturally for a limited circle, members of which had to pay for it beforehand. Such a small number of books was bound to lead to pirating, and in Shanghai, Ping Jinya 平襟亞, the head of Zhongyang Shudian 中央書店, got hold of a copy and in 1934 made a reprint of 100 copies, identical to the Beiping ones. Since the book was forbidden, the sales had to be kept secret, and the deal was not very profitable (Sun Chao 2021: 66).

Zheng Zhenduo 鄭振鐸, at the time editor for a book series, was well aware of both the cultural and commercial value of JPM and wanted to make the book more available. He therefore edited and published an expurgated version, serialized in the World Library (Shijie wenku 世界文庫) put out by Shenghuo shudian 生活書店. Unfortunately, production was interrupted when only 33 chapters of the book had come out (Sun Chao 2021: 66, 68).

The commercial value of an expurgated JPM attracted others as well. Two publishers, the Shanghai Journal Company (Shanghai Zazhi Gongsi 上海雜誌公司) and the Central Bookstore (Zhongyang Shudian 中央書店), starting out as competitors but ending up cooperating, both published in late 1935 a bowdlerised version of JPMCH, annotated by Shi Zhecun 施蟄存, a well-known essayist. Both editions were illustrated with old woodcuts and included in fancy book series at each company, which further enhanced the legitimate air of the publication. The places where text had been censored were marked with the number of missing characters. The price was kept low, only 1,5 yuan for the whole set. The success was immediate and enormous; both companies put out several reprints throughout the 1940s, and further publishers followed suit (Sun Chao 2021: 67).

Another economic success was the publication of the expurgated parts of the JPMCH. Ping Jinya was the first to put the little volume on the market, titling it *An Appendix to the Expurgated Parts of* Jin Ping Mei (Jin Ping Mei *shanwen buyi* 金瓶梅刪文補遺). The Shanghai Journal Company marketed a similar volume, *The Little Book of the Expurgated* Jin Ping Mei (Jin Ping Mei *shanben xiao ce* 金瓶梅刪本小冊). These books could not be sold openly, but they made good business. The volume could be given a cover with advertisements for medicines and made available only for those who had already bought or ordered the JPMCH (Sun Chao 2021: 67, 69).

Hide! Fake! Restrict! Bowdlerize! Extort! – People's Republic of China (PRC)

Did JPM exist at all? The writer Sun Li 孫犁 has pointed out that the literary histories of the PRC left out any mention of JPM, nor was the book presented in literature classes at universities. Professors treated it as a closely guarded secret, although in private many were curious to read it, while too embarrassed to ask to borrow it (*Du tianxia* 2012: 64).

In the early PRC, no one dared to publish JPM until Mao Zedong 毛澤東 had encouraged it. Mao's comments on JPM are cherished even today: who else would have dared to do it? At a 1957 meeting with high-level cadres, Mao is quoted as having said: 'JPM can be used for reference, but the episodes where

JIN PING MEI AS FORBIDDEN FRUIT

women are humiliated are bad. Province Party secretaries can have a look at it.' (*Du tianxia* 2012: 64; Song Chundan 2016: 69). This was the start of a series of publications with very restricted distribution and with censorship. No one seemed to ask the question why only high cadres could read 'harmful' literature.

In November 1957, after consultations with the ministries of Culture and Propaganda, the People's Publishing House (Renmin wenxue chubanshe 人民文學出版社), using a fake name, 'Publishing House for Ancient Literary Works' (Wenxue guji kanxingshe 文學古籍刊行社), put out an unexpurgated photo printed JPMCH in 2,000 sets of 21 volumes. It was based on *Re-Engraved Jin Ping Mei in Verse and Prose* (*Xin ke Jin Ping Mei cihua* 新刻金瓶梅詞話), commissioned in 1933 and considered to represent the oldest text version of JPM in the PRC. The publisher stated that the book was produced 'for researchers of classical novels'. The book could be sold to people in or above 'the rank of vice ministers, province vice party secretaries, well-known full professors in universities and research units and other famous people in the cultural sphere. The names of buyers were to be registered'. Zhou Enlai 周恩來 demanded that the editor-in-chief of the publisher must sign every purchase. The project was shrouded in secrecy; not even the editors of the People's Publishing House were allowed to read the book, much less to buy it. It came to be called the 'high cadre edition' (*gaoganban* 高幹版) (Zhang Yuanfang 2012: 30; Song Chundan 2016: 69), or the 'minister version' (*buzhangben* 部長本) (*Du tianxia* 2012: 64).

When the People's Publishing House received permission in the 1980s to reprint the 1957 book, a market-minded strategy was applied to restrict access: the book was priced at 2000 RMB.[4] People of the rank of senior editors and above were allowed to buy the book. Another reprint in 1991 could be bought by people with the professional rank of provincial and city office leader or above, with the support of a letter of introduction from their work unit proving that the purchase was for academic purposes. It could not be sold abroad, and each purchase had to be signed by the director of the publishing house (Song Chundan 2016: 70; *Du tianxia* 2012: 66). A further reprint in 2013 was priced at 3000 RMB.

In 1957 Mao had suggested to Zhou Yang 周揚 that he tell the People's Publishing House to start planning an expurgated version of JPM, but this was delayed by a multitude of political campaigns. Only after 1978 did a specialist of classical literature, Dai Hongsen 戴鴻森, edit a collated version of JPMCH, in which sexually explicit parts were cut out, paragraphs separated, and punctuation added. Over 19,000 characters were deleted, and notes were added to mark the deletions. The publisher applied to the Chinese Communist

---

4   In 1985, the average annual income of employees in state units was 1213 RMB. Wikipedia.

199

Party Central Committee to publish 20,000 volumes of the 'clean' version (*jieben* 潔本), but Deng Liqun 鄧力群 approved only 10,000 volumes. Set in simplified characters, they came out in 1983,[5] and were priced at 12 RMB. Dai Hongsen stated that the sexual descriptions could harm young people's bodies and minds and contaminate 'mental hygiene' in society (Song Chundan 2016: 70; *Du tianxia* 2012: 65), a formulation that has become the standard conservative argument against JPM. Despite expurgation, access to this book was very restricted: internal distribution limited to persons of the rank of province or city office leader, members of All-China Federation of Writers, and people working with classical literature. All purchases had to be supported by identification documents (*Du tianxia* 2012: 65).

Around this time, a publisher in Xi'an put out a JPM picture-story book but received a punishment (Song Chundan 2016: 71). In May 1988, Han Yingshan 韓英珊, a writer in the army, abridged – 'disinfected' – JPM into *Jin Ping Mei Stories* (*Jin Ping Mei gushi* 金瓶梅故事), and published it in a journal.[6] The matter was brought to the attention of the authorities, who punished the author so that he lost his military status, and the journal was discontinued. However, Han did not give up. He added more stories, and convinced the Writers Publishing House (Zuojia Chubanshe 作家出版社) to publish it. The book was printed in 300,000 copies, and was on its way to bookshops when it was stopped. The writer Cong Weixi 叢維熙 was then the supervisor at the publishing house, and he wrote an open letter to the Press and Publication Administration (Xinwen Chubanshu 新聞出版署), which summoned a meeting of experts. The outcome was that the book had 'faults' but it was not a 'bad book' or a 'pornographic book', so the author should not be punished. The book itself would be dealt with in 'low key' and distributed internally (Yan Zhen 1993: 59. Song Chundan 2016: 71).

Only gradually were more versions allowed to be published. When, in 1989, Qilu Press (Qilu Shushe 齊魯書社) printed an uncensored, reset version of *Jin Ping Mei, Newly Carved and Illustrated, with Commentary* (*Xin kan xiuxiang piping Jin Ping Mei* 新刻繡像批評金瓶梅), the Shandong provincial Press and Publication Department was so concerned about the work that they posted police guards outside the publishing house, which led to ironic comments in the media: printing JPM was more secret than printing university-entrance exam questions! This version, 8,000 sets, was made available to people with the rank of associate professor or above, with work unit identification card and

---

5 Song 2016, 70, gives the year 1985. Several other details differ in the sources.

6 It was published in the Shaanxi 陝西 literary journal *Spirit of the Sword* (*Jianhun* 劍魂) 1985 No. 1.

JIN PING MEI AS FORBIDDEN FRUIT

a letter of introduction from the unit (Song Chundan 2016: 71; *Du tianxia* 2012: 66). When Qilu Press reapplied for another print run of 8,000 sets, the national Press and Publication Administration turned down the application: 'There are enough of this book for the needs of research; further copies would flow into society and poison young people' (Song Chundan 2016: 71).

In 1993, a lively debate broke out after Cao Sibin 曹思彬 published an article in which he wished that JPM could be found on bookstore shelves just like *Dream of the Red Chamber* (*Honglou meng* 紅樓夢). Soon the People's Publishing House reprinted the 'clean version' of JPM and changed it from 'internal distribution' to public access, which finally brought it to the shelves of Xinhua 新華 bookstores all over the country (*Du tianxia* 2012: 66).

After the Tiananmen massacre on 4 June 1989, the atmosphere in the PRC was tense and this led to various state measures for increased control. One of them was the 'Crack down on pornography and illegal publishing' (*Sao huang da fei* 掃黃打非) campaign. It began with a telephone meeting organized by the Central Ministry of Propaganda on 24 August 1989 and resulted in what is called today the 'National small group for "crackdown on pornography" work' (*Quanguo 'sao huang' gongzuo xiaozu* 全國'掃黃'工作小組). The group was made up of representatives from the Ministry of Propaganda, the Press and Publication Administration, the Ministries of Culture, of Radio, Film and Television, of Railways, of Post and Telecommunications, the State Administration of Industry and Commerce, the General Administration of Customs, and the Beijing municipal government (Xu Huansheng 1998). This was the start of a huge, institutionalized organization that would become permanent and extend its activities all over the country.[7]

During this protracted campaign, JPM has appeared in various contexts. In the early 1990s, an editor of *Chengdu Evening News* (*Chengdu Wanbao* 成都晚報) named Wu Hong 吳紅, who had published JPM research, got together with another writer, Deng Shuxun 鄧樹勛, and the owner of a printing shop, and reprinted 2,000 sets of JPMCH from an original by Hong Kong Taiping Shuju 太平書局. This was a photoprint of the uncensored Wanli engraved version. It is unclear whether Taiping had authorized the printing, but Wu is said to have had a book number, and the printing was done in the name of a *Jin Ping Mei* Research Association. But then suddenly the *Sao huang* campaign started, Wu was deemed to have pirated the book, and he ended up in jail for years. Another case was Zhang Jun 張軍, a book seller in Liaoning 遼寧, who

---

7   Its work can today be followed from its website, *Zhongguo Sao huang da fei wang* 中國掃黃打非網 (China Net for Crackdown on Pornography and Illegal Publishing), www.shdf.gov.cn.

pirated a large number of copies of JPM and was therefore executed (Song Shinan 2017: 101).

With the Chinese Copyright Law of 1991 and the arrival of the internet in 1994, much of the work of the group has since then focused on electronic publications – and still does. As JPM has been adapted for film at least four times since 1968, all of them outside the PRC,[8] there have been many cases of millions of videos, VCDs, and DVDs being pirated in or smuggled into China, mostly by groups active in Guangdong. For example, in one case, in 2002–2003, a man named Chen Songbo 陳松波 imported 11.3 million DVDs, of which 7.5 million were 'obscene and pornographic', while the rest, DVDs of JPM and *Xi Shi* 西施, were 'illegal'. He had managed to sell 5.07 million DVDs by the time he was caught, earning merely 0,07 RMB per product. But since the number of DVDs involved was enormous, he could expect a harsh punishment, confiscation of his property, and years in jail (Quanguo 2004). Often the confiscated merchandize was publicly destroyed by bulldozers. Cases such as this appear to mean that JPM's reputation sells even if the contents are non-sensational – or perhaps the buyers thought they would be.

Today JPM is by no means 'liberated' from the censors' opinions and actions. Just as it was in the past, price is used to restrict the circulation of versions of JPM. This applied to a reprint of a JPM cartoon *Jin Ping Mei in Pictures* (*Jin Ping Mei quan tu* 金瓶梅全圖) by Cao Hanmei 曹涵美, who in 1936 started drawing it for the Shanghai journal *Cartoons of Our Times* (*Shidai manhua* 時代漫畫). The war interrupted the project, and it was only in 1943 that the National News and Book Printing Company (Guomin xinwen tushu yinshua gongsi 國民新聞圖書印刷公司) was able to produce the entire series. A reprint was made in 2002 by Zhejiang People's Publishing House (Zhejiang renmin chubanshe 浙江人民出版社) after the General Administration of Press and Publication (Xinwen chuban zongshu 新聞出版總署) had given its permission to publish a limited edition of a 'luxurious version aimed at collectors' (Zhu Shuirong 2003: 27). It may be that the printing paper was fancy and the work exquisite, but the price for the set of 10 small volumes was indeed intimidating: 1800 RMB (Zhang Qiming, 2003: 26).

JPM continues to cause controversy wherever it appears. During the period 2006–2010, a heated debate ensued when two places in Shandong 山東, Yanggu county 陽谷 and Linqing city 臨清, made or were planning to make

---

8   In 1968 in Japan as *The Concubines*; in 1974 in Hong Kong by Li Han-hsiang as *The Golden Lotus*; in 1982 in South Korea by Kim Ki-young as *Ban Geum-ryeon* (Pan Jinlian); and in 2008 in Hong Kong by Qian Wenqi as *The Forbidden Legend Sex and Chopsticks* (wikipedia.org/wiki/Jin_Ping_Mei).

JIN PING MEI AS FORBIDDEN FRUIT

huge investments in JPM theme parks (Xiao Fuxing 2006). Yanggu, the place where Wu Song killed the tiger, had in 2003 invested 30 million RMB in Lion Tower Tourist City, where a 'JPM Culture Area' was the main attraction, together with a 'Shuihu Culture Area' and a 'Song Dynasty Culture Area'. Pan Jinlian 潘金蓮 was the mascot of the JPM Culture Area and could be seen as a wax statue, together with Ximen Qing 西門慶, at their first meeting in Auntie Wang's teahouse, opposite Wu Dalang's 武大郎 house, next to Ximen Qing's pharmacy, salt, silk, and pawn shops (He Yong 2006a).

Since some scholars agreed that Linqing was the place where the JPM story occurred, the town, with their help, came up with a 5-year plan to increase tourism by building a 'JPM Culture City', where Ximen Qing's house with its seven courtyards, Auntie Wang's tea house, Wu Dalang's bun shop, a JPM wax cabinet, a cultural exhibition hall and a centre for international conferences would entice visitors. There would be performances of Ximen Qing's and Pan Jinlian's first meeting, and of Wu Da catching the paramour, where tourists could get to play the roles for a fee. As the main target group was newlyweds, there would also be a 'Newlyweds' Mandarin Duck Tower' with 'sex education facilities' where 'newlyweds could live, learn and experience' (He Yong 2006a).

After some rounds of fierce opposition with various arguments, the province and the two localities explained their stand. Shandong pointed out that development of tourism had been decentralized, and that all places were encouraged to make use of their local cultural capital, albeit of a 'sound' nature. It also remarked that it was rather a question of 'Shuihu' culture, but that the province would 'strengthen its guidance'. Linqing pointed out that so far they only had a plan, while Yanggu promised to adapt its guides and information to 'mainstream values' (He Yong 2006.07.21).[9] Not all the locals were convinced, either, even though 69% of them thought that the stories in JPM 'can be counted as history'. Local interviewees agreed that the government needed to have a 'moral bottom line' (Qin Junyong 秦俊勇 2006: 53–54).

Later, some more dispassionate voices declared that the localities involved were poor and lacked resources to improve people's lives, so the local leaders ended up in a desperate search for ways of economic development, which the central government strongly encouraged. In July 2010, the Ministry of Culture and the State Cultural Relics Bureau declared that it was forbidden to use

---

9 A Yanggu homepage video, 'The Yanggu Home of Wu Dalang' (Yanggu Wu Dalang jia 陽谷武大郎家) presents all the buildings, constructed in 'Song style', where the story took place, such as where Wu Dalang 武大朗 was poisoned, Ximen Qing and Pan Jinlian 潘金蓮 killed, as well as Ximen Qing's pharmacy where the arsenic came from, his pawn shop, silk store, etc. See baike.baidu.com/item/阳谷县/2461704.

203

'negative' historical or fictional characters in the development of tourism projects (Zhang He 2010).

JPM's reputation seems to be incurable. To an observer it seems that a very conservative attitude towards sex still prevails in many parts of Chinese society, despite the ubiquity of sex in urban popular culture. With the development of a greater tolerance toward popular culture in the past decades, and a more modern attitude towards sex as one aspect of culture, one might expect the critical views on JPM to have abated. Scholars of history or literature who study JPM often find many positive aspects of the book, in relation to its description of manners, material culture, even sexual culture, religion etc., and its many literary merits. However, many academics still today end their articles on JPM with a warning about its negative effects on the morals of the general public. It is conceivable that this is done to ward off more conservative criticism. Whatever those reasons may be, *Jin Ping Mei* remains as sensitive as a thorn in the flesh.

References

Da Qing lüli 大清律例 (*The Great Qing Code*)

2010. Available at <u>kuscholarworks.ku.edu/bitstream/handle/1808/3635/ qingcode00.pdf?sequence=1&isAllowed=y</u> Downloaded 2021.12.10.

Du tianxia bianjibu 读天下编辑部 (Editorial Department of *Du tianxia*)

2012. '*Jin Ping Mei* dangnei zhubu jiejin 60 nian《金瓶梅》党内逐步解禁 60 年' (60 Years of Unprohibiting *Jin Ping Mei* within the Party). *Du Shu Wenzhai* 读书文摘 (*Book Readers' Digest*) 1 November: 63–68. Originally published in *Du Tianxia* 读天下 (*Reading the World*) 14.

Egerton, Clement

1988. *The Golden Lotus.* 4 vols. Singapore: Graham Brash (PTE) Ltd.

Grube, Wilhelm

1909 [1902]. *Geschichte der chinesischen Litteratur.* Leipzig: Amelang.

He Yong 何勇

2006a. 'Shandong liang di zheng xiang jie *Jin Ping Mei* kaifa wenhua lüyou yinfa zhengyi 山东两地争相借《金瓶梅》开发文化旅游引发争议' (Two Locations in Shandong in Strife Over Use of *Jin Ping Mei* for Tourism Development Cause Controversy). *Renmin Ribao* 人民日报 (People's Daily) 19 July.

2006b. 'Shandong youguan fangmian huiying: Dujue bu jiankang lüyou xiangmu 山东有关方面回应杜绝不健康旅游项目' (Response from Concerned Parties in Shandong: Stop Unsound Tourism Projects). *Renmin Ribao* 人民日报 (People's Daily) 21 July.

JIN PING MEI AS FORBIDDEN FRUIT

Idema, Wilt and Lloyd Haft

1997. *A Guide to Chinese Literature*. Ann Arbor: Center for Chinese Studies, University of Michigan.

Johnson, David

1985. 'Communication, class and consciousness in late imperial China.' In Johnson, D., A.J. Nathan and E. S. Rawski (eds), *Popular Culture in Late Imperial China*. Berkeley, Los Angeles, London: University of California Press., pp. 34–72

Kaikkonen, Marja

2006. 'Becoming literature: Views of popular fiction in twentieth-century China.' In Anders Pettersson (ed.), *Notions of Literature Across Times and Cultures,* pp. 36–69. Vol. 1 of Gunilla Lindberg-Wada (ed.), *Literary History: Towards a Global Perspective*, (4 vols.). Berlin, New York: Walter de Gruyter.

Lévy, André

2000. *Chinese Literature, Ancient and Classical*. Bloomington and Indianapolis: Indiana University Press.

Li Mengsheng 李梦生

2008. *Jinhui xiaoshuo yetan* 禁毁小说夜谭 (Evening Talks on Prohibited Novels). Shanghai: Shanghai Shudian Chubanshe.

Ma, Tai-loi

1980. 'Novels prohibited in the literary inquisition of Emperor Ch'ien-lung, 1722–1788.' In Yang, Winston L. Y. and Curtis P. Adkins (eds), *Critical Essays on Chinese Fiction*. Hong Kong: The Chinese University Press, pp. 201–212.

Qin Junyong 秦俊勇

2006. 'Shandong Yanggu: Zhengfu kaifa *Jin Ping Mei*' 山东阳谷：政府开发"金瓶梅" (Yanggu, Shandong: Government Will Develop *Jin Ping Mei*). *Xiao Kang* 小康 (*Comfortable Life*) 9: 52–54.

Quanguo 全国

2004. 'Quanguo zui dazong yinhui seqing chubanwu an tiqi gongsu 全国最大宗淫秽色情出版物案提起公诉' (Public Charge Brought to Largest National Case of Obscene and Pornographic Publications). *Zhongguo sao huang da fei wang* 中国扫黄打非网 (China Net for Crackdown on Pornography and Illegal Publishing) 18 March. Available at www.shdf.gov.cn. Downloaded 2022.01.08.

Song Chundan 宋春丹

2016. '"Jin shu" *Jin Ping Mei* de tuomin zhi lü ' 禁书"《金瓶梅》的脱敏之旅' (The Desensitization of the 'Forbidden Book' *Jin Ping Mei*). *Dong xi nan bei* 东西南北 (*East West South North*) 15 December: 69–71. Slightly abridged from original in *Zhongguo xinwen zhoukan* 中国新闻周刊 (*Chinese News Weekly*) 12 October 2016: 778. Available at kknews.cc/culture/jvolzge.html. Downloaded 2021.12.07.

Song Shinan 宋石男

2017. '*Jin Ping Mei* chuban xiao shi: Shijie zheme da, xiangyao kandao quanben *Jin Ping Mei* bing bu nan 金瓶梅出版小史: 世界這麼大, 想要看到全本金瓶梅並不難' (A Short History of the Publication of *Jin Ping Mei*: In a World This Big, It Is Not At All Hard to Get to Read the Entire *Jin Ping Mei*). *Zhongguo Qiyejia* 中國企業家 (*Chinese Entrepreneur*) 20 January: 100–101.

Sun Chao 孙超

2021. '1930 niandai *Jin Ping Mei* cihuaben de paiyin chuban ji qi yiyi 1930 年代《金瓶梅》词话本的排印出版及其意义' (The Course and Significance of *Jin Ping Mei* Published in Shanghai in 1930s). *Zhongguo wenxue yanjiu* 中国文学研究 (*Chinese Literary Research*) 4: 65–70.

'Wan Qing jin shu zhengce ji dui wenxue chuban de yingxiang' 晚清禁书政策及对文学出版的影响 (Late Qing Book Banning Policy and Its Effect on Literary Publishing), n.d. Available at LunWenData.Com论文网.m.lunwendata.com/show.php?id=68114. Downloaded 2021.12.10.

Wang Fan-sen

2016. 'Political pressures on the cultural sphere in the Ch'ing period.' In Willard J. Peterson (ed.), *The Cambridge History of China* Vol. 9, Cambridge: Cambridge University Press, pp. 606–648.

Xiao Fuxing 肖复兴

2006. 'Hai you duoshao "wenhua" ke zaota 还有多少"文化"可糟蹋' (How Much More 'Culture' Is There to Ravage). *Renmin Ribao* (People's Daily) 21 July.

Xiu Yun 秀云

2015. 'Man yi *Jin Ping Mei* yanjiu pingshu 满译《金瓶梅》研究述评' (A Review of Research on the Manchu Translation of *Jin Ping Mei*). *Chifeng xueyuan xuebao* 赤峰学院学报 (*Journal of Chifeng University*) 1: 194–6.

Xu Huansheng 徐焕生

1998. 'Li ci quanguo "sao huang" "da fei" huiyi' 历次全国"扫黄" 打非' 会议' (All the Past National Meetings of 'Crackdown on Pornography', 'Crackdown on Illegal Publishing'). *Chuban Faxing Yanjiu* 出版发行研究 (*Publishing Research*) 81 (Feb.): 16–17.

Yan Zhen 严真

1993. 'Xiao yi *Jin Ping Mei* chuban zhi kanke 小议《金瓶梅》出版之坎坷' (On the Frustrations of Publishing *Jin Ping Mei*). *Henan Tushuguan xuekan* 河南图书馆学刊 (*Henan Journal of Library Science*) 2: 58–59.

Yang Hongtai 杨鸿台

1991. 'Qingdai jinhui "yinshu" deshi yu dangqian "saohuang" douzheng de sikao' 清代禁毁"淫书"得失与当前"扫黄"斗争的思考' (Some reflections on the successes and failures of Qing Dynasty bans and destructions of "obscene books" and the contemporary struggle to "crack down on pornography"). *Fan zui yanjiu* 犯罪研究 (*Chinese Criminology Review*) 5:26–30.

Yang Qi 杨杞

2006. 'Qingchao qianqi dui yinshu de chajin 清朝前期对淫书的查禁' (Early Qing Dynasty Suppression of Obscene Books). *Falü Wenxian Xinxi yu Yanjiu* 法律文献信息与研究 (*Legal Document News and Research*) 2: 65, 57.

Zhang He 张贺

2010. 'Mingren guli zhi zheng weihe yu yan yu lie? 名人故里之争为何愈演愈烈?' (Why Is the Fight Over Notables' Domiciles Worsening?). *Renmin Ribao* 人民日报 (*People's Daily*) 29 October.

Zhang Qiming 张奇明

2003. 'Cangjia jingpin – *Jin Ping Mei quan tu* 藏家精品—《金瓶梅全图》' (Artwork for Collectors – *Jin Ping Mei Picture Story Book*). *Meishu zhiyou* 美术之友 (*Friends of Art*) 1: 26.

Zhang Xia 张霞

2014. 'Qing mo xiaoshuo chajin ji minjian shufang de huiying 清末小说查禁及民间书坊的回应' (Late Qing Bans on Fiction and Private Booksellers' Response). *Qingchun suiyue* 青春岁月 (*Time of Youth*) 9: 15.

Zhang Xiansheng 张弦生

1994. 'Qingdai chajin "yinci xiaoshuo" yu Ding Richang de tongchiling 清代查禁"淫词小说"与丁日昌的通饬令' (Qing Dynasty Ban on 'Obscene Novels' and Ding Richang's General Order). *Zhongzhou xuebao* 中州学报 (*Zhongzhou Academic Journal*) 6: 90–92.

Zhang Yuanfang 张远方

2012. '*Jin Ping Mei* jiejin 60 nian neimu 《金瓶梅》解禁 60 年之内幕' (The Inside Story of Lifting the 60-Year Ban on *Jin Ping Mei*). *Wanbao wencui* 晚报文萃 (*Evening Paper Digest*) 23: 30–31.

Zhao Xingqin 赵兴勤 and Zhao Wei 赵韡

2016. '*Shenbao* suo zai wan Qing Minguo *Jin Ping Mei* de liubo 《申报》所载晚清民国《金瓶梅》的流播' (The Circulation of *Jin Ping Mei* During the Late Qing and the Republic as Recorded by *Shenbao*). *Shehui Kexue Luntan* 社会科学论坛 (*Tribune of Social Sciences*) 3: 169–188.

Zhu Shuirong 朱水蓉.

2003. 'Gu wei jin yong, yang wei Zhong yong – *Jin Ping Mei quan tu* lianhuanhua chuban 古为今用洋为中用—《金瓶梅》连环画出版' (Make the Past Serve the Present and Foreign Things Serve China – *Jin Ping Mei Picture Story Book* published). *Meishu zhi you* 美术之友 (*Friends of Art*) 1: 27.

Zi Yang 滋阳

1985. '*Jin Ping Mei* shanjieben《金瓶梅》删节本' (Expurgated Editions of *Jin Ping Mei*). *Jilin Daxue shehui kexue xuebao* 吉林大学社会科学学报 (Jilin University Journal of Social Sciences) 4: 95–96.

Note on Contributor

Marja Kaikkonen is Professor Emerita of Sinology, Stockholm University, Sweden. Main interests: traditional popular culture, storytelling, popular literature, publishing, censorship, and propaganda.

CHAPTER 14

The Portrayal of Sex in *Jin Ping Mei*

KEITH MCMAHON

Explicit portrayals of sexual acts occur throughout *Jin Ping Mei*, beginning in early chapters and continuing for the entire novel. The same is true of obscene and explicit sexual language. The content that has been counted obscene and explicit, and that has been censored in modern editions of the novel, in all amounts to around 2% percent of the whole, or about 19,000 of 800,000 characters in a 1985 edition.[1] Yet this relatively minor portion has given the novel a notorious reputation. Few have subjected the language and style of these parts to close examination, though it is clear that what we may call the pornographic content of the novel has much to say. It is inherent to the telling of the story, is full of thematic meaning, and is linguistically and aesthetically rich. The portrayals of sex in *Jin Ping Mei* both inherit from the past and invent new spaces of their own. It was a lucky author who could write so freely about the sexual relations of the polygamous household that is at centre of the novel. The author had the benefit of living during a period, the last century of the Ming, in which authors could be as creative in this way as their talents and resources allowed.[2]

Examining these parts of the novel necessitates considering how *Jin Ping Mei* makes use of what it inherits from the past and where it diverges and creates its own type of writing, including what it shares and does not share with other pornographic works of the Ming and Qing. From the past, the novel inherits a linguistic style that employs metaphor and euphemism to describe sexual acts. Where *Jin Ping Mei* diverges is in its graphic and explicit descriptions of sexual acts, a kind of depiction that became a key feature of *xiaoshuo* 小說 fiction from the Ming dynasty to sometime in the mid-Qing, after which it passed from the scene and has not experienced any significant resurgence and renewal in modern times. *Jin Ping Mei*'s contribution remains a high point, whose brazenness marks the beginning of an early modern challenge to established patterns of political and cultural authority. It was a challenge that the new and

---

1 See Liu Yongqiang 劉勇強 2007: 291; and Qi Lintao 2018: 15–16, on the history of modern editions and difficulty of access to the novel.

2 See Ge Fei 格非 2014: 158, who argues that the novel belongs to a 'wave' of such production.

expanded growth of late Ming print culture helped enable. The appearance of *Jin Ping Mei* was part of a wave of both literary and commercial productivity that eroded attempts to maintain traditional social and moral hierarchies.[3]

Passing Detail in *Jin Ping Mei*

Before going into *Jin Ping Mei*'s inheritance from the past and its innovations, let me cite an example of its approach to sexual affairs, which comes from a brief episode that shows how casually the novel inserts even mere passing detail that is ribald and obscene. This is in Chapter 85, just after Pan Jinlian 潘金蓮 has aborted her illegitimate fetus from her affair with Chen Jingji 陳敬濟, and just after the affair has been discovered and they have been abruptly separated on the orders of Wu Yueniang 吳月娘. Jinlian is in poor spirits, as her maid Chunmei 春梅 can tell, and because of which Chunmei tries to cheer her up. At that moment, the go-between, Auntie Xue 薛嫂 (Xue *sao*), arrives to deliver a welcome love message from Chen Jingji, who is eager to see Jinlian again and has persuaded Xue to deliver his message by giving her money.[4] Just before Xue arrives, Chunmei consoles Jinlian, telling her that her misfortunes will pass, and, anyway, how can Wu Yueniang 'control our private affairs' (他也難管你我暗地的事).[5] Her point is: 'During our life on earth, we should get all the days of romance that we want!' (人生在世，且風流了一日是一日). Just then, Chunmei sees two dogs copulating nearby and says, 'Even animals enjoy this kind of pleasure. Why should we humans enjoy any less?' (畜生尚有如此之樂，何況人而反不如此乎). When Auntie Xue arrives, she laughs in glee when she sees the same two dogs, saying, 'What an auspicious omen for this house of yours! Just the sight of it should dispel all grief among your ladyships!' (你家好祥瑞，你娘兒每看怎不解悶).[6]

The reason I cite this passage is to point to the everyday quality of such things as Chunmei's remarks or of the appearance of the dogs copulating nearby. It is not an exaggeration to say that sex is everywhere in the novel, or

---

3   See Wang 2021: 9.

4   For a good commentary on the scene, see Ge Fei 2014: 189–90.

5   I will supply *pinyin* for cases of four characters or fewer. Translations are my own unless otherwise indicated.

6   I have quoted what the Chongzhen 崇禎 and *cihua* 詞話 editions share here, but the passage in the latter is slightly longer. See *Lanling xiaoxiao sheng* 蘭陵笑笑生 1990: 85.1217–18. This is the edition that I will usually cite. For the *cihua* edition I will cite *Lanling xiaoxiao sheng*, Bu Jian 卜鍵, ed., 2010 85.2049–50, hereafter abbreviated JPMCH. This edition is convenient because it includes both Chongzhen and Zhang Zhupo 張竹坡 (1670–1698) commentaries.

THE PORTRAYAL OF SEX IN *JIN PING MEI*

at least something that keeps taking place and to which characters easily and openly refer. When Chen Jingji first approaches Auntie Xue in his attempt to get back in touch with Pan Jinlian, he admits with no hesitation that he and Jinlian have been 'carrying on together for quite a while' (*gouda ri jiu* 勾搭日久). He is open about this in spite of the fact that their affair would normally be thought of as incestuous. But go-between Auntie Xue is just the type of person to whom such affairs are not a matter of shame or embarrassment. She laughs uproariously and says, 'Whoever heard of a son-in-law cavorting with his mother-in-law?! Where in the world have you ever seen such a thing?!' (誰家女婿戲大母? 世間那裡有此事?). (85.1217)[7] When he gives her more silver than he first offered, she in turn has no hesitation in going to see Pan Jinlian with his message, written in the form of a love poem.

Sexual teasing like this is common in the novel. On Meng Yulou's 孟玉樓 birthday, Wu Yueniang decides that Ximen Qing should go to Meng's room for the night, though she usually has no control over such activities, nor does she usually try to exert control. Pan Jinlian escorts Meng to her room, on the way to which, in jest, she pretends to be Meng's mother, saying, 'Go to bed now, my child, be good and sleep tight. Mummy will come back to see you tomorrow. Don't be naughty!' (我兒, 好好兒睡罷。你娘明日來看你, 休要淘氣). (21.279) Since people having sex make noise, and since others in the household, servants in particular, know about and can often hear what is going on, it is not surprising when two maids tease Li Ping'er 李瓶兒 one morning, saying, 'Is it true that yesterday the emperor dispatched four border agents (*yebushou* 夜不收) to ask you to seek an alliance with the barbarians?' (昨日朝廷差四箇夜不收, 請你往口外和番, 端的有這話麼). When Li Ping'er is baffled about what they mean, the maid replies: 'People say that you are good at calling out "*dada*"' (說你老人家會叫的好達達). *Dada* is a word that women cry out during the heat of sexual passion, but it is also a *double-entendre* with the word for 'Tartar', here meaning barbarians.[8] Not as clever at repartee as someone like Pan Jinlian, Li Ping'er 'reddens and blanches in utter embarrassment' (羞的臉上一塊紅, 一塊白). (20.256) Not only are others present in nearby places, but they may even intrude when Ximen Qing is having sex. Ying Bojue 應伯爵 barges into the room where Ximen Qing is having sex with the courtesan Li Guijie 李桂姐, and says, 'Hurry and throw water on the two huggers! They are all stuck together!' (快取水來, 潑潑兩箇摟心的, 摟到一答里

---

7   The *cihua* writes *zhangmu* 丈母 instead of *damu* 大母; see JPMCH 85.2049.

8   *Yebushou* is a Ming dynasty term for border agent or scout. The word *dada* relates to the word *die* 爹, 'father'. Tartar is *dada* 韃靼, also written *tata* 塔塔. See Zhang Huiying 张惠英 1992: 138.

211

KEITH MCMAHON

了). (52.686)[9] He goes up to kiss her, and then tells Ximen Qing to '[...] bang her all you want! Bang the bottom out of her for all I care!' (兩箇儘著搗，儘著搗，搗吊底也不關我事). (52.687)[10] In a final act of foolery, before leaving the room, he asks for some breath lozenges that Ximen Qing had promised him.

Scenes such as these do not involve drawn-out portrayal of sex in action, merely brief but explicit reference to sexual matters or the use of sexually explicit language, as in Ying Bojue's use of the word *dǎo* 搗, to pound or beat, for 'bang'.[11] The novel is, of course, better known for its lengthier portrayals, which can be divided into two general types. The first involves the style inherited from the past that I mentioned above, in which *Jin Ping Mei* uses elegant and figurative language to describe sexual acts. The second is the novel's graphic style, in which raw and direct language describes unfiltered excess.[12]

The Tradition of the Art of the Bedchamber

In the first type, *Jin Ping Mei* looks back to a sexual culture whose earliest texts date to sex manuals found in the Mawangdui 馬王堆 tombs of the third century B.C.E. The same tradition of texts, called *fangzhong shu* (房中術), the 'art of the bedchamber', extends through the Six Dynasties, the Tang, and into the Ming and Qing, and includes illustrated albums, the last of which – though not the term *fangzhong shu* – appear in the novel.[13] These texts treat sex as a noble act, in which the man masterfully and considerately attends to the woman in her successive stages of arousal, never pushing ahead until she is ready. Though pleasure is central, the partners avoid rash, unchecked excess. The language is never vulgar but is instead artful and refined. In scores of instances, *Jin Ping Mei* likewise refrains from vulgarity and instead uses artful and figurative language, though its characters in general ignore the prohibition against excess. In addition, the novel largely confines its inheritance from the art of the bedchamber to the utilization of aphrodisiacs and sex tools and to the

---

9   Probably referring to a custom of throwing water on two copulating dogs to get them to separate.

10   '[...] bang the bottom out of her for all I care' comes from Roy 2006: 52.276.

11   It is common vulgar slang that is a level above the crudest word, *ri* 曰 ('fuck', the two commonly occurring together as *ridao*).

12   I discuss these styles at greater length in *Saying All That Can Be Said: The Art of Describing Sex in Jin Ping Mei*, forthcoming, Harvard Asia Center.

13   A shortened form of this term, *fangshu* 房術, appears once in *Jin Ping Mei*, when Ximen Qing refers to the aphrodisiac that he is about to receive as 'the drug for the art of the bedchamber' (*fangshu yao* 房術藥; see JPM 49.638). This is a narrow use of the term, which does not comprise the art of the bedchamber in the sense I am using here.

THE PORTRAYAL OF SEX IN *JIN PING MEI*

alternation between various sex positions, though the names of the positions are different in *Jin Ping Mei* and other fiction of the Ming and Qing.

Besides aphrodisiacs, sex tools, and sexual positions, thrusting techniques are also part of the classic tradition, but appear in reduced form in *Jin Ping Mei*, in which they are never as carefully executed as in the art of the bedchamber. Ximen Qing thrusts aggressively and likes forcing the woman into a helpless state of arousal. With Wang Liu'er 王六兒, for instance, he performs a series of 'shallow pulls and deep thrusts' (*qian shou shen song* 淺抽深送). (50.645) Each of these words derives from the ancient tradition. But in that tradition, a man would perform a specific series of 'nine shallow thrusts and one deep' (*jiu qian yi shen* 九淺一深), for example, only after engaging in foreplay by caressing the woman's body with hands and mouth, and only then proceeding to stimulate the 'shallow' areas of her vulva. He would not yet enter deeply, never go to a depth that the art of the bedchamber considers too deep, and would never enter deeply all at once.[14] Similarly, in another scene with Wang Liu'er, Ximen Qing rubs aphrodisiac ointment on his 'turtle's head' (*guitou* 龜頭), a slang word for the glans that does not occur in the art of the bedchamber. He causes her 'unbearable stimulation' (*mayang buneng dang* 麻癢不能當), after which he 'plays and prods with her flower's heart, holding back and refusing to go deeper' (又挑弄其花心,不肯深入). (79.1140)[15] In titillating the 'flower's heart' and dallying at the entrance or 'shallow' parts of the woman's genitals, Ximen Qing does indeed echo the method of the classic sex manuals, but not according to the original style and intent. In the original teaching, as just mentioned, dallying at the shallow opening and not going deeper is part of the gradual buildup of arousal in the woman, whom the man never forces or rushes. Instead, Ximen Qing takes advantage of the woman's sensitivities and relishes making her lose control.

In short, Ximen Qing's focus is on not stopping, which is precisely what the art of the bedchamber discourages. A brief passage sums up his style: 'He pulls out all the way to the tip, then thrusts back all the way to the root, continuing for hundreds of times' (抽徹至首, 復送至根, 又數百回). (78.1140) The drive is all the more unstoppable after he acquires the marvelous, but dangerous, aphrodisiac from the monk. Ximen Qing's penis becomes a swollen and bulging thing, as described in this reaction after taking the drug: 'His word flew into a violent rage. Like a melon bursting open, its sunken eye bulged wide, and from its surrounding whiskers it bounded straight up' (那話登時暴怒起

---

14   On the notion of 'too deep', see Li Ling 李零 and Keith McMahon 1992: 165–66; and Li Ling 1993: 195–96 (from the Ming text *Sunü miaolun* 素女妙論).

15   Using Roy's translations – see Roy 2001: 38.388 and Roy 2011:79.635.

来,裂瓜頭凹眼睜圓,落腮鬍挺身直豎). (28.360) A further comment on this passage will follow below, but for now let me note one of the novel's common euphemisms for penis, *nahua* 那話, which I translate as 'word,' though it could also be translated as 'thing' or 'unmentionable'. Although vulgar words for the genitals occur elsewhere in the novel, they usually do not appear in descriptions of sexual activity, but instead when characters use them to curse or refer jokingly or mockingly to the sexual organs.

The Tradition of Erotic Poetry

Another inheritance from the past is from the literature of erotic poetry, which Li Xiaorong calls the literature of the 'fragrant and bedazzling' (*xiangyan* 香艷), which continued into the Ming and Qing.[16] This is the art of using polished and euphemistic language to write about the pleasures and passions of sex, a prominent example of which is a work that was lost for centuries and only re-found in modern times, the late Tang *Rhapsody on the Grand Pleasure* (*Dale fu* 大樂賦).[17] It is an example of elegant and tasteful erotica, which comes from a social milieu in which sexual pleasure is an inherent part of the life of elite cultural refinement.[18] The difference between *Jin Ping Mei* and works such as the *Rhapsody* lies in the contrast between the semi-literate Ximen Qing, on the one hand, and the connoisseur of pleasure featured in *xiangyan* literature, on the other. In *Jin Ping Mei*, a gap always exists between the polished and lofty tones of the novel's high erotic style and the surrounding narrative, which is about the complex relations of the polygamous household. Those relations are constantly marked by rivalry and jealousy between women, by secrecy and deception, and by the deal-making that women commonly engage in while serving Ximen Qing sexually.

An example of a *xiangyan*-like moment occurs when Li Ping'er gives Ximen Qing fellatio. The maid readies the bed for them, as is common in situations in which other members of the household are present when sex is taking place. 'They sit shoulder to shoulder, thigh over thigh, drinking and amusing themselves in conversation.' Here, Ximen Qing is engaging in the type of behaviour

---

16 See Li Xiaorong 2019 (*xiangyan*); Qi Lintao 2018: 200–207 (regarding metaphor and euphemism in *Jin Ping Mei*'s language, especially in terms of how this affects translation); and Yao Ping 2013.

17 See the text of *Dale fu* by Bai Xingjian 白行簡 (776–826), in Li Ling 1993: 93–99, especially 94–96 (wife and concubines); and van Gulik 2004, in relation to parts 5 and 6 of *Dale fu*.

18 See Yao Ping 2013, who discusses this milieu in its late Tang form; and Michael Nylan 2018: 17–18, in relation to the tradition of pleasure in terms of the incorporation of sensuality and aestheticism into a life centred around erudition and refinement.

THE PORTRAYAL OF SEX IN *JIN PING MEI*

associated with the refined gentleman-connoisseur of pleasure, which as a rule must be spread out and enjoyed in intervals, never spent all in a rush. 'Soon, yearning spreads across their faces and lust begins to ripple through their bodies' (並肩疊股, 飲酒調笑. 良久, 春色橫眉, 淫心蕩漾). They do 'clouds and rain' (*yunyu* 雲雨) for a while, an ancient euphemism for having sex, after which they stop and he has her 'play the flute' (*pin xiao* 品簫) for him, another commonly appearing euphemism, referring to fellatio. Then come four lines of poetry:

> The sounds are like neither flute, zither, nor stone; the carnal notes resonate in a way like no other.
> The tassels of the bed curtains swish and sweep; you can't quite tell the note, is it do, re, mi, or fa...?

不竹不絲不石, 肉音別自唔咿. 流蘇瑟瑟碧紗垂, 變不出宮商角徵

(17.208)[19]

A connoisseur, even a pretend one such as Ximen Qing, should enjoy special moments of the acts of sex, not merely engage in driven frenzy. One day, instead of 'clouds and rain', Ximen Qing has Pan Jinlian 'play the flute' for him, knowing that this is a specialty of hers. As he enjoys himself, 'he lowers his head to watch the marvel of it going in and out' (垂首覘其出入之妙). (10.125) However brief such a moment may be, it functions as a self-contemplative aside that attempts to capture and extend the moment of pleasure instead of blindly letting it pass. The same gesture takes place in the *Rhapsody on the Grand Pleasure* of many centuries before, as well as in the earlier 16th-century novel, *Ruyijun zhuan*, 如意君傳 (The Lord of Perfect Satisfaction), from which *Jin Ping Mei* often copies, including in this case.[20]

But *Jin Ping Mei* cannot be said to strive for the literary quality of the *xiangyan* style of language and imagery, though the author at times writes as a *xiangyan* poet (or at least imitates or copies from them). The following line of adumbration appears three times in the novel, twice on occasions of a man's first sex with a virgin: 'As spring enlivens the peach tree's blossoms, their red buds split open. As the breeze teases the willows, their green waists bend' (春點桃花紅綻蕊, 風欺楊

---

19   The lines in the *cihua* edition makes no mention of 'carnal notes', but otherwise end with the same 'I never knew the magic rhinoceros horn could feel so good' (不覺靈犀味美). See JPMCH 17.322–23; and, on 'rhinoceros horn' as euphemism for penis, see Roy 1993: 13.514, note 13.

20   See *Dale fu*, in Li Ling 1993: 95 (*kan chu kan ru*, 看出看入); and *Ruyijun zhuan*, in Xu Changling 徐昌齡 1995: 44, 51. For the latter's influence on *Jin Ping Mei*, see Hanan 1963: 43–47, and Stone 2003: 121–22.

215

柳綠翻腰).[21] Compare this with a line from a *xiangyan* poem by a Ming poet: 'Covered in dew, the crabapple is still fresh in colour./ Greeting the wind, the orchid-musk fragrance still emits from flickering light.' (承露海棠犹带色, 迎風蘭麝尚浮光). The Ming poem refers to a night of lovemaking, in which dew is a metaphor for semen. In both *Jin Ping Mei* and the poem, the image of the wind's effect on flower blossoms represents the man having sex with the woman.[22] Other shared language includes instances in which the sounds of sex are compared to the warbling of birds such as swallows or orioles, and the use of flower imagery to refer to the female body, such as *rui* (蕊 pistil) for female genitalia.

What Does *Jin Ping Mei* Do That is New?

The novel's use of graphic description sets it apart from earlier literature and constitutes a new space of creative exploration. Graphic in this case means straightforward, raw, and direct, though not necessarily vulgar. Vulgar language does not usually occur during descriptions of acts of sex, but mainly as I have said when characters utter such words in curses and bouts of anger.[23] Raw, graphic sex is about heated frenzy, which takes place when Ximen Qing is with his most wanton women, such as Pan Jinlian, Wang Liu'er, Song Huilian 宋惠蓮, or Lady Lin 林太太 (Lin Taitai). Moreover, such descriptions do not necessarily carry a negative tone. As in more elegant portrayals, graphic ones present sexual acts as having an all-encompassing energy with a beauty of their own, even if the language is no longer elegant or euphemistic. Such portrayals do not occur with main wife Wu Yueniang, nor with Meng Yulou or Li Ping'er after the latter becomes a mother. The novel represents these women as standing above the kind of sex that Ximen Qing has with his wanton women.

At times such description can verge on the grotesque, but again not necessarily. The first view of the naked Pan Jinlian describes her as having a 'woman's

---

21 The first time is from Ximen Qing's sex with Pan Jinlian (10.126), the second from his first time with courtesan Zheng Aiyue 鄭愛月 (who is supposedly a virgin, but may not be; 59.778), and the third when Chen Jingji consummates with his new wife, Ge Cuiping 葛翠屏 (97.1379).

22 See Li Xiaorong 2019: 123–24 (slightly modifying her translation), 133, from Zeng Rulu 曾汝魯 (late Ming), 'Rising Late' (*Yan qi* 晏起):

23 For example, Dai'an 玳安 uses the word 'cum' for semen (*song* 屄) when he mocks the servant Huatong 畫童, Ximen Qing's catamite (50.644). Pan Jinlian curses Li Ping'er, saying 'What fucking Sister Ping?!' (*shemma Ping diao yi* 甚麼瓶鳥姨, 18.228), using the slang word for 'dick' or 'prick', *diao*. (鳥, 屌). On women who use such words, see the comment by Zhang Zhupo to that effect, in Hou Zhongyi 侯忠義 and Wang Rumei 王汝梅 (eds) 1985: 38 (referring to both Pan Jinlian and Wang Liu'er).

216

THE PORTRAYAL OF SEX IN *JIN PING MEI*

gate devoid of hair, pure and fragrant and plump to fullness, just like a risen bun' (牝戶上並無毳毛. 猶如白如馥馥,鼓蓬蓬發酵的饅頭). (4.60–61) In the first view of courtesan Zheng Aiyue, her vagina is 'immaculate and hairless, like a white steamed cake, soft and tender and delightful to behold' (牝淨無毛,猶如白麵蒸餅一般,柔嫩可愛). (59.778) But a scene with wet-nurse Ruyi 如意 carries a note of the grotesque:

> Ximen Qing's organ was so thick that it completely filled the woman's vagina. The action of its going in and out turned the color of her flower's heart rouge like the tongue of a parrot, dark like the wings of a bat, moving back and forth in a delightful way. Ximen Qing wrapped her legs around his waist, as the two hugged tightly and pressed closely together. His word plunged to the root, leaving not a hairsbreadth outside. The woman's eyes fell into a stare, she lost her voice, and her wanton waters flowed out in waves. When his passion reached the height of ecstasy, his semen erupted like the gush of a fountain.
>
> Little knowing that the tidings of spring had already arrived, all they felt was the melting sensation of body and bone.

> 西門慶那話粗大,撐的婦人牝戶滿滿,往來出入,帶得花心紅如鸚鵡舌, 黑似蝙蝠翅, 翻覆可愛. 西門慶於是把他兩股扳抱在懷內,四體交匝, 兩相迎湊,那話盡沒至根,不容毫髮. 婦人瞪目失聲, 淫水流下. 西門 慶情濃樂極,精邈如湧泉. 正是: 不知已透春消息,但覺形骸骨節鑠.

> (78.1121)

Such a passage shows how *Jin Ping Mei* combines the graphic and the elegant, the latter of which occurs in the last lines, which suddenly elevate what has just been portrayed in one of the rawest, most frenzied descriptions in the novel, which occurs not long before Ximen Qing's gruesome death.

Jin Ping Mei and Ming and Qing Pornography

What does *Jin Ping Mei* share and not share with pornographic works of the Ming and the Qing? Such a question comes down to, how pornographic is *Jin Ping Mei*? The main difference is one that might be expected, that the more purely pornographic works engage in explicit description primarily for entertainment. *Jin Ping Mei* also entertains, but not to the extent to which the others go to shock and titillate. They enjoy breaking taboos, and engage in a narrative drive that matches the very drive of the high-powered sex that they portray. Though not above stand-alone scenes portraying heights of passion and pleasure, *Jin Ping Mei* ultimately subordinates such portrayals to the complexities that come before and after, and in general undermines its characters by depicting them in a way that

217

KEITH MCMAHON

is 'divested of heroism and grandeur' (Hsia 1968: 138).[24] Another difference lies in the absence of certain kinds of scenes and characters that appear in the more purely pornographic works, such as: 1) the stock scene of sex in one bed between a polygamist and a number of his wives (though a minor form of this scenario occurs in Chapter 83 with Chen Jingji, Pan Jinlian, and Chunmei); or 2) the young man whom a husband sodomizes and in return allows him to sleep with the husband's wife; or 3) the sex-starved widow who succumbs to desire when she sees a well-endowed man or animals or insects mating; or 4) a virgin who becomes lascivious once exposed to sexual lure; or 5) games that men and women play to see which man can do the most thrusts, which man has the largest penis, or which woman can produce the most sexual fluids.[25] To the author of *Jin Ping Mei*, such scenes would be both gratuitous and superfluous.

Finally, pornographic fiction of the Ming and Qing shares a common focus on occult Daoist practices, which is when characters resort to powerful drugs and internal techniques in order to strengthen themselves in sexual battle. Characters try to rob each other of vital essence.[26] For example, a woman in *The Pornographic Story of the Embroidered Couch* (*Xiuta yeshi* 繡榻野史) 'can open and close her vagina, take [the man's] prick and inhale and exhale it, lock down on him while alternating between fast and slow', and in this way finally make him ejaculate (會開, 又會夾, 把毛+亂吞進吐出, 緊抽緊鎖, 慢抽慢鎖). (1.116)[27] In the male countermove, a man can control his movements as if his penis was like a head with a moving mouth or like an arm extending from his groin. Recall the quote above from *Jin Ping Mei*, 'His word flew into a violent

---

24 That descriptions of sexual activity in *Jin Ping Mei* have a thematic purpose and do not simply cater to pleasing the reader, see also Tian Xiaofei 2003: 138.

25 See, respectively, 1) *Taohua ying* 桃花影, *Xinghua tian* 杏花天 and *Naohua cong* 鬧花叢; 2) *Xiuta yeshi* 繡榻野史, *Taohua ying*, *Naohua cong*, and *Taohua yanshi* 桃花艷史; 3) *Chanzhen houshi* 禪真後史 (ch. 1), *Shidian tou* 石點頭, Story 4, *Jingshi tongyan* 警世通言, Story 35, *Pai'an jingqi* 拍案驚奇, Story 31, and *Wushan yanshi* 巫山艷史; 4) *Chundeng mishi* 春燈迷史, *Zuichun feng* 醉春風, and *Shenlou zhi* 蜃樓志; and 5) *Bie you xiang* 別有香, Story 4, *Zhaoyang qushi* 昭陽趣史, *Guwangyan* 姑妄言 (chs. 14, 24), and *Xingshi hengyan* 醒世恆言, Story 23 (about Prince Hailing, Hailing wang 海陵王).

26 See Pan Jianguo 潘建國 1997 and Wan Jingchuan 萬晴川 2000.

27 For discussions of the novel, see Li Mengsheng 李夢生 1994: 80–87; Idema 2004: xxix–lix; Wong 2007; and Lü Tiancheng 呂天成 1995, trans. by Lenny Hu 2001 as *The Embroidered Couch* (Hu 2001). The same skill appears in *Zhaoyang qushi*, in which the woman can 'clamp down tightly' (*jiade jinjinde* 夾得緊緊的) or 'lock down' on the man (鎖). (1.106) See Yanyan sheng 艷艷生 1995: 1.74; and further examples in McMahon, forthcoming, Chapter 4 on sex as battle (*Chanzhen yishi* 禪真逸史 and *Zhulin yeshi* 朱林野史). Please, note that 毛+亂 means that 毛 and 亂 should be pushed together as one character. This is a Wu dialect slang for penis, but is not found among computerized characters.

rage. Like a melon bursting open, its sunken eye bulged wide, and from its surrounding whiskers it bounded straight up' (28.360). But although Ximen Qing uses powerful aphrodisiacs, neither he nor any of the women resort to other occult practices. The Indian monk is the only character from the world of occult arts that pervades other works of the late Ming and after.[28] In those works, characters engage in a kind of sexual battle in which they use their sexual organs as if they were dueling weapons. *Jin Ping Mei* only portrays such battles in the verse passages that accompany the scenes of Ximen Qing's sex with Pan Jinlian, Wang Liu'er, and Lady Lin.[29]

To call *Jin Ping Mei* an 'erotic novel', as has often been done, is too kind and circumspect. *Jin Ping Mei* is a brazen book beyond the sense allowed by the usual sense of the word erotic. Its pornographic passages are a sign of that. But neither is the novel simply a work of pornography, or rather we should say that even its pornography is deeply thematic, not to mention linguistically brilliant. At the same time, as many have observed, the author often indulges in an exuberance of description that overflows his thematic intent.[30] Further, the novel at times contradicts itself, at one moment issuing didactic condemnations of its characters, at another celebrating the pleasure that the characters enjoy.[31] The two main versions of the novel, the *Cihua* 詞話 and the Chongzhen 崇禎, differ in this regard. Though the two are similarly pornographic, the Chongzhen edition removes or softens much of the didacticism that the *Cihua* contains and in terms of literary quality in general creates a superior text that irons out many of the superfluities and contradictions found in the *Cihua*.[32] Both versions differ from *Shuihu zhuan* (*Water Margin*, 水滸傳), from which *Jin Ping Mei* borrows the episode of the adulterous affair of Ximen Qing and Pan Jinlian, the latter of whom the two later versions portray more sympathetically than before.[33]

---

28 See Xue Yingjie 薛英傑 2017.

29 See Chapters 29, 37, and 78.

30 See Ding Naifei 2002: 161–62, ('glossolalia', 'taking pleasure in its own sounds'); Shang Wei 2005: 63–92, 83, 91 ('the robust appetites of his characters become manifest in his own narrative'); and Qi Lintao 2018: 190, reference to passages that are 'independent from the realistic presentation of the scene'.

31 As noted by Liu Yongqiang 1996: Chapter 10, p. 71, for example, in which a poem celebrates Ximen Qing having a good time in the brothel (see also the introductory poem for chapter 20).

32 Many have commented on this, but see Tian Xiaofei 2002: 348, 352, 377–78, 387; Ge Fei 2014: 195, 197, 293; and Qi Lintao 2018, 24–27 (for example, less vulgarity and better diction in chapter titles).

33 See Tian Xiaofei 2003: 16–17.

Conclusion: Reception and Translation

Two final points are worth brief mentioning. The first is that there has been a change in the reception of the novel since its earliest appearance, especially in terms of how readers view its pornography. The Chongzhen commentator appreciates the scenes of sexual pleasure, complimenting passages that later would be censored and condemned, including the one in Chapter 27, which is usually considered the most obscene chapter of the book. The commentator Zhang Zhupo instead favours the moral message of the book and what he promotes as the correct way to read it.[34] Zhang set a tone that has endured to the present, as characterized by modern writers such as Mao Dun 茅盾 (1896–1981), Lu Xun 鲁迅 (1881–1936), Hu Shi 胡適 (1891–1962) and others, who can be summed up by Hu Shi's characterization of the novel's sexually explicit passages as portraying nothing but 'bestial desire'.[35] As Ding Naifei writes, readings of the novel are 'socially framed', depending on the positionality of the readers and the collective and institutional contexts that they represent.[36] Such variables affect not only the evaluation of the novel but also the range of things that can be said about it, including how explicitly it can be discussed. Ding is particularly interested, for example, in the 'situational complexities' of the women in the novel, whether bondservant, concubine, courtesan or main wife, and in how differently each character acts depending on such things as whether in marrying Ximen Qing she transitions from bondservant to concubine (Pan Jinlian), courtesan to concubine (Li Jiao'er 李嬌), or main wife to concubine (Meng Yulou, Li Ping'er).[37] Such variables affect the way Ximen Qing has sex with each and the way the novel describes sex with each. Portrayals are more extensive and graphic with Pan Jinlian than Meng Yulou, sex with whom hardly occurs at all. The most detailed scene in her case is the one in which Ximen Qing forces himself on her when she is ill and in discomfort (75.1053). Descriptions are extensive and graphic in scenes with Song Huilian, Wang Liu'er, Lady Lin and Ruyi, but less so in

---

34 See Liu Yongqiang 1996: 73–74. Zhang condemns the behaviour in chapter 27; see Hou Zhongyi and Wang Rumei 1985: 100.

35 See Ding Naifei 2002: 3 (Hu Shi's words, *shouxing de rouyu* 獸性的肉慾), 6 and 19.

36 See Ding Naifei 2002: xxv, xxvi (how the novel 'had to be made literary, and its place determined through successive readings, editorial polishing, published notational comments, and commentary editions'; and Qi Lintao 2018: 27–31, on the history of the study of the novel.

37 See Ding Naifei 2002: xxi (situational complexities), 44 (women 'struggling for power and survival by whatever means necessary, with sex and sexuality their primary and perhaps only weapon of choice'); and Liu Yongqiang 1996: 75.

portrayals of Ximen Qing and Wu Yueniang, Meng Yulou, or with Li Ping'er after pregnancy and motherhood.

My second final point is that the very explicitness of the novel, including its language of sex, has affected its translation into other languages, which do not necessarily share the range and depth of language that the author both had at hand and invented. Languages differ in terms of their lexicons of sex. Eras differ in terms of what can or cannot be translated.[38] The contrast between Clement Egerton's 1939 translation and that of David Roy in the late 20th and early 21st centuries is instructive. Egerton had to struggle with the threat of censorship, although the effects of this were not as severe with many of the poetic passages in the novel, which are not as explicit as prose passages. Poetic language tends to reticence. It is refined and full of metaphor, which results in the softening of pornographic effects. In contrast, more explicit passages, whether in prose or poetry, had either to be cut or translated into Latin (the portions of which have now been translated into English). Though Egerton's version is highly readable, it is in general more allusive and paraphrastic, whereas Roy's is more literal and explicit.[39]

Problems of translation are also a matter of the lack of equivalent words and images, or the mismatch between them. It is safe to say that the repertoire of the language of sex in late Ming China is richer than that of the contemporary English-speaking world, whose lexicon tends to either scientific terminology (the clinical-sounding language just referred to), or else profanity. There are few equivalents for such terms as 'flower's heart', 'woman's gate', 'turtle's head', 'jade stalk', or 'rhinoceros horn'. The mid-18th-century *Fanny Hill* is more imaginative in this regard than modern texts. Some languages, as well as some translators, are better at reflecting *Jin Ping Mei*'s original style and language. Moreover, as Qi Lintao writes, Chinese is a 'high context' language with a great deal of implicit meaning, whereas English is low-context and prone to be more explicit.[40] But the bridging between Chinese and other languages

---

38 See Qi Lintao 2018: 47–79, in relation to translation and adaption of *Jin Ping Mei* into European languages; and Nam Nguyen 2017: 6, 8 9, 10, in relation to the fact that readers in Japan and Korea read the novel in Chinese at first, not translating it until three centuries later. Similarly, Vietnamese read it in English and French until 1969, when the first Vietnamese translation appeared, which was expurgated.

39 On Egerton, see Qi Lintao 2018: 80–108; and on Roy, see ibid.: 109–134; see also 171–72, 194–95, 200–202; also see André Lévy's French translation (Lévy 1985a) and his 'Introduction' to this (Lévy 1985b: xxxix), which has references to other prior translations and to the fact that Egerton left out most of the verse and tempered the coarseness, removing about a quarter of the original.

40 See Qi Lintao 2018: 2–3, 200. In other words, in the Chinese, much 'remains linguistically implicit,' whereas English must spell things out.

in this context is something that I leave for future thought. Let it suffice for now to pose the questions of why and how such differences exist, what is their nature and meaning, and what do they tell us about comparative cultural and linguistic history?

References

Ding Naifei
>**2002.** *Obscene Things: Sexual Politics in Jin Ping Mei*. Durham: Duke University Press.

Ge Fei 格非
>**2014.** *Xueyin lusi: Jin Ping Mei de shengse yu xuwu* 雪隐鹭鸶：《金瓶梅》的声色与虚无. Nanjing: Yilin chubanshe.

Hanan, Patrick
>**1963.** 'The sources of the *Chin P'ing Mei*.' In *Asia Major* 10(2): 23–67.

Hou Zhongyi 侯忠義 and Wang Rumei 王汝梅
>**1985.** *Jin Ping Mei ziliao huibian* 金瓶梅資料滙編. Beijing: Beijing daxue chubanshe.

Hsia, C. T.
>**1968.** *The Classic Chinese Novel: A Critical Introduction*. New York: Columbia University Press.

Hu, Lenny
>**2001.** *The Embroidered Couch. An Erotic Novel of China*. Vancouver: Arsenal Pulp Press.

Idema, Wilt L.
>**2004.** '"Blasé literati": Lü T'ien-ch'eng and the lifestyle of the Chiang-nan elite in the final decades of the Wan-Li period.' In Robert van Gulik, *Erotic Colour Prints of the Late Ming Period*, pp. xxix–lix. Leiden: Brill.

Lanling xiaoxiao sheng 蘭陵笑笑生
>**1990.** *Xinke xiuxiang piping Jin Ping Mei* 新刻繡像批評金瓶梅. Hong Kong: Sanlian shudian.
>**2010.** Edited by Bu Jian 卜鍵. *Shuanggexie chongjiao ping pi Jin Ping Mei* 雙舸榭重校評批金瓶梅. Beijing: Zuojia chubanshe.

Lévy, André (trans.)
>**1985a.** *Fleur en Fiole d'Or (Jin Ping Mei cihua)*. Paris: Gallimard. 2 vols.
>**1985b.** 'Introduction.' In André Lévy, *Fleur en Fiole d'Or (Jin Ping Mei cihua)*. Paris: Gallimard, vol. 1: xxxvii–lxxi.

Li Ling 李零

1993. *Zhongguo fangshu gaiguan* 中國方術概觀. Beijing: Renmin Zhongguo chubanshe.

Li Ling 李零 and Keith McMahon

1992. 'The contents and terminology of the Mawangdui texts on the arts of the bedchamber.' *Early China* 17: 145–85.

Li Mengsheng 李夢生

1994. *Zhongguo jinhui xiaoshuo baihua* 中國禁毀小說百話. Shanghai: Shanghai guji chubanshe.

Li Xiaorong

2019. *The Poetics and Politics of Sensuality in China; The 'Fragrant and Bedazzling' Movement (1600–1930).* Amherst: Cambria Press.

Liu Yongqiang 劉勇強

1996. '*Jin Ping Mei* benwen yu jieshou fenxi 《金瓶梅》本文與接收分析'. *Beijing daxue xuebao* 4: 68–76.

2007. *Zhongguo gudai xiaoshuoshi xulun* 中國古代小說史敘論. Beijing: Beijing daxue chubanshe.

Lü Tiancheng 呂天成

1995. *Xiuta yeshi* 繡榻野史. In Vol. 2 of Chen Qinghao and Wang Qiugui (eds), *Siwuxie huibao.* Taipei: Taiwan daying baike.

Martinez, Marc (trans.)

1985. 'Introduction to the French translation of *Jin Ping Mei cihua.*' *Renditions* 24: 109–29.

McMahon, Keith

2019. 'The art of the bedchamber and *Jin Ping Mei* 金瓶梅.' *Nan Nü: Men, Women and Gender in China* 21(1): 1–37.

Forthcoming. *Saying All That Can Be Said. The Art of Describing Sex in Jin Ping Mei.* Harvard Asia Center.

Nam Nguyen

2017. '"Are we talking about the same *Jin Ping Mei*?" Examining the reception of the novel in Vietnam from a cultural translation studies perspective.' *Asia Pacific Translation and Intercultural Studies* 4(1): 3–21.

Nylan, Michael

2018. *The Chinese Pleasure Book.* New York: Zone Books.

Pan Jianguo 潘建國

1997. '*Daojiao fangzhong wenhua yu Ming Qing xiaoshuo zhong de xing miaoxie* 道教房中文化與明清小說中的性描寫'. *MingQing xiaoshuo yanjiu* 3: 57–70.

Plaks, Andrew

1987. *The Four Masterworks of the Ming Novel. Ssu ta ch'i-shu.* Princeton: Princeton University Press.

Qi Lintao

2018. *Jin Ping Mei English Translations: Texts, Paratexts, and Contexts.* London: Routledge.

Roy, David T. (trans.)

1993. *The Plum in the Golden Vase or, Chin P'ing Mei. Volume One: The Gathering.* Princeton: Princeton University Press.

2001. *The Plum in the Golden Vase or, Chin P'ing Mei. Volume Two: The Rivals.* Princeton: Princeton University Press.

2006. *The Plum in the Golden Vase or, Chin P'ing Mei. Volume Three: The Aphrodisiac.* Princeton: Princeton University Press.

2011. *The Plum in the Golden Vase or, Chin P'ing Mei. Volume Four: The Climax.* Princeton: Princeton University Press.

2013. *The Plum in the Golden Vase or, Chin P'ing Mei. Volume Five: The Dissolution.* Princeton: Princeton University Press.

Shang Wei

2005. 'The making of the everyday world: *Jin Ping Mei cihua* and encyclopedias for daily use.' In David Der-wei Wang and Shang Wei (eds), *Dynastic Crisis and Cultural Innovation: From the Late Ming to the Late Qing and Beyond*, pp. 63–92. Cambridge, MA.: Harvard University Press.

Stone, Charles

2003. *The Fountainhead of Chinese Erotica. The Lord of Perfect Satisfaction (Ruyijun zhuan).* Honolulu: University of Hawaii Press.

Tian Xiaofei 田曉菲

2002. 'A preliminary comparison of the two recensions of *"Jinpingmei".'* *Harvard Journal of Asiatic Studies* 62(2): 347–388.

2003. *Qiushui tang lun Jin Ping Mei* 秋水堂論金瓶梅. Tianjin: Tianjin renmin chubanshe.

Van Gulik, Robert

2004. *Erotic Colour Prints of the Ming Period. With an Essay on Chinese Sex Life from Han to the Ch'ing Dynasty, B.C. 206–A. D. 1644.* Leiden: Brill Publishers (reprint of privately issued edition of 1950).

Wan Jingchuan 萬晴川

2000. 'Lun fangzhongshu dui Ming Qing xiaoshuode yingxiang 論房中術對明清小說的影響.' *Jinyang xuekan* 晉陽學刊 1: 70–73.

THE PORTRAYAL OF SEX IN *JIN PING MEI*

Wang, Yvon

2021. *Reinventing Licentiousness: Pornography and Modernity in China at the Turn of the Twentieth Century.* Berkeley: University of California Press.

Wong, Ka F.

2007. 'The anatomy of eroticism: Reimagining sex and sexuality in the late Ming novel *Xiuta Yeshi.*' *Nan Nü: Men, Women and Gender in China* 9(2): 284–389.

Xu Changling 徐昌齡

1995. *Ruyijun zhuan* 如意君傳. In Chen Qinghao and Wang Qiugui (eds), *Siwuxie huibao*, vol. 24. Taipei: Taiwan daying baike.

Xue Yingjie 薛英傑

2017. Wenren shenfen yu tazhe xiangxiang: wanMing he Qingchude 'yinseng' gushi 文人身份與他者想象: 晚明和清初的 '淫僧' 故事. Ph.D. dissertation, The University of Hong Kong.

Yanyan sheng 艷艷生

1995. '*Zhaoyang qushi* 昭陽趣史.' In Chen Qinghao and Wang Qiugui (eds), *Siwuxie huibao*. Taipei: Taiwan daying baike. Vol. 3.

Yao Ping

2013. 'Historicizing great bliss: Erotica in Tang China (618–907).' *Journal of the History of Sexuality* 22(2): 207–229.

Zhang Huiying 张惠英

1992. *Jin Ping Mei lisu nanci jie* 金瓶梅俚俗难词解. Beijing: Shehui kexue wenxian chubanshe.

Note on Contributor

Keith McMahon is Professor of Chinese, Department of East Asian Languages and Cultures, University of Kansas, USA. He studies the history of sexuality in China from ancient times to the verge of modernity and has most recently published a two-volume study of the history of imperial marriage and women rulers. A new book by Prof. McMahon will appear in 2023, published by the Harvard Asia Center, *Saying All That Can Be Said. The Art of Describing Sex in Jin Ping Mei*. His other areas of interest include polygamy and gender characterization in fictional narrative of late imperial China, mythical and historical narrative from ancient times to the end of the last dynasty, and the culture of opium smoking in 19th century China. His next project will be about immortals, demons and cosmic geography in the 16th-century novel, *Journey to the West*.

CHAPTER 15

The Adaptation of Sex and Sexy Adaptations

Rewriting *Jin Ping Mei* for the Mid-20th Century Anglophone Market

LINTAO QI

An adaptation, according to Sanders (2006), involves omissions, rewritings, and maybe additions, but is still recognizable as the work of the original writer. The recognisability of the final product of adaptation, in the field of translation studies, is likely to lead many target-text (TT) readers who are illiterate in the source language to consume the adaptation as the source text (ST), or leave the readers with the impression that the adaptation is an accurate representation of the ST. In adaptation, a literary work is transferred from one historical context into another, and the TT, which is produced for the target culture, also carries with it properties of the source context. In adapting a classic Chinese novel like *Jin Ping Mei* (hereafter JPM),[1] the TT producer has to carry out two different types of dialogue, both cross spatio-temporal in nature. One is a dialogue with the ST, in which the translator has to make sense of the world in and of the ST; and the other a dialogue with the target context, in the sense that the final translation product has to resonate with the target culture (Qi 2016). In other words, the TT represents the ST on one hand and the translator's response to their target context on the other.

It should, however, be emphasized that many of the English adaptations of JPM are products of indirect translation. As such, they are relay-translated from existent translated versions of JPM (either in English or other languages such as German), rather than from a Chinese ST.[2] Consequently, the concept of ST

---

1 The content, features and literary merits of *Jin Ping Mei* (JPM) are well elucidated in the other chapters of this collection.

2 The concept of ST is relative and hierarchical. The Chinese ST of JPM could be considered the primary ST. If an English TT is not produced from a Chinese version of the JPM, then its ST is deemed secondary (i.e. its ST is already a translation, but that translation is made

THE ADAPTATION OF SEX AND SEXY ADAPTATIONS

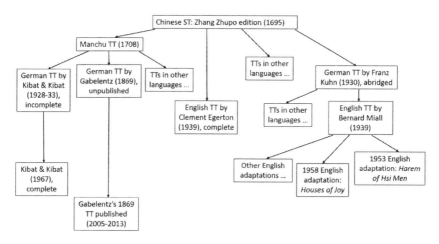

Figure 15.1. Translations from the Zhang Zhupo edition of JPM

becomes rather complicated in the translation history of JPM. To visualise the genealogy of the relationship between the Chinese ST and their TTs (which very often become the ST for later translations), Figure 15.1 and Figure 15.2 are prepared here to provide a sketchy history of the translations of the Zhang Zhupo edition and the *Cihua* edition, respectively.[3]

If translations are contextualised in terms of dialogues with either the ST or the target context, as mentioned above, then direct translations of JPM are often predominantly immersed in the first type of dialogue, i.e. with their Chinese ST, where fidelity is foregrounded and usually considered the touchstone of quality of the TT. Among the early translations into English, Clement Egerton's *The Golden Lotus*, first published in 1939, is an example of this process (even though he sometimes overstepped the limits of translation and entered the terrain of adaptation). However, in the typical *adaptations* of JPM, the constraint of the ST is to be dialectically viewed. The cross spatio-temporal dialogue between the ST and the historical context of its translation enables translators (i.e. authors of the adaptations) to creatively circumvent some of the ST constraints and adapt

---

   directly from a Chinese version of the novel) or tertiary (i.e. its ST is a translation, and that translation is in turn relayed from a previous translation). Examples can be found in Figure 15.1. Of course, there is a similar relationship within the many editions of JPM in Chinese, where the editions have a primary, secondary or tertiary etc., relationship vis-à-vis each other. However, for the purposes of the present chapter it is not necessary to go too deeply into this question.

3 It is worth noting that not all texts presented in Figure 15.1 and Figure 15.2 will be discussed in this chapter, but the figures provide a panoramic view of the translation history of JPM in some of the major languages and are also of reference value in relation to the other chapters in this collection. For Japanese translations, see Qi and Shani (2022).

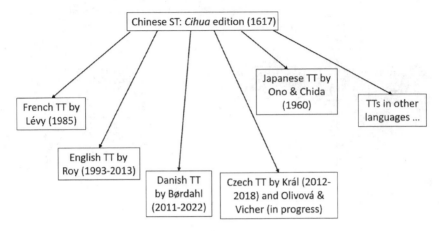

Figure 15.2. Translations from the *Cihua* edition of JPM

the novel according to their own historical context in the target culture (Qi 2018). Our primary example of this process is Franz Kuhn's (1884–1961) well-founded and well-translated, but significantly abridged and adapted, German version of JPM, *Kin Ping Meh oder die abenteuerliche Geschichte von Hsi Men und seinen sechs Frauen* (1930). Kuhn adapted from the Zhang Zhupo 張竹坡 (1670–1698) edition of JPM, a version with commentary that was first published in 1695 and promptly superseded all previous versions in popularity. Kuhn's adaptation, which was an immense success, later became the ST for a number of translations and adaptations into other (mainly European) languages. In this chapter we concentrate on two English adaptations that were (indirectly) based on Kuhn's German adaptation, examining the interactions of the adaptations with their target context, and the effect of these interactions on the reception of JPM in the Anglophone world.

Omissions in Adaptation: From Kuhn and Miall to *Harem of Hsi Men*[4]

In translation, the translator's creativity is constrained in multifarious ways: not only is it curtailed by the translator's personal interpretation and idiosyncratic re-presentation of the ST, but it is also subject to the influence of the ideological, aesthetic and social climate of the TT. When the translator surrenders to any of these factors and proceeds to tamper deliberately with

---

4   When quoting from a certain edition, we use the transcription or spelling of names that is used in the given edition (e.g. *Hsi Me*n), but elsewhere we shift to the *pinyin* transcription (e.g. *Ximen Qing*).

THE ADAPTATION OF SEX AND SEXY ADAPTATIONS

the ST, he/she assumes the role of an adaptor. A most commonly employed technique in adaptation is *omission*.

The year of 1939 witnessed the birth of two English translations of JPM. One was *The Golden Lotus,* a fairly complete translation produced by Clement Egerton (1884–ca.1960). Published in four volumes amounting to about 1,500 pages, Egerton's English version was translated directly from the Chinese version by Zhang Zhupo, the same as that used by Kuhn (Xiaoxiaosheng and Egerton 1939). The other was a translation by Bernard Miall (1939), from Kuhn's German version. Miall's edition, entitled *Chin P'ing Mei: The Adventurous History of the Mandarin and his Six Wives,* was about half the length of Egerton's TT. In the Anglophone world, Miall's version became the basis for several further adaptations of JPM (Qi 2018, 2021). In these TTs adapted from Miall's translation, large-scale omission and abbreviation were undertaken. To illustrate how omission was employed as an adaptation technique, we need to bring in some lengthy excerpts from the respective works. We shall first quote a passage (see Figure 15.3) from JPM in the popular edition of Zhang Zhupo (1695) that served as ST for the first translations, into Manchu, German and English, after which we will introduce the English translations by Egerton (excerpt 1), Miall (translated from Kuhn, excerpt 3), and the adaptation of Miall as appeared in *Harem of Hsi Men* (excerpt 2). The reason why the excerpt from Miall is quoted after the *Harem* will be explained below.

Excerpt 1. *Golden Lotus,* Chapter 37:

When they had taken a few cups together, the woman moved her seat nearer to Hsi-men's, and they passed their wine from mouth to mouth. After making sure that there was no one about, Hsi-men threw his arms around her, kissed her and caressed her tongue with his own. She took the jade sceptre into her hand. Their passions were stirred into flame. They drank no more, but saw to the fastenings upon the door. Then both took off their clothes, and the woman prepared the coverlets upon the bed. It was the hour before sunset. The wine had set Hsi-men Ch'ing on fire. He took the silver clasp from its case, and put it in position, while the woman fondly touched him with her slender hands. *She thought his weapon looked magnificent; the veins swelled with dark red blood, and the flesh was firm and powerful.* She sat on his knees; they threw their arms round each other's necks and kissed again. Then she raised one of her legs, and, with her hand, helped that sword to find its scabbard. For a while they jousted together. Hsi-men Ch'ing allowed his hands to wander over the woman's body. It was very soft but firm. The hair was fine and delicate. *Eventually he told her to lie on the bed; he pulled her legs around his body and threw himself fiercely into the struggle.*

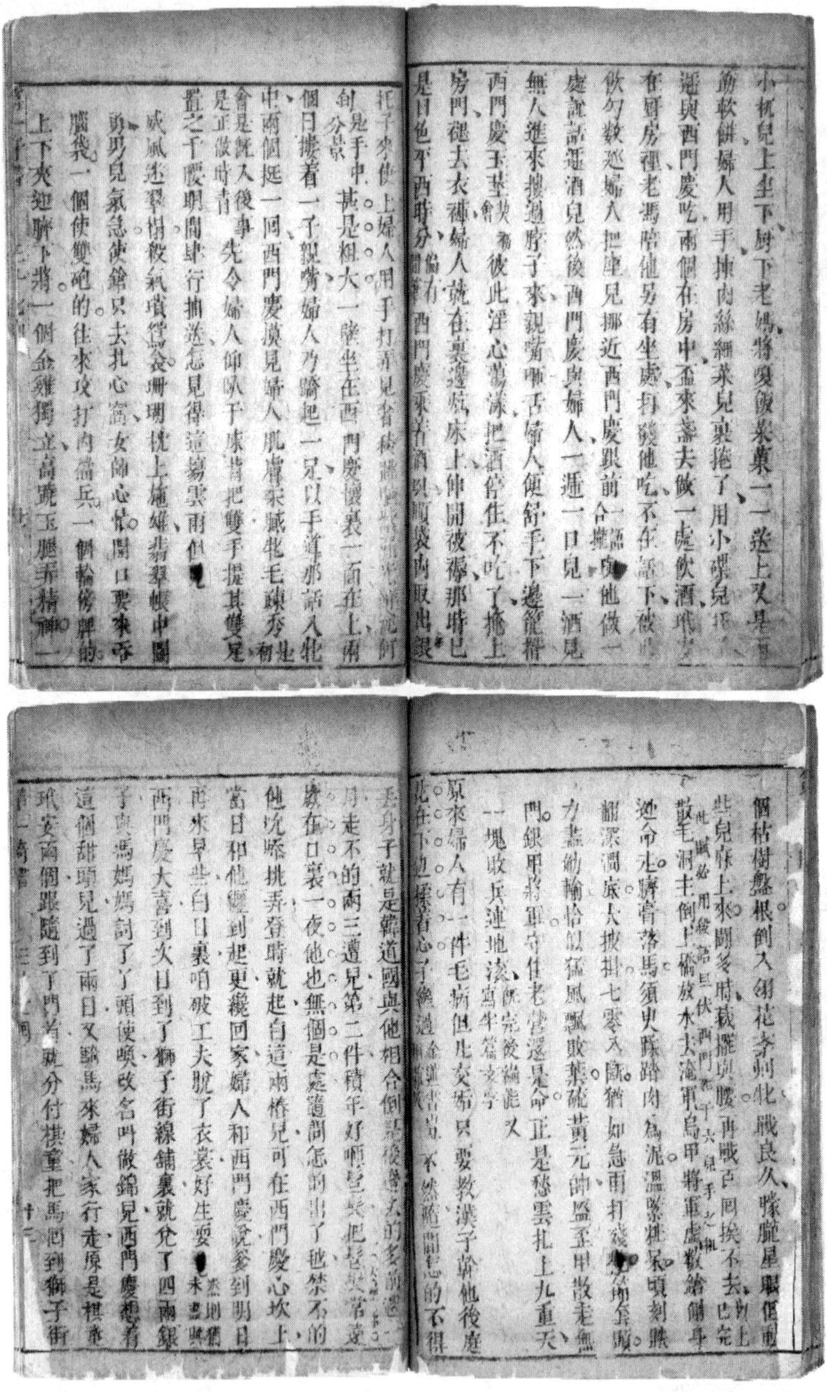

Figure 15.3. Chinese ST for English excerpts 1, 2 and 3

THE ADAPTATION OF SEX AND SEXY ADAPTATIONS

The god of battle now holds sway over the green-clad bed.

The coverlets, with silk-embroidered love birds, feel the press of strife.

Heroes display their prowess on the coral pillows

Striving for victory within the silken curtains.

The hero dashes madly to the fray, plunges his spear with fury home.

The heroine's heart beats wildly. She yawns and gapes and fain would
all devour him.

Then up he brings his pair of culverins, and lets them loose upon the
enemy skulking in the trousers.

The other raises her shield to meet the mad attack of the great general
stationed beneath the navel.

One plays the golden cockerel, standing on single leg, raising the other
high, to show his mettle

The other, like a stripped tree, with roots that spread in all directions,
thrusts forth to meet the foe.

When they have fought a while, the shining eyes are dimmed

A single movement makes them squirm and quiver.

Though their limbs tremble, they still fight on

Clashing a hundred times, they cannot break away,

Then, letting loose the dam, the captain of the scanty hair would
drown his enemy in the flood.

The general in black armour feigns to make a thrust, but turns aside
and seeks to fly.

The warden of the navel is unhorsed, thrown down and ground to dust
in but a moment.

Lord 'warm and tight' now plays the fool, tumbling he falls to the far
depths of the abyss.

The heavy mail is broken into pieces, like faded blossoms when the
storm breaks on them

The silken cap gives way beneath the strain, like fallen leaves before the
raging winds

And Marshal 'sulphurous', his crest awry, can find no place to flee.

Prince 'Silver Armour' holds his ground, and swears he'll stand till
death.

The skies are hidden by a sad dark cloud

The warriors roll stricken on the field.

*Porphyry liked one game more than any other. When she had joined with him
as lovers do, she wanted him to enjoy the flower in her bottom while she played
with the flower in her womb. Satisfied in this way she reached the blissful oblivion
which is the aim of lovers. She used to practise this game so often that in thirty
days Han Tao-kuo would take his pleasure at the front gate no more than three*

LINTAO QI

times. Apart from this she titillated his ivory sceptre with her lips and fondled it all night with never-failing desire; if its master flagged, her lips returned his strength.

Nothing could have given Hsi-men Ch'ing greater pleasure. All that day they played, till the watchman gave his first warning. Then he went home.

Before Hsi-men left her, Porphyry asked him to come again the next day, and to come early. She promised that if he did so he should not go away unsatisfied. Hsi-men could have asked for nothing better. The next day [...]

Xiaoxiaosheng and Egerton 1972: 147–149) (italics mine)

This is one of the many graphically explicit sexual scenes in JPM, quoted from a 1972 reprint of Egerton's translation, and the sections in italics were in Latin in Egerton's original translation published in 1939. The passage provides a verisimilar depiction of a case of sexual intercourse where the couple indulge themselves in passionate foreplay, enthusiastic coition, and happy agreement for future rendezvous. The language – especially the lyrical description, which clad the erotic in flowery metaphors, is highly euphemistic, but at the same time expressions like 'jade sceptre', 'weapon', and 'helped that sword to find its scabbard' so permeate the passage that it leaves nothing to imagination. The alternate use of prose and poetry in the excerpt makes the text a double-coded one: the prose furnishes a realistic presentation of the couple's behaviour, especially in the foreplay; the lyric, a figurative description of sexual intercourse. The latter is an effective supplement to the former, by suspending the story line and highlighting the sexual components of the novel.

Note that the lyric passage is devoid of reference to either Ximen Qing or Wang Liu'er (variously translated as Wang the Sixth, Sixth Wang, or Porphyry), and that absence distances the figurative description from the readers and to some degree even separates it from the two lovers' behaviour, endowing the passage with some universality (Qi 2018: 169), and therefore independence from the realistic presentation of the scene. The effect of the alternate use of prose and poetry, in this case, is comparable to the camera work in film shooting. The prosaic text provides a close-up of what is happening to the characters in the film, and the shift to lyrics is similar to a change of shot. In order to avoid realistically filming how the two characters copulate, the camera is artistically or figuratively directed to, for example, an erotic painting on the wall, which, on top of maintaining the continuity of the narrative, also adds variation and thus vitality to the story. With the sudden shift from prose to lyric, the two characters are temporarily zoomed out of the story or screen. The lyric presentation, as an alternative shot of the realistic intercourse, romanticizes the scene, in which the absence, or rather the implied presence, of the characters is the ingenious design. The narrative is consequently made melodramatically hierarchical rather than monotonous. These characteristics of the Chinese ST are all faithfully and stylistically well rendered in Egerton's translation.

Totalling ca. 880 Chinese characters in the Chinese ST, corresponding to 717 words in the Egerton edition, the same scene is drastically shorter in the English translation by Miall (and its ST, i.e. Kuhn's German version) and subsequent adaptations. In the pulp edition *The Harem of Hsi Men*, a 1953 anonymous adaptation from Miall's translation, we find the passage compressed to 139 words:[5]

> Excerpt 2. *Harem of Hsi Men*, Chapter 12:
>
> [*The Sixth Wang offered him a brimming bowl of tea with a beaten-up mixture of walnuts and bamboo shoots; then she herself sat down on the edge of the bed. They spoke briefly or at greater length of various domestic matters.*]
> After a few goblets of wine, the conversation was becoming more intimate. First, they drank together from the same side of the goblet. Then the young woman moved nearer and nearer. He laid his arm about her neck and kissed her with a passionate tongue-kiss, while she let her hand fall as though by accident on his lap. In mutual desire the hot waters of their passion bubbled over. Now she unsheathed herself, and he too stripped off his clothes. With a sense of blissful relief, he was conscious of her soft flesh, her smooth skin. The Sixth Wang was acquainted with variations of the game of love which offered even the greatly experienced Hsi Men unfamiliar delights. It was with high satisfaction that he parted from his new darling as the night was falling. On the following day [...] (Anonymous 1953: 171)

In sequence of time, an adaptation comes *after* its ST, but it may not be treated and presented as secondary or derivative. In the *Harem of Hsi Men*, there is no indication of either the ST author or the TT producer; and the only reference to its source is on the front cover, where it is promoted as 'a great Chinese classic – renowned for centuries' (ibid.: n.p.). With no supplementary bibliographical details, the book is encouraging or deliberately misleading its readers to treat it as an 'English replacement of the ST': for readers without access to the Chinese ST, it 'attains the status of the original'; and for those without any knowledge of its paternal English text by Miall (not to mention Miall's ST, i.e. the German version by Kuhn), it becomes *the translation* (Qi 2018: 61).

The excerpts above, particularly the one from *Harem of Hsi Men*, are clearly much more reticent in sexual description than the Chinese ST. In *Harem*,

---

5   This particular paragraph remains the same in Miall's translation (and its parent text by Kuhn) and the *Harem*. What has been changed is the co-text, which will be discussed in more detail later in this section.

the metaphorical lyric expressions of the erotic are nowhere to be found, but the realistic depictions are also greatly simplified in the process from Kuhn > Miall > *Harem*. In the Egerton version, the heroine 'took the jade sceptre into her hand', but the metonymical manipulation in the adaptation of *Harem* makes the scene much less amorous: she is said to 'let her hand fall as though by accident on his lap'. The voluptuous female character, who is lustful and even somewhat aggressive in her sensuous pursuit in the original Chinese ST, as well as in Egerton's version, has through the metamorphosis of Kuhn and Miall finally changed into a somewhat reserved and unadventurous lady in the TT of *Harem*. The use of 'as though by accident' is out of character for Wang the Sixth, who is outspokenly prurient in JPM; and the replacement of 'jade sceptre' with 'the lap' betrays the reluctance to make reference to the male sexual organ, even in a metaphorical manner.

In the adaptation, the passionate foreplay is banally toned down, the enthusiastic sexual act is only vaguely implied, and the happy agreement to a future rendezvous simply disappears. Furthermore, instead of clarifying that the heroine is infatuated with sodomy and fellatio, *Harem*'s euphemistic text merely indicates that she is 'acquainted with variations of the game of love', which, together with the 'unfamiliar delights' the protagonist derives, leaves the interpretation of the bizarre erotic scene largely to chance. The adaptation turns a major sexual encounter of the hero, which gives that chapter its title, into a minor event.

This toning down of sexually explicit details is apparently not entirely the product of *Harem*'s adaptation, when the passage above is compared with Miall's, and indeed, Kuhn's translation. As a matter of fact, the quoted passage (i.e. Excerpt 2) remains largely unchanged from Kuhn to Miall to *Harem*. What made *Harem*'s adaptation unique is how it omits the context of this sexual encounter. In between the two paragraphs quoted above in Excerpt 2, a number of details from Miall's translation, which help to contextualise the two lovers' sexual intercourse, have been deleted. In order to illustrate the scale of omission in this case, Miall's text is quoted below, in Excerpt 3, with the passages *Harem* deleted underlined.

Excerpt 3. *The Adventurous History of Hsi Men and His Six Wives*, Chapter 25

[*The Sixth Wang offered him a brimming bowl of tea with a beaten-up mixture of walnuts and bamboo shoots; then she herself sat down on the edge of the bed. They spoke briefly or at greater length of various domestic matters.*]

Hsi Men did not like to see her busying herself with the tea tray.

'You really must have a young maid,' he said.

THE ADAPTATION OF SEX AND SEXY ADAPTATIONS

'Well, I cannot deny,' she promptly agreed, 'that since my daughter has left me I find it very trying to have to do everything with my own hands.'

'That can easily be avoided. I will commission Mother Fong to engage a young maid for you tomorrow. Let me see to paying her wages.'

'But how I take still further advantage of your goodness! Already I am deeply indebted to you.'

He was secretly delighted to note how easily and correctly she spoke. And at this moment old Fong brought in the ready-laid table.

'Hey, Mother Fong, a young maid is wanted in this house,' he said. 'See if you can find one tomorrow!'

'Oh, you ought to thank him nicely for that, little lady!' said Mother Fong, turning to the Sixth Wang. 'And I know where I can find one. My sister-in-law Chow in the southern city would be glad to find a situation for her thirteen-year-old daughter, but she wants four bars of silver. If the noble gentleman is agreeable ....'

'That's settled,' said Hsi Men, and the young woman thanked him with a hasty *Wan fu*.

Now they proceeded to dine. The Sixth Wang was about to hand her noble guest the first goblet of wine with a new-fashioned ceremonial curtsy, but this he would not allow.

'Enough of ceremonies!' he said, gallantly raising her, on which she smilingly breathed another *Wan fu*. After old Fong had cleared the table she discreetly withdrew to the kitchen, where with the assistance of Tai A she did justice to the abundant remains of the meal.

Meanwhile, in the bedroom, after a few goblets of wine, the conversation was becoming more intimate. First, they drank together from the same side of the goblet. Then the young woman moved nearer and nearer. He laid his arm about her neck and kissed her with a passionate tongue-kiss, while she let her hand fall as though by accident on his lap. In mutual desire the hot waters of their passion bubbled over. Now she unsheathed herself, and he too stripped off his clothes. With a sense of blissful relief, he was conscious of her soft flesh, her smooth skin. The Sixth Wang was acquainted with variations of the game of love which offered even the greatly experienced Hsi Men unfamiliar delights.

It was with high satisfaction that he parted from his new darling as the night was falling. On the following day [...] (Xiaoxiaosheng and Miall 1982: 368–369: quoted from a 1982 reprint of Miall's 1939 translation)

It is worth pointing out at this stage that the discussion in this chapter will not be based on fidelity to the ST, as 'there are many and varied motives behind adaptation and few involve faithfulness' (Hutcheon 2006: xiii). To be sure, any adaptation has to be built on a prior text, but the word 'adapt' is explicitly reminiscent of changes made to that ST (to avoid a profusion of terms, the prior text will hereafter be invariably branded ST, including when it points to 'derived' texts that are already translations or adaptations, such as Kuhn and Miall – cf. Figure 15.1.) To use Hutcheon's words, 'adaptation is repetition, but repetition without replication' (ibid.: 7). In other words, adaptation connotes both familiarity and difference, both preservation and change. Infidelity to the ST is in the gene of adaptation. The familiarity, or faithful component, makes the text recognizable as the afterlife of the ST, while the difference gives it a renewed life in the contemporary world, appealing to a new audience with a new lifestyle.

JPM is a *magnum opus* open to a multitude of interpretations: some read it as history, others read it as pornography, still others learn about Chinese business culture or interactions in officialdom; but in adapting it, all the different facets of JPM will not be retained intact (Qi 2018: 61). The work of the adaptor is in no way an innocent one; even a seemingly careless omission has profound implications. The act of omitting may itself be rooted in ideological constraints, economic considerations or intellectual concerns, but an omission is by no means mechanical. It is, rather a creative process (ibid.). Cutting away part of the story is diametrically opposite to preserving it intact, but the work of the adaptor is in general to achieve both a shorter version and a version that looks complete.

Let us first, with a view to length and completeness, compare the three English translations/adaptations that we have so far analysed – Miall, Egerton and *Harem*. The 316 pages of *The Harem of Hsi Men*, when compared to the 1500 plus pages of Egerton's *Golden Lotus*, represents only a quarter of the length of the latter. *Harem* begins with the beginning of JPM and ends with the end, and between the covers, the book keeps the flow of the story with smooth transitions. However, since it cannot expect to keep the multifarious themes intact with only a quarter of the capacity of the complete translation by Egerton, the adaptor has to decide which episodes (of its immediate predecessor, i.e. Miall's English TT in this case) are to be transposed into the adaptation.

By removing the lead-in to the sexual intercourse between Hsi Men (the master) and Wang the Sixth (the wife of a servant of Hsi Men), the adaptation loses an important opportunity to situate the love affair in the sociocultural context of Ming China, in which the relationship between male and female, between people from different social classes, and between sensual pleasure and the materialistic culture, are highly sophisticated. However, the title of *The Harem of Hsi Men* is axiomatic of the focus of the incarnated text, and therefore anything sexually related in its ST is transported as it is into the new textual universe, and the historical narrative, the commercial activities and the interactions in the officialdom are simplified, minimized, or expurgated.

THE ADAPTATION OF SEX AND SEXY ADAPTATIONS

In this way, *Harem* is autotelic in that it achieves what its title has purported to present. And indeed, in assessing what *Harem* does to the text of JPM, one has to refer back to its immediate ST, i.e. Miall's English version, instead of to the Chinese ST, even though *Harem* promotes itself as 'a great Chinese classic'.

Additions in Adaptation: *Houses of Joy*

In 1958, Olympia Press in Paris published *Houses of Joy,* another adaptation from Miall's English translation. Olympia Press was the publisher who first brought to the world such 'once mind-boggling, now canonical works' as *Lolita* and *Naked Lunch* (De St. Jorre 1994: 12). *Houses of Joy* was included in the publisher's well-known, indeed notorious, 'Traveller's Companion' series. Printed uniformly in an 'ugly plain green cover', the series consists mainly of pornographic books in English (Girodias 1965: 20). The only information on the cover of this book other than the title and the name of the publisher is the name 'Wu Wu Meng',[6] an apparent pseudonym.

Houses of Joy is the version of JPM that 'most Westerners are familiar with' (Xiaoxiaosheng and Egerton 2008: n/p). With only 238 pages, it exercises omission to an extreme degree and neither begins with the beginning of the original Chinese story, nor ends with the original ending. The opening of the novel is the meeting of Pan Jinlian and her tiger-slaying brother-in-law Wu Song, which involves much erotic fantasy on the part of the female character, and it concludes with the horrendous death of Ximen Qing from an overdose of aphrodisiac (Meng 1958). But what is more significant in the case of *Houses* is that it makes equal recourse to the techniques of omission and addition, to foreground and amplify the sexual descriptions. First, let us look at a passage from Miall's version:[7]

Excerpt 4. *The Adventurous History of Hsi Men and his Six Wives,* Chapter 11:

Sadly, Gold Lotus went back to her pavilion. The time passed with intolerable slowness. An hour seemed to her a month. At last, she made up her mind. Hsi Men would not come home that night, she was certain. As soon as it was dark, she sent her two maids to bed. Then Gold Lotus went into the park, as though she were going to take one of her nightly strolls. But this time she had a definite goal: the cottage of the young gardener, Kin Tung. Quietly she invited him to

---

6   Wu Wu Meng proved to be the South African beat poet Sinclair Beiles (Qi 2018: 63). This is a name coined by Beiles, and no corresponding Chinese characters have ever been used for this pseudonym.

7   Since *Houses of Joy* has no relationship to any original Chinese edition of JPM, we shall only bring the relevant passages from its ST, Miall 1939 – see Table 15.1.

come to her pavilion. She let him in, carefully bolted the door, and set wine before him. She pressed him to drink until he grew tipsy. Then she loosened her girdle, disrobed, and abandoned herself to him.

> Eternal rules she disregards,
> Rules that nature herself proclaims:
> The high must ever shun the low,
> Noble from base be strictly severed.
> Emboldened by her desires,
> She fears not her master's wrath.
> Hot with unbridled desire
> She obeys only her own voice.
> In the park of the hundred flowers
> She allows her base impulse to rule her,
> Making a brothel of the house
> Where chastity should prevail.
> But what is honor, what reputation?
> Love is her pastime.
> The ignoble seed of an ass
> Is allowed to defile her jasper body.

Every night from now onwards Gold Lotus admitted the gardener's boy to her pavilion. Early in the morning, before it grew light, she sent him away.

(Miall 1959: 84–85)

The excerpt from Miall's translation describes how Pan Jinlian, during the absence of Ximen Qing, seduces a teenage gardener of the Ximen household and initiates an illicit love affair with him. The language is stylistically similar to the first excerpt quoted in this chapter, in which the pre-intercourse behaviour of the characters is described in a realistic way, while the act itself is figuratively presented in lyrical language. In *Houses*, the same episode undergoes dramatic rewriting with *amplification*.

Excerpt 5. *Houses of Joy*, Chapter 12:

Sadly, Gold Lotus went back to her pavilion. The time passed with intolerable slowness. An hour seemed to her a month. At last, she made up her mind. Hsi Men would not come home that night, she was certain. As soon as it was dark, she sent her two maids to bed. Then Gold Lotus went into the park, as though she were going to take one of her nightly strolls. But this time she had a definite goal: the cottage of the young gardener *who was frightened by her smile when she saw him clipping a tree through the window of her bedchamber.* Quietly she invited him to come to her pavilion. She let him in, carefully bolted the door,

THE ADAPTATION OF SEX AND SEXY ADAPTATIONS

and set wine before him. She pressed him to drink until he grew tipsy. Then she loosened her girdle, disrobed, and abandoned herself to him.

When a woman, such as Gold Lotus, who has given herself over utterly to sensuality and longs for offspring by her acts, finds that her husband's seed refuses to take root in her, she desires to play the part of a man by sticking a portion of herself, as large as a male truncheon, into his body. Lacking this portion, she plumbs his starfish with her little fingers but soon finds this insufficient satisfaction. But she dares not go further for fear of offending his virility. This was not the case with the young gardener.

Nature is strange. Sometimes when its demands are not satisfied it behaves unreasonably. It drives a woman who fears barrenness to regard her mate as female and to behave as if she is able to impregnate him with a mere instrument! Hsi Men's absence had driven Gold Lotus to extremes, and after she had satisfied herself in one or another of the usual ways with the gardener, she got the docile boy to kneel over, with his buttocks above her face and his brown starfish exposed to her view. Then she took up a brush, which lay on the table close to hand, and plunged its smooth ebony handle deep into the brown orifice. She had oiled it well, so it slipped smoothly into the firm tunnel. Then she commanded the bewildered boy to place his tongue between the lips of her love-purse, and while he let it dally there in the moistness with her hair scratching his chin and lips, she drove the bit of oiled ebony furiously in and out of his hole.

By these means Gold Lotus raised herself to a terrible pitch of fervour, and a heat of such intensity overtook her that she felt as if her body had been cast into fire.

She clasped his head so tightly between her thighs and rammed the ebony so hard into his starfish that the boy gave a smothered cry. Then she withdrew it, tossed it away, and made him turn round. He leaped between her thighs, lunging his pulsing thruster into her palpitating wetness, and while he pounded away, she sank her teeth deeper and deeper into his shoulder. His lunges threw her body into a series of ecstatic convulsions, so strong that when at last she felt his fire-juice spurting into her, she could bear it no longer, and in her agony, she cast the frightened boy aside and lay alone writhing and whimpering [...]

> Eternal rules she disregards,
> Rules that nature herself proclaims.

Every night from now onwards Gold Lotus admitted the gardener's boy to her pavilion. Early in the morning, before it grew light, she sent him away.

(Meng 1958: 124–125)

Amounting to 596 words (of which only 162 are from its immediate source text, i.e. Miall's translation), the adapted version more than doubles the length of this passage in Miall's translation. The adaptor, the South African Beat poet

Sinclair Beiles, replaces the metaphorical depiction of the act of coitus in lyric with an extended realistic scene encompassing a series of sexual variations, spiced with narratorial comments. To better interpret the changes made to its immediate textual source, the Miall translation, the social, institutional and individual background will be recounted at some length in the following.

Firstly, there is the great (if not the greatest) monetary impetus behind the adaptor and publisher's production of the erotic adaptation. Maurice Girodias, the legendary owner of the Olympia Press, once frankly recalled his publishing technique:

> When I had completely run out of money I wrote blurbs for imaginary books, invented sonorous titles and funny pen names (Marcus van Heller, Akbar del Piombo, Miles Underwood, Carmencita de las Lunas, etc.) and then printed a list which was sent out to our clientele of booklovers, tempting them with such titles as *White Thighs, The Chariot of Flesh, The Sexual Life of Robinson Crusoe, With Open Mouth,* etc. they immediately responded with orders and money, thanks to which we were again able to eat, drink, write, and print. I could again advance money to my authors, and they hastened to turn in manuscripts which more or less fitted the descriptions. (Girodias 1965: 19)

Therefore, financial concern is the overriding driving force for the publisher, and his authors, mainly the 'beatniks and expatriates lying about in the Left Bank hotels and flophouses' (Server 2002: 169), are scarcely better off than Girodias himself, who usually paid a flat fee for his author's manuscript, which, 'although modest, formed the substance of many an expatriate budget' (Girodias 1965: 19). Sinclair Beiles was one such expatriate in Paris and 'translated' JPM partly out of a need for money. Girodias reminisced thus about the adventure:

> A young South African appeared one day in our office. His name was Sinclair Beiles [...]. He explained to us [... that he] was presently translating a rare Chinese novel, of a voluptuousness and sensuality that only the Chinese could achieve. For a price, he would continue the translation for Olympia Press, and at an agreed price, would bring us a new chapter every week. [...] This arrangement continued until we had all of *Houses of Joy,* an extremely amusing and delicately indelicate book. (ibid.: 597)

The hunger for money brings the publisher and the adapter together. As the previous quotation clearly shows, the erotic writing is what the publisher was after, and the adapter, in order to sustain the cooperation, has to pander to that taste. The result is the 'extremely amusing and delicately indelicate' *Houses of Joy,* to which the above excerpt belongs.

In the additions Beiles made to his source text, Pan Jinlian (Gold Lotus) sadistically sodomized Qintong (the young gardener) with first her finger and

THE ADAPTATION OF SEX AND SEXY ADAPTATIONS

then a brush; meanwhile, she 'commanded' the boy to perform oral sex on her. The titillating scene is then consummated with an intercourse between the two. Both the details and the variations of the sexual description in the excerpt, which are in line with the requirement of the publisher, would have contributed to the commercial success of the novel.[8] Here the pressure from the economic consideration is not a restricting factor but a creative one in the shaping up of the adaptation: it drives the adapter to flesh out the story with invented obscenity, directing the characters to do things they did not do and would not do in the original Chinese ST environment.

Indeed, the addition of a female character sodomizing a male and a male performing cunnilingus is an anachronism in both time and space as far as the Chinese ST is concerned. They are the creation of the adapter who, partly out of commercial concern, invented them to cater to contemporary taste. To be sure, oral sex and buggery are not unheard of in JPM and even enjoyed some popularity in the erotic writings in the Ming and Qing dynasties, but when sadism is involved, the agent is more often than not the male, and the female is usually described as the victim of this behaviour (Ding 2007: 199). The sadism of the male and the masochism of the female as demonstrated in JPM – for example, Ximen Qing's habitual incense-burning on his sexual partner's vagina and Pan Jinlian's offering to drink Ximen's urine to save him from the trouble of going to toilet in the cold winter night – are unmistakably the hallmarks of the androcentric ST society.[9] The adapter's creative description, however, somewhat democratizes that society with regard to sexual practice, obscuring the novel's historical value.

Secondly, in 1960, together with the other Beat poets William Burroughs, Brion Gysin, and Gregory Corso, Beiles co-authored *Minutes to Go*, the 'now legendary book of cut-up writing' (Cummiskey 2009: 13). Beiles may magnify the sensual aspect of JPM out of a desire for economic benefit, but as a writer of literary genius, he is likely to simultaneously attach some importance to the intellectual virtue of his adaptation. For instance, apart from anal coitus and cunnilingus, Beiles also dramatically appeals to psychology to justify his invention of Pan Jinlian's sexual behaviour.

In the excerpt, the adapter uses the following as a lead-in to Pan's sodomizing of the young gardener: 'When a woman, such as Gold Lotus, who has

---

8   The success of the book is confirmed by Beiles himself in an interview in the 1990s (Holmes 2009: 59).

9   One might argue that I am reading personal opinion and modern viewpoints into how far these practices were sadistic or nasty vis-à-vis the female partner in ancient China. There are indeed many indications in JPM that the female partners were in fact stimulated by moxa burning and somehow did like it, but then classical Chinese novels on the topic of sexuality were often works of male authors.

given herself over utterly to sensuality and longs for offspring by her acts, finds that her husband's seed refuses to take root in her, she desires to play the part of a man [...]'. The connection between the psychological motives of Pan and her ensuing behaviour seems a bit far-fetched, but Beiles's effort to establish a psychological basis for Pan's behaviour in his adaptation is undoubtedly an intellectual endeavour that functions, to a certain extent, to prevent the final product from completely falling into the abysm of 'sex for sex's sake'.

Indeed, the adapter's recourse to the character's psychological world not only enables him to comment on, intervene in and direct the development of the story, but it also enriches the image of his characters, and therefore multi-dimensionally presents Pan Jinlian as a sophisticated female rather than merely a prurient woman. For instance, his presentation of Pan's behaviour demonstrates sympathy with the heroine: 'Nature is strange. Sometimes when its demands are not satisfied it behaves unreasonably. It drives a woman who fears barrenness to regard her mate as female and to behave as if she is able to impregnate him with a mere instrument!', with a tinge of accusation of the patriarchal society: 'Hsi Men's absence had driven Gold Lotus to extremes [...]'.

Omission as an adaptation technique is mainly a constraint imposed upon the creativity of the ST, though the decision as to what to omit is in itself a creative activity. The various reasons for doing so, whether they are ideological, intellectual or economic, are often interdependent and interrelated. For instance, the choice of deleting explicit sexual description is often out of concern for legality, but it is also to avoid potential financial risk: if a book is deemed by the censors to be obscene and is subsequently prosecuted, the publisher might be fined, and the book proscribed from circulation. However, the other adaptation technique, addition and amplification, is usually employed for exactly the same types of reasons (e.g. ideological, intellectual or economic), albeit as a demonstration of creativity against various constraints (e.g. in the context of literary censorship or as an activist approach to rebelling against socio-historical constraints).

Concluding remarks

In literary adaptations, the adapter re-interprets and re-presents his/her ST[10] in response to his/her own historical context by either conforming to it or rebelling against it. The choice, which betrays the adapter's political reaction to the milieu of his own society, is usually materialized through the technique of omission or addition, both being typical forms of rewriting. The adapter's

---

10 For the complexity of the concept ST, please refer to footnote 2 in this chapter.

choices are ineluctably constrained by the immediate ST, the agents involved in the production of the TT (e.g. the publisher) and their legal and commercial considerations, as well as their intellectual orientation. However, as the examples in this chapter reveal, these constraints can also be creatively exploited to the advantage of the adapter's final textual product. Whether the resulting 'opus' should be considered 'pulp' or 'creative writing' is another question, and one that we shall leave out of consideration here. To be sure, an adaptation is born out of its parental text or ST, but that does not mean that it is derivative, secondary or inferior. It is, by definition, supposed to better adapt to the new TT environment, with all its similarity to, and difference from, the ST. It reflects a need of the TT milieu for the TT audience. Fidelity to the ST, particularly if the ST is itself a translation, is not a major concern. Consideration for the original ST in the work's original language and setting is not even a minor concern.

The process of interlingual, cross-cultural, usually transnational and sometimes trans-historical translation and adaptation is one similar to what Said (1983: 226–227) proposes in relation to recurrent patterns by which ideas or theories travel. It consists of four stages – namely, a point of origin that enables the birth and circulation of the idea or theory; a spatio-temporal distance traversed; a set of conditions of acceptance (or resistance); and transformation in the new time and place. All the four stages are present in translation as well as in adaptation, each imposing its specific constraints, which in turn stimulates the creativity of the translator/adapter. Translation and adaptation are, therefore, immanently sites where constraints and creativity encounter, combat, negotiate, compromise and reconcile.

References

Anonymous
> 1953. *The Harem of Hsi Men*. New York: Universal Publishing and Distributing Corporation (Royal Books).

Cummiskey, Gary and Eva Kowalska (eds.)
> 2009. *Who was Sinclair Beiles?* Sandton, South Africa: Dye Hard Press.

De St. Jorre, John
> 1994. *Venus Bound: The Erotic Voyage of the Olympia Press and its Writers*. New York: Random House.

Ding, Fengshan
> 2007. *Ming Qing xing ai xiao shuo lun gao*. Taibei: Da an chubanshe.

Børdahl, Vibeke
2019. *Jin Ping Mei – i vers og prosa*. Kbh: Vandkunsten.

Gabelentz, Hans Conon von der and Martin Gimm
2012. *Jin Ping Mei Teil 7*. Berlin: Staatsbibliothek zu Berlin.

Girodias, Maurice
1965. *The Olympia Reader; Selections from the Traveller's Companion Series*. New York: Grove Press.

Holmes, Earle
2009. 'The beat goes on.' In G. Cummiskey and Eva Kowalska (eds), *Who was Sinclair Beiles?* Sandton, South Africa: Dye Hard Press.

Hutcheon, Linda
2006. *A Theory of Adaptation*. New York: Routledge.

Kibat, Otto, Artur Kibat and Herbert Franke
1989. *Djin Ping Meh: Schlebenblüten in goldener Vase: ein Sittenroman aus der Ming-Zeit*. Zürich: Diogenes.

Král, Oldřich
2012. *Jin Ping Mei, aneb, Slivoň ve zlaté váze*. Lásenice: Maxima.

Kuhn, Franz
1930. *Kin Ping Meh oder die abenteuerliche Geschichte von Hsi Men und seinen sechs Frauen. Aus dem Chinesischen übertragen von Franz Kuhn*. Leipzig: Insel-Verlag.

Lévy, André
2004. *Fleur en Fiole d'Or = Jin Ping Mei*. Paris: Gallimard.

Meng, Wu Wu
1958. *Houses of Joy*. Vol. 75, The Traveller's Companion Series. Paris: Olympia Press.

Miall, Bernard
1939. *Chin P'ing Mei: The Adventurous History of the Mandarin and his Six Wives*. London: The Bodley Head.
1959. *Chin p'ing Mei: The Adventurous History of Hsi Men and his Six Wives*. London: The Bodley Head.

Ono, Shinobu, and Kuichi Chida (trans.)
1960. *Jin Ping Mei* 金瓶梅. 3 vols. Tokyo: Heibonsha.

Qi, Lintao
2016. 'Agents of Latin – An archival research on Clement Egerton's English translation The Golden Lotus.' *Target: International Journal of Translation Studies* 28 (1): 39–57.

2018. *Jin Ping Mei English Translations: Texts, Paratexts and Contexts. Routledge Advances in Translation and Interpreting Studies.* Abingdon and New York: Routledge.

2021. 'Translating sexuality in the context of Anglo-American censorship: The case of *Jin Ping Mei*.' *Translation and Interpreting Studies* 16 (3): 416–433. doi. org/10.1075/tis.19010.qi.

Qi, Lintao and Shani Tobias

2022. 'Japanese translations of *Jin Ping Mei*: Chinese sexuality in the socio-cultural context of Japan.' In Lintao Qi and Shani Tobias (eds), *Encountering China's Past: Translation and Dissemination of Classical Chinese Literature,* pp. 125–144. Singapore: Springer.

Said, Edward W.

1983. *The World, the Text and the Critic.* Cambridge, Mass.: Harvard University Press.

Sanders, Julie

2006. *Adaptation and Appropriation. The New Critical Idiom.* London, New York: Routledge.

Server, Lee

2002. *Encyclopedia of Pulp Fiction Writers.* Facts on File Library of American Literature. New York: Facts on File.

Xiaoxiaosheng and Bernard Miall

1982. *Chin P'ing Mei: The Adventurous History of Hsi Men and His Six Wives.* New York: Perigee Books.

Xiaoxiaosheng and Clement Egerton

1939. *The Golden Lotus: A Translation, from the Chinese Original, of the Novel Chin P'ing Mei.* 4 vols. London: Routledge and Kegan Paul.

1972. *The Golden Lotus: A Translation, from the Chinese Original, of the Novel Chin P'ing Mei.* 4 vols. Vol. 2. London: Routledge and K. Paul.

2008. *Jin Ping Mei (The Golden Lotus).* Silk Pagoda.

Xiaoxiaosheng and David Tod Roy

2013. *The Plum in the Golden Vase or, Chin P'ing Mei.* Vol. 5. Princeton, New Jersey: Princeton University Press.

Contributor

Lintao Qi is Lecturer in the Masters of Interpreting and Translation Studies at Monash University, Australia. His research interests include literary translation theory and practice, translation and cultural diplomacy, and sexuality and censorship in translation. He is the author of *Jin Ping Mei English Translations: Texts, Paratexts, and Contexts* (Routledge, 2018) and co-editor (with Leah Gerber) of *A Century of Chinese Literature in Translation: English Publication and Reception* (Routledge, 2020). His most recent book is *Encountering China's Past* (co-edited with Shani Tobias, Springer 2022). Lintao Qi has published widely in internationally recognized journals such as *Target, Translation and Interpreting Studies*, and *Perspectives*. He is a NAATI-certified translator and Co-editor of *New Voices in Translation Studies*.

CHAPTER 16

Sex-related Expression or Vulgarism?

On the Occurrences of the Word 合 in the Two Main Editions of *Jin Ping Mei*

ONDŘEJ VICHER

It is widely known that, among the classic Chinese novels, *Jin Ping Mei* (JPM) became infamous for the relatively large number of explicit sex scenes. Naturally, there must be a corresponding number of sex-related expressions in the text, and as Robert van Gulik (2003: 287) observed, '[...] the terminology used in those passages is derived from the slang of that day', which applies to both main editions. The *cihua* 詞話 edition (also called the *Wanli* edition 萬曆本) will henceforward be referred to as JPMa, and the *xiuxiang* 繡像 (*Chongzhen* edition 崇禎本) as JPMb.

Many erotic expressions may be considered euphemisms, while others, in contrast, express blunt sex-related realities in an undisguised, explicit and vulgar manner. This chapter introduces the usage and specifics of the character 合 and its occurrences in the two editions, with a brief comparison and assessment of the semantic level of this expression, in an attempt to determine the boundary between the sexual and the vulgar.

The character 合 is not included in most dictionaries and there is no entry for it in traditional dictionaries such as the *Kangxi zidian* 康熙字典 (*Kangxi* dictionary), or the *Zihui bu* 字彙補 (*Zihui* supplement), where it is explained that 合 is a variant of *cái* 財 (wealth, property, valuables). According to the *Jin Ping Mei jianshang cidian* 金瓶梅鑒賞辞典 (*Jin Ping Mei* Dictionary for Connoisseurs) (Sun Xun and Wei Tongxian 1993: 507), it is a slang expression with a meaning synonymous with the modern vulgarisms *cào* 肏, *rù* 入 or *rì* 日, which are equivalents to the English verb 'to copulate' or the more vulgar translation variants

---

Work on this chapter was supported financially by the student project *Research of the Novel Jin Ping Mei and a Comparison of its Two Main Editions* (IGA_FF_2021_047) at Palacký University in Olomouc, Czech Republic.

247

ONDŘEJ VICHER

such as 'to fuck' or 'to screw'. This dictionary does not, however, supplement entries with *pinyin* transcription to provide a definitive answer to the reading of this character. According to the entry in *Hanyu Da Zidian* 漢語大字典 (2010: 149), it can be read in two ways. In addition to the reading *cái* with the meaning of 'wealth', the character can also be pronounced *rì*, the same as 日, mentioned above. Due to the 日 component, this reading may be considered the proper one[1] for 合 in its sex-related meaning and when used as a vulgarism. According to Zhang Huiying (2016: 33–34), there are also other synonymous variants of the character 合 based on their mutual homophony in some of the dialects of Wu language (*Wúyǔ* 吳語)[2] written with the characters 值 or 直 (*zhí*), which is something else that supports the correctness of the proposed pronunciation *rì* rather than *cái*.

Zhang further argues that 'JPM is a vernacular novel, not a novel written in Shandong dialect.' (ibid.: 122–143) This does not, however, answer the question as to whether 合 originally belonged to the Shandong dialect or to the Wu language.[3] The above-mentioned *Jin Ping Mei jianshang cidian* (Sun Xun and Wei Tongxian 1993: 507) included this expression in the dialects and slang section (*fāngyán súyǔ* 方言俗語); regrettably, that does not explain, either, whether it pertains to certain specific dialects, or is simply a vernacular (or slang) expression. However, solving the question of possible affiliation of 合 to any particular dialect is not absolutely essential, since in the occurrences in question this does not affect its meaning in any way.[4]

A Needle in a Haystack

A thorough search for occurrences of 合 in each of the 100 chapters of the two editions of JPM, without the help of an electronic search engine, would be like

---

1   An example from Chapter 51 of JPM in Keith McMahon's article (2019: 33) and its *pinyin* transcription also supports the correctness of this pronunciation: *Wǔ'ér risile* 五兒合死了. Just a brief aside here: as Keith McMahon states (ibid.: n. 77), this example comes from JPMb, since 合 does not appear in the JPMa source text in this sole instance.

2   Zhang specifically mentions dialects of Wu language spoken in the Suzhou and Shanghai areas.

3   Zhang does not directly discuss this, writing only about 合 in the context of language puns based on homophony with other words in the Wu language. Discussion on this topic has involved a good deal of controversy. According to Andrew Plaks (1987: 63), there are several 'scholars who claim to have identified examples of Wu-dialect expressions in the novel', and he lists their names and works below on page 63 in footnote 33.

4   Apart, perhaps, from the example from Chapter 15, 合八; see section 'Questionable or Contextual Instances'.

248

SEX-RELATED EXPRESSION OR VULGARISM?

trying to look for a needle in a haystack. This part introduces helpful digital tools and briefly describes the setbacks encountered during the search process. In order to navigate faster in the printed editions of JPM,[5] web-based corpora accessible at ctext.org and wikisource.com were used. Both websites enable the user to look up characters in the entire corpus of texts as well as within other relevant works of literature, which is a handy tool. It also has certain disadvantages, however, as typing errors often occur during digitalization. The following words of Paul Vierthaler illustrate the situation very well: 'It is very difficult to find high quality digital transcripts of The Plum in the Golden Vase. There are a lot of them floating out there on the internet, but if you compare them character for character with "good scholarly" editions, there are differences.' (Cesta 2017: t. 18:34–18:47) Therefore, it is always beneficial to *sānsī' érxíng* 三思而行, 'to think thrice before acting', or in this instance 'to count thrice before issuing a final declaration'.

Printed editions

Table 16.1 clearly shows that 合 appears exclusively in all instances in the printed editions, whereas 肏 does not appear in printed editions at all. The final number of occurrences of 合 in both editions was 54 in JPMa and 45 in JPMb.

Digitalized editions

Digitalized source texts (ST) have both 合 (Ctext JPMa and JPMb) and 肏 (Ctext JPMb, Wikisource both JPMa and JPMb). Further examination of other lines for the occurrence of 合 or its synonymous proxy 肏 indicates that the numbers do not add up. There are several reasons for this discrepancy between the number of occurrences in the printed SOURCE TEXT (ST) and the digitized STs from Ctext and Wikisource.

Ctext

The number of total occurrences of 合 on Ctext for JPMa is 51. There is one extra instance of 合 in JPMa digitized ST in Chapter 42 that does not appear in the printed edition.[6] If we consider this instance invalid and therefore exclude

---

5   *Jin Ping Mei cihua xiaozhu* 金瓶梅詞話校註 (Lanling Xiaoxiaosheng 1998) for JPMa and *Xinke Xiuxiang Piping Jinpingmei* 新刻繡像批評金瓶梅 (Lanling Xiaoxiaosheng 1990a and 1990b) for JPMb. As for Ctext.org, see Chinese Text Project (中國哲學書電子化計劃), in the following shortened as Ctext.

6   The sentence 西門慶和老婆足幹搗有兩頓飯時，纔了事。 (Lanling Xiaoxiaosheng 1998: 1034) has 合 instead of 有 on Ctext.

249

ONDŘEJ VICHER

Table 16.1. The number of occurrences of 仺 and 肏 in different sources of both editions

Source / edition	JPMa	JPMb
Printed 仺	54	45
Ctext 仺	51	26
Wikisource 仺	0	26
Printed 肏	0	0
Ctext 肏	0	16
Wikisource 肏	55	16

it from the final count, we have a final tally of 50 occurrences, which is still four occurrences short of the final count in the printed edition. The reason for this is the four occurrences of other proxy variants of 仺[7] in both editions. When divided into components *rù* 入 and *rì* 日 / *yuē* 曰, character 仺 provides a possible proxy variant. As suspected, one instance of *rùyuē* 入曰 appeared in Chapter 23, and the remaining three were occurrences of *hé* 仺 (two in Chapter 27 and one in Chapter 38).

For JPMb, there are only 26 results when searching for 仺. There are, however, 16 occurrences of 肏 used in sentences that have 仺 in the printed edition.[8] The sum of 26 + 16 is 42, which means that the final count for JPMb (i.e. 44) is still short of two occurrences. These were eventually discovered in Chapter 99, where character 入 appears instead of 仺.

Wikisource

There are no results for 仺 when searching the digitized JPMa ST at Wikisource, and the result from JPMb ST is identical to that from Ctext (i.e., 26). There are no occurrences of 仺 in the JPMa ST available at Wikisource, but there are, instead, 55 occurrences of 肏 substituting for 仺. The reason for this is one extra instance of 肏 from Chapter 32, which is undoubtedly a typographical

---

7   Those are graphically similar characters *rù* 入, *rì* 日 (or their combination *rùrì* 入日; *rùyuē* 入曰), and *hé* 仺.

8   Chapters 4, 75 (3x), 76, 78 (3x), 81, 82, 86 (2x), 89, 93, 94 and 99.

SEX-RELATED EXPRESSION OR VULGARISM?

Table 16.2. The number of occurrences of 㿗 and 㞘 in the
digitized sources (including variants and additions)

Character / source	JPMa Ctext	JPMa Wikisource	JPMb Ctext and Wikisource
㿗	51	55	26
㞘	0	0	16
Variants	4	0	2
Additions	-1	-1	0
Total	54	54	44

error that occurred during the optical character recognition (OCR) process.[9] The Wikisource version of JPMb ST is identical to the one from Ctext. There is therefore no need to discuss it further.

Table 16.2 provides the final overview of occurrences in the digitized sources, supplemented by the count of variants and the negative number of additions. The total count is now equal to the number of occurrences subsequently found and confirmed in printed editions of JPMa and JPMb.

Several revisory methods were applied when it became clear that the numbers did not add up. In order to find the missing pieces from Ctext, digitized STs were also checked to see whether any 'proxy variants' form a combination with the characters, with which 㿗 seemed to create a compound most often in printed editions, i.e. 搗 *dǎo* and 窝 *wō*. Although there were no results for 入搗 and 日搗, there was one occurrence of 合搗 in Chapter 27. *Rìdǎo* 合搗 (literally 'to fuck and pound') occurs in both printed editions seven times.[10] There were no results for the combination of proxy variants with the character 窝 on Ctext. 合窝 *rìwō* (literally 'to fuck the hollow')[11] occurs only once, in Chapter 75 of JPMa and Roy (2011: 458) translates this instance rather euphemistically using the expression 'go at it'. To conclude, although the results are not 100% reliable, it is helpful to work with digitized corpora. Therefore, the application of vari-

---

9   The sentence in question from the JPMa printed edition ST is 只是一味白鬼 (Lanling Xiaoxiaosheng 1998: 872). Wikisource has 㞘 instead of 白鬼, which created this discrepancy.

10 In Chapter 13 (2x), Chapter 16 (2x), Chapter 27 (as 合搗 on Ctext), Chapter 68 and Chapter 75; see section 'Sex-Related Instances' for detailed examples.

11 According to a note in the JPMa edition (Lanling Xiaoxiaosheng 1998: 2267, n. 12), the meaning of the constituent 㿗 is *jiāogòu* 交媾 (to copulate) and of 窝 is *nǚyīn* 女陰 (vagina).

251

ONDŘEJ VICHER

ous control mechanisms is highly advisable since even the best computer-based algorithms cannot assess the small nuances that an experienced JPM scholar or translator recognizes at a glance.

Analysis

Table 16.3 provides data on the chapters and editions of respective occurrences, the type of incidence, and who the speaker is. It is an extract of the spreadsheet that has been created for this research. A full-scale version of this spreadsheet, which is too extensive to present here, also contains the relevant passages from the printed Chinese STs and their target texts (TT), the English translations (Roy's and Egerton's), including paginal references.

The incidence of 膣 is distributed throughout the novel in 30 different chapters, with several occurrences in each of the ten-chapter units. The only exceptions are the more numerous clusters between Chapters 23–28, 31–38, and 75–78,[12] mainly caused by multiple usages of 膣 in one utterance or even by its reduplication in a single sentence.[13] In the following sections, the occurrences will be introduced in greater detail.

Who is the Speaker?

Table 16.3 also shows that 21 different characters (11 male and 10 female) utter 膣 at least once. The narrator is the 22nd speaker who utters the word four times.[14] Male characters utter the word 20 times altogether, completely outnumbered by the 10 female characters, who utter the word 31 times. It should be noted, however, that the 'female team' leads these statistics thanks to 19 utterances on the part of the main female protagonist Pan Jinlian, whereas other female characters use the word only twice at the very most. There are two leaders among the male protagonists: Ximen Qing and Liu the Second (both have four utterances), followed closely by Chen Jingji (with three).

The usage of 膣 pertains to persons of questionable moral character, as it is a vulgar and sex-related expression. One would assume that such foul language

---

12 As Hu Yannan pointed out (2014: 216), between Chapters 72 and 79, only 50 days elapse (after Ximen Qing arrives from the capital until his death), and during this time, 15 sex scenes take place. Most of them are explicitly described, and others are mentioned in passing. The occurrences of the word 膣 thus mirror the frequency of the sex scenes. There are 11 occurrences in total, of which 10 convey sexual meaning and only in one case is 膣 used as a vulgarism (by Pan Jinlian at Chapter 75).

13 This occurs in Chapters 16, 78, and 86.

14 In Chapter 69, twice in Chapter 75 and once in Chapter 82.

SEX-RELATED EXPRESSION OR VULGARISM?

would be used predominantly by men, but that is not the case, as was noted above. What connects the speakers is their origin or occupation. Among female speakers, there are singing girls (prostitutes) such as Li Guijie and Zheng Aiyue, matchmakers Auntie Yang and Dame Wang, and the maidservants Chunmei, Ruyi, and Xiaoyu. The base conduct and sexual debauchery of Song Huilian and Wang Liu'er is in many ways similar to Pan Jinlian's, who is neither of decent origin nor a woman of unwavering morality (unlike Wu Yueniang), as evidenced by her heinous actions throughout the novel. It is no secret that Pan Jinlian is a 'nymphomaniac constantly unable to gratify herself' (Hsia C. T. 2015 [1968]: 173) and 'her bedroom talk is unparalleled' (Qi Lintao 2018: 186). Therefore, it is not very surprising that her lexicon matches her character and that she ranks first in usage of 含, and probably also in the usage of other indecent expressions. As Zhang Zhupo had already pointed out in his celebrated *Jin Ping Mei dufa* 金瓶梅讀法 (How to Read *Jin Ping Mei*), '[...] lewd language is used more often by Pan Jinlian and Wang Liu'er than by anyone else [...]' (Roy 1990: 230–231; Zhang Zhupo 1986: 38).

The number of occurrences, in contrast, uttered by Ximen Qing is intriguing. One would expect a higher number of occurrences due to the frequency of his direct involvement in sex scenes and other relevant situations in the novel. In the male category, the expression is used by servants, swindlers, and profiteers, boorish and not very virtuous characters of questionable morals, which is demonstrated in the novel not only by their utterances but above all by their actions. That is the case with Ximen Qing, Chen Jingji and Ying Bojue, characters who are mere 'pigs and dogs in the guise of men', as Ding Naifei notes (2002: 128) paraphrasing the words of Zhang Zhupo in note 47 of *Jin Ping Mei dufa* (1986: 37).

Occurrences in the Various Editions

The general differences between the JPMa and JPMb are well known to sinologists thanks to a number of landmark works.[15] 'Textually, the two editions differ drastically.' (Tian Xiaofei 2002: 347) What is missing in JPMb are often unimportant details; however, in some places the changes and modifications add logic to characters or events (Hu Yannan 2014: 224–225). It is evident from Table 16.3 that there are 44 occurrences in total in the two editions, of which 10 are in JPMa only and one is in JPMb only. Table 16.4 presents the 10

---

15 See the works of Patrick Hanan (1962 and 1963), Andrew Plaks (1987), Tian Xiaofei (2002), and especially the review by Zhou Lu (2016), which summarizes studies on JPM comparing the two main editions.

ONDŘEJ VICHER

Table 16.3. The occurrence of 肏 in respective chapters and editions, type of incidence, and its speaker

Chapter	JPMa, JPMb or both?	Sex related, vulgarism or questionable?	Speaker
4	Both	Vulgarism	Dame Wang
7	Both	Questionable	Auntie Yang
7	Both	Sex	Auntie Yang
13	Both	Sex	Pan Jinlian
13	Both	Sex	Pan Jinlian
15	JPMa	Questionable	Sun Guazui
16 (2x)	Both	Sex	Pan Jinlian
23	Both	Sex	Pan Jinlian
24	Both	Sex	Xiaoyu
25	JPMa	Questionable	Song Huilian
25	Both	Sex	Laiwang
25	Both	Questionable	Pan Jinlian
27	Both	Sex	Ximen Qing
27	Both	Sex	Pan Jinlian
28	Both	Vulgarism	Pan Jinlian
31	Both	Vulgarism	Xiaoyu
31	JPMa	Sex	Pan Jinlian
31	JPMa	Vulgarism	actor in role Jing
32	Both	Vulgarism	Li Guijie
34	JPMa	Sex	Pan Jinlian
35	Both	Questionable	Pan Jinlian
35	Both	Sex	Ping'an
38	Both	Sex	Wang Liu'er
50	Both	Sex	Daian
50	Both	Vulgarism	Daian

SEX-RELATED EXPRESSION OR VULGARISM?

51	Both	Sex	Pan Jinlian
51	JPMb	Sex	Pan Jinlian
61	Both	Questionable	Pan Jinlian
61	Both	Sex	Pan Jinlian
68	Both	Sex	Ying Bojue
68	Both	Vulgarism	Zheng Aiyue
69	JPMa	Sex	Narrator
75	JPMa	Sex	Pan Jinlian
75	Both	Sex	Narrator
75	Both	Sex	Narrator
75	Both	Vulgarism	Pan Jinlian
75	Both	Sex	Chunmei
76	Both	Sex	Chunmei
78 (2x)	JPMa	Sex	Ximen Qing
78	Both	Sex	Ximen Qing
78	Both	Sex	Ruyi
78	Both	Questionable	Pan Jinlian
81	Both	Sex	Hu Xiu
82	Both	Vulgarism	Pan Jinlian
82	JPMa	Sex	Narrator
86 (2x)	Both	Sex	Chen Jingji
89	Both	Vulgarism	Chen Jingji
93	Both	Vulgarism	Yang Erfeng
94	Both	Vulgarism	Liu the Second
99	Both	Vulgarism	Liu the Second
99	Both	Vulgarism	Liu the Second
99	Both	Vulgarism	Liu the Second

cases from JPMa and the single case from JPMb, supplemented with the page references (to respective Chinese and English editions) and relevant details about the other edition.

Types of Expression

合 mainly functions as a verb denoting the sex-related 'to fuck'; it also functions as a vulgarism, when the meaning usually has no relation to sexual activity at all.[16] Whether it is the former or the latter depends on the context of the individual cases; whichever is the case, it is, as Zhang Huiying affirms (2016: 33), a *xiècí* 褻词 (indecent word). Nevertheless, the boundary between the sexual and vulgar is sometimes not so unambiguous as it may seem. In several cases, which meaning is intended is not entirely clear, as 合 displays characteristics of both meanings, and the translation solutions are also sometimes contradictory.

Sex-Related Instances

Logically, one would expect sex-related instances of 合 to occur mainly during or around sex scenes, or in scenes where the protagonists talk about sexual affairs.[17] There are 33 instances in which 合 has a sex-related meaning. That includes the four occurrences uttered by the narrator (see Table 16.3), the 12 occurrences uttered by Pan Jinlian, the four occurrences uttered by Ximen Qing, the two uttered by Chen Jingji and the two by Chunmei,[18] and other occurrences uttered only once by other characters. Verbs denoting sexual activity are far more often used by men than by women (Cameron and Kulick 2003: 30). Why is it, though, that Pan Jinlian uses 合 more than most of the male characters? The answer lies in paying closer attention to the meaning of each sentence and assessing various small nuances. The examples below therefore demonstrate the usage of the expression in its sexual meaning. The last example introduces the usage of 合 in a homosexual context.

---

16 Depending on the context, it possesses different degrees of expressivity.

17 Pan Jinlian is usually the person who comments on the affairs of others. E.g., in Chapter 13 and Chapter 16 (four occurrences), Pan Jinlian speaks of Ximen Qing (and to Ximen Qing) having sex with Li Ping'er; in Chapter 23, she scolds Ximen Qing about having an affair with Song Huilian, in Chapter 27 speaks again to him about amusing himself with Li Ping'er, in Chapter 31 speaks about page boys and maidservants screwing around and fornicating with each other, in Chapter 34 she refers to the homosexual adventures of Ximen Qing with servant Shutong, Chapter 75 Pan Jinlian is again scolding Ximen Qing for having a sexual affair with wet-nurse Ruyi using the word 合 to describe their screwing around.

18 Note that Ximen Qing, Chunmei, and Chen Jingji only utter 合 in a sexual, not in a vulgar meaning.

SEX-RELATED EXPRESSION OR VULGARISM?

Table 16.4. Details on the ten occurrences of 合
that appear only in one of the editions

Chapter	Edition	Chinese ST	English TT	Situation in the other edition
15	JPMa	Lanling 1998: 442	Roy 1993: 309	Missing sentence
25	JPMa	Lanling 1998: 679	Roy 2001: 86	Several sentences missing
31	JPMa	Lanling 1998: 838	Roy 2001: 229	Almost identical[a]
31	JPMa	Lanling 1998: 842	Roy 2001: 238	Missing passage (888 characters)[b]
34	JPMa	Lanling 1998: 952	Roy 2001: 307	Missing sentence
69	JPMa	Lanling 1998: 1983	Roy 2011: 251	Almost identical[c]
75	JPMa	Lanling 1998: 2231	Roy 2011: 458	Missing sentence
78	JPMa	Lanling 1998: 2360	Roy 2011: 584	Almost identical[d]
78	JPMa	Ditto	Ditto	Question form (合不合)
82	JPMa	Lanling 1998: 2496	Roy 2013: 34	Missing sentence
51	JPMb	Lanling 1990a: 666	Egerton 2011a: 610	Almost identical[e]

a Only 合 is missing: JPMa 把人合遍了也休要管他！(Lanling Xiaoxiaosheng 1998: 838); JPMb 把人說遍了，也休要管他！(Lanling Xiaoxiaosheng 1990a: 380)

b This whole passage consists of a theatrical play in verse. Such passages were usually not included in JPMb.

c In JPMb the 施 shī is used instead of 合: JPMa 深閨內合毴的菩薩。(Lanling Xiaoxiaosheng 1998: 1983); Roy has 'A veritable bodhisattva of coition' (2011: 253); JPMb 深閨內施 的菩薩 (Lanling Xiaoxiaosheng 1990b: 948); Egerton has 'a goddess who, as it were, made sacrifice of her body for the love of men' (2012b: 224). Also notable is the character 毴 bī (vagina), a variant of 屄 (Sun Xun and Wei Tongxian 1993: 561).

d The sentence is slightly altered in JPMb. This example is further discussed in detail in the following subsection: see section 'Sex–related instances' in relation to Chapter 78.

e This is the unique case of occurrence of 合 in JPMb only. Pan Jinlian utters the word during sex with Ximen Qing. In JPMa, 合 is missing from the sentence. See the respective passages from both editions for a comparison: JPMb 那話直抵牝中，只顧揉搓，沒口子叫：「親達達，罷了，五兒合死了！」(Lanling Xiaoxiaosheng 1990a: 665–666); Egerton: …and pressed the whole penis inside herself. Then she whispered gently, 'Darling, finish it off or I'll die.' (2012a: 610); JPMa 沒口子叫：「親達達，罷了！五兒的死了。(Lanling Xiaoxiaosheng 1998: 1350); Roy: 'My own daddy!' she cried out inarticulately. 'That's enough. Your Fivey is dying.' (2006: 240)

ONDŘEJ VICHER

Chapter 13

JPMa and JPMb ST (identical):

嗔道教我那裡沒尋，原來把這行貨子悄地帶出，和那淫婦合搗去了。

(Lanling Xiaoxiaosheng 1990a: 168; 1998: 373)

The Plum:

'No wonder I turned the place upside down looking for it, and all the time it was you who had spirited the thing away in order to screw around with that whore.' (Roy 1993: 270)

The Golden Lotus:

'There cannot be another like you in all the world. You take this thing with you on the sly when you go to play with that wicked creature.' (Egerton 2011a: 179)

This instance of 合 uttered by Pan Jinlian does not occur during a sex scene, but during her conversation with Ximen Qing shortly after he climbs over the wall, back from visiting Li Ping'er.[19] At this point in the novel, Ximen Qing is already meeting secretly with her, and her husband, Ximen Qing's neighbour and sworn brother Hua Zixu does not suspect anything. Pan Jinlian, however, knows all about it, decides to take advantage of the situation, and therefore she incites Ximen Qing with the following words:

JPMa and JPMb ST (identical):

等你過那邊去，我這裡與你兩個觀風，教你兩個自在合搗。

(Lanling Xiaoxiaosheng 1990a: 168; 1998: 374)

The Plum:

'When you go over there in the future, I'll act as a lookout, so the two of you can screw away to your hearts' content.' (Roy 1993: 270)

The Golden Lotus:

'Indeed, when you go to call on her, I'll keep a lookout for you on this side, and the pair of you can enjoy yourselves in peace.' (Egerton 2011a: 180)

---

19 The thing Pan Jinlian was searching for is 'a silver clasp' *yín tuozi* 銀托子, which Egerton translates with artful euphemism ('warrior' for his 'penis' 那話 and 'armour' for the 'clasp'), and the 'whore' is Li Ping'er.

SEX-RELATED EXPRESSION OR VULGARISM?

Chapter 75

JPMa and JPMb ST (identical):

這西門慶真個把胞膈尿都溺在老婆口內，當下兩個婍妮溫存，萬千囉躁，合搗了一夜。　　(Lanling Xiaoxiaosheng 1990b: 1041; 1998: 2236)

The Plum:

Hsi-men Ch'ing then actually pissed a whole bladderful of his urine into the woman's mouth. The two of them continued their:

> Impassioned lovemaking,
> In all its myriad forms,
> as they went at it together all night long.　　(Roy 2011: 464)

The Golden Lotus:

[...] and Ximen made water in her mouth. They made love in every possible way.
(Egerton 2011b: 307)

This is the second occurrence in the novel of the infamous 'urophilia' scene. This time, Ximen Qing urinates in Ruyi's mouth, imitating the act from Chapter 72 with Pan Jinlian.[20] Note that in both instances from Chapter 13 and this one, 合 forms the compound 合搗.

Chapter 78

JPMa ST:

這西門慶口中喃喃吶吶，就叫：「葉五兒！不知道口裏令合不合？」

(Lanling Xiaoxiaosheng 1998: 2360)

The Plum:

Hsi-men Ch'ing muttered to himself, saying, 'Yeh the Fifth, I don't know whether you are familiar with oral intercourse, or not.'　　(Roy 2011: 584)

Uttered by Ximen Qing, this scene contains two occurrences of 合 due to its reduplication in one sentence. It is also the only instance in the novel of 合 in connection with fellatio. Although this scene occurs both in JPMa and JPMb,

---

20　This rare case of paraphilia has been further discussed by many; see Gulik 2003: 167; Ruan and Matsumura, 1991: 95–96; Ding 2002:195; Lévy 2000: 141–142; Plaks 1987: 145; Liu 2015: 495.

ONDŘEJ VICHER

in JPMb 合 is expunged, and the meaning of this sentence is thus slightly altered:

西門慶口中喃喃呐呐，就叫「葉五兒」不絕。

(Lanling Xiaoxiaosheng 1990b: 1112)

The Golden Lotus:

After that, Ximen Qing kept murmuring: 'Ye the Fifth, Ye the Fifth.'
(Egerton 2011b: 369)

Chapter 50

Although Ximen Qing usually indulges in heterosexual intercourse, he occasionally yields to homosexual desires with his pageboys. Ximen Qing's relations with his pageboys aptly demonstrate this unequal power dynamic. For example, Shutong, one of Ximen Qing's pageboys, gains influence and certain privileges in return for satisfying his master's sexual desires (Hinsch 1992: 135). In Chapter 50, there are several scenes where other household members tease Shutong for his intimate relationship with his master. They often call him *yínfù* 淫妇 (lascivious woman), a title that usually pertains to women, which makes it even more degrading, as Hu Yannan aptly remarks (2014: 87). In addition, his fellow servant Daian jokes about engaging in sodomy with him and with the words *yào rì nǐ de pìgu* 要合你的屁股 threatens to 'fuck him in the ass'. Note that Egerton's translation solution is again much more euphemistic than Roy's:

JPMa and JPMb ST (identical):

玳安罵道：「秫秫小廝，你也回嘴。我尋你要合你屁股！」

(Lanling Xiaoxiaosheng 1990a: 643; 1998: 1324)

The Plum:

'Why you "sweetie" of a page boy!' cursed Tai-an. 'You have the nerve to talk back to me, do you? I was looking for you so I could fuck you in the ass.'
(Roy 2006: 207)

The Golden Lotus:

'Little boy', Daian said, 'would you bandy words with me? I was looking for you because I want to do some business with your behind.' (Egerton 2011a: 591)

260

Instances of Vulgarisms

Vulgarisms are negatively expressive profane or obscene words used to convey a wide range of negative emotions. 'The Chinese have always been regarded as highly imaginative in their abusive language [...]' (Huang and Eberhard 1968: 25), and '[...] the swearwords in Chinese are often constructed using words originally describing body parts, especially the intimate ones and those of sexual activities [...]' (ibid.: 36), which probably also applies to other languages. Such activities have even inspired taboos and inhibitions in all societies from the earliest periods of human history (Burridge 2015: 271). Semantically, there is a thin line, however, between what is sexual and what is already a vulgar and abusive expression. Based on context, the meaning of 合 shifts from sexual to vulgar, and the expression takes on the semantic function of vulgarism. There are dozens of abusive expressions in JPM. Many are substantives with the original meaning of intimate body parts or verbs originally describing sexual activity. Speakers use 合 as a vulgarism in 15 instances to abuse somebody.[21] Notably, Ximen Qing does not use this expression in a vulgar manner at all. The first two examples below demonstrate how is the expression used as a vulgarism during an argument between two protagonists.

Chapter 4

In this situation from the beginning of the novel, Dame Wang tries to hush up the affair between Ximen Qing and Pan Jinlian in front of the young Yunge, who notices that something is suspicious and tries to enter Wu Da's house to catch them red-handed. Dame Wang prevents him from entering, and they start to quarrel and abuse each other.

JPMa and JPMb ST (identical):

婆子罵道：「賊合娘的小猢猻！你敢高則聲，大耳刮子打出你去！」

(Lanling Xiaoxiaosheng 1990a: 62; 1998: 143)

The Plum:

'You lousy mother-fucking little monkey!' the old lady cursed. 'If you raise your voice again I'll drive you out of here with a couple of good boxes on the ear!'

(Roy 1993: 95)

---

21 Liu the Second (4x), Pan Jinlian (3x), others just once. Again, see Table 16.3 for reference.

The Golden Lotus:

'You son of a thief, you little monkey, make a noise like that and I'll trash you out of the place.'　　　　　　　　　　　　　　　　　　　(Egerton 2011a: 88)

Chapter 99

In this scene, one of the key protagonists of the last 20 chapters – Liu the Second – abuses Magnate He. An analogous instance of this expression also occurs in Chapter 31 of JPMa (see section below, '合娘 and its Variations').

JPMa and JPMb ST (identical):

那劉二罵道：「你？你這狗合！」

　　　　　　　　　　　　　　(Lanling Xiaoxiaosheng 1990b: 1397; 1998: 2825)

The Plum:

'You'll come after me, will you, you dog-fucked creature!' Liu the Second cursed at him.　　　　　　　　　　　　　　　　　　(Roy 2013: 374)

The Golden Lotus:

'Going, are you, you dog?' Tiger Liu said, in a furious temper.

　　　　　　　　　　　　　　　　　　　　　　(Egerton 2011b: 617)

Chapter 68

The following example demonstrates the usage of 合 as a vulgarism when describing a specific individual to a third person. In this instance, Zheng Aiyue remonstrates with Ximen Qing about Zhang the Second (Zhang Maode 張懋德).[22]

JPMa and JPMb ST (identical):

愛月兒道：「那張懋德兒好合的貨！

　　　　　　　　　　　　　　(Lanling Xiaoxiaosheng 1990b: 934; 1998: 1954)

22　Roy again translated the vulgarism to the letter: 'fucking Zhang Maode', while Egerton decided for the euphemism 'ugly fellow'. Of course, this is related to the morals and general feeling of the readership of the times when the respective translations were published. For more discussion on that topic and censorship of English editions of JPM, see the recent works of Qi Lintao (2016, 2018, 2021).

The Plum:

'Why that fucking Chang Mao-te!' exclaimed Cheng Ai-yüeh.

(Roy 2011: 232)

The Golden Lotus:

'No,' Aiyue said, 'not that ugly fellow.' (Egerton 2011b: 213)

合娘 *and its Variations*

The examples below possess the common denominator *rì niáng* 合娘 (fuck mother):

a) Chapter 31: *gǒu rì niáng* 狗合娘 (Lanling Xiaoxiaosheng 1998: 842), translated as 'mother-fucking dog' (Roy 2001: 238), missing in JPMb.

b) Chapter 94: *rì nǐ Dàoshi shúshú niáng* 合你道士秋秋娘 (Lanling Xiaoxiaosheng 1990b: 1330; 1998: 2730), translated by Roy: 'Fuck you, you "sweetie" of a Taoist priest', (2013: 272), and by Egerton: 'I'll pound your mother's rice for her, you priest', (2011b: 560).

c) Chapter 99 (2x): First occurrence; *Zéi gǒunánnǚ, wǒ rì nǐ niáng!* 賊狗男女, 我合你娘！ second occurrence; *Rì nǐ yínfù niáng* 合你淫婦娘 (both Lanling Xiaoxiaosheng 1990b: 1397; 1998: 2825). First translated by Roy as: 'I'll fuck your mother!' and second as 'You whore, I'll fuck your mother!' (both 2013: 374). Egerton does not translate the 我合你娘 in the first part, just has 'Ha, you doggish pair!' and the second one translates as: 'Who are you, strumpet?' (2011b: 617).

d) Chapter 50: *Wǒ rì nǐ niáng de yǎn* 我合你娘的眼 (Lanling Xiaoxiaosheng 1998: 1327; 2012: 646), Roy translates as: 'I'll fuck your mother's hole!' (2006: 213) and Egerton as: 'My dagger to your mother's cunt' (2011a: 594).[23]

e) Chapter 93: *Rì nǐ niáng yǎn* 合你娘眼 (Lanling Xiaoxiaosheng 1990b: 1318; 1998: 2706) Roy: 'I'll fuck your mother's cunt!' (2013: 245), Egerton: 'I'll shove my spade in your mother's eye' (2011b: 549).[24]

---

23 Note that *yǎn* 眼 (eye) in this instance has the meaning of 'hole,' i.e. it serves as a euphemism for 'vagina'.

24 This occurrence is almost identical to one of the previous examples from Chapter 50. The overall tone of Egerton's translation is vulgar, but still the euphemistic 'spade' and 'eye' are used to meliorate the sentence.

ONDŘEJ VICHER

Questionable or Contextual Instances

Since 合 can have both a sexual and a vulgar meaning, in some instances it is difficult to make a clear distinction and decide whether it is a sex-related term or a vulgarism. Below, there is a summary and discussion of several instances where there is a question mark related to this.

合八

<u>JPMa only:</u>

孫寡嘴道：「我是老實說，哥如今新敘的這個表子，不是裏面的，是外面的表子，還把裡邊人合八。」　　(Lanling Xiaoxiaosheng 1998: 422)

<u>The Plum:</u>

'To tell the truth', interposed Blabbermouth Sun, 'this new tart that Brother's taken up with isn't even an inhabitant of the quarter. She's an outsider who doesn't give a fuck for the insiders.'　　(Roy 1993: 309)

This is an instance from Chapter 15. In JPMb, the last sentence in question is missing; therefore, the following discussion regards JPMa only. In this scene, Ximen Qing and his companions are visiting the brothel of the Li family, and they are talking about Li Guijie. The question arises as to whether Roy's translation is entirely accurate and whether the meaning is not purely sexual in this case, i.e., not 'who doesn't give a fuck for the insiders', but 'who does not fuck with insiders', as the translator of the JPMa Czech edition Oldřich Král understood it (2013: 193). Both of these solutions are then entirely overthrown by Zhang Huiying (2016: 33), who claims that the *rì bā* 合八 is an example of *chāizì* 拆字 (a pun based on composition-decomposition of characters). According to Zhang, in the Wu language the character 合 has an identical reading to the characters *rù* 入, *rì* 日, and *shí* 十. 合八 is then read as *shí bā* 十八 (18), which is part of a crafty word-play. Consequently, 十八 is referring to *shíbāzi* 十八子 from Chapter 16, literally translated by Roy as the 'Eighteenth Youngster' (1993: 331), which is a pun consisting of the three characters. Combined, they form the character *lǐ* 李 (plum), which refers only to a woman of such family name, and according to Roy (1993: 522, n. 16) as well as Král (2013, p. 222, n. 8), this is either Li Ping'er or Li Guijie. Zhang Huiying further claims (2016: 33) that 合八 refers exclusively to Li Ping'er (he does not mention Li Guijie). Based on that claim, the sentence uttered by Sun Guazui (Blabbermouth Sun) may therefore be understood in the sense that the new lady of Ximen Qing's

264

SEX-RELATED EXPRESSION OR VULGARISM?

interest is not a prostitute (the insider 裏面的), but someone from outside of the licensed quarter (外面的表子), and that her family name is also Li.[25]

There is another point of view provided, however, by the Russian translation of this sentence:

> Сказать правду, — вмешался в разговор Сунь Молчун, — брат завел себе такую, которая без мамашиного надзору живет. Будет он теперь с поднадзорными путаться?!   (Manukhin 1993: 315)

'To tell you the truth', Sun Molchun[26] intervened in the conversation, 'my brother got himself one who lives without her mother's supervision. Would he get mixed up with the supervised ones now?!'   (my translation)

Based on this translation solution, a proximate meaning of the last sentence would be: 'does he (Ximen Qing) now need to visit one of the Li girls in here?' This translation does not convey either a sexual or vulgar meaning and points to the girls from the Li family bordello (Li Guijie and Li Guiqing) rather than Li Ping'er, which directly opposes Zhang Huiying's theory.

In conclusion, if Zhang Huiying's theory is accepted and 合八 is further considered a language pun, the meaning of the last sentence completely shifts, and this occurrence of 合 does not have either a sexual or vulgar meaning, as is conveyed in the Russian translation (in contrast to the English and Czech translations). It is not easy, however, to assess correctly and impartially which of the translation solutions presented is the most accurate one.

合遍街搗遍巷

There are three occurrences of 合 in the phrase *rì biàn jiē dǎo biàn xiàng* 合遍街 搗遍巷 (verbatim: fucked in every street, pounded in every alley), in Chapters

---

25 Another question is whether the words 還把裡邊人 preceding 合八 in the last sentence do not form an enigmatic pun in the Wu topolect as well, which would further change or clarify the meaning of the sentence. Zhang Huiying, however, does not elaborate on this. He neither elaborates on whether the expression 合 specifically originates from the Wu topolect or other dialects.

26 Just a quick aside: it is also notable how Russian translation dealt with the anthroponym Sun Guazui 孫寡嘴, which Roy translates as 'Blabbermouth Sun'. In Russian, a similar translation method is applied, combining the transliteration of the family name Sun 孫, i.e., Сунь and translation of the cryptonym Guazui 寡嘴, i.e. Молчун. However, the meaning of Молчун (Molchun) is the exact opposite of 'Blabbermouth', since it denotes a person who does not like to speak much, and it could therefore be loosely translated as 'silent man' or 'mute'.

ONDŘEJ VICHER

61, 75 and 76. Whether the final meaning of each is sex-related or vulgar depends on the context.[27]

Chapter 61

<u>JPMa and JPMb (identical):</u>

你早是個漢子，若是個老婆，就養遍街，合遍巷。

(Lanling Xiaoxiaosheng 1990b: 810; 1998: 1682)

<u>The Plum:</u>

'It's a good thing you're a man. If you were a woman, you'd be:

> Laid by every man in the street, and
> Fucked by every guy in the alley.'   (Roy 2011: 15)

<u>The Golden Lotus:</u>

You shameless scoundrel! It is a good thing you are a man. If you were a woman, you would be carrying on with every man in the street.   (Egerton 2011b: 97)

Chapter 75

<u>JPMa and JPMb (identical):</u>

春梅越發惱了，罵道：「賊合遍街搗遍巷的瞎淫婦！

(Lanling Xiaosheng 1990b: 1045; 1998: 2241)

<u>The Plum:</u>

This only made Ch'un-mei angrier than ever, and she continued to curse her, saying, 'You lousy blind whore! You're ready to be:

> Laid by every man in the street, and
> Fucked by every guy in the alley.'   (Roy 2011: 471)

<u>The Golden Lotus:</u>

This made Chunmei more angry still. 'You wandering vagabond of a strumpet!'

(Egerton 2011b: 311)

---

27 The occurrence in Chapter 61 is slightly different from the other two in the ST; there, it is *yǎng biàn jiē, rì biàn xiàng* 養遍街，合遍巷 instead of 合遍街搗遍巷.

SEX-RELATED EXPRESSION OR VULGARISM?

Chapter 76

JPMa and JPMb (identical):

做甚麼為這合遍街搗遍巷的賊瞎婦，教大娘這等罵我！

(Lanling Xiaoxiaosheng 1990b: 1077; 1998: 2293)

The Plum:

'Merely on behalf of that lousy blind whore, who has been:

> Laid by every man in the street, and
> Fucked by every guy in the alley,

why should I deserve to be so reviled by the First Lady?'   (Roy 2011: 524)

The Golden Lotus:

'Why should I be insulted because I told that blind vagabond what I thought about her? And the Great Lady found fault with my mother too, and said that she didn't keep me in order. Is it right that I should be punished because I cursed that blind scamp?'   (Egerton 2011b: 340)

The example from Chapter 61, where *yǎng* 養 (to support, to provide for) and 合 function as verbs, has a sexual meaning, which is also expressed in both English translations.[28] In Chapters 75 and 76, the phrase has the attributive function, and is used as a vulgarism, albeit with sexual overtones.[29]

髻髮合的

There are two occurrences of *jiba rì de* 髻髮合的 in JPM.[30] The examples below demonstrate how two identical expressions can carry different meanings depending on the context of a sentence. While the first example from Chapter

---

28 It is worth noting that while Roy uses the passive voice, as if he were following the theory that 'only men can be active sexual subjects, while the role of women is to be passive objects of male desire' (Cameron and Kulick 2003: 29), Egerton retains the active voice and, in addition, uses the meliorative 'carrying on'.

29 Note that Roy's translation is identical in all three instances, even though the one from Chapter 61 varies from the other two. Egerton's solutions, on the other hand, vary with each instance, and in Chapters 75 and 76 the content and original meaning of the phrase is considerably reduced, to 'wandering vagabond' and 'blind vagabond'.

30 髻髮 is a homophonous variant of *jiba* 雞巴 (cock, penis). Notable, again, is Egerton's euphemistic translation solution, 'champion', from Chapter 61, whereas Roy uses the coarse term 'prick.'

267

51 has a sexual meaning, in the second from Chapter 89 the meaning is vulgar, which is also expressed in the English translations.

Chapter 51

<u>JPMa and JPMb (identical):</u>

俺每是雌剩鬏髻合的，你還說不偏心哩！

(Lanling Xiaoxiaosheng 1990b: 664; 1998: 1349)

<u>The Plum:</u>

'Am I only fit to be fucked by what's left of that spent prick of yours?'
(Roy 2006: 236)

<u>The Golden Lotus:</u>

'I have to content myself with the defeated champion.'   (Egerton 2011a: 608)

Chapter 89

<u>JPMa and JPMb (identical):</u>

經濟便道：「我鬏髻合的才是丈母。

(Lanling Xiaoxiaosheng 1990b: 1263; 1998: 2616)

<u>The Plum:</u>

'Some fucking excuse for a mother-in-law!' exclaimed Ch'en Ching-chi.
(Roy 2013: 152)

<u>The Golden Lotus:</u>

'Curses on my mother-in-law!' Jingji cried.   (Egerton 2011b: 501)

Occurrences in Other Works

Xingshi Yinyuan Zhuan

The *Xingshi Yinyuan Zhuan* 醒世姻緣傳 (hereinafter XSYYZ) (The Story of a Marital Fate to Awaken the World)[31] is a novel from the late Ming or early Qing dynasty. Although the exact publication date is unknown, it is believed that it was published later than JPM. The pen name of XSYYZ's author is Xizhou Sheng 西周生 (Scholar of the Western Zhou) (Berg 2001: 660; Wu Yenna 1991: 55). JPM greatly influenced XSYYZ, and the examples below of several conspicuous similarities prove that:

1) Both JPM and XSYYZ are 100-chapter novels of manners written anonymously.

2) The authors of both novels title themselves as 'scholars'. As David Roy claims (1986: 33; 1993a: xxiii), Lanling Xiaoxiaosheng 蘭陵笑笑生 (The Scoffing Scholar of Lanling) may have been an admirer of Xunzi, since Xunzi ended his career in Lanling. This similarity between two pseudonymous 'scholars', authors of novels that resemble each other, seems to be correlative when juxtaposed to the 'Scholar of the Western Zhou' since Xunzi was a philosopher and author from the Eastern Zhou period.

3) There is a great deal of sexual and scatological expressions both in JPM and in XSYYZ. In contrast to the explicit pornographic descriptions of sexual acts in JPM, however, in XSYYZ, as Andrew Plaks pointed out (1985: 563–564), the author is 'noticeably restrained in treatment of these scenes'.

4) Similarly to JPM, the lexicon of XSYYZ contains expressions from the Shandong dialect, and the novel depicts the life of local society in the Shandong province on a grand scale (Berg 2001: 660; Wu Yenna 1991: 55).

5) The plot of XSYYZ is permeated by Buddhist and Confucian philosophies (Wu Yenna 1999: 55–56), which is also considered to be one of the thematic features of JPM.[32]

Since it is not the primary subject of this study, only examples of occurrences of 𡳞 from Chapter 32 and multiple occurrences from Chapter 72 have been confirmed. The total number of occurrences of 𡳞 in XSYYZ is therefore

---

31 Or according to Yenna Wu (1986) 'Marriage Destinies to Awaken the World.'

32 See Carlitz 1984: 398; Plaks 1987: 156; and especially Tian Xiaofei 2002: 351 and further for a detailed discussion on the Confucian and Buddhist values in JPM. For a comprehensive study of the XSYYZ, especially the discussion on authorship and dating, see Wu Yenna 1986.

unknown. It might prove worthwhile to look closer into the sex-related lexicon of XSYYZ and to compare it with JPM's. Identification of occurrences was further hampered by the quality of the second volume.[33] The wording of these examples is listed below, and the degree of their lexical similarity to examples from JPM is quite remarkable.[34]

Chapter 32: 再要拉他的，我合他媽那眼! (Xizhou Sheng 2017: 390)

Chapter 72: 裁縫老婆喬聲怪氣的罵哩：『偷雞的叫驢子雞巴合你媽！叫駱駝雞巴合你媽！我還不叫驢子合駱駝合哩，我只叫周龍皐使雞巴合！』(Xizhou Sheng 2022: 8/46)

In addition to XSYYZ, other works known to be related to JPM in some ways were also examined for the occurrence of 合.

Ruyijun Zhuan

It is a long-established fact that *Ruyijun Zhuan* 如意君傳 (The Lord of Perfect Satisfaction) was in many ways an inspiration and source for JPM (see Hanan 1963: 43). Although there are no occurrences of 合, the verb *rù* 入 (enter) is used extensively instead, and the novel is replete with expressions such as *quán rù zhǔ bǐng* 全入麈柄 (to plunge in the broom handle), *rù lú* 入爐 (to enter the furnace) and *chārù pìn zhōng* 插入牝中 (to insert into the vagina).

Honglou Meng

In *Honglou Meng* 紅樓夢 (Dream of the Red Chamber), the character 肏 is used instead of 合. There are at least 15 occurrences, and five of them can be found in Chapter 9:

這里茗煙先一把揪住金榮，問道：我們肏屁股不肏，管你紅樓夢生字{毛+几}{毛+巴}[35]相干，橫豎沒肏你爹去罷了！　(Cao Xueqin 2005: 137)

---

33 The photographic edition of the non-digitalized second volume of XSYYZ was only available to me from ctext.org, where the quality is relatively poor and barely readable. It was possible, however, to identify the character 合 in the relevant passage.

34 To compare, 合你媽 in Chapter 32 of XSYYZ is 合你娘 in JPM and 合他媽那眼 in Chapter 72 of XSYYZ is 合你娘 (的) 眼 in JPM – see the JPM examples discussed in the section 'Instances of Vulgarisms', '合娘 and its variations'; furthermore, the 雞巴合 from Chapter 72 of XSYYZ is 鬐髿合 in JPM, see section 'Questionable or contextual Instances', '鬐髿合的'.

35 These two characters, consisting of the elements 毛 and 几 and 毛 and 巴, are not part of Unicode and are therefore presented separately in the digital texts. The pronunciation and

Shan'ge

A collection of folk songs by Feng Menglong 馮夢龍 (1574–1646), *Shan'ge* 山歌 (The Mountain Songs), is another possible target to check for occurrences of 屄. There is again no incidence of 屄 anywhere in the text. There are, however, many occurrences of *cào* 操 and its homophone 肏, which are, according to Oki and Santagelo (2011: 283, 338), 'used in vulgar language and swearing with the meaning of fucking'.

There may be more works of literature from the Ming and Qing era worth exploring for occurrences of 屄.[36] Every study has its limitations, however, and I can only hope that this list included the most relevant candidates.

Conclusion

'First thing we come in contact with when reading a literary work is language' (Meng Xianzhang 1991: 121). Therefore, it must be of a certain value to study the language of the given literary work to a deeper level and wider extent, as was the purpose of this paper. This is in all probability, however, the first study that provides a systematic comparison of the two JPM editions from the perspective of sex-related and profane vocabulary, focusing closely on the occurrences of one selected expression. Apart from a few occurrences in XSYYZ, 屄 pertains almost exclusively to JPM and therefore may be considered the novel's 'signature lexeme'. The indecency of the word seems to reflect the moral character of the protagonists, who use the word most often in the novel, and it is probably no surprise that Pan Jinlian, the archetypal femme fatale of Chinese fiction, ranked first among them.

The comprehensive search for 屄 in the STs of both editions proved to be extremely arduous, and although web-based digitalized corpora were enormously helpful with locating the occurrences, it became apparent that it is advisable not to rely on them entirely.

In the 'Analysis' section of this paper, the details of the search results have been presented, and from the ensuing discussion several questions arise, of which two can be considered fundamental:

---

meaning of this word are synonymous to the previously mentioned 鬌髟 or 雞巴, i.e., *jiba* (cock, penis).

36 Luo Junjie (2010: 150) mentions, for example, *Weishuixuan Riji* 味水軒日記 (Diary of *Weishui* Study) by Li Rihua (李日華; 1565–1635) referring to it as a novel that 'uses vulgar language derived from the conversations and jokes of the lower social classes'. According to the digital search on Ctext, however, there is no occurrence of 屄 or 肏 in the text of the novel.

271

Is there a definitive answer as to what type of expression 弇 is? Based on the type of occurrence in the samples examined, the sex-related context prevails, as it is used as a verb denoting not only heterosexual coitus but also fellatio and homosexual (anal) intercourse. The characteristics of this expression in a sentence are greatly influenced, however, not only by the meaning of the given sentence but also by the overall context of the surrounding sentences, the broader context of a conversation, episode, or even the whole chapter. Therefore, as demonstrated by the examples presented, the meaning is questionable in some cases.

Does this study confirm any drastic textual differences between JPMa and JPMb? Moreover, is JPMb, compared to JPMa, somehow emasculated in this respect? The answer to both questions is negative. Apart from the 11 instances that occur only in one edition and not the other one (which is still less than 20% of occurrences), the two editions are almost identical in this respect. Either one or more sentences are missing in the other edition, or the sentences are identical, but 弇 is omitted in one of the editions (substituted by another, usually synonymous expression). In only one case is an entire passage containing 弇 missing from one edition – a passage depicting a theatrical performance, which is in JPMa but is completely missing from JPMb. However, this is nothing unusual, since the editor of JPMb deleted a significant number of passages written in verse. It is only circumstantial that, in this instance, the editor also deleted the occurrence of 弇. If he had been trying to somehow purge the text of colloquialisms and dialects, he would in all probability have gotten rid of or also replaced all the instances of 弇, which, as we now know, did not happen.

I hope that that the type of lexical analysis undertaken here, based on a comparison of occurrences of 'rare expressions' between JPM and other contemporary works of literature, may prove to be of particular value. Perhaps it may bring new insights that will aid in identifying the author of the novel – something that has been disputed for the past 400 years and undoubtedly an aim that is worth pursuing.

References

Berg, Daria

> **2001.** 'Traditional vernacular novels: Some lesser known works.' In Victor Mair (ed.), *The Columbia History of Chinese Literature,* pp. 659–674. New York: Columbia University Press.

Burridge, Kate

> **2015.** 'Taboo words.' In John R. Taylor, *The Oxford Handbook of The Word,* pp. 401–415. Oxford: Oxford University Press.

SEX-RELATED EXPRESSION OR VULGARISM?

Cameron Deborah and Don Kulick

2003. *Language and Sexuality.* Cambridge: Cambridge University Press.

Cao Xueqin 曹雪芹

2005. *Honglou Meng* 红楼梦 (Dream of the Red Chamber). Vol. 1. Beijing: Renmin wenxue chubanshe.

Carlitz, Katherine

1984. 'Family, society and tradition in *Jin Ping Mei.*' *Modern China* 10(4): 387–413.

Cesta, Stanford

2017. *Digital Research into the Authorship of the Jin Ping Mei.* Online Youtube video, total length 1:38:14. Published February 15, 2017 (filmed February 9, 2016). Accessible from: youtu.be/hZYiDdYyYlc.

Ding Naifei

2002. *Obscene Things: Sexual Politics in Jin Ping Mei.* Durham, NC: Duke University Press.

Egerton, Clement (trans.)

2011a. *The Golden Lotus: A translation, from the Chinese original, of the novel Chin P'ing Mei* (Vol. 1). London: Routledge and Kegan Paul Ltd.

2011b. *The Golden Lotus: A translation, from the Chinese original, of the novel Chin P'ing Mei* (Vol 2). London: Routledge and Kegan Paul Ltd.

Gulik, Robert van

2003. *Sexual Life in Ancient China: A Preliminary Survey of Chinese Sex and Society from ca. 1500 B.C. till 1644 A.D.* Leiden: Brill.

Hanan, Patrick

1962. 'The text of the Chin P'ing Mei.' *Asia Major* 9(1): 1–57.

1963. 'Sources of the Chin P'ing Mei.' *Asia Major* 10(2): 43–47.

Hanyu Da Zidian Weiyuanhui 漢語大字典委員會 (eds)

2010. *Hanyu Da Zidian* 漢語大字典, Vol 1. (9 Vols., 2nd Ed.) Hubei Dictionaries Press.

Hinsch, Bret

1992. *Passions of the Cut Sleeve: The Male Homosexual Tradition in China.* Oakland: University of California Press.

Hsia, C. T.

2015 [1968]. *The Classic Chinese Novel: A Critical Introduction.* Revised Edition Hong Kong: The Chinese University of Hong Kong. (Original Edition © C. T. Hsia 1968)

ONDŘEJ VICHER

Huang, Frank and Wolfram Eberhard

1968. 'On some Chinese terms of abuse.' *Asian Folklore Studies* 27(1): 25–40.

Hu Yannan 胡衍南

2014. *Jin Ping Mei yinshinannü* 《金瓶梅》飲食男女 (*Jin Ping Mei* – Wine, Food and Sex). Taibei: Taiwan xuesheng shuju.

Král, Oldřich (trans.)

2013. *Jin Ping Mei aneb Slivoň ve zlaté váze. Svazek druhý.* (*Jin Ping Mei*, or The Plum in the Golden Vase.) Vol. 2. Lásenice: Maxima. (Czech edition)

Lanling Xiaoxiaosheng 蘭陵笑笑生

1990a. *Xinke Xiuxiang Piping Jinpingmei* 新刻繡像批評金瓶梅 (New Annotated and Illustrated Edition of *Jin Ping Mei*). Qi Yan 齊煙 and Wang Rumei 王汝梅 (eds). Vol 1. Hong Kong and Jinan: Sanlian shudian and Qilu shushe.

1990b. *Xinke Xiuxiang Piping Jinpingmei* 新刻繡像批評金瓶梅 (New Annotated and Illustrated Edition of *Jin Ping Mei*). Qi Yan 齊煙 and Wang Rumei 王汝梅 (eds). Vol 2. Hong Kong and Jinan: Sanlian shudian and Qilu shushe.

1998. *Jin Ping Mei cihua xiaozhu* 金瓶梅詞話校註 (Edited and annotated edition of *Jin Ping Mei cihua*). Feng Qiyong 馮其庸, Bai Weiguo 白維國 and Bu Jian 卜鍵 (eds). Changsha: Yuelu shushe.

Lévy, André

2002. *Chinese Literature Ancient and Classical*. Bloomington and Indianapolis: Indiana University Press.

Liu Dalin 劉達臨

2015. *Zhongguo xingwenhua shi* 中國性文化史 (History of Chinese Sex Culture). Wuhan: Wuhan daxue chubanshe.

Liu Hui 劉輝 (ed.)

1991. *Jin Ping Mei yanjiu* 金瓶梅研究 (Studies on *Jin Ping Mei*). Shanghai: Jiangsu guji chubanshe.

Luo Junjie

2010. *Desire and Redemption: The Two Worlds in Jin Ping Mei*. University of Illinois at Urbana-Champaign.

Manukhin, V. S. (transl.)

1993. *Цзинь, Пин, Мэй, или Цветы сливы в золотой вазе.* Пер. В.С.Манухин и др.; Сост. и отв. ред. А.И. Кобзев; Прим. А.И. Кобзева, В.С.Таскина и Б.Л. Рифтина. Т. 1, кн. 1. М.: ИВ РАН (Jin, Ping, Mei, or Plum Flowers in a Golden Vase. Translated by V. S. Manukhin et al.; compiled and edited by A. I. Kobzev, V. S. Taskin and B. L. Riftin. Vol. 1, Book. 1. Moscow: IV RAN).

McMahon, Keith

2019. 'The art of the bedchamber and *Jin Ping Mei*.' *Nan Nü* 21(1): 1–37.

Meng Xianzhang 孟憲章

1991. 'Lun Jin Ping Mei yuyan moshi yu Shandong fangyan shuo 論金瓶梅語言模式與山東方言說' (On the language pattern of *Jin Ping Mei* and the Shandong dialect). In Liu Hui 劉輝 (ed.), *Jin Ping Mei yanjiu* 金瓶梅研究 (Studies on *Jin Ping Mei*), pp. 121–133. Shanghai: Jiangsu guji chubanshe.

Oki Yasushi and Paolo Santagelo (eds)

2011. *Shan'ge, the 'Mountain Songs': Love Songs in Ming China.* Leiden and Boston: Brill.

Plaks, Andrew H.

1985. 'After the fall: Hsing-Shih Yin-Yüan Chuan and the seventeenth-century Chinese novel.' *Harvard Journal of Asiatic Studies* 45(2): 543–580.

1987. *The Four Masterworks of the Ming Novel.* Princeton, NJ: Princeton University Press.

Qi Lintao

2016. 'Agents of Latin: An archival research on Clement Egerton's English translation of *Jin Ping Mei*.' *Target* 28(1): 42–60.

2018. *Jin Ping Mei English Translations – Texts, Paratexts and Contexts.* London and New York: Routledge.

2021. 'Translating sexuality in the context of Anglo-American censorship: The case of *Jin Ping Mei*.' *Translation and Interpreting Studies* 16(3): 416–433.

Roy, David T. (trans.)

1993–2013. *The Plum in the Golden Vase or, Chin P'ing Mei* (Vols. 1– 5). Princeton, NJ: Princeton University Press. (Volume 1 1993, Volume 2 2001, Volume 3 2006, Volume 4 2011, Volume 5 2013)

1986. 'The case for T'ang Hsien-Tsu's authorship of the *Jin Ping Mei*.' *Chinese Literature: Essays, Articles, Reviews (CLEAR)* 8(1/2): 31–62.

1990. 'How to read the Chin P'ing Mei.' In David L. Rolston (ed.), *How to Read the Chinese Novel,* pp. 196–243.Princeton, NJ: Princeton University Press.

1993a. 'An Introduction.' In *The Plum in the Golden Vase or, Chin P'ing Mei (Vol. 1 – The Gathering),* pp. xvii–xlviii. Princeton, NJ: Princeton University Press.

Ruan Fangfu and Molleen Matsumura (eds)

1991. *Sex in China: Studies in Sexology in Chinese Culture.* New York: Plenum Press.

Sun Xun 孫遜 and Wei Tongxian 魏衛賢 (eds)

1993. *Jin Ping Mei jianshang cidian* 金瓶梅鑒賞辭典 (*Jin Ping Mei* Appreciation Dictionary). Shanghai: Shanghai guji chubanshe.

ONDŘEJ VICHER

Tian Xiaofei

2002. 'A preliminary comparison of the two recensions of "Jinpingmei".' *Harvard Journal of Asiatic Studies* 62(2) (Dec): 347–388.

Wu Yenna

1986. 'Marriage Destinies to Awaken the World: A Literary Study of Xing-shiyinyuan zhuan'. Ph.D. dissertation, Harvard University.

1991. 'Repetition in Xingshi yinyuan zhuan.' *Harvard Journal of Asiatic Studies* 51(1): 55–87.

1999. *Ameliorative Satire and the Seventeenth-Century Chinese Novel, Xingshi Yinyuan Zhuan-Marriage as Retribution, Awakening the World.* Lewiston: E. Mellen Press.

Xizhou Sheng 西周生

2017. *Xingshi Yinyuan Zhuan* 醒世姻缘传 (Marriage Destinies to Awaken the World) (Vol. 1). Tuanjie chubanshe.

2022. *Xingshi Yinyuan Zhuan* 醒世姻缘传 (Marriage Destinies to Awaken the World) (Photographic copy) 10 vols. Ctext.org,online.Available at: ctext.org/library.pl?if=gbandfile=92811andpage=46andremap=gb

Zhang Huiying 張惠英

2016. Jin Ping Mei zhong zhide zhuyi de yuyan xianxiang 《金瓶梅》中值得注意的語言現象 (Notable Linguistic Phenomena in *Jin Ping Mei*). In Zhang Huiying 張惠英 and Zong Shouyun 宗守雲 (eds), *Jin Ping Mei yuyan yanjiu wenji* 《金瓶梅》語言研究文集 (An Anthology of Linguistic Studies on *Jin Ping Mei*), pp. 28–41. Beijing: Zhongguo shehui kexue chubanshe.

Zhang Zhupo 張竹坡

1986. Piping diyi qishu Jin Ping Mei dufa 批評第一奇書金瓶梅讀法 (A Treatise on How to Read the First Marvellous Book *Jin Ping Mei*). In Hou zhongyi 侯忠義 and Wang Rumei 王汝梅 (eds), *Jin Ping Mei ziliao huibian* 金瓶梅資料彙編 (Compilation of Materials on *Jin Ping Mei*), pp. 24–46. Beijing: Beijing daxue chubanshe.

Zhou Lu 周璐

2016. Jin Ping Mei cihuaben yu chongzhenben bijiao yanjiu shuping 《金瓶梅》詞話本與崇禎本比較研究述評. (A Review of Studies on *Jin Ping Mei* Comparing the Cihua and Chongzhen Editions). *Neijiang Shifan Xueyuan Xuebao* 9(31): 8–14.

Note on Contributor

Ondřej Vicher is a Doctoral Candidate at the Department of Asian Studies at Palacký University in Olomouc, Czech Republic, where he currently teaches courses on the Ancient History of China and delivers a literary lecture on The Four Masterworks of the Ming dynasty Novel. Before turning to an academic career, he worked as a translator and interpreter from Chinese. His research focuses primarily on *Jin Ping Mei*, particularly on the differences between its main editions. For this purpose, he has translated the first chapter of the *Chongzhen* edition into Czech. Additionally, he is working on completing the translation of the last 30 chapters of the *Wanli* edition into Czech with Lucie Olivová, after the novel's original translator Prof. Oldřich Král passed away in 2018. Apart from the research-in-translation of *Jin Ping Mei*, he analyses the sex-related vocabulary and historical and cultural references in the novel. He also recently started working on the complete and unabridged translation of *Sanguo Yanyi* into Czech.

CHAPTER 17

A Book that Invites Lust

The Fate of *Jin Ping Mei* during the Edo Period in Japan

KAWASHIMA YUKO

Translated by Megan Seal

Mori Ōgai 森鴎外's (1862–1922) *Vita Sexualis* ヰタ・セクスアリス includes a scene in which a 15-year-old boy discovers the novel *Jin Ping Mei* 金瓶梅 beneath the desk of his teacher Bunen-sensei, from whom he had been learning classical Chinese in Mukojima:

> One day I looked at the Chinese book peeking out from under the teacher's desk, and it was *Jin Ping Mei*. I had only read Bakin's *Jin Ping Mei,* But I knew that the Chinese *Jin Ping Mei* was very different. 'How can a teacher read a novel of this kind?' I thought to myself.

Why was *Jin Ping Mei* peeking out from 'under the teacher's desk'? And why did the boy think, 'How can a teacher read a novel of this kind?' For Ogai to include further explanations was unnecessary; at the time there was a shared awareness of the kind of work that *Jin Ping Mei* was. What kind of work *was it*? Kyokutei Bakin 曲亭馬琴 (1767–1848), who wrote *Shinpen Kinpeibai* 新編金瓶梅, an adaptation of *Jin Ping Mei*, said the following about it in the introduction to the first volume of his edition:

> This book depicts the lust-filled life of Ximen Qing 西門慶, a wealthy Song era merchant. [...] It is a book that invites lust and includes much content that should not be read by sovereigns, subjects, fathers, and children. [...] In essence, it is like what is called 'popular entertainment' (*ukiyo monomane*) in Japan, and it does not have a single clever storyline.

This work is a revised version of my article in *Intriguing Asia*, Vol. 105 (Bensei Shuppan, 2007). This work was supported by JSPS KAKENHI Grant Number 16K02589. The translation was produced by Megan Seal on the basis of an English version provided by the author.

According to Bakin, *Jin Ping Mei* 'does not have a single clever storyline'. It is a book about 'the lust-filled life of Ximen Qing', which 'leads to lust'. Was this perception commonly shared in the Edo period?

In what follows I will explore, on the basis of relevant documents, how our ancestors read and received this text that had crossed the ocean to come to Japan in the Edo period.

The Importation of *Jin Ping Mei* to Japan

Jin Ping Mei is a 100-chapter full-length vernacular novel published approximately 400 years ago during the Wanli 万暦 era (1573–1620) of the Ming Dynasty in China. It was introduced to Japan several decades later during the early 17th century. The oldest published edition, which has an introduction from the 45th year of the Wanli reign (1617) (commonly referred to as the *cihua* 詞話 version or the *Wanli* version), was the first to come to Japan. As a very valuable text, it was only in the possession of temples and the households of feudal lords; few people ever came into contact with it.

The version that later became widely available in Japan through more general distribution channels was the Zhang Zhupo 張竹坡 version or the *Di yi qi shu* 第一奇書 (*No.1 Marvelous Book*) version. The Zhang Zhupo version consists of a revision of *Jin Ping Mei* that was created at the end of the Ming Dynasty in the Chongzhen years (1628–1644) (referred to as the 'revised' version or the Chongzhen 崇禎 version) and a critique by the Qing literary scholar Zhang Zhupo (1670–1698). Looking at documents from the Edo period regarding the importation of Chinese texts, we find records of the Zhang Zhupo version being frequently brought into Japan. In the 4th year of the Kan'en reign (1751) alone, 11 copies of it were imported, despite each copy having 100 (Ōba [ed.] 1967; 1972).

From the 1754 publication *Tōsei Kuruwa Dangi* 当世花街談義, we can gain a glimpse of how *Jin Ping Mei* was received at the time:

> Young people who have educated themselves a bit write Chinese and Japanese poems with pride. Of them, those beardless Chinese student scholars talk about the concubine Pan Jinlian in *Jin Ping Mei* and the handsome man Miosei 未央生 in *Kakugozen* 覚悟禅, about whether the liver is pronounced *gan* or *kan* in Chinese, and so on. (Mizuno 1978)

This text says that there are young men who boastfully talk about Chinese novels such as *Jin Ping Mei* and *Kakugozen* (*Rouputuan* 肉蒲団, described below), to women in entertainment districts. Putting aside the question of how much they had actually read of these books, we can infer that *Jin Ping Mei* was already fairly well-known. As a novel, *Jin Ping Mei* had begun its wide circulation in Japan.

The Reception of *Jin Ping Mei* in the Edo Period

It appears that Japanese people have liked *Shui Hu Zhuan* 水滸伝 since the Edo period, as demonstrated by the many commentaries and translations that were published after its arrival in Japan (Takashima 1991). By contrast, the popularity of *Jin Ping Mei*, which came out of *Shui Hu Zhuan*, was very limited. The Chinese literature scholar Sawada Mizuho 澤田瑞穗 (1912–2002) explains this as follows:

> At the end of the Edo period in Japan, the popular fiction writer Bakin released his own adaptation, entitled *Shinpen Kinpeibai*. However, this is basically the only example of *Jin Ping Mei* being publicly promoted. It was not as widely familiar to the masses and did not have as great an influence on Japanese literature as *Shui Hu Zhuan* or *Xi You Ji* 西遊記. Above all, being judged as the foremost 'obscene book', it was probably not something that could be read or discussed by gentlemen, and at most only read furtively under desks by the Chinese studies scholars who could read or speak *Towa* 唐話 (Chinese / vernacular Chinese writing of the time). Its shady status as an 'under-the-desk book' continued from the Edo period into the Meiji and Taisho, as well as the Showa. During the prewar period, one could not openly engage in research on it. This was because, along with intellectual oppression, the curse of it being an 'obscene book' had not gone away.   (Sawada 1965)

In other words, because of *Jin Ping Mei*'s content, from the Edo to the Showa period it had a shady status as an 'under-the-desk book', and this became a fetter that slowed research on it. This view is not limited to Sawada: in Japan this has been the generally shared viewpoint when it comes to the reception of *Jin Ping Mei* (Xiaoxiaosheng 1973–8; Kusaka 1996). Of 'China's Four Classic Novels', *Sanguo Yanyi* 三国演義, *Shui Hu Zhuan* and *Xi You Ji* were translated during the Edo period, while not a single translated version of *Jin Ping Mei* was published during that period. Only in the Meiji period was a vernacular translation published (and it was only of the first 11 chapters). However, was this really because it was an 'obscene book'?

During the Edo period, there was a commentary on *Jin Ping Mei*. It was never published but examining it may shed some light on this issue.

Okaminami Kankyō's 岡南閑喬 'Kinpeibai Yakubun' (*Jin Ping Mei*)

From the Shotoku era (1711–1716) to the Hōreki era (1751–1764) in the Edo period, there was a man in Osaka (with the family name Oka 岡 and first name Minami 南) who went by the courtesy name Kankyō Nanasuke 閑喬七介. A doctor by profession, his translation 'Kinpeibai Yakubun' is the oldest existing

Jin Ping Mei commentary in Japan as well as the only one from the Edo period that still exits.

In 18th-century Japan, Chinese vernacular novels became hugely popular. During this period, many commentaries and Chinese character reference works for a variety of Chinese vernacular novels, including *Shui Hu Zhuan*, were compiled. Some of them quote *Jin Ping Mei*, and others clearly state that they refer to it. This reveals the popularity of *Jin Ping Mei* among scholars of vernacular novels at the time (Kawashima 2010; 2019b). Under such circumstances, it would have been entirely natural for commentaries to be made on this text. However, Okaminami's commentary is the only one that has been discovered, and it only exists in manuscript form.

Looking at 'Kinpeibai Yakubun', we first find words related to architectural structures: 到底七進 referring to a large house, 穿堂 to a through hall, 儀門 to a ritual gate, and 角門 to a corner gate. Then we find an array of *xiehouyu* 歇後語 riddles, such as 提傀儡兒上場還少一口気兒哩 and 両隻脚還趕不上一張嘴哩. This is followed by explanations of words and expressions from the first chapter of the novel. At the beginning of the Zhang Zhupo version – though there are some differences between printings – we find supplements, such as 西門慶房屋 (about the 'Structure of the Ximen House') and 金瓶梅趣談 (about the '*Xiehouyu* Riddles' in the novel). This suggests that Okaminami's commentary was based on the Zhang Zhupo version, which was circulating at the time. Additionally, we can sense his determination to read the book from cover to cover.

However, he encountered difficulties from the beginning, with unannotated characters and characters described as 'unclear' (*fushō* 不詳), as can be seen from Figure 17.1. In addition, of the 62 *xiehouyu* riddles, approximately half remained completely unannotated. *Xiehouyu* are a type of *chengyu* 成語 (idiom) or idiomatic expression, composed of two parts. They are a kind of wordplay in which one is made to infer the second half from the first part. Many of them are very hard to decipher.

One example: 夾道売門神——看出来的好画児. 夾道 is a narrow alleyway and 門神 is an image of a god hung on a gate that serves as an amulet. When a 門神 is on a main road it does not stand out; however, when it is being sold in a dreary, narrow alleyway, one is made to realize that it is a pretty good picture (看出来的好画児). This phrase therefore means 'reconsidering something's merits'. Looking at 'Kinpeibai Yakubun', we find the following explanation:

夾道売門神看出来的好画児　化粧ヲシタル面ノコトヲ云不詳

'A face with makeup applied' makes no sense. Okaminami probably thought that was strange, and therefore followed it with 'unclear'.

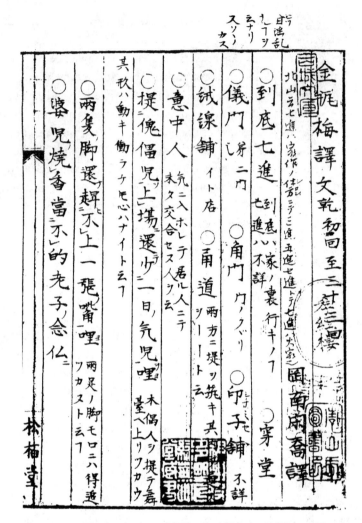

Figure 17.1. The beginning of 'Kinpeibai Yakubun' (Hatano Taro's library) A reproduction is found in Chinese literature language studies compilation 中国文学語学集成 (Fuji Shuppan, 1988).

The scholar of Chinese literature Kuraishi Takeshirō 倉石武四郎 (1897–1975) likened translating the *Jin Ping Mei* to deciphering the Rosetta stone (Ono 1979). *Jin Ping Mei* is truly difficult. Kyokutei Bakin himself pointed out multiple times that *Jin Ping Mei* was a difficult-to-read book that included a lot of colloquial language and idioms:

小説中の手とり物ニて、よみ易からず候 (It is hard to read, even for a novel; letter to Jōsai from the 28th day of the first month of the 13th year of Bunsei), 金瓶梅ハ、俗語中にてよミ得がたきもの也 (*Jin Ping Mei* is

A BOOK THAT INVITES LUST

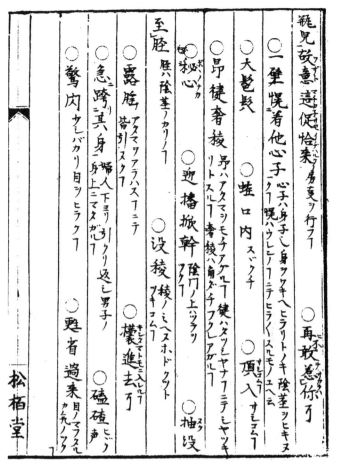

Figure 17.2. 'Kinpeibai Yakubun' Chapter 27 (Hatano Taro's library)

difficult even for a vernacular novel; letter to Jōsai from the 26th day of the third month of the 13th year of Bunsei), and 彼書中ニハ方言洒落、ほのめかしたることもある (That book includes idioms, riddles, slang, and so on; introduction to *Shinpen Kinpeibai*). (Shibata 2002)

Looking at 'Kinpeibai Yakubun' as a whole, we can see that it includes unannotated words, as well as ones described as indecipherable using compounds such as 不詳 (unclear), 不解 (incomprehensible) and 待考 (to be examined). It is not hard to imagine that with no dictionaries to rely on, Okaminami's work involved considerable difficulties. Nevertheless, he did not give up, and made commentaries on all 100 chapters of the novel.

283

Next, how did he handle the sexual descriptions that gave *Jin Ping Mei* the reputation of being an 'obscene book'? As shown in Figure 17.2, he provided notes in a very straightforward fashion without giving them any special treatment. There is no major difference between his approach to these expressions and his approach to other difficult-to-understand words.

As mentioned above, 'Kinpeibai Yakubun' is only available in manuscript form. However, the reason why it has not been published does not appear to be the novel's obscene reputation. Instead, it is perhaps due to the fact that Okaminami was only able to create an imperfect commentary – in other words, the novel was too difficult, and he was unable to read it with precision.

After 'Kinpeibai Yakubun'

Though incomplete, Okaminami's work would make a great contribution to the subsequent reception of *Jin Ping Mei*. In a letter, Kyokutei Bakin wrote:

> During the Bunka years, I purchased the rare book 'Kinpeibai Yakubun'. However, I no longer have it because I exchanged it for another book. It was the original manuscript by the compiler himself. There is only one in the world.
>
> (Letter to Jōsai 篠斎 on the twenty-sixth day of the third month of the 13th year of Bunsei, i.e. 1830)

Here, Bakin noted that he had been in possession of 'Kinpeibai Yakubun' for some time. When Bakin read *Jin Ping Mei*, Okaminami's 'Kinpeibai Yakubun' was near at hand.

There are several manuscript copies of this 'Kinpeibai Yakubun'. In the copy that was part of the library of the late Chinese literature scholar Hatano Taro 波多野太郎 (1912–2003),[1] we find the following next to its title characters: 北山先生題簽 (title characters [written] by Hokuzan-sensei) (see Figure 17.3). 'Hokuzan-sensei' probably refers to Confucian scholar Yamamoto Hokuzan 山本北山 (1752–1812) of the late Edo period. Furthermore, next to Okaminami's explanation of the phrase *daodi qijin* (到底七進), which appears at the beginning of the book (到底ハ家ノ裏行キノコト七進ハ不詳), *daodi* (到底) refers to the depths of a house. As for *qijin* (七進) (I do not know what it means), we find Hokuzan's explanation: 北山云、七進ハ家作ノ仕方ニシテ、三進、五進、七進トテ、七進ハ大家也 'Hokuzan says that *qijin* is a building method. There is *sanjin* (三進), *wujin* (五進), and *qijin*. *Qijin* refers to a large house.' (see Figure 17.1) Based on this, Hatano Tarō writes that Okaminami was a 'scholar in the Hokuzan school'. However, in the manuscript in Kyoto University's library that I reviewed, there were neither Hokuzan's title

---

1 A reproduction is found in Hatano (1988), see part 1, volume 1.

A BOOK THAT INVITES LUST

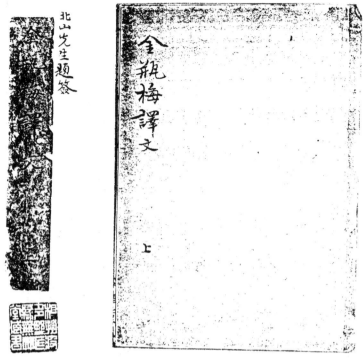

Figure 17.3. Title characters of *Kinpeibai Yakubun* (Hatano Taro's library)

characters nor any added explanation 北山云 (Hokuzan's inscription). Also, the handwriting of the notes to the main text was completely different. Those appear to be only in the manuscript that was part of Hatano's library.

In the first place, Yamamoto Hokuzan was active long after the creation of 'Kinpeibai Yakubun', which was estimated to be around 1750. Therefore, it is unlikely that Okaminami was a scholar in the Hokuzan school. Rather, it is more natural to think that Hokuzan, or someone related to him, acquired 'Kinpeibai Yakubun' (either the author's original manuscript or a copied manuscript), and wrote this therein (or that the book in Hatano's library was copied by someone related to Hokuzan). Allowing our imagination to run further, based on the expression 北山云 (Hokuzan's inscription) we can entertain the possibility that multiple people, including Hokuzan, read *Jin Ping Mei* alongside 'Kinpeibai Yakubun'.

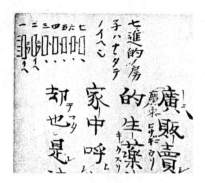

Figure 17.4. Headnotes of *Jin Ping Mei* Chapter 1 (The Tamazato Collection of Kagashima University Library)

A *Jin Ping Mei* Reading Group

During the Edo period, there was a *Jin Ping Mei* reading group. In the Kagoshima University Library's Tamazato Collection, there is a manuscript of *Jin Ping Mei* with Japanese reading marks for classical Chinese (*kunten* 訓点) and annotations (referred to below as the 'Tamazato 玉里' version) (Tokuda 1987). This appears to be a record of a *Jin Ping Mei* reading group led by the Chinese-language scholar Tōyama Katō 遠山荷塘 at the end of the Edo period.[2] Over the course of five years, one of his disciples did transcription work, added Japanese reading marks for classical Chinese, and wrote down Katō's understanding and explanations of the words. In these explanations, we find quotations from a wide range of books: not only classical Chinese novels and vernacular Chinese novels but also *Zhuangzi* 荘子 and *Wuzazu* 五雑組. At some points, diagrams have even been provided for ease of understanding. *Jin Ping Mei* was read very seriously in this group (see Figure 17.4).

Even for the sexual expressions, truly detailed explanations have been added in a straightforward fashion, as can be seen in Figure 17.5. There is no sense of even the smallest amount of shame stemming from reading *Jin Ping Mei*. From this 'Tamazato' version, we can see that this group read *Jin Ping Mei* precisely. Notwithstanding their academic approach, there are vague explanations and misinterpretations – *Jin Ping Mei* was indeed difficult. However, was it not for this very reason that this book was valued as an advanced text for readers of vernacular Chinese novels (Kawashima 2009; 2013)?

---

2 Regarding Tōyama Katō, see Ishizaki 石崎又造 1967; Aoki 青木正児 1970; Iwaki 岩城秀夫 1979; Tokuda 徳田武 1990; Fan 樊可人 2017, 2018.

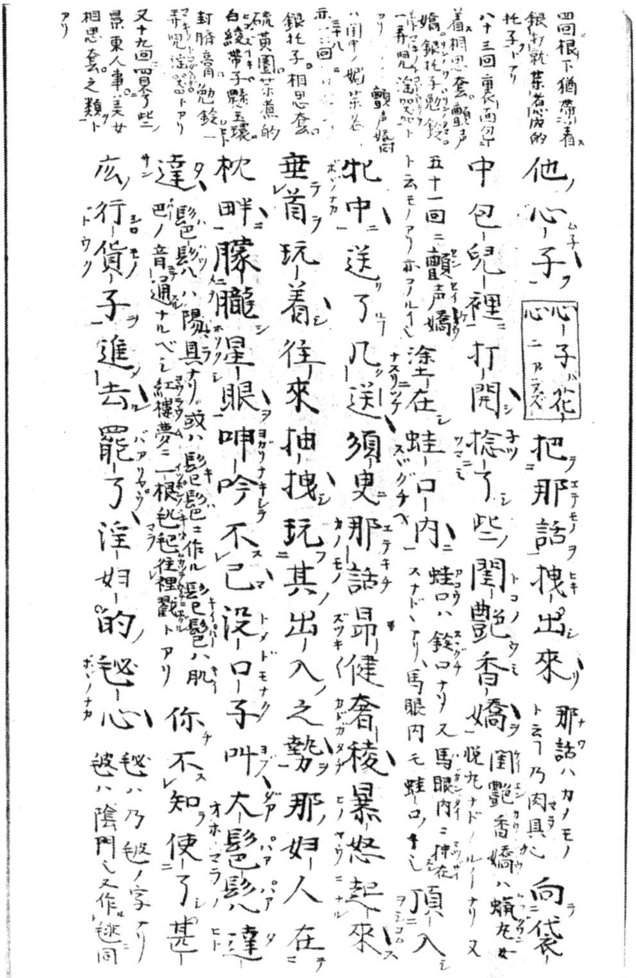
他心子把那話拽出來向袋
中包兒裡打開捻了些閨艷香嬌
塗在蛙口內頂入
牝中送了几送須臾那話昂健奢稜暴怒起來
垂首玩着往來抽拽玩其出入之勢那婦人在
枕畔朦朧星眼呻吟不已沒口子叫大鬃鬁達
達你不知使了甚
麼行貨子進去罷了淫婦的屄心

Figure 17.5. *Jin Ping Mei* Chapter 27 (The Tamazato Collection of Kagashima University Library)

People of the Edo Period and 'Obscene Books'

To what extent were people during the Edo period resistant to 'obscene books' from China? For example, the famous *Rouputuan*, towards the end of the Ming dynasty and at the beginning of the Qing dynasty, is a genuinely 'obscene book', which depicts the sexual history of its main character Weiyangsheng. However, a translation with explanations was published in the second year of the Hōei era (1705), and subsequently an adaptation was also published. This book is also known for having been liked by Okajima Kanzan 岡島冠山 (1674–1728), a famous Chinese-language scholar from the Edo period. Never separated from *Rouputuan*, Kanzan read it morning and evening. He learned Chinese through using this book (Amenomori 1928).

Such 'obscene books' from China were not banned by the government. Banned books during the Edo period were primarily ones related to politics and Christianity; bans were not issued for *Jin Ping Mei* or *Rouputuan* (Konta 1981; *Ōba* 2003). Perhaps the people of the Edo period approached *Jin Ping Mei* and *Rouputuan* more openly than we think? Many studies have pointed out that *Jin Ping Mei* is an obscene book, but does that really mean much? People who lived in the Edo period treated this book more naturally than we did.

Next, let us turn to the question of why a Japanese translation with explanations of *Rouputuan* was published, but not one of *Jin Ping Mei*. Where did the difference between these two books lie? Compared to *Rouputuan*, *Jin Ping Mei* is different in various ways, such as in its considerable length. However, the decisive difference is that it is very difficult to read. Considering the circumstances we looked at above, it is reasonable to conclude that a translation of *Jin Ping Mei* appeared much later than translations of other novels not because it was 'obscene' but because it was difficult, at least during the Edo period. For the Chinese studies scholars of the Edo period, putting aside their minor individual differences, *Jin Ping Mei* was entirely an 'on-the-desk book', so to speak.

However, it appears that, for ordinary people, the circumstances were a little different. In a letter to a friend, Bakin writes the following:

> The book title *Jin Ping Mei* is widely known in the world, and there are therefore people who talk about it. However, in reality, there are few people who have actually read it. It is this kind of obscene book. However, since its title is widely known, I created an adaptation, and, this year, made it into a *gōkan* [a type of picture book popular in the late Edo period].
>
> (Letter to Jōsai dated the 26th day of the third month
> of the 13th year of the Bunsei era, i.e. 1830)

Bakin writes that while the book's name was well-known, few people had read it. It may have been the subject of gossip in Japan. In China, it had been a well-known sexual book ever since its creation. Or it may have been well known because it is one of 'China's Four Classic Novels'. At any rate, around the time of Bakin it appears that its name was widely known.

Bakin, capitalizing on the popularity of *Jin Ping Mei*, created an adaptation of it. However, he loathed its erotic elements and completely removed such 'poison', to make '唐本の金瓶梅とはいたくちがひ候もの' (something completely different than the original *Jin Ping Mei*) (Letter to Jōsai dated the 25th day of the 11th month of the third year of the Tenpō era, i.e. 1833). Through the *Shinpen Kinpeibai* mentioned at the beginning of this chapter, he advertised widely that *Jin Ping Mei* was an 'obscene book'.

From the Meiji period onwards, *Jin Ping Mei* would become established as an 'under-the-desk book'. This was probably due to the success of the publicity Bakin created.

Conclusion: The Subsequent Path of *Jin Ping Mei*

In closing, I will briefly summarize the path of *Jin Ping Mei* from the Meiji period onwards. Between the 15th and 18th years of the Meiji period (1882–1885), Matsumura Misao 松村操 published the first vernacular translation of *Jin Ping Mei*. However, due to the translator's death, it was cut off in the middle of the 11th chapter. In the 12th year of Taishō (1923), Inoue Kōbai 井上紅梅 published *Jin Ping Mei and the State of Chinese Society* 金瓶梅と支那の社会状態 (up to Chapter 67), and in 1925 Ka Kin'i 夏金畏 and Yamada Masato 山田正人 published a joint translation entitled *A Complete Translation of the Jin Ping Mei* 全訳金瓶梅 (up to Chapter 22). However, all of these were abbreviated translations, omitting or censoring sexual depictions. Despite this, both books were banned in 1925. We can see how society's suppression of 'obscene books' had become strict to an extent incomparable with that of the Edo period. Perhaps in a reflection of human nature, to desire to read a book once it is banned, Akutagawa Ryūnosuke 芥川龍之介 (1892–1927) wrote the following in a postcard dated October 19th, 1916, to Ishida Mikinosuke 石田幹之介 (1891–1974): 'I pray that you are safe in your travels [in China]. If there are no other 'obscene books', then buy the cheapest *sekiin* (lithographic print) of *Jin Ping Mei* for me'. It appears that at the time a cheap *sekiin* version of the original was circulating and people who could understand older vernacular Chinese enjoyed reading it 'under the desk'. On the other hand, it seems that, for those who could not read it, its image as an enigmatic 'obscene book' grew stronger and stronger (Kawashima 2019a).

Subsequently, in 1932, the '*cihua*' version, thought to be the oldest woodblock print version of *Jin Ping Mei*, was discovered in Shanxi province (after the appearance of the more popular 'Zhang Zhupo' version, the '*cihua*' version disappeared, and even the fact that it existed was completely forgotten). Then a version belonging to the Tokuyama Domain was found in the Nikko mountain Rinnō-ji temple in Japan. This instantly invigorated research on *Jin Ping Mei*, and multiple translations and scholarly works were published. The translation by Ono Shinobu 小野忍 and Chida Kuichi 千田九一 (Xiaoxiaosheng 1973–8), based on the '*cihua*' version, covers the entire book (although sexual depictions are left out to a great degree).[3] This has been published multiple times and is still widely used. Later, a detailed translation, focusing on the incomplete sexual depictions in the Ono-Chida translation, was published (Sakato [ed. and trans.] 1999; Tsuchiya 2007), as was Tanaka Tomoyuki 田中智行's *A New Translation of the Jin Ping Mei* 新訳金瓶梅 (Tanaka 2018; 2021).[4] We can finally read this difficult work in Japanese without much trouble.

There is no doubt that *Jin Ping Mei* is a novel that includes graphic and relentless depictions of sex. However, that is not the only topic that *Jin Ping Mei* covers in great detail. All aspects of everyday life are spelled out, from room furnishings, clothing and accessories and banquet games to song lyrics. Sexual depictions are one (major) element; however, they are by no means the sole focus of *Jin Ping Mei*.

Is *Jin Ping Mei* an 'obscene book'? This question has been constantly asked ever since the novel's appearance. *Jin Ping Mei* critic Zhang Zhupo offered an answer long ago, in the Qing dynasty: 'Those who say that *Jin Ping Mei* is an obscene book are only looking at its obscene parts.'

References

Amenomori, Hoshu 雨森芳洲

1928. 'Kisso sawa 橘窓茶話', Vol. 1. In *Nihon zuihitsu taisei* 日本随筆大成 (*Compilation of Japanese Zuihitsu Essays*). Tōkyō: Yoshikawa Kōbunkan.

Aoki, Masaru 青木正児

1970. 'Denki shōsetsu o kōji geko zen shitaru, Tōyama Katō Ga den no sen 伝奇小説を講じ月琴を善したる, 遠山荷塘が伝の箋' (Annotations on the Biography of Tōyama Katō, who was skilled in interpreting Chinese romance novels with the yueqin). In *Aoki Masaru zenshū* 青木正児全集 (*Complete Works of Aoki Masaru*) 2. Tōkyō: Shunjūdō.

---

3   In 1948, Tōhō Shokyoku published the first volume of this translation (up to and including Chapter 40). Subsequently, the publisher was changed to Mikasa Shobō and Kawade Shobo. It was then again changed to Heibonsha, which in 1959 published all 100 chapters in *Complete Collection of Chinese Classical Literature* 中国古典文学全集 vols. 15–17; subsequently *Chinese Classical Literature Compendium* 中国古典文学大系 vols. 35–37. In addition, Iwanami Shoten published a revised edition in 1973.

4   Currently, only the first two volumes (up to chapter 66) have been published. There are plans to publish the third volume as well.

Fan, Keren 樊可人

2017. 'Tōyama Katō *Genkai Kōchū Kohon Seishōki* no seiritsu ikisatsu ni tsuite 遠山荷塘『諺解校注古本西廂記』の成立経緯について' (On the compilation of the *Genkai Kōchū Kohon Seisōki* by Tōyama Katō). *Nihon Chūgoku Gakkaihō* 69: 242–256.

2018. 'Tōyama katō no *Jōga Seiin* ni tsuite – edo kōki no minshingaku juyō ni kansuru ichikōsatsu 遠山荷塘の『嫦娥清韻』について—江戸後期の明清楽受容に関する一考察—' (*The Jōga Sei'in* by Tōyama Katō: An Inquiry into the reception of Minshingaku in the late Edo period). *Tōhōgaku* 東方学 (*Tōhōgakkai*) 136: 42–65.

Hatano, Taro 波多野太郎 (ed.)

1988. *Chūgoku bungaku gogaku shūsei* 中国文学語学集成 (Chinese Literature Language Studies Compilation). Tōkyō: Fuji Shuppan.

Ishizaki, Matazo 石崎又造

1967. *Kinsei Nihon ni okeru shina zokugo bungaku-shi* 近世日本に於ける支那俗語文学史 (A History of Chinese Vernacular Literature in Early Modern Japan). Tōkyō: Shimizu Kōbundo Shobō.

Iwaki, Hideo 岩城秀夫

1979. 'Sō Ikkei to Kamei Shōyō' 僧一圭と亀井昭陽 (The priest Ikkei and Kamei Shōyō). In 森三樹三郎博士頌寿記念東洋学論集 (*Collection of Eastern Studies Articles Celebrating the Long Life of Dr. Mori Mikisaburō*). Kyōto: Hōyū Shoten.

Kawashima, Yuko 川島優子

2009. 'Edo jidai ni okeru hakuwashōsetsu no yoma re-kata – Kagoshimadaigaku fuzoku toshokan Tamasato bunkogura *Kinpeibai* 江戸時代における白話小説の読まれ方—鹿児島大学付属図書館玉里文庫蔵「金瓶梅」' (How vernacular Chinese novels were read during the Edo period: Focusing on the *Jin Ping Mei* in the Tamasato Collection of Kagashima University Library). *Chūgoku chūsei bungaku kenkyū* 56: 59–79.

2010. 'Edo jidai ni okeru *Kinpeibai* no juyō – jisho, zuihitsu, sharebon o chūshin to shite 江戸時代における『金瓶梅』の受容—辞書、随筆、洒落本を中心として—' (The reception of *Jin Ping Mei* in the Edo period: Focusing on dictionaries, essay collections and late Edo period *sharebon*). *Bulletin of Ryukoku University* 32(1): 1–20.

2013. Edo jidai ni okeru 'shiryō' to shite no *Kinpeibai* – Takashina Masatsune no yomi o tōshite 江戸時代における「資料」としての『金瓶梅』—高階正巽の読みを通して' (The *Jin Ping Mei* as a form of 'material' in Edo Japan: With reference to Takashina Masatsune's reading of the *Jin Ping Mei*). *Tōhōgaku* 125: 107–122.

2019a. 'Meiji Taishō-ki no *Kinpeibai* – sanshu no yakuhon o chūshin to shite 明治・大正期の『金瓶梅』—三種の訳本を中心として—' (*Jin Ping Mei* during the Meiji and Taisho: Three translations). In *Nitchū hikaku bunka ronshū*

日中比較文化論集 (*Collection of Japan–China Comparative Culture Articles*). Tōkyō: Hakuteisha.

2019b. *Kinpeibai no kōsō tosonojuyō* 『金瓶梅』の構想とその受容 (*The Conception and Reception of Jin Ping Mei*). Tōkyō: Kenbun Shuppan.

Konta, Yōzō 今田洋三

1981. *Edo no kinsho* 江戸の禁書 (*The Banned Books of the Edo Period*). Tokyo: Yoshikawa Kōbunkan.

Kusaka, Midori 日下翠

1996. *Kinpeibai Tenkadaiichi no kisho* 『金瓶梅』– 天下第一の奇書―(*Jin Ping Mei: The Most Curious Book in the World*). Tōkyō: Chūkō Shinsho.

Mizuno, Minoru 水野稔 (ed.)

1978. *Sharebon taisei daiikkan* 洒落本大成第一巻 (*Compilation of Sharebon Vol. 1*). Tōkyō: Chūō Kōron-sha.

Ōba, Osamu 大庭脩

2003. *Nitchū kōryū shiwa – Edo jidai no nitchūkankei o yomu* 日中交流史話―江戸時代の日中関係を読む―' (*Historical Tales of Exchange Between Japan and China*). Ōsaka: Nenshōsha.

Ōba, Osamu 大庭脩 (ed.)

1967. *Edo jidai ni okeru tōsenmochiwatarisho no kenkyū* 江戸時代における唐船持渡書の研究 (*Research on Books that Came on Boats from China During the Edo Period*). Kansai: Kansai Daigaku Tōzai Gakujutsu Kenkyūsho.

1972. *Kunaichō shoryōbu zō hakusai shomoku fu kaida* 宮内庁書陵部蔵舶載書目附改題 (*Holdings of the Imperial Household Agency's Archives and Mausolea Department*). Kansai: Kansai Daigaku Tōzai Gakujutsu Kenkyūsho.

Ono, Shinobu 小野忍

1979. *Michishirube – Chūgoku bungaku to watashi* 道標―中国文学と私―(*Guideposts: Chinese Literature and Me*). Tōkyō: Ozawa Shoten.

Sakato, Minomushi 坂戸みの虫 (ed. and trans.)

1999. *Kinpeibai shi-banashi – in no sekai* 金瓶梅詞話―淫の世界―(*Jin Ping Mei: The World of Sexual Desire*). Tōkyō: Taihei Shooku.

Sawada, Mizuho

1965. *Kinpeibai no kenkyū to shiryō* 『金瓶梅』の研究と資料 (*Jin Ping Mei* research and materials). In *Chūgoku no hachi dai shōsetsu* 中国の八大小説 (China's Eight Great Novels), pp. 262–273. Tōkyō: Heibonsha.

Shibata Mitsuhiko 柴田光彦 and Kanda Masayuki 神田正行

2002. *Bakin shokan shūsei daiikkan* 馬琴書翰集成第一巻 (*Compilation of Bakin's Correspondence, Vol. 1*) Tōkyō: Yagi Shoten.

Takashima, Toshio 高島俊男

1991. *Suikoden to Nihonjin – Edo kara Shōwa made* 水滸伝と日本人—江戸から昭和まで— (*Shui Hu Zhuan and Japanese people: From Edo to Showa*). Tōkyō: Taishūkan Shoten.

Tanaka, Tomoyuki 田中智行 (trans.)

2018. *Kinpeibai* 新訳金瓶梅 (*A New Translation of the Jin Ping Mei*), vol.1. Nagano: Chōeisha.

2021. *Kinpeibai* 新訳金瓶梅 (*A New Translation of the Jin Ping Mei*), vol.2. Nagano: Chōeisha.

Tokuda, Takeshi 徳田武

1987. 'Tōyama Katō and *Jin Ping Mei* 遠山荷塘と『金瓶梅』' in 日本近世小説と中国小説 (*Japan's early modern novels and Chinese novels*), Tokyo: Seishōdō Shoten.

1990. 'Tōyama Katō to Hirose Tansō Kamei Shōyō 遠山荷塘と広瀬淡窓・亀井昭陽' (Tōyama Katō to Hirose Tansō, Kamei Shōyō). In *Edo kangaku no sekai* 江戸漢学の世界 (*The World of Edo Chinese Studies*). Tōkyō: Perikansha.

Xiaoxiaosheng 蘭陵笑笑生 (1530–1600)

2007. *Kinpeibai* 金瓶梅 (*Jin Ping Mei*). Edited and translated by Tsuchiya Hideaki 土屋英明. Tōkyō: Tokuma Shoten.

Xiaoxiaosheng 蘭陵笑笑生 (1530–1600)

1973–8. '*Kinpeibai*' no hōyaku•Ō-yaku 『金瓶梅』の邦訳・欧訳 (Japanese and European Translations of *Jin Ping Mei*). Translated by Ono Shinobu 小野忍. Tōkyō: Iwanami Shoten.

Note on Contributors

Dr. Kawashima Yuko is Professor of Chinese literature at the Graduate School of Humanities and Social Sciences, Hiroshima University, Japan.

Megan Seal is currently studying for a Masters of Interpreting and Translation Studies at Monash University, Melbourne, Australia, which she will complete this year. Looking at the translation of Japanese works into English, her research interests include the translation of culturally specific symbolism in literary works, with particular focus on the relationship between this symbolism and religion.

CHAPTER 18

The Game of Official Advancement, *Shengguan tu*

A Macaronic Folk Ballad from the Middle of the Qing Dynasty

MARTIN GIMM

Translated and re-arranged by Vibeke Børdahl

*S*hengguan tu 陞官圖 (The Game of Official Advancement) is first and foremost the name of a traditional Chinese game of chance going back to the Tang dynasty. The play is based on the Chinese conviction that power and riches are obtainable for almost every person who passes the imperial examinations and enters the world of officialdom, leading directly to 'ascendance to the White Clouds', *qingyun zhishang* 青雲直上. Throwing dice, the players seek to advance from one 'official position' to another, ascending to ever higher positions. The playing board, made of paper or wood, has 64 or 66 squares, arranged in groups according to 'ministries' and 'institutions' [...][1] *The game has a certain affinity to the old European 'Game of the Goose', which was already known in the 14th century and has been popular from the 16th century until today, mostly as a family entertainment.*[2] [...] It is far from clear how best to understand the connection between the old dice game and the folk ballad of

---

1 Omission of passages in Martin Gimm's original text are marked [...].

2 Passages in *italics* are summaries rather than translations.

Editor's note: Chapter 18 is based on Martin Gimm: *Shengguan tu*, 'Tafel der Beamten-karriere', eine makkaronische Volksballade aus der mittleren Qing-Zeit, in: *Oriens Extremus*, Vol. 44 (2003/04), pp. 211–252. It is a translation from the German original into English of excerpts from the introduction as well as a re-arrangement and translation of the ballad text from German and Chinese by Vibeke Børdahl. Notes and references are generally omitted, and the Introduction is much shortened. For the full scientific treatment of the *Shengguan tu*, please consult the original article by Martin Gimm. *The notes in the following are all by the translator/editor.*

294

the same name that is the topic of the following description. Maybe the text functions as a kind of travesty of the well-known 'Advancement' game, turning moments of coincidence into focused determination with erotic boorishness.

The Chinese Folk Ballad and the *Zidi Shu* 子弟書

It is generally believed that the present folk ballad belongs to the Chinese category of *shuochang wenxue* 說唱文學 (literature for telling and singing), formerly also called *shuoshu* 說書 (storytelling) or more specifically *danchang guci* 單唱鼓詞 (drum ballads for solo singing) [...]. In this case the text belongs to the subgenre of *zidi shu* (tales of the bannermen gentry) [...] for which the origin is to be sought in former cultic songs of the Manchu bannermen of the three North-eastern Provinces. The *zidi shu* originally arose in the capital of Beijing as a special form of ballad singing in which a solo singer performing the ballad with pantomime and gesticulation was accompanied by a drum-player of the *bajiao gu* 八角鼓 (octagonal drum) (man or woman) adding varied rhythmic accentuation [...]

The genre of zidi shu, *flowering during the middle of the Qing dynasty, especially 1750–1850, and forming an appreciated entertainment form for the aristocratic youngsters,* zidi, *of Manchu society, was instrumental in integrating the new dominant class with the traditional culture of the Chinese population and further seems to have had a certain influence on Chinese* shuochang wenxue. *Later the genre sank more and more into oblivion and became at times a kind of livelihood for blind street musicians.* [...] The subject matter of the ballads was primarily taken from well-known works of fiction and drama, such as the novels *Jin Ping Mei* 金瓶梅 (*Jin Ping Mei*), *Sanguo yanyi* (Three Kingdoms), *Honglou meng* (A Dream of Red Mansions) and drama *Xixiangji* (The West Chamber). Secondarily, themes from contemporary social life were popular.

The *zidi shu* were formally characterized by a verse structure of unequal length, but mainly heptasyllabic, arranged in chapters and sharing the same rhyme throughout the chapter. As with current usage in other folk ballads, it was possible – according to the chosen melodic model – to insert portions of recitation into the song sequences. Mainly the even verse lines rhyme. Moreover, the rhymes were based on the system of the '13 rhyme-groups', *shisan zhe* 十三轍 that were generally applied during the Ming dynasty for folk theatre and ballad singing [...] Verse lines containing 'padding words', *chenzi* 襯字, enlarging the lines beyond the heptasyllabic model, were performed with melismatic freedom, which tended to restore each line according to the heptasyllabic rhythm. So, despite the unequal length of the verse lines, a musical and metric equilibrium was attained.

Apparently, there were no firm rules for the length of *zidi shu* ballads. There were very short items like the *Shengguan tu* and there were long works divided into several dozen chapters, which would stretch over many evenings of performance.

The Textual Corpus of *Zidi Shu*

Apart from a few exceptions, the corpus of *zidi shu* texts that has been preserved up to our time – *about 600 texts* – has been anonymously transmitted. They can be divided into two types: A. Written in Chinese only – by far the larger part of the corpus. B. Hybrid texts written in a mixture of Chinese and Manchu. No *zidi shu* texts written purely in Manchu are known so far. [...] *The number of hybrid texts (B.), which is the focus of this study, is very small. The mixture of Chinese and Manchu takes different forms, being either integrated or separated. The structure of the present text is written in integrated form, where Chinese and Manchu words can be found side by side in the same verse line, and moreover the Manchu words are written in Chinese characters (not in Manchu letters). The texts written in the separated form, where one line is in Chinese and another line in Manchu, are easily understandable by both Chinese- and Manchu-speaking audiences. But the texts written in integrated form are mainly understandable by a bilingual audience. There seems to be a tendency for this kind of text to develop into a burlesque macaronic style, which was also seen in other genres during the Qing dynasty, such as folk songs in a mixed language. Only five texts of category B., hybrid texts, are found among the total corpus. The present text is number (5.):*[3]

(5.) The Game of Official Advancement
Chinese title: *Shengguan tu* 陞官圖
No Manchu title (but called **hafan wesire durugan**[4] in an external source)
Author anonymous, manuscript
Probably from ca 1800 or somewhat earlier
Form: Integration of Chinese and Manchu phrases, written with Chinese characters exclusively

The *Shengguan Tu* Ballad

The folk ballad of Shengguan tu *cannot be accurately dated, but linguistic evidence points to the end of the 18th century. This was a time of rigorous suppression of*

---

3   These five texts are all discussed in Gimm 2003/4: 220–222.

4   For transcription of Manchu, cf. the 'Arrangement of the English Translation of the Ballad Text', below.

THE GAME OF OFFICIAL ADVANCEMENT, *SHENGGUAN TU*

licentious literature under the Qing emperor. How could a burlesque erotic text like this ballad have survived under these conditions? Apparently, the Manchu gentry who enjoyed such songs and ballads were relatively isolated from the general Chinese population. The bannermen were not allowed to mix with Chinese comedians and entertainment troupes or to perform their own ballads in public. Therefore their 'private' amusement was not considered dangerous for the people of the empire. It is worth noting in this connection that Jin Ping Mei had already been translated into Manchu in 1708 and printed in the imperial workshops – at a time when the expurgation of lascivious literature was particularly intense. The survival of the present ballad seems, however, a rare coincidence, since such erotic ballads and songs were generally kept secret in the Manchu milieu.

The present ballad is found in 6 manuscript versions altogether.[5] The translation is according to version (1.) and (2.):

(1.) Manuscript, Fu Ssu-nien Library, 傅斯年圖書館, Institute of History and Philology, Academia Sinica, Taibei.
Signature: T 27–336; 5 double pages with pagination
Size: 10.8 x 21.9 cm

(2.) Manuscript, almost identic with (1.), same place.
Signature: T 27–337, T 27–338; 5 double pages, no pagination.
Size: 10.5 x 22.7 cm

The subject matter of the *Shengguan tu* ballad is from the well-known novel *Jin Ping Mei*, which was also the background of several other *zidi shu*, in spite of the fact that the novel was explicitly forbidden several times under the Kangxi emperor (1662–1723). The anonymous author avails himself of two main characters and two secondary roles: 1. Ximen Qing 西門慶, and 2. Pan Jinlian 潘金蓮, his beloved concubine, 3. Wu Yueniang 吳月娘, Ximen Qing's first wife, and 4. Wang Pozi 王婆子, the old neighbour who arranges the first meeting between Ximen Qing and Pan Jinlian.

The ballad text of *Shengguan tu*, a rare document written for a bilingual audience in the daily vernacular of the 18th century, is publicly made available in print here for the first time[6] – testifying to the language of a traditional genre that, despite the utterly profane contents, must nevertheless be characterized as a piece of artistry [...] Here we shall only give a brief summary of some conspicuous features.

---

5   Cf. Gimm 2003/4: 223–224.

6   Cf. Gimm 2003/4: 224, note 78.

(A) External structure:

(1) Length of verses:
The ballad text consists of 72 verses of unequal length – the number of syllables per verse line is between 7 and 17. However, the performance practice normally leads to a metric rhythm of 7 beats per verse line.[7] *The habit of doubling some characters in the column and diminishing their size is a way of indicating the basic heptasyllabic structure of the verse.* So far, little more is known about the performance practice.

(2) Rhyme:
Alliteration of verse beginnings, typical of Manchu poetry, is not in use here, since all the verses begin in Chinese language. End rhyme in Chinese style is the general rule. All even verses rhyme on *-a* in 'level tone' (*ping* 平),[8] i.e., verse no. 2, no. 4 [...] up to no. 72, including verse no. 1. This is the rhyme *fa, hua zhe* 發花轍 of the '13 rhyme-groups'.[9]

(B) Internal structure:

The present ballad text belongs to the kind of word play called *paronomasia*, i.e., the text includes puns based on the similarity of sound between words of different meaning. Each verse line flaunts an 'official title' and thus the text appears *prima facie* as harmless, but fairly incomprehensible. In order to understand these key words, half of which are in Manchu, one must substitute them with phonetically similar words of a very different origin, creating 'double entendre' puns [...].[10]

[*Translator's note:* This paragraph of Martin Gimm's article explains the arrangement of the ballad text *Shengguan tu* as rendered in Chinese, Manchu, and German translation. Professor Gimm explicitly states that many portions of the translation must be considered tentative. Each entry has elaborate explanations, often with several suggestions for the translation. The reader who wants to understand these aspects more in depth is referred to the original article, which is the background for the present simplified version. The following 'Arrangement of

---

7   Cf. above section 2.

8   The traditional four tone names, *ping* 平, *shang* 上, *qu* 去, and *ru* 入, do not correspond exactly to the tones of Modern Standard Chinese. *Ping* corresponds to MSC first and second tone.

9   Cf. above Section 2.

10 For further phonetic, grammatical and semantic explanation of the textual puns, see Gimm 2003/4: 225–226.

the English Translation of the Ballad Text' explains how the translator has chosen to present the text. It is not a translation from German. As for the text proper, the *Shengguan tu* ballad, the English translation is based on the German translation as well as on the Chinese original. The Manchu words are all translated directly from German, since the translator has no education in Manchu.]

Arrangement of the English Translation of the Ballad Text

Line 1:
The original verse line of 'The Game of Official Advancement' bannermen's ballad, numbered from 1–72. The Chinese characters are rendered as in the original, according to Gimm 2004: 227–242; Manchu-words, written with Chinese characters, are marked in **grey colour**. The 'double entendre' words are underlined. To the right of the verse line, the embedded official title is given in translation after the sign ♦, e.g., for the first verse line: ♦ **Grand Historian**.

Line 2:

Pinyin transcription of Chinese characters in *italics*, with underlining of the 'double entendre' words, i.e., in the first verse line *da shi*, embedding the official title. Manchu-words are in **bolded, roman font**; the transcription is according to Gimm 2003/4, e.g., the second verse line: **booi da** = **Master of the House**.

Line 3:
Explanation of the 'double entendre' pun. Meaning of the underlined written characters of the original verse line, e.g., for the first verse line as written and read: 大史 *da shi* = **Grand Historian**; for the first verse line as heard and understood in the context: *ba qian da shihua* = spent a lot of money.

Line 4:
Translation of the line as understood 'by the ear', i.e., according to the meaning of the sentence as 'heard' and interpreted on the basis of the pun.

The Ballad Text of 'The Game of Official Advancement'

1) 西門慶調情把錢大史花 ♦ Grand Historian
Ximen Qing tiaoqing ba qian da shi hua
da shi = Grand Historian; *ba qian da shi hua* 把錢大使花 = spent a lot of money, i.e., *huaqian* 花錢 = spend money; *shi(yong)* 使(用) = spend
Ximen Qing spent a lot of money on his sexual escapades

2) 請潘金蓮去裁那**包亦達** ◆ **Master of the House**
qing Pan Jinlian qu cai na **booi da**
booi da = **Master of the House**; **booi** = vaguely points to *yifu* 衣服 = gown
he asked Pan Jinlian to take off **her gown**

3) 王婆子他倒上門軍躲出去 ◆ Janitor
Wang Pozi ta dao shang menjun duo chuqu
menjun = Janitor; the first syllable puns with *men* 門 = door
Granny Wang entered the door but withdrew at once

4) 西門慶他色膽如天把司獄發 ◆ Prison Governor
Ximen Qing ta sedan ru tian ba siyu fa
siyu = Prison Governor; punning with *ba siyu fa* 把私慾發 = his lust was ignited
Ximen Qing gave free rein to his passions, and his lust was ignited

5) 走到跟前伸砲手 ◆ Cannoneer
zou dao genqian shen paoshou
paoshou = Cannoneer; punning on the last syllable with *shou* 手 = hands
he went over to her and stretched his hands towards her

6) 將潘金蓮的袖子一**蘇拉** ◆ **Sinecure Post**
jiang Pan Jinlian de xiuzi yi **sula**
sula = **Sinecure Post**; the last syllable puns with *la* 拉 = pull or drag
and **pulled up** the sleeves of Pan Jinlian

7) 滿臉嘻嘻那們護軍校 ◆ Leader of the Palace Guard
manlian xixi namen hujun xiao
hujun xiao = Leader of the Palace Guard; the last syllable puns with *xiao* 笑
= laugh
He was smiling all over his face and laughing

8) 說趁著沒人偺們**烏真极哈** ◆ **Heavy-Armed Bannerman**
shuo chenzhe moren zanmen **ujen cooha**
ujen cooha = **Heavy-Armed Bannerman**; probably only the syllable coo is
relevant, recalling *chuo* 連 = fight it out, do it
He said: 'Since nobody is around, **let's do it!**'

9) 這淫婦春心難按把協尉動 ◆ Chief Constable

THE GAME OF OFFICIAL ADVANCEMENT, *SHENGGUAN TU*

zhe yinfu chunxin nan an ba xieyu dong
xieyu = Chief Constable; punning with *xieyu* 邪慾 = evil desire
Driven by lust, the wanton woman abandoned herself to evil desire

10) 心裏覺著艾什拉密 ◆ Colonel
xinli juezhe **aisilambi**
aisilambi = **aisilame kadalara da** = **Colonel**; the first syllable puns with *ai*愛
= love
and her heart was full of love

11) 那話頭兒相畫稿的占音他會湊達 ◆ **Secretary**
na huatouer xiang huagao de **janggin** *ta hui couda*
janggin = **Secretary**; punning with *shengyin* 聲音 = sound
He harmonized to the sound of her beautiful voice

12) 說你這有情有義一等子 ◆ Count of First Grade
shuo ni zhe you qing you yi yideng zi
yideng zi = Count of First Grade; *yideng zi*: a first-class person
She said: 'You are a first-class man, full of passion and loyalty,

13) 我情愿意一輩子給你當個郭什哈 ◆ **Bodyguard**
wo qing yuanyi yi beizi ji ni dang ge **gosiha**
gosiha = **Bodyguard**; perhaps Manchu loanword in Chinese: *guoshi* 果實 =
be in love with
my wish is to be your intimate lover all my life.'

14) 門慶說你模樣長的比嘎巴什先官學生還俊 ◆ **Vanguard**
Men Qing shuo ni moyang chang de bi **gabsihiyan** *guan xuesheng huan jun*
gabsihiyan = **Vanguard**; the Manchu word also means **good-looking, smart**
Ximen Qing said: 'You look much smarter than a student from the Palace School,

15) 恰好似員外郎新開一朵探花 ◆ Deputy Director
qiahao si yuanwailang xin kai yiduo tanhua
yuanwailang = Deputy Director of a Ministerium; the first syllable *yuan* puns
with *yuan* 園 = garden; *tanhua* = third on the list of candidates for the Hanlin
academy, punning on the syllable *hua* 花 = flower
you are just like a flower opening in the garden.

301

16) 怪不浔王婆子在我的跟前保你卓異 ◆ Promised Position
guaibude Wang pozi zai wo de genqian bao ni zhuoyi
bao = Promised Position; *zhuoyi* = extraordinary

No wonder, that Madam Wang promised me something extraordinary.

17) 你真是個養漢的木昆呢達 ◆ **Chieftain**
ni zhen shi ge yanghan de **mukǒn-i da**
mukǒn-i da = **Chieftain of a Clan**.

You are truly a **master** in the art of seducing men.

18) 怎耐吳月娘作我的治儀正 ◆ Supervisor
zen nai Wu Yueniang zuo wode zhiyi zheng
zhiyi zheng = Supervisor of the Imperial Coaches

How can I tolerate that Wu Yueniang acts as my supervisor?

19) 娶了你算一個阿拉哈占音你混著罷 ◆ **Deputy Chief**
quliao ni suan yige **araha janggin** *ni hunzhao ba*
araha janggin = **Deputy Chief of a Bannermen Regiment**

Since I have married you, you are the **deputy head of the family**, do you get it?'

20) 金蓮說多謝官人的恩騎尉 ◆ Cavalry Chief
Jinlian shuo duo xie guanren de en qiwei
Qiwei = Cavalry Chief; the word *en* = kind, kindness is relevant for the pun

Jinlian said: 'Thank you for your kindness!'

21) 我入夫外單就不怕他 ◆ **Battle Company Chief**
wo ru fu waidan jiu bu pa ta
faidan = **Battle Company**

'Since I have entered your **company**, I'm not scared by her anymore.'

22) 兩個人眉來眼去動了額色 ◆ **Master of a Banner Company**
Liangge ren mei lai yan qu dongliao ese
ese probably refers to Manchu *ejen* = **Master (of a Banner Company)**; *ese* 額色
= forehead, punning with *ese* 惡色 = evil lust

Both of them exchanged glances and stirred up their **evil lust**.

23) 男貪女愛要京察 ◆ Beijing Official's Evaluation
nan tan nü ai yao jingcha

THE GAME OF OFFICIAL ADVANCEMENT, *SHENGGUAN TU*

Jingcha probably refers to the evaluation of the officials, taking place every third year in the capital; the pun is unclear; maybe punning on the expression *jincha* 進岔 = get into the trousers, do it

When the man is full of desire and the woman is in love, they want to do it.

24) 西門慶那**達拉密**起了興 ◆ Headman
Ximen Qing na **dalambi** *qiliao xing*
dalambi = Headman; punning on the Beijing dialect word *dala* 耷拉 = dangle, droop

That **dangling thing** of Ximen Qing was raising.

25) 潘金蓮那未入流的浪水亂滴達 ◆ Orderly
Pan Jinlian na **weiru liu** *de lang shui luan dida*
weiru liu = *orderly/companion*; *dida* 滴達 seems to be a mistake for 滴答 = drip

Pan Jinlian, his companion, was dripping wet.

26) 官人說這床上無有**教習**可怎麼幹 ◆ Instructor
Guanren shuo zhe chuangshang wu you **jiaoxi** *ke zenme gan*
jiaoxi = Instructor; the second syllable of *jiaoxi* puns with *xi* 席 = a mat/sleeping mat

The gentleman said: 'There is no sleeping mat on the bed. What shall we do?'

27) 淫婦說那不是**多鱉呢占音**你墊上他 ◆ Keeper of the Seal
yinfu shuo na busbi **doron-i janggin** *ni dian shang ta*
doron-i janggin = Keeper of the Seal; the sound is close to *duoluoni* = woollen blanket

The wanton woman said: 'Isn't there a **woollen blanket** over there? Spread it out!'

28) 解開了**牛彔**脫下了銀紅襖 ◆ Banner Company
jiekailiao **niru** *tuoxialiao yinhong ao*
niru = Banner Company; the first syllable puns with *niu* 紐 = button

She undid the **buttons** and took off her red silver embroidered jacket.

29)那**烏克身**子白淨像那棉花瓜 ◆ Armour
Na **uksin** *zi bo jing xiang na mianhuagua*

303

uksin = **armour**; the syllable *shen* 身 in *shenzi* 身子 = body is relevant for the pun.

Her **body** was white and clean like a cotton boll.

30) 西門慶接住金蓮的**撥什戶** ◆ **Corporal**
Ximen Qing jiezhu Jinlian de **bosoko**
bosoko = **Corporal**; the first syllable **bo** puns with *bo* 脖 in *bozi* 脖子 = neck
Ximen Qing touched Jinlian's **neck**,

31) 連忙的拿把總去摸唖唖 ◆ Squadron Leader
lianmang de na bazong qu mo zaza
bazong = Squadron Leader; *bazong* puns with *bazhang* 巴掌 = hands; *zaza* 唖唖 = female breasts

and quickly fingered her breasts with his hands.

32) 隔著司庫就摸一下 ◆ Storekeeper
gezhu siku jiu mo yixia
siku = Storekeeper; the syllable *ku* puns with *ku* 褲 = trousers
He felt her body all over, only covered by her trousers.

33) 金蓮說**阿拉**你別鬧**克伊夫**快幹罷 ◆ **Arrow**
Jinlian shuo **ara** *ni bie nao* **keifu** *kuai gan ba*
keifu = **arrow** (?); **ara** = *aiyo* 哎喲 = Oh, dear! The pun on **keifu** is unclear.
Jinlian said: 'Oh, dear! Don't waste time! Let's get going!'

34) 回手解開紅黃帶 ◆ Red or Yellow Belt
hui shou jiekai honghuang dai
honghuang dai = Carrying the Red or Yellow Belt of the Imperial Clan; the pun is on *dai* 帶 = belt
He withdrew his hands and loosened her belt.

35) 就往那邊駕司里爬 ◆ Minister of Arms
jiu wang nabian jiasi li pa
jiasi = Minister of Arms; punning with *jiazi* 架子 = bedstead
Then he climbed onto the bedstead,

36) 又脫下柘榴紅的**額折庫** ◆ **Secretary**
you tuoxia shiliu hong de **ejeku**

THE GAME OF OFFICIAL ADVANCEMENT, *SHENGGUAN TU*

ejeku = Secretary; punning with *ku* 褲 = trousers
and took off her trousers as red as pomegranate.

37) 他身上連知縣全無把人愛殺 ◆ District Magistrate
ta shenshang lian zhixian quan wu ba ren aisha
zhixian = District Magistrate; punning with *zhi xian* 只線 = a single thread
She had not a single thread on, and he was getting mad with lust.

38) 喀吧播的毛那們扎蘭呢達 ◆ **Leader of a Banner-Troupe**
kabadang de mao namen **jalan-i da**
jalan-i da = Leader of a Banner-Troupe; the first syllable puns with *zha* 扎 = to
rip open; *kabadang* 喀吧播 = Beijing dialect: the opening between the thighs
The fine hair between her thighs were suddenly visible,

39) 仰把插像布庫吃了個多活洛 ◆ Storekeeper of Fabrics
yang ba cha xiang buku chi liao ge doholo(mbi)
buku = Storekeeper of Fabrics; doholo(mbi) = wrestle
facing upwards, she looked ready to wrestle.

40) 漏出了小肚子低下的喀達拉巴 ◆ **Bailiff**
louchu liao xiao duzi dixia de kadalaba
kadalaba = kadalambi = Bailiff; the word puns with gadarambi = to get stiff
Under his belly something was getting stiff.

41) 毛烘烘四面都是藍翎長 ◆ Official of the Sixth Rank
mao honghong simian dou shi lanling chang
lanling = Official of the Sixth Rank (carrying a featherhat with blue feathers);
lan ling = blue feathers
His pubic hair was growing profusely all over like blue feathers.

42) 當中間你睄罷好像那八旗合操的仰山窪 ◆ Eight Banners
dang zhongjian ni shao ba haoxiang na baqi hecao de Yangshan wa
baqi = Eight Banners of the Manchu Bannermen troops; there is no pun, just
a metaphor
Look at it! It is like the Eight Banners drilling on the slopes of Yangshan!

43) 東西別名叫花戶 ◆ A Registered Family
dongxi bie ming jiao huahu

305

huahu perhaps same as *huji* 戶籍 = A Registered Family; punning with *huahu* = 'flower door' = vagina

Her parts are called by another name, the 'flower door',

44) 好像胡子嘴可無有四街 ◆ The Four Departments
haoxiang huzi zui ke wu you siya
siya = *si yamen* = Four Departments of the imperial government; the syllable *ya* puns with *ya* = tooth

it looks like a mouth with beard, but no teeth.

45) 官人連忙翻譯舉 ◆ Candidate of Translation
guanren lianmang fanyi ju
fanyi ju = *fanyi juren* = Candidate of Translation; the pun is on the syllable *fan* 翻 = turn over

The gentleman jumped over in a hurry,

46) 像過馬的一般往上爬 ◆ Horse
xiang guo ma de yiban wang shang pa
ma = horse; only the word *ma* = horse seems to serve as 'official title' here.

he climbed upon her like mounting a horse,

47) 把淫婦兩條腿那們一分洿撥什户 ◆ **Lieutenant of the mounted forces**
ba yinfu liang tiao tui namen **funde bosoko**
funde bosoko = **Lieutenant of the Mounted Forces**; the pun is on **fun** = *fen* = separate

and **separated** the thighs of the wanton woman.

48) 西門慶把挺硬的遊擊往裏插 ◆ Brigadier
Ximen Qing ba tingying de youji wang li cha
Youji = Brigadier; the syllable *ji* puns with *ji* 雞 = male member
Ximen Qing inserted his hardened male member into her innermost.

49) 金蓮害怕伸守備 ◆ Deputy Brigadier
Jinlian haipa shen shoubei
shoubei = Deputy Brigadier; the syllable *shou* puns with *shou* 手 = hand
Jinlian became so afraid that she stretched out her hands in defence.

50) 荒忙托主了夸蘭達 ◆ **Storekeeper**

THE GAME OF OFFICIAL ADVANCEMENT, *SHENGGUAN TU*

Huangmang tuozhu liao **kowaran-i da**
kowaran-i = Storekeeper; the pun is on the syllable *kua* 跨 = hip reminding of **kowa**

But then in haste she supported him with her **hips**.

51) 説你摺烏搶雄壯我耽不住 ♦ Gun
Shuo ni zhe wuqiang xiongzhuang wo danbuzhu
wuqiang = gun, weapon
She said: 'Your unfolded weapon is so strong that I can hardly take it.'

52) 西門慶說你把陰門柏唐阿 ♦ **Employé**
Ximen Qing shuo ni ba yinmen **baitangga**
baitangga = Employé; the first syllable puns with *bai* 掰 = open, divide with the fingers.
Ximen Qing said: 'Please, **open** your female door **with your fingers**.'

53) 手頭兒招呼著内廷館 ♦ Official of the Imperial Court
shou tou'er zhaohu zhe neiting guan
neiting guan = Official of the Imperial Court; the syllable *ting* punning with *ting* 挺 = stiff, erect
With his hands, he wielded his stiff member,

54) 慞兒上的海巡亂串達 ♦ Leader of the Coast Defence
Huang'er shang de haixun luan chuanda
haixun = Leader of the Coast Defence; punning on the syllable *xun* = inspect, visit
and excited, he was wildly thrusting himself into rounds of inspection.

55) 金蓮說你比射撥遂艾罕的還不准 ♦ **Target for Gunnery Training**
Jinlian shuo ni bi she **bosoi aigan** *de hai bu zhun*
bosoi aigan = Target for Gunnery Training
Jinlian said: 'You are far off the mark! Much more than when shooting at a **target!**

56) 你底下沖著中書加勁呀 ♦ Palace Secretary
ni dixia zhong zhe zhongshu jiajing ya
zhongshu = Palace Secretary; punning with *zhongshu* 中樞 = the middle point
You must be more energetic when you enter me down there right in the middle!

307

57) 你睄睄傳官急的青筋叠暴 ♦ Officer in Charge of Communication

Ni qiaoqiao chuanguan ji de qingjin die bao

chuanguan = Officer in Charge of Communication; punning with *ganguan* 感官 = sense organ?

Look! How the blue veins of your organ stand out!'

58) 低下跑暈了兩個嘎來達 ♦ **Commander of the Wing of a Banner Company**

dixia pao yun liao liangge gala-i da

gala-i da = **Commander of the Wing of a Banner Company**; the word is used as a metaphor for the testicles

Below his two '**commanders of the wing**' were jumping wildly.

59) 西門慶說雀兒上有榜眼 ♦ Secondary on the List of Candidates

Ximen Qing shuo qiao'er shang you bangyan

bangyan = Secondary on the List of Candidates; punning with *yan* = eye; *qiao'er* = sparrow, nickname for a boy's penis

Ximen Qing said: 'My 'sparrow' has only one eye,

60) 睄著倒像個頭等瞎 ♦ **Imperial Guard of the First Class**

qiaozhe dao xiang ge toudeng hiya

hiya = **Imperial Guard of the First Class**; hiya puns with *xia* 瞎 = blind

but is able to look and poke about like a blind.'

61) 金蓮說少不得我當喀達拉密 ♦ **Administrator**

Jinlian shuo shaobude wo dang kadalambi

kadalambi = administrate, lead;

Jinlian said: 'I have to lead him.'

62) 西門慶說得了莫几格就進了瞎衣巴 ♦ **Messenger**

Ximen Qing shuoliao mejige jiu jinliao hiya-i ba

mejige = **Messenger**; punning with *maichi* 麥齒 = labia minora; hiya-i ba = drill ground

Ximen Qing said: 'As soon as I feel your labia, I am right at the **drill ground!**'

63) 兩個卵子像柏拉拿門的一般樣 ♦ **Guard Soldier**

liangge luanzi xiang bayara na men de yiban yang

bayara = **Guard Soldier**; *luanzi* = twin, testicle

His twin balls looked like two **guard soldiers** standing at the gate.

THE GAME OF OFFICIAL ADVANCEMENT, *SHENGGUAN TU*

64) 几老八出來進去他得了**專呢達** ◆ **Lieutenant of the Imperial Guard**
jilaoba chulai jinqu ta deliao **juwan-i da**
jilaoba = jiba 雞巴 = penis; **juwan-i da = Lieutenant of the Imperial Guard**;
only the syllable **-i** in **juwan-i da** functions as a pun with the syllable *yi* = 意 in
deyi 得意 = obtain satisfaction

His cock went in and out, and he was obtaining great satisfaction.

65) 金蓮說我是捐納**監**生假金頂兒 ◆ A Fourth Grade Student
Jinlian shuo wo shi juanna jiansheng jia jinding
jiansheng = fourth grade student with a false golden knob; the expression is
used as a metaphor

Jinlian said: 'I am only a purchased fourth grade student with a false golden
knob.

66) 八子里比秀才還酸你慢著罷 ◆ Candidate of the Imperial Examinations
bazi li bi xiucai hai suan ni manzhe ba
bazi = imperial concubine; punning with *bazi* 把子 = female organ, cunt;
xiucai = Candidate of the Imperial Examinations

My cunt feels sorer than a candidate of the imperial examinations! Please, slow
down a bit!'

67) 官人得意他**哈撒**的更**托錦** ◆ **Official of the Fifth Rank**
guanren deyi ta hasa *de geng* tojin
hasa = fast; tojin = peacock, symbol of an Official of the Fifth Rank; the
syllable *jin* is punning with *jin* 緊 = excited

The gentleman, satisfying his desire, moved faster and was even more excited,

68) 把京奇呢章京出了一大窪 ◆ **Officer of Banner Troops**
ba jingkini janggin *chuliao yi da wa*
janggin = Officer of Banner Troops; gin 京, in Chinese *jing*, puns with *jing*
精 = sperm

and he ejaculated a big puddle of sperm.

69) 歇息了一會纔拔貢 ◆ Selection of Candidates
xiexi liao yihui cai bagong
bagong = Selection of Candidates; only the syllable *ba* 拔 = to draw out is relevant

After a short rest, he drew it out.

309

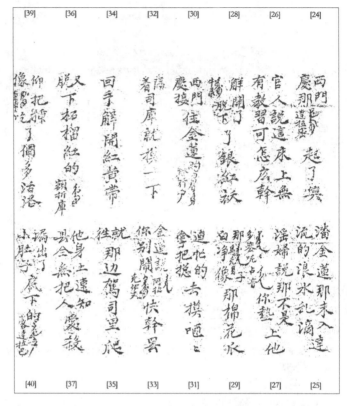

Figure 18.1 Manuscript No. 2, double page showing verses 24–40 of the *Shengguan tu*

70) 好像回了圍的喀蘭幾達更覺乏 ◆ **Brigade of Tigerhunters**
Haoxiang hui liao wei de **karan gida** *geng jue fa*
karan gida = **Brigade of Tigerhunters**; 'tigerhunter' = elite hunter of the imperial hunts
He felt more exhausted than a '**tigerhunter**' returning from the hunt.

71) 金蓮說這箄帖式可怎麼好 ◆ **Clerk**
Jinlian shuo zhe **bithesi** *ke zenme hao*
bithesi = **Clerk**; the syllable *shi* 式 in **bithesi** is punning with *shi* 淫 = fluid, stain
Jinlian said: 'How do we get rid of the **stains**?'

72) 門慶說你不必著急拿出敖尒布搭 ◆ **Hunter's Jacket**
Men Qing shuo ni bu bi zhaoji nachu **olbu** *cha*

THE GAME OF OFFICIAL ADVANCEMENT, *SHENGGUAN TU*

olbu = Hunter's Jacket; the syllable *bu* 布 = cloth is relevant for the wordplay
Ximen Qing said: 'You need not worry! Just take a cloth and wipe it up!'

完
wan
The End

Note on Contributors

Martin Gimm, Professor Emeritus, Department of East Asian Studies, University of Cologne, Germany

Vibeke Børdahl, Ph.D., Dr. Phil. of Sinology, Senior Researcher, Nordic Institute of Asian Studies, University of Copenhagen, Denmark

CHAPTER 19

A Wild Horse in the History of Chinese Literature

The Value and Influence of *Jing Ping Mei*

LIU ZHEN

Translated by Hu Yaowen and Vibeke Børdahl

Shijing 詩經 (The Odes), *Chu Ci* 楚辭 (The Songs of Chu), *Han Fu* 漢賦 (The Rhyme-Prose of the Han dynasty), *Liuchao pianwen* 六朝駢文 (The Parallel Prose of the Six dynasties), *Tang shi* 唐詩 (The Poetry of the Tang dynasty), *Song Ci* 宋詞 (The Song-lyrics of the Song dynasty), *Yuan Qu* 元曲 (Yuan Drama) – these genres are all 'representative of the literature of a certain dynastic era and unequalled by later generations'.[1] As a summary and generalization we may say that every period is represented by a certain genre. In every period representative works and authors come to the fore and contribute to the literary blossoming of the epoch. Literary development follows the rule of gradual growth – from small beginnings to larger forms, from a lower level to a higher level, and from simple to complex. During the Ming and Qing dynasties, vernacular fiction and drama blossomed and thrived. The novels *San guo yanyi* 三國演義 (Romance of the Three Kingdoms), *Shuihu zhuan* 水滸傳 (Water Margin), *Xiyou ji* 西遊記 (Journey to the West), *Rulin waishi* 儒林外史 (The Scholars) and *Honglou meng* 紅樓夢 (A Dream of Red Mansions) – one after another saw the day of light, and thus the novel reached a sublime level during this period.

It was also during this time that *Jin Ping Mei* came galloping like a wild horse, making turmoil in late imperial China. The work was received with a mixture of love and hate, and the critics did not know what course to take. It was condemned both in speech and writing, but after the initial criticism, its

---

1   Wang Guowei 2007, 1.

Editors' note: We gratefully acknowledge the assistance of David Rolston in revising the pre-final version of this chapter.

literary worth and its value for the Chinese vernacular fiction were gradually recognized and accepted. And thus, the early unanimous moralistic criticism of the novel's lechery began to swerve towards its literary creativeness.

In *Jin Ping Mei cihua xu* 金瓶梅詞話序 (Preface to *Jin Ping Mei cihua*), Xinxin zi 欣欣子 (The Master of delight) writes that in this work the author 'has focused his attention on the manners of the age'.[2] In a second preface *Jin Ping Mei xu* 金瓶梅序 (Preface to *Jin Ping Mei*), Dongwu Nongzhu ke 東吳弄珠客 (The Pearl-juggler of Eastern Wu) declares that '*Jin Ping Mei* is an obscene work'.[3] Different readers had different opinions. Some people 'felt a strong compassion' for the characters, others 'felt a strong aversion', some 'felt a great happiness', while others 'wanted to follow suit'.[4] *Jin Ping Mei* (JPM) was, from the beginning, not readily accessible. Xie Zhaozhe (1564–1624) wrote: 'Since there were no printed versions, and the work circulated only in manuscript, copies differed, and parts got lost.'[5]

With the beginning of the modern period, opinions about JPM were still divided and the debate was furious. Gradually, as the times and society progressed, scholarly circles began to go beyond morality and ethics and to focus more on the literary merits of the work and its historical significance. Hu Shi 胡適 (1891–1962) remarked that JPM 'from a literary viewpoint was absolutely devoid of value. Why? Aesthetics is one of the key factors of literature. Let me ask you, gentlemen, when you read *Jin Ping Mei*, are you able to find any aesthetic value in it?'[6] Chen Duxiu 陳獨秀 (1879–1942) replied:

'You and Mr. Xuantong 玄同 both praise *Shuihu zhuan* and *Honglou meng* as the best novels we have ever had. So why is it that none of them can compete with *Jin Ping Mei*? Because this book describes the old society just like the depictions of evil creatures on the bronze tripods of the sage emperor Yu, no detail is left out. *Honglou meng* was born from *Jin Ping Mei*, but as for clear, forceful and natural language, it cannot compete with it. Should we discard it just because it depicts illicit behavior? Can *Shuihu zhuan* and *Honglou meng* be exempted from such criticism?'

---

2   Huang Lin 黄霖: *Jin Ping Mei ziliao huibian* 金瓶梅资料汇编 (Collected Material on the *Jin Ping Mei*), Beijing: Zhonghua shuju, 1987, 1; henceforward, JPMZLHB. English translation quoted from Roy 1993, 3.

3   JPMZLHB, 2. English translation quoted from Roy 1993, 6.

4   Dongwu Nongzhu ke, *Jin Ping Mei xu*, JPMZLHB, 2–3.

5   Xie Zhaozhe 谢肇淛, *Jin Ping Mei ba* 金瓶梅跋 (Postscript to *Jin Ping Mei*), JPMZLHB, 4.

6   Hu Shi 'Reply to Qian Xuantong' ('Da Qian Xuantong shu' 答錢玄同書), in Hu Shi 1993, 253.

A WILD HORSE IN THE HISTORY OF CHINESE LITERATURE

In Chen's view, 'even the famous Chinese drama *Xixiang ji* 西廂記 (The Story of the West Wing) and *Mudanting* 牡丹亭 (The Peony Pavilion) are also not suitable books for young people, and this is one of the shortcomings of our literature.'[7] Qian Xuantong 錢玄同 (1887–1939) held the opinion that 'if we free ourselves of moralistic bias and only consider literary value, then *Jin Ping Mei* must be counted among the very best'.[8] He placed JPM at the same level as *Honglou meng, Shuihu zhuan, Rulin waishi, Xiyou ji* and the modern works of Li Boyuan 李伯元 (1867–1906) and Wu Jianren 吳趼人 (1866–1910): 'All of these are novels of great value in Chinese literature.'[9] Lu Xun 魯迅 (1881–1936) in his *Zhongguo xiaoshuo shi lue* 中國小說史略 (Brief History of Chinese Fiction), wrote that when the novels about gods and devils flourished, the novels of manners, describing human affairs, also appeared: 'Among all the novels of manners, *Jin Ping Mei* is the most famous.' This was the outcome of literary evolution and the revolution of literature. In the contemporary period, there have been both ups and downs in our research on literary history. However, both in *Zhonghua wenxue tongshi* 中華文學通史 (Comprehensive History of Chinese Literature, ten volumes) edited by the Institute of Literature and Institute of Ethnic Literature of CASS (Chinese Academy of Social Sciences) (1997), and in the *Zhongguo wenxue shi* 中國文學史 (History of Chinese Literature, three volumes) by Zhang Peiheng 章培恒 and Luo Yuming 駱玉明 (1996), JPM's important place in Chinese literature was confirmed.

The reason why I call JPM 'a wild horse' is because it came like a bolting horse running wild over 10,000 miles, shaking off and trampling the morals and principles that people had stuck to scrupulously for ages. Frankly and without shame, the work displays the secrets of human nature and a life of sensual delight and disreputable acts. Together with the other three novels, *Sanguo yanyi, Shuihu zhuan*, and *Xiyou ji*, JPM was ranked as the '*Si da qi shu* 四大奇书 (Four Extraordinary Books)' of the Ming Dynasty, and '*Jin Ping Mei* is the most extraordinary among them'.[10] Because of this 'extraordinary' quality, JPM was able to keep its position in the history of Chinese literature, but this was also the reason why the work was called an 'obscene book' and a 'lecherous book'.

---

7   Chen Duxiu, 'Reply to Hu Shi', JPMZLHB, 342.

8   Qian Xuantong, 'Reply to Hu Shi', JPMZLHB, 346.

9   Qian Xuantong, 'Reply to Chen Duxiu', JPMZLHB, 343.

10 Preface to the Manchu translation of *Jin Ping Mei*, JPMZLHB, 5. On this translation and its preface, see Chapter 20 below.

LIU ZHEN

The Ideas of *Jin Ping Mei* in a Turbulent Age

The plot of JPM is developed from the story in *Shuihu zhuan* of Wu Song 武松 killing his sister-in-law. The novel stands as a breakthrough since it is neither historical fiction nor fiction about gods and devils. Taking as point of departure the apothecary Ximen Qing 西門慶, a descendent from an impoverished landlord family in Qinghe District, the novel displays a family history of sin and evil. Within the family, the relationships and lives of Ximen Qing and his wives and other women such as Pan Jinlian 潘金蓮, Li Ping'er 李瓶兒, Wu Yueniang 吳月娘 and Pang Chunmei 龐春梅 are in focus; outside the family there are types such as local officials, monks and Daoists, prostitutes and actors, of every possible variety. Together they constitute a full and complete picture of society.

Prior to JPM, the content of Chinese fiction mainly focused on historical or mythical legends. Some short stories were about love between men and women, but JPM displayed a canvas of family life and human relations of the mundane world. The work not only described in detail and with frankness sexual behaviours, but it also treated relationships that were contrary to moral ethics and described both in minute detail. This is something that was hardly obtained in any literary work before it, and this is also one of the reasons why it was called 'extraordinary'. In the Preface to the before mentioned manuscript of the Manchu translation of JPM (1708) it is stated that in JPM:

> '... the rotten habits are compiled to serve as a warning for 10,000 generations. Everything is described in full detail, from the daily life of ordinary couples, monks and nuns, doctors and witches, fortunetellers and musicians, sing-song girls and jugglers, as well as all kinds of merchandise and delicacies, articles of daily use, bantering and ridicule; even the smallest details from the remotest places are not left out. The reader feels as if the whole world is clearly displayed in front of his own eyes.'[11]

The novel describes in a completely naturalistic way topics that were absolutely taboo in traditional culture – the most secret sexual lovemaking, violating usual ethical norms – revealing the details without restraint. Moreover, the description is characterized by a kind of appreciation and enjoyment. Such passages are not just few and scattered; they are the general motif and form the structural framework of the entire novel. Certainly, this work struck like a bolt from the blue and shattered traditional views on Confucian morality, revealing the sordid side of human nature.

---

11 Preface to the Manchu Script of *Jin Ping Mei*, JPMZLHB, 6.

The appearance of JPM did not, however, result from a stroke of paranoia on the part of the author Lanling Xiaoxiao Sheng 蘭陵笑笑生. The reasons why this work could see the light of day are to be found in contemporary society, namely the commercial and cultural development in Chinese urban areas of the 16th century.

Who Lanling Xiaoxiao Sheng actually was remains very difficult to find out. Academic opinions vary and there is no consensus as yet. Wang Shizhen 王世貞, Li Yu 李漁, Lu Nan 盧楠, Xue Yingqi 薛應旗, Li Zhi 李贄, Xu Wei 徐渭, Li Kaixian 李開先, Feng Weimin 馮惟敏 and Shen Defu 沈德符 have all been proposed as the author.[12] Regarding the time when it was written, some scholars favour the period of the Jiajing reign (1522–1567), some that of the Wanli reign (1573–1620); most scholars tend to favour the latter period.[13]

In the Song and Yuan dynasties, Neo-Confucian ideas developed into a new idealism, and after getting approval from the central powers, this idealism became more secularized and closer to daily life, as expressed by Zhu Xi 朱熹 (1130–1200):

'Sticking to the etiquette of sprinkling and sweeping the courtyard, entertaining guests properly and understanding the rules of advance and retreat, following the rule to love and respect one's relatives, masters, and friends, this is the foundation of self-cultivation, of organizing the family, of governing the country, and of keeping the world at peace.'[14]

These principles were even more striking for ordinary people and their behaviour in daily life. 'Preserving heavenly principles' (*cun tianli* 存天理) was thought to be a superior pursuit to self-centered desire (*renyu* 人欲), which was rejected as lowly physiological cravings. During the Jiajing reign, the philosophical school of Wang Yangming 王陽明 (1472–1529), called the Wang School (*Wangxue* 王學), which had been considered unorthodox, gained more influence (see Chapter 8 in this book). As a result of urban and commercial development, enormous ideological and social changes took place. 'During the Jiajing reign, with less moral restraint and state control, civil activities were given more space, urban lifestyle tended to be more diverse, the shackles of moral uniformity became less heavy, and the control of the authorities was more relaxed.'[15] The newly acquired wealth of merchants and landlords had

---

12 *Editor's note:* Famous personalities from the 16th and 17th century.

13 Zhonghua wenxue tongshi, volume 3, Beijing: Huayi chubanshe,1997, 620–62.; Zhongguo wenxue shi (Second Part) Shanghai: Fudan Press,1996, 311.

14 *Zhu Wen Gong wenji* 朱文公文集, *juan* 67, '*Ti xiaoxue* 題小学', p. 21–A.

15 Ge Zhaoguang 2001, 300.

changed their experience and aesthetic standards, and the School of Wang Yangming had led to even more ideological freedom. This was a period when people were fighting to free themselves of traditional shackles and, trying to win ideological freedom, a period of dramatic social change during which people pursued more liberty and personal indulgence. Wang Yangming pointed out that 'there are no principles outside the mind, there are no affairs outside the mind' (心外无理，心外无事), 'the form of the mind is its true nature, and its nature is the same as its principle. How can there exist any nature apart from the mind? How can there be any mind separate from the principles?' (心之体，性也，性即理也，天下宁有心外之性？宁有性外之理乎？宁有理外之心乎？)[16] He emphasized the unity of the earthly and the transcendental mind. Speaking objectively, this might lead to abandonment (of self-control) and a collapse of faith in reason. The theories of his followers in the *Taizhou Xuepai* 泰州學派 (School of Taizhou) went even further:

> 'Their purpose was to attack and destroy all the historical traditions of veneration and social status. They mixed up the laity and the sages, secular life and the ideal realm, normal earthly desire and the sublime understanding of congenial spirits. They permitted the standards of daily life and normal earthly desire, conflating the natural attitude of the soul with the sublime attitude of the ideal, and considering the laity as sages. Thus, they wanted to affirm the worth of life and the meaning of life.'[17]

Their bold idealism and radical naturalism exercised an enormous influence on the social atmosphere and the philosophical trends of the late Ming dynasty: 'Lots of scholars, including open-minded and courageous younger scholars, followed them with admiration and enthusiasm.'[18] In *A Brief History of Chinese Fiction*, Lu Xun wrote that later readers gave JPM a bad name, condemning it as pornography, but as he said: 'Actually, at that time, such descriptions were the fashion.'[19]

---

16 *Shu zhu Yang juan* 书诸阳卷, *Wang Wencheng gong quanshu* 王文成公全書 (Collections of Wang Yangming) Vol. 8, 12A.

17 Ge Zhaoguang 2001, 317.

18 Shen Zan 沈瓚, *Jin shi cong can* 近事丛残, quoted in *Li Zhi yanjiu cankao ziliao* 李贽研究参考资料 (Research Materials on Li Zhi), ed. by Xiamen University Department of History, volume 1, Fuzhou: Fujian renmin chubanshe,1975, 74.

19 Lu Hsun 1964, 238.

The Value of *Jin Ping Mei* and Its Influence on Chinese Literature

JPM has had an important influence on the history of Chinese literature, particularly on the development of fiction. First and foremost, this work opened the way for realistic depiction in Chinese novels of real life. The Chinese fiction tradition can be traced back to the 'tales of the miraculous' (*zhiguai xiaoshuo* 志怪小說) during the Wei, Jin, and Southern and Northern Dynasties. However, in traditional fiction, it was mainly historical or legendary heroes, emperors, nobles, scholars, beautiful ladies, or unrealistic ghosts and demons that were described. In JPM these old conventions changed overnight, and the focus turned towards real life. It described every trade and profession of townspeople; their daily occupations, their eating and drinking habits, their clothes and accessories, and the ways in which their lives unfolded in a hundred ways.

Centering on Ximen Qing and his family with their connections to other family members as well as their social circles, a grand canvas was unfolded presenting a fresh, lively, variegated, truthful, and realistic picture of contemporary society. No other work of fiction had so far ever been able to attain this profound realistic power, neither in breadth nor in depth. This was also a result of rapid urban development, the liberation of ideas and a new freedom arising during this turbulent age. The former oppression of peoples' minds and hopes was lessened, and they were able to indulge in sensual passion without scruples, and their most secret desires were no longer hidden.

The description of love and sex is an important part of the work. Passages on this topic are both frequent and detailed, constituting the most despised and controversial part, while attaining a kind of extreme naturalism. Describing love and sensual enjoyment is an everlasting theme of literature around the world, and literary beauty belongs here. In China this tradition dates back to the *Shijing*, as recorded in the airs of the states of Zheng 鄭 and Wei 衛. In later periods, works with such languorous tones were never lacking; there were even depictions of sexual scenes in certain classical works. However, due to the development of society and people's striving for good morals, descriptions of lust and sex were gradually suppressed and gave way to a veiled and bashful treatment in literature. Only the feelings and thoughts could be described. This was true especially after the Song dynasty, when Neo-Confucianism rose to its zenith and theories of desire were rationalized to the point of 'eliminating human desire' (*mie renyu* 滅人欲). JPM stands as a striking breakthrough, providing a structured and systematic exposition of love and lust that was truly astonishing. In the prefaces to JPM, Xinxin zi defended it as 'illuminating the cardinal human relationships, discouraging sexual promiscuity, distinguishing between the pure and the impure, edifying both the good and the un-good, and expounding the secrets of flourishing and decay, failure and success, through the inexorable working of karmic cause and effect, in such a way that they lie utterly revealed before the reader's eyes'[20] and Dongwu Nongzhu ke suggested that the author's 'intentions are admonitory rather than hortatory'.[21] While it is hard to deny a 'warning to the world' behind the sexual descriptions, the fact that the author lacked a critical attitude toward those descriptions is as clear as can be. Nevertheless, the content of its thought and the topics of its descriptions makes the JPM merit the title given it by Xu Shuofang 徐朔方 (1923–2007) as 'the first and foremost among the erotic novels'.[22]

In JPM people from diverse trades and backgrounds are profoundly brought to life so that their human nature and spirit is unmasked. This is probably what Yuan Zhongdao 袁中道 (1570–1624) had in mind when he wrote:

> 'Once, in the capital, a prefectural military official, whose family name was Ximen, employed an old scholar from Shaoxing. In his idle hours, the elderly scholar recorded the unseemly affairs taking place in his master's family. In these notes, he modelled Ximen Qing and his concubines on what he saw in the character gallery of his master's house'.[23]

From this we can imagine the author's great efforts to observe the daily life and capture the features of every person, so that no matter what status or role a character has, no matter whether he or she is described in a few strokes or in detail, they all come out in vivid individuality; indeed, they come alive in just a few words. The former two-dimensional, flat characters of fiction are changed into individual, multi-dimensional, complicated and vivid persons. In general, there are no uniformly positive characters. According to Xie Tao 解弢 in *Xiaoshuo hua* 小說話 (On fiction)(1919):

> 'There are no positive characters in *Jin Ping Mei* and not in *Honglou meng* either; those who come close to this are You Erjie 尤二姐 and Li Ping'er 李瓶儿, who resemble each other in that respect.'[24]

---

20 Lanling Xiaoxiao Sheng, *Jin Ping Mei Cihua*, 1992, 1. *Editor's note:* The translation is from Roy 1993, 3.

21 Lanling Xiaoxiao Sheng, *Jin Ping Mei Cihua*,1992, 4. *Editor's note:* The translation is from Roy 1993, 6.

22 Xu Shuofang 徐朔方, *Huijiao huiping Jin Ping Mei xu* 会校会评金瓶梅序 (Collection of Commentaries to the Prologues of *Jin Ping Mei*), Hong Kong: Tiandi tushu gongsi,1998,1.

23 JPMZLHB, 229.

24 JPMZLHB, 352.

A WILD HORSE IN THE HISTORY OF CHINESE LITERATURE

Under the tidal wave of intellectual liberation during the last period of the Ming dynasty, the author of the novel was able to free himself from the shackles of traditional thought and morality, starting from real life in his depiction of the characters. Life itself was his source and model which he used to sculpt the realistic, vivid, richly-facetted characters, so lively that they seem on the point of materializing in front of the reader – and few of them could claim to be 'positive characters'. They are not types or flat characters, but persons with a strong flavour of reality. This exerted an important influence on later novels of manners.

If we look at the structure of the novel, JPM was innovative in changing the previous linear development of the plot. Centering on Ximen Qing and his manifold activities and moving from his family out into society in all directions, a vast web of combinations was created linking the characters with nodes connecting plot chains and social situations. Creating this kind of structure and description implies certain difficulties: How to depict the characters as individual personalities when they belong to a host of people with similar status, sex and social position? How to unfold the plot, sometimes aptly condensing, sometimes elaborating the details, at times concentrating on minor episodes without becoming too wordy, accomplishing the creation of the narrative discourse, logical tiers, the changing of time and space, and shifting between strong and weak strokes of the brush? All this shows the author's deep life experience and his great narrative ability. This is surely what Xinxin zi had in mind when he wrote:

> 'The strands of the plot are as intricately articulated as the conduits of the circulatory system and are like myriad skeins of silk that flutter in the wind without ever becoming entangled'.[25]

Let us take the relationship between Pan Jinlian and Chen Jingji 陳經濟 as an example. Chen is the second most important man to Pan except for Ximen Qing. This extra storyline starts with Chen Jingji's first appearance in the novel, where there are already hints implying the complicated and chaotic constellations between the family members, foreshadowing the later decay and collapse of the family that Ximen Qing will not live to see. Observing the structure and style, we notice how 'the complete picture is not revealed at first sight' and 'feelings are not brought out at once', but the development and changing of the relationships between the characters are keeping step with the progress of the entire narrative. The dynamics between Pan and Chen follows the shift in family circumstances. The attitude of the characters to each other and to their

---

25 Lanling Xiaoxiao Sheng, *Jin Ping Mei cihua*, 1992, 1. *Editor's note*: Translation from Roy 1993, 3.

surroundings constitute the dynamics of their fate. At the same time, the cases of Chunmei 春梅 and Qiuju 秋菊 are naturally and artfully interlocked in the process. Thus, the author's elevated artistic skills are obvious, and this is an important reason for the success of this novel in applying the style of realism.

The reason why the characters of JPM give you the feeling that if you 'called out to them they would answer' is also aided by the author's strength when it comes to mastering language. Xinxin zi's evaluation was: 'One finds sentences of such amazing novelty that they will attract readers of the most varied tastes'.[26] Chen Duxiu was of the opinion that '*Honglou meng* was born from *Jin Ping Mei*, but as for clear, forceful and natural language, it cannot compete with it.' The language of the novel abounds with vernacular and colloquial expressions from the daily life in the cities. The language of people's conversations is particularly lively, as though it had been overheard there and then. Furthermore, the author uses a wealth of proverbs and sayings, including *xiehouyu* 歇後語.[27] The language matches the status, character and thinking of each character, and provides a vivid picture of urban life.

The attractive force of the realism of JPM also lies in meticulous descriptions and documentary records of the social manners and customs of the time, written as if by a historian. The author's penetrating insight into life and his gift of expression are highly convincing. His realistic depictions are not restricted to the different characters and events, but are also manifested in the descriptions of rituals, customs, festivals, banquets, weddings, funerals, marriages, sales, plays, amusements, and artifacts, which would have been difficult to achieve without personal experience. From a purely literary point of view, Chen Duxiu once remarked that 'such detailed description of food, clothing, and luxury is rather boring'.[28] However, as a realistic description, this work, just like the painted scroll of *Qing Ming Shang He Tu* 清明上河圖 (Spring Festival Along the River), must be considered the most 'authentic documentary record' of contemporary social customs. Such a depiction and such a record are, indeed, well worth historical research.

As the first groundbreaking novel in China, of encyclopedic dimensions, JPM has been greatly influential in Chinese literature. For long periods it has been proscribed because of its explicit love scenes and its violation of general morals. However, as a masterpiece of realism, its radiance could not be concealed in the long run, and it has exerted a deep and lasting influence on

---

26 *Editor's note:* The translation is based on Lévy 1985, Vol. 1, 3.

27 A kind if riddle in which the first part of a saying is given, and the hearer has to guess what was left out; the meaning of the riddle can also be dependent on a pun.

28 Chen Duxiu, ibid., JPMZLHB, 342.

A WILD HORSE IN THE HISTORY OF CHINESE LITERATURE

later Chinese literature. Of course, the most notable example is *Honglou meng*. This great work of realism was indeed created under the influence of JPM. Cai Yuanpei 蔡元培 (1868–1940) thought that with Meng Yulou 孟玉樓 the author hinted at the Ministry of Rites of the Ming dynasty and that this was also 'at the root of *Honglou meng*'.[29] Chen Duxiu declared, as we have seen, that '*Honglou meng* was born from *Jin Ping Mei*.' Xie Tao likewise declared that *Honglou meng* was taking after JPM in its depiction of the inconstancy of the world. The birth of *Honglou meng* was tightly connected to JPM, and thus Chinese fiction reached its zenith in our history of literature.

References

Ge Zhaoguang 葛兆光

2001. *Zhongguo sixiang shi* 中国思想史 (History of Chinese Philosophy), Vol. 2, Shanghai: Fudan Press.

Hu Shi

1993. 'Reply to Qian Xuantong', in: *Hu Shi xueshu wenji – Xin wenxue yundong* 胡适学术文集新文学运动 (Collected academic writings of Hu Shi – The New Literary Movement), Beijing: Zhonghua shuju.

Huang Lin 黄霖 ed.

1987. *Jin Ping Mei ziliao huibian* 金瓶梅资料汇编 (*Jin Ping Mei* Collections), Beijing: Zhonghua shuju. Shortened: JPMZLHB.

JPMZLHB, see Huang Lin.

Lanling Xiaoxiao Sheng

1992. *Jin Ping Mei Cihua*, Beijing: People Literature Press.

Lu Hsun

1964. *A Brief History of Chinese Fiction*, Yang Hsien-yi and Gladys Yang, translators, Beijing: Foreign Languages Press.

Shen Zan 沈瓉

1975. *Jin shi cong can* 近事丛残, quoted from *Li Zhi yanjiu cankao ziliao* 李贽研究参考资料 (Research Materials on Lizhi), ed. by Xiamen University Department of History, volume 1, Fuzhou: Fujian renmin chubanshe.

Wang Guowei 王國維

2007. *Song Yuan xiqu shi* 宋元戲曲史 (History of Song and Yuan Drama), Nanjing: Jiangsu wenyi chubanshe.

---

29 JPMZLHB, 341.

Xiaoxiao Sheng, and David Tod Roy

1993. *The plum in the golden vase: or, Chin P'ing Mei.* Princeton, New Jersey: Princeton University Press.

Xu Shuofang 徐朔方

1998. *Huijiao huiping Jin Ping Mei xu* 会校会评金瓶梅序 (Collection of Commentaries to the Prologues of *Jin Ping Mei*), Hong Kong: Tiandi tushu gongsi.

Note on Contributors

Liu Zhen 刘祯, Doctor of Literature, Research fellow, Curator of Mei Lanfang Memorial Museum under Ministry of Culture and Tourism, Beijing, China.

Hu Yaowen 胡耀文, Doctoral Candidate in comparative literature and cross-cultural studies at Beijing Foreign Studies University, China.

Vibeke Børdahl, Ph.D., Dr. Phil. of Sinology, Senior Researcher, Nordic Institute of Asian Studies, University of Copenhagen, Denmark.

CHAPTER 20

The Manchu Edition of 1708, *Gin ping mei bithe*

The Earliest Translation of the Novel *Jin Ping Mei*

MARTIN GIMM

Translated by Zhenzhen Lu

The Manchu version of the Chinese novel *Jin Ping Mei* 金瓶梅 (JPM) of 1708 is among the most sophisticated texts of Manchu literature.[1] Unlike the Mongols, the Manchus did not produce significant works of literature in their own language apart from those in genres of folk literature, which were passed down primarily through oral transmission. Yet in the course of their assiduous efforts to adapt to Chinese culture, the Manchus distinguished themselves as authors of literary works in the Chinese language. All these works emerged during the cultural heyday of the Qing dynasty in the 18th to early 19th centuries.

Within the diarchic structure of the Manchu ruling system, with its general bilingualism, translation played an extraordinarily important role in both the official and private realms. In this context, Manchu elites tried to develop their linguistic proficiency and prepare themselves for the Chinese educational system by diligently practising the translation of Chinese texts. They were aware that the Chinese traditional administrative and educational system had to be transformed into a bilingual one were they to rule the empire in the long run.

Of note is the special interest that grew at this time in the translation of Chinese entertainment literature – this came to be a popular private activity among educated Manchus, through which one endeavoured not only to improve one's linguistic proficiency but also one's knowledge of Chinese tradition. Although Manchu readers ostensibly tried to observe the proprieties, their marked preference for 'entertainment literature' at times gained the

---

1 In addition to this chapter, see Gimm 2005.

MARTIN GIMM

upper hand, so that – despite what appear to have been heavy losses – there are still some 77 Manchu translations of novels and short stories preserved in manuscript form, either in full or in fragments.[2]

The famous novel on the history of the Three Kingdoms, *Sanguo zhi yanyi* 三國志演義 (Romance of the Three Kingdoms), occupies a privileged position in this context. According to lore, it was especially favoured by the dynasty founders Nurhači/Nuerhazhi 奴爾哈赤 (1559–1626) and Hông Taiji/Huang Taiji 皇太極 (1592–1643).[3] Allegedly, the Manchu rulers believed that they could detect the military stratagems of the Chinese from this text and use it for their own purposes. The book was thus regarded as a historical source rather than as a work of entertainment literature.

A Novel of Manners and Erotic Literature

As a widely cherished work of erotic literature, the novel of manners *Jin Ping Mei* 金瓶梅 (hereafter: JPM) presents us with a different picture. Given its numerous sensual depictions, its fame could grow only in secret. Wilhelm Grube (1855–1908) passed on this saying in his history of Chinese literature: 'No one will admit owning it, but everyone has it; no one will confess to having read it, but everyone is acquainted with it.'[4] According to the findings of R. H. van Gulik, the novel, probably written at the end of the 16th century, came to be especially popular during the Kangxi period.[5]

Gin ping mei bithe

JPM acquired a special status in the period after 1700 with the appearance of the accomplished translation of the novel into Manchu. This was the only Chinese novel in Manchu translation to have appeared in print.

Title: *Gin ping mei bithe*

Imprint without title page (being a palace edition); preface dated Kangxi 47 (1708), the fourth month (June 18–July 17); Marginal title: *Gin ping mei bithe*; chapter and page numbering in Chinese; text in 100 *juan* (volumes);

---

2 Huang Runhua (1983) provides an overview; see also Gimm 1988. Approximately one tenth of the Chinese titles recorded in Sun Kaidi's well-known catalogue of this literature (Sun 1957 [1933]: n. p.) has been preserved in Manchu.

3 The Manchu version of the novel, *Ilan gurun-i bithe*, was published in three different editions.

4 Grube 1902: 430.

5 Van Gulik 1951: Vol. 1, 128; Gimm 2005: 62–63.

THE MANCHU EDITION OF 1708, *GIN PING MEI BITHE*

(depending on the binding) 4 or 6 *tao* (cases), 40, 43 or 80 volumes; format ca. 26 x 17 (printed area: 19.5 x 13.5) cm, 9 columns per page. Columns to be read from left to right. No woodblock illustrations.[6]

The special design of this Manchu edition featured a most unusual sight: the Chinese terms and phrases that have been rendered phonetically into Manchu in the main text – such as transcriptions of names of persons, places, titles, certain terms and idiomatic expressions – are inserted interlineally in Chinese.[7]

The relatively late and frequently reprinted edition of Zhang Zhupo 張竹坡 (i.e. Zhang Daoshen 張道深, 1670–1698), which had appeared in print only a decade earlier than the Manchu version, was used as the base text, with its preface and printing dated 1695 and the text in 100 *hui* with abridged verse sections.[8] The original text is slightly trimmed in many places in the translation, and the prefaces, commentary, and instructions to the reader that lie at the beginning of the Chinese edition have also been omitted. The publication of the Chinese edition of 1695 seems, however, to have provided the impetus for the preparation of the 1708 Manchu translation, as well as serving as the source text.

The Preface in Manchu

A peculiar feature of the Manchu edition is the preface preceding the novel proper, written by an anonymous author in his native language of Manchu, and dated to the fourth lunar month (June 18 to July 17) of the year 1708 (Kangxi 47).[9] The detailed circumstances of its origin are to date unknown.

In a rather unusual manner, the author of the preface postulates that the original Chinese text of the JPM was written by the retired eccentric Lu

---

6   For a reprint of the original text, reproduced on a reduced scale, see *Gin Ping Mei bithe* 1975, altogether 5804 pages in 10 volumes. See review in Walravens 1979.

7   For example, at the beginning of the text, the Manchu syllable *kim* is glossed with 琴, and the syllable *lioi* with 呂. The translation is somewhat uneven (from Chapter 95 onwards, there are sections printed graphically differently), so that at least two persons must have been involved in the preparation of the blocks.

8   Two facsimile reprints of the 1695 edition are available in the work *Jin Ping Mei* 1975, 8 vols.

9   *Gin Ping Mei bithe sioi*. See the provisional German translation by Hans Conon v. d. Gabelentz (1807–1874) (Gabelentz 2013). Since the 1980s, two modern Chinese translations of the preface have become widely known, namely (1) by Huang Runhua and Wang Xiaohong (1983: 2–4), and (2) Liu Housheng (1985: 356–357). These translations at times differ considerably from each other.

MARTIN GIMM

Nan 盧柟 (1507–1560)[10] in order to denounce the reprehensible deeds of the father-and-son pair, Yan Song 嚴嵩 (1480–1565) [11] and Yan Shifan 嚴世蕃 (1513–1565). [12] According to a passage in the preface, Lu Nan had composed JPM with the aim of criticizing the prodigal lives of his two contemporaries and to leave behind this picture of the times 'as an admonition for 10,000 generations'.[13] The anonymous author of the preface does not mention any source for his identification of the author of JPM, but qualifies his statement by adding: *inu waka be warkô* – 'whether this is true or not, I do not know'.

While the veracity of this attribution of the authorship of JPM cannot be ascertained, it is plausible that it was an attempt to justify the publication of the new translation of the novel with all its detailed scenes of illicit and immoral actions. Its elaborate accounts of mores and manners were to be interpreted as warnings in disguise, demonstrating the necessity of prohibitions (Manchu: *targacun*; Chinese: *jie* 戒; Sanskrit: śila) according to Buddhist teachings and admonishing readers with turns of events that inevitably lead to retribution. 'The hundred chapters [of JPM] come with a hundred cautionary lessons.' The protagonist Ximen Qing 西門慶, who dies miserably from illness at the age of 33 at the end of the story, was an instructive case.[14] It seems likely that the newly conceived preface was appended to the printed edition to formally make the case for its publication – presenting the work, according to this new analysis, as a work of admonition; for the laws of the time prohibited the dissemination of obscene texts in any form.

To date the author behind the preface is unknown.[15] The manner in which the preface is formulated seems to rule out the translator of the novel, pointing rather to the patron or initiator of the translation as its probable author. As noted in the preface: 'Since the cautionary intention [in JPM] is clear and evident, I arranged to have it translated (*ubaliyambubumbi*). I have perused it in my spare time and revised it.'[16]

10　Goodrich and Fang Chaoying 1976: 995–997; Lu Nan is known for his work *Miemeng ji* 蟻蠓集.

11　Goodrich and Fang Chaoying 1976: 1586–1591 etc.

12　Goodrich and Fang Chaoying 1976: 1586 etc.

13　Gimm 2005: 64, 37–38.

14　Manchu translation, *Gin ping mei bithe* 1975: Chapter 79, 42.

15　See also Gimm 2005: 64.

16　*gônin ilibuha targacun obuhangge. getuken iletu ofi. tuttu ubaliyambubufi. bi šolo de dasatame toktobuha.* – *ubaliyambumbi:* 'to translate'; causative: *ubaliyambubumbi* ('to have something translated'); Hauer 2007: 488.

THE MANCHU EDITION OF 1708, *GIN PING MEI BITHE*

Censorship

After its conquest of the Ming dynasty, with the establishment of the *Aisin gurun-*/Houjin 後金 state in 1616 and the reign of the first Qing emperor Fulin/Shunzhi 順治 (1638–1661), which commenced in 1644 in Beijing, the new Qing state was anxious to maintain the Confucian legal character of the traditional Chinese political and administrative system, regarded as the most important of all official doctrines.[17] This required enforcing and safeguarding moral principles in the upbringing of the populace. Sexual promiscuity, referred to as *jian* 奸 or *yin* 淫, was considered, along with political infractions, acts of disloyalty, crimes, and other offenses, as a sign of social disorder and anarchy, or *luan* 亂, a subversive phenomenon that must be eliminated.[18] The Manchus, as the new ruling class who comprised less than 1% of the population, saw it as their duty to ensure stability in this respect.

The enforcement of Confucian moral ideas demanded the promotion of imperially sanctioned educational texts integral to the state, which went hand in hand with the demotion of 'entertaining' texts of all kinds, considered 'tools for instructing thieves and licentious women'; for 'they destroy the mind and annihilate the conscience'.[19] The literature of fiction was thus officially relegated to the sphere of useless popular entertainment. Emperor Qianlong called these writings 'books of filth and harm', *huiwu zhi shu* 穢惡之書, which were 'of no use', *wuyi* 無益, and 'robbed the people of good morals', *xisu zhi tou* 習俗之偷.[20] An era of persecution followed. The repeated expurgation campaigns proved effective in the sense that the so-called literary inquisition against 'forbidden books', *jinshu* 禁書, and 'obscene books', *huishu* 穢書, allowed for the elimination of other writings that were subversive or hostile to the dynasty. In official sources, three kinds of content were named:

(1) Books with content that promoted rebellion and glorified lawlessness and banditry, *huidao* 誨盜.

(2) Books with heretical or subversive ideas, especially those texts that expressed sentiments against the Qing Dynasty, the Manchus and their northern predecessors.

---

17 For details see Gimm 2018: 25–33; on the reception of the Chinese model of governance, see Gimm 2021: 226; the Ming code of 1397 was borrowed almost unchanged from the beginning of Manchu rule.

18 Sommer 2000: 30–37.

19 Gimm 2005: 69.

20 Gimm 2005: 72.

331

(3) Literature with morally offensive content.

The last group included texts that openly depicted sexuality with 'obscene words', *yinci* 淫詞, in particular those of the promiscuous variety, which was seen as damaging and destructive to the Confucian social order. Compared to the previous dynasty, the Qing state insisted much more strongly on the marital ideal of female fidelity and on sexual discretion.[21]

Moral transgressions led to severe punishments of various kinds, as well as to inquisitions of erotic literature and, in a number of instances, the destruction of such texts. Among them were Manchu translations of Chinese 'novels with obscene words'. The scholar Asitan (ca. 1650–1683/4), father of the translator Hesu mentioned below, addressed petitions to the emperor on a number of occasions, requesting clarification of the rules relating to such prohibitions.[22]

The books in question undoubtedly included JPM, which Shen Hanguang 申涵光 (1618–1677) had criticized: 'books like JPM destroy the conscience and shatter the virtue' (金瓶梅等書喪心敗德).[23] According to P. H. Rushton,[24] the JPM presents 102 erotic scenes, 47 of which are described in detail, 21 partially delineated, and 34 only hinted at.

For the period around 1700 the following bans have been recorded:

1687: General ban on obscene books (*yinshu* 淫書).

1701: General ban on 'novels with obscene words' (*yinci xiaoshuo* 淫詞小說), 'for all time' (*yongxing yanjing* 永行嚴禁).

1709, 6th month: General ban on obscene novels (*yinci xiaoshuo* 淫詞小說) and on private medicinal recipes. This ban was issued only one year after the printing of the Manchu edition of JPM!

1713: Order to destroy relevant books and printing blocks. Non-compliers threatened with caning and banishment.

1714, 4th Month: General ban on obscene novels, *xiaoshuo yinci,* including the JPM;

1725: Ban on the JPM.[25]

---

21 Van Gulik 1951: Vol. 1, IV.

22 *Baqi tongzhi* 1985 [1739]: *juan* 237, 5339–5340; Linke 1982: 160–161, Gimm 2005: 85.

23 *Jingyuan xiaoyu* 1996: j.6, 12b.

24 Rushton 1978: 253, cited in Zibet 1996: 68, 80.

25 Ma Tai-loi 1980: 203.

THE MANCHU EDITION OF 1708, *GIN PING MEI BITHE*

Dates of other literary bans in this era:[26]

1635 (4th month), 1644, 1645, 1652, 1653, 1663, 1687, 1701, 1706 (9th month), 1709 (4th and 6th months), 1714 (4th month), 1724 (4th, 11th and 12th months), 1725 (4th and 5th months), 1727 (4th month), 1728 (3rd and 7th month), 1729 (9th month), 1735, 1736 (5th month), 1738, 1740, 1753 (29th day of the 7th month), 1754, 1762, 1764, 1769, 1777, 1780, 1786.

The age of censorship of immoral and obscene writing reached its height in the Qianlong era (1735–1796).

1850: The total number of banned titles: 268, including JPM.[27]

Beyond the Law

The restrictions and regulations concerning prohibited books that applied to the majority of the population did not, however, apply to the ruling class or to members of the imperial family. The world of Manchu nobility carried on beyond the law, *extra legem*. Moreover, discussion of the sexual mores of the court was subject to the strictest taboo.[28]

'Prohibited books' as far as the population at large was concerned may well have been available to the rulers and high officials of the time. This is confirmed somewhat later by Prince Zhaolian 昭槤 (1776–1830),[29] a member of the imperial *Aisin gioro* clan, in his jottings *Xiaoting zalu* 嘯亭雜錄: 'All the noblemen and high officials take pleasure in displaying [copies of prohibited books such as] *Shuihu zhuan* and *Jin Ping Mei*.'[30] The possession of erotic literature was

---

26 See *Da Qing Shengzu (Kangxi) huangdi shilu : juan* 238, 7b; *juan* 258, 17a; *Xuezheng quanshu* 1970 [1783]: *juan* 7, 1a–2a; Wylie 1902: 202–203; Ou Itaï 1933: 174–175; Fuchs 1936: 40–41; Wang Xiaozhuan 1958: 21, 23; Goodrich 1966 : XXI, 19–29; Bodde and Morris 1967: 67, 274–275; Durrant 1979: 273–274; Ma Tai-loi 1980; Wang Liqi 1981 [1958]: 212–214 etc; Huang Runhua 1983: 9, 11; Gimm 1988: 80 note 10, 87 note 35; Sommer 2000 : 32–35, (contains the routine entries of the Ministry of Justice); Zimmer 2002: Vol. 2/1, 34; Zimmer 2003: 48–55 ; Gimm 2005: 67–72.

27 Xie Taofang 1994: 32–34.

28 I was told in September 2004 by a senior staff member in the department of Palace History at the Palace Museum in Beijing that research into the entire complex of courtly sexual life had only recently begun, and only tentatively. The relevant archival materials were still kept undisclosed at that time.

29 Zhaolian was an eighth-generation descendant of Daišan 代善 (1583–1648), the second son of the dynasty founder Nurhači (1559–1626). See Fang Chao-ying, in Hummel 1943/4: Vol.1, 78–80.

30 Zhaolian 1980 [1880], *juan* 2, 427, 士大夫…無不陳水滸傳金瓶梅以為把玩.

among the privileges of the upper class. For the outside world, however, such texts had to be kept hidden.

As far as we know, no copy of JPM can be found in the accessible areas of the libraries in the palace. The title is also missing from the exquisite collection of the Library of the Palace Museum, 故宮博物院圖書館, at present located in the Palace of Longevity and Peace, Shou'an gong 壽安宮, in the northwestern part of the Forbidden City. The library currently houses some 400 titles in Manchu, including 36 translations of works of fiction, which are preserved in the form of manuscripts.[31]

For the emperor and his kin, the laws in force did not apply; they also enjoyed exemption from punishment.[32] The Manchu aristocracy, the members of the high nobility, the imperial princes and their affiliates formed a distinct class of prestige and privilege. Only in urgent legal cases did the emperor, who was considered a sacred being, the 'son of heaven' and mediator between Heaven and Man, personally make decisions on punitive or restrictive measures.

Translation into Manchu

As the popularity of JPM grew among the Manchu aristocracy, the desire arose to have the novel translated into the Manchu national language. The hitherto unknown initiator of the translation must have commanded enough power and influence to counter the prohibitions in force at that time. It is only natural that the sources are silent on this matter. A person of high position, a privileged member of the nobility, likely one of the princes, who had the means and licence to finance and publish the translation, is a probable candidate. This person was most likely also responsible for the writing of the preface in Manchu, with which he tried to justify the risqué content of the novel by establishing its underlying admonitory and moralizing intentions.

Yinreng's role

Yinreng 胤礽/In Ceng (1674–1724) the second son of Emperor Kangxi, *huang erzi* 皇二子/*jai age*, may have been the *spiritus rector* behind the translation.[33]

---

31 See the overview in Qu Liusheng 1981: 61–64.

32 Weggel 1980: 138.

33 Yinreng, Prince Limi Qinwang 理秘親王, was the 7th son of Kangxi (counting sons who died young, Kangxi had a total of 55 children); he was later also given the name of Yunreng 允礽/Yôn Ceng, for reasons related to the observance of taboos in names. (The Manchu syllable *ceng* is not the transliteration of the Chinese syllable *reng*, but it is based on an early

THE MANCHU EDITION OF 1708, *GIN PING MEI BITHE*

He was a connoisseur of literature and himself composed poems.[34]

After his stay together with the emperor Kangxi in the Summer Palace of Jehol (6th day of the 5th month [June 23] to the 9th month of 1708),[35] Yinreng stood in imperial favour in spite of several conflicts, so that in the period before the completion of the preface in the 5th month of 1708, i.e., during the year 1707[36] and the first half of 1708, he was the crown prince, and certainly possessed the power to carry out or support the actions necessary for the publication of the JPM in Manchu. The author of the preface claims to have commissioned the translation. Unfortunately, the preface and other Chinese sources are all silent on the details. From the 9th month of 1708 to the 3rd month of 1709, Yinreng fell briefly into disgrace. Whether the translation of the JPM completed in the same year counted as one of his 'misdeeds' remains to be investigated.[37]

Possible Candidates for the Translator

The name of the translator is not given in the printed Manchu edition of JPM. The sophisticated quality of the text suggests the involvement of elite court circles in choosing the translator, who was among the distinguished experts of both languages of that time. A hint is given here by Prince Zhaolian in his

---

Manchu name that was adopted in this case.) His mother, who died upon his birth, was the first empress Xiaochengren 孝誠仁 (d. 1674) of the Heseri clan. In Ceng had a troubled relationship with his father for a long time because of his disloyal deeds and excesses. Possibly the reasons also included his homoeroticism; P. Kilian Stumpf S. J. (1655–1720) called him 'Ganymedes' (in Greek mythology, the name of a young handsome man whom Zeus made his cupbearer and lover). For this see Collani 1985: 141, note 136. Yinreng had been promoted to crown prince at the age of two in 1675 and enjoyed Kangxi's goodwill for a time – during the military campaigns of 1696/97, when the emperor was absent from the capital, he acted in his stead in Beijing – but he fell into disgrace after several incidents in the ninth month of 1708. He was rehabilitated in the third month of 1709 and demoted again in the tenth month of 1712. From then until his death, he lived under house arrest in the Xian'an palace 咸安宫. See Prandi 1846: 96. For the original version, see Ripa 1852: Vol. I, 453. For Yinreng's biography, see Fang Chao-ying in Hummel 1943: 924–925; Spence 1966: 129–132; Spence 1974: 111, 120, 124–139; Kessler 1976: 56, 127–128; Gimm 2005: 53–54, 93; Yu Zhenmin 1997 [1938] vol. 6: 78.

34 See the collection *Xichao yasong ji* 熙朝雅頌集 1992 [1805]: *juan* 26, 106, Appendix, *juan* 2, etc; as well as *Wanqing yi shihui* 晚晴簃詩匯 1990 [1929].

35 Lin Tiejun 1988: Vol. 3, 308.

36 In 1707, from the 22nd day of the 1st month to the 22nd day of the 5th month, Emperor Kangxi completed his sixth southern tour, *nanxun* 南巡; see Gimm 2015: 29.

37 See Gimm 2012: Part VII, I–IV; Gimm 2014: Introduction, 99–101.

MARTIN GIMM

Xiaoting zalu mentioned above.[38] In these jottings, the official Hesu 和素[39] (1652–1718) is credited for his success in translating the drama *The Western Wing* (*Xixiang ji* 西廂記; preface dated 1710) and the novel JPM. He was a Manchu of the Wanggiya/Wanyan 完顏 clan of the Bordered Yellow Banner, son of the renowned scholar Asitan/Ashitan 阿什壇[40] (c.1650–1683/4) and a descendant of the dynasty founder Nurhači – a background that certainly endowed him with power.

After passing the civil service examinations, Hesu assumed a variety of official positions. He was a tutor to the crown prince, an Academician Reader-in-Waiting at the Grand Secretariat (*neige shidu xueshi* 內閣侍讀學士) and held the title of Erudite *baksi/bakeshi* 巴克什 (< Mongol *baγsi* < *boshi* 博士). He earned much renown through his translations.[41] The *Conversations with*

---

38   Zhaolian 1980 [1880], *juan* 1, 397, *Fanshu fang:* 有戶曹郎中和素者. 翻譯絕精. 其翻西廂記. 金瓶梅諸書. 疏節字句. 咸中...肯. 人人爭誦焉

39   On his biography, see *Baqi tongzhi* 1985 [1739]: *juan* 237, 5341–2; *Baqi manzhou shizu tongpu* 1989 [1744]: Chinese *juan* 28, 8a., Manchu *juan* 28, 11b; Li Huan 1976 [1883]: *juan* 75, XI; *Enhua Yongchun* 1935: *juan* 1, 4a; *Qing bai leichao* (reprint), vol. 8, 4031; also *Qing bai leichao xuan*: extracts from the section on *wenxue* etc., 178, ff.; Fuchs 1936: 25–30, 33, 43; also in Hummel 1943: 281 (see also the Chinese sources cited there); Linke 1982: 166, 216, 251, 232, 262–266, 283; Huang Runhua 1983: 11; Hu Wenbin 1986: 91; Wang Rumei 1986: 217–219; Fang Ming 1986: 190–191; Huang Lin 1987: 262, 301; Wang Lina 1988: 134; Gimm 1988: 87; Teng Shaozhen 1989: 198; Huang Lin 1991: 1016.

40   Asitan, who was a descendant of the Jürchen imperial clan, passed the *jinshi* examination in 1652. Fuchs 1936 describes him as one of the 'most significant translators of the early [Qing]' (Fuchs 1936: 42). After a series of setbacks, he earned the esteem of the Kangxi emperor, who once called him 'a great scholar of our dynasty'; see *Baqi tongzhi* 1985 [1739]: *juan* 237, 5340. The sources cited below record him as having translated, among other texts, *Daxue* 大學, *Zhongyong* 中庸, *Xiaojing* 孝經, *Tongjian zonglun* 通鑑總論 and *Taigong jiajiao* 太公家教 – on this see *Baqi tongzhi* 1985 [1739]: *juan* 237, 5338–5341; *Enhua Yongchun* 1935: 4b, 5a, 9a; Fuchs 1936: 42 (with further references); see also Hummel 1943: Vol. 1, 13–14; Linke 1982: 158–168; Gimm 1988: 81 note 11. Hesu's younger brother was Hesihen/Heshiheng 赫世亨 (c. 1645–1708), well-known as an intermediary between Christian missionaries and the court, whose name also appears in the missionaries' accounts as Heschgen and under the 'confidential name' Henkama as well; *Baqi tongzhi* 1985 [1739]:, *juan* 237, 5341; *Baqi manzhou shizu tongpu* 1989 [1744]: *juan* 28, 8a ; Rosso 1948: 137, 138, 140, 157 etc; Linke 1982: 166; Collani 1985: 60, note 272; for details see Gimm 2016: 101–136.

41   'Esteemed as one of the most able Manchu translators'; Fuchs in: Hummel, 281. According to the *Baqi yiwen bianmu* (Enhua Yongchun 1935: *juan* 1, 4a, 31a, 31b, 38b) he had also translated the following books into Manchu: *Zuozhuan* 左傳, *Huangshi gong sujing* 黃石公素經 and *Caigen tan* 菜根譚. For additional titles see Walravens 2014: No. 68–74, 157.

336

THE MANCHU EDITION OF 1708, *GIN PING MEI BITHE*

Figure 20.1. Hesu 和素 (1674–1724), the most likely translator of *Jin Ping mei* into Manchu, at the age of 45; painted on silk by an anonymous palace artist, dated November, Kangxi 34 (1695); with three inscriptions; Palace Museum, Beijing, 1.59 × 1.15 m.

MARTIN GIMM

the Hundred and Twenty Elders remarked of his work, 'his style in Manchu is extraordinary'.[42]

He enjoyed the goodwill of the emperor.[43] In an edict dated to the 1st day of the 3rd month (April 18) of the year 1711 (Kangxi 50), Kangxi ranked him, together with Xu Yuanmeng, discussed below, among the 'unsurpassed translators of Chinese literature in the present day'.[44] Jesuit scholars of his time also extolled him as a bilingual scholar. Around 1735, Father Dominique Parrenin S.J. (1665–1741) praised him thus in a letter to Father Jean Baptiste du Halde S. J. (1674–1743): 'The translator is named Hosu [Hesu], a most famous name in this empire –precisely the person to whom the great Emperor Cham-hi [Kangxi] entrusted most of his sons to be taught the Chinese and Tartar (Manchu) languages. This man is reputed to be among the most skilled teachers of his time in both languages; his death was most untimely.'[45]

During his time in office, Hesu was associated with two institutions that are of particular importance for the preparation and production of the JPM in Manchu:

---

42 *manju gisun ici dembei sain*; se Stary 1983: 250 and 458.

43 The First Historical Archive of China, *Zhongguo diyi lishi dang'anguan* 中國第一歷史檔案 館 in Beijing, preserves ca. 400 dated (and ca. 10 undated) Manchu works by Hesu in the period from the 2nd day of the 5th month of 1711 to the 7th day of the 2nd month of 1715 alone, many of which deal with diverse printed editions in various stages of preparation; on this, see the Chinese translations in *Kangxi chao manwen zhupi zouzhe quanyi* 1996, from no. 1716 onwards. Among other things, Hesu was part of the editorial team that was responsible for preparing the literary concordance *Peiwen yunfu* 佩文韻府 of 1711 and the imperial selection of Tang poems *Yuxuan tangshi* 御選唐詩 of 1713 (see the list of staff there).

44 *Baqi tongzhi* 1799 imprint, section *shou, juan* 8, 12b. Two Chinese imprints and a Manchu translation by Hesu were also submitted to the emperor; see *Kangxi chao manwen zhupi zouzhe quanyi* 1996: nos. 2155 and 2169, dated to the 22nd and 28th of the intercalary 5th month of Kangxi 52 (i.e., 14 and 22 July 1713).

45 *Welt-Bott:* 1755, No. 623, 1–2. The letter is undated; Pfister 1932: 615, gives the year 1740. On this see also *Lettres édifiantes et curieuses concernant l'Asie, l'Afrique et l'Amérique, avec quelques relations nouvelles des missions* [...], Paris 1843, vol. 3, 750. In his letter, Father Parrenin preoccupied himself with a detailed description of a 'piece' that contains 'rules of the house and useful moral teachings', which was written 'in Chinese language' and translated into 'Tartar' by Hesu; he also appended a long series of passages (2–12) that he had translated into French and marked with annotations. It can be inferred that this is the above-mentioned, well-known collection of aphorisms and maxims, the *Caigen tan* 菜根 譚 of 1600, by the Ming author Hong Yingming 洪應明, whose translation into Manchu, *Z'ai gen tan bithe*, appeared in a bilingual imprint in 1708. On this, see also the German translation of selections from the French version of this letter in Voiret (ed.)1996: 259–274. On Parrenin see Pfister 1932: no. 233; Dehergne 1973: no. 611.

THE MANCHU EDITION OF 1708, *GIN PING MEI BITHE*

- From 1688 he was Supervisor of the Imperial Translation Office, *Nei fanshu fang guanli dachen* 內翻書房管理大臣[46]; see below.

- From about 1706 until at least 1712 he held the post of Director of the Imperial Printing Office, *Wuying dian zongjian* 武英殿總監[47]; his brother Hesihen probably held the same post a few years earlier.[48]

- On the Imperial Printing Office, *Wuying dian*, see the next section.

The Imperial Translation Office, *Nei fanshu fang* 內翻書房,[49] established in 1670, was attached to the Grand Secretariat, *Neige* 內閣, which was the topmost advisory organ in the government. Bannermen distinguished for their proficiency in both Chinese and Manchu were gathered here at an office affiliated with the government, located near the main gate south of the Forbidden City, *Taihe men* 太和門/*amba hôwaliyambure duka*. The office served mainly to translate official writings, imperial decrees, inscriptions, government documents, and court diaries, but it also oversaw the translation of collections of literature and works of philosophy and history initiated by the emperor, as well as official dictionaries. Unfortunately, very little is known about the detailed activities and number of employees of this office. It is also unclear whether the translation of a 'prohibited' book was even possible in a government office – and whether Hesu had to search for other means to publish his translation.

Another source names Xu Yuanmeng 徐元夢/Sioi yuwan meng (1655–1741)[50] as the translator of the JPM. Xu, a Manchu of the Šumuru/Shumulu 舒穆祿 clan of the Plain White Banner, from Liaoyang 遼陽 (Liaoning Province), was the eldest son of Sirtai/Xi'ertai 席爾泰. He was a well-known scholar (*jinshi*

---

46 Wu Changyuan 1848: *juan* 2, 25; *Xiaoting zalu xulu*: *juan* 1, 397; Fuchs, in Hummel, Vol. 1: 281; Hucker: no. 4172.

47 See his entries in *Kangxi chao manwen zhupi zouzhe quanyi* 1996: no. 979 (21st of the 8th month of 1706), nos. 1890–1892, 1943, 2146, 2147, 3889–3896 etc.; Hucker: nos. 2630, 7091, 7840; Brunnert and Hagelstrom 1961 [1912]: no. 94.

48 *Kangxi chao manwen zhupi zouzhe quanyi* 1996: nos. 3873–3876; texts undated; Gimm 2016: 112.

49 *Xiaoting zalu, xulu, juan* 1, 397; *Qingbai leichao* 1984–87: *juan* 70, 215, reprint, 4030. The examinations for Mongolian and Manchu translators had been newly established in 1651; see *(Qinding) Fanyi kaoshi tiaoli*: 1a. Translator examinations were highly prestigious, as they were at times presided over personally by Emperor Kangxi and were held in 1663, 1671, 1673, 1685, 1694, 1712 in his garden palace Changchun yuan 暢春園; see Gimm 2015: 101.

50 Li Huan 1976 [1883]: *juan* 12, 6a–10a.; *Baqi manzhou shizu tongpu* 1989 [1744]: Chinese, *juan* 6, 19ab, Manchu, *juan* 6, 26a; Fuchs 1936: 25, 49, 52, 55–56; Suter and Fang Chaoying, in Hummel 1943/4, 659; Linke 1982: 78, 242, 353; Huang Runhua 1983: 11; Gimm 1988: 88 note 37; Huang Lin 1991: 1016.

1673), a high official (his posts included Chief of the Ministry of Finance), and a member of the Hanlin Academy; he was involved in several literary projects, and also served as tutor to several princes for some three decades from 1687. Emperor Kangxi praised him for his abilities: 'Xu Yuanmeng is presently unsurpassed in his translations.'[51]

The only known source for Xu's alleged authorship of the Manchu JPM is an anonymous commentary[52] to the famous jottings of Yuan Mei 袁枚 (1716–1798), *Suiyuan shihua* 隨園詩話, j. 5 (entry no. 50), titled *Piben Suiyuan shihua* 批本隨園詩話. The commentary reveals (without giving further sources)[53] that 'The translation of the JPM comes from the hand of Xu Dieyuan 徐蝶園 [i.e., a sobriquet of Xu Yuanmeng].'

Hesu, who held a higher position of power, is more likely to be the translator of JPM.

Guesswork that appears exclusively in European sources can be disregarded here. They consider a direct connection to the imperial family to be possible, given the special status of JPM, and speculate that a brother of Kangxi or Qianlong might be the initiator and/or translator.[54]

Printing by the Court

At the beginning of the Qing, the official printing office and its facilities were taken over from the Ming court and placed under the control of the Bureau of Imperial Household Affairs (*Neiwu fu* 內務府).[55] Around 1671, a separate entity emerged from it, and established itself from around 1680 as a workshop (*zaoban chu* 造辦處) in the Hall of Martial Grace (*Wuying dian* 武英殿/ *Horonggo yangsangga deyen*) in the southwestern part of the Forbidden City, a facility responsible for the manufacturing of a wide variety of things used in the palace.[56] Significantly expanded under Emperor Kangxi, from 1729

---

51 *Xu Yuanmeng fanyi xianjin wuneng guozhi* 徐元夢翻譯現今無能過之; cited in Huang Runhua 1985: 209, but the source is not given there.

52 According to the afterword, the author of this commentary may be a son of Ulana/Wulana 伍拉納 (1739–1795, executed). Possibly this is the literatus Shu Dun 舒頓, a brother of the better known Shu Min 舒敏 (1777–1803). On this see *Yuan Mei quanji* 1993: vol. 3, 837. For further details see Ye Dejun 1979, 622; Huang Lin 1987: 263; Huang Lin 1991: 1112.

53 *Yuan Mei quanji* 1993: Vol. 3, 815.

54 For details see Gimm 2005: 86–96.

55 Hucker 1985: no. 4291.

56 *Da Qing huidian shili*: *juan* 1173, 7b; Gimm 1993: 29–30; Gimm 2005: 67, 77, 84. For a detailed introduction to the printing activities of Wuying dian, see the appendix to Weng Lianxi 2004. Of special note is the collection of records published 2014 in the *Qinggong*

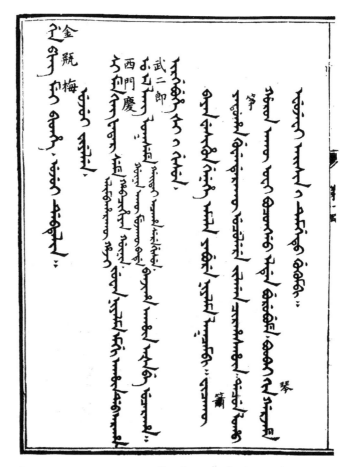

Figure 20.2. Gin ping mei, officially printed edition of 1708, beginning of the first chapter.

onwards the printing facility was known as the Office for the Compilation of Books at the Hall of Martial Grace (*Wuying dian xiushu chu* 武英殿修書處/*Bithei weilere ba*). By the Qianlong period, it had grown into an advanced technical facility, whose established processes were enhanced by innovations.

The imperial printing office at the Hall of Martial Grace was responsible for almost all areas of court book production, including the compilation of manuscripts, the production and carving of printing blocks, the preparation of paper, the process of manually printing the pages, the stitching and binding,

---

Wuying dian xiushuchu dang'an in 11 volumes; a monograph is under preparation. Unfortunately, none of the equipment used for printing has survived in the Wuying dian; a museum of art and calligraphy was established there in 2008.

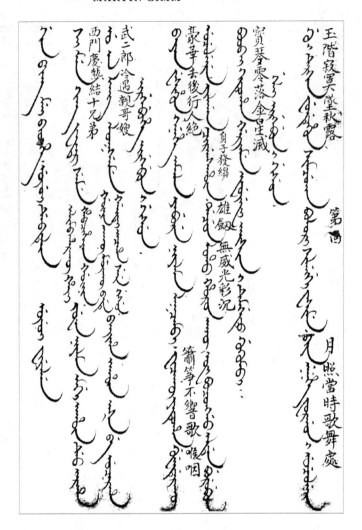

Figure 20.3. *Gin ping mei bithe* (the Manchu translation of *Jin Ping Mei*), manuscript, beginning of the first chapter. From the holdings of WANG Yintai 王蔭泰 (1886–1961), who studied in Berlin since 1912 and during the 1920s was employed at the Ethnological Museum of Berlin (Völkerkundemuseum); later he occupied diplomatic positions in China (W. FUCHS (1966), S. 122, Nr. 229). The manuscript belongs today to the Department of East Asian Studies, Freie Universität, Berlin.

THE MANCHU EDITION OF 1708, *GIN PING MEI BITHE*

and the official distribution of books. This printing office also gained renown for its production of literature in Manchu and other languages. The centre of imperial book production was thus established in Beijing, and only when work was occasionally overtaxing was the court production of Chinese-language imprints transferred to other places, including Yangzhou[57] and Nanjing. In the Kangxi period, approximately 100 works were printed, some of which were exceedingly voluminous.[58]

The carefully checked imprints produced in the imperial workshops were known as 'palace editions' (*dianben* 殿本 or *neifu ben* 內府本); the Manchu JPM belonged among them.[59] These imprints enjoyed a reputation for outstanding textual reliability and superior printing quality, which are also discernable in the case of the JPM imprint.[60]

The books, printed from woodblocks made of pear wood, *limu* 梨木, or jujube wood, *zaomu* 棗木, were distinguished from other books by one peculiarity, namely their missing title pages.[61] The palace editions were not for sale

---

57 This was the case with the famous literary concordance *Peiwen yunfu* 佩文韻府 and the large poetry collection *Quan Tangshi* 全唐詩.

58 Weng Lianxi 2004: Appendix, 5.

59 Lowe and Bodde 1983 [1940/1]: Vol. 2, 177: '[...] the famous *Tian Pan* or 'Palace Block Editions' indicating royal favours in the past when emperors found time to take part in the literary enterprise of book publications.' Dun Yi 1911 explicitly referred to the copy of the Manchu JPM purchased a century later by a Japanese man at the price of 40 *jin* 金 as a 'palace edition' (*neifu ben* 內府本); see the entry based on it in the collection *Qingbai leichao* (preface dated 1916), reprint, issue 8, 4031, and likewise in the *Qingbai leichao xuan*, *wenxue*: 178; Mao Guangsheng 1873–1959 also refers to the imprint as a *neifu keben* 內府刻本 (1911: 2a), while the *Qingbai leichao* refers to it similarly as a *neifuwu keben* 內府務刻本. Additionally, see Gimm 1988: 87 and note 36; see also Huang Runhua 1983: 11; Hu Wen-bin 1986: 91 (no sources given); Fang Ming 1986: 190–191; Huang Lin 1987: 262, 301; Wang Lina 1988: 134; Huang Lin 1991: 1016.

60 As for page design, size, paper quality, etc., the Manchu JPM imprint resembles other court imprints of the period. The printed area marked by a double border (*sizhou shuangbian* 四週雙邊) converging at the 'seam' (*banxin* 版心), which contained a 'simple black fishtail' (*heidan yuwei* 黑單魚尾) placed between the Manchu title *Gin Ping Mei* and the chapter and page numbers in Chinese. See Weng Lianxi 2004: Figures 26–50, 245–248; see the figures in this chapter.

61 The title pages (*fengmian* 封面) of commercially printed books typically contain the name of the print shop, combined with terms like *cangban* 藏板, *bancun* 板存 or *zixing* 梓行, and references to the possibility of purchase in addition. In contrast, 'the palace editions of the period under Manchu rule [...] never contain a title page'; see Fuchs 1956: 37. See also Schubert 1929/1930: 59–73. The title page is to be distinguished from the so-called 'cover title', *fengmian ti* 封面題, which can often be found handwritten on the covers of palace editions.

343

and were above all not intended for the book market. Through an established process of distribution, they found their way to government and educational institutions or served as treasured imperial gifts. It was the usual practice for printing to take place immediately after prefaces had been written. In the case of the Manchu JPM, the preface was dated 1708, so that the printing can be dated to the time around 1708/1709. The print runs of these imprints were small and manageable, usually only a few hundred copies and only in exceptional cases exceeding a thousand copies.[62] The Manchu JPM probably had a print run somewhere in between.[63]

For understandable reasons, there is no direct evidence of the Hall of Martial Grace being involved in the printing of the Manchu JPM.[64] Yet the fact that it was the only Chinese novel of manners to be deemed worthy of a printed translation into Manchu suggests that the entire undertaking – the planning of the project, the compilation, the editing, the translation, the block-carving, the printing and distribution – had been carried out under the auspices of the upper echelons of the court. As far as we know, the chief supervisor of the imperial printing facilities, *zongcai guan* 總裁官/ *uheri tuwara amban*[65] in the Kangxi period was for the most part under the charge of one of the princes.[66] This person, appointed by the emperor for specific tasks, was involved in a

---

62 It is difficult to obtain information on the print runs of palace editions; the *Peiwen yunfu* 佩文韻府 had one thousand copies (see Gimm 1983: 170). Apparently, as with the book trade, print production was purely 'on-demand'.

63 Notably, a relatively large number of the original imprints have been preserved in archives, although some are incomplete. Thus, in China, they can be found in Beijing (among other places at the College for Minority Languages (*Zhongyang minzu daxue* 中央民族大學) and the National Library of China (*Guojia tushuguan* 國家圖書館), and in Inner Mongolia in Huhehot; in Germany: Berlin, Leipzig; in England: Cambridge and London (several copies), Manchester; in France: Paris; in Holland: Leiden; in Italy: Vatican; in Japan: Osaka, Tenri, Tokyo; in Mongolia: Ulaan Bator; in Russia: Irkutsk, Moscow (several copies), St. Petersburg (several copies), Vladivostok; in Sweden: Stockholm; in Hungary: Budapest; in USA: Baltimore, Cambridge Mass. (Harvard), etc. In addition, a number of manuscripts can be traced back to the printed edition of 1708. In them, the Manchu text is expanded in places with modern synonyms, and the Chinese glosses are supplemented by additions. These manuscripts can be found in China in Beijing and Dalian/Dairen (titled *Shitai yanliang* 世态炎凉/*Jalan de wenjehun andahŏri-i goiman bithe*), in Jilin University (*Jilin daxue* 吉林大學); in Germany: Berlin; in Japan: Tenri; in Mongolia: Ulaan Bator; in Russia: St. Petersburg; in Canada; in USA: Harvard.

64 In records such as the *Qing neifu keben dang'an shiliao huibian*, Volume 1, one finds no hints.

65 Hucker: no. 7156.

66 Brunnert and Hagelstrom 1961 [1912]: No. 94, 23: 'In charge of the Printing Office is a Prince or Minister of the Household, styled 管理武英殿修書處事務.'

THE MANCHU EDITION OF 1708, *GIN PING MEI BITHE*

secondary capacity in the commission of major literary projects, whose titles contain the prefix *yuzhi* 御制 or *qinding* 欽定 (imperially ordered). In the list of staff involved in these compilations, *zuanji* 纂輯, the prince's name always appears at the beginning.

As the emperor's confidant, the prince in question had direct influence on the activities of the Hall of Martial Grace. One can imagine that a person with distinct privileges, in this case probably Prince Yinreng, possessed the power and licence to set into action the printing of a forbidden book that was to be kept secret from the outside world.

The Reception of the Manchu JPM in Europe

Both the Chinese and Manchu versions of JPM probably first found their way into European libraries around 1740 in St. Petersburg.[67] In France, J. P. Abel-Rémusat (1788–1832) mentioned the Manchu version in 1816 and described it as '*un chef-d'œuvre d'élégance et de correction*' (a masterpiece of elegance and style).[68] Julius Klaproth (1783–1835) was also among those who early on (around 1830) owned a copy of the Manchu JPM.[69] Since then, several translations into European languages have been attempted, such as the earliest partial translation of JPM into French by Antoine P. L. Bazin (1799–1863) in 1853, and the anonymous German translation of 1924.[70]

For a long time it was unknown to the world that the famed linguist Hans Conon von der Gabelentz (1807–1874),[71] father of the sinologist Georg von

---

67 Both the Chinese and the Manchu versions are mentioned in the *Journal von Russland* 2 (1794). The entry is based on an earlier list by Aleksej L. Leontev from 1741. On this, see Walravens 2006: 560.

68 Remusat 1816: 59.

69 Klaproth 1839: part 2, 61, no. 244.

70 The translator was possibly Hans Rudelsberger (1868–1940). In the German language, the brothers Artur Kibat (1878–1961) and Otto Kibat (1880–1956) followed in 1928 and 1932 with the first two volumes of their complete translation of the JPM, which was, however, not published in its entirety until 1967/83 due to censorship (Kibat and Kibat 1967–1983 [1928, 1929]). Unbeknownst to them (and unaware of them), Franz Kuhn (1884–1961) had attempted the same task at about the same time and published his well-known, if significantly abridged, German translation in 1930, which, thanks to its accessible length, provided the basis for further translations into other languages and for various adaptations. See Gimm 2005: 47–48.

71 The Thuringian private scholar descended from Meissen nobility had worked with some 80 languages in the course of his studies, and installed libraries containing writings in some 200 languages at his two residences, the Poschwitz Castle near Altenburg and Lemnitz Castle near Triptis; see Gimm 2005: 7–26.

345

der Gabelentz (1840–1893), who was renowned for his *Chinesische Grammatik* (Chinese Grammar) of 1881, was already preoccupied with the Manchu JPM during 1861–1869, and within seven years – probably mostly as an exercise for himself – completed a translation of the entire work.[72] On February 2, 1869, he finished the manuscript of his translation of the novel from Manchu, totaling approximately 3800 pages, which nevertheless could not be published given the constraints in the moral climate at that time. It was the earliest translation of the novel in its entirety into a European language. The manuscript, long considered lost, was rediscovered by chance in 1998 in the Thuringian State Archives in Altenburg/Thuringia. Apparently, it had been overlooked by the Red Army Trophy Commission at the end of the war in 1945, when the majority of the books and art objects in the Gabelentz collection was transferred from Poschwitz Castle to the Soviet Union.

Important Dates in the History of the *Jin Ping Mei* before the 20th Century

1596 and 1606: Earliest mentions of the Chinese JPM.

1617: First verifiable printing of the JPM, the *cihua* edition.

1650: Printing of the Manchu version of the novel *Sanguo zhi* 三國志.

1687: General ban on obscene books, *yinshu* 淫書.

1695: Printing of the Zhang Zhupo edition of JPM.

1701: General ban on 'novels with obscene words', *yinci xiaoshuo* 淫詞小說, condemned as 'strictly forbidden for all time', *yongxing yanjing* 永行嚴禁;

ca. 1700–1708: Preparation of the Manchu translation of JPM, probably by the scholar Hesu (1652–1718).

1703: Earliest evidence for the existence of a Manchu translation of JPM.

1708, 5th month: Preface to the Manchu edition by an anonymous author.

1709, 1st day of 7th month: General ban on obscene novels, *yinci xiaoshuo* 淫詞小說, private medicinal recipes, etc. This ban took place only one year (!) after the printing of the Manchu JPM.

---

72 In a letter to Stanislas Julien from around March 1870, H. Conon wrote: 'Most useful for me, though, was a complete translation of the *Jin Ping Mei*, a work in a splendid style by a Manchu prince, and, as far as one can judge without having the original in hand, it cannot be more faithful in reproducing the spirit of the original text [...]. It is a pity that its teeming frivolities prevent it from being published. It would be a wonderful aid in learning the language and even in learning about the Chinese life.' Translated here from Walravens 2021: 75.

1725: JPM banned.

1741: Evidence of a Manchu JPM imprint in the St. Petersburg Library.

1816: Earliest Western European mention of the JPM in Chinese and Manchu by J. P. Abel-Rémusat (1788–1832).

1862: Hans Conon v. d. Gabelentz (1807–1874) begins translating the JPM from Manchu.

Summary

The novel JPM, in its extant Manchu version, is one of the most important texts of Manchu literature, which reached its height in the period between the 17th to 18th centuries. In 1816, J. P. Abel-Rémusat (1788–1832) described the JPM translation as 'un chef-d'œuvre d'élégance et de correction',[73] followed by Alexander Wylie (1815–1887) in 1855.[74] The translator H. Conon v. d. Gabelentz (1807–1874) remarked in 1870 that 'the work is written in a splendid style'.[75] Berthold Laufer (1855–1908) called it 'a brilliant achievement of Manchu language and literature. [...] In artistic achievement, this work belongs [...] amongst the best of its genre.'[76] Erich Haenisch (1880–1966) observed: 'The translation, which reflects the living language in its diction, simple and smooth, is unmatched by any other work of Manchu literature'.[77]

Since JPM was a 'forbidden book', there is no direct documentation of the circumstances of its printing left. The pertinent official records are missing; they were presumably destroyed after the fact. One has to rely largely on speculation while comparing information from different sources. We can be sure that the translation was initiated and carried out by a powerful person, probably a prince, who possessed the interest and insight as well as the authority, power and means to realize such a project against the current of the times. It was necessary both to find a competent translator to carry out the work in secret, *intra muros*, and to persuade the powerful head of the Imperial Printing Office to make the necessary preparations for the finished text to be taken to press. All the steps in the process – conceivably with the covert approval of the emperor – were kept secret from the outside world.

---

73 Rémusat 1816: 59.

74 Wylie 1855: xlii.

75 See note 72.

76 Laufer 1908: 32.

77 Haenisch 1961.

References

Abel-Rémusat, Jean Pierre

1816. *Le livre des récompenses et des peines, traduit du chinois, avec des notes et des éclaircissemens.* Paris : Antoine-Augustin Renouard.

Baqi tongzhi 八旗通志 [Gazeteer of the Eight Banners]

1985 [1739]. Compiled by Ortai/Eertai 鄂爾泰. Changchun. 8 vols.

Baqi manzhou shizu tongpu 八旗滿洲氏族通譜/*Jakůn gůsai Manjusai mukůn hala be uheri ejehe bithe*

1989 [1744]. Imperially commisioned work, compiled 1735–1744, in Manchu and Chinese. 1989 reprint in Chinese only. Shenyang: Liaoshen.

Bodde, Derk and Clarence Morris

1967. *Law in Imperial China Exemplified by 190 Ch'ing Dynasty Cases.* Cambridge, Mass.: Harvard University Press.

Brunnert, H. S. and V. V. Hagelstrom

1961 [1912]. *Present Day Political Organization of China.* Taipei. Original publication Shanghai: Kelly and Walsh.

Collani, Claudia von

1985. *P. Joachim Bouvet S. J., sein Leben und sein Werk.* Nettetal: Steyler Verlag (Monumenta Serica Monograph Ser., XVII).

Da Qing huidian shili 大清會典事例

1,220 j. Revised in 1899 during the *Guangxu* reign, printed 1904. Reprint Taipei: Xinwen feng 1963, Beijing 1976.

Da Qing Shengzu (Kangxi) huangdi shilu 大清聖祖康熙皇帝實錄

300 j. Revised 1723/31, revised again 1732 in *Da Qing lichao shilu* 大清歷朝實錄. Reprint Taipei: Taiwan zhonghua 1963/4.

Dehergne, Joseph S. J.

1973. *Répertoire des Jésuites de Chine de 1552 à 1800.* Rome and Paris : Institut. Histor. (Bibliotheca Instituti Historici, Serie I., vol. 37).

Dun Yi, cf. *Qingbai leichao.*

Durrant, Steven W.

1979. 'A Note on the Translation of Chinese Historical Romances into Manchu and Mongolian.' *Chinese Literature: Essays, Articles, Reviews* 1 S. : 273–274.

Enhua Yongchun 恩華詠春

1935. *Baqi yiwen bianmu* 八旗藝文編目 No place, no year (postface 1935). 2 vols. (*Qinding*) *Fanyi kaoshi tiaoli* 欽定翻譯考試條 Printed 19th century.

THE MANCHU EDITION OF 1708, *GIN PING MEI BITHE*

Fang Ming 方銘

1986. *Jin Ping Mei ziliao huilu* 金瓶梅資料匯錄. Hefei : Huangshan shushe.

Fuchs, Walter

1936. *Beiträge zur Mandjurischen Bibliographie und Literatur* (Mitteilungen d. Deutschen Gesellschaft f. Natur- u. Völkerkunde. Ostasiens, Suppl. Bd. 14). Tōkyō: Deutsche Ges. f. Natur- u. Völkerkunde. Ostasiens.

1956. 'Miszellen zum Druckjahr chinesischer Palastausgaben'. *Nachrichten d. Gesellsch. f. Natur- u. Völkerkunde Ostasiens* 79–80: 37–40.

Gabelentz, Hans Conon v. d.

2013. *Jin Ping Mei, Chinesischer Roman, erstmals vollständig ins deutsche übersetzt,* Berlin: Staatsbibliothek zu Berlin, Neuerwerbungen der Ostasienbibliothek, Sonderheft 34, Teil VIII, Anhang S. I–IV.

Gimm, Martin

1983. Zur Entstehungsgeschichte der chinesischen Literaturkonkordanz P'ei-wen yün-fu 佩文韻府. *T'oung Pao* 69: 159–174.

1988. The Manchu Translations of Chinese Novels and Short Stories: An Attempt at an Inventory. *Asia Major* 3 ser. 1(2): 77–114. Chinese version in *Zhongguo chuantong xiaoshuo zai yazhou* 中國傳統小說在亞洲, Beijing 1989, pp. 130–190, translated by Yan Bao 顏保 et al.

1993. *Kaiser Qianlong (1711–1799) als Poet.* Sinologica Coloniensia 15. Stuttgart: Steiner.

2005. *Hans Conon von der Gabelentz und die* Übersetzung *des chinesischen Romans* Jin Ping Mei. Sinologica Coloniensia 24. Wiesbaden: Harrassowitz.

2012. Ein Nachtrag zum Druckjahr der manjurischen *Jin Ping Mei*-Ausgabe. In Hans Conon von der Gabelentz (1807–1874), *Jin Ping Mei, Chinesischer Roman, erstmalig vollständig ins Deutsche* übersetzt, *Teil VII,* pp. I–IV. Berlin: Staatsbibliothek zu Berlin, Neuerwerbungen der Ostasienabteil, Sonderheft 30.

2014. Ein Kapitel aus der ersten vollständigen *Übersetzung* des chinesischen Romans *Jin Ping Mei* ins Deutsche. *Studia Orientalia Slovaca,* 12(1): 99–118 (Introduction). Bratislava.

2015. *En Monat im Privatleben des chinesischen Kaisers Kangxi Gao Shiqis Tagebuch Pengshan miji aus dem Jahre 1703.* Sinica Coloniensia 34. Wiesbaden: Harrassowitz.

2016. Henkama, 'Väterchen Heng', ein Mediator zwischen Kaiser Kangxi und den Jesuitenmissionaren in der Epoche des Ritenstreites im 18. Jahrhundert. *Monumenta Serica,* 64(1): S. 101–136.

2018. *Der geheime Schamanismus der Qing-Kaiser und der Schamanentempel Tangzi in Beijing.* Sinologica Coloniensia 35. Wiesbaden: Harrassowitz.

MARTIN GIMM

2021. *P. Johann Adam Schall von Bell S. J. und die Geheimakten zum Gerichtsprozeß der Jahre 1664–1666 in China.* Sinologica Coloniensia 37. Wiesbaden: Harrassowitz.

Gin Ping Mei bithe, A Manchu Edition of the Chin P'ing Mei
1975. San Francisco: Chinese Materials Center. 10 vols.

Goodrich, Luther Carrington
1966. *The Literary Inquisition of Ch'ien-lung.* 2nd ed. New York: Paragon.

Goodrich, Luther Carrington and Fang Chaoying
1976. *Dictionary of Ming Biography 1368–1644* 明道名人傳, New York, London: Columbia University Press.

Grube, Wilhelm
1902. *Geschichte der chinesischen Literatur.* 2nd edition. Leipzig: Amelang.

van Gulik, Robert Hans,
1951. *Erotic Colour Prints of the Ming Period with An Essay on Chinese Sex Life from the Han to the Ch'ing Dynasty, B. C. 206–A. D. 1644/Mixi tukao* 秘戲圖考. Privately published in 50 copies in Tokyo. 3 vols. Reprints: Plainsboro N. J. (ca. 1987); Taipei (1988), (1993); without place and year (Hong Kong, ca. 1990); Boston (2003); Authorized reprint, with Introductions by James Cahill, Wilt Idema and Sören Edgren (Sinica Leidensia, 62), Leiden : Brill (2004).

Haenisch, Erich
1961. *Mandschu-Grammatik mit Lesestücken und 23 Texttafeln.* Leipzig: Enzyklopädie.

Hauer, Erich
2007. *Handwörterbuch der Mandschusprache, 2., durchgesehene und erweiterte Auflage.* Edited by Oliver Corff. Wiesbaden: Harrassowitz.

Hu Wenbin 胡文彬
1986. *Jin Ping Mei shulu* 金瓶梅書錄. Liaoning: Renmin chubanshe.

Huang Lin 黃霖
1987. *Jin Ping Mei ziliao huibian.* Beijing: Zhonghua shuhu.
1991. *Jin Ping Mei da cidian* 金瓶梅大辭典. Chengdu: Bashu shushe.

Huang Runhua 黃潤華
1983. Manwen fanyi xiaoshuo shulue 滿文翻譯小說述略. *Wenxian* 文獻 16: 6–23.
1985. Lue tan manwen yiben, Jin Ping Mei 略談滿文譯本《金瓶梅》. *Wenxian* 18: 204–215.

Huang Runhua 黃潤華 and Wang Xiaohong 王小虹
1983. 'Manwen yiben "Tangren xiaoshuo", "Liaozhai zhiyi" deng xuwen ji yiyin "Sanguo yanyi" yuzhi 滿文譯本《唐人小說》《聊齋志異》等序文及譯印《三國演義》諭旨.' *Wenxian* 文獻 16: 1–5.

350

THE MANCHU EDITION OF 1708, *GIN PING MEI BITHE*

Hucker, Charles O.

1985. *A Dictionary of Official Titles in Imperial China,* Stanford: Stanford University Press.

Hummel, Arthur W.

1943. *Eminent Chinese of the Ch'ing Period (1644–1912).* Washington: Government Printing Office. 2 vols.

Jin Ping Mei

1975. Guyi xiaoshuo yanjiu hui 古佚小說研究會. 8 vols. Hong Kong.

Jingyuan xiaoyu 荊園小語

Vers. Shen Hanguang 申涵光. Ed. Zhaodai congshu 昭代叢書.

Kangxi chao manwen zhupi zouzhe quanyi 康熙朝滿文朱批奏折全譯

1996. Beijing: Zhongguo shehui.

Kessler, Lawrence D.

1976. *K'ang-hsi and the Consolidation of Ch'ing Rule 1661–1684.* Chicago, London: University of Chicago Press.

Kibat, Artur and Otto Kibat

1967–1983 [1928, 1932]. *Djin Ping Meh, Schlehenblüten in goldener Vase. Ein Sittenroman aus der Ming-Zeit mit 200 Holzschnitten einer Ausgabe von 1775.* 5 volumes + an extra volume of commentary, with an introduction by Herbert Franke. Hamburg, Zürich: Waage. Originally published in 1928 and 1932 as *Djin Ping Meh, Unter weitgehender Mitwirkung von Artur Kibat aus dem ungekürzten chinesischen Urtext übersetzt und mit Erläuterungen versehen von Otto Kibat.* Gotha: Engelhard-Reyher in 2 vols. (Vol. 1: Chapters 1–10, Vol. 2: Chapters 11–23). This was later banned; the erotic passages were printed in a private edition of 4 pages (Vol. 1) and 8 pages (Vol, 2) with the message Nicht zur freien Verbreitung!' [Not for free distribution!]. It also exists in abridged versions published in Frankfurt (1987) and in Zürich (1989).

Klaproth, Julius

1839. *Catalogue des livres imprimés, des manuscrits et des ouvrages chinois, tartares, japonais etc., composant la bibliothèque de feu M. Klaproth.* Preface to the second part by C. Landresse. Paris: Merlin (1839).

Laufer, Berthold

1908. 'Skizze zur manjurischen Literatur.' *Keleti Szemle* 9: 1–53.

Li Huan 李桓

1976 [1883]. *Guochao qixian leizheng* 國朝耆獻類徵. 720 j., 7 vols. Taipei: Mingwen.

351

Lin Tiejun 林鐵均 et al.

1988. *Qingshi biannian* 清史編年. Beijing: Zhongguo renmin daxue.

Linke, Bernd-Michael

1982. *Zur Entwicklung des mandjurischen Khanats zum Beamtenstaat. Sinisierung und Bürokratisierung der Mandjuren während der Eroberungszeit.* Sinologica Coloniensia Vol. 12. Wiesbaden: Harrassowitz.

Liu Housheng 劉厚生

1985. Chinese translation of preface to the Manchu translation of JPM. In *Jin Ping Mei ziliao huibian* 金瓶梅資料匯編, pp. 356–357. Shanghai: Nankai daxue

Lowe H. Y. [Lu Xingyuan] and Derk Bodde

1983 [1940/1]. *The Adventures of Wu, The Life Cycle of a Peking Man.* Princeton. Originally published in The Peking Chronicle.

Ma Tai-loi (Ma Tailai 馬泰來)

1980. Novels Prohibited in the Literary Inquisition of Emperor Ch'ien-lung, 1722–1788. In Winston L. Y. Yang and Curtis P. Adkins, *Critical Essays on Chinese Fiction.* Hong Kong: Chinese University Press.

Mao Guangsheng 冒廣生 (Nickname: Dun Huan 鈍宦)

1911. Manwen Jin Ping Mei 滿文金瓶梅. In: *Guocui xuebao* 國粹學報 Jg. 7, 2 (Nr. 75): 2a–2b. Reprint Nanjing: Guangling shushe, 2006, pp. 10359–10360.

Ou Itaï (Wu Yitai) 吳益泰

1933. *Le roman chinois.* Paris: Editions Véga.

Pfister, Louis S.J.

1932–34. *Notices biographiques et bibliographiques sur les Jesuites de l'ancienne mission de Chine 1552–1773.* Shanghai: Mission Catholique.

Prandi, Fortunato

1846. *Memoirs of Father Ripa during Thirteen Years Residence at the Court of Peking.* New York S. 96; for Italian original cf. Ripa.

Qingbai leichao 清稗類鈔

1984–87. Compiled by Xu Ke 徐珂. 13. Vols. Beijing: Zhonghua shuju

Qinggong Wuying dian xiushuchu dang'an 清宮武英殿修書處檔案

2014. Beijing: Gugong chubanshe. 11 vols.

Qu Liusheng 曲六生

1981. *Gugong cang manwen tushu* 故宮藏滿文圖書. *Gugong bowuyan yuankan* 故宮博物院院刊 1: 61–64.

Ripa, Matteo

1852. *Storia della fondazione della congregazione e del collegio de Cinesi sotto il*

titolo della Sacra Famiglia di G.C. scritta dallo stesso fondatore Matteo Ripa e de' viaggi da lui fatti. 3 vols. Napoli: Tipografia Manfredi.

Rosso, Antonio Sisto.

1948. *Apostolic Legations to China in the eighteenth century*. New York: South Pasadena, P.D. and I. Perkins.

Rushton, Peter Halliday

1978. 'The Narrative Form of Chin P'ing Mei'. Ph.D. dissertation, Stanford University.

Schubert, Johannes

1929/1930. Die Gestaltung des chinesischen Titelblattes. *Buch und Schrift*, Jg. 3: 59–73. Leipzig.

Sommer, Matthew Harvey

2000. *Sex, Law and Society in Late Imperial China*. Stanford: Stanford University Press.

Spence, Jonathan D.

1966. *Ts'ao Yin and the K'ang-hsi Emperor, Bondservant and Master*. New Haven, London: Yale University Press.

1974. *Emperor of China. Self-Portrait of K'ang-hsi*. New York: Vintage.

Stary, Giovanni (ed.)

1983. *Emu tanggû orin sakda-i gisun sarkiyan, Erzählungen der 120 Alten* (Asiatische Forschungen, Bd. 80). Wiesbaden.

Sun Kaidi 孫楷第

1957 [1933]. *Zhongguo tongsu xiaoshuo shumu* 中國通俗小說書目. Beijing: Zuojia chubanshe.

Teng Shaozhen 滕紹箴

1989. *Qingdai baqi zidi* 清代八旗子弟. Beijing: Zhongguo Huaqiao chubanshe.

Voiret, Jean-Pierre (ed.)

1996. *Gespräch mit dem Kaiser und andere Geschichten. Auserlesene Stücke aus den 'Erbaulichen und seltsamen Briefen' aus dem Reich der Mitte*. (Schweizer Asiatische Studien, Bd. 25). Bern, Berlin.

Walravens, Hartmut

1979. 'Rezension [Review] of *Gin Ping Mei bithe* 1975.' *Orientalistische Literaturzeitung* 74: 502.

2006. 'Rezension [Review].' *Orientalistische Literaturzeitung* 101, 4–5, p. 560.

2014. *Chinesische und manjurische Handschriften und seltene Drucke, Teil 8: Mandschurische Handschriften und Drucke im Bestand der Staatsbibliothek* *zu Berlin* (Verzeichnis der orientalischen Handschriften in Deutschland, vol. XII, 8). Stuttgart: Steiner.

2021. *Stanislas Julien – wissenschaftliche Korrespondenz über China mit Schilling von Canstadt, Klaproth, Endlicher, Gabelentz und A. von Humboldt.* Norderstedt: Bod.

Wanqing yi shihui 晚晴簃詩匯

1990 [1929]. Compiled by Xu Shichang 徐世昌. Beijing: Zhonghua (1990). 10 vols.

Wang Lina 王麗娜

1988. *Zhongguo gudian xiaoshuo xiqu mingzhu zai guowai* 中國古典小說戲曲名著在國外, pp. 28–29. Beijing: Xuelin.

Wang Liqi 王利器 (ed.)

1981 [1958]. *Yuan Ming Qing sandai jinhui xiaoshuo xiqu shiliao* 元明清三代禁毀小說戲曲史料. Published originally in Beijing (1958); reprint Hong Kong (1970), under the name Wang Xiaozhuan 王曉傳. *Zengding ben* 增訂本 [expanded edition] published in Shanghai 1981.

Wang Rumei 王汝梅

1986. *Jin Ping Mei tansuo* 金瓶美探索. Beijing: Jilin daxue chubanshe.

Wang Xiaozhuan, see Wang Liqi.

Weggel, Oskar

1980. *Chinesische Rechtsgeschichte* (Handbuch der Orientalistik). Leiden: Brill.

Welt-Bott

1676–1843. *Allerhand So Lehr- als Geist-reiche Brief/Schrifften und Reis-Beschreibungen/Welche von denen Missionariis der Gesellschafft Jesu Aus Beyden Indien/und andern Über Meer gelegenen Ländern/Seit An. 1642 biss auf das Jahr 1726 in Europa angelangt seynd.* Vol. 1, Parts I–VIII, edited by Joseph Stöcklein S. J. [1676–1733], Augsburg and Grätz (1728); Vol. 4, Parts XXV–XXVII, edited by Franz Keller, Wien (1755). Title on the copperplate of the 1st Vol.: *Der Neüe Welt-Bott mit allerhand nachrichten deren Missionariorum Soc. Iesu.* Hierzu s.a. *Lettres édifiantes et curieuses concernant l'Asie, l'Afrique et l'Amérique, avec quelques relations nouvelles des missions.* Paris (1843), Vol. 3.

Weng Lianxi 翁連溪

2004. *Qingdai neifu keshu tulu* 清代內府刻書圖錄. Beijing: Beijing chubanshe.

Wu Changyuan 吳長元

1848. Preface. In : *Chenyuan shilüe* 宸垣識略.

Wylie, Alexander

1855. *Translation of the Ts'ing wan k'e mung, a Chinese Grammar of the Manchu*

Tartar Language; with Introductory Notes on Manchu Literature. Shanghai : London Mission Press.

1902. *Notes on Chinese Literature: With Introductory Remarks on the Progressive Advancement of the Art; and a List of Translations from the Chinese Into Various European Languages.* American Presbyterian Mission Press.

Xichao yasong ji 熙朝雅頌集

1992 [1805]. Compiled by Tie Bao 鐵保 (1752–1824). Anthology of Tribal Poetry, 134 j.1. Reprinted Shenyang (1992) : Liaoning minzu chubanshe.

Xie Taofang 謝桃坊

1994. 'Zhongguo jindai jinhui xiaoshuo xiqu de deshi 中國金代禁毀小說戲曲的得失.' *Wenxian* 文獻 3 : 30–45.

Xuezheng quanshu 學政全書

1970 [1783]. Compiled by Surna 素爾納 (18th century.) et al.; 80 *j.* Reprint Taipei: Wenhai.

Ye, Dejun 葉德均

1979. *Xiqu xiaoshuo congkao* 戲曲小說叢考. Beijing : Zhonghua shu ju : Xin hua shu dian.

Yu Zhenmin 裕振民 (ed.)

1997 [1938]. *Aixin jiaoluo zongpu* 愛新覺羅宗譜/*Aixin gioro da sekiyen mafa ejere bithe.* Beijing. 30 volumes with index, ca. 17.000 pages. Cf. Parts *jia* 甲, *yi* 乙, *bing* 秉, *ding.* Original publication in 1938 in 8 volumes.

Yuan Mei quanji 袁枚全集 [Yuan Mei complete works]

1993. Edited by Wang Yingzhi 王英志. 8 vols. Nanjing: Jiangsu guji chubanshe.

Zhaolian 昭棟

1980 [1880]. *Xiaoting zalu* 嘯亭雜錄. Beijing: Zhonghua shuju.

Zibet, U. L. G.

1996. 'Laterna stimulans, tsuipa, Kung Fu und Ritsch-ratsch. Anmerkungen zu einer wirklich frühen *Jin Ping Mei-Übersetzungsprobe* der zwanziger Jahre und einer angeblichen *Über*setzung der mandjurischen *Jin Ping Mei*-Fassung ins Deutsche.' In v. W. v. Murat (ed.), *Erotische Literatur, Mitteilungen zu Erforschung und Bibliographie*, Vol. 3, pp. 63–89. Berlin: Bell.

Zimmer, Thomas

2002. 'Der chinesische Roman der ausgehenden Kaiserzeit.' In W. Kubin (ed.), *Geschichte der chinesischen Literatur*, Vol. 2, parts 1–2. München: K. G. Saur.

2003. 'Zensierte "Kleinigkeiten". Eine Bewertung der Erfolge und Mißerfolge staatlicher Verbote gegenüber der Erzählliteratur der xiaoshuo in den Dynastien Ming und Qing.' In Bernhard Führer (ed.), *Zensur, Text und Autorität in China in Geschichte und Gegenwart, Referate der Jahrestagung 2000 der Deutschen Vereinigung für Chinastudien* (DVCS), pp. 46–57. Wiesbaden: Harrassowitz.

Note on contributors

Martin Gimm is Professor Emeritus, Department of East Asian Studies, University of Cologne, Germany.

Lu Zhenzhen 陸珍楨 received her PhD from the University of Pennsylvania and is Assistant Professor of Chinese at Bates College (Maine, USA). Her research focuses on popular literature and manuscript culture in late imperial China. She has published articles on scribal publishing and entertainment literature in 19th century Beijing (particularly in the genre of *zidi shu*), and is currently at work on her first book, *The Vernacular World of Pu Songling.*

CHAPTER 21

About the Life of My Brother and Me

ARTUR KIBAT
Translated by Veronika Bauer

Born the son of a mid-level postal officer, Rudolf Kibat, in Lyck (East Prussia), on October 8, 1878, I was given the first names Artur Rudolf Ferdinand. I was the third of his five children; my brother Otto Friedrich Wilhelm was born as the fourth child on March 11, 1880, in Lyck. We also had three sisters. Our mother was of the Fabricius family from Gambinnen (East Prussia). Before I was even old enough to attend school, my father passed away at the age of 52. We had already lost our mother. This meant our small flock had already been orphaned twice in early childhood. My father's brother, also a civil servant, welcomed us into his family in Insterburg (East Prussia). This is where my brother and I first started to attend school. However, we only lived for three and a half years in Insterburg. The cost of supporting us became too high, which is why my mother's siblings in Gambinnen took us into their house, which included a commercial business and a store. But only three months later I was accepted as a ward in the Royal Orphanage in Königsberg in Prussia. One and a half years after me, my brother came there as a ward as well, while our sisters stayed in Gambinnen until they grew up and married. The Royal Orphanage in Königsberg was the remarkable establishment of the first Prussian King Frederick I, founded on the occasion of his coronation as 'King in Prussia' on 18 January 1701. In golden letters the small tower of the orphanage bore an inscription of gratitude *'Ad majorem Dei gloriam pro data a coelo corona'*. During my time, the orphanage was also a *Progymnasium*, i.e. a humanistic grammar school, which, as was usual, included Latin and Greek lessons, but without the *Prima*. It was the custom, when the classes had been

---

Editor's note: This chapter is a translation from German from the original autobiographical preface by Artur Kibat in Kibat, Otto and Artur Kibat (trans.), Herbert Franke (ed.) 1967. *Djin Ping Meh, Schlehenblüten in goldener Vase.* 5 Vols + Vol 6, Hamburg: Die Waage, Vol. 6, 9–17.

completed, to choose a couple of the most capable among the wards and allow them to attend the *Prima* of another royal *Gymnasium* (grammar school) until they achieved their qualification for entry into higher education, i.e. the *'Abiturium'*. I was lucky enough to be one of those sponsored. So, for eight and a half years until my *Reifeprüfung* (school-leaving examination) in 1897, the house became a second home for me. My brother was only a ward at the orphanage for four years, because at that time the *Gymnasium* was discontinued, and everything was re-organised. Consequently, my brother returned to Gambinnen, but was also able to complete the remaining *Gymnasium*-classes there until he completed his *Abiturium* at Easter 1899.

I pushed myself to continue my scientific studies, which meant attending university. But it was impossible to raise funds from the house in Gambinnen. I was advised, as there was a vacancy for an apprenticeship at the pharmacy on the market square in Gambinnen, to take the job as an apprentice. I did so, but gradually realised that this kind of employment was not in line with my expectations of life. I had already lost one and a half years. Then, in spite of all the difficulties, I dared, in the autumn of 1898, to start studying at the Alma Mater Albertina, i.e., the University of Königsberg. I had only managed to raise a very small amount of money, but I believed in myself and managed to get by with work on the side, especially by giving private lessons. This was so successful that I advised my brother to follow my example when he had passed his *Reifeprüfung*. In those early years we lived together. He chose to study law and was later able to get by all on his own with the help of savings and loans.

The University of Königsberg had been founded by Duke Albrecht of Prussia, who had been the last Grand Master of the German Teutonic Order, on the occasion of and at the same time as the transformation of his domain (i.e., the German Teutonic Order) into a secular duchy on the advice of Dr Martin Luther. While my brother finished his studies very soon after his sixth semester, passed his first law examination and was then already professionally active as a *Gerichtsreferendar* (junior lawyer), initially in Gambinnen and later in Gotha, I was still a student in Königsberg. For I was so captivated by the scientific spirit, the *aura academica*, that prevailed at the university, that I, unperturbed by concerns about my professional future, preferred to pursue purely scientific goals. I studied Indo-European linguistics, especially the ancient Indian and Iranian part, i.e. Sanskrit and the language of the Rigweda, but also the Zen language of the Iranian Avesta, i.e. the sacred script of the Zarathustrians, and chose a linguistic question from the Rigweda for my doctoral dissertation. Only after obtaining my doctorate did I turn my full attention to the scholarship that my later profession required, although I had by no means completely neglected this side of my studies beforehand either. Therefore, German, English and phi-

ABOUT THE LIFE OF MY BROTHER AND ME

losophy became my expert subjects, among them philosophy, above all. I studied with great intensity the works of Immanuel Kant, by far the most important philosophical thinker since the time of Aristotle, and turned them all into my personal intellectual property, both during this time and also in the later years of my life. Kant himself had, during the first half of the 18th century, been one of the pupils at the same *Gymnasium* that I had been allowed to attend. His bust in the assembly hall of the *Gymnasium* and his statue near the university building were time and again the object of my reverent contemplation.

After I had passed my state examinations in 1906, and completed the *Wanderzeit* (preparatory travelling time), I was, in 1908, permanently employed as a teacher at the humanistic grammar school in the district town of Osterrode in East Prussia. However, my chosen disciplines were better suited to *Realanstalten* (schools for modern sciences). For this reason, I exchanged Osterrode for Glogau in Silesia in 1909, and moved back to Wilhelmshaven in 1910. I got married around Christmas 1907. My wife had been one of the first female full-time students in Königsberg and had graduated from the same humanistic *Gymnasium* as me, as an external student.

My year of compulsory military service had fallen in the period prior to this. While I enlisted in my local fusilier regiment in Gambinnen, my brother, however, enlisted at almost the same time in the third naval battalion in Wilhelmshaven, i.e., the naval infantry of that time. This is how he arrived at the garrison of Tsingtau (Qingdao) in China, which was at the time Chinese territory leased by Germany. When his military service was over, he exchanged his legal profession for a position in a large German company in the German–Chinese trade. Over the next few years, he got to know Chinese life, thinking and behaviour both in the big seaside cities and deep in the interior of China. He also learned the language and its difficult written characters with the help of a Chinese teacher.

In order to follow my brother to China, I applied to the authorities of the *Reichsmarine* (German navy) for a position at the German School of Higher Learning in Tsingtau. I was told that I had been registered, but that there was no vacancy for the time being. That was as far as things progressed, because the First World War broke out in 1914. I was called up for military service in the training of infantry replacement troops in villages on the left bank of the Rhine and also on the military training grounds of the Bitche Fortress. Towards the end of the war, I was also enrolled at the military equipment office in Hanau, which was under the command of a colonel. My ranks during the war were lieutenant, then first lieutenant and finally captain.

In January 1918, after the armistice, I returned to my civilian job in Wilhelmshaven. At the outbreak of the war, my brother, like other German conscripts in China, had boarded a ship destined for Tsingtau. However, the military authorities in Tsingtau waived the recruitment of those who reported there and cancelled their enlistments. Tsingtau fell into the hands of the Japanese. The Chinese, on the other hand, were well-disposed towards the Germans at the time and refrained from any hostile actions. However, under fierce pressure from the English side, all Germans and their trading companies were expelled from China towards the end of the war. My brother was therefore also forced to return to Germany. In Gotha he resumed his former work as a *Gerichtsreferendar* (junior lawyer), but not long afterwards he registered for the second legal examination, i.e., the assessor's examination, passed it, married and settled as a lawyer in Gotha. This happened during the devastating years of inflation in Germany. The considerable savings my brother had been able to make in China disappeared rapidly and completely. So, it was only natural for him to return to China after the peace treaty. The old trade connections had been destroyed. However, because of his prior experience he found a suitable connection in another, new enterprise and travelled to China with his wife and their little first-born. My brother's second stay there was about five years; his first had lasted almost thirteen. In China, he became the father of a little girl, later followed by a second daughter.

During his first long stay in China, he had already told me (on the occasion of a holiday in his homeland) about his plan to translate the novel *Djin Ping Meh* (*Jin Ping Mei*, JPM), the most important of all Chinese novels, into German, because it had never been completely translated into an occidental language, and certainly not to a standard equal to the original. If he were indeed to embark on this undertaking, he needed – and was looking for – a collaborator. In me he found a willing helper. I immediately began to study the Chinese characters without any professional help. But this was an unusually difficult task and took many years.

When my brother had finally given up China and remained permanently in Germany as a lawyer and soon afterwards as a notary in Gotha, we energetically continued our planned work. My brother found understanding in the then respected Gotha printing house Engelhard-Reyher, that did particularly good work in the field of cartography. And so this printing house agreed to publish the first small volume of JPM, which appeared in 1928. It comprised only the first ten of the one hundred chapters that make up the entire novel. It was my brother's first work and was later revised and repeatedly improved and corrected by me and my brother. This first volume was, however, well received and widely distributed. As soon as we had finished the second volume, Chapters 11–23 of the complete novel, our publisher also accepted this for printing. Compared to the first, we succeeded in achieving a much higher quality in the

ABOUT THE LIFE OF MY BROTHER AND ME

second volume. It was published in 1932, shortly before the National Socialists came to power in Germany. There were mass public book burnings of books from all literary genres that were liberal and independent or did not seem to fit with their direction. Our Chinese novels also fell victim to the ban and the printed materials were destroyed.

It seemed that everything was lost. We got together and thought, 'What now?' We both made up our minds: 'Continue the work!' Of course, in defiance of the ban, but quietly, without drawing attention to ourselves. And so, we did. Now we were no longer under any time pressure with regard to the publication of the following parts of the novel. We translated, interpreted, and slowly and tenaciously shaped the entire work with scientific precision and thoroughness, almost up to the end of the 100th chapter, often meeting each other and consulting, but mainly through extraordinarily lively postal correspondence. For a better understanding of the whole, we also created a supplementary explanatory volume, completely new and entirely of our own making. This was the auxiliary final volume, which brings together details scattered throughout the work that require further explanation. It introduces the reader to the peculiarities, customs, traditions, history, religious and spiritual culture of Daoism and Buddhism and everything else that is worth knowing.

About this time, the Second World War broke out. My brother's son, now a young man, fell as a soldier in Russia. My wife died of heart failure in 1944. The countless bombs falling over Wilhelmshaven had taken a slow but inexorable toll on her heart and vitality. The house where my brother lived and worked in Gotha was destroyed during an air raid. Our manuscripts were saved, but lost were the Chinese pictures which, although without connection to the Chinese author of JPM, had been created in later times and proved how widely known the novel was in China and in what high esteem it was held.

When the nightmare of Nazi rule ended in 1945 with the armistice after the Second World War, the possibility of publishing the Chinese novel JPM in a translation into German opened up again. At that time, after the long years of the Nazi ban, we had calmly and without haste completed the work almost as far as the 100th chapter. Only a small part was still missing. Most importantly, our unprecedented arrangement of the explanatory notes. We needed to transform the original jumble of random notes into a well-organised and useful resource. This happened over the next few years. There was no shortage of people advising us to publish the finished translation in the Russian-occupied zone, to which Gotha also belonged and still belongs. However, the communist intention to exploit the work politically was unmistakable. That is why I refused the advice, and my brother agreed with the refusal, since in the Russian-occupied zone individual human development no longer exists.

361

ARTUR KIBAT

After 1953, my brother's health began to fail. The increasing failure of the nerves in his back forced him to become bedridden. He died in the summer of 1956 at the age of 76. He, who had provided the impetus for our many years of difficult, always scientific and complete translation, was denied the opportunity to see the printing and publication of our joint work. My task henceforth was to take care of whatever remained and, in this way, to do my best to honour his memory.

Dr. Artur Kibat

Wilhelmshaven, August 1958[1]

References

Kibat, Otto and Artur Kibat (trans.), Herbert Franke (ed.)
   1967. *Djin Ping Meh, Schlehenblüten in goldener Vase*. 5 Vols + Vol 6, with 'Commentary' by Herbert Franke. Hamburg: Die Waage.

Note on Contributors

Artur Kibat (1878–1961), teacher at a *Gymnasium* in Wilhelmshaven, Germany. Self-taught sinologist, translator with his brother Otto Kibat of the *Jin Ping Mei* edition by Zhang Zhupo, *Diyi qishu* (1695) into German as *Djin Ping Meh. Schlehenblüten in goldener Vase* (1928–1967).

---

1   *Editorial note:* The publisher of the full edition of Otto and Artur Kibat's German translation of *Jin Ping Mei*, Herbert Franke, wrote the following in the 'Commentary' Vol. 6, p. 9:

As the publisher of this great complete series of volumes by two German scholars who had worked tirelessly towards its completion for over 30 years despite the most severe political and economic adversities, without ever having the certain prospect of a worthy publication in the near future or being able to see on the horizon an economic remuneration for their work that might be somewhat commensurate to the effort involved, I, fortunately, had in time asked the surviving brother, Artur Kibat, for an account from his own pen, before he passed away in 1961 (Otto Kibat died in 1956). May this document provide scholars with reliable material on the lives and working conditions of these two extraordinary people. For the attention of those who are interested, I present here a verbatim account of Artur Kibat's autobiographical reminiscences.

Despite their best efforts, the editors have been unable to locate and make contact with the current copyright holder of the original German text that is translated in this chapter. The publisher and editors welcome being contacted by the copyright holder and undertake to add any missing attribution statement to all copies subsequently printed.

ABOUT THE LIFE OF MY BROTHER AND ME

Veronika Bauer is a teaching associate at Monash University, Melbourne, Australia. She is a German and English translator and educator. She is currently completing the Master of Interpreting and Translation at Monash University and has collaborated on historic publications such as *The Finsters – From the Beginning of the 14th Century to the Present.*

CHAPTER 22

The Strategy and Process of David Tod Roy's English Translation of *Jin Ping Mei*

DAVID L. ROLSTON

In 2013, David Tod Roy finally saw the last volume of his translation of *Jin Ping Mei* 金瓶梅 (hereafter JPM) into English appear in print from Princeton University Press (hereafter PUP). I was fortunate to have him for my advisor for the 11 years (1977–1988) that it took me to complete my graduate education and finish my dissertation (he wrote 40 pages of corrections by hand for the latter), and to have been in touch regularly with him until he died in 2016. That decade-plus during which I was his student and the following close to three decades during which he kindly thought of me as a colleague gave me a lot of insight into how he prepared for and completed his monumental translation of JPM.[1]

Before turning to Professor Roy and his translation, I beg the reader's indulgence as I provide more details about my relationship to both. Unlike some of Roy's other doctoral advisees, such as Paul Martinson, Katherine Carlitz, and Indira Satyendra, my dissertation did not include JPM in its title, but it did include two substantial sections on it (one of which I later expanded into a long article[2]). I came along too late to participate in the famous conference on Chinese narrative held in 1974 (the papers were edited by Andrew Plaks and published by PUP in 1977, see Plaks 1977), but did become involved in a project that was first broached at that conference and appeared in print as *How to Read the Chinese Novel* in 1990 from PUP (Rolston 1990). Roy and John C. Y. Wang had agreed to edit that collection of translations of 'how to read' (*dufa* 讀法) essays, but after asking perhaps too many times when the project was going to be finished, the job of editing the submissions (two from Roy) and ushering the volume into print was given to me. When the first volume of Roy's translation was under review, the same PUP editor that I had worked with for

---

1 I have also written on this topic in Chinese under my Chinese name, Lu Dawei (see Lu Dawei 陸大偉 2016).

2 An extract appears in this volume. See Chapter 6.

364

DAVID TOD ROY'S ENGLISH TRANSLATION OF *JIN PING MEI*

How to Read asked me to be one of the pre-publication reviewers. I raised the problem that my connections to Roy were rather too close, but was assured that that was not a problem and that they really wanted me to do the work; however, surely because of the problem I raised, I was not quoted on the jacket when the volume appeared. Although the other pre-publication reviewer, Andrew Plaks, had once studied under Roy while the latter was still at Princeton, that was only for a short period and he had rightly become very famous since, while my time as Roy's student was still very recent. I came into intimate contact with Roy's translation again when I published a translation of Chapter 100 designed to reproduce the effects of reading that chapter as it appears in the famous commentary edition by Zhang Zhupo 張竹坡 (1670–1698; Rolston 2014), for which Roy kindly shared his as yet unpublished version of that chapter for me to modify.

During most of the years that Professor Roy taught at the University of Chicago, it was quite unique among American universities for having more graduate than undergraduate students and for the number of small-enrollment graduate seminars that the professors were allowed to teach. Roy regularly taught graduate seminars on the *Jin Ping Mei* and on works that preceded that novel that he wanted to examine more closely as part of his translation project (this included, for instance, a three-quarter class reading 'plain tales' [*pinghua* 平話], works that he admitted were quite lacking in literary merit and apologized for making us read; I didn't mind, the paper that I turned into my Master's thesis came out of that class). Roy was extraordinarily well read in a wide variety of Chinese literature that had appeared before the JPM, but less so for those that appeared after (my choice of a Qing dynasty novel to put into the title of my doctoral thesis caused him to read that novel for the first time, which he did not resent because the experience convinced him that the JPM had been very influential with regard to it).

I took one of Roy's *Jin Ping Mei* seminars for credit and was able to sit in for a certain amount of time for two more of them.[3] The academic year was

---

3   In 2013, when his voice was still up to it (he was suffering from ALS, the disease that finally ended his life), Roy gave a series of workshops at the University of Chicago on the novel, which were video recorded. I pushed very strongly to persuade the sponsor, the Department of East Asian Literatures and Civilizations, to make the recordings widely available, but to no avail; however, Blu-Ray DVD copies can be watched in the University of Chicago Library (catalog.lib.uchicago.edu/vufind/Record/11802285). For those who would like to hear him speak about the novel and his work on it, the 2013 interview that he did with Carla Nappi after the publication of the last volume is available at newbooksnetwork.com/ david-tod-roy-the-plum-in-the-golden-vase-or-chin-ping-mei-princeton-up-1993-2013. Conferences to commemorate him were held at the University of Chicago in 1999 and

broken into quarters rather than semesters, and when I was a student there it was common for a single course to be taught over the three quarters of the regular academic year and for students to take an 'incomplete' for all of them and write up a substantial paper during the summer. Two of the JPM seminars by Roy that I attended stretched through all three quarters of an academic year, while the third actually extended into the next academic year as well. In the years that I was a graduate student, all of Roy's classes were held in his office in the three-story converted house that lodged the Department of East Asian Literatures and Civilizations. His office was one of the larger ones in the building, but it was stuffed with books, whose number was continually supplemented by new purchases at such a rate that he was unable to keep up with their processing (which involved signing and dating them and finding a place for them on his bookshelves) and instead they were piled up on the table around which the students sat, in front of his desk, and we had to lay out the stuff we needed to have access to in class on top of them. At one point the backlog got so bad and the piles got so high that we students wondered if, eventually, we would not be able to see each other across the ever rising piles of books or if we would come to class to find out that Professor Roy had ended up buried under a book avalanche. During class he loved to pull down from the shelves his copies of books that were mentioned in our discussions and pass them around; each class was a lesson in how to do scholarship in a very practical and hands-on way.

After I graduated, the department moved out of that house and into the southwest corner of the quadrangle at the very centre of campus. His books were too many for his office there and spilled out into shared space in the department. After he retired, he and his books were moved to an upstairs office in the same basic building, and then later to a building on the east side of campus, and then eventually sold or donated, a process I tried to help with as much as I could. A portion of them ended up in the collection of Notre Dame,[4] where they are integrated into the general collection rather than kept separate. While attending a conference there, I had the pleasure of guessing which ones were his and verifying my guesses by looking for his signature.

The most striking thing about Professor Roy's translation of JPM is without a doubt the amount of paratextual material that he provides. Qi Lintao has

---

at Harvard University in 2019. Papers were presented at both but were not published as conference volumes. I was honoured to give the first speech, on the topic 'What to Do with All the Sex in the *Jin Ping Mei*', at the former, but only chaired a panel at the latter.

4 A good friend and colleague in the department was a graduate of Notre Dame and made the arrangements.

provided a table listing all of the types of paratextual material in volume one of the translation, which includes the percentage of pages given over to each (2018: 117, Table 4.1). In terms of the percentage of the volume they take up, the seven biggest items are notes (13.2%), cast of characters (7.8%), illustrations (5.6%), index (5.3%), introduction (4.5%), bibliography (4.2%), and appendices (2.7%); notes come in first by a wide margin. As students, we were first introduced to Roy's interest and care with regard to annotating the novel from the handwritten notes in the order that the items glossed appeared in the photo-reprint of the earliest extant version of the novel (the one whose full title includes *cihua* 詞話[5] at the end), which were provided to us at minimal cost (see Figure 22.1 for a sample page, chosen at random).

The sample page of glosses (Figure 22.1) contains three historical/cultural notes identifying two historical figures and one place name, but the bulk of the items are either simple glosses of characters or phrases, sometimes with Romanization added, and attempts to deal with problematic characters by identifying them as phonetic or sight loans for characters that make more sense. If we compare the 54 endnotes (Roy 1993: 473n77–476n17) given in the translation for the text covered in the sample page (Roy 1993: 37–50), only the first category of notes in the sample page noted above are reflected, in expanded form, in the translation. There is no sign of the category of notes, those identifying other occurrences in the novel or pre-existing sources of the same or similar language defined by Roy to be of interest, that constitute the vast bulk of Roy's endnotes.

Professor Roy had his own personal copy of the photo-reprint (Xiaoxiao sheng 1963) and on it he kept track of both his textual emendations and text in the

---

5   When these two characters, or their expanded form of *shuochang cihua* 說唱此話, appear in the titles of other works, those works are almost always *chantefables* in which the ratio of verse to prose approaches one to one and the verse often has narrative functions. Roy discounted the appearance of *cihua* in the title of the edition of the novel that he translated (the term, for instance, is never glossed or discussed in the translation), despite the fact that the *shuochang cihua* published in the 15th century, buried in a tomb, and not rediscovered until last century, are among the sources he lists for language in the novel, published an article on formulas in them (Roy 1981), and one of his students, Gail Oman [King], translated one of the longer of them in her 1982 dissertation and the 1989 book that came out of it (King [trans.] 1989). For my own opinion on whether it is useful to consider the JPM as belonging to the genre of *cihua*, see Rolston 1994: 33–34. Vibeke Børdahl, however, in her Danish translation of the novel, recently completed, takes the appearance of *cihua* in the title of the earliest edition of JPM very seriously, as did also André Lévy, who completed an almost complete translation into French of the *cihua* edition, and according to Børdahl (2003: 303–304), gave a speech in 2002 in which he argued that the author of the novel might have been a woman because they were 'mainly used' to perform *cihua* and another *chantefable* genre, *tanci* 彈詞.

367

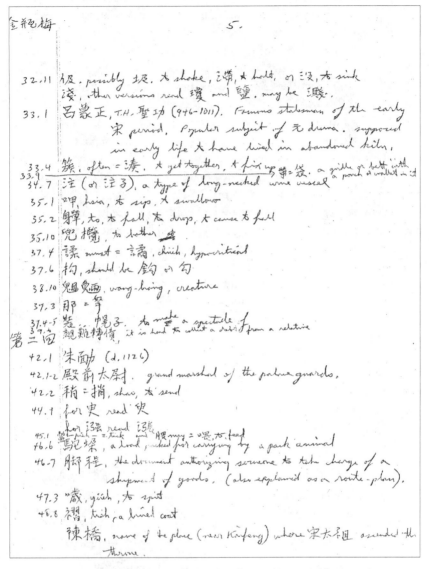

Figure 22.1. Page from handwritten notes on the JPM prepared by David Roy and distributed to his students. The numbers in the right-hand column give first the modern pagination of the photo-reprint of the novel (Xiaoxiao sheng 1963) followed by a period and then the line number. The page covers things that appear at the end of Chapter 1 and the beginning of Chapter 2.

DAVID TOD ROY'S ENGLISH TRANSLATION OF *JIN PING MEI*

novel for which he had found sources. It did not take me very long to realize how valuable that information was and I eventually persuaded him to lend his copy to me so that I could transcribe all the annotations onto my copy (see Figure 22.2; see Figure 22.3 for the corresponding pages on Roy's copy in its final form).

The text of the earliest edition of the novel is in very bad shape, either because the author never got a chance to finish or revise it, or those who prepared the edition did not know what they were doing, or both. Carefully edited and collated typeset editions of the novel only appeared much later. As someone who spent a lot of time on the novel and knew it as well as anyone, Roy's textual emendations are quite worthy of consideration by anyone seriously interested in the novel, but they are never mentioned in his endnotes to his translation.[6] His extensive work documenting where bits of text reappear in the novel and in works that predated its appearance is carefully documented in his endnotes, but those same endnotes have been underused by Chinese scholars, many of whom have been interested in such borrowings for a long time (see Rolston 1994: 15–18). It bothered me that the information on Roy's personal copy was both very valuable and inaccessible, especially to those who cannot read English.

By the time I decided it was imperative to have the personal copy scanned and made available, it had already been donated by Professor Roy to the University of Chicago East Asian Library, where it was sitting, honoured but ignored, safe but hidden out of sight. Decades of constant use had weakened the bindings of the five volumes to the point that one of Roy's graduate students who was a book binder, Charles Stone, rebound each of them, but in the process some of Roy's annotation got swallowed up in the new, tighter gutters. The then Curator of the Library, Zhou Yuan, was understandably reluctant to unbind the volumes so that good scans could be made, but after months of persuasion he gave in (Figure 22.4 shows how the rebinding obscured some of the annotation and Figure 22.5 shows the same two pages as they were scanned after the unbinding). The scans are openly accessible for downloading on the 'Ten Thousand Rooms Project' website[7] (only single images can be downloaded at

---

6   Interestingly enough, the card catalogue information for the De Gruyter Princeton University Press e-Book Package Backlist electronic copies of Vols. 2–5 lists Roy as the editor, which is true to the extent that he emended characters in the *cihua* text when he translated it. When he signed my copy of Volume 1 of his translation, Roy wrote 'with the best wishes of the author (or at least the translator)', which probably points toward the degree to which he identified with the implied author he found in the novel (on the importance of traditional commentary editions with regard to readers' increasingly sharper and more detailed conceptions of the implied authors of premodern novels, see Rolston 1997: 105–30).

7   tenthousandrooms.yale.edu/project/david-tod-roys-personal-annotated-copy-plum-golden-vase

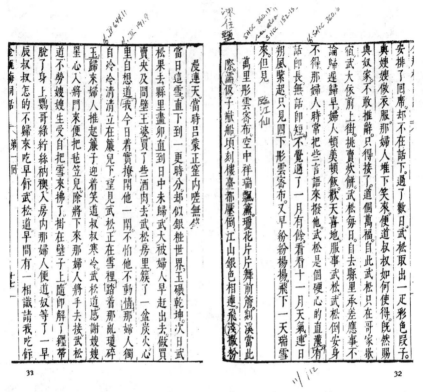

Figure 22.2. Scan of pp. 32–33 of my personal copy of Xiaoxiao sheng 1963, with some notes transcribed from Roy's copy as it looked in the 1980s. It is very likely that I did not transcribe everything that he had written on those pages, but another reason for the large disparity between the number of notes that can be seen in these two figures is that Roy kept finding new sources and annotating them. The temporal note (11/ /12 [11th month of year 12]) that appears in the bottom margin on Figure 22.2 appears in the upper margin on Figure 22.3 refers to a line that includes the news that over a month passed. This is how Roy kept track of mentions of the passing of time in the novel.

a time) and through the University of Chicago Library website[8] (there are ten files, each covering approximately one tenth of the novel). Roy kept track of the acronyms he used for sources by working up a 3 by 5 card for each (see Figure 22.6 for the first of them and Figure 22.7 for the acronym on it). These have been scanned and posted on the 'Ten Thousand Rooms Project' website (click on the 'Index Cards of Bibliographic Acronyms' button, ignore the bewildering display of the 875 jpeg files that appears, and click on any one of the jpeg files to get into a single file that you can more easily move around in).

---

8   catalog.lib.uchicago.edu/vufind/Record/10811949#

DAVID TOD ROY'S ENGLISH TRANSLATION OF *JIN PING MEI*

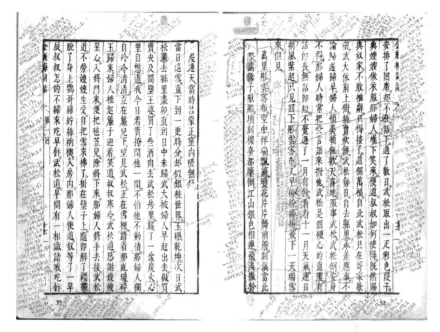

Figure 22.3. Scan of the equivalent pages in Figure 22.2 to pp. 32–33 of Roy's personal copy of the novel with annotations. Chunks of text in brackets have notes detailing the works (identified by acronyms) and pages where the same chunk of text also appears (a checkmark appears in the upper margin to make clear that a block of text has been put in brackets). Characters that Roy identified as problematic are circled and characters that should or could, he felt, replace them are given in the upper margin above them. I have highlighted the problematic characters and their replacements. These two pages show the pages that pertain to the first four items glossed in Figure 22.1. Additional problematic characters have been identified at 32.11 and 33.3 and the one originally glossed in Figure 22.1 for 33.9 is not circled or provided with a replacement.

Professor Roy is famous for the drawers of 3 by 5 cards that he compiled to help him keep track of aspects of the novel as he worked on his translation. One set of cards was compiled with one card for each chunk of language in the novel that he wanted to monitor for reoccurrences in the novel and occurrences in other texts that predated it[9] (besides indicating where in the novels these linguistic chunks or variants of them occur, no further information is provided; to see if or where Roy found occurrences in works that predated the novel, you have to consult his personal copy or the notes to his translation or the separate sets of cards he compiled for specific sources). This and all of the other sets of

---

9   This set includes almost 2300 cards. I scanned them all to preserve them but have not found an online site interested in posting them.

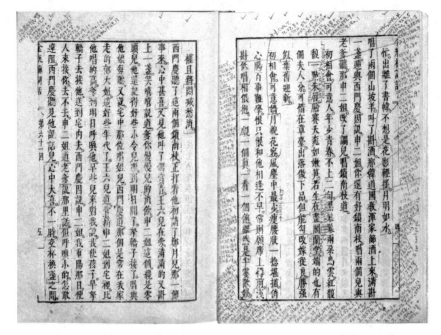

Figure 22.4. Pages 8–9 of vol. 4 of Roy's personal copy of Xiaoxiao sheng 1963, part of a set of exploratory scans that I made before the decision was made to scan the entire copy. Some of the annotation in the bottom part of the right-hand margin of p. 9 got swallowed up into the gutter when the volume was rebound.

3 by 5 cards Roy compiled as part of his work on the novel and its translation are now archived in the University of Chicago Library.[10]

Recurrences of identical or similar chunks of text were important to Roy for two reasons. One was that he thought they often purposely invited readers to compare widely separated sequences in the novel. An example would be how Pan Jinlian 潘金蓮 'sat astride Wu the Elder's body' (*qi zai Wu Da shenshang* 騎在武大身上) when she is murdering him in Chapter 5 (Xiaoxiao sheng 1963: 1, 119; Roy 1993: 107) and then 70-odd chapters later 'sat astride his [Ximen Qing's 西門慶] body' (*qi zai ta shenshang* 騎在他身上) after she has given him the overdose of his aphrodisiac that leads to his death in Chapter 79 (Xiaoxiao sheng 1963: 4, 753; Roy 2011: 638). Besides using the same language to translate

---

10 According to the copy of the 'Accession Form' I was given after Roy's 'papers' were removed to the Archives section of the University of Chicago Library, they filled 29 boxes that took up a total of 43.5 linear feet and included 65 3 by 5 card catalogue drawers with cards. Of interest to scholars will be the four boxes of correspondence. No inventory is publicly available, but one is promised if you visit the Special Collections Research Center where the cache is held (catalog.lib.uchicago.edu/vufind/Record/11560087).

DAVID TOD ROY'S ENGLISH TRANSLATION OF *JIN PING MEI*

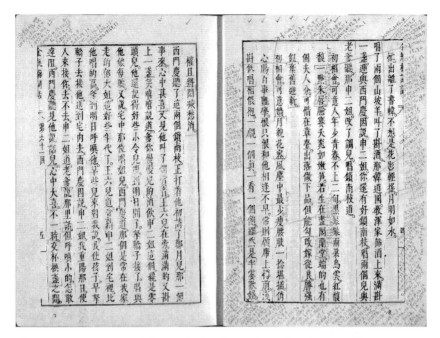

Figure 22.5. Pages 8–9 of the professional scanning of Roy's personal copy made after the volumes were unbound.

the two occurrences of the same basic language (the only difference being who she was astride), Roy also provided notes right after each of the two phrases that draw the reader's attention to how the two sequences echo each other. In the note to the earlier appearance of the phrase (Roy 1993: 487n23), Roy notes how this sequence 'foreshadows the death of Ximen Qing'[11] and in the note to the later occurrence (Roy 2011: 845, n18) he stresses how this scene 'recalls' the earlier one. Interestingly enough, the language for the two notes also include a lot of 'verbal correspondences'.

The other reason why Roy was interested in monitoring special language in the JPM was that he thought that doing so provided valuable clues as to how, he believed, the author of the novel had purposely borrowed from pre-existing works in order to set his own novel off from them by ironic contrast. The biggest such source, of course, was the *Water Margin* (*Shuihu zhuan* 水滸傳), from which came the majority of the text for the first 10 chapters.

When almost 15% of a translation is given over to endnotes, as in the case of Professor Roy's translation of JPM, it is important that the benefits of such a substantial investment are clear. This was one of my concerns when I wrote my

---

11 I have changed the Wade-Giles Romanization of the original to *pinyin*.

373

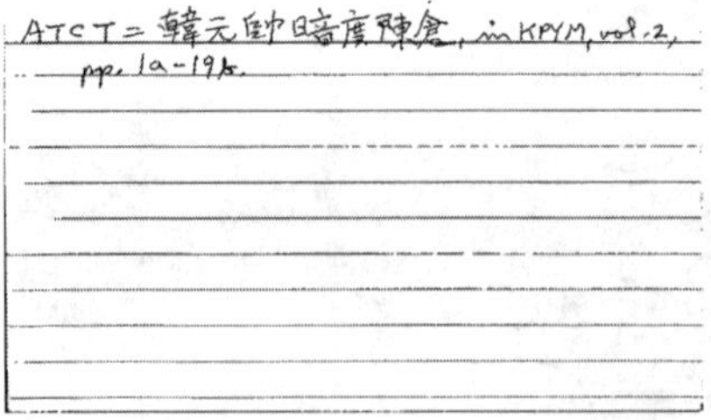

DAVID L. ROLSTON

Figure 22.6. First of 875 acronym cards made by David Roy.

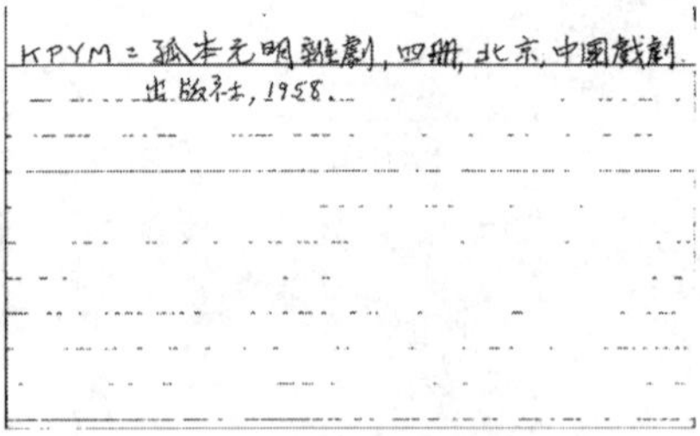

Figure 22.7. Acronym card for the acronym in the first acronym card (Figure 22.6).

pre-publication review of the first volume. I noted that the 'sheer bulk' and 'the generally dry and specialist nature of much of it [the annotation]' were problems that needed to be addressed, and it was important, for instance, to show more clearly 'the kind of relevance the annotated sources have to the reading of the novel'. Roy responded by presenting, in the notes, his annotation to the preface to the novel signed by the Master of Delight (Xinxin zi 欣欣子; he is the only writer who claimed to know the author and some have argued that he himself was the author) as a model showing the novel's use of sources and borrowed language. Unfortunately, for the reader to be exposed to that argument they had to read both the preface and its annotation (notes are skipped by a lot of readers, especially when they are hidden at the end of a volume as endnotes; prefaces are often skipped by readers and even by translators). Another way that Roy tried to justify all the scholarly apparatus of his translation was to argue that the JPM was just as complicated and worthy of such treatment, in order to be properly understood, as are James Joyce's *Ulysses* and Vladimir Nabokov's *Lolita* (Roy 1993: xlvii), but did not mention any specific examples of annotated editions of those two works. There are indeed a lot of separately published reader's guides to *Ulysses*, but no heavily annotated editions that I am aware of. An annotated edition of *Lolita*, however, appeared as early as 1970 (in the revised edition, Appel 1991, the pages devoted to the endnotes take up almost one-third of the volume).

Many reviewers of Professor Roy's translation complained about the number of endnotes in the translation and it has, indeed, been very hard to get the undergraduates to whom I assign the first volume to read for class to pay attention to them. Before Roy died I got his permission to approach PUP about doing a 'classroom' edition designed to reduce the bulk and cost so that teachers would be more likely to assign it in classes. The hope is to get the translation down to two volumes by posting almost all of the paratextual material online on PUP's website, and to convert the off-putting Wade-Giles Romanization

374

DAVID TOD ROY'S ENGLISH TRANSLATION OF *JIN PING MEI*

to the now more familiar *pinyin* system, as was done with the new edition of the Clement Egerton translation edited by Robert Hegel (Egerton 2011). I promised Roy that I would make sure that no part of the translation would be cut and will insist on that. PUP was interested but no contract has as yet been signed, and it has taken me this long to get out from other projects enough to begin to think about getting down to doing the necessary work. The plan is to keep the endnote numbers in the main text of the translation and to code both those numbers and the endnotes themselves so that the reader will know which of the notes are cultural, which list sources, and which should not be missed.

Another thing that Professor Roy did so as to indicate when the text made use of borrowed language was to use indentation. In the section in the introduction to the translation under the heading 'Creative Use of Traditional Formulaic Material', he explains that all poetry and song is indented one step (the same as for the first-line indentation for each paragraph), while the material referred to as 'traditional formulaic material' is indented two steps. To my knowledge, Roy is the only translator of traditional Chinese fiction to take this step, which he justifies by claiming that the material is used creatively and thus worthy of attention. Many reviewers just find the practice irritating or even inconsistent (by their lights), but since I personally believe that Roy's translation is the most 'transparent' (reflects most clearly the highest percentage possible of what is going on in the text), and because I also research and teach traditional Chinese drama, translations of which have traditionally used different levels of indentation to distinguish arias from poems, I personally appreciate this aspect of the transla-tion, which is heavily reliant on all the effort Roy put into tracking the circulation of such language. Some might object that of course I favour Roy's approach to the novel since I am his student and I first read the novel under his tutelage. But we did not always see eye to eye. He, for instance, stressed the idea that the novel was written by a genius who always made careful and thought-out choices in his planning and execution of his novel,[12] but I have always been more struck by how experimental and 'unperfected' the first edition of the novel was.[13] It was the

---

12 This is certainly the impression that traditional fiction commentators wanted the readers to get of the authors of the novels they commented on (see Rolston 1997: 105–30).

13 We can both, however, be considered members of the Princeton–Chicago school of 'over-reading' pre-modern Chinese fiction who have collectively valorized traditional fiction commentary, as opposed to the C. T. Hsia (of Columbia) school, which took Western fiction as the model by which to judge Chinese fiction, and whose approach could be called a school of 'under-reading' (his students, whose number includes Robert Hegel, did not tend to agree with either of those aspects of his scholarship; his 'school' was small but influential, since he was the first to write a book on the Chinese novel). Rolston 1990 and Rolston 1997 are essentially 'anti-Hsia', although he did not seem to realize that; the only

first domestic novel set within one household, the first major novel that did not originate in oral storytelling but was primarily the creation of one author (even as he chose to make extensive use of pre-existing popular literature), and the first in which dialogue (including gossip) was so important; many of the devices and approaches that would make those choices read more naturally had not yet been worked out. The author of the JPM was also quite willing to make creative use of storytelling techniques and forms from outside the genre of vernacular fiction.[14] Many of these rather anarchic aspects were toned down or eliminated in the 'illustrated' edition of the novel usually dated to the Chongzhen reign period (1627–1644), whose version of the text became the only one read until the *cihua* edition was rediscovered in the 20th century.

While 3 by 5 cards were a critical way that Professor Roy kept track of linguistic aspects of the novel as an aid to his teaching and translation of it, he used notebooks to keep track of other things, such as the appearance of characters in the novel (Figure 22.8 shows sample pages) and names that were just mentioned in the novel. The first set were surely fundamental to Roy's compilation of the 'Cast of Characters' for each volume of his translation. The idea of providing lists of characters for each volume surely derived from David Hawkes' translation of *The Story of the Stone* (*Shitou ji* 石頭記) (Hawkes [trans.] 1973, 1977),[15] but whereas Hawkes' are short and concise, one review referred to the entry in Volume 5 on Pan as a 'synopsis of the whole novel, from the perspective of Pan

---

time I got a chance to talk with him about the second book, his only comment was that the font size was too small.

14 See Rolston 1994: 27–36. *Editors' note*: the relevant sections of Rolston's (1994) paper are reprinted in this book in abbreviated form; please refer to Chapter 6 for more details.

15 Roy cites Hawkes' work on *The Story of the Stone* as a model when it comes to translating *everything* (Roy 1993: xlviii), but their use/non-use of footnotes/endnotes could not have been more different. Hawkes adds precisely four footnotes to his translations of the chapters in his first volume, three of which just point the reader to the appendix on the riddles in Chapter 5. In his preface to his second volume, he wrote that 'reading a heavily annotated novel would seem to me rather like trying to play tennis in chains' (Hawkes 1977: 18). There are times, however, when a footnote would have helped. For instance, in Chapter 1 Huo Qi 霍啓, the name of the servant whose negligence is blamed for the loss of Zhen Shiyin's 甄士隱 daughter, is translated by Hawkes as Calamity (Hawkes 1973: 61) because his name is homophonous with two characters whose names include that meaning, *huo qi* 禍起 (more literal translations would be 'Calamity Arises' or 'Source of Calamity'). The idea that any pre-modern Chinese family would be okay with having a servant named Calamity and would be glad enough to say in effect 'Come Calamity' every time they summoned him is quite 'rich'. In the other complete English translation of the novel, Huo Qi's name is just transliterated and the reader is not alerted to the pun (Yang and Yang 1994: 19), despite the fact that four other such phonetic puns in this chapter (Chapter 1) are explained in endnotes (645).

376

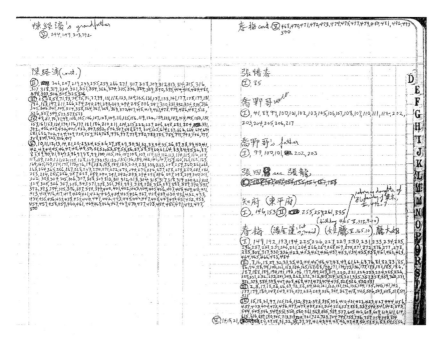

Figure 22.8. Sample pages from a notebook in which Roy kept track of the appearance of characters in the novel. The entry for Chen Jingji ends on the left-hand page, while the one for Pang Chunmei begins at the bottom of the right-hand page and concludes in the upper margin of that same page. The five volumes of Xiaoxiang 1963 are indicated by roman numerals that are circled; the Arabic numerals are the modern page numbers added by Daian.

Jinlian' (Qi Lintao 2016: 217). If we compare Roy's entries for her with that which Hawkes gives for the most important female character in the first volume of *The Story of the Stone,* Roy gives Pan Jinlian's entry for the first volume 19 lines of text (Roy 1993: lxxx; shortened to 18 lines for the other volumes), while Hawkes gives Lin Daiyu 林黛玉 only two lines (Hawkes 1973: 538; the same for the other four volumes). It has been objected that Chinese novels did not include such casts of characters, but at least one was published with such a list, several unpublished lists were compiled for *The Story of the Stone,* and many novels incorporated rosters of characters into their main texts (a famous example is the list of the 108 heroes in *Shuihu zhuan*).[16] If fact, Zhang Zhupo 張竹坡 (1670–1698) included a number of lists in the paratexts to his commentary edition of JPM, even if they are quite quirky (one is a list of Ximen Qing's sexual conquests, includes three women whom he lusted after but never succeeded in seducing, while another is of Pan Jinlian's sexual partners).

---

16 See Rolston 1990: 62 and Rolston 1997: 95.

DAVID L. ROLSTON

Dear readers, it has probably occurred to you already that nowadays electronic editions can be globally searched individually and databases such as the one for traditional Chinese popular literature provided by Erudition (Airusheng 愛如生), Zhongguo Suwen Ku 中國俗文庫, allow you to do global searches of a very large number of texts at once (this database includes an 'illustrated' edition and a Zhang Zhupo commentary edition of JPM, but not the *cihua* edition). Although many of us are not yet competent in digital humanities techniques, we have at least heard of them and of examples of their use (there has been, for instance, an attempt to establish the identity of the author of the JPM through such techniques, which, because of a paucity of searchable texts and the unique 'pastiche' nature of the novel, was not very convincing; things will improve). Professor Roy did use a computer to write his translation, but he used the same computer and software (WordPerfect) throughout, which was only kept operational through the valiant efforts of his bookbinding student, Charles Stone. He only got a new computer after the translation was finished and was never very happy with it. I can sympathize with him; I have, for instance, sworn off all use of social media until my next incarnation.

The exact methods I have described Professor Roy as having used to produce his translation, such things as handwritten notes on his copy of the novel, huge sets of 3 by 5 cards, and notebooks, certainly no longer need to be emulated when this same general effect can be produced by more electronic means. Be that as it may, his commitment to the novel and his conception of its author, his erudition, and his superb control of and use of a huge English vocabulary in order to reproduce the different tones and levels of language in the original novel should be models for us all, forever.

References

Appel, Alfred.
    1991. *The Annotated Lolita, Revised and Updated.* New York: Vintage Books.

Børdahl, Vibeke
    2003. 'Review of David Tod Roy, trans., *The Plum in the Golden Vase or, Chin P'ing Mei: Volume Two: The Rivals.*' *Acta Orientalia* 64: 303–308.

Egerton, Clement (trans.)
    2011. *Golden Lotus.* Edited by Robert E. Hegel. Rutland, VT: Tuttle Publishing.

Hawkes, David (trans.)
    1973. *The Story of the Stone, Volume One: The Golden Days.* London: Penguin Books.

1977. *The Story of the Stone, Volume Two: The Crab-Flower Club*. London: Penguin Books.

King, Gail Oman (trans.)

1989. *The Story of Hua Guan Suo*. Tempe, AZ: The Center for Asian Studies, Arizona State University.

Lu Dawei 陸大偉 (David L. Rolston)

2016. 'Rui Xiaowei Yingyi *Jin Ping Mei cihua* de celüe yu jingguo 芮效衛英譯《金瓶梅詞話》的策略與經過' [The strategy and process of the translation of *The Plum in the Golden Vase* by David Tod Roy]. *Jin Ping Mei yanjiu* 金瓶梅研究 [Studies on the *Jin Ping Mei*] 12: 13–22.

Oman, Gail

1982. 'A Study of *Hua Guan Suo zhuan*: A Prosimetric Narrative Printed in 1478'. University of Chicago doctoral thesis.

Plaks, Andrew H. (ed.)

1977. *Chinese Narrative: Critical and Theoretical Essays*. Princeton: Princeton University Press.

Qi, Lintao.

2016. 'Review of David Tod Roy, trans., *The Plum in the Golden Vase or, Chin P'ing Mei: Volume Five: The Dissolution*.' *Chinese Literature: Essays, Articles, and Reviews* 38: 214–18.

2018. *Jin Ping Mei English Translations: Texts, Paratexts, and Contexts*. London and New York: Routledge.

Rolston, David L.

1994. 'Oral Performing Literature in Traditional Chinese Fiction: Nonrealistic Usages in the *Jin Ping Mei Cihua* and Their Influence.' *CHINOPERL Papers* 17: 1–110.

1997. *Traditional Chinese Fiction and Fiction Commentaries: Reading and Writing Between the Lines*. Stanford: Stanford University Press.

Rolston, David L. (trans.)

2014. 'The Number One Marvelous Book: *Jin Ping Mei*, commented by Zhang Zhupo from Pengcheng [Xuzhou], Chapter 100.' *Renditions* 81–82: 85–128.

Rolston, David L. (ed.)

1990. *How to Read the Chinese Novel*. Princeton: Princeton University Press.

Roy, David Tod

1981. 'The fifteenth-century *Shuo-chang Tz'u-hua* as examples of written formulaic composition.' *CHINOPERL Papers* 10: 97–128.

Roy, David Tod (trans.)

1993. *The Plum in the Golden Vase or, Chin P'ing Mei. Volume One: The Gathering*

Xiaoxiao sheng 笑笑生

1963. *Jin Ping Mei cihua* 金瓶梅詞話. Tokyo: Daian.

Yang Xianyi and Gladys Yang (trans.)

1994. *A Dream of Red Mansion*. Vol. 1. Beijing: Foreign Languages Press.

Note on Contributor

David L. Rolston is Professor of Chinese Language and Literature in the Department of Asian Languages and Cultures at the University of Michigan. After working and publishing on traditional Chinese fiction (with an emphasis on traditional Chinese fiction commentary), he turned his attention primarily to traditional Chinese theatre in general and *Jingju* (Peking opera) in particular.

CHAPTER 23

The Architecture of Ximen Qing's Residence

Visualizing the General Layout and Translating it into a European Language and Culture

Lucie Olivová

This article is not a scholarly piece about architecture; it is, rather, an essay built up from observations and reflections on how the design and shape of the Ximen 西門 residence are presented in the novel *Jin Ping Mei* 金瓶梅, and how they can be made intelligible to readers from a different cultural background living centuries later. I am using the *Jin Ping Mei cihua* 金瓶梅詞話 version (the so-called A edition) as my principal text source (*Jin Ping Mei cihua* 1981). The set of 200 woodcut illustrations from the Chongzhen 崇禎 edition constitute another important source. Many of them show partial views of various buildings seen from outside and projecting inside. I have decided to ignore them because I am mainly interested in the general layout of the residence and the role it plays in the plot. The illustrations reveal how the individual structures looked, but that is not relevant to my concerns here. Besides, what they show is the product of the illustrator's imagination, however familiar the illustrator was with late Ming architecture. Last but not least, without the proper expertise on Ming book illustration, I would rather not investigate them.

The novel needs no introduction in the context of this miscellany. It is generally agreed that, on the surface at least, it tells the story of the Ximen family and household. However, the architecture of the mansion receives little attention, unlike, for example, food and clothing. Occasionally, there are detailed descriptions of particular interiors, usually from the perspective of a visiting outsider astonished by their luxuriousness. In Chapter 67, Ximen Qing's study inside the Hidden Spring Pavilion (*Cangchunge* 藏春閣) is typically described in the following way:

381

During the winter months, Ximen Qing spent his leisure time in the studio in the Hidden Spring Pavilion.[1] On the surface of the bed frame over the *kang*, which was heated by an underground firebox, there was also a brazier of yellow brass. Warmth was retained in the room by a hanging portiere of thin oiled silk, decorated with a motif of the moon amid the plum branches. The outer parlour was embellished with an oleander, a variety of chrysanthemums.

> Cool slender bamboos, and
> Turquoise-hued orchids.
> The studio itself was furnished with:
> Brushes, inkstones, and a plum in a vase;
> Zither and books were elegantly displayed.
> On the bed frame over the *kang* there were:
> A madder red strip of felt lying on top of,
> A brocade mat figured with silver flowers.
> The pillow was decorated with water birds;
> The hanging curtains were of mermaid silk.[2]

> (*The Plum in the Golden Vase or, Chin P'ing Mei.*
> *Volume Four: The Climax* 2011: 175)

Such glimpses of a few interiors do not, however, compensate for the lack of an overall portrayal of the residence (*zhai* 宅), neither do they gratify the reader who seeks some basic sense of orientation. With all due respect, facts about the architectural setting seem deficient, and the topic has consequently remained relatively understudied. Those scholars who have taken an interest in the architecture of the residence have usually focused on the garden alone and, unsurprisingly, approached it from the literary criticism point of view. An exception is Mary Scott (1986) who attempted a remarkable reconstruction of the layout of the residence, despite the fact that the information that can be extracted from the novel is meagre, fragmentary, and scattered across the text. Independently of Scott, in his monograph Meng Qingtian (2001: 159–199) presented the residence as well as a number of other houses, gaudy and plain, where the plot took place. He selected and cited the relevant passages and created plans for some of the houses. Both Scott and Meng paid a lot of attention to the garden and compared it with the garden dwelling in the novel *Honglou meng* 紅樓夢. An online article from the same year (2021), written under the pseudonym Cyber (Cyber 2021), relates Ximen Qing's 西門慶 garden to the

---

1 In D. T. Roy's translation the name is rendered as 'the Hidden Spring Grotto'; however, the grotto (*Cangchunwu* 藏春塢) and the pavilion were probably two separate buildings. See Sun Xun and Wei Tongxian 1993, 901 and 902.

2 A passage from chapter 67, translated by David T. Roy, with my editing.

horticultural aesthetics of the late Ming. Descriptions of general building types and also of some particular buildings from the novel are provided in the dictionary compiled by Sun Xun and Wei Tongxian (Sun Xun and Wei Tongxian 1993: 898–907).

Gradual Introduction of the Residence

The large walled residence consisted of *two* entities: a mansion with a garden beside it. They were juxtaposed not only in terms of architecture but also in terms of the contents of the novel, as is known. In the next paragraph, I shall summarize the facts about the mansion as they emerge during the plot. Immediately after his first appearance in Chapter 2, readers learn who Ximen Qing is, and that he is rich, spoilt and influential. It is not explicitly stated what kind of a house he lives in, but it is naturally assumed that it is a very fine one. In the opening chapters of the novel, the plot unfolds elsewhere. Then, at the beginning of Chapter 7, Auntie Wang 王 is looking for Ximen Qing in his home, but she only makes it to the gate. In the apothecary's, located in the front of the residence, she is told where to find Ximen Qing, and goes away. It is not until the end of Chapter 7 that readers get a glimpse of it. Ximen Qing's bride Meng Yulou 孟玉樓 leaves her former dwelling in an uproar and enters the safety of her new home. She is given a suite of three rooms in the west wing (*xixiang fang sanjian* 西廂房三間) to live in. Chinese readers readily understood the circumstances and there was no need to go into explanations or details. Not being the principal wife, she lived in a building on the side (*xiang* 廂), and this building was oblong, of a regular size, numbering three rooms. Nothing specific about Ximen Qing's residence has been communicated at this point. Only when the fifth wife, Pan Jinlian 潘金蓮, moves there, in Chapter 9, does the reader learn – through the description of her luxurious room – that the whole residence must be very opulent. In this vein, one discovers the house gradually, and learns more about it step by step. This gradational mode of getting beyond the entrance gate and randomly entering first one place and then another may be intentional, but it also means that there is no systematic description of the Ximen residence, as if the author always assumes that the reader already knows or can easily imagine what it is like. Descriptions of the residence emerge in fragments, depending on the plot, or due to the author's desire to reveal some stunning details about a particular interior. Finally, the spatial setting plays a specific role in the structural symmetry of the plot; as observed by Plaks (1987: 75), the opening and the closing twenty chapters happen outside the residence, whereas the core of the narrative takes place within.

LUCIE OLIVOVÁ

The Mansion

Despite this method of presentation, scholars have succeeded in reconstructing the shape of the residence, taking advantage of certain general rules that applied to the housing of the better off during the late Ming. It is therefore accepted that the Ximen mansion was a compound laid out in the traditional, symmetrical, courtyard style.[3] With seven bays (*jian* 間)[4] across the front, it was wider than an average dwelling, which would have had five or three bays, and it had four, five or perhaps six courtyards (*yuan* 院) in sequence. As such, it was quite large by everyday standards, but not quite large enough given the number of its residents, including the many servants.

The main gate opened onto the first courtyard. On the left (west), and the right (east) sides, there were stables and servants' quarters, and on the opposite side there was the ceremonial gate (*yimen* 義門) leading to the next courtyard. This second court was dominated by a large reception hall (*dating* 大廳), which occupied the whole of the building on its north side. To the west it was flanked by Ximen Qing's study (*shufang* 書房), and to the east by the apartment of his son-in-law Chen Jingji 陳經濟. This part of the front of the residence was designed for the social use of male residents, whereas the adjoining courtyards in the rear of the compound were residential. This arrangement is standard and corresponds with the classification of outer (*wai* 外) and inner (*nei* 內) spaces; in the novel, however, the terms 'front' (*qian* 前) and 'rear' (*hou* 後) are preferred when referring to the outer and inner parts of the residence. Consequently, the reception hall is also frequently called 'the front room' (*qianting* 前廳), the apartment of Wu Yueniang 吳月娘 is also called 'the rear apartment' (*houfang* 後房), etc. It may be noted that there is a lateral passage or lane (*jiadao* 夾道) running on the side of the outer, or front walled area, making it possible to reach the private quarters without going through the front courtyards, and so without being seen there. Servants use this passage on various errands and, as one would expect, characters engaging in some kind of debauchery also take advantage of this hidden shortcut (e.g. Song Huilian 宋惠蓮 in Chapter 23, or Ximen Qing in Chapter 78).

Separated by a second ceremonial gate (*yimen* 義門) is the part of the house inhabited by women, which no male visitor (except family members) was supposed to enter. Ying Bojue 應伯爵, a close friend of Ximen Qing, repeatedly asks him for permission to go inside in order to pay respects to the First Lady,

---

3   The basic description presented further agrees with Scott 1986: 83–84.

4   *Jian* means the distance between two columns, it is commonly translated as 'bay' or, in this case, 'bay width'.

384

THE ARCHITECTURE OF XIMEN QING'S RESIDENCE

and he is repeatedly denied it; she is also very reluctant to receive Doctor Ren 任 in her apartment when he comes there to check on her health (Chapter 75).[5] Just like the other buildings in this residence (or any other residence, in fact), her apartment was a suite of three rooms, entered via the central room (*mingjian* 明間). The central room was used as a living room, while the side rooms (*wu* 屋, also *cijian* 次間), equipped with a built-in heating system (*kang* 炕), were used as bedrooms. Being the dwelling of the principal wife, Wu Yueniang's apartment displayed its special status in the household hierarchy by its south-facing position on the central axis of the residence, and also by its size. The central room was big enough to accommodate all female relatives and visitors during performances by Buddhist nuns and during other festivities. Last but not least, her apartment was frequently referred to as 'the principal apartment' (*shangfang* 上房), i.e. the apartment belonging to the woman of the highest status (Sun Xun and Wei Tongxian 1993: 899). The second and third wives of Ximen Qing lived in individual apartments on the east and west sides of the third courtyard. The lateral position of these apartments reflected the family hierarchy, as was usual in large traditional houses. The fourth wife, Sun Xue'e 孫雪娥, formerly a servant, lived in the rear courtyard near the main kitchen. Her lowly position among the other wives was clearly indicated by the location of her quarters; it was also her duty to run the kitchen and supervise the cooking.

It is possible to sketch the rough layout of the mansion, although the reconstruction is of necessity tentative and imprecise because the information we have is incomplete, and what is said is not always clear. When it comes to specifics, various questions arise that cannot be readily answered. For instance, how many courtyards were there? Is the second courtyard a part of the garden, as Scott (1986: 84) and sodeog.com (2020) claim, or not? Consequently, did 'the open-sided pavilion' (*juanpeng* 捲棚)[6] stand in the courtyard behind the reception room, or in the garden? The answers are at best unclear, and it has to be accepted that there are gaps in what is known.

The Garden

The garden is more difficult to reconstruct than the mansion. The mansion followed the customary arrangement for houses. The design of the garden, however, was based on abstract principles: a garden was a formalized representation of nature with all its irregularities. Each garden was unique; there

---

5   A similar situation also occurs in Chapter 54, when Doctor Ren examines one of the wives.

6   As translated by Scott 1986: 84.

was no generally accepted plan to rely on. Therefore, any reconstruction of Ximen Qing's garden and its layout is hypothetical. It is nevertheless assumed that the garden was located to the west of the front part of the mansion area. Visitors would have entered it through the main entrance in the west side of the first courtyard. A small side or lateral gate (*jiaomen* 角門) located in the back linked it to the courtyard inhabited by the first, second and third wives, possibly on the level of the inner ceremonial gate. Within the whole residence, the garden occupied a space in the front, alongside the front part of the house; the apartment of Pan Jinlian is consequently referred to as 'the front apartment' (*qianfang* 前房), much to the confusion of readers, I daresay. Relatively early in the story, the garden was enlarged. It was first merged with the neighbouring property (Chapter 14), and then redesigned (Chapter 16). This only took six months. At this point, we know roughly what kind of buildings there were,[7] and we know where some of them stood in relation to others. Nevertheless, the place remains a kaleidoscope of garden architecture, the components of which cannot be unambiguously put together. In the novel, there are two remarkable depictions of the garden, although they do not really help to clarify its layout. One lengthy passage, numbering 1045 characters, occurs in Chapter 19 after the reconstruction had been completed. On this occasion, the First Lady invited the other wives to take a stroll there. The description, it may be said, is relatively complex. Buildings are conveniently referred to by their names, specific flowers and plants are admired, and the atmosphere of the place is convincingly captured. The second comparable passage occurs in Chapter 96, when Chunmei 春梅 (once Pan Jinlian's maid but now the concubine of commandant Zhou Xiu 周休) comes to visit her former 'home'. It is her wish to go into the garden, which was no longer being used then and had fallen into a state of dilapidation. The neglect and gloomy atmosphere are viewed as if through her eyes.

Plans of the Ximen Residence

It is helpful to draw a plan in order to understand the arrangement of the residence. I was able to compare three, one published in the book by Meng Qingtian (2001: 182) and two posted on the websites sodeog.com (2020) and zhuanlan.zhihu.com (see Cyber 2021), respectively. They agree on many points but disagree on many others. Their approaches also differ. Meng Qingtian drew a simplified layout, strictly based on the facts mentioned in the novel; he

---

7   Despite the fancy appearance of garden buildings, their basic structure was not different from that of ordinary houses (Keswick 1978: 117).

THE ARCHITECTURE OF XIMEN QING'S RESIDENCE

did not, however, include the lateral passage leading from the main gate to the women's quarters. Zhuanlan.zhihu.com tried to reconstruct the residence in more detail, and therefore could not avoid a certain amount of invention, although within the rules of Ming vernacular architecture. Somewhere between is sodeog.com, neither sparse nor too detailed, but with some extraordinary deviations from the general conception of the residence. First of all, on the sodeog.com plan, the garden is located in the eastern part of the residence. This seems wrong. It is possible to deduce its orientation from Chapter 14, when Hua Zixu's 花子虛 valuables were transferred, on the advice of Wu Yueniang, over the west wall into the Ximen garden. The story evolves in the Ximen residence; it is therefore assumed that the narrator views the situation from there. If that is correct, then the garden must have been laid out to the west of the residence. Next, on the sodeog.com plan the garden merges into the mansion; this assumption is questionable, too. As Scott (1986: 84) observed, the courtyard behind the main reception hall was part of the original garden. This does not imply, however, that the courtyard had not been separated from the reconstructed garden by a wall. In Chapter 96, Wu Yueniang had to fetch keys to open the side gate and enter the garden, so evidently the mansion and the garden were separated. All the plans show the garden with straight borders. In theory, garden perimeters had no typical shape, but the new Ximen garden occupied the area of a former house, which explains its straight borders. This fact also has implications for the size of the garden. It must have been quite large, but not extending beyond the front part of the Ximen mansion. In this respect, Meng Qingtian's version, with the garden stretching along the full depth of the mansion, seems exaggerated.

As for the mansion, Meng presents a simplified layout with four courtyards, while the other two versions have six. They place one between the main reception hall and the inner ceremonial gate, and the other additional courtyard is at the rear of the mansion. Zhuanlan.zhihu has the fifth courtyard with Sun Xue'e's dwelling, the kitchen and the kitchen garden, including the Hibiscus Kiosk (*Furongting* 芙蓉亭) on an elevation. In the sixth courtyard there are bungalows for female servants, and also a back gate leading outside (*houmen* 後門). Sodeog.com has the fifth courtyard with Sun Xue'e's dwelling on the axis and two unspecified dwellings on each side. Such an arrangement does not, however, fit with Sun Xue'e's lowly position. In the sixth courtyard, there are the kitchen, bungalows for female servants, and the back gate. Meng Qingtian has no back gate, although it is spoken of at least 40 times in the novel. It may be mentioned in passing that the Hibiscus Kiosk stands in the grounds of the garden in the other two versions: close to the kitchen in Meng Qintian's plan, but in a remote part of the garden in sodeog.com (2020). Sun Xun and Wei

Tongxian (1993: 899) claim that the Hibiscus Kiosk stood in a garden at the back of the residence. These inconsistencies only confirm how little we know about the placement of the garden buildings, as noticed above. One could argue that the author wished the garden to be enigmatic.

Hidden Meaning

Together with the ostentatious display of wealth, the image of the Ximen residence yields many associations. Foremost, it resembles a courtesan's house. As Li Hsiao-t'i wrote, the rooms and courts in the house of the famous Ming courtesan Li Daniang were of extreme splendour; inside, the music and singing were performed nonstop (Li Hsiao-t'i 2008: 87). A corridor ran through the mansion of another famous courtesan (ibid.), possibly a kind of the passage *jiadao* mentioned earlier. Ximen Qing's guests, and the readers, too, would perceive the setting in this way.

The division of the residence into two contrasted parts, a mansion and a garden, provides ample material for symbolism. Many odd things happened in the mansion, but it was organized more or less according to normal rules.[8] The garden, on the other hand, becomes the place where Confucian norms were violated, both literally and in other ways; it was the place of bureaucratic bribery (e.g. Chapter 49) and inappropriate sex (e.g. Chapter 27).

It is worth noting that the garden does not have a name; the ponds and mounds, which represent the chief elements of garden design, *shan shui* 山水, remain nameless, too. In contrast, the sumptuous and elegant buildings are identified by names. This conveys an impression that this garden was not created in admiration of nature, but in appreciation of artificial worldly gains.

Rather than in the women's quarters, Ximen Qing had his two favourite concubines, Pan Jinlian and Li Ping'er 李瓶兒, accommodated in the garden. Each one stayed in a storeyed pavilion, on the upper floor of which there were repositories of items from Ximen Qing's shops in the front of the house: the apothecary's and the pawnshop, respectively. Medicines allude to the untimely end of Ximen Qing (Chapter 79) and pawned valuables allude to the riches transferred over the wall from Hua Zixu's neighbouring estate (Chapter 14), the same estate where the new garden was built. Hua Zixu was the deceased husband of Li Ping'er, whose ill fate and ultimate death she caused indirectly

---

8   One of the oddities was accommodating Chen Jingji and his wife, i.e. the son-in-law and the daughter of the master of the house, in the outer part of the residence. They moved into the inner part, as was appropriate, as late as Chapter 83, when the First lady Wu Yueniang tried to get things in the house under control.

THE ARCHITECTURE OF XIMEN QING'S RESIDENCE

(Chapter 14), whereas Pan Jinlian murdered her husband with her own hands (Chapter 5).

These evil doings opened the garden to them, and the taint of evil lingers over it. The place is doomed, like the Emperor Huizong's 徽宗 park on Gen Yue 艮嶽 hill, which Ximen Qing possibly emulated, and which was repeatedly referred to in the novel, e.g. in Chapter 70. The extravagance of the emperor was dearly paid for, just as were the violations of moral codes Ximen Qing committed. In Chapter 77, Ximen Qing pays a visit to his new colleague and protégé He Yongshou 何永壽 who has just bought a residence in the town and is about to move there with his family. They inspect the place together. Finally arriving in the back yard, they discover a garden pavilion standing in an empty, devastated space. On Ximen Qing's advice, He Yongshou decides to reconstruct the garden. He Yongshou is one of the few pure characters in the novel, and his plan to have the garden reconstructed alludes to the possible moral restoration of society. Nonetheless, He Yongshou is a secondary character, and readers never find out what happened with his house and his garden.

Remarks on Translating Building Terminology

Together with my colleague Ondřej Vicher, we are currently translating the novel *Jin Ping Mei* into Czech.[9] In the course of our work, we are facing various challenges, and not only ones relating to architecture (Olivová and Vicher 2022). Since I am addressing readers in English here, I will not dwell on the problems arising from the nature of the two languages, the source language, Chinese, and the target language, Czech. Rather, I shall focus on the problems created by different cultural background and habits and try to explain them in English. In fact, the very word 'house' presents a challenge when used in a translation. There is a significant difference between what constitutes 'house'/'home' in Chinese architecture, and what it means in European terms. In the Czech tradition, house (*dům*) means a single building, large or small. In sharp contrast, the traditional Chinese house (*siheyuan* 四合院) is made up of several courtyards arranged along a central axis, with small single buildings surrounding one or more square and oblong courts (Olivová 2008: 82–85). In other words, the traditional house is a compound composed according to given rules that Europeans are usually not familiar with. It would therefore be misleading to use the word *dům* (Eng. *a*

---

9   Specifically, we are translating the last 30 chapters of the novel, following up with the translation of 70 chapters (*Jin Ping Mei aneb Slivoň ve zlaté váze* 2012–2018) by Oldřich Král, who passed away leaving his project unfinished. Volume 8 in our translation is to be published in Autumn 2022; volumes 9 and 10 will follow later.

house), and the expression 'residence' is a better choice, because it implies a large layout as well as wealth. The neutral 'dwelling' is also a possibility, as well as the term 'atrium house', which is, however, a specific term borrowed from classical Roman culture. Despite similarities, it is not the exact equivalent of *siheyuan*, and in fact may, if anything, confuse better-informed readers.

Separate buildings, standing independently around the Chinese courtyard, are translated according to their usage and particular context. Each wife of Ximen Qing had her private building (*fang* 房, also *fangwu* 房屋), be it a suite of three rooms or something more substantial. There is no need to go into details. It may be rendered as *příbytek* (Eng. *dwelling*), or *apartmá* (Eng. *apartment*), none of which has quite the meaning of the source language. Similarly, the seemingly unobtrusive word 'door' (*men* 門) can, in the Chinese tradition, mean not only 'door' (i.e. an opening in a wall) but also 'gatehouse', representing a building. In the Czech architectural tradition, however, the word *dveře* (Eng. *door*) or *brána* (Eng. *gate*) implies merely the opening in the wall, equipped with one or more door leaves, regardless of its size. In the novel, characters often stand or hide inside a *men* 門, something hard for a Czech reader to imagine. This can be solved with the help of the word 'vestibule' which may be understood as a small anteroom. (But it can also be understood as a large hall, for example in a palace. The context should be of assistance in this case.) When it comes to specialist terms, there are many cases and options. Take the word *yimen* 義門, literally 'the gate of righteousness', which is an ornamental gate, but still a common structure. It is so called because righteousness is one of the chief Confucian principles to which a family, and an individual too, must adhere. The term *yimen* is generally known to a Chinese reader, but for the foreign reader unfamiliar with Chinese traditional architecture it creates doubts; the term 'righteousness' seems exaggerated in an ordinary household. We therefore render it as *slavnostní* brána (Eng. *ceremonial gate*), a term that is descriptive and implies the status of such a gate as well as its decoration.

In addition, the principal apartment, where the mistress of the house Wu Yueniang lived, is frequently referred to as *houfang* 後房, i.e., 'the back dwelling', or *zadní příbytek* in Czech. This expression sounds a little awkward; it implies something lowly and not quite dignified. We therefore translate it as 'the apartment of the First Lady' or 'the principal apartment'. It is helpful to explain the peculiarities of Chinese housing tradition to the readers in the foreword, as we have done for Volume 8, or even to provide them with a plan of a traditional Chinese house, as we have not done, since the reconstruction of Ximen Qing's residence remains partly hypothetical.

Garden architecture presents another challenge. In the novel, there are various structures called *lou* 樓, *ge* 閣, *xuan* 軒, *ting* 亭, *juanpeng* 卷棚, etc. In

THE ARCHITECTURE OF XIMEN QING'S RESIDENCE

technical terms, both *lou* and *ge* are storeyed buildings, *xuan* is an exposed building located on high ground (Guo Qinghua 2002: 86), *ting* a small pavilion for respite and the appreciation of views (ibid.: 79) and *juanpeng* is a pavilion with a roof that sweeps smoothly over the entire space, without any ridge (ibid.: 50). However, in the novel, the term *ge* is used for ground-floor structures, as in the case of the Hidden Spring Pavilion, mentioned earlier. There seems to be an adequate counterpart for *xuan* in European garden architecture, namely 'gloriette', which is also an exposed building located on high ground, supported by columns but no walls. We did not use this term, first because it evokes the European baroque garden and secondly because Ximen Qing's study, called the Kingfisher Pavilion (*Feicuixuan* 翡翠軒), the interior of which is described through Ying Bojue's eyes in Chapter 34, undoubtedly had walls. Overall, Vicher and I looked for Czech terms from garden architecture that did not sound too technical and were not limited to European gardens. We tried to use general, commonly-used Czech terms for garden houses, synonyms like *pavilonek* (Eng. *pavilion*), *altánek* (Eng. *kiosk*) or *besídka* (Eng. *arbour*), sometimes in a roundabout way, e.g. 'summer pavilion' to indicate an open-sided building. Finally, garden buildings were given fanciful names.[10] For example, the large pavilion (*juanpeng*), which embodied Ximen Qing's wealth and social pretensions, was called the Hall of Assembled Scenic Views (*Jujingtang* 聚景堂). Typically, the 'Assembled Scenic Views' do not create as much problems as the term *tang* 堂 does. To Chinese readers, *tang* at once indicates that this was the principal hall, but it does not have a proper equivalent in European architecture or, in fact, culture.

References

Guo Qinghua

> **2002.** *A Visual Dictionary of Chinese Architecture*. Victoria: Images Publishing Group.

Jin Ping Mei cihua 金瓶梅詞話

> **1981.** Wang Han 王寒, Gao Shuo 高碩, Qin Zhen 秦蓁 and Ling Yin 凌殷 (eds). 3 vols. Taibei: Zengnizhi wenhua shiye.

Jin Ping Mei aneb Slivoň ve zlaté váze

> **2012–2018.** Translated by Oldřich Král. 7 vols. Lásenice: Maxima.

---

10 For the sake of the unity of the complete Czech translation, we (Ondřej Vicher and Lucie Olivová) took over most of the fanciful names which our predecessor O. Král had already chosen.

Keswick, Maggie

1978. *The Chinese Garden: History, Art, and Architecture.* New York: Rizzoli International Publications.

Li Hsiao-t'i

2008. 'Bidding Farewell to Late Ming Nanjing: Literary Accounts of Politics, Pleasure and Disruption.' In Olga Lomová (ed.). *Paths Toward Modernity.* Praha: The Karolinum Press, pp. 61–97.

Meng Qingtian 孟庆田

2001. *Honglou meng he Jin Ping Mei zhong de jianzhu* 红楼梦和金瓶梅中的建筑 (Architecture in *Honglou meng* and *Jin Ping Mei.*) Qingdao: Qingdao chubanshe.

Olivová, Lucie

2008. *Tradiční čínská architektura.* Praha: Dokořán.

Olivová, Lucie and Ondřej Vicher

2022. 'On Translating *Jin Ping Mei* into Czech.' In Lintao Qi and Shani Tobias (eds.), *Encountering China's Past: Translation and Dissemination of Classical Chinese Literature.* Singapore: Springer, pp. 207–232.

Plaks, Andrew H.

1987. *The Four Masterworks of the Ming Novel. Ssu ta ch'i shu.* Princeton, N.J.: Princeton University Press.

The Plum in the Golden Vase or, Chin P'ing Mei. Volume Four: The Climax

2011. Translated by David T. Roy. Princeton, N.J.: Princeton University Press.

Scott, Mary

1986. 'The image of the garden in *Jin Ping Mei* and *Hongloumeng.*' *Chinese Literature: Essays, Articles, Reviews (CLEAR)* 8(1/2) (July): 83–94.

sodeog.com (Qinhetangyx)

2020. *Ximen Qing jia pingmiantu* 西门庆家平面图 (The ground plan of Ximen Qing's house). Shuang ou wang 双偶网. Available at www.tspweb.com/key/西门庆家平面图.html

Sun Xun 孫遜 and Wei Tongxian 魏衕賢 (eds)

1993. *Jin Ping Mei jianshang cidian* 金瓶梅鑒賞辭典 (*Jin Ping Mei* Appreciation Dictionary). Shanghai: Shanghai guji chubanshe.

Cyber

2021. 西门庆的书房: 是附庸风雅, 还是真有讲究? – 从西门庆的造园看明人的生活情趣及工匠精神. (Ximen Qing's study, frivolous or truly elegant? Lifestyle and the craftsman spirit of the Ming people seen from Ximen Qing's garden creation). zhuanlan.zhihu.com 知乎专栏. Available at zhuanlan.zhihu.com/p/367343383

Note on Contributor

Lucie Olivová is Associate Professor in the Department of Chinese Studies, Masaryk University, Czech Republic. Main interests: art and culture in late imperial China. Translator of *Jin Ping Mei cihua* (1617) into Czech.

CHAPTER 24

Jin Ping Mei in the World
Its Translation into Foreign Languages

WU GAN
Translated by Celine Zhijie Ren and Daniel Haocheng Cui

The 16th century Ming dynasty vernacular novel *Jin Ping Mei* is a monumental work in Chinese literary history. The novel was first translated into Manchu in 1708. Since then, *Jin Ping Mei* has been translated into over 20 languages. The rediscovery of the first edition of the novel, the *cihua* 詞話 edition of 1617 in the 1930s brought about a series of fruitful research publications by renowned scholars such as Zheng Zhenduo 鄭振鐸 and Wu Han 吳晗. In the mid-20th century, a publication wave of *Jin Ping Mei* in Taiwan and Hong Kong turned that region into the third centre of *Jin Ping Mei* Studies, after Japan and Euro-America. The open publication of *Jin Ping Mei* in Mainland China in the 1980s then gave rise to a gradual flourishing of studies on the novel there, duly establishing China as the leader of *Jin Ping Mei* studies. The translation of the Chinese novel into other languages, which is carried out by sinologists around the world, is an integral part of the scholarship on *Jin Ping Mei*. The recent addition of the Danish translation to an ever-expanding roster is another important step in the global dissemination and reception of the novel.

Written in the Ming dynasty, the vernacular novel *Jin Ping Mei* (also known as *The Golden Lotus* or *The Plum in the Golden Vase*; hereafter JPM) is a milestone in China's literary history. The book received praise from intellectuals as soon as it began to circulate in manuscript. Yuan Hongdao 袁宏道, a literatus and the head of the Gong'an school of writing, praised what he read as 'pages full of an erotic haze' (*yunxia manzhi* 雲霞滿紙), and as greatly superior to Mei Sheng's *Qifa'* 七发 (Seven Stimulations). Xie Zhaozhe 謝肇淛, a Ming dynasty scholar of wide learning and interests, commented that the novel contains

[the state of government affairs in the capital and the provinces,] connections between the official and the private, intimate exchanges in the boudoir, vulgar gossip in the market place; and, what is more, obsequious and profit-seeking conduct, winning, losing, and gloating mentalities, a fin-de-siècle promiscu-

JIN PING MEI IN THE WORLD

ity, conversations at drinking parties and in bedrooms, the imperious temperaments of traders and merchants, women ingratiating themselves with their beautiful looks, frequenters of brothels and sycophants fawning for favours, and servants and maids bickering and quibbling. All of the portrayals are vivid and graphic in the extreme. They set off one's imagination and delight one's heart. It can be compared to a sculptor moulding with clay. As regards the pretty, the ugly, the old, and the young, humans and ghosts as different as can be, the book manages not only to faithfully convey their looks but also to transmit their spirits. Therefore, the book truly belongs to fiction of the first class and demonstrates an expertise in literary refinement. [1]

It was not long before Feng Menglong 馮夢龍 and Li Yu 李漁 listed JPM as one of the 'Four Marvellous Books', alongside *Sanguo yanyi* 三國演義 (*Romance of the Three Kingdoms*), *Shuihu zhuan* 水滸傳 (*Water Margins*), and *Xi you ji* 西遊記 (*Journey to the West*). In 1695, the book was named *diyi qishu* 第一奇書 'The Number One Marvellous Book' by the literary critic Zhang Zhupo. *Hong lou meng* 紅樓夢 (*Dream of the Red Chamber*), arguably the best-known novel written in the Qing dynasty, was considered in a comment to it to have 'greatly attained the hidden mysterious techniques of the *Jin Ping Mei*'. In his *A Brief History of Chinese Fiction*, Lu Xun 魯迅, the leading figure of modern Chinese literature in the 20th century, said that 'of all the novels of manners, the *Jin Ping Mei* is the most famous ... no novel of the period surpassed it'.

JPM is a novel that features a distinctive new artistic style, as well as a profound depth of thought. It depicts the process of the rise and fall of the Ximen household, as the epitome of the society the author lived in. The creation of the classic character Ximen Qing, who is simultaneously a merchant, scoundrel, and bureaucrat, introduced a new archetypal figure to Chinese novels.

By the time the novel was conceived, 'feudal' Chinese society was rife with flaws, after two millennia, lacking signs of advancement; yet new economic factors (referred to as 'sprouts of capitalism' by some) continued to develop, and new social classes began to emerge. The historical responsibility for depicting the state of this new society fell on the shoulders of literary and artistic works. JPM was the first to really shoulder such a responsibility.

The depiction of the Ximen household and the changes that it underwent reveal a corrupt political system under which 'through the description of one man the author has described an entire district' (item 84 of *Jin Ping Mei dufa* [How to read *Jin Ping Mei*] by Zhang Zhupo), depicting a single household to represent the whole nation was referred to by Lu Xun (2010: 169) as 'presentation of such a family is in effect a condemnation of the whole ruling class'.

---

1   The translation of this quotation is cited from Yan Liang (2014: 67)

The novel also depicts a marital system under which wives and concubines are overcome with jealousy, and a system of slavery where masters and slaves are pitted against each other. Through descriptions of the evils of these two systems, the author of JPM, without realising it, presented a broad overview of the socio-political reality of his time.

The emergence of JPM shifted the subject of storytelling away from emperors and governors, heroes and outlaws, demons and other mystical beings in a groundbreaking manner. The novel portrays families as social units, and its narrative is centred on commoners, depicting realities through descriptions of banal normality. Thus, the novel can be seen as an encyclopaedia of interpersonal relationships of late-stage 'feudal' society in the mid-to-late Ming dynasty.

Unlike previous novels such as *Romance of the Three Kingdoms*, *Water Margin*, and *Journey to the West*, which had linear and sequential narrative structures, the narrative of JPM follows Ximen Qing, which is then interwoven with the stories of Pan Jinlian, Li Ping'er and Chunmei, revolving around Ximen's household to form a complex and intricate social network connecting people of all levels of society within and outside of Qinghe County. While this later became the classic narrative structure followed by *Dream of the Red Chamber* and other modern novels, JPM was the first Chinese novel to use such a structure to achieve relative success.

JPM includes several hundred characters, and those with complete storylines amount to several dozens at the least. Aren't the plotlines too many, and won't this make the reader confused? Zhang Zhupo said, 'The author has invented the three characters [elements of whose names make up the title], Pan Jinlian, Li Ping'er, and Chunmei. Notice how he brings them together in one place and then disperses them again. In the first half of his work the focus is on Pan Jinlian and Li Ping'er, but in the second half it is on Chunmei. In the first half Ximen Qing manages, by hook or by crook, to obtain for himself the gold (Jinlian) and the vase (Ping'er) which had belonged to other men; but in the second half the plum blossom (Chunmei) that was his to begin with falls easily into the hands of another man.' (Zhang and Roy 1990). By concentrating on the main points (and characters), making the topics clear and then filling out the details, the author was able to ingeniously resolve the issue of overwhelming intricacy. From this point of view as to how the narrative and its characters are broached and resolved, Chapter 1 of JPM can be seen as an overview of the novel and Chapter 79 as the pivot for the last half of the novel, which provides quite a lot of balance to the structure of the novel.

JPM employs social classes as units, depicting the twisted and abnormal family life of Ximen Qing. The core character Pan Jinlian is a woman who is at the same time lewd, jealous and fierce. Furthermore, sex was a popular

JIN PING MEI IN THE WORLD

topic of discussion at the time when the novel was written. As a result, JPM inevitably had some naturalist depictions of sex (some of which are essential for characterization). Such depictions, which take up fewer than 20,000 Chinese characters, can be considered a minor flaw of the novel.

The development of JPM studies (a.k.a. Jin studies or Jin-ology) has been a gradual process, with eminent scholars, monumental works and a pool of researchers all being crucial to the process. By the end of 2020, during the modern and contemporary periods, hundreds of monographs on JPM had been published, and thousands of research essays have appeared.

The scholars in the ranks of researchers of the novel number in the hundreds. Divided by their countries of origin or residence they include Lu Xun, Wu Han and Zheng Zhenduo from China; Hans Conon von der Gabelentz, Otto Kibat and Franz Walther Kuhn from Germany; Arthur Waley and Clement Egerton from the U.K.; Shinobu Ono, Torii Hisayasu and Mizuhō Sawada from Japan; Patrick Hanan, David Tod Roy and Katherine Carlitz from the U.S.; Sergey Manukhin, Olga Fishman and Boris Riftin from the Soviet Union; André Lévy from France; and Yong-chul Choe and Taekwon Kang from Korea, to name but a few.

Since the first International Conference on JPM Studies, which was held in Xuzhou in 1989, the term *jin xue* 金學 (JPM Studies, or Jin-ology) began to appear with some frequency. Not only has it been recognized by the academic sphere, but it has also grown into a trending area of research, on a par with 'Redology' (*Hong xue* 紅學, *Honglou meng* studies).

However, the study of JPM is by no means a recent phenomenon. Hundreds of notes and comments from the Ming and Qing dynasties already have the air of research on the novel. Although most are brief anecdotes, records or comments, they already involve many of the future directions of JPM research, with valuable insights and contributions. In the history of commented editions of the JPM in the pre-modern era there are three major figures: the anonymous commentator of the illustrated Chongzhen edition, Zhang Zhupo and Wen Long 文龍. Their works constituted the three peaks of an interconnected tradition that continued throughout the Qing dynasty. The commentary on the illustrated edition pointed out how the novel reflected the ways of the world, its principles, and techniques, setting a high standard for future commentators. Wen Long's commentary expanded on previous points, corrected misconceptions, and proposed emendations, representing the culmination of JPM commentary. Zhang Zhupo's commentary, in particular, following in the footsteps of Jin Shengtan 金聖嘆[2] (1608–1661) and Mao Zonggang 毛宗

---

2   The most famous commentator of *Shuihu zhuan*.

剛[3] (1632–1709), built on the past and paved the way for the future. Widely considered the most effective representative example of classical Chinese novel commentary, Zhang Zhupo's work is a harbinger of modern fiction theory. The study of JPM in the Ming and Qing dynasties must be given credit for setting precedents and inspiring future improvements.

JPM Studies, in its modern sense and form, appeared in the 20th century. The publication of Lu Xun's *A Brief History of Chinese Fiction* in 1924 [2010] marked the end of the classical period of JPM research and the beginning of the modern period. The photo-reprinting of a copy of the *cihua* edition of JPM in 1933 foretold that the modern stage of JPM Studies would advance in a comprehensive manner. The publication of essays by a number of renowned scholars from the 1930s to 1950s initiated new academic areas of JPM research. The prosperity of JPM Studies in our contemporary era can be best evidenced by the emerging of the four major research circles: in Mainland China, in Hong Kong and Taiwan, in Japan and Korea and in the West (particularly the U.S., the Soviet Union, France and Britain). This period also witnessed the formation and expansion of a multitude of research topics, including but not limited to authorship, literary significance, characterization, linguistic style and theoretical criticism, as well as translation, publication and dissemination.

As noted above, the history of the translation of JPM began in 1708. Since then, it has been translated (including fragment translations) into more than 20 languages, including Manchu, Mongolian, Japanese, French, German, English, Dutch, Belgian, Czech, Swedish, Finnish, Italian, Korean, Russian, Vietnamese, Polish, Hungarian, Danish, Yugoslavian, Latin, and Romanian. Earlier translations were mostly rewritings, partial translations or abridged translations; but of late, complete translations have become more common.

The Manchu translation was produced from a copy of Zhang Zhupo's commentary edition (first published in 1695); most early translations into other languages were made from Zhang's edition or the Manchu translation of this edition. Franz Kuhn's abridged German version *Kin Ping Meh; oder, Die Abenteuerliche Geschichte von Hsi Men und seinen sechs Frauen,* for example, was translated from the former. First published in 1930 and reprinted multiple times, Kuhn's German version subsequently became the source text for many translations into other European languages including English and French. Recent translations have mostly been produced from the *cihua* edition (Wu Gan 2015).

Among the many translated versions, the following, each with different characteristics, are the most famous: the German complete translation *Gin-Ping-Mei,*

---

3   One of the best-known commentator of *Sanguo yanyi*.

translated from the Manchu version by Hans Conon von der Gabelentz and his two sons between 1862 and 1869 (edited by Martin Gimm and published by Staatsbibliothek zu Berlin between 2005–2013). *Djin Ping Meh, Schlehenblüten in Goldener Vase*, translated sentence-by-sentence into German from *The Number One Marvellous Book* by the Kibat brothers (Otto Kibat and Artur Kibat). The first volume of their translation was published in 1928, and the second, in 1932, covering the first 23 chapters of the Chinese novel. Although it was announced that the third book would be published the following year, this did not go as planned due to the cultural totalitarianism imposed by Hitler. However, this did not prevent the Kibat brothers from continuing their translation enterprise. In 1946, they finally completed the translation and annotation of the whole novel in 6 volumes, which was accepted for publication by the Swiss publisher Verlag die Waage. The first volume appeared in 1967, and the final one in 1983.[4]

Clement Egerton produced the first basically complete English translation of JPM, *The Golden Lotus,* based on Zhang Zhupo's edition, with the help of Lao She. The first edition of Egerton's translation was published by Routledge and Kegan Paul in London in 1939, and the version has since been reprinted many times around the world. In 2008, it was introduced to China in bilingual format by the People's Literature Publishing House. The first complete Japanese translation (based on the *cihua* edition), under the title of *Kinpeibai*, was jointly produced by Shinobu Ono and Chida Kuichi. The first forty chapters (in four volumes) were published by Tōhō Shokyoku from 1948 to 1949, while the complete translation was not finished until 1959. It was later included in *Sekai Fuuryuu Bungaku Zenshuu* published by Kawade Shobo Shinsha, *Chuugoku Koten Bungaku Taikei* and *Chuugoku Koten Bungaku Zenshuu*, published by Heibonsha, and in *Chuugoku no Meicho* published by Keisoshobo and *Iwanami Bunko* published by Iwanami Shoten (this edition was reprinted many times; by 1974 it had had six impressions).

The complete Russian translation, based on *Jin Ping Mei cihua*, by V. Manukhin (В. Манухин 1926–1974) was published by Moscow Literary Publishing House in 1977, with a print run of 50000 copies. When it was reprinted in 1986, another 75000 copies were produced. The first complete French translation *Fleur en Fiole d'Or* by André Lévy[5] was published by Gallimard in Paris in 1985. The first truly complete English translation *The Plum in the Golden Vase* Or, *Chin P'ing Mei* by David Tod Roy[6] was published by Princeton University Press in 5 volumes from 1993 to 2013. The first Korean

---

4   For the translational history of JPM, refer also to Chapter 15 of this book.

5   See Chapter 1 of this book by André Lévy.

6   Refer to Chapter 22 of this book for further details about Roy's translation of JPM.

translation, *Wan Yeog Geumbyeongmae – Cheonhajeilgiseo Sososaeng*, was produced by relying on both the *cihua* and Chongzhen editions of the novel. This translation, made by Taekwon Kang, was published by Solbook in 10 volumes in 2002. Most recently, Vibeke Børdahl published her complete Danish translation of *Jin Ping Mei cihua*. All but one of the translations mentioned in this paragraph were completely based on the *cihua* edition.

In conclusion, we can say that the rediscovery of the *cihua* edition in the 1930s brought about a new series of substantial research. In the mid-20th century, there was a wave of JPM studies in Taiwan and Hong Kong, followed by the open publication of JPM in Mainland China in the 1980s, after which Mainland China once again became the leader of JPM Studies. Needless to say, the translation of the Chinese novel into other languages, which is carried out by sinologists around the world, is an integral part of the scholarship on JPM. The recent completion of the Danish translation published by Vandkunsten Publishers, Copenhagen, in ten volumes, 2011–2022, will bring this work to the attention of the Scandinavian readers and represents a new achievement of JPM Studies that will significantly expand the dissemination of JPM.

Today, JPM Studies is no longer an 'ivory tower' but is a 'garden' in which all are welcome to roam. Hundreds of monographs, essays and graduate theses have been written on it. From the jottings of the Ming dynasty to the latest works of JPM studies, we can say that JPM is a discussion topic that is inexhaustible. The ever-expanding reader base – those introduced to the novel by either the various Chinese editions of JPM or their translations into other languages – will only increase and widen the discussion.

Written on 4 June 2021, at Minbaoxuan, Pengcheng
Wu Gan

References

Børdahl, Vibeke
> **2019.** *Jin Ping Mei i vers og prosa. Syvende Bog.* Copenhagen: Vandkunsten Publishers.

Gabelentz, Hans Conon von der and Martin Gimm
> **2012.** *Jin Ping Mei Teil 7.* Berlin: Staatsbibliothek zu Berlin.

Kibat, Otto, Artur Kibat and Herbert Franke
> **1989.** *Djin Ping Meh: Schlebenblüten in goldener Vase: ein Sittenroman aus der Ming-Zeit.* Zürich: Diogenes.

JIN PING MEI IN THE WORLD

Kuhn, Franz

1930. *Kin Ping Meh oder die abenteuerliche Geschichte von Hsi Men und seinen sechs Frauen. Aus dem Chinesischen übertragen von Franz Kuhn.* Leipzig: Insel-Verlag.

Lévy, André

2004. *Fleur en Fiole d'Or = Jin Ping Mei.* Paris: Gallimard.

Lu, X. (2010). *Zhongguo xiaoshuo shi lue* 中國小說史略 (A Brief History of Chinese Fiction). Nanchang: 21 shiji chubanshe.

Ono, Shinobu, and Kuichi Chida (trans.)

1960. *Jin Ping Mei* 金瓶梅. 3 vols. Tokyo: Heibonsha.

Wu Gan 吴敢

2015. 'Jin Ping Mei fanyi shi lue' 金瓶梅翻译史略. *Hua xi yuwen xuekan* (*Acta Linguistica et Litteraturaria Sinica Occidentalia*). (1): 78–86.

Xiaoxiaosheng and Clement Egerton

1939. *The Golden Lotus: A Translation, from the Chinese Original, of the Novel Chin P'ing Mei.* 4 vols. London: Routledge and Kegan Paul.

Yan Liang

2014. 'Reflections on a braised pig's head: Food and vernacular storytelling in *Jin Ping Mei.*' *Journal of the American Oriental Society* 134(1): 51–68.

Zhang, Zhupo and Roy, David Tod

1990. 'How to Read the Chin P'ing Mei'. In D. L. Rolston (Ed.), *How to Read the Chinese Novel* (pp. 196–243). Princeton, NJ: Princeton University Press.

Note on Contributors

Wu Gan 吴敢 is Dean at Xuzhou Education College, Jiangsu, and Vice-president of the Chinese *Jin Ping Mei* Research Society, China. He was also formerly the head of the Xuzhou Cultural Bureau.

Celine Zhijie Ren is a student translator currently completing her masters in interpreting and translation studies at Monash University, Australia. Before her masters, Celine studied archaeology and linguistics at the University of Melbourne, where she produced a typology of mirativity in Quechua.

Daniel Haocheng Cui is a student translator currently completing his masters of interpreting and translation studies at Monash University, Australia. He majored in Chinese translation during his undergraduate studies, when he focused on the development of the Chinese language and of Chinese society.

Index

f=figure, n=footnote, t=table; **bold**=extended discussion or key reference

Abbot Wu 吳道官 (leader of the *daoist* temple outside Qinghe) **19–20**, 47–48

adaptation: definition (Sanders) 226

adaptation of sex and sexy adaptations additions (*Houses of Joy*) **237–242** alternate use of prose and poetry **229–233** omissions **228–237** rewriting *JPM* for Anglophone market **226–246**

Aisin gioro 愛新覺羅 clan 333

Aisin gurun (or Houjin 後金 state) foundation (1616) 331

Akutagawa Ryūnosuke 芥川龍之介 (1892–1927) 289

Aleksejew, W.M. 137

All-China Federation of Writers 200

alternative names **101**

Ambrosiani, Inga Nyman xxi(n6)

Anhui School. *See* Huizhou School

aphrodisiacs 212n13, 213, 219, 372 death of Ximen Qing 237

Appel, Alfred 374

arias 92n17, 99, 103

Aristotle 359

artistic conception **171–176**

artwork **xxxiii–xxxiv**

Asitan 阿什壇 (*c.*1650–1684) 332, 336, **336n40**

Au bord de l'eau (1978) 2 *see also Shuihu zhuan*

Auntie Wang (matchmaker in Qinghe), 203, 253, 254t, 383 *see also* Dame Wang

authority (political and cultural): *JPM's* challenge **209–210**

Bai Laiqiang 白來創 (member of Ximen Qing's brotherhood) 20

baihua 白話 (vernacular language) xx

baihua 白畫 (ink outline drawings) 140

baimiao 白描 (ink outline drawings) 140

baishi 稗史 (works of fiction) 79

baiwen 白文 49

baixi 百戲 (skits) 117

Baiyin, Zen Master 白隱 180

baizhang qi 百丈旗 (dance with flag) 119

bajiao gu 八角鼓 (octagonal drum) 295

Bakin, Kyokutei 曲亭馬琴 (1767–1848) xxxvi, **278–279**, 282, 284, **288–289** *Shinpen Kinpeibai* (adaptation of *JPM*) 280

banchang 搬唱 (sing) 93

bangqiang 幫腔 (choral amplification) 116n4

bankuang 板框 (printed area) 153, 153n28

bannermen 295, 297, **299–311**, 339

banxin 版心 (seam) 343n60

Bao Zhishui 包知水 (character in the drama Yuhuan ji) **107–108**

Bao zhuanghe 抱妝盒 (Carrying Dressing Case) 98n2, 102, 103

Baojian ji 寶劍記 86, 88, 90n13, 92n17, **99–100**, 102, 105

baojuan 寶卷 (寶眷) 25, 33n, **87**; definition 87

403

JIN PING MEI – A WILD HORSE IN CHINESE LITERATURE

Bazin, Antoine P.L. (1799–1863) 345
Beijing **101–102**, 131, 149n18, 179, 180, 295, 331, 343, 344n63
    College for Minority Languages 344n63
    National Library of China 344n63
    Palace Museum 333n28, 334, 339n
Beijing University Library 153, 161n
Beiles, Sinclair 237n6, 240
Beiping 北平 197
Beiqu 北曲 (Northern songs) 119
Bell in Still of Night 149n18
Ben Dichuan 贲地傳 (manager on the staff of Ximen Qing) 110, 111
Berättelser från träskmarkerna (Malmqvist) xxi
Bergman, Pär **xxi–xxii**
Berlin: Völkerkundemuseum 342n
bì 毴 (vagina) 257n
Bian er chai 弁而釵 150, 150n23
biao 表 (performance) 38, 39, 39n, 50
Bishop, John 10
block printing 138
book graphics **129–139**
book illustrations: Chongzhen edition **140–159**
book that invites lust (*JPM*) **278–293**
Børdahl, Vibeke **xiii–xiv**, **xxvii–xxxix**, 1, 11, 367n, 400
    note on contributor **xi**, 28, **57**, **64**, 311, 326
    Danish translation (2011–2022) of *JPM* xiii, **xv–xvii**, xxii, xxix
    game of official advancement **294–311**
    language shifting and narrating instance **29–57**
    Pan Jinlian **58–64**
    pinghua and *cihua* **19–28**
    stock phrases **29–57**
    wild horse **315–326**
bribery 175, 388
Brulotte, Gaëtan 7
Bu Jian 卜健 13n35, 88n3, 94n27

bu yan 不言 ('no more of this') 42
Buddenbrooks (Mann) xxviii
Buddhism xxxii, 87, 129, 130, 131, 138, 146n, 166, 169, 175, 269, 269n32, 330, 361
bufang 補方 (badge of rank) 136
Bunen-sensei 278
Burroughs, William 241
Burton, Sir Richard xx, xx(n3)
buxi 步戲 (skit) 116

Cai Bojie (from the drama *Pipa ji*) 85
Cai Yuanpei 蔡元培 (1868–1940) 325
Cailou ji 彩楼记 (drama, *Story of Painted Pavilion*) 86, 109
caizi shu 才子書 (works of genius) 79
calligraphy ('idle art') 165, 183
camera work (film shooting) 232
cao 肏 [expletive] 247, 249, 250, 250–251t, 251n9, 270, **271**, 271n36
Cao Hanmei 曹涵美 202
Cao Sibin 曹思彬 201
Cao Xueqin 曹雪芹 (1715–1763) 182, 270
    Dream of Red Chamber (*Honglou meng* 紅樓夢) 182
Cao Yin 曹寅 (1658–1712) 182
captions 132, 135, 140, 145
Carlitz, Katherine 85, 94n28, 364, 397
cartoon version of *JPM* 202
Censor Song Qiaonian 宋乔年 (official in the universe of *JPM*) 118, 123
censorship 196, 197, 221, 242, 262n, **331–333**, 345n70
Cervantes, M. de
    Don Quixote (1615) xxviii, 7, 12
chāizi 拆字 (pun) 264, 265, 265n25
changci 唱詞 (story-singing genre) 32, 50–51, 52
changci pinghua 唱詞評話 (verse for singing and prose storytelling) 25
chantefable genre 12, 25, 30, **32–33**, 35, 50, 367n
chapter titles **135**

404

INDEX

Chen Duxiu 陳獨秀 (1879–1942) **316–317,** 324

Chen Henghe 陳恆和 (1883–1937) 183

Chen Henghe shulin 陳恆和書林 (Chen Henghe Book Forest) 183

Chen Hongshou 陳洪綬 (1599–1652) 133, 134, **150,** 150n24

Chen Jingji 陳敬濟 (son-in-law of Ximen Qing) 89, 92–93, 110, 111, 140n2, 210–211, 216n21, 218, 252, 253, 255t, 256, 256n18, 268, 377f, 384, 388n
  book illustrations **152**
  relationship with Pan Jinlian **323–324**
  son-in-law to Ximen Qing 384
  songs 95

Chen Kailiang 陳開良 184

Chen Liao 陳遼 49n

Chen Lin 陳琳 102, 103

Chen Songbo 陳松波 202

Chen Yishi 陳義時 184

Chen Zhengchun 陳正春 184

Chengdu Wanbao 成都晚報 (*Chengdu Evening News*) 201

Chenghua reign 成化 (1465–1487/8) **23–24,** 32, 94, 94n26

Chenghua shuochang cihua 成化說唱詞話 24

chengyu 成語 (idiom) 281

chenzi 襯字 (paddling words) 295

chi nüzi 痴女子 (infatuated woman) 62

Chicago Manual of Style xxv

Chida Kuichi 千田九一 289, 290, 399

Chin P'ing Mei: Adventurous History of Mandarin and Six Wives (Miall translation, 1939) 229

Chinese Academy of Social Sciences (CASS): Institute of Literature 317

Chinese Communist Party Central Committee 199–200

Chinese folk ballad **295–296**

Chongzhen 崇禎 edition (of *JPM*) **xxxiii–xxxiv,** xxxv, 22, 160, 160n2,

162, 170, 172–173, 189, 210n6, 219, 220, 277, 279, 376, 381, 397, 400
  also called *Illustrated Version* **185**
  deletions and revisions 163
  illustrators **148–153**
  woodcuts **166–168,** 170
  see also cihua edition

Chongzhen edition illustrations **140–159**
  decorative objects 143
  emotions 143
  physical violence 143
  private spaces 142
  sexual activity ('excessively explicit') 143
  what we see **142–148**

Chongzhen reign (1627–1644) 376

chuanqi 傳奇 drama/opera 99, 104, 109, 116, 117, 118, 122

Chunmei 春梅 (Pan Jinlian's maid) 89, 89n5, 90, 120, 148, 210, 218, 253, 255t, 256, 256n18, 266, 318, 324, 377f
  book illustrations **143, 152**
  concubine of commandant Zhou Xiu 周休 386
  plum blossom 396
  songs 89
  see also Hongniang

ci 詞 poetry (sung) 26, 80, 81, 92n17, 94

cihua 詞話 19, 93
  element '*ci*' in name of genre 24
  extant works calling themselves ~ 94
  meaning in *JPM cihua* **25**
  prosimetric storytelling xxxi, 46
  pseudo-genre of *JPM cihua* **23–25**
  story-singing genre 32, 50

cihua edition (of *JPM* 金瓶梅詞話 1617) **xxxi–xxxii,** xxxiii, xxxv, xxxviii, **2–3,** 33, 46, 142, 160n2, 163, 195, 201, 210n6, 210n6, 219, 247, 277, 279, 289, 346, 367, **367n,** 381, 394, 398
  also called *Verse and Prose* version 185, 189

405

chapter thirty-nine **48f**

cihua as pseudo-genre **23–25**

differences from Chongzhen edition 253, **254–255t**

'high cadre' edition (1957) **199**

narrator (storyteller persona) **22–23**

nonrealistic usages 77–97

pinghua and *cihua* **19–28**

preface 316

rediscovery (1930s) 400

uncensored engraved version 201

words *cihua* 詞話 in title of novel 93

see also expurgated editions

cihua manner 27, **46–51**

cijian 次間 (side rooms) 385

circular network (*JPM*) 101

Classic Chinese Novel (1968) **6–7**

collective authorship 93n24

coloured set printing 186, **187–188f, 188–189**

Columbia University 375n13

Commandant Zhou , Zhou Xiu 周休 (local military commander, colleague of Ximen Qing) **102–103**

commentarial mode (Hanan) 92

Comprehensive History of Chinese Literature 中華文學通史 (CASS, 10v, 1997) 317

Confucian norms 331, 332, 388

undermined by *JPM* 318

Confucianism 131, 137, 169, 269, 269n32

Confucius 孔子 114

Cong Weixi 叢維熙 200

Copenhagen Symposium (2022) xiii, **xxix**, xxxii

Copyright Law (1991) 202

corruption **193–194**, 395

Corso, Gregory 241

Covid-19 pandemic xiii, xxix

crown princes **103**

ctext.org 249–250, 250–251t, 270n33, 271n36

cun tianli 存天理 (preserving heavenly principles) 319

cuodianjuan 撮墊圈 (gasket tricks) 119

Cyber (pseudonym) 382–383

da dao kuo fu 大刀闊斧 (big knife, broad axe) method 132

Da Qing lüli 大清律例 (*Great Qing Code*, 2010 edition) 195, 204

da shu 大書 (great repertoires) 50

Da Tang Qinwang chihua 大唐秦王詞話 94, 94n26

dada 達達 ('Tartar', darling) 211, 211n8

dadao 打稻 ('threshing' dance) 117

Dai Buzhang 戴步章 (1925–2003) 42n, 46n12

Dai Hongsen 戴鴻森 **199–200**

Dai'an 玳安 (Ximen Qing's trusted page) 89, 92n18, 216n23 254t, 260

Dale fu 大樂賦 (*Rhapsody on Grand Pleasure*) 214, 214n17, 215

Dame Wang 王婆子 (teahouse owner and mathchmaker) 92, 253, 254t, 261

see also Auntie Wang; Madam Wang

dan dao 單道 (marker, 'Here it is specially expressed') 34t, 35

danchang guci 單唱鼓詞 (drum ballads for solo singing) 295

dǎo 搗 (to pound or beat) 212, 251

dao 道 (way) 114

Daoism xxxii, 82, 166, 169, 175, 218, 361

daoqing 道情

Daoist equivalent of *baojuan* 寶卷 87

dashu 大書 11

dating 大廳 (reception hall) 384

death penalty 195, 202

demons 225, 321, 396

Deng Guangdou 邓光斗 58n3

Deng Liqun 鄧力群 200

Deng School of Water Margin 邓门水浒 58n3

Deng Shuxun 鄧樹勛 201

INDEX

desire **123–124**

Di yi qishu 第一奇書 ('Number One Marvellous Book') xxxiv, 395

Diamond Sutra (*Jin'gangbanruojing* 金剛般若經) 130, 170n10

dianben 殿本 (palace editions) **343–344**

Ding Naifei 220, 253

Ding Richang 丁日昌 (1823–1882) Provincial Governor in Jiangsu (1867–1870) 196n

Dixiong xiangfeng 弟兄相逢 ('Brothers meet again') 60

Djin Ping Meh, Schlehen-bluten in goldener Vase (1928–32, 1967) xxxvii

doctors **99–102**
Ren 任 385, 385n5
Zhao 趙, Zhao Longgang 趙龍岗 (quack doctors of the Ximen family) 90, 90n13, **99–102**

Dong Jieyuan 董解元 (fl. 1190–1208) 79

Dong Qichang 董其昌 (1555–1636) 8, **163**

Dongping Prefecture 118

Dongwu Nongzhu ke 東吳弄珠客 (Pearl-juggler of Eastern Wu) 316, 322

Drömmen om röda gemak xxi

Du Fu 杜甫 xx

Du Xinfu 杜信孚 162n3

Duan Chengshi 段成式
Youyang zazu 酉陽雜俎 10

dufa 讀法 ('how to read') essays 364

duirou 堆肉 ('added flesh') 62

důn (Czech, 'house') 389

Eckermann, J.P. 7

Edo period (Japan, 1603–1867) xxxvi
fate of *JPM* **278–293**
'obscene books' **286–289**
reception of *JPM* **280**

education **194**

Egerton, Clement xxxv, xxxviii, **221**, 252, 257t, 375, 397, 399

Egerton translation (*Golden Lotus*, 1939) 227, **229–234** (*230*), **258–268**
length (1500 pages) 236

El Greco (1541–1614) 162

elegance **121–123**

elites 176
classical ~ (losing their voice) 175

Elvin, Mark 143n10

Encyclopedia of Chinese Classical Fiction 中國古代百科全書 4

Encyclopedia of Erotic Literature (Brulotte and Phillips, 2006) 7, 12

engraving knife (for woodcutting) **181–182**

entrances (Chinese drama) **90–91**
Doctor Zhao **99–101**

erotic images **154–155**, 166

erotic literature **328–329**, 332, 333–334

erotic novels 166
JPM 'first and foremost' 322

erotic poetry tradition **214–216**

erotic scenes: woodcuts 137

Eunuch He 何太監 (character in *JPM*) 120

Eunuch Huang 黃太尉 (character in *JPM*) 118

Eunuch Liu 劉太監 (character in *JPM*) 84, **102–104**, 122

Eunuch Xue 薛内相 (character in *JPM*) 84, 102, **103–104**, 118, **122–123**

eunuchs 86, 117, 117n5

euphemism 209, 214, 215, 215n19, 216, 232, 234, 247, 251, 258n19, 260, 262n, 263n23–24, 267n30

expurgated editions (of *JPM*) **193–201**
'bowdlerised versions' **xxxv**, 198
'clean' edition (PRC, 1983) 200, 201
separate publication of censored parts 198
see also Lanling Xiaoxiaosheng edition

fanben 繁本 editions 34, 38, 52

fang 房 (private building) 390

407

fang ke 坊刻 (commercial engraving)
182, **183**

fangwu 房屋 (private building) 390

fangzhong shu 房中術 (art of bedchamber) **212–214**

Fanny Hill 221

Färden till Västern xxi

Fei Junliang 費駿良 53n

Fei Li 費力 53n

Feng Menglong 馮夢龍 (1574–1646) 164, 395

   Shan'ge 山歌 (Mountain Songs) **271**

   Yushi mingyan 喻世明言 24

Feng Weimin 馮惟敏 319

fengmian 封面 (title pages) 343n61

fengmian ti 封面題 (cover title) 343n61

Fengyun hui 風雲會 (drama) 91n, 98

fiction: low status in China **194**

film adaptations (of *JPM*) 202, 202n

forbidden fruit xxxi, **xxxiv–xxxvi**, 4, **191–311**

   fake book titles **196**

   ineffectiveness of bans **196**

   JPM in Imperial China **194–197**

   JPM in Republican China **197–198**

   JPM's first banning (1611, before earliest extant edition) 195

   lists of banned books 195, 196, 197

   portrayal of sex in *JPM* **209–225**

   PRC **198–204**

   punishments **195–197, 201–202**

forgeries (of *JPM*) 165

Forster, E.M. 13

Four Classic Novels 288

   Japanese translations 227n3, 280

Four Marvellous Books 395

France 345, 397, 398

Franke, Herbert **362n**

Fu Ming (manager of Ximen Qing) 110, 111

Fu Ssu-nien Library 傅斯年圖書 297

Fulin or Shunzhi 順治

   first Qing Emperor (1638–1661) 331

Fuzhou pinghua 福州平話 50

Gabelentz, Albert von der (1834–1892) 2n2, 399

Gabelentz, Georg von der (1840–1893) 2n2, 345–346, 399

   Chinesische Grammatik (1881) 346

Gabelentz, Hans Conon von der (d. 1874) xxxvii, 2, 2n2, 329n9, **345–346**, 346n, 347, 397, 399

Gao Ming 高明 (c.1301–c.1371): *Pipa ji* 琵琶記 (drama, *The Lute*) 79

Gao Qiu 高俅 (high official during Northern Song, a villain in *Shuihu zhuan* and *JPM*) **86**

Gao Xingjian 高行健 xxii

gaoganban 高幹版 ('high cadre edition' of *JPMCH*, 1957) **199**

ge 閣 (storeyed building) 390, 391

Ge Liangyan 葛良彥, 29n, 33n, 45, 48, note on contributor 28

   pinghua and *cihua* **19–28**

General Administration of Press and Publication 202

Genette, Gérard 31n, 93n21

Germany 2, 129, 130, 397

Giles, Herbert

   History of Chinese Literature **xix-xx**

Gimm, Martin xxv, xxxvi, xxxvii, 2, **294–311, 327–356**, 399

   note on contributor 311, 356

Gin ping mei bithe. See Manchu edition

Girodias, Maurice **240**

Goethe, J.W. von xxii, 7

Golden Lotus. See Egerton translation

Gong'an school of writing 394

gonghua 拱花 (embossed printing) 184

Gotha 358, 360, 361

Gou Dong 苟洞 5

Great Master Jianzhen 鑒真 (688–763) 180

Grube, Wilhelm (1855–1908) 193, 328

Gu Qiyuan 顧啟元 (1565–1628) 119

Guan'ge 官哥 (Ximen Qing's son) 88

   literally, 'Office Boy' 84

INDEX

premature death 84

Guangling guji keyin she 廣陵古籍刻印社(Guangling Ancient Books Engraving and Printing Society) **180–181**, 184

Guangling Shushe 廣陵書社 (Guangling Book Society of Yangzhou) xxix, xxxiv

guangyin ru jian 光阴如箭 ('time passed like arrow') 42, 46, 46n12

guantu 冠圖 (capping illustration) format 140n1, 141n6, 142

guci 鼓詞 (story-singing genre) 50

Gulik, Robert H. van 154n33, 247, 328

Guo Licheng 郭立誠 93n23

guojin 過錦 (sketch) 117

Gysin, Brion 241

Haenisch, Erich (1880–1966) 347

Haiyan qiang 海鹽腔 (Haiyan style of opera/theatre) 116, **116n3**, **121–123**

Haiyan troupe 104, **110–111**

Halde S.J., Father Jean Baptiste du (1674–1743) 338

Han Aijie 韓愛姐 (daughter of Han Daoguo) 50, 89

Han Daoguo 韩道國 (manager of Ximen Qing) 231–232

Han Yingshan 韓英珊 (writer) **200**

Hanan, Patrick (1927–2014) 10n26, 11, 24, 94n27, 162n4, 171n12, 397

handwritten copies (relevance of text) **163–165**

Hangji Yang Bang 杭集揚幫 (Yang Gang of Hangji [engravers]) **182–184**

Hangzhou 133, 149, 149n18, 170

Hanlin Academy 301,340

Hanyu Da Zidian 漢語大字典 248

Harem of Hsi Men (Anonymous, 1953) 229, *230*, **233–234**, **236–237**, 243

Harvard University 366n3

Hatano Taro 波多野太郎 (1912–2003) **284**, *285*

Hawkes, David 376, 376n15, 377

hé 合 (singing in harmony) 91, 250, 250n7

Hegel, Robert E. 46, 133n, **140–159**, 375, 375n13

note on contributor **159**

heidan yuwei 黑單魚尾 (simple black fishtail) 343n60

heqian 合前 (insertion of refrains) 91

Heshiheng (Hesihen) 赫世亨 (c.1645–1708) 336n40

Hesu 和素 (1652–1718)

biographical sources **336n39**

Director of Imperial Printing Office 339

portrait (painted on silk) **337f**

son of Asitan (*qv*) 332

Supervisor of Imperial Translation Office 339

translator of *JPM* **336–340**, 346

History of Chinese Literature 中國文學史 (Zhang and Luo, 3v, 1996) 317

Hōei era 287

Homer 7–8, 14, 31n

homosexual context 256, 256n17, **260**, 272, 335n33

Hong Guoliang 洪國良 134, 145, 152, 170

also known as Hong Wenyuan 洪聞遠 149, 149n19

illustrator of Chongzhen edition 148, **149**, 150

Hong Kong xxxiii, 11, 202n, 394, 398, 400

editions of *JPM*: (1906) 139; (1990) 140n1

Hong Kong Taiping Shuju 太平書局 201

Hông Taiji: same as Huang Taiji 皇太極 (1592–1643) 328

Hong xue 紅學, ('Redology') 397

Honglou meng 紅樓夢 (Dream of Red Mansions, 1792) xxi, **xxxvi**, 4, 80,

409

104, 201, **270**, 316, 317, 322, **325**, 382, 395

'born from *JPM*' (Chen Duxiu) 324, 325

Hongniang 紅娘 (heroine's maid in *Xixiang ji*) 90

see also maidservants

Hōreki era (1751–1764) 280

hou 後 (rear) 384

houfang 後房 (rear apartment) 384, 390

Houses of Joy (1958)

   economic motives **237–242**

   short version (238 pp) of *JPM* 237

   techniques of omission and addition **237–242**

Hsi-men Ch'ing *230*, **233–234**

   same as Ximen Qing (*qv*) 228n, 229

Hsia, C.T. **6–7**, **12–13**, 253, 374n13

Hu Shi 胡適 (1891–1962) **3–4**, 5, 220, 316

Hu Wenbin 胡文彬 153n28–29

Hu Yannan 胡衍南 252n12, 260

Hu Zhengyan 胡正言 (1584–1674) 185

hua 話 (story) 22, 38

hua shuo 話說 ('story goes') 29–30, 42

hua xiu raoshe 話休饒舌 ('let us not waste more words on that') 21n3

hua xiu xufan 話休絮煩 ('let us not get lost in unnecessary details') 21n3

Hua Zixu 花子虛 (husband of Li Ping'er, member of Ximen Qing's brotherhood) 258, 387, 388–389

huaben 話本 (stories) 31

Huainan shuju 淮南書局 (Huainan Book Bureau) 182

Huang Junqian 黃君倩 (artisan) 150

Huang Runhua 黃潤華 328n2, 329n9

Huang Ruyao 黃汝耀 (artisan) 134, 148, 170, 185

Huang Yibin 黃一彬 (artisan)133, 148

Huang Yisong 黃一松 (b. 1599)

   professional name 'Ruguang' 148n15

Huang Zihe 黃子和 (artisan) 149n18

Huang Zili 黃子立 (b. 1611) (artisan) **150–152**, 170, 185

   illustrator of Chongzhen edition 148

   pseudonym of Huang Jianzhong 建中 **133–134**

Huatong 畫童 (servant in the family of Ximen Qing) 111, 216n23

Huaying jinchen 花營錦陣 142n7, 154n33

huazan 畫贊 46n13

hui 回 (session) **32n**

Hui *pai* 徽派. *See* Huizhou School

huidao 誨盜 (promotion of rebellion) 331

huishu 穢書 (obscene books) 331

huiwu zhi shu 穢惡之書 (books of filth and harm) 331

Huizhou 5, 134, 170

Huizhou School (of book illustration) **132–133**, 141, 141n5, 149, 149n18, 171n13

Huizong 徽宗 (Emperor) 389

human nature

   sordid side (depicted in *JPM*) 318

Huo Xianjun 霍現俊 **98–113**

note on contributor **113**

huqin 胡琴 (fiddle) 120

Idema, Wilt 23

illustration titles (placement) 132

illustrations (for *JPM*) **129–139**

Imperial Printing Office 347

ink tablets **133**

Inoue Kōbai 井上紅梅

   JPM and Chinese Society (1923) 289

Institute for Zen Studies (Japan) 180

International Conference on *JPM* Studies (Xuzhou, 1989) 397

internet xiii, 202, 249

interpolations: prose ~ 91, 91n; song 92n17

intertextuality **xxxii–xxxiii**, **75–126**

irony xxvii, 8, 12, 109, 111, 194

INDEX

Ishida Mikinosuke 石田幹之介 (1891–1974) 289

Japan **xxxvi**, 2, 3, 153n29, 202n, 221n38, 394, 397
    commentary (on *JPM*) **280–284**
    fate of *JPM* during Edo period **278–293**
    importation of *JPM* 279–280
    JPM reading group **285–286**
Jensen, Minna Skafte **xv–xvii**
jia ke 家刻 (private engraving) 182, **183**
Jia Sanjin 賈三近 5
jiaban 家班 (private troupes) **120–121**
jiadao 夾道 (lateral passage) 384, 388
Jiajing reign 嘉靖 (1522–1567) 120, 319
jian 間 (bays) 384, 384n4
jian 奸 (sexual promiscuity) 331
jianben 簡本 editions (of *Shuihu zhuan*) 38
Jiangnan region 141, **148**, 149, 153
jiankou 剪口 ('cut story short') 59, 59n6
Jianyang (建陽) School
    same as 'Fujian School' 141
jiaoben 腳本 (*aides-mémoire,* story-teller's script) 30, 32
jiaodai 交待 ('let me explain') 42, 45
Jiaofang si 教坊司 (Music Office) **117–120**
jiaogou 交媾 (to copulate) 251n11
jiaomen 角門 (lateral gate) 386
Jiaqing reign 嘉慶 (1796–1820) 196
jiayue 家樂 (private troupes) **120–121**
jileide 積累的 (cumulative) 4
Jin Ping Mei 金瓶梅 (*JPM; Plum in Golden Vase*) xxvii
    adherence to text, control over text **165–168**
    anonymous novel (late C16) xiii
    artistic conception (enhancement) **171–176**
    author controversy **xxvii, 52–53**
    in China and in world **xxxvi–xxxix, 313–401**

'complete picture of society' 318, **321–324**
composition: (date) 319; (place) 5
even passing detail 'ribald' **210–212**
forbidden fruit **191–311**
ideas of ~ in turbulent age **318–320**
important dates (1596–1862) **346–347**
length (3,000 pages) xv
main problem **9**
notoriety xvi, **202–203**
'number one extraordinary book' xiii
oral storytelling **1–74**
plays mentioned (function) **98–113**
pornographic aspects **217–219**
portrayal of Ming drama **114–126**
portrayal of sex **209–225**
self-contradiction 219
sequels 165
story of novel **xxvii–xxviii**
strategy and process **364–380**
structure **323**
text refined by images **168–171**
value and influence **315–326**
'wild horse' in Chinese literature **xxix-xxx, 315–326**
'wild horse' metaphor (reason) **317**
Jin Ping Mei banhua 金瓶梅版画 (*JPM* woodcuts) xxxiv
Jin Ping Mei cihua xu 金瓶梅詞話序 (Preface to *JPM cihua*) 316
Jin Ping Mei xu 金瓶梅序 (Preface to *JPM*) 316
Jin Ping Mei zhuan 金瓶梅傳 (*JPM* chronicle) **xxxi–xxxii**, 23
Jin Shengtan 金聖歎 (1608–1661) xxxii, 61n, 79, 397, 397n
jin xue 金學 ('*JPM* Studies') xxix-xxx, 397
Jin Yong 金庸 (Louis Cha, 1924–) **5**
jing 淨 (comic-villain role) **107**
Jingshi tongyan 警世通言 81–82
Jinlian xishu 金蓮戏叔 ('Jinlian flirts with brother-in-law') 61

411

Jinling 金陵 School (of book illustration) **132–133**, 141, 170, 179
jinshi 進士 (scholar) 339
jinshu 禁書 (forbidden books) 331
jitide 集體的 (collective) 4
Jiucun village: woodcutters (Huang clan) **133–134**
Joking Scholar from Lanling. *See* Lanling Xiaoxiaosheng
Joyce, James: *Ulysses* 7, 8, 9, 12, 33, 374
*JPM*a: identical to *cihua* edition (*qv*) 247
*JPM*b: same as Chongzhen edition (*qv*) 247
JPMCH: abbreviation for *cihua* edition (*qv*) 160n2
juan 卷 (scroll) 23, 139; (sections) 153
juanpeng 捲棚 (pavilion) 385, 390, 391
Julien, Stanislas 346n

Kagoshima University Library 285–286, **287f**
Kaikkonen, Marja xiv, **160–208**
note on contributor **178**, 190, 208
Kakugozen (*Rouputuan* 肉蒲团) 279
kan 看 (to see) 32n
Kan'en reign (Japan) 279
Kang Taekwon 397, 400
kang 炕 (heated bed) 385
kanguan 看官 (audience)12
kanguan ting shuo 看官聽說 (marker, 'Listen, dear audience') 40
Kangxi, Emperor (1662–1723) 1, 2, 196, 297, 334–335, 336n40, 338, 339n49, 340
Kangxi reign 康熙 182, 185, 328, 343, 344
Kankyō Nanasuke 閑喬七介 280
Kant, Immanuel 359
Karlgren, Bernhard **xx-xxi**
Kawade Shobo 289–290n3
Kawashima, Yuko 川島優子 **278–293**
note on contributor **293**
ke 刻 (carved by) 149

ketou 磕頭 (polite greeting) xvi
Kibat, Artur (1878–1961) xxi(n5), xxv, xxxiii, xxxvii, 2, 22, 345n70, **357–363**, 399
Kibat, Otto (1880–1956) xxi(n5), xxxiii, xxxvii, 2, 22, 345n70, **357–363**, 397, 399
Kin Tung (gardener) **237–238**
same as 'Qintong' 琴童 240–241
King, Gail Oman 367n
Klaproth, Julius (1783–1835) 345
Kōgetsu Sōgan 江月宗玩 180n2
Korea 202n, 221n38, 397
Král, Oldřich (1930–2018) xxxviii, 264, 389n, 391n
ku shuo 苦說 4
'Kuaizui Li Cuilian ji' 快嘴李翠記 (story) 81
Kuhn, Franz (1884–1961) xxxv, **xxxvii–xxxviii**, 136, 228, 229, 233, 236, 345n70, 397, 398
Kuraishi Takeshirō 倉石武四郎 (1897–1975) 282
Kyoto University Library 284

Laiqingge 來青閣 and Cuihua 粹華 bookshops 197
landscape (in book illustrations) 141, 142n6
language within language **33–40**
language shifting 29–57
Lanling 蘭陵 (Shandong) 5
Lanling Xiaoxiaosheng 蘭陵笑笑生 ('Scoffing Scholar of Lanling') xxvii, 19, 24, 137, 269
attempts to identify real name **319**
Lanling Xiaoxiaosheng edition (1990, 1998) **257t, 258–268**, 274
see also Manchu edition
Lao She 老舍 (1899–1966) xxxviii
Larsson, Hans Emil
Kinesiska dikter på svensk värs (1894) xix
Laufer, Berthold (1855–1908) 347

INDEX

Leontev, Aleksej L. 345n67

Lessing, E.G. (1729–1781) 162

Letter Papers from Ten Bamboo Studio 189

Lévy, André (1925–2017) xxv, xxxi, xxxiii, **xxxviii**, **1–18**, 21-23, 47, 47n15, 193, 221n39, 259n20, 324n26, 367n, 397, 399
note on contributor **18**
stock phrases **21–22**

li 李 (plum) 264

Li Bai 李白 xx

Li Boyuan 李伯元 (1867–1906) 317

Li Guijie 李桂姐 (courtesan from the brothel quarter of Qinghe) 82, 86, 88, **107–108**, 211, 253, 254t, 264, 265

Li Hsiao-t'i 388

Li Jiao'er 李娇兒 108, 220
second wife of Ximen Qing 82

Li Kaixian 李開先 (1502–1568) 11, 13n35, 99–100, 319
Baojian ji 寶劍記 (Precious Sword) **86**, 88n3

Li Lüyuan: *Qiludeng* 歧路燈 (novel, *Lantern at Crossroads*) **166**

Li Ming 李銘 (young musician on the staff of Ximen Qing) 82, **120**, 122

Li Ping'er 李瓶兒 86, 99, **108–110**, 120, 211, 214, 216, 220, 221, 256n17, 258, 264, 265, 318, 322, 388–389, 396
death 104, **105–106**, 122
mother of Guan'ge 84
premature death 84
sixth wife of Ximen Qing 82
songs 89, 89n4

Li Rihua 李日華 (1565–1635) 271n36

Li Ruzhen 李如真 185

Li Shiren 李時人 94n27

Li Xiaorong 214, 216, 223

Li Xifan 李希凡 13

Li Yu 李漁 (1611–1680) 79, 163, 319, 395

Rouputuan 11

Li Zhi 李贄 (1527–1602) 170, 319

Liang Qichao 梁啟超 (1873–1929) 79

Liangshi yinyuan 兩世因緣 88

Liangshi yinyuan Yuhuan ji 兩世姻缘 玉环记 (Marriage of Two Lifetimes) 122

liangyi suo 良醫所 (good medical clinics) 102

Liaoning 遼寧 201–202, 339

licentiousness 163, 166

limu 梨木 (pear wood) 343

Lin Shu 林紓 (1852–1894) 79

Lin Taitai 林太太 (Lady Lin , mistress of Ximen Qing) **147f**, 216, 219, 220

Ling Mengchu 凌濛初 (1580–1644) 79

Linqing city 臨清 (Shandong) 202–203

Linqing: *JPM* Culture City 203

literary art (*JPM*) **160–178**

literary bans (1687–1850) **332–333**

literary criticism xxii, 3, 161, 175, 382, 395

literary *noumena* (Kant) 162

literati xxxi, 183, 194

literati novels (Plaks) 6

literati style (文人化) 168

Liu Bang 劉邦 21

Liu Housheng 劉厚生 329n9

Liu Hui 劉輝 4, 93n21, 93n23, 94n26

Liu Jingting 柳敬亭 (1592–1674) 20, **49–50**, 80

Liu Junyu 刘君裕 171n13

Liu Kun 劉坤 xxxiv
apprenticeship **179–182**
background **179–180**
engraving of *JPM* **184–189**
future work 189
JPM workload 189
master artist (newly re-cut blocks for illustrations of *JPM*) **179–190**
methods **185–186**
note on contributor 190
principle (used in engraving work) **186–189**

413

JIN PING MEI – A WILD HORSE IN CHINESE LITERATURE

tools **189**

woodcuts according to Chongzhen
Edition **187–188f**

works 185

'Yang Gang of Hangji' **182–184**

Liu Qixian 劉啟先 134, 149n18, 170,
185

   illustrator of Chongzhen edition
148, **152**

Liu the Second 劉二 (owner of a
restaurant) 252, 255t, 262

Liu Shaoqi 刘少奇 11n31

Liu Shide 劉世德 **4–5**, 7

Liu Yingzu 劉應祖 134, 170, 185

   of Xin'an; illustrator of Chongzhen
edition 148

Liu Zhen 刘祯 xiii, **315-326**

   note on contributor **326**

lixue 理學 (School of Principle) 114

Lodén, Torbjörn **xix-xxiv**

Lotus d'or (1912) xxxvii

Lou 樓 (storeyed building) 390, 391

Lu Dawei 陸大偉 (David Rolston)
364n1

Lu Nan 盧 楠 (1507–1560) 319,
329–330, 330n10

Lü Tiancheng 呂天成 110n

Lu Wuqing 陸武清 (artisan) 149, **150**,
150n23

Lu Xun 魯迅 (1881–1936) 86, 162n3,
176, 220, 317, 320, 397

   Zhongguo xiaoshuo shi lue 中國小說
史略 (Brief History of Chinese
Fiction) 317, 320, 395, 398

Lu Zhenzhen 陸珍楨 xiv, **327–356**

   note on contributor **356**

Lü Zhi'an 呂止庵 (14th century) 102n

luan 亂 (anarchy) 331

Luo Junjie 271n36

Luo Rufang 羅汝芳 (1515–1588) 114

Luo Yuming 駱玉明 317

Ma editions 馬版 (Yangzhou book
engraving) 183

Ma Ronggen 馬榮根 197

Ma Wei 马伟 **58–74**

   note on contributor **63–64**, 74

Ma Zhijun 馬之駿 164

macaronic folk ballad **294–311**

mai guanzi 卖关子 (high suspense) 59,
59n6

maidservants 120, 138

   see also Chunmei; Hongniang;
Qiuju; Ruyi, Yuxiao

Malmqvist, Göran xxi

Manchu bannermen 295, 297, **299–311**,
339

Manchu edition of *JPM* (*Gin ping mei
bithe*, 1708) xxxv, xxxvii, xxxviii, 1,
196, 229, 297, 318, **327–356**, 398

   based on 1695 Chinese edition 329

   beyond law (Manchu nobility)
333–334

   censorship **331–333**

   earliest translation of *JPM* **327–356**

   first chapter **341–342f**

   instigator (unknown; but probable
type of person) **334**, 347

   library holdings (worldwide)
344n63

   page design, size, paper quality
343n60

   preface (1708) **329–330**, 335, 346

   print run **344**, 344n63

   printing by court **340–345**

   reception in Europe **345–346**

   translator candidates **335–340**

   Yinreng's role **334–335**

   see also neifu ben

Manchu language **296–311**

Manukhin, V. (В. Манухин
1926–1974) 265, 397, 399

Mao Dun 茅盾 (1896–1981) 220

Mao Guangsheng 冒廣生 (1873–1959)
343n59

Mao Zedong 毛澤東 **198–199**

Mao Zonggang 毛宗剛 (1632–1709)
397–398, 398n

414

INDEX

Mawangdui 馬王堆 (tombs) 212

mayang buneng dang 麻癢不能當 (unbearable stimulation) 213

McMahon, Keith 149n19, 150n23, 248n1
  note on contributor **225**
  portrayal of sex in *JPM* **209–225**

'Meeting at Swan Gate' (*Hongmenhui* 鴻門會) **20–21**, 47

Mei Jie 梅節 (b. 1928) 162n4

Mei Sheng 枚生
  Qifa' 七发 (*Seven Stimuli*) 163, 165, 394

Meiji period (1868–1912) xxxvi, 289

men 門 (door; gatehouse) 390

Mencius 孟子 114

Meng Qingtian 孟庆田 382, **386–387**

Meng Yulou 孟玉樓 85, 89, 105, 107, 108, 211, 216, 220, 221, 325, 383
  fourth wife of Ximen Qing 82
  plays *pipa* 82

meta-narrative markers: functions **33**

Miall, Bernard 229, 244

Miall translation (from Kuhn) 229, *230*, **234–240**

mie renyu 滅人欲 (eliminating human desire) 321

Mikasa Shobō 289n

Miner, Earl 94

Ming Chenghua shuochang cihua 明成化 說唱詞話 (1471–1478) 32

Ming code (1397) 331n17

Ming drama customs
  historical value of *JPM* **114–126**

Ming Dynasty (1368–1644) xxvii, xxviii, 78, 83, 99, 166

Ming novel 35
  see also zhanghui xiaoshuo

mingjian 明間 (central room) 385

Ministry of Culture 203–204

Ministry of Propaganda 201

Ministry of Rites 325; Board of Rites 195

Minutes to Go (Burroughs *et al.*) 241

Mo Yan 莫言 xxii

monks 26, 87, 95, 129, 130, 213, 219, 318

Morant, G.S. de (1878–1955) xxxvii

Mori Ōgai 森鴎外 (1862–1922)
  Vita Sexualis 278

Mudanting 牡丹亭 (drama, *Peony Pavilion*) 317

music 105, 107, **117–121**

Nabokov, Vladimir: *Lolita* 7, 237, 374

nahua 那話 (euphemism for 'penis') 214

naked bodies **12–13**, 142, 143n10

Naked Lunch 237

Nanjing 132, 180, 343
  Jinling Sutra Engravery (*Jinling ke jing chu*) 金陵刻經處 179, 184
  School. *See* Jinling School

nanxi 南戲 (Southern drama) 99, 116

Nappi, Carla 365n

narrating instance **29–57**
  definition 31n

narrative
  perspective (of *JPM*) **115–116**
  pinghua and *cihua* (new template) **25–27**
  transition **36–37t**

narrator xvi–xvii, **22–23**, **39t**, **44t**, 78, 81, 255t, 256

National News and Book Printing Company 202

National Register of Intangible Heritage 58n1

nei 内 (inner spaces) 384

Nei fanshu fang guanli dachen 內翻書 房管理大臣 (Imperial Translation Office) **339**

neifu ben 內府本 (palace editions) **343–344**
  see also Qilu Shushe

Neige 內閣 (Grand Secretariat) 339

Neiwu fu 內務府 (Bureau of Imperial Household Affairs) 340

neiyue 內樂 (palace music) 117

415

Neo-Confucianism 319, 321
nonrealistic usages 77–97
   two main categories **95**
Nordisk familjebok xx
Northern Song Dynasty (960–1126/7)
   xxvii, xxviii, 21, 78, 53
novel of manners (*JPM*) 167, 175, 316,
   317, 323, **328–329**, 330, 344, 395
Nurhači: same as Nuerhazhi 奴爾哈赤
   (1559–1626) 328, 333n29, 336
nüyin 女陰 (vagina) 251n11
Nylan, Michael 214n18

oral sex 214–215, 232, 234, 239, 241,
   259, 272
obscenity **xxxiv–xxxvi**
official engraving (*guan ke* 官刻)
   182–183
Oka Minami 岡南
   'Kinpeibai Yakubun' [*JPM* com-
     mentary] 岡南閑喬 **280–284**
     (**282–283f**)
Okajima Kanzan 岡島冠山 (1674–1728)
   287
Olivová, Lucie xxxviii, 277, **381–393**
   note on contributor **393**
Olympia Press (Paris) 237, **240**
Ono Shinobu 小野忍 289, 290, 397, 399
optical character recognition (OCR)
   251
oral literature: versus written literature
   9
oral performing literature **77–97**
   content-centred, non-experimental
     uses **84–88**
   experimental, formal uses **88–95**
   non-realistic uses in *JPM cihua*
     84–95
   uses (in *JPM cihua*) **82–83**
   uses (pre-*JPM*) **80–82**
oral storytelling xvi–xvii, **xxxi–xxxii**,
   46–51
oral tradition 19, 51

Wang School of Water Margin
   58–64
Oslo Symposium (2007) xxxi, 1n
outlaws xxviii, 149n18, 396

page: folded ~ versus single ~ **134–135**,
   141–142n6
pai 牌 (tune matrixes) 91
painting 129, 140, 169, 170, 176
   'idle art' 165
Painting Manual of Ten Bamboo Studio
   189
Pan Jinlian 潘金蓮 (Golden Lotus)
   26–27, **65–74**, **108–110**, **254–255t**,
   256n17
   abortion 210
   'archetypal *femme fatale* of Chinese
     fiction' 271
   book illustrations **135–136**, 139,
     140n2, **144f**, **144–145**, **146f**,
     152–153
   death 171 (grave 89)
   fifth wife of Ximen Qing 82, 383
   Golden Lotus 3, **12–14**, **237–242**
   knowledge of drama and song 87
   'main character' in *Shengguan tu*
     297, **300–310**
   main female protagonist (*JPM*)
     xxxii
   miscellaneous xxvii, xxxv, 59, 59n7,
     92, 105, 107, 120, 136, 171–173,
     211, 215– 220 *passim*, 237, 253,
     261, 318, 376–377, 386, 388, 396
   murder of husband (Wu the Elder)
     61–62, 142, 372
   songs 82, 85, **89**, 91, 92n18
   'sophisticated female rather than
     prurient woman' 242
   tourist mascot 203
   use of vulgarism 252n12
   Wang School of Water Margin
     58–64
Pan Kaipei 潘開沛 10, 17
Pang Chunmei 龐春梅. *See* Chunmei

INDEX

Paris workshop (2017) 29n

Park, J.P. 143

paronomasia 298

Parrenin S.J., Father Dominique
(1665–1741) 338

Pei Jingong huandai ji 裴晋公还带记
(Story of Pei Du's Return of Belts)
118–119

People Online 人民網 4

People's Publishing House **199**, 201,
399

personality **104–108**

Petronius 1, 7

Phillips, John 7

ping 平 (level tone) 298, 298n8

Ping Jinya 平襟亞 197, 198

pinghua 評話 (评话) or 平話 **19–21**, 22,
39, 52, 58
  'folk books' 平話 129, 130, 131, 132
  'oral storytelling' 評話 47
  'plain storytelling without music' 評
    話 xxxii
  'plain tales' 平話 30, 32, 35, 46, 365
  'storytelling with commentary' 評
    話 xxii
  see also Yangzhou *pinghua*

pinghua jieshuo 評話捷說 ('speed up
your storytelling') **21–22**, 25, 38,
40, 49

pinyin xxvi, 210n5, 248, 373n, 375

pipa 琵琶 (lute) 120, **145**, **146f**, 152

Pipa ji 琵琶記 (drama, *The Lute*), 79, 85,
98, 148
  see also Gao Ming

plain tales 平話 32, 43n, 45, 47n14, 52,
365

Plaks, Andrew H. **6**, 94n28, 162n4,
248n3, 269, 364, 365, 383

plays 78, 79, 84
  mentioned in *JPM* (function)
    98–113
  mentioned in *JPM* (lists) **98n1–2**

plum blossoms 111, 176, 185
  Chunmei (*qv*) 396

Plum in Golden Vase (*JPM*) 249, 394

poetry 81, 92, 93, 168, 169n8, 375

popular literature (Ming and Qing) 162

pornography 209, **217–219**

pornography crackdown work (*Sao
huang* 掃黃 campaign, PRC)
201–202

Porphyry: same as Wang Liu'er (*qv*) 232

Press and Publication Administration
(Xinwen Chubanshu 新聞出版署)
200

price 198, 200; use to restrict *JPM*
circulation **199**, 199n, 202

Prime Minister Cai Jing 蔡京, **120–121**

Princeton University Press
  Roy translation of *JPM* **364–380**

print culture **xxxiii–xxxiv**, **127–190**

printing blocks 153
  Destruction Order (1713) 332

prohibited books
  ruling class versus general popula-
    tion 333

prosimetric storytelling xxxi, 12, 24, 46,
51, 78, 79, 93, 94

prostitutes 82, 85, 86, 88, 104n, 108,
111, 117n5, 253, 318

psychology 241–242

public morals 196, 204

puns 264, 265, 265n25, **298–310**,
324n27, 376n15

Qi Lintao 齐林涛 **xiii–xiv**, **xxvii–xxxix**,
209n1, 214n16, 219-221, **226–246**,
253, 262, 366, 377
  note on contributor **xi**, **245–246**

qian 前 (front) [of residence] 384

Qian Daxin 錢大昕 (1728–1804) 5–6,
6n13

qian shou shen song 淺抽深送 (shallow
pulls and deep thrusts) 213

Qian Xuantong 錢玄同 (1887–1939)
3–4, 5, 316, 317

Qian Zhongshu 钱钟书 (1910–1998)
169n8

qianfang 前房 (front apartment) 386

Qianlong reign 乾隆 (1735/6–1795/6) 183, 195, 331, 333, 340, 341

qianqiang 前腔 91

qianting 前廳 (front room) 384

qie 切 (cutting) 182

qie shuo 且說 ('meanwhile, let's tell') 42, 46, 46n12

Qilu deng 歧路燈 [novel] 80

Qilu Shushe 齊魯書社 (Qilu Press) uncensored edition (1989) **200–201** *see also* Zhang Zhupo edition

Qin Dynasty 195

Qin Ruolan 秦弱兰 **111**

qinding 欽定 (imperially ordered) 345

Qing Dynasty xxx, 183 notorious for book bans 195, 195n1

Qing Ming Shang He Tu 清明上河圖 (Spring Festival Along River) 324

qingchang 清唱 (unstaged singing) 99

Qingfengzha 清風閘 (Qingfeng Sluice) (1819) 53n

Qinggong yuan 清宮怨 (Tragedies at Qing Court) 11

Qinghe County 60, 68, 101, 118, 120, 144, 318

Qinglou meng 青樓夢 (novel) 79

qingyun zhishang 青雲直上 (Ascendance to White Clouds) 294

Qiuju 秋菊 (maid) 140n2, 152, 324 *see also* maidservants

qu 曲 poetry (sung) 81, 92n17, 94

quotation and allusion 87

Rare Editions Project (PRC) 180

real life xvii, xxi, 52, 130, **321–325**

realism **166**

Rémusat, J.P. Abel (1788–1832) 1, 7, 345, 347

renyu 人欲 (self-centred desire) 319

Renzong 仁宗 (Emperor, r.1023–1064) 103

reputation (of *JPM*) **204**, 209

revised version

same as 'Chongzhen version' 279

ri 日 (to copulate) 247, 248, 250, 250n7, 264

ri 𡆧 [expletive] **xxxv** occurrences in works other than *JPM* **269–271** variant of *cai* 財 (wealth) 247, 248

ri 𡆧 (occurrences in *JPM*) **247–277** ctext.org 249–250, 250–251t digitalised editions 249, 251t *JPM*'s 'signature lexeme' 271 needle in haystack **248–252** occurrences in only one of *JPM* editions 253[–]256, **257t**, 272 occurrences in various *JPM* editions **253–256** printed editions 249, 250t questionable instances **264–268** sex-related instances **254–255t**, **256–260** speakers **252–253** types of expression 256, 272 use as vulgarism **254–255t**, 256, **260–263** variations **263** Wikisource 250–251t

Riftin, Boris (1932–2012) xxv, **xxxiii**, **129–139**, 397 note on contributor **139**

Rolston, David L. xiv, xxv, 31, 35, 37–38, 47n15, 51n, 77–**97**, 98n, 114n, **118–123**, 315n, **364–380** note on contributor **97** disagreements with Roy 375 editor, *How to Read Chinese Novel* (1990) 364–365

Rongyutang 容與堂 edition (of *Water Margin*, 1610) 23, 34, 34n, 56, 149n18, 157

Rouputuan 肉蒲團 (*Carnal Prayer Mat*) 11, 279, **286–288**

Roy, David Tod xxviii, xxxiii, xxxviii, 7, 11, **13**, 21, 22n5, 47n15, 98n, 140n1,

418

INDEX

221, 251, 252, 269, 382n1–2, 397, 399
annotations 369, **370f**
cards **370–372**, 374f, 376, 378
death (2016) 364
endnotes 367, 369, **373–375**, 376n15
notebooks 376, **377f**, 378
personal copy of *JPM* 371, **371–373f**
sample page of glosses 367, **368f**
stock phrases 21, 21n3
textual emendations (of *JPM*) 369, 369n6
traditional formulaic material 375
translation of *JPM* **258–268**
use of indentation 375
ru 入 (to copulate, to enter) 247, 250, 250n7, 264, 270, 298n8
Ruan Dacheng 阮大鋮 (1587–1646): *Yanzi jian* 燕子笺 (drama, *Swallow's Letter*) 149
Rudbeck, Carl xxii
Rudelsberger, Hans (1868–1940) 345n70
rui 蕊 (pistil; female genitalia) 216
Rulin waishi 儒林外史 (The Scholars) 315, 317
ruling class xxviii, xxxv, 331, 333, 395
Rushton, P.H. 332
Ruyi 如意 (nurse of Ximen Qing's son) 217, 220, 253, 256n17
see also maidservants
Ruyijun zhuan 如意君傳 (Lord of Perfect Satisfaction) 215, **270**

Said, Edward W. 243
Sakyamuni's teachings 170n10
Sanders, Julie 226
Sanguo zhi yanyi 三國志演義 (Romance of Three Kingdoms, 1650) xxxvi, 19, 25–26, 315, 317, 328, 346, 395, 396, 398n
sanyue 散樂 (free music) 119
satire xvi, 86, 137

Sawada Mizuhō 澤田瑞穂 (1912–2002) 280, 292, 397
Scheffer, Carl Fredrik (1715–1786) xix
School of Mind. *See xinxue*
Scoffing Scholar. *See* Lanling xiaoxiaosheng
Scott, Mary 382, 385, 387
sekiin (lithographic print) 289
Selected Yuan Dramas 133
sex **209–225**
art of bedchamber **212–214**
conservative attitudes 204
erotic poetry tradition **214–216**
euphemism 209, 214, 214n16, 215, 215n19, 216
explicit scenes (tiny proportion of *JPM*) **193**, 209
graphic description (*JPM* point of departure) **216–217**
lengthier portrayals (general types) 212
naturalist depictions 'minor flaw of novel' 397
reception **220–221**
translation **221–222**
Sha sao ji xiong 杀嫂祭兄 ('Killing Sister-in-law as Sacrifice to Elder Brother') 59
Shandong 202–203
dialect 248, 269
Press and Publication Department 200
Province xxvii, 144, 179–180
shangfang 上房 (principal apartment) 385
Shanghai 197, 248n2
Shanghai Journal Company 198
Shanpo yang 山坡羊 (song, 'Sheep on Mountain Slope') 38, 89, 89n6, 93n23
Shanxi province 197, 289
shen 身 (body) 143n10
Shen Cai 沈采 110n
Shen Defu 沈德符 **164–165**, 319

Shen Hanguang 申涵光 (1618–1677) 332

sheng 生 (male role) 107

Shengguan tu 陞官圖 (game of official advancement) **294–311**

    ballad text **299–311**

    ballad text (conspicuous features) **297–298**

    double meanings (underlined) **299–311**

    English translation (arrangement) **299**

    Manchu words (grey colour) **299–311**

    puns **298–310**

    rhyme **298**

    structure (external) **298**

    structure (internal) **298**

    subject matter from *JPM* 297

    verses (length) **298**

    verses twenty-four to forty **310f**

Shenghuo shudian 生活書店 198

shengqiang 聲腔 (vocal styles) 121

Shi Nai'an 施耐庵 (Yuan) 61n

Shi yu huapu 詩餘畫譜 (*Pictures Beyond Poems*) 175

Shi Zhecun 施蟄存 (essayist) 198

Shijing 詩經 321

Shinpen Kinpeibai 新編金瓶梅 (Japanese adaptation of *JPM*) 278, 280, 283, 288

Shitou ji 石頭記 (Story of Stone) 79, **376–377**

    see also Honglou meng

shizan 詩讚

    even line poetry 94

    panegyric verses 24

Shotoku era (1711–1716) 280

Shrew (novel, *Cu hulu* 醋葫蘆) 149

Shu Dun 舒頓 340n52

Shu Min 舒敏 (1777–1803) 340n52

shuchang 书场 (storyteller's house) 59n5

shufang 書房 (study) [room] 384

Shui Hu Zhuan 水滸伝 279, 280, 281

Shuihu 水滸 (Water Margin in Yangzhou storytelling) **58–64**

Shuihu zhuan 水滸傳 (Water Margin; Chronicle of Marshlands) **xxvii–xxviii**

    fanben 繁本 edition 34

    illustrations 130, 134, **172f**

    miscellaneous xxi, xxix–xxxvi *passim*, 2, 9, 11, 19, 23, 26, 30, 46, 79, 100, 166–175 *passim*, 219, 315–318 *passim*, 333, 373, 377, 395, 396, 397n

    Sanduozhai 三多齋 edition 171

    storyteller's manner 41t

shumian 書面 style 35

shunga 春畫 (Japanese prints) 143n10

shuo 說 (telling) 38, 39, 42

shuochang 說唱 (telling and singing arts) 31, 37n, 38, 50

shuochang cihua 說唱詞話 (ballad-stories) 23, 30, 32, 33, 40, 94n26, 367n

shuochang wenxue 說唱文學 ('literature for telling and singing') 295

shuohua 說話 (professional oral story-telling) 22n5, 30

shuohuade 說話的 (storyteller) **22–23**, 25, 40, 41t

shuoshu 說書 (professional oral story-telling) 22n5, 30, 37n, 49–50, 295

shuoshu yiren 說書藝人 (professional storyteller) 41t

shuoshude 說書的 (professional story-teller) 20, 47

Shutong 書童 (servant) 82, **151f**, 151–152, 256n17, 260

si da qi shu

    四大奇书 (four extraordinary books) 317

    四大奇書 (amazing four books) 14

Sibao 四堡 (Fujian Province) 180

Sichuan Province 101, 104n

siheyuan 四合院 (Chinese house) 389, 390

INDEX

Sijie ji 四节记 (drama, *Story of Four Seasons*) **110–111**

Six Classics (pre-Qin) 169, 169n9

Six Script Styles 185

Sixth Wang. *See* Wang Liu'er

sizhou shuangbian 四週雙邊 (bookmaking, double border) 343n60

skits 7, 8, 9, 81, 84, 91, 116, 117, 119

Small Group for Reparation and Binding of Ancient Books (Yangzhou, 1960–) 184

social class 175, 236, 271n36, 395, 396
see also ruling class

social customs: *JPM* 'documentary record' 324

sodeog.com 387

sodomy 231, 234, 239, 240–241, 260

Sommardal, Göran xxii

Song 宋 Dynasty 23, 53, 83, 99, 111, 115, 130, 136, 170, 175, 176, 194, 319, 321

Song Huilian 宋惠蓮 (mistress of Ximen Qing) 216, 220, 253, 254t, 256n17, 384

Song Jiang 宋江 (bandit leader during the late Song, character in *JPM*) 46n13

Song Jiang 宋江 [repertoire of Yangzhou storytelling] 58n3

song suites 31, 85, 92n17, 102n9, 103, **108–109**, 120, 122

songs 26–27, 35[–]38, **49**, 50, 81, **84**, **86**, **91**, 92, **102**, 175, 375
private troupes **120–121**
used as dialogue or soliloquy **88–90**

source text (ST) **226–243**, 249, 251, 252, **257t**, 266n27, 271

Southern drama **122–123**

Soviet Union 397, 398

St. Petersburg 345, 347

State Cultural Relics Bureau 203–204

Stein, Gertrude xxviii

stock phrases **21–22**, 26, **29–57**

Stone, Charles 369, 378

Story of Marital Fate to Awaken World (XSYYZ) **269–270**, 271

storyteller's manner xxxii, 29, 31, **32t**

storytelling **1–18**
'simulating' versus 'representing' ~ **30–33**
storyline pushed forward **108–110**

Stumpf S.J., P. Kilian (1655–1720) 335n33

su 俗 (vulgar) 155

Su Dongpo 蘇東坡 176
see also Su Shi

Su Shi 蘇軾 (1037–1101) 80, 169n8

Sui Shusen 隋樹森 92n17

sujiang 俗講 (oral sermons) 131

Sun Chang, Kang-i 孫張康宜 90n9

Sun Chao 孫超 193

Sun Guazui 孫寡嘴, Blabbermouth Sun (member of Ximen Qing's brotherhood) 254t, 265n26

Sun Kaidi 孫楷第 (1898–1986) 4, 328n2

Sun Li 孫犁 198

Sun Molchun 265, 265n26

Sun Wukong 孫悟空 92n17
see also Xiyou ji

Sun Xue'e 孫雪娥 (fourth wife of Ximen Qing) 385, 387

Sun Xun 孫遜 383, 387

Sun Yen-Mee xv

surroundings: adding colour **110–112**

Suzhou 50, 164, 248n2
printing of *JPM* illustrations 133

Suzhou 蘇州 style 141

Suzong 肅宗 period (756–761) 170n10

Svenska Dagbladet xxi(n6)

Sytschow, L.P. 136

Tagore, R. (1861–1941) 161–162

Taihu rock 149, 152, 154

Taishō era 289

Taiwan xxxiii, 394, 398, 400

taiyi 太醫 (royal doctor) 102

Taizhou School of Mind 114

421

Taizhou Xuepai 泰州學派 (School of Taizhou) 320

Tale of Genji (1010) xxviii, 7

Tanaka Tomoyuki 田中智行: *New Translation of JPM* 新訳金瓶梅 (2018, 2021) 290, 290n4

tanci 彈詞 (*chantefable* genre) 49, 50–51, 79, 367n

Tang 唐 Dynasty (618–907) 24, 104n, 117n5, 130, 170, 170n10, 212, 294

Tang shi huapu 唐詩畫譜 (*Illustrations of Tang Poems*) 175

Tang Xianzu 湯顯祖 (1550–1616) 11, **114–115**

Tao Gu 陶谷 **111**

taoyu 套語 (stock phrases) 33, **45**

target text (TT) 226–243 *passim*, 252, **257t**

Ten Thousand Rooms Project 369, 370

Tenpō era 288

theatre 53, **94**, 132

Thuringian State Archives 346

tian 填 (to set [a song]) 91

Tiananmen massacre (1989) 201

Tianjin Library 161n

Tianxia ming shan sheng gaiji 天下名山勝概記 (*Mountains of World*) 170

tiao 挑 (raising, wood block engraving) 181

tiao duizi 跳隊子 (group dance) 119

tiedan 貼旦 (secondary female role) 105

ting 聽 (to listen) 32n

ting 亭 (small pavilion) 390, 391

Tōhō Shokyoku 289n

Toi Kuyasushi 鳥居久靖 162n4

Tokuyama Domain 289

tone names 298n8

tonggan 通感 (synesthesia) **169**

Tōsei Kuruwa Dangi 当世花街談義 279

tourism **203–204**

Tōyama Katō 遠山荷塘 286

translations (of *JPM*) **394–401**
attempts at prevention 2
from *cihua* version 227, *228*

into a European language and culture **381–393**

indirect ~ **226–227**, *227*, 228, 229

nearly 30 languages (listed) xxxviii

from Zhang Zhupo version *227*, 227, 228

translations (into specific languages)
Czech xxxviii, 264, 265, 277, 389, 389n
Danish xi, xiii, xv, xvii, xxii, xxiii, xxix, 54, 57, 367n5, 394, 400
English xxxiii, xxxvii, xxxviii, 47n15, **221**, 221n40, 227, **228–243**, 252, **257t**, **258–265**, **364–380**, 399
European languages xxi
French xxxi, xxxiii, xxxvii, xxxviii, 2, 3, 47n15, 221n39, 345, 367, 399
German xxxiii, **xxxvii–xxxviii**, 2, 226, 228, 229, 233, 329n9, **345–346**, **360–362**, **398–399**
Japanese 3, 221n38, 289–290, 399
Korean 221n38, 399–400
Latin sections 221, 232
Russian **265**, **265n26**, 399
Swedish (1950) xxi, xxii
Vietnamese 221n38
see also Manchu edition

translator examinations (1651–) 339n49

troupes: private **120–121**

Tsingtau (Qingdao) **359–360**

tu 圖 (pictures) 139

ukiyo monomane (popular entertainment) 278

ukiyo-e 浮世繪 (Japanese colour prints, "pictures of the floating world") 143n10

Ulana 伍拉納 (1739–1795) 340n52

United Kingdom 397, 398

United States 397, 398

University of Chicago **365–366**, 369, 370, 372, 375n13

University of Königsberg **358–359**

422

INDEX

Uppsala University xix

vase (Ping'er) 396
vernacular fiction 7, 8, 19, 26, 78, 376
Verse and Prose Version. *See cihua*
 edition
verse-introductory markers 34t
Vicher, Ondřej xxxviii, **247–277**, 389,
 391
 note on contributor 277
Vierthaler, Paul 249
virgins 215–216, 216n21, 218
visualizing general layout **381–393**
vulgarism **247–277**, **254–255t**
vulgarity **121–123**

wa 挖 (gouging) 181–182
Wade-Giles Romanization 373n, 374
wai 外 (outer spaces) 384
walengmao 瓦楞帽 (tile-shaped cap) 136
wan 完 (The End) 311
Wan, Margaret 29n
wan fu 萬福 (greeting) 235
Wang, John C.Y. 364
Wang, Madam 王婆子 (owner of
 teahouse, matchmaker) **61**, **66–74**
 see also Auntie Wang; Dame Wang
Wang Bo 王勃 (650–676) 84–85, 91
Wang Daokun 汪道昆 5
Wang Family Memorial Hall of Gaoyou
 58
Wang Gen 王艮 (1483–1541) **114**
Wang Huangqin 王皇親 (Imperial
 Relative Wang, rich man in Qinghe)
 120, 122
Wang Jide 王驥德 (1540–1623) 170
Wang Liqi 王利器 (1912–1998) 162n4
Wang Liu'er 王六兒 (mistress of Ximen
 Qing) xxxv, **213**, 216, 219, 220, 233,
 234–235, 236, 253, 254t
 variously translated (Porphyry, Sixth
 Wang, Wang the Sixth) 232
Wang Pozi 王婆子

'Granny Wang' 300
'secondary role' in *Shengguan tu* 297,
 300, 302
 see also Auntie Wang; Dame Wang;
 Madam Wang
Wang Rumei 王汝梅 (b. 1935) 162n4
Wang School of Water Margin **58–64**
Wang Shaotang 王少堂 (1889–1968)
 xxxii, 58n3
 Shuihu 水滸 (Water Margin) 53n
 Wu Song 62
Wang Shizhen 王世貞 (1526–1590) 163,
 319
Wang the Sixth: same as Wang Liu'er
 (*qv*) 232
Wang Wei 王維 (poet, 701–761), 169n8
Wang Wei 王蔚, 150, 157
Wang Xiaohong 王小虹 329n9
Wang Yangming 王陽明 (1472–1529)
 114, 115, 123, **319–320**
Wang Yilong 王義龍 (Master Wang,
 artisan of wood block cutting) 184
Wang Yintai 王蔭泰 (1886–1961) 342n
Wang Zhijun 王致軍 149n18–19
Wangxue 王學 (School of Wang
 Yangming) **319–320**
Wanli version (of *JPM*, 1617)
 same as *cihua* edition (*qv*) 247
Wanli reign 萬曆 (1573–1620) 21, 24,
 25–26, 120, 121, 141, 165, 171, 174,
 185, 195, 279, 319
Water Margin. See Shuihu zhuan
Water Margin (*Shuihu* in Yangzhou
 storytelling) **58–64**
water-colour block printing (*shuiyin* 水
 印, *douban* 餖版) 184
Wei Tongxian 魏衕賢 383, 387–388
Wen Long 文龍 397
 see also Zhang Zhupo
'Wenjing yuanyang hui' 刎頸鴛鴦會
 (story) 81
wenyan 文言 (literary language) xx, 30,
 33, **34–35**, 42, 45

423

Western Han (oral tradition) **20–21**, 40, 51
    markers of narrative transition **44t**
    narrator's appeal to audience 44t
    stock phrases **42–46**
    verse-introductory markers **43t**
wikisource.com 249, 250–251t
wild horse xxxvi, **317**
Wilhelmshaven 359, 361
wineshops 142–143, 145
wisecracks **99–104**
wō 窩 (nest, pit, hollow part of the human body) 251
women 199, 211–220 *passim*, 252–253, 256, 267n28, 279, 367n
woodblock engraving (*JPM*) **160–178**
    artistry **186–188**
    Liu Kun **179–190**
    practice 181, 182, 184
    qualities required **181–182**
    stages **182**
woodblock printing process 142n9
woodblock repair **184**
woodcuts **xxxiv, 129–139**, 381
    'refining' function 168
    straight and curved lines (combination) **174–175**
wordplay 264, 281, 298, 311
    see also puns
World Intangible Cultural Heritage 180
Writers Publishing House 200
wu 屋 (side rooms) 385
Wu, Captain. *See* Wu Song 武松
Wu Da (Wu the Elder) 武大 26, 71, 73, 74, 203, 261
    house 142, 172
    murdered by Pan Jinlian **60–62**, 372
Wu Da jiehun 武大结婚 ('Wu the Elder gets married') 59
Wu Dalang 武大郎 173, 203
    see also Wu Da
Wu Gan 吳敢 23, **394–401**
    note on contributor **401**

Wu Guanyin 舞觀音 (Guanyin dance) 119
Wu Han 吳晗 (scholar) 394, 397
Wu Hong 吳紅 (publisher of *JPM cihua* during campaign against pornography), 201
    see also pornography crackdown work
Wu Jianren 吳趼人 (1866–1910) 317
Wu shi hui 武十回 (*Ten Chapters on Wu Song*) xxvii
Wu Song 武松 26, 58n3, 80, 138, 172, 171, 173
    book illustration **172–173f**
    brother-in-law of Pan Jinlian **60–62**
    'Captain Wu' 65, **69–74**, 173f
    killing of sister-in-law (in *Shuihu zhuan*) 318
    tiger-slayer 237
    'Wu the Second' 69, 110–111
Wu Song
    also called *Wu shi hui* 武十回 (Ten Chapters on Wu Song) 58n3
Wu Song (Yangzhou storytelling) 58, 59, **65–74**
Wu Song da hu 武松打虎 (Wu Song Fights Tiger) 11, 37n, 50, 136, 203
Wu Song saga **xxvii–xxviii**, xxxii, 34n
Wu Wu Meng (pseudonym) 237, 237n6
Wu Yueniang 吳月娘 **87, 89, 108–110**
    first wife of Ximen Qing 82
    miscellaneous 85–86, 90n12, 92–93, 93n23, 107, 210, 211, 216, 221, 253, 318, 384, 385, 387, 388n, 390
    'secondary role' in *Shengguan tu* 297, 302
Wu Zuxiang 吳組緗 (1908-1994) 86
Wulin 武林 (famous place for woodcut engraving) 170–171
Wulin 武林 style 141
Wuxing 吳興 (famous place for woodcut engraving) (141

INDEX

Wuying dian zongjian 武英殿總監 (Imperial Printing Office, 1670–) 339

Wuying dian 武英殿 (Hall of Martial Grace) **340–341**, 344, 345

Wúyǔ 吳語 (Wu language) 248, 248n3, 264, 265n26

Wuzong 武宗 (Emperor, r.1506–1521/2) 103, 136

Wylie, Alexander (1815–1887) 347

Xi Shi 西施 (famous beauty of ancient China), 202

Xi You Ji 西遊記 (novel, *Journey to the West*) 280

Xia Chunhao 夏春豪 92n19

xianci 弦詞 (story-singing) 50

xiang 象 (appearance, portrait) 139, 169

Xiang Nanzhou 項南洲 (artisan, also known as Xiang Zhonghua 項仲華) 149, **150**

Xiang Yu 項羽 (232–202 BC, Hegemon-King during the Chu–Han contention) 21

xiangyan 香艷 'fragrant and bedazzling' literature 214, 215–216

xianzi 弦子 (banjo) 120

xiao shu 小書 (small repertoires) 50

xiaochang 小唱 (unstaged singing of arias) 116

xiaoshu 小書 (minor tales) 11

xiaoshuo 小說 (fiction) xxxi, 5–6, 11, 79, 194, 209

Xiaoxiaosheng 笑笑生 5

Xiaoxue 笑學 (scoffing studies) 5

Xiaozong 孝宗, religious name of the Hongzhi Emperor 弘治 (1488–1505) 136

Xie Tao 解弢

Xiaoshuo hua 小說話 (On Fiction, 1919) 322, 325

Xie Xida 謝希大 (member of Ximen Qing's brotherhood) 109

Xie Zhaozhe 謝肇淛 (d. 1624) **115–116**, 316, **394–395**

xieci 褻词 (indecent word) 256

xiehou yu 歇後語
'riddles' 281, 324, 324n27
'words that come after a pause' **87–88**

xieshi 寫實 (realistic style) 86

xieyi 寫意 (writing about the essential idea) 187

xiju 戏剧 (theatre) 58

Ximen Qing 西門慶 xxviii, **12–14**, **61–62**, 73
affairs **256n17**
alternative name (*Siquan* 四泉 Four Springs) 101
archetypal figure (merchant, scoundrel, bureaucrat) 395
book illustrations **135–136**, 137, 138, 139, **144–145**, **147f**, 152
death 14, 84, 137, 171, 237, 330, 372
homosexual desires (occasional) **260**
interest in plays **110–111**, 122
'main character' in *Shengguan tu* 陞官圖 297, **299–311**
miscellaneous 20, 26, 47, 82, 85, 89, 172, 175, 211, 216n21, 219, 252, 253, 255t, 256, 256n18, 261, 373, 377
personality **105–107**
six wives xv–xvi

Ximen Qing's mansion xxxviii, **381–393**
building terminology (translation) **389–391**
garden 382–386, 387, 388, 389
gradual introduction (in opening chapters of *JPM*) 383
hidden meaning **388–389**
plans **386–388**

Xin'an 新安 (Anhui Province) 134, 170
another name for Shexian 歙縣 148, 185

Xingshi hengyan 醒世恆言 82

see also Feng Menglong

Xingshi Yinyuan Zhuan 醒世姻緣傳 (XSYYZ) **269–270**, 271

Xinxin zi 欣欣子 (Master of Delight) 316, **321–322**, 323, 324, 374

xinxue 心學 (School of Mind) **114–115** rise **115–116**

Xiuta yeshi 繡榻野史 (*Pornographic Story of Embroidered Couch*) 218, 218n27

xiuxiang 繡像 version (of *JPM*) same as Chongzhen edition (*qv*) 247

Xixiang ji 西廂記 (*Story of Western Wing*) 79, 88, 90, 91, 120, 131, 295, 317, 336
full-page illustrations (1573 edition) **132**
zhugongdiao and *zaju* versions 92n20

Xiyou ji 西遊記 (novel, *Journey to the West*) xxi, xxxvi, 19, 26, 315, 317, 395, 396

Xizhou Sheng 西周生 ('Scholar of Western Zhou', author of *Xingshi Yinyuan Zhuan*) 269

Xu Shuofang 徐朔方 (1923–2007) 11, 11n28, 322

Xu Wei 徐渭 (1521–1593) 170, 319

Xu Wenzhen 徐文貞 164, 165

Xu Yuanmeng 徐元夢 (Sioi yuwan meng, 1655–1741) 338, **339–340**

xuan 軒 (building on high ground) 390, 391

xuan 旋 (swirling) 181

Xuanhe 宣和 reign (1119–1125) xxviii

Xuanhe yishi 宣和遺事 (*Legends of Xuanhe Reign*) 35, 42, 44, 46n13

Xunzi 荀子 (philosopher) 11n28, 269

Xuwan 許灣 (Jiangxi Province) 180

Yamamoto Hokuzan 山本北山 (1752–1812) **284–285**

Yan Fu 嚴復 (1853–1921) 79

Yan Shifan 嚴世蕃 (1513–1565) 330

Yan Song 嚴嵩 (1480–1565) 330

yǎn 眼 (eye, hole)
euphemism for 'vagina' 263n23

yanbiao 言表 (performance) 38, 39

yanchang 演唱 (act) 93

yǎng 養 (to support, to provide for) 267

Yang Erfeng 陽二風 (gambler and bad element in the universe of *JPM*) 255t

Yanggu 陽谷 (township) 60, 101
Lion Tower Tourist City 202, 203

Yanggu County 陽谷 101, 202–203, 203n

Yangzhou xxxii, **179–180**, 343

Yangzhou *pinghua* 扬州评话 or 揚州評話 (Yangzhou storytelling tradition) xxxii, 21, 30, 44, 52, 58, 58n1
'manner' **40–41**
oral performance and written script **40–41**
see also pinghua

Yangzhou shiju 揚州詩局 (Yangzhou Poetry Bureau) 182

Yangzhou storytelling xvi, 42–43, 45, 49, 51
Pan Jinlian **58–64**

yanyi 演義 (novel, romance) 46

Yao Ping 214n18

Yao Xinnong 姚莘農 (1905–1991) 11

Ye Dejun 葉德均 (1911–1956) 24

yebushou 夜不收 (border agent, scout) 211, 211n8

Yi qiang: abbreviation for *Yiyang qiang* 弋陽腔 (*qv*) 116n4

yimen 義門 (ceremonial gate) 384, 390

yin 淫 (lewd) 155; (sexual promiscuity) 331

yinci 淫詞 (obscene words) 332

yinci xiaoshuo 淫詞小說 (novels with obscene words) 332, 346

yínfu 淫妇 ('lascivious woman') **59–61**, 260

Ying Bojue 應伯爵 (member of Ximen Qing's brotherhood) 85, 86, 100, **107–111**, 145, 211, 253, 255t, 384, 391

INDEX

'best friend' of Ximen Qing 82

Ying'er 迎兒 (daughter of Wu Da) 89n4, 172

see also Wu Da

Yinreng 胤礽 (1674–1724) **334–335**, 345

yinshu 淫書 (obscene books) 154, 332, 346

Yixian 邑縣 (Shandong) 5

Yiyang qiang 弋陽腔 (Yiyang style of opera) 116, **116n4, 121–123**

Yongxi yuefu 雍熙樂府 102, 109

Yongzheng, Emperor 雍正 1, 117n5, 183

you fen jiao 有分教 ('it was predestined' marker) 34t, 35

youxi wenxue 遊戲文學 (light and vulgar literature) 9

Yu Yue 俞樾 (1821–1907) 163

yuan 院 (courtyards) 384, 385

Yuan Dynasty (1279–1368) xxvii, 23, 99, 315, 319

Yuan Dynasty *zaju* 雜劇 83

Yuan Hongdao 袁宏道 (1568–1610) xxxiv, 8, 154, **163**, 165, 394

Yuan Mei 袁枚 (1716–1798): jottings 340

Yuan shi 元史 (History of Yuan Dynasty) 93

Yuan Zhongdao 袁中道 (1570–1624) 8, 154, **163–164**, 165, 322

Yuan Zongdao 袁宗道 (1560–1600) 154

yuanben 院本 (dramatic skit) 81, 119

yuanlai 原來 (marker, 'in fact') 39t, 39, 39n

Yue family bookshop (Beijing) 131

yuequ 樂曲 ('musical verses') 24

Yuhuan ji 玉環記 (Story of Jade Ring) 85, 86, 88, 90n14, 98n1, **104–107** plot **104–105n**

Yujia ao 漁家傲 (song suite, Fisherman's Pride) 123

yunxia manzhi 雲霞滿紙 (pages full of erotic haze) 163, 394

yunyu 雲雨 ('clouds and rain') 215

Yuxi jian 禦戲監 (Drama Supervision Bureau) 117

Yuxiao 玉簫 (maid of Wu Yueniang, first wife of Ximen Qing) 107, 108, 120

see also maidservants

Yuxiao 玉簫 (prostitute, heroine of the drama *Yuhuan ji*) 86, **104–105n**, 107, 108

Yuyao qiang 余姚腔 (Yuyao style) 121, **121n11**

yuzhi 御制 (imperially ordered) 345

zaju 雜劇 (drama, plays, comedies) 88, 98–99, 103, 116, 117, 119, 122

zaomu 棗木 (jujube wood) 343

zashua 杂耍 (acrobatics) 116

zen jian 怎見 (marker, 'how did it look') 34t, 35n4

zen jiande 怎見得 ('how did it look', 'what a sight!') 34t, 35n4, 42, 44t

zhai 宅 (residence) 382

Zhang Dai 張岱 (1597–1689) 49

Zhang Daoshen 張道深 (1670–1698) same as Zhang Zhupo (*qv*) 329

Zhang Huiying 张惠英 248, 248n2–3, 256, **264–265**, 265n25

Zhang Jun 張軍 (bookseller in Liaoning, executed for pirating and selling JPM) 201–202

Zhang Min 张敏 **160–190** note on contributor **178, 190**

Zhang Peiheng 章培恒 317

Zhang Tingting 張婷婷 **114–126** note on contributor **126**

Zhang Xiumin 張秀民 149n19

Zhang Yuanfen 張遠芬 (1939–) 162n4

Zhang Zhupo 張竹坡 (1670–1698) xxxiv, xxxvii, xxxviii, 2, 4, 9, 161, 216n21, 220, 253, 289, 290, 395, 396, 397–398

Zhang Zhupo edition (of *JPM*; 1695) 160n2, 185, 189, 210n6, 229, **230f,**

427

279, 281, 329, 346, 365, 377, 378, 398, 399

see also Chongzhen edition

zhanghui xiaoshuo 章回小說 (Ming novels) 30, 31, 32, 46, 174

zhanjiao 展角 (wings of official's caps) 136

Zhao Guangyao 赵广耀 (bookseller severely fined for selling *JPM*) 197

Zhao Longgang 99

see also doctors: Zhao

Zhao Qimei 趙琦美 (1563–1624) 10

Zhaolian, Prince 昭槤 (1776–1830) *Xiaoting zalu* 嘯亭雜錄 (jottings) 333, 333n29, 335–336

Zhejiang People's Publishing House 202

zheng 箏 (zither) 120

Zheng Aiyue 鄭愛月 (Ximen Qing's preferred prostitute) 216n21, 217, 253, 255t, 262–263

Zheng Zhenduo 鄭振鐸 (1898–1958) 24, 161n, 162n3, 198, 394, 397

zhenge shi 真個是 (marker, 'Truly') 34t, 35n4

Zhenzong, Emperor 真宗 (r.998–1022) 103

zhi jian 只見 (marker, 'just look') 37t, 37n

zhi shuo 只說 ('let us just tell') 42

zhi yan 只言 ('let's now tell about') 42

zhiguai xiaoshuo 志怪小說 (tales of the miraculous) 321

Zhonggu si 鐘鼓司 (Bell and Drum Office) 117, 117n5

Zhongguo wenxue shi 中國文學史 (Zhang and Luo, 3v, 1996) 317

Zhonghua wenxue tongshi 中華文學通史 (CASS, 10v, 1997) 317

Zhongyang Shudian 中央書店 197

Zhou Enlai 周恩來 199

Zhou Wu 周蕪 141n5, 148n15, 149n18, 150n20, 21, 23, 25, 158,162n3, 171, 171n13, 178

Zhou Xinhui 周心慧 149n18–19, 162n3

Zhou Yang 周揚 199

Zhu Shenglin 諸聖鄰 *Da Tang Qin Wang cihua* 大唐秦王 詞話 24, 94

Zhu Xi 朱熹 (1130–1200) 114, 319

Zhu Xing 朱星 9

zhuan 傳 (chronicle, tale) 23, 46

zhuanlan.zhihu.com 386, 387

zhugongdiao 諸宮調 (medley with interpolated prose) 80–81
prosimetric style 24, 79

zidi shu 子弟書 9, 356
characteristics 295
'gentry tale' xxxvi
'literary style of storytelling' 80
'tales of bannermen gentry' **295–296**
textual corpus **296**
types 296

Zui Xihu Xinyue Zhuren 醉西湖心月主人 149n19